A FIRST BOOK OF C++
From Here to There

A FIRST BOOK OF C++
From Here to There

Gary J. Bronson
Fairleigh Dickinson University

West Publishing Company
Minneapolis/Saint Paul New York Los Angeles San Francisco

PRODUCTION CREDITS

Text design: *David Farr, Imagesmythe, Inc.*
Copyeditor: *Sheryl Rose*
Composition: *Alexander Teshin Associates, Mountain View, CA*

West's Commitment to the Environment

In 1906, West Publishing Company began recycling materials left over from the production of books. This began a tradition of efficient and responsible use of resources. Today, up to 95 percent of our legal books and 70 percent of our college and school texts are printed on recycled, acid-free stock. West also recycles nearly 22 million pounds of scrap paper annually—the equivalent of 181,717 trees. Since the 1960s, West has devised ways to capture and recycle waste inks, solvents, oils, and vapors created in the printing process. We also recycle plastics of all kinds, wood, glass, corrugated cardboard, and batteries, and have eliminated the use of styrofoam book packaging. We at West are proud of the longevity and the scope of our commitment to our environment.

Production, Prepress, Printing and Binding by West Publishing Company.

 TEXT IS PRINTED ON 10% POST CONSUMER RECYCLED PAPER

British Library Cataloguing-in-Publication Data. A catalogue record for this book is available from the British Library.

Copyright ©1995   By WEST PUBLISHING COMPANY
                    610 Opperman Drive
                    P.O. Box 64526
                    St. Paul, MN 55164-0526

Library of Congress Cataloging-in-Publication Data

Bronson, Gary J.
  A first book of C++ : from here to there / Gary J. Bronson.
    p.   cm.
  Includes index.
  ISBN 0-314-04236-9 (soft)
  1. C++ (Computer program language)   I. Title.
QA76.73.C153B76 1994
005.13'3—dc20   94-28503
                                                         CIP

dedicated to

Rochelle,
David,
Matthew,
Jeremy,
and
Sparky

Contents

Preface

. . . in the long term to get the most out of something like C++ you will need to use it in an object-oriented manner. You need to use object-oriented programming and to do object-oriented design. However, you also have to get from here to there.[1]

Object-oriented software development has been credited with many benefits, among which are reduced software development time and significant code reuse. Within the programming community, however, there has been serious debate as to how best to move to a complete object-oriented environment. Such an environment requires the integration of three inter-related areas: object-oriented requirements analysis (OOR), object-oriented design (OOD), and object-oriented programming (OOP).

One approach maintains that object-oriented design should be learned before object-oriented programming is introduced. A second approach, and the one taken by this text, introduces object-oriented programming (OOP) first as an entry point into object-oriented design and requirements analysis. I feel that this approach is especially relevant to learning C++ because C++ is not a "pure" object-oriented programming language, but a hybrid that has all of the features of its procedural ancestor, C.

Specifically, my own experience is that it is much easier and more rewarding to work from C++ into object-oriented programming and then learn to design rather than the other way around. Doing so permits one to more easily master the syntax and features of the language and then move on, in a natural

---

[1] "Interview with Bjarne Stroustrup," *C++ Journal*, vol. I, no. 3 (1991), pp. 16–25.

progression, to a proficiency in object-oriented programming. The text does this in two distinct steps:

- First, C++ is introduced as a language in its own right, not as an add-on to C, but as a better version of C. As such the procedural elements of C++ are initially stressed with object concepts touched on for input (`cin`) and output (`cout`).
- Only after the syntax and semantics of C++ are learned are classes introduced. Proficiency in creating and using objects is then developed, which includes encapsulation and simple inheritance features.

Distinctive Features of This Book

Writing Style. I firmly believe that introductory texts do not teach students—professors teach students. An introductory textbook, if it is to be useful, must be the primary "supporting actor" to the "leading role" of the professor. Once the professor sets the stage, however, the textbook must encourage, nurture, and assist the student in acquiring and "owning" the material presented in class. To do this the text must be written in a manner that makes sense to the student. My primary concern, and one of the distinctive features of this book, is that it has been written for the student. Thus, first and foremost, I feel the writing style used to convey the concepts presented is an important aspect of the text.

Software Engineering. Rather than simply introduce students to programming in C++, this text introduces students to the fundamentals of software engineering, from both a procedural and an object-oriented viewpoint. This begins with a discussion of these two programming approaches in Section 1.1 and is reinforced throughout the text.

Introduction to References and Pointers. One of the unique features of my previous text, *A First Book of C*, was the early introduction of pointer concepts. This was done by displaying the addresses of variables and then using other variables to store these addresses. This approach always seemed a more logical and intuitive method of understanding pointers than the indirection description in vogue at the time *A First Book of C* was released.

I have since been pleased to see that the use of an output function to display addresses has become a standard way of introducing pointers. Although this approach, therefore, is no longer a unique feature of this book, I am very proud of its presentation and continue to use it in this text. Additionally, references are also introduced early, in Chapter 2.

Program Testing. Every single C++ program in this text has been successfully compiled and run under Borland's Turbo C++ Compiler. A source diskette of all programs is included with the text. This permits students to both experiment and extend the existing programs and more easily modify them as required by a number of end-of-section exercises.

Pedagogical Features

To facilitate the goal of making C++ accessible as a first-level course, the following pedagogical features have been incorporated into the text:

End of Section Exercises. Almost every section in the book contains numerous and diverse skill builder and programming exercises. Additionally, solutions to selected odd-numbered exercises are provided in an appendix.

Pseudocode Descriptions. Pseudocode is stressed throughout the text. Flowchart symbols are presented, but are only used in visually presenting flow-of-control constructs.

Common Programming Errors and Chapter Review. Each chapter ends with a section on common programming errors and a review of the main topics covered in the chapter.

Appendices and Supplements

An expanded set of appendices are provided. These include appendices on operator precedence, ASCII codes, I/O redirection, program entry and compilation, floating point number storage, and linked list examples using classes.

Additionally, a solutions manual to selected odd- and even-numbered exercises on a 3 1/2" IBM-PC compatible diskette (containing both ASCII and WordPerfect formats) is available to adopters.

Acknowledgments

This book began as an idea. It became a reality only due to the encouragement, skills, and efforts of many people. I would like to acknowledge their contribution.

First, I would like to thank Richard Mixter, my editor at West Publishing Company. His encouragement and handling of numerous scheduling and review details permitted me to concentrate on the actual writing of the text. I would also like to express my gratitude to the individual reviewers listed on the next page. Each of these individuals supplied extremely detailed and constructive reviews of both the original manuscript and a number of revisions. Their suggestions, attention to detail, and comments were extraordinarily helpful to me as the manuscript evolved and matured through the editorial process.

Once the review process was completed, the task of turning the final manuscript into a textbook again depended on many people other than myself. For this I especially want to thank the production editor, Poh Lin Khoo, the copy editor, Sheryl Rose, and the compositor, Mary Austin from Teshin Associates. The dedication of these three people was incredible and very important to me. Almost from the moment the book moved to the production stage these three individuals seemed to take personal ownership of the text and I am very grateful to them. I am also very appreciative of the suggestions and work of the promotion manager at West, Ellen Stanton.

The direct encouragement and support of my dean at Fairleigh Dickinson University, Dr. Paul Lerman, must also be acknowledged. Without his support and the support of my chairman, Dr. Naadimuthu, this text could not have been written.

Finally, I deeply appreciate the patience, understanding, and love provided by my friend, wife, and partner, Rochelle.

Gary Bronson

Acknowledgments

The author thanks these reviewers for their knowledgeable help in the completion of this book.

Thomas J. Ahlborn	*West Chester University*
Rhoda Baggs	*Florida Institute of Technology*
John Connely	*Cal Poly, San Luis Obispo*
H. E. Dunsmore	*Purdue University*
Carl Eckberg	*San Diego State University*
Krystof Frankowski	*University of Minnesota*
Mike Holland	*Northern Virginia Community College*
Peter Isaacson	*University of Northern Colorado*
Christopher C. Jones	*Utah Valley State College*
Edward M. Keefe	*Des Moines Area Community College*
Robert A. McDonald	*East Stroudsburg University*
Charles McDowell	*University of California, Santa Cruz*
Mike Michaelson	*Palomar College*
Allan M. Miller	*College of San Mateo*
Kathy Newman	*University of California, Los Angeles*
Mike Parker	*Shoreline Community College*
Richard Reid	*Michigan State University*
Greg Riccardi	*Florida State University*
Hamilton Richards, Jr.	*University of Texas*
John Riedl	*University of Minnesota*
Peter Rosenbaum	*Framingham State College*
Arline Sachs	*Northern Virginia Community College*
Bryan G. Scarbeau	*Lake Sumter Community College*
Vasant Shambhogue	*Wichita State University*
Steven Stepanek	*California State University, Northridge*
Martha Tillman	*College of San Mateo*
Huaqing Wang	*California State University, Bakersfield*

Getting Started

Chapter One

1.1   Introduction to Programming

A computer is a machine and like other machines, such as an automobile or lawn mower, it must be turned on and then driven, or controlled, to do the task it was meant to do. In an automobile, for example, control is provided by the driver, who sits inside of and directs the car. In a computer, control is provided by a computer program. Formally, a *computer program* is a structured combination of data and instructions that is used to operate a computer. *Programming* is the process of writing a computer program in a language that the computer can respond to and that other programmers can understand. The set of instructions, data, and rules that can be used to construct a program is called a *programming language*.

Programming languages are usefully classified by level and orientation. Languages that use instructions resembling written languages, such as English, are referred to as *high-level languages*. FORTRAN, BASIC, COBOL, and Pascal are all examples of high-level languages. The final program written in such languages can be run on a variety of computers. In contrast, *low-level languages* use instructions that are directly tied to one type of computer, such as IBM, Apple, or DEC. Although programs written in low-level languages are limited in that they can only be run on the computer type they were written for, they do permit using special features of the computer that are different from other machines. They also can be written to execute faster than programs written in high-level languages.

C++, as well as its immediate predecessor, C, is conventionally classified as a middle-level language. The term *middle-level* is used to convey the fact that although C++ can be used as a high-level language, it also can be used to take advantage of features associated with low-level languages.

A second classification of programming languages makes use of the distinction between procedure-oriented and object-oriented languages. In a *procedure-*

TABLE 1–1   High-Level Programming Language Instruction Summary

Operation	FORTRAN	BASIC	COBOL	Pascal	C++
INPUT (Get the data)	READ	INPUT READ/DATA	READ ACCEPT	READ READLN	cin cin.get scanf()
PROCESSING (Use the data)	= IF/ELSE DO	LET IF/ELSE FOR	COMPUTE IF/ELSE PERFORM	:= IF/ELSE FOR WHILE REPEAT	= if for while do
OUTPUT (Display the data)	WRITE PRINT	PRINT PRINT/ USING	WRITE DISPLAY	WRITE WRITELN	cout printf()

oriented language the available instructions are used to create a logically consistent set of directions, called a procedure, that is meant to produce a specific result from the data. For example, consider Table 1–1, which lists the fundamental set of instructions provided in FORTRAN, BASIC, COBOL, Pascal, and C++. Notice that the instructions all resemble English words, which is indicative of high-level languages, and that the instructions can be conveniently grouped into input, processing, and output operations. These groupings are common to a procedure-oriented approach because they support the processing typically associated with a procedure-based program, which, as illustrated in Figure 1–1, is to accept data (input), to manipulate the data (process), and to produce a result (output).

For the last twenty-five years all programming languages have predominately been procedure-oriented. Within the past few years a second orientation, referred to as object-oriented, has evolved to become a second major form for programming applications.

One of the motivations for *object-oriented languages* has been the development of graphical screens capable of displaying multiple windows. In such an environment each window on the screen can conveniently be considered as an object, with associated characteristics, such as color, position, and size. Under an object orientation a program must first define the objects it will be manipulating; this includes describing both the characteristics of the object and the procedures that can be used to manipulate and alter these characteristics. The remaining parts of the program are then concerned with activating each object as required. This is accomplished by passing information, called messages, to each object. As a message is passed to an object the object responds and alters its characteristics using its previously defined procedures. For now it is sufficient to understand that these two distinct approaches to programming currently exist. This is because C++ contains features found in both procedure- and object-oriented languages.

The reason for C++'s dual nature is that it began as an extension to C, which is a procedure-oriented language developed in the 1970s at AT&T Bell Laboratories. In the early 1980s, Bjarne Stroustrup (also at AT&T) used his simulation language background to develop C++. A central feature of simulation languages is that they model real-life situations as objects that respond to stimuli in well-defined ways. This object orientation, along with other procedure-oriented improvements, was combined with existing C language features to form the C++ language.

FIGURE 1–1 Procedure-Oriented Program Operations

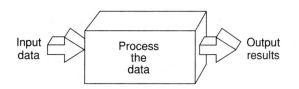

Algorithms and Procedures

As algorithms are central to C++'s procedure-oriented side, it will serve us well to understand what an algorithm is. From a procedural point of view, before writing a program, a programmer must clearly understand what data is to be used, the desired result, and the procedure to be used to produce this result. The procedure to be used is referred to as an algorithm. More precisely, an *algorithm* is defined as a step-by-step sequence of instructions that describes how a computation is to be performed.

Only after we clearly understand the data that we will be using and the algorithm (the specific steps required to produce the desired result) can we write the program. Seen in this light, procedure-oriented programming is the translation of a selected algorithm into a language that the computer can use.

To illustrate an algorithm, we shall consider a simple problem. Assume that a program must calculate the sum of all whole numbers from 1 through 100. Figure 1–2 illustrates three methods we could use to find the required sum. Each method constitutes an algorithm.

Clearly, most people would not bother to list the possible alternatives in a detailed step-by-step manner, as is done in Figure 1–2, and then select one of the algorithms to solve the problem. But then, most people do not think algorithmically; they tend to think intuitively. For example, if you had to change a flat tire on your car, you would not think of all the steps required—you would simply change the tire or call someone else to do the job. This is an example of intuitive thinking.

Unfortunately, computers do not respond to intuitive commands. A general statement such as "add the numbers from 1 through 100" means nothing to a computer, because the computer can only respond to algorithmic commands written in an acceptable language such as C++. To program a computer successfully, you must clearly understand this difference between algorithmic and intuitive commands. A computer is an "algorithm-responding" machine; it is not an "intuition-responding" machine. You cannot tell a computer to change a tire or to add the numbers from 1 through 100. Instead, you must give the computer a detailed step-by-step sequence of instructions that, collectively, forms an algorithm. For example, the sequence of instructions

Set n *equal to 100*
Set a = 1
Set b *equal to 100*
Calculate sum $= \dfrac{n * (a + b)}{2}$

forms a detailed method, or algorithm, for determining the sum of the numbers from 1 through 100. Notice that these instructions are not a computer program. Unlike a program, which must be written in a language the computer can respond to, an algorithm can be written or described in various ways. When English-like phrases are used to describe the algorithm (the processing steps),

Method 1. *Columns:* Arrange the numbers from 1 to 100 in a column and add them:

$$
\begin{array}{r}
1 \\
2 \\
3 \\
4 \\
\cdot \\
\cdot \\
\cdot \\
98 \\
99 \\
+100 \\
\hline
5050
\end{array}
$$

Method 2. *Groups:* Arrange the numbers in convenient groups that sum to 100. Multiply the number of groups by 100 and add any unused numbers to the total:

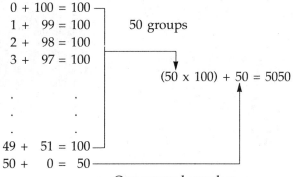

Method 3. *Formula:* Use the formula

$$
\text{Sum} = \frac{n(a + b)}{2}
$$

where

n = number of terms to be added (100)
a = first number to be added (1)
b = last number to be added (100)

$$
\text{Sum} = \frac{100(1 + 100)}{2} = 5050
$$

FIGURE 1–2 Summing the Numbers 1 through 100

as in this example, the description is called *pseudocode*. When mathematical equations are used, the description is called a *formula*. When diagrams that employ the symbols shown in Figure 1–3 are used, the description is referred to as a *flowchart*. Figure 1–4 illustrates the use of these symbols in depicting an algorithm for determining the average of three numbers.

FIGURE 1–3 Flowchart Symbols

SYMBOL	NAME	DESCRIPTION
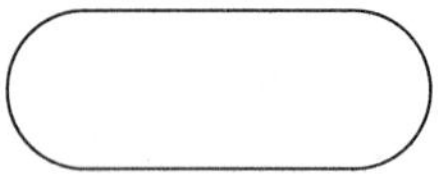	Terminal	Indicates the beginning or end of an algorithm
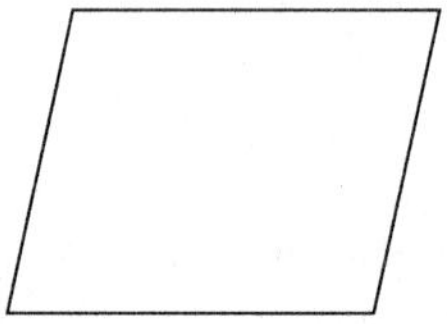	Input/output	Indicates an input or output operation
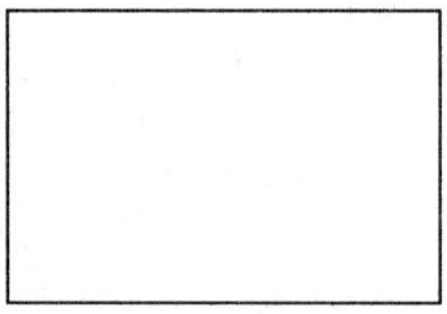	Process	Indicates computation or data manipulation
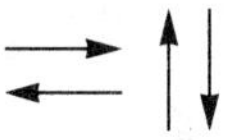	Flow lines	Used to connect the flowchart symbols and indicated the logic flow
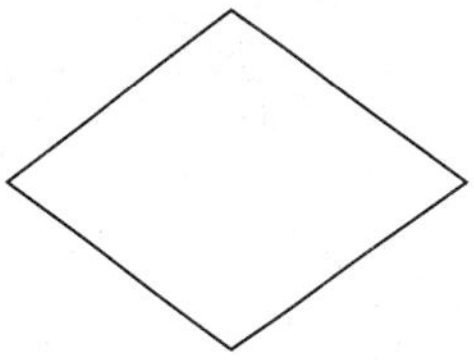	Decision	Indicates a decision point in the algorithm
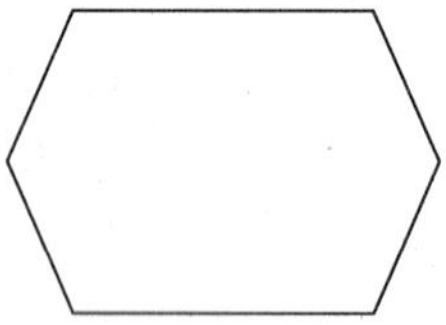	Loop	Indicates the initial, final, and increment values of a loop
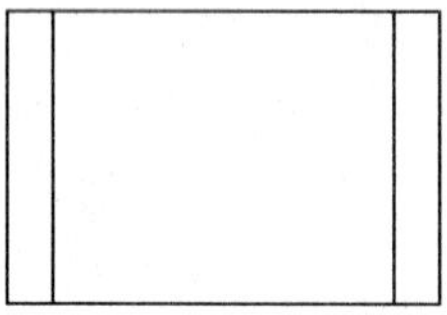	Predefined process	Indicates a predefined process, as in calling a sorting process
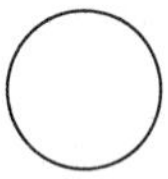	Connector	Indicates an entry to, or exit from another part of the flowchart

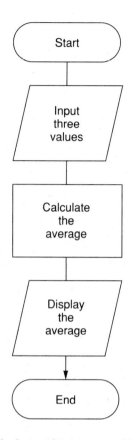

FIGURE 1–4 Flowchart for Calculating the Average of Three Numbers

Because flowcharts are cumbersome to revise and can easily support unstructured programming practices, they have fallen out of favor among professional programmers, while the use of pseudocode to express the logic of algorithms has gained increasing acceptance. In describing an algorithm using pseudocode, short English phrases are used. For example, acceptable pseudocode for describing the steps needed to compute the average of three numbers is:

> *Input the three numbers into the computer*
> *Calculate the average by adding the numbers and*
> *   dividing the sum by three*
> *Display the average*

Only after an algorithm has been selected and the programmer understands the steps required can the algorithm be written using computer-language statements. The writing of an algorithm using computer-language statements is called *coding* the algorithm (see Figure 1–5).

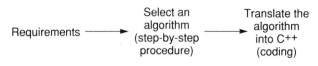

FIGURE 1–5 Coding an Algorithm

Classes and Objects

Just as algorithms are central to procedure-oriented languages, classes are central to object-oriented languages, because objects are created from classes. As illustrated in Figure 1-6, an object consists of both data and the specific procedures that can be applied to the data within the object. These procedures are also referred to as methods, and we will use these terms interchangeably when talking about classes and objects.

Classes are broad categories that define both the characteristics of the data that an object can contain and the methods that can be applied to this data. An *object* is a specific item from a class. The relationship of an object to a class is similar to the relationship of a specific geometric shape to a class of shapes. For example, Rectangles is a class of four-sided shapes whose opposite sides are equal in length and adjacent sides are perpendicular. A specific rectangle, for example, one having a measurement of two inches by three inches, is an object of the class Rectangle. This particular object is a specific case, or instance, of the defined class Rectangles.

As a further example, consider the type of data that we call integers. If we expand the definition of integers to be all whole numbers plus the allowable methods that can be applied to integers (the operations of addition, subtraction, multiplication, etc.) we have, in object-oriented terms, defined a class. A number such as 5 that is a specific item from this class, in object-oriented terminology, is called an object. Again, an object is simply a particular instance of a class.

Notice that a true class includes not only a data type, but the methods, or operations, that can be applied to the data in the class. A particular method is activated, or invoked, by sending the object a message (see Figure 1–6). For example, in object-oriented terms, the plus sign in an expression such as 5 + 2 is not considered an addition operation, but a message: a message to the 2 object that it is to be added to the 5 object.

The important aspect of objects for our current purposes is that a message to an object triggers a well-defined response. Although we will create our own

FIGURE 1–6 An Object Consists of Data and Methods

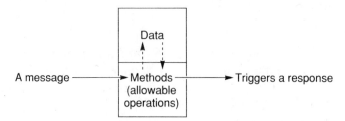

classes and objects as we become more fluent with C++, we can use any objects that are provided with C++ as long as we know the correct messages to trigger the appropriate responses. As we will see shortly, two objects, named cin and cout, respectively, have been provided with C++ for the input and output of data values. We will use these two objects extensively in our early work.

Program Translation

Once an algorithm or class is written in C++ it still cannot be executed on a computer without further translation. This is because the internal language of all computers consists of a series of 1s and 0s, called the computer's *machine language*. To generate a machine language program that can be executed by the computer requires that the C++ program, which is referred to as a *source program*, be translated into the computer's machine language (see Figure 1–7).

The translation into machine language can be accomplished in two ways. When each statement in the source program is translated individually and executed immediately, the programming language used is called an *interpreted language*, and the program doing the translation is called an *interpreter*.

When all of the statements in a source program are translated before any one statement is executed, the programming language used is called a *compiled language*. In this case, the program doing the translation is called a *compiler*. C++ is a compiled language. Here, the source program is translated as a unit into machine language. The output produced by the compiler is called an object program. An *object program* is simply a translated version of the source program that can be executed by the computer system with one more processing step. Let us see why this is so.

Most C++ programs contain statements that use preprogrammed routines, for input and output and for finding such quantities as square roots, absolute values, and other commonly encountered mathematical calculations. Additionally, a large C++ program may be stored in two separate program files. In such a case, each file can be compiled separately. However, both files must ultimately be combined to form a single program before the program can be executed. In both of these cases it is the task of a linker program, which is frequently called automatically by the compiler, to combine all of the preprogrammed routines and individual object files into a single program ready for execution. This final program is called an *executable program*. (See Appendix C for a complete description of entering, compiling, and running a C++ program.)

FIGURE 1–7 Source Programs Must Be Translated

Exercises 1.1

1. Define the following terms:
   a. computer program
   b. programming language
   c. programming
   d. algorithm
   e. pseudocode
   f. flowchart
   g. procedure
   h. object
   i. method
   j. message language
   k. response
   l. class
   m. source program
   n. compiler
   o. object program
   p. executable program
   q. interpreter

2. Determine a step-by-step procedure (list the steps) to do these tasks:

Note: There is no one single correct answer for each of these tasks. The exercise is designed to give you practice in converting intuitive commands into equivalent algorithms and understanding the differences in the thought processes involved.
   a. Fix a flat tire.
   b. Make a telephone call.
   c. Go to the store and purchase a loaf of bread.
   d. Roast a turkey.

3. Determine and write an algorithm (list the steps) to interchange the contents of two cups of liquid. Assume that a third cup is available to hold the contents of either cup temporarily. Each cup should be rinsed before any new liquid is poured into it.

4. Write a detailed set of instructions, in English, to calculate the dollar amount of money in a piggybank that contains h half-dollars, q quarters, n nickels, d dimes, and p pennies.

5. Write a set of detailed, step-by-step instructions, in English, to find the smallest number in a group of three integer numbers.

6. a. Write a set of detailed, step-by-step instructions, in English, to calculate the change remaining from a dollar after a purchase is made. Assume that the cost of the goods purchased is less than a dollar. The change received should consist of the smallest number of coins possible.
   b. Repeat Exercise 6a, but assume the change is to be given only in pennies.

7. a. Write an algorithm to locate the first occurrence of the name MIXTER in a list of names arranged in random order.
   b. Discuss how you could improve your algorithm for Exercise 7a if the list of names was arranged in alphabetical order.

8. Determine and write an algorithm to sort three numbers in ascending (from lowest to highest) order. How would you do this problem intuitively?

9. Define an appropriate class for each of the following specific objects:
   a. the number 5
   b. a square that is 4" by 4"
   c. this C++ textbook
   d. a 1995 Ford Thunderbird car
   e. the last ballpoint pen that you used

10. a. What operations should the following objects be capable of doing?
   i. a 1955 Ford Thunderbird car
   ii. the last ballpoint pen that you used
   b. Do the operations determined for Exercise 10a apply only to the particular object listed or are they more general and apply to all objects of the type listed?

1.2 Function and Class Names

A well-designed program is constructed using a design philosophy similar to that used in constructing a well-designed building; it doesn't just happen, but depends on careful planning and execution for the final design to accomplish its intended purpose. Just as an integral part of the design of a building is its structure, the same is true for a program.

Programs whose structure consists of interrelated segments arranged in a logical order to form an integrated and complete unit are referred to as *modular programs* (Figure 1–8). Modular programs are easier to develop, correct, and modify than programs constructed otherwise. In general programming terminology, the smaller segments used to construct a modular program are referred to as *modules*. In C++ the modules can be either classes or functions. We have already encountered classes. More formally, we can define a class as a unit containing a data structure and the procedures that can be applied to the data structure. A *function* is a simpler unit that only contains a sequence of operations.

FIGURE 1–8 A Well-Designed Program Is Built Using Modules

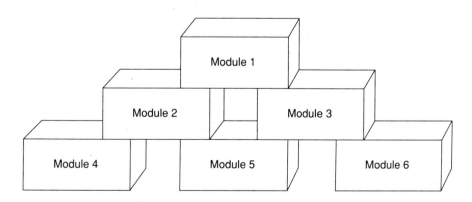

It helps to think of a function as a small machine that transforms the data it receives into a finished product. For example, Figure 1–9 illustrates a function that accepts two numbers as inputs and multiplies the two numbers to produce a result.

As illustrated in Figure 1–9, the interface to the function is its inputs and results. How the inputs are converted to results is both encapsulated and hidden within the function. In this regard the function can be thought of as a single unit providing a special-purpose operation. A similar analogy is appropriate for a class. A class, which encapsulates both data and operations, can be thought of as a small dedicated computer. As such, each class contains all of the elements required for the input, output, and processing of its objects.

One important requirement for designing a good function or class is to give it a name that conveys to the reader some idea about what the function or class does. The names permissible for functions and classes are also used to name other elements of the C++ language, and are collectively referred to as *identifiers*. Identifiers can be made up of any combination of letters, digits, or underscores (_) selected according to the following rules:

1. The first character of an identifier must be a letter or underscore (_).
2. Only letters, digits, or underscores may follow the initial letter. Blank spaces are not allowed; use the underscore to separate words in an identifier consisting of multiple words.
3. An identifier cannot be one of the keywords listed in Table 1–2.
   (A *keyword* is a word that is set aside by the language for a special purpose and should only be used in a specified manner.)[1]
4. On most systems only the first 31 characters of an identifier are actually used and recorded by the computer. (However, some systems recognize and use more than the first 31 characters.)

FIGURE 1–9 A Multiplying Function

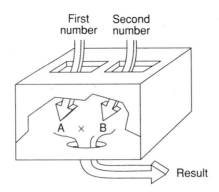

First number   Second number

A × B

Result

---

[1] Keywords in C++ are also reserved words, which means they must be used only for their specified purpose. Attempting to use them for any other purpose will generate an error message.

Examples of valid C++ identifiers are:

```
grosspay    tax_calc    add_nums    deg_to_rad
mult_two    salestax    netpay      bessel
```

Examples of invalid identifiers are:

```
1AB3    (begins with a number, which violates Rule 1)
E*6     (contains a special character, which violates Rule 2)
while   (this is a keyword, which violates Rule 3)
```

Besides conforming to C++'s identifier rules, a good function or class name should also be a mnemonic. A *mnemonic* is a word or name designed as a memory aid. For example, the name deg_to_rad is a mnemonic if it is the name of a function that converts degrees to radians. Here, the name itself helps to identify what is being done.

Examples of valid identifiers that are not mnemonics are:

```
easy    c3po    r2d2    theforce    mike
```

Nonmnemonic identifiers should not be used because they convey no information about what their purpose is.

Notice that all identifiers have been typed in lowercase letters. This is traditional in C++, although it is not absolutely necessary. Uppercase letters are usually reserved for symbolic constants, a topic covered in Chapter 3. It should be noted that C++ is a *case-sensitive* language. This means that the compiler distinguishes between uppercase and lowercase letters. Thus, in C++, the names TOTAL, total, and TotaL represent three distinct and different names. For this reason, we will type all names in the same case, which traditionally is lowercase in C++.

TABLE 1–2   C++ Keywords

auto	default	goto	public	this
break	do	if	register	template
case	double	inline	return	typedef
catch	else	int	short	union
char	enum	long	signed	unsigned
class	extern	new	sizeof	virtual
const	float	overload	static	void
continue	for	private	struct	volatile
delete	friend	protected	switch	while

The **main** Function

A distinct advantage of using functions and classes in C++ is that the overall structure of the program, in general, and individual modules, in particular, can be planned in advance, including provision for testing and verifying each module's operation. Each function and class can then be written to meet its intended objective.

To provide for the orderly placement and execution of modules, each C++ program must have one and only one function named main. The main function is referred to as a driver function because it drives, or tells, the other modules the sequence in which they are to execute (Figure 1–10).[2]

Figure 1–11 illustrates a structure for the main function. The first line of the function, in this case void main (void), is referred to as a *function header line*. A function header line, which is always the first line of a function, contains three pieces of information:[3]

FIGURE 1–10 The main Function Directs All Other Modules

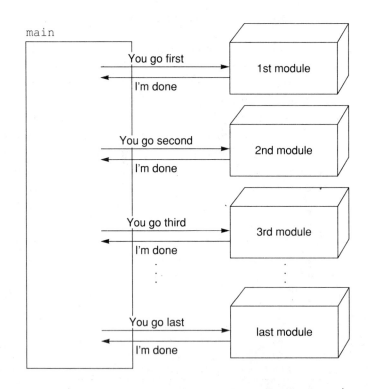

---

[2] Modules executed from main may, in turn, execute other modules. Each module, however, always returns to the module that initiated its execution. This is true even for main (), which returns control to the operating system in effect when main was initiated.

[3] As we will see in Chapter 11, a class must also begin with a header line that adheres to these same rules.

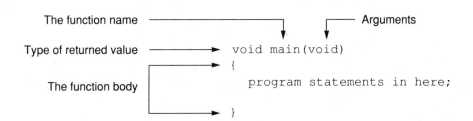

FIGURE 1–11 The Structure of a `main` Function

1. What type of data, if any, is returned from the function

2. The name of the function

3. What type of data, if any, is sent into the function

The keyword before the function name defines the type of value the function returns when it has completed operating. When placed before the function's name the keyword `void` (see Table 1–2) designates that the function will return no value. Similarly, when placed within parentheses following the function name, `void` signifies that no data will be transmitted into the function when it is run. (Data transmitted into a function at run time are referred to as arguments of the function.) The braces, { and }, determine the beginning and end of the function body and enclose the statements making up the function. The statements inside the braces determine what the function does. Each statement inside a function must end with a semicolon (;).

You will be naming and writing many of your own C++ functions. In fact, the rest of this book is primarily about the statements required to construct useful functions and how to combine functions and data into useful classes and programs. Each program, however, must have one and only one `main` function. Until we learn how to pass data into a function and return data from a function (the topics of Chapter 6), the header line illustrated in Figure 1–11 will serve us for all the programs we need to write. In the next section we will use this header line to complete our first working C++ program.

Exercises 1.2

1. State whether the following are valid identifiers. If they are valid, state whether they are mnemonic names. A mnemonic identifier conveys some idea about its intended purpose. If they are invalid identifiers, state why.

```
m1234          new_bal      abcd        A12345      1A2345
power          abs_val      invoices    do          while
add_5          taxes        net_pay     12345       int
new_balance    a2b3c4d5     salestax    amount      $taxes
```

2. Assume that functions with the following names have been written:

```
retrieve_old_bal   enter_sold_amt   calc_new_bal   report
```

   a. From the functions' names, what do you think each function might do?
   b. In what order do you think a `main` function might execute these functions (based on their names)?

3. Assume that the following functions have been written:

```
input_bill   calc_salestax   calc_balance
```

   a. From the functions' names, what do you think each function might do?
   b. In what order do you think a `main` function might execute these functions (based on their names)?

4. Determine names for functions that do the following:
   a. Find the maximum value in a set of numbers.
   b. Find the minimum value in a set of numbers.
   c. Convert a lowercase letter to an uppercase letter.
   d. Convert an uppercase letter to a lowercase letter.
   e. Sort a set of numbers from lowest to highest.
   f. Alphabetize a set of names.

5. Just as the keyword `void` can be used to signify that a function will return no value, the keywords `int`, `char`, `float`, and `double` can be used to signify that a function will return an integer, character, floating point number, and double precision number. Using this information, write header lines for a `main` function that will receive no arguments but will return:
   a. an integer
   b. a character
   c. a floating point number
   d. a double precision number

1.3 The cout Object

One of the most versatile and commonly used objects provided with C++ is named `cout` (pronounced "see out"). This object, whose name was derived from Console OUTput, is an output object that sends data given to it to the standard system display device. For most systems this display device is a video screen. The `cout` object prints out whatever is passed to it. For example, if the data `Hello there world!` is passed to `cout`, this data is printed (or displayed) on your terminal by the `cout` object. The data `Hello there world!` is passed to the `cout` object by simply putting the insertion ("put to") symbol, <<, before the message and after the object's name (see Figure 1–12).

    Now let's put all this together into a working C++ program that can be run on your computer. Consider Program 1-1.

```
cout << "Hello there world!";
```

FIGURE 1–12 Passing a Message to cout

 Program 1-1

```
#include <iostream.h>
void main(void)
{
  cout << "Hello there world!";
}
```

The first line of the program:

```
#include <iostream.h>
```

is a preprocessor command. Preprocessor commands begin with a pound sign (#) and perform some action before the compiler translates the source program into machine code. Specifically, the #include preprocessor command causes the contents of the named file, in this case iostream.h, to be inserted where the #include command appears. The file iostream.h is referred to as a *header file* because it is placed at the top, or head, of a C++ program using the #include command. In particular, the iostream.h file provides two classes, *istream* and *ostream*, that contain the actual data definitions and operations used for data input and output.[4] This header file must be included in all programs that use cout. As also indicated in Program 1-1, preprocessor commands do not end with a semicolon.

Following the preprocessor command is the start of the program's main function. The main function begins with the header line developed in the previous section and the body of the function consists of only one statement. Remember that all statements end with a semicolon (;). The statement in main passes one message to the cout object. The message is the string "Hello there world!"

Since cout is a prewritten object, we do not have to write it; it is available for use just by activating it correctly. Like all C++ objects, cout was written to do a specific task, which is to output results. It is a versatile object that can display results in many different forms. When a string of characters is passed to cout, the object sees to it that the string is correctly printed on your terminal, as shown in Figure 1–13.

---

[4] Formally, cout is an object of the class ostream.

```
Hello there world!
```

FIGURE 1–13 The Output from Program 1-1

Strings in C++ are any combination of letters, numbers, and special characters enclosed in double quotes (`"string in here"`). The double quotes are used to mark the beginning and end of the string and are not considered part of the string. Thus, the string of characters making up the message sent to `cout` must be enclosed in double quotes, as we have done in Program 1-1.

Let us write another program to illustrate `cout`'s versatility. Read Program 1-2 to determine what it does.

 Program 1-2

```cpp
#include <iostream.h>
void main(void)
{
  cout << "Computers, computers everywhere";
  cout << "\n    as far as I can C";
}
```

When Program 1-2 is run, the following is displayed:

```
Computers, computers everywhere
        as far as I can C
```

You might be wondering why the \n did not appear in the output. The two characters \ and n, when used together, are called a newline escape sequence. They tell `cout` to send instructions to the display device to move to a new line. In C++, the backslash (\) character provides an "escape" from the normal interpretation of the character following it by altering the meaning of the next character. If the backslash was omitted from the second `cout` statement in Program 1-2, the n would be printed as the letter n and the program would print out:

```
Computers, computers everywheren    as far as I can C
```

Newline escape sequences can be placed anywhere within the message passed to `cout`. See if you can determine the display produced by Program 1-3.

Program 1-3

```
#include <iostream.h>
void main(void)
{
    cout << "Computers everywhere\n as far as\n\nI can see";
}
```

The output for Program 1-3 is:

```
Computers everywhere
as far as

I can see
```

Exercises 1.3

1. a. Using cout, write a C++ program that prints your name on one line, your street address on a second line, and your city, state, and zip code on the third line.
b. Run the program you have written for Exercise 1a on a computer. (*Note:* You must understand the procedures for entering and running a C++ program on the particular computer installation you are using.)

2. a. Write a C++ program to print out the following verse:

```
Computers, computers everywhere
  as far as I can see
I really, really like these things,
  Oh joy, Oh joy for me!
```

b. Run the program you have written for Exercise 2a on a computer.

3. a. How many cout statements would you use to print out the following:

```
PART NO.            PRICE

T1267               $6.34
T1300               $8.92
T2401               $65.40
T4482               $36.99
```

b. What is the minimum number of cout statements that could be used to print the table in Exercise 3a?
c. Write a complete C++ program to produce the output illustrated in Exercise 3a.
d. Run the program you have written for Exercise 3c on a computer.

4. In response to a newline escape sequence, cout positions the next displayed character at the beginning of a new line. This positioning of the next character actually represents two distinct operations. What are they?

5. a. Most computer operating systems provide the capability for redirecting the output produced by cout either to a printer or directly to a floppy or hard disk file. Read the first part of Appendix D for a description of this redirection capability.
b. If your computer supports output redirection, run the program written for Exercise 2a using this feature. Have your program's display redirected to a file named poem.
c. If your computer supports output redirection to a printer, run the program written for Exercise 2a using this feature.

1.4 Programming Style

C++ programs start execution at the beginning of the main function. Since a program can have only one starting point, every C++ language program must contain one and only one main function. As we have seen, all of the statements that make up the main function are then included within the braces { } following the function name. Although the main function must be present in every C++ program, C++ does not require that the word main, the parentheses (), or the braces { } be placed in any particular form. The form used in the last section

```
void main(void)
{
   program statements in here;
}
```

was chosen strictly for clarity and ease in reading the program.[5] For example, the following general form of a main() function would also work:

```
void main
(
void
) { first statement;second statement;
         third statement;fourth
statement;}
```

Notice that more than one statement can be put on a line, or one statement can be written across lines. Except for strings, double quotes, identifiers, and keywords, C++ ignores all whitespace (whitespace refers to any combination of one or more blank spaces, tabs, or newlines). For example, changing the

---

[5] If one of the program statements uses cout, the #include <iostream.h> preprocessor command would have to be used.

whitespace in Program 1-1 and making sure not to split the string `Hello there world!` across two lines results in the following valid program:

```
#include <iostream.h>
void main
(void
){
cout <<
"Hello there world!";
}
```

Although this version of `main` does work, it is an example of extremely poor programming style. It is difficult to read and understand. For readability, the `main` function should always be written in standard form as:[6]

```
void main(void)
{
   program statements in here;
}
```

In this standard form the function header line starts in column 1 and is placed on a line by itself. The opening brace of the function body follows on the next line and is placed under the first letter of the line containing the function name. Similarly, the closing function brace is placed by itself in column 1 as the last line of the function. This structure serves to highlight the function as a single unit.

Within the function itself, all program statements are indented at least two spaces. Indentation is another sign of good programming practice, especially if the same indentation is used for similar groups of statements. Review Program 1-2 to see that the same indentation was used for both `cout` object calls.

As you progress in your understanding and mastery of C++, you will develop your own indentation standards. Just keep in mind that the final form of your programs should be consistent and should always serve as an aid to the reading and understanding of your programs.

Comments

Comments are explanatory remarks made within a program. When used carefully, comments can be helpful in clarifying what the complete program is about, what a specific group of statements is meant to accomplish, or what one line is intended to do. C++ supports two types of comments: line and block. Both types of comments can be placed anywhere within a program and have no effect on program execution. The computer ignores all comments—they are there strictly for the convenience of anyone reading the program.

---

[6] If the `main` function returns an integer value to the operating system, the appropriate first line would be `int main(void)`. Similarly, data can be passed into `main` when the program is executed, as discussed in Appendix E.

A line comment begins with two slashes (//) and continues to the end of the line. For example,

```
// this is a comment
// this program prints out a message
// this program calculates a square root
```

are all comment lines. The symbols //, with no white space between them, designate the start of the line comment. The end of the line on which the comment is written designates the end of the comment.

A line comment can be written either on a line by itself or at the end of the same line containing a program statement. Program 1-4 illustrates the use of line comments within a program.

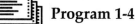

Program 1-4

```
#include <iostream.h>
void main(void)      // this program prints a message
{
  cout << "Hello there world!"; // a call to cout
}
```

The first comment appears on the same line as the function name and describes what the program does. This is generally a good location to include a short comment describing the program's purpose. If more comments are required, they can be placed, one per line, between the function name and the opening brace that encloses the function's statements. If a comment is too long to be contained on one line, it can be separated into two or more line comments, with each separate comment preceded by the double slash symbol set //. The comment

```
// this comment is invalid because it
    extends over two lines
```

will result in a C++ error message on your computer. This comment is correct when written as:

```
// this comment is used to illustrate a
// comment that extends across two lines
```

Comments that span across two or more lines are, however, more conveniently written as block comments rather than as multiple line comments. Block comments begin with the symbols /* and end with the symbols */. For example,

```
/* This is a block comment that
   spans
   across three lines */
```

In C++, a program's structure is intended to make the program readable and understandable, making the use of extensive comments unnecessary. This is reinforced if function, class, and variable names, described in the next chapter, are carefully selected to convey their meaning to anyone reading the program. However, if the purpose of a function, class, or statement is still not clear from its structure, name, or context, include comments where clarification is needed. When the program must be maintained or read by others, obscure code with no comments is a sure sign of bad programming. Similarly, excessive comments are also a sign of bad programming, because they imply that insufficient thought was given to making the code self-explanatory.

Exercises 1.4

1. a. Will the following program work?

```
#include <iostream.h>
void main(void){cout << "Hello there world!";}
```

b. Why is the program given in Exercise 1a not a good program?

2. Rewrite the following programs to conform to good programming practice:

a.
```
#include <iostream.h>
void main(void
){
cout             <<
"The time has come"
;}
```

b.
```
#include <iostream.h>
void main
(void){cout << "Newark is a city\n";cout <<
"In New Jersey\n"; cout <<
"It is also a city\n"
; cout << "In Delaware\n"
;}
```

c.
```
#include <iostream.h>
void main(void){cout << Reading a program\n";cout <<
"is much easier\n"
;cout << "if a standard form for main is used\n")
;cout
<<"and each statement is written\n";cout
<<          "on a line by itself\n")
;}
```

```
d. #include <iostream.h>
   void main
   (void){cout << "Every C++ program"
   ;cout
   <<"\nmust have one and only one"
   ;
   cout << "main function"
   ;
   cout <<
   "\n the escape sequence of characters")
   ;cout <<
   "\nfor a newline can be placed anywhere"
   ;cout
   <<"\n within the string passed to cout"
   ;}
```

3. a. When used in a message, the backslash character alters the meaning of the character immediately following it. If we wanted to print the backslash character, we would have to tell cout to escape from the way it normally interprets the backslash. What character do you think is used to alter the way a single backslash character is interpreted?

b. Using your answer to Exercise 3a, write the escape sequence for printing a backslash.

4. a. A token of a computer language is any sequence of characters that, as a unit, with no intervening characters or whitespace, has a unique meaning. Using this definition of a token, determine whether escape sequences, function names, and the keywords listed in Table 1–2 are tokens of the C++ language.

b. Discuss whether adding white space to a string alters the message. Discuss whether strings can be considered tokens of C++.

c. Using the definition of a token given in Exercise 4a, determine whether the statement "Except for tokens of the language, C++ ignores all whitespace" is true.

1.5 Common Programming Errors

Part of learning any programming language is making the elementary mistakes commonly encountered as you begin to use the language. These mistakes tend to be frustrating, since each language has its own set of common programming errors waiting for the unwary. The more common errors made when initially programming in C++ are:

1. Omitting the parentheses after main.
2. Omitting or incorrectly typing the opening brace { that signifies the start of a function body.
3. Omitting or incorrectly typing the closing brace } that signifies the end of a function.

4. Misspelling the name of an object or function; for example, typing `cot` instead of `cout`.

5. Forgetting to close a string sent to `cout` with a double quote symbol.

6. Omitting the semicolon at the end of each statement.

7. Forgetting the `\n` to indicate a newline.

Our experience is that the third, fifth, sixth and seventh errors in this list tend to be the most common. We suggest that you write a program and specifically introduce each of these errors, one at a time, to see what error messages are produced by your compiler. Then, when these error messages appear due to inadvertent errors, you will have had experience in understanding the messages and correcting the errors.

1.6 Chapter Summary

1. A C++ program consists of one or more modules. One of these modules must be the function `main`. The `main` function identifies the starting point of a C++ program.

2. The simplest C++ program consists of the single function `main` and has the form:

```
#include <iostream.h>
void main(void)
{
   program statements in here;
}
```

This program consists of a preprocessor `#include` statement, a header line for the `main` function, and the body of the `main` function. The body of the function begins with the opening left-facing brace, {, and ends with the terminating right-facing brace, }.

3. All C++ statements within a function body must be terminated by a semicolon.

4. Many functions and classes are supplied in a standard library provided with each C++ compiler. One such set of classes, which are used to create input and output capabilities, is defined in the header file `<iostream.h>`

5. The `cout` object is used to display text or numerical results. A stream of characters can be sent to cout by enclosing the characters in double quotes and using the insertion ("put to") operator, <<, as in the statement `cout << "Hello World!";`. The text in the string is displayed directly on the screen and may include newline escape sequences for format control.

Data Types, Declarations, and Displays

Chapter Two

C++ programs can process different types of data in different ways. For example, calculating the bacteria growth in a polluted pond requires mathematical operations on numerical data, while sorting a list of names requires comparison operations using alphabetical data. In this chapter we introduce C++'s elementary data types and the operations that can be performed on them. Additionally, we show how to use the `cout` object to display the results of these operations.

2.1 Data Constants

There are three basic data values used in C++: integer, floating point, and character. Each of these data values is described below.

Integer Values

An integer value is any zero, positive, or negative number without a decimal point. Examples of valid integer values are:

5   –10   +25   1000   253   –26351   +36

As these examples show, integers may be signed (have a leading + or – sign) or unsigned (no leading + or – sign). No commas, decimal points, or special symbols, such as the dollar sign, are allowed. Examples of invalid integer constants are:

$255.62   2,523   3.   6,243,892   1,492.89   +6.0

Different computer types have their own internal limit on the largest (most positive) and smallest (most negative) integer values that can be used in a program. These limits depend on the amount of storage each computer sets aside for an integer. The more commonly used storage allocations are listed in Table 2–1. (Review Section 2.8 if you are unfamiliar with the concept of a byte.) By referring to your computer's reference manual or using the `sizeof` operator introduced in Section 2.5, you can determine the actual number of bytes allocated by your computer for an integer value.[1] To store integer values greater than those supported by the memory allocations shown in Table 2–1 requires use of integer qualifiers. These qualifiers are described in Section 2.5.

---

[1] The limits imposed by the compiler can also be found in the `limits.h` header file. The values listed are in hexadecimal notation and are defined as the constants `INT_MAX` and `INT_MIN`.

TABLE 2–1 Integer Values and Byte Storage

Storage Area Reserved	Maximum Integer Value	Minimum Integer Value
1 byte	127	−128
2 bytes	32767	−32768
4 bytes	2147483647	−2147483648

Floating Point Numbers

A *floating point number*, which is also called a *real number*, is any signed or unsigned number having a decimal point. Examples of real numbers are:

+10.625   5.   −6.2   3251.92   0.0   0.33   −6.67   +2.

As with integers, special symbols, such as the dollar sign and the comma, are not permitted in real numbers. Examples of invalid real numbers are:

5,326.25   24   123   6,459 $10.29

C++ supports three different categories of floating point numbers: float, double, and long double. The difference between these numbers is the amount of storage that a computer uses for each type. Most computers use twice the amount of storage for doubles than for floats, which allows a double to have approximately twice the precision of a floating point number (for this reason floats are sometimes referred to as *single precision* numbers). Similarly, long double numbers typically use twice the storage used for doubles, with a consequent increase in precision. The actual storage allocation for each data type, however, depends on the particular computer. In computers that use the same amount of storage for double and single precision numbers, these two data types become identical. The same is true for long doubles. The sizeof operator introduced in Section 2.5 will allow you to determine the amount of storage reserved by your computer for each of these data types. A float number is indicated to the computer by appending either an F or f after the number and a long double is created by appending either an L or l to the number. In the absence of these suffixes, a floating point number is considered a double. For example:

9.234 indicates a double
9.234f indicates a float
9.234L indicates a long double

The only difference in these numbers is the amount of storage the computer may use to store them. For numbers having more decimal digits to the right of the decimal point, this storage becomes important. Appendix F describes the binary storage format typically used for real values and its impact on number precision. The exact difference, if any, in allocated storage is compiler dependent. The only requirement made by C++ is that a long double must provide at least the same precision as a double and that a double must provide at least the same precision as a float.

Exponential Notation

Floating point numbers can be written in exponential notation, which is commonly used to express either very large or very small numbers in compact form. The following examples illustrate how numbers with decimal points can be expressed in exponential notation.

Decimal Notation	Exponential Notation
1625.	$1.625e3$
63421.	$6.3421e4$
.00731	$7.31e{-}3$
.000625	$6.25e{-}4$

In exponential notation the letter e stands for exponent. The number following the *e* represents a power of 10 and indicates the number of places the decimal point should be moved to obtain the standard decimal value. The decimal point is moved to the right if the number after the *e* is positive, or moved to the left if the number after the *e* is negative. For example, the *e*3 in the number 1.625*e*3 means move the decimal place three places to the right, so that the number becomes 1625. The *e*–3 in the number 7.31*e*–3 means move the decimal point three places to the left, so that 7.31*e*–3 becomes .00731.

Character Constants

The third basic type of value recognized by C++ is characters. Characters include the letters of the alphabet, the ten digits 0 through 9, and special symbols such as + $. , – !. A *character constant* is any one letter, digit, or special symbol enclosed by single quotes. Examples of valid character constants are:

'A'   '$'   'b'   '7'   'y'   '!'   'M'   'q'

Character constants are typically stored in a computer using either the ASCII or EBCDIC codes. ASCII, pronounced "as-key," is an acronym for American Standard Code for Information Interchange. EBCDIC, pronounced either "ebb-sah-dick" or "ebb-see-dick," is an acronym for Extended Binary Coded Decimal Interchange Code. Each of these codes assigns individual characters to a specific pattern of 0s and 1s. Table 2–2 lists the correspondence between bit patterns and the uppercase letters of the alphabet used by the ASCII and EBCDIC codes.

TABLE 2–2   The ASCII Uppercase Letter Codes

Letter	ASCII	EBCDIC	Letter	ASCII	EBCDIC
A	01000001	11000001	N	01001110	11010101
B	01000010	11000010	O	01001111	11010110
C	01000011	11000011	P	01010000	11010111
D	01000100	11000100	Q	01010001	11011000
E	01000101	11000101	R	01010010	11011001
F	01000110	11000110	S	01010011	11100010
G	01000111	11000111	T	01010100	11100011
H	01001000	11001000	U	01010101	11100100
I	01001001	11001001	V	01010110	11100101
J	01001010	11010001	W	01010111	11100110
K	01001011	11010010	X	01011000	11100111
L	01001100	11010011	Y	01011001	11101000
M	01001101	11010100	Z	01011010	11101001

Using Table 2–2, we can determine how the character constants 'M', 'I', 'X', 'T', 'E', and 'R', for example, are stored inside a computer that uses the ASCII character code. Using the ASCII code, this sequence of characters requires six bytes of storage (one byte for each letter) and would be stored as illustrated in Figure 2–1.

Escape Sequences

When a backslash (\) is used directly in front of a select group of characters, the backslash tells the computer to escape from the way these characters would normally be interpreted. For this reason, the combination of a backslash and these specific characters are called escape sequences. We have already encountered an example of this in the newline escape sequence, \n. Table 2–3 lists C++'s most commonly used escape sequences.

FIGURE 2–1   The Letters MIXTER Stored Inside a Computer

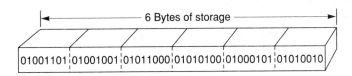

TABLE 2–3   Escape Sequences

Escape Sequence	Meaning
\b	move back one space
\f	move to next page
\n	move to next line
\r	carriage return
\t	move to next tab setting
\\	backslash character
\'	single quote
\"	double quotes

Although each escape sequence listed in Table 2–3 is made up of two distinct characters, the combination of the two characters with no intervening white-space causes the computer to store one character code. Table 2–4 lists the ASCII code byte patterns for the escape sequences listed in Table 2–3.

TABLE 2–4   The ASCII Escape Sequence Codes

C++ Escape Sequence	Meaning	Computer Code
\b	backspace	00001000
\f	form feed	00001100
\n	new line	00001010
\r	carriage return	00001101
\\	backslash	01011100
\'	single quote	00100111
\"	double quote	00100010

Exercises 2.1

1. Determine data types appropriate for the following data:
  a. the average of four grades
  b. the number of days in a month
  c. the length of the Golden Gate Bridge
  d. the numbers in a state lottery
  e. the distance from Brooklyn, N.Y. to Newark, N.J.

2. Convert the following numbers into standard decimal form:

$$6.34e5 \qquad 1.95162e2 \qquad 8.395e1 \qquad 2.95e{-}3 \qquad 4.623e{-}4$$

3. Convert the following decimal numbers into exponential notation:

$$126. \qquad 656.23 \qquad 3426.95 \qquad 4893.2 \qquad .321 \qquad .0123 \qquad .006789$$

4. Using the system reference manuals for your computer, determine the character code used by your computer.

5. *a.* Using the EBCDIC code, determine the number of bytes required to store the letters KINGSLEY.
   b. Show how the letters KINGSLEY would be stored inside a computer that uses the EBCDIC code. That is, draw a figure similar to Figure 2–1 for the letters KINGSLEY.

6. *a.* Repeat Exercise 5a using the ASCII code.
   b. Repeat Exercise 5b using the ASCII code.

7. *a.* Repeat Exercise 6a using the letters of your own last name.
   b. Repeat Exercise 6b using the letters of your own last name.

8. Since most computers use different amounts of storage for integer, floating point, double precision, and character values, discuss how a program might alert the computer to the amount of storage needed for the various data types in the program.

9. Although the total number of bytes varies from computer to computer, memory sizes of 65,536 to more than several million bytes are not uncommon. In computer language, the letter K is used to represent the number 1024, which is 2 raised to the 10th power. Thus, a memory size of 64K is really 64 times 1024, or 65,536 bytes, and a memory size of 512K consists of 512 times 1024, or 524,288 bytes. Using this information, calculate the actual number of bytes in:
   a. a memory containing 64K bytes
   b. a memory containing 128K bytes
   c. a memory containing 192 bytes
   d. a memory containing 256 bytes
   e. a memory consisting of 64K words, where each word consists of 2 bytes
   f. a memory consisting of 64K words, where each word consists of 4 bytes
   g. a floppy diskette that can store 360K bytes

2.2 Arithmetic Operators

Integers and real numbers may be added, subtracted, divided, and multiplied. Although it is usually better not to mix integers and real numbers when performing arithmetic operations, predictable results are obtained when different data types are used in the same arithmetic expression. Somewhat surprising is the fact that character data can also be added and subtracted with both character and integer data to produce useful results.

The operators used for arithmetic operations are called arithmetic operators and are listed below:

Operation	Operator
Addition	+
Subtraction	−
Multiplication	*
Division	/
Modulus	%

A *simple arithmetic expression* consists of an arithmetic operator connecting two operands of the form:

```
operand operator operand
```

Examples of simple arithmetic expressions are:

$$3 + 7$$
$$18 - 3$$
$$12.62 + 9.8$$
$$.08 * 12.2$$
$$12.6 / 2.$$

The spaces around the arithmetic operators in these examples are inserted strictly for clarity and may be omitted without affecting the value of the expression. When evaluating simple arithmetic expressions, the data type of the result is determined by the following rules:

1. If both operands are integers, the result is an integer.
2. If any operand is a floating point value, the result is a floating point value.

An expression that contains only integer operands is called an *integer expression*, and the result of the expression is an integer value (Rule 1). Similarly, an expression containing only floating point operands is called a *floating point* or *real expression*, and the result of the expression is a floating point value (Rule 2). An arithmetic expression containing both integer and noninteger operands is called a *mixed-mode* expression. The result of a mixed-mode expression is always a floating point value (Rule 2).

It is worth noting that the arithmetic operations of addition, subtraction, multiplication, and division are implemented differently for integer and floating point values. Specifically, whether an integer or floating point arithmetic operation is performed depends on what types of operands (integer or floating point) are contained in the arithmetic expression. In this sense, the arithmetic operators are considered to be overloaded. More formally, an *overloaded operator* is a symbol that represents more than one operation and whose execution depends on the types of operands encountered. Although the overloaded nature of the arithmetic operators is rather simple, we will encounter the concept of overloading many more times in our journey through C++.

Integer Division

The division of two integers can produce rather strange results for the unwary. For example, dividing the integer 15 by the integer 2 yields an integer result. Since integers cannot contain a fractional part, a result such as 7.5 cannot be obtained. In C++, the fractional part of the result obtained when dividing two integers is dropped (truncated). Thus, the value of 15/2 is 7, the value of 9/4 is 2, and the value of 17/5 is 3.

There are times when we would like to retain the remainder of an integer division. To do this C++ provides a nonoverloaded arithmetic operator that is only implemented for integers. This operator, called the modulus operator, has the symbol %, and is used to capture the remainder when two integers are divided. For example,

$$9 \% 4 \text{ is } 1$$
$$17 \% 3 \text{ is } 2$$
$$14 \% 2 \text{ is } 0$$

Negation

Besides the binary operators for addition, subtraction, multiplication, and division, C++ also provides unary operators. One of these unary operators uses the same symbol that is used for binary subtraction (–). The minus sign used in front of a single numerical operand negates (reverses the sign of) the number.

Table 2–5 summarizes the six arithmetic operations we have described so far and lists the data type of the result produced by each operator based on the data type of the operands involved.

Operator Precedence and Associativity

Besides such simple expressions as 5 + 12 and .08 * 26.2, we frequently need to create more complex arithmetic expressions. C++, like most other programming languages, requires that certain rules be followed when writing expressions containing more than one arithmetic operator. These rules are:

1. Two binary arithmetic operator symbols must never be placed side by side.

   For example, 5 * %6 is invalid because the two operators * and % are placed next to each other.
2. Parentheses may be used to form groupings, and all expressions enclosed within parentheses are evaluated first.

   For example, in the expression (6 + 4) / (2 + 3), the 6 + 4 and 2 + 3 are evaluated first to yield 10 / 5. The 10 / 5 is then evaluated to yield 2.

   Sets of parentheses may also be enclosed by other parentheses. For example, the expression (2 * (3 + 7)) / 5 is valid. When parentheses are used within parentheses, the expressions in the innermost parentheses are always evaluated first. The evaluation continues from innermost to outermost parentheses until

TABLE 2-5 Summary of Arithmetic Operators

Operation	Operator	Type	Operand	Result
Addition	+	Binary	Both integers	Integer
			One operand not an integer	Floating point
Subtraction	−	Binary	Both integers	Integer
			One operand not an integer	Floating point
Multiplication	*	Binary	Both integers	Integer
			One operand not an integer	Floating point
Division	/	Binary	Both integers	Integer
			One operand not an integer	Floating point
Remainder	%	Binary	Both integers	Integer
Negation	−	Unary	Integer	Integer
			Floating point	Floating point

the expressions of all parentheses have been evaluated. The number of right-facing parentheses, (, must always equal the number of left-facing parentheses,), so that there are no unpaired sets.

3. Parentheses cannot be used to indicate multiplication. The multiplication operator, *, must be used.

For example, the expression (3 + 4) (5 + 1) is invalid. The correct expression is (3 + 4) * (5 + 1).

Parentheses should be used to specify logical groupings of operands and to indicate clearly to both the computer and programmers the intended order of arithmetic operations. In the absence of parentheses, expressions containing multiple operators are evaluated by the priority, or precedence, of the operators. Table 2-6 lists both the precedence and associativity of the operators considered in this section.

The precedence of an operator establishes its priority relative to all other operators. Operators at the top of Table 2-6 have a higher priority than operators at the bottom of the table. In expressions with multiple operators, the operator with the higher precedence is used before an operator with a lower precedence. For example, in the expression 6 + 4 / 2 + 3, the division is done before the addition, yielding an intermediate result of 6 + 2 + 3. The additions are then performed to yield a final result of 11.

TABLE 2–6 Operator Precedence
and Associativity

Operator	Associativity
unary −	right to left
* / %	left to right
+ −	left to right

Expressions containing operators with the same precedence are evaluated according to their associativity. This means that evaluation is either from left to right or from right to left as each operator is encountered. For example, in the expression 8 + 5 * 7 % 2 * 4, the multiplication and modulus operator are of higher precedence than the addition operator and are evaluated first. Both of these operators, however, are of equal priority. Therefore, these operators are evaluated according to their left-to-right associativity, yielding

$$8 + 5 * 7 \% 2 * 4 =$$
$$8 + 35 \% 2 * 4 =$$
$$8 + 1 * 4 =$$
$$8 + 4 = 12$$

Exercises 2.2

1. Following are algebraic expressions and incorrect C++ expressions corresponding to them. Find the errors and write corrected C++ expressions.

Algebra	*C++ Expression*
a. (2)(3) + (4)(5)	(2)(3) + (4)(5)
b. $\dfrac{6 + 18}{2}$	6 + 18 / 2
c. $\dfrac{4.5}{12.2 - 3.1}$	4.5 / 12.2 − 3.1
d. 4.6(3.0 + 14.9)	4.6(3.0 + 14.9)
e. (12.1 + 18.9)(15.3 − 3.8)	(12.1 + 18.9)(15.3 − 3.8)

2. Assuming that amount = 1, $m = 50$, $n = 10$, and $p = 5$, evaluate the following expressions:

a. $n / p + 3$

b. $m / p + n - 10 * $ amount

c. $m - 3 * n + 4 * $ amount

d. amount $/ 5$

e. $18 / p$

f. $18 \% p$

g. $-p * n$

h. $-m / 20$

i. $-m \% 20$

j. $(m + n) / (p + $ amount$)$

k. $m + n / p + $ amount

3. Repeat Exercise 2 assuming that amount = 1.0, $m = 50.0$, $n = 10.0$, and $p = 5.0$.

4. Determine the value of the following integer expressions:

    a. 3 + 4 * 6

    b. 3 * 4 / 6 + 6

    c. 2 * 3 / 12 * 8 / 4

    d. 10 * (1 + 7 * 3)

    e. 20 − 2 / 6 + 3

    f. 20 − 2 / (6 + 3)

    g. (20 − 2) / 6 + 3

    h. (20 − 2) / (6 + 3)

5. Determine the value of the following floating point expressions:

    a. 3.0 + 4.0 * 6.0

    b. 3.0 * 4.0 / 6.0 + 6.0

    c. 2.0 * 3.0 / 12.0 * 8.0 / 4.0

    d. 10.0 * (1.0 + 7.0 * 3.0)

    e. 20.0 − 2.0 / 6.0 + 3.0

    f. 20.0 − 2.0 / (6.0 + 3.0)

    g. (20.0 − 2.0) / 6.0 + 3.0

    h. (20.0 − 2.0) / (6.0 + 3.0)

6. Evaluate the following expressions and list the data type of the result. In evaluating the expressions be aware of the data types of all intermediate calculations.

    a. 10.0 + 15 / 2 + 4.3

    b. 10.0 + 15 % 2 + 4.3

    c. 10.0 + 15.0 / 2 + 4.3

    d. 3.0 * 4 / 6 + 6

    e. 3.0 * 4 % 6 + 6

    f. 3 * 4.0 / 6 + 6

    g. 20.0 − 2 / 6 + 3

    h. 10 + 17 % 3 + 4

    i. 10 + 17 % 3 + 4.

    j. 10 + 17 / 3. + 4

2.3 Numerical Output Using cout

In addition to displaying strings, the cout object allows us to display the numerical result of an expression on the standard output device. To do this we must pass the desired value to cout. For example, the statement

```
cout << (6 + 15);
```

yields the display 21. Strictly speaking, the parentheses surrounding the expression 6 + 15 are required to indicate that it is the value of the expression, which is 21, that is being placed on the output stream. In practice most compilers will accept and correctly process this statement without the parentheses.

In addition to displaying a numerical value, a string identifying the output can also be displayed by passing the string to cout as we did in Chapter 1. For example, the statement:

```
cout << "The total of 6 and 15 is " <<  (6 + 15);
```

causes two pieces of data to be sent to cout, a string and a value. Individually, each set of data is sent to the cout preceded by its own insertion symbol (<<). Here, the first data sent to the stream is the string "The total of 6 and 15 is ", and the second item stream is the value of the expression 6 + 15. The display produced by this statement is:

```
The total of 6 and 15 is 21
```

Notice that the space between the word is and the number 21 is caused by the space placed within the string passed to cout. As far as cout is concerned, its input is simply a set of characters that are then sent on to be displayed in the order they are received. Characters from the input are queued, one behind the other, and sent to an output stream for display. Placing a space in the input causes this space to be part of the output stream that is ultimately displayed. For example, the statement

```
cout << "The sum of 12.2 and 15.754 is " <<  (12.2 + 15.754);
```

yields the display

```
The sum of 12.2 and 15.754 is 27.954
```

Note that insertion of data into the output stream can be made over multiple lines and is only terminated by a semicolon. Thus, the prior display is also produced by the statement

```
cout << "The sum of 12.2 and 15.754 is "
     <<  (12.2 + 15.754);
```

The requirements for using multiple lines are that a string contained within double quotes cannot be split across lines and that the terminating semicolon appear only on the last line. Within a line multiple insertion symbols can be used.

As the last display indicates, floating point numbers are displayed with sufficient decimal places to the right of the decimal place to accommodate the fractional part of the number. This is true if the number has six or fewer decimal digits. If the number has more than six decimal digits, the fractional part is rounded to six decimal digits, and if the number has no decimal digits, neither a decimal point nor any decimal digits are displayed.[2]

Character data can also be displayed using cout. For example, the statement

```
cout << "The first letter of the alphabet is an " << 'a';
```

causes the display

```
The first letter of the alphabet is an a
```

Program 2-1 illustrates using cout to display the results of an expression within the statements of a complete program.

---

[2] Note that none of this output is defined as part of the C++ language. Rather, it is defined by a set of classes and routines provided with each C++ compiler.

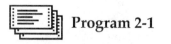 **Program 2-1**

```
#include <iostream.h>
void main(void)
{
  cout << "15.0 plus 2.0 equals " << (15.0 + 2.0) << '\n'
       << "15.0 minus 2.0 equals " << (15.0 - 2.0) << '\n'
       << "15.0 times 2.0 equals " << (15.0 * 2.0) << '\n'
       << "15.0 divided by 2.0 equals " << (15.0 / 2.0) << '\n';
}
```

The output of Program 2-1 is:

```
15.0 plus 2.0 equals 17
15.0 minus 2.0 equals 13
15.0 times 2.00 equals 30
15.0 divided by 2.0 equals 7.5
```

Formatted Output[3]

The format of numbers displayed by cout can be controlled by field width manipulators included in each output stream. Table 2–7 lists the most commonly used manipulators available for this purpose.

For example, the statement

```
cout << "The sum of 6 and 15 is" << setw(3) << 21;
```

TABLE 2–7   Commonly Used Stream Manipulators

Manipulator	Action
setw(n)	Set the field width to *n*
setprecision(n)	Set the floatingpoint precision to *n* places
setiosflags(flags)	Set the format flags (see Table 2–9 for flag settings)
dec	Set output for decimal display
hex	Set output for hexadecimal display
oct	Set output for octal display

---

[3] The material in this section may be omitted on first reading with no loss of subject continuity.

causes the printout

The sum of 6 and 15 is 21

The setw(3) field width manipulator included in the stream of data passed to cout is used to set the displayed field width. The 3 in this manipulator sets the default field width for the next number in the stream to be three spaces wide. This field width setting causes the 21 to be printed in a field of three spaces, which includes one blank and the number 21. As illustrated, integers are right-justified within the specified field.

Field width manipulators are useful in printing columns of numbers so that the numbers in each column align correctly. For example, Program 2-2 illustrates how a column of integers would align in the absence of field width manipulators.

 Program 2-2

```
#include <iostream.h>
void main(void)
{
  cout << '\n' << 6
       << '\n' << 18
       << '\n' << 124
       << "\n---"
       << '\n'<< (6+18+124);
}
```

The output of Program 2-2 is

```
  6
 18
124
---
148
```

Since no field width manipulators are given, the cout object allocates enough space for each number as it is received. To force the numbers to align on the units digit requires a field width wide enough for the largest displayed number. For Program 2-2, a width of three suffices. The use of this field width is illustrated in Program 2-3.

Program 2-3

```
#include <iostream.h>
#include <iomanip.h>
void main(void)
{
  cout << '\n' << setw(3) << 6
       << '\n' << setw(3) << 18
       << '\n' << setw(3) << 124
       << "\n---"
       << '\n'<< setw(3) << (6+18+124);
}
```

The output of Program 2-3 is:

```
  6
 18
124
---
148
```

Notice that the field width manipulator must be included for each occurrence of a number inserted into the data stream sent to cout, and that the manipulator only applies to the next insertion of data immediately following it. Also notice that if manipulators are to be included within an output display, the iomanip.h header file must be included as part of the program. This is accomplished by the preprocessor command #include <iomanip.h>.

Formatted floating point numbers require the use of two field width manipulators. The first manipulator sets the total width of the display, including the decimal point; the second manipulator determines how many digits can be printed to the right of the decimal point. For example, the statement

```
cout << '|' << setw(10) << setprecision(3) << 25.67 << '|';
```

causes the printout

```
|     25.67|
```

The bar symbol, |, in the example is used to mark the beginning and end of the display field. The setw manipulator tells cout to display the number in a total field of 10, while the setprecision manipulator tells cout to display a maximum of three digits to the right of the decimal point. Since the number contains only two digits to the right of the decimal point, only two decimal digits are displayed.

For all numbers (integers, floating point, and double precision), cout ignores the setw manipulator specification if the total specified field width is too small, and allocates enough space for the integer part of the number to be printed. The fractional part of both floating point and double precision numbers is displayed up to the precision set with the setprecision manipulator (in the absence of a setprecision manipulator, the default precision is set to 6 decimal places). If the fractional part of the number to be displayed contains more digits than called for in the setprecision manipulator, the number is rounded to the indicated number of decimal places; if the fractional part contains fewer digits than specified, the number is displayed with the fewer digits. Table 2–8 illustrates the effect of various format manipulator combinations. Again, for clarity, the bar symbol, |, is used to clearly delineate the beginning and end of the output fields.

In addition to the setw and setprecision manipulators, a field justification manipulator is also available. As we have seen, numbers sent to cout are normally displayed right-justified in the display field, while strings are displayed left-justified. To alter the default justification for a stream of data, the setiosflags manipulator can be used. For example, the statement

```
cout << '|' << setw(10) << setiosflags(ios::left) << 142 << '|';
```

causes the following left-justified display:

|142 |

TABLE 2–8   Effect of Format Manipulators

Manipulators	Number	Display	Comments
setw(2)	3	| 3|	Number fits in field
setw(2)	43	|43|	Number fits in field
setw(2)	143	|143|	Field width ignored
setw(2)	2.3	| 2.3|	Field width ignored
setw(5) setprecision(2)	2.366	| 2.37|	Field width of 5 with 2 decimal digits
setw(5) setprecision(2)	42.3	| 42.3|	Number fits in field
setw(5) setprecision(2)	142.364	|142.36|	Field width ignored but precision specification used
setw(5) setprecision(2)	142.366	|142.37|	Field width ignored but precision specification used
setw(5) setprecision(2)	142	| 142|	Field width used, precision irrelevant

As we have previously seen, since data passed to cout may be continued across multiple lines, the previous display would also be produced by the statement

```
cout << '|' << setw(5)
        << setiosflags(ios::left)
        << 142 << '|';
```

As always, the field width manipulator is only in effect for the next single set of data passed to cout. Right-justification for strings in a stream is obtained by the manipulator setiosflags(ios::right).

In addition to the left and right flags that can be used with the setiosflags() manipulator, other flags may also be used to affect the output. The most commonly used flags for this manipulator are listed in Table 2–9.

For example, the output stream

```
cout << setiosflags(ios::showpoint) << setprecision(4)
```

forces the next number sent to the output stream to be displayed with a decimal point and four decimal digits. If the number has less than four decimal digits it will be padded with trailing zeros.

In addition to outputting integers in decimal notation, the ios::oct and ios::hex flags permit conversions to octal and hexadecimal, respectively. Program 2-4 illustrates the use of these flags. Since decimal is the default display, the dec manipulator is not required in the first output stream.

TABLE 2–9 Format Flags for Use with setiosflags()

Flag	Meaning
ios::showpoint	Always show the decimal point with a default of 6 decimal digits
ios::showpos	Display a leading + sign when the number is positive
ios::fixed	Display up to 3 integer digits and 2 digits after the decimal point. For larger integer values revert to exponential notation
ios::scientific	Use exponential display on output
ios::dec	Display in decimal format
ios::oct	Display in octal format
ios::hex	Display in hexadecimal format
ios::left	Left-justify output
ios::right	Right-justify output

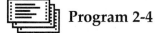 **Program 2-4**

```
#include <iostream.h>
#include <iomanip.h>
void main(void) // a program to illustrate output conversions
{
  cout << "The decimal (base 10) value of 15 is " << 15
       << "\nThe octal (base 8) value of 15 is "
       << setiosflags(ios::oct) << 15
       << "\nThe hexadecimal (base 16) value of 15 is "
       << setiosflags(ios::hex) << 15;
}
```

The output produced by Program 2-4 is:

```
The decimal (base 10) value of 15 is 15
The octal (base 8) value of 15 is 17
The hexadecimal (base 16) value of 15 is f
```

In place of the conversion flags ios::dec, ios::oct, and ios::hex, three simpler manipulators, dec, oct, and hex are provided in <iostream.h>. These simpler manipulators, unlike their longer counterparts, leave the conversion base set for all subsequent output streams. Using these simpler manipulators, Program 2-4 can be rewritten as:

```
#include <iostream.h>
void main(void)  // a program to illustrate output conversions
{
  cout << "The decimal (base 10) value of 15 is " << 15
       << "\nThe octal (base 8) value of 15 is " << oct << 15
       << "\nThe hexadecimal (base 16) value of 15 is " << hex
       << 15;
}
```

The display of integer values in one of the three possible number systems (decimal, octal, and hexadecimal) does not affect how the number is actually stored inside a computer. All numbers are stored using the computer's own internal codes. The manipulators sent to cout simply tell the object how to convert the internal code for output display purposes.

Besides displaying integers in octal or hexadecimal form, integer constants can also be written in a program in these forms. To designate an octal integer constant, the number must have a leading zero. The number 023, for example, is an octal number in C++. Hexadecimal numbers are denoted using a leading 0x. The use of octal and hexadecimal integer constants is illustrated in Program 2-5.

Program 2-5

```
#include <iostream.h>
void main(void)
{
   cout << "\nThe decimal value of 025 is " << 025
        << "\nThe decimal value of 0x37 is "<< 0x37;
}
```

When Program 2-5 is run, the following output is obtained:

```
The decimal value of 025 is 21
The decimal value of 0x37 is 55
```

The relationship between the input, storage, and display of integers is illustrated in Figure 2–2.

FIGURE 2–2 Input, Storage, and Display of Integers

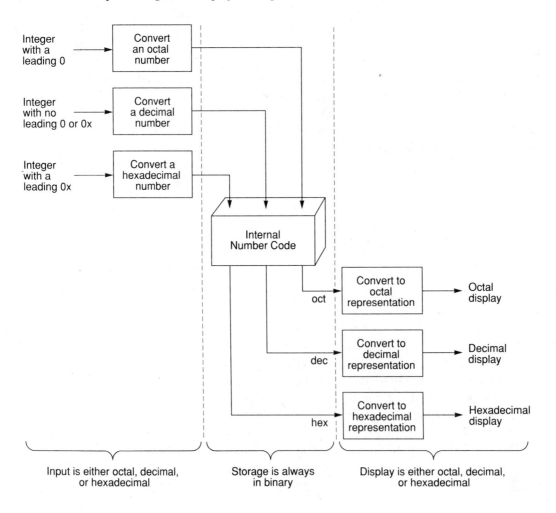

Exercises 2.3

1. Determine the output of the following program:

```
#include <iostream.h>
void main(void)   // a program illustrating integer truncation
{
   cout << "answer1 is the integer " << 9/4
        << "\nanswer2 is the integer " << 17/3;
}
```

2. Determine the output of the following program:

```
#include <iostream.h>
void main(void)   // a program illustrating the % operator
{
   cout << "The remainder of 9 divided by 4 is " << 9 % 4
        << "\nThe remainder of 17 divided by 3 is " << 17 % 3;
}
```

3. Write a C++ program that displays the results of the expressions 3.0 * 5.0, 7.1 * 8.3 – 2.2, and 3.2 / (6.1 * 5). Calculate the value of these expressions manually to verify that the displayed values are correct.

4. Write a C++ program that displays the results of the expressions 15 / 4, 15 % 4, and 5 * 3 – (6 * 4). Calculate the value of these expressions manually to verify that the display produced by your program is correct.

5. Determine the errors in each of the following statements:
   a. cout << "\n << " 15)
   b. cout << "setw(4)" << 33;
   c. cout << "setprecision(5)" << 526.768;
   d. "Hello World!" >> cout;
   e. cout << 47 << setw(6);
   f. cout << set(10) << 526.768 << setprecision(2);

6. Determine and write out the display produced by the following statements:
   a. cout << '|' << 5 <<'|';
   b. cout << '|' << setw(4) << 5 << '|';
   c. cout << '|' << setw(4) << 56829 << '|';
   d. cout << '|' << setw(5) << setprecision(2) << 5.26 << '|';
   e. cout << '|' << setw(5) << setprecision(2) << 5.267 << '|';
   f. cout << '|' << setw(5) << setprecision(2) << 53.264 << '|';
   g. cout << '|' << setw(5) << setprecision(2) << 534.264 << '|';
   h. cout << '|' << setw(5) << setprecision(2) << 534. << '|';

7. Write out the display produced by the following statements:
   a. cout << "\nThe number is " << setw(6)
            << setprecision(2) << 26.27;
       cout << "\nThe number is " << setw(6)
            << setprecision(2) << 682.3;
       cout << "\nThe number is " << setw(6)
            << setprecision(2) << 1.968;

b. cout << '\n' << setw(6) << setprecision(2) << 26.27;
   cout << '\n' << setw(6) << setprecision(2) << 682.3;
   cout << '\n' << setw(6) << setprecision(2) << 1.968;
   cout << "\n--------";
   cout << '\n' << setw(6) << setprecision(2)
       << 27.27 + 682.3 + 1.968;
c. cout << '\n' << setw(5) << setprecision(2) << 26.27;
   cout << '\n' << setw(5) << setprecision(2) << 682.3;
   cout << '\n' << setw(5) << setprecision(2) << 1.968;
   cout << "\n--------";
   cout << '\n' << setw(5) << setprecision(2)
       << 27.27 + 682.3 + 1.968;
d. cout << '\n' << setw(5) << setprecision(2) << 36.164;
   cout << '\n' << setw(5) << setprecision(2) << 10.003;
   cout << "\n-----";

8. The following table lists the correspondence between the decimal numbers 1 through 15 and their octal and hexadecimal representation:

Decimal:	1	2	3	4	5	6	7	8	9	10	11	12	13	14	15
Octal:	1	2	3	4	5	6	7	10	11	12	13	14	15	16	17
Hexadecimal:	1	2	3	4	5	6	7	8	9	A	B	C	D	E	F

Using the above table, determine the output of the following program:

```
#include <iostream.h>
#include <iomanip.h>
void main(void)
{
  cout << "\nThe value of 14 in octal is " << oct << 14
       << "\nThe value of 14 in hexadecimal is " << hex << 14
       << "\nThe value of 0xA in decimal is " << dec << 0xA
       << "\nThe value of 0xA in octal is " << oct << 0xA;
}
```

2.4 Variables and Declarations

All integers, real numbers, and other values used in a computer program are stored and retrieved from the computer's memory unit. Conceptually, individual memory locations in the memory unit are arranged like the rooms in a large hotel. Like hotel rooms, each memory location has a unique address ("room number"). Before high-level languages existed, memory locations were referenced by their address. For example, to store the integer values 62 and 17 in memory locations 1321 and 2649 (see Figure 2–3), respectively, required instructions equivalent to

put a 62 in location 1321
put a 17 in location 2649

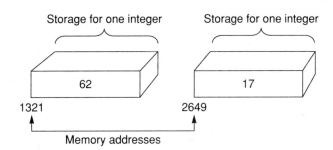

FIGURE 2–3   Enough Storage for Two Integers

To add the two numbers just stored and save the result in another set of memory locations, for example at location 45, required a statement comparable to

add the contents of location 1321
to the contents of location 2649
and store the result in location 45

Clearly this method of storage and retrieval is a cumbersome process. In higher-level languages like C++, symbolic names are used in place of actual memory addresses. Symbolic names used in this manner are called *variables*. A variable is simply a name given by the programmer that is used to refer to computer storage locations. The term variable is used because the value stored in the variable can change, or vary. For each name that the programmer uses, the computer keeps track of the actual addresses. In a hotel room analogy, this is equivalent to putting a name on the door of a hotel room and referring to the room (or suite of rooms) by this name, such as the Blue Room, rather than using the actual room number.

In C++ the selection of variable names is left to the programmer, as long as the variable name is chosen according to the rules given for selecting identifiers in Section 1.2. Thus, a variable name can consist of any number of letters, digits, or underscores, the first of which must be a letter or underscore, and cannot be a keyword (Table 1–2).

As with all identifier names, variable names should be mnemonics that give some indication of the variable's use. For example, a variable named `total` indicates that this variable will probably be used to store a value that is the total of some other values. As with function names, all variable names are typed in lowercase letters. This again is traditional in C++, although not required.

Now assume that the first memory location previously illustrated in Figure 2–3, which has address 1321, is given the variable name `num1`. Also assume that memory location 2649 is given the variable name `num2` and that memory location 45 has been given the name `result`, as illustrated in Figure 2–4.

Using these variable names, the operation of storing 62 in location 1321, storing 17 in location 2649, and adding the contents of these two locations is accomplished by the C++ statements

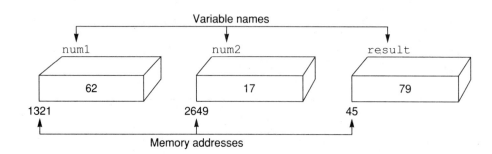

FIGURE 2–4 Giving Storage Locations Names

```
num1 = 62;
num2 = 17;
result = num1 + num2;
```

These statements are called *assignment statements* because they tell the computer to assign (store) a value into a variable. Assignment statements always have an equal (=) sign and at least one variable name immediately to the left of this sign. The value on the right of the equal sign is determined first and this value is assigned to the variable immediately to the left of the equal sign. The blank spaces in the assignment statements are inserted for readability. We will have much more to say about assignment statements in the next chapter, but for now we can use them to store values in variables.

A variable name is useful because it frees the programmer from concern over where data is physically stored inside the computer. We simply use the variable names and let the computer worry about where in memory the data is actually stored. Before storing values into variables, however, C++ requires that we clearly declare the type of data that will be stored in each variable. We must tell the computer, in advance, the names of the variables that will be used for characters, the names that will be used for integers, and the names that will be used to store the other data types supported by C++.

Declaration Statements

Naming and defining the data type that can be stored in each variable is accomplished by using *declaration statements*. A declaration statement for variables has the general form:

data-type variable-name;

where `data-type` designates a valid C++ data type and `variable-name` is a user-selected variable name. For example, variables used to hold integer values are declared using the keyword `int` to specify the data type and have the form:

`int` *variable-name;*

Thus, the declaration statement

```
int total;
```

declares `total` as the name of a variable capable of storing an integer value. Variables used to hold single precision floating point values are declared using the keyword `float`, variables that will be used to hold double precision values are declared using the keyword `double`, and long doubles are declared by using the keywords `long double`. For example, the statement

```
float firstnum;
```

declares `firstnum` as a variable that can be used to store a floating point number. Similarly, the statement

```
double secnum:
```

declares that the variable `secnum` will be used to store a double precision number and the declaration

```
long double thirdnum
```

declares that the variable `thirdnum` will be used to store a long double value.

Although declaration statements may be placed anywhere within a function, most declarations are typically grouped together and placed immediately after the function's opening brace. In all cases, however, a variable must be declared before it can be used, and like all C++ statements, declaration statements must end with a semicolon. If the declaration statements are placed after the opening function brace, a simple `main` function containing declaration statements would have the general form

```
#include <iostream.h>
void main(void)
{
    declaration statements;

    other statements;
}
```

Program 2-6 illustrates this form in declaring and using four floating point variables, with the `cout` object used to display the contents of one of the variables.

Program 2-6

```
#include <iostream.h>
void main(void)
{
  float grade1;   // declare grade1 as a float variable
  float grade2;   // declare grade2 as a float variable
  float total;    // declare total as a float variable
  float average;  // declare average as a float variable

  grade1 = 85.5;
  grade2 = 97.0;
  total = grade1 + grade2;
  average = total/2.0;  // divide the total by 2.0
  cout << "\nThe average grade is " << average;
}
```

The placement of the declaration statements in Program 2-6 is straightforward, although we will shortly see that the four individual declarations can be combined into a single declaration. When Program 2-6 is run, the following output is displayed:

        The average grade is 91.25

Notice that when a variable name is sent to cout, the value stored in the variable is placed on the output stream and displayed.

Just as integer and real (floating point, double precision, and long double) variables must be declared before they can be used, a variable used to store a single character must also be declared. Character variables are declared using the reserved word char. For example, the declaration

                char ch;

declares ch to be a character variable. Program 2-7 illustrates this declaration and the use of cout to display the value stored in a character variable.

Program 2-7

```
#include <iostream.h>
void main(void)
{
  char ch;       // this declares a character variable

  ch = 'a';      // store the letter a into ch
  cout << "\nThe character stored in ch is " << ch;
  ch = 'm';      // now store the letter m into ch
  cout << "\nThe character now stored in ch is "<< ch;
}
```

When Program 2-7 is run, the output produced is:

```
The character stored in ch is a
The character now stored in ch is m
```

Notice in Program 2-7 that the first letter stored in the variable ch is a and the second letter stored is m. Since a variable can only be used to store one value at a time, the assignment of m to the variable automatically causes a to be overwritten.

Multiple Declarations

Variables having the same data type can always be grouped together and declared using a single declaration statement. The common form of such a declaration is:

```
data-type variable list;
```

For example, the four separate declarations used in Program 2-6,

```
float grade1;
float grade2;
float total;
float average;
```

can be replaced by the single declaration statement

```
float grade1, grade2, total, average;
```

Similarly, the two character declarations,

```
char ch;
char key;
```

can be replaced with the single declaration statement

```
char ch, key;
```

Notice that declaring multiple variables in a single declaration requires that the data type of the variables be given only once, that all the variables names be separated by commas, and that only one semicolon be used to terminate the declaration. The space after each comma is inserted for readability, and is not required.

Declaration statements can also be used to store an initial value into declared variables. For example, the declaration statement

```
int num1 = 15;
```

both declares the variable num1 as an integer variable and sets the value of 15 into the variable. When a declaration statement is used to store a value into a variable, the variable is said to be *initialized*. Thus, in this example it is correct to say that the variable num1 has been initialized to 15. Similarly, the declaration statement

```
float grade1 = 87.0, grade2 = 93.5, total;
```

declares three floating point variables and initializes two of them. Constants, expressions using only constants (such as 87.0 + 12 − 2), and expressions using constants and previously initialized variables can all be used as initializers within a function. For example, Program 2-6 with declaration initialization would appear as Program 2-6a.

 Program 2-6a

```
#include <iostream.h>
void main(void)
{
  float grade1 = 85.5, grade2 = 97.0, total, average;

  total = grade1 + grade2;
  average = total/2.0;  // divide the total by 2.0
  cout << "\nThe average grade is " << average;
}
```

Notice the blank line after the declaration statement. Placing a blank line after the variable declarations placed at the top of a function body is a common programming practice that improves both a program's appearance and its readability. We will adopt this practice in subsequent programs.

A nice feature of C++ is that variable declarations may be freely intermixed and contained with any other statement; the only requirement is that a variable must be declared prior to its use. For very large programs this is a plus, because it allows variables to be to declared close to where they will be used. Using the fact that variables may be declared anywhere within a program permits Program 2-6a to be written as follows:

```
#include <iostream.h>
void main(void)
{
   float grade1 = 85.5, grade2 = 97.0;

   float total = grade1 + grade2;
   float average = total/2.0;  // divide the total by 2.0
   cout << "\nThe average grade is " << average;
}
```

This last version of the program is inferior to Program 2-6a because it needlessly disperses the declarations. In general, it is preferable to keep all declarations together, as concisely and clearly as possible.

Reference Variables[4]

Once a variable has been declared it may be given additional names. This is accomplished using a reference declaration, which has the form:

$$data\text{-}type \; \&new\_name = existing\_name;$$

For example, the reference declaration

```
float &sum = total;
```

equates the name sum to the name total—both now refer to the same variable, as illustrated in Figure 2–5.[5]

FIGURE 2–5 sum Is an Alternative Name for total

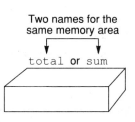

Two names for the same memory area

total or sum

---

[4] This section may be omitted on first reading without loss of subject continuity.

[5] Knowledgeable C programmers should not confuse the use of the ampersand symbol, &, in a reference declaration with the address operator or with using a reference variable as a pointer. A reference variable simply equates two variable names.

Once another name has been established for a variable using a reference declaration, the new name, which is referred to as an alias, can be used in place of the original name. For example, consider Program 2-8:

Program 2-8

```
#include <iostream.h>
void main(void)
{
    float total = 20.5;     // declare and initialize total
    float &sum = total;     // declare another name for total

    cout << "sum = " << sum << '\n';
    sum = 18.6;                  // this changes the value in total
    cout << "total = " << total << '\n';
}
```

The following output is produced by Program 2-8:

```
sum = 20.5
total = 18.6
```

Since the variable sum is simply another reference to the variable total, it is the value stored in total that is obtained by the first call to cout in Program 2-8. Changing the value in sum then changes the value in total, which is displayed by the second call to cout in Program 2-8.

In constructing references, keep the following consideration in mind: the reference should be of the same data type as the variable it refers to. For example, the sequence of declarations

```
int num = 5;
double &numref = num;
```

does not equate numref to num, since they are not of the same data type. Rather, since the compiler cannot correctly associate the reference with a variable, it creates an unnamed variable of the reference type first, and then references this unnamed variable with the reference variable. Such unnamed variables are called *anonymous variables*. For example, consider Program 2-9, which illustrates the effect of creating an anonymous variable.

Program 2-9

```cpp
#include <iostream.h>
void main(void)
{
  int num = 10;
  float &numref = num;// this does not equate numref to num
                      // instead, it equates numref to an
                      // anonymous floating point variable

  numref = 23.6;
  cout << "The value of num is " << num << '\n'
       << "The value of numref is " << numref << '\n';
}
```

The output produced by Program 2-9 is:

```
The value of num is 10
The value of numref is 23.6
```

Notice that the value of num is not affected by the value stored in numref. This is because numref could not be created as a reference for num; rather, it is another name for an unnamed (anonymous) floating point variable that can only be reached using the reference name numref.

Just as declaring a reference to an incorrect data type produces an anonymous variable, so does equating a reference to a constant. For example, the declaration

```cpp
int &val = 5;   // an anonymous variable is created
```

creates an anonymous variable with the number 5 stored in it. The only way to access this variable is by the reference name. Clearly, creating references to anonymous variables should be avoided. Once a reference name has been equated to either a legal variable or an anonymous one, the reference cannot be changed to refer to another variable.

As with all declaration statements, multiple references may be declared in a single statement as long as each reference name is preceded by the ampersand symbol. Thus, the declaration

```cpp
float &sum = total, &mean = average;
```

creates two reference variables named sum and average.[6]

---

[6] Reference declarations may also be written in the form `data-type& new_name = existing name;`, where a space is placed between the ampersand symbol and the reference variable name. This form, however, becomes error prone when multiple references are declared in the same declaration statement and the ampersand symbol is inadvertently omitted after the first reference name is declared. In order to more easily accommodate multiple references in the same delcaration and clearly mark a variable as a reference, we will adhere to the convention that places the ampersand directly in front of each reference variable name.

As we learn more about C++, we will have occasion to use reference variables in more detail, primarily as function arguments or as a function return type. Reference variables used in this manner are described in Section 6.3.

Specifying Storage Allocation

The declaration statements we have introduced perform both software and hardware tasks. From a software perspective, declaration statements always provide a list of all variables and their data types. In this software role, variable declarations also help to control an otherwise common and troublesome error caused by the misspelling of a variable's name within a program. For example, assume that a variable named `distance` is declared and initialized using the statement

```
int distance = 26;
```

Now assume that this variable is inadvertently misspelled in the statement

```
mpg = distnce / gallons;
```

In languages that do not require variable declarations, the program would treat `distnce` as a new variable and either assign an initial value of zero to the variable or use whatever value happened to be in the variable's storage area. In either case a value would be calculated and assigned to `mpg`, and finding the error or even knowing that an error occurred could be extremely troublesome. Such errors are impossible in C++, because the compiler will flag `distnce` as an undeclared variable. The compiler cannot, of course, detect when one declared variable is typed in place of another declared variable.

In addition to their software role, declaration statements can also perform a distinct hardware task. Since each data type has its own storage requirements, the computer can allocate sufficient storage for a variable only after knowing the variable's data type. Because variable declarations provide this information, they can be used to force the compiler to reserve sufficient physical memory storage for each variable. Declaration statements used for this hardware purpose are also called *definition statements*, because they define or tell the compiler how much memory is needed for data storage.

All the declaration statements we have encountered so far have also been definition statements. Later, we will see cases of declaration statements that do not cause any new storage to be allocated and are used simply to declare or alert the program to the data types of variables that are created elsewhere in the program.

Figure 2–6 illustrates the series of operations set in motion by declaration statements that also perform a definition role. The figure shows that definition statements (or, if you prefer, declaration statements that also cause memory to be allocated) "tag" the first byte of each set of reserved bytes with a name. This

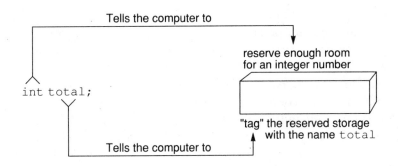

FIGURE 2–6a Defining the Integer Variable Named `total`

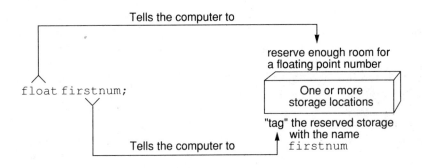

FIGURE 2–6b Defining the Floating Point Variable Named `firstnum`

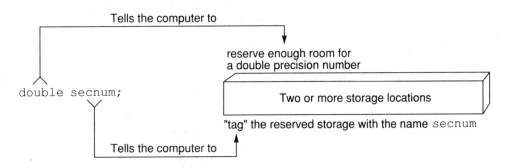

FIGURE 2–6c Defining the Double Precision Variable Named `secnum`

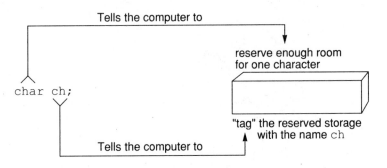

FIGURE 2–6d Defining the Character Variable Named `ch`

name is, of course, the variable's name and is used by the computer to correctly locate the starting point of each variable's reserved memory area.

Within a program, after a variable has been declared, it is typically used by a programmer to refer to the contents of the variable (that is, the variable's value). Where in memory this value is stored is generally of little concern to the programmer. The compiler, however, must be concerned with where each value is stored and with correctly locating each variable. In this task the computer uses the variable name to locate the first byte of storage previously allocated to the variable. Knowing the variable's data type then allows the compiler to store or retrieve the correct number of bytes.

Exercises 2.4

1. State whether the following variable names are valid or not. If they are invalid, state the reason why.

```
prod_a      c1234      abcd        -c3         12345
newbal      while      $total      new bal     a1b2c3d4
9ab6        sum.of     average     grade1      fin_grad
```

2. State whether the following variable names are valid or not. If they are invalid, state the reason why. Also indicate which of the valid variable names should not be used because they convey no information about the variable.

```
salestax    a243    r2d2    first_num   cc_a1
harry       sue     c3p0    average     sum
maximum     okay    a       awesome     goforit
3sum        for     tot.a1  c$five      netpay
```

3. a. Write a declaration statement to declare that the variable `count` will be used to store an integer.
b. Write a declaration statement to declare that the variable `grade` will be used to store a floating point number.
c. Write a declaration statement to declare that the variable `yield` will be used to store a double precision number.
d. Write a declaration statement to declare that the variable `initial` will be used to store a character.

4. Write declaration statements for the following variables:
a. `num1`, `num2`, and `num3` used to store integer numbers
b. `grade1`, `grade2`, `grade3`, and `grade4` used to store floating point numbers
c. `tempa`, `tempb`, and `tempc` used to store double precision numbers
d. `ch`, `let1`, `let2`, `let3`, and `let4` used to store character types

5. Write declaration statements for the following variables:
a. `firstnum` and `secnum` used to store integers
b. `price`, `yield`, and `coupon` used to store floating point numbers
c. `maturity` used to store a double precision number

6. Rewrite each of these declaration statements as three individual declarations:
   a. `int month, day = 30, year;`
   b. `double hours, rate, otime = 15.62;`
   c. `float price, amount, taxes;`
   d. `char in_key, ch, choice = 'f';`

7. *a.* Determine what each statement causes to happen in the following program:

```cpp
#include <iostream.h>
void main(void)
{
   int num1, num2, total;

   num1 = 25;
   num2 = 35;
   total = num1 + num2;
   cout << "The total of" << num1 << " and "
        << num2 << " is " << total;
}
```

   b. What is the output that will be printed when the program listed in Exercise 7a is run?

8. Write a C++ program that stores the sum of the integer numbers 12 and 33 in a variable named `sum`. Have your program display the value stored in `sum`.

9. Write a C++ program that stores the integer value 16 in the variable `length` and the integer value 18 in the variable `width`. Have your program calculate the value assigned to the variable `perimeter`, using the assignment statement

`perimeter = 2 * length + 2 * width;`

and print out the value stored in the variable `perimeter`. Make sure to declare all the variables as integers at the beginning of the `main()` function.

10. Write a C++ program that stores the integer value 16 in the variable `num1` and the integer value 18 in the variable `num2`. (Make sure to declare the variables as integers.) Have your program calculate the total of these numbers and their average. Store the total in an integer variable named `total` and the average in an integer variable named `average`. (Use the statement `average = total/2.0;` to calculate the average.) Use the `cout` object to display the total and average.

11. Repeat Exercise 10, but store the number 15 in `num1` instead of 16. With a pencil, write down the average of `num1` and `num2`. What do you think your program will store in the integer variable that you used for the average of these two numbers? How can you ensure that the correct answer will be printed for the average?

12. Write a C++ program that stores the number 105.62 in the variable `firstnum`, 89.352 in the variable `secnum`, and 98.67 in the variable `thirdnum`. (Make sure to declare the variables first as either float or double.) Have your program calculate the total of the three numbers and their average. The total should be stored in the variable `total` and the average in the variable `average`. (Use the statement `average = total /3.0;` to calculate the average.) Use the `cout` object to display the total and average.

13. Every variable has at least two items associated with it. What are these two items?

14. *a.* A statement used to clarify the relationship between squares and rectangles is "All squares are rectangles but not all rectangles are squares." Write a similar statement that describes the relationship between definition and declaration statements.

b. Why must a variable be defined before any other C++ statement that uses the variable?

Note for Exercises 15 through 17:

Assume that a character requires one byte of storage, an integer two bytes, a floating point number four bytes, a double precision number eight bytes, and that variables are assigned storage in the order they are declared (review Section 2.8 if you are unfamiliar with the concept of a byte).

15. *a.* Using Figure 2–7 and assuming that the variable name rate is assigned to the byte having memory address 159, determine the addresses corresponding to each variable declared in the following statements. Also fill in the appropriate bytes with the initialization data included in the declaration statements (use letters for the characters, not the computer codes that would actually be stored).

```
float rate;

char ch1 = 'w', ch2 = 'o', ch3 = 'w', ch4 = '!';

double taxes;

int num, count = 0;
```

b. Repeat Exercise 15a, but substitute the actual byte patterns that a computer using the ASCII code would use to store the characters in the variables `ch1`, `ch2`, `ch3`, and `ch4`. (*Hint:* Use Table 2–2.)

FIGURE 2–7 Memory Bytes for Exercises 15, 16, and 17

Address:	159	160	161	162	163	164	165	166

Address:	167	168	169	170	171	172	173	174

Address:	175	176	177	178	179	180	181	182

Address:	183	184	185	186	187	188	189	190

16. a. Using Figure 2–7 and assuming that the variable named `cn1` is assigned to the byte at memory address 159, determine the addresses corresponding to each variable declared in the following statements. Also fill in the appropriate bytes with the initialization data included in the declaration statements (use letters for the characters and not the computer codes that would actually be stored).

```
char cn1 = 'a', cn2 = ' ', cn3 = 'b', cn4 = 'u', cn5 = 'n';

char cn6 = 'c', cn7 = 'h', key = '\\', sch = '\'', inc = 'o';

char inc1 = 'f';
```

b. Repeat Exercise 16a, but substitute the actual byte patterns that a computer using the ASCII code would use to store the characters in each of the declared variables. (*Hint:* Use Table 2–2.)

17. Using Figure 2–7 and assuming that the variable name `miles` is assigned to the byte at memory address 159, determine the addresses corresponding to each variable declared in the following statements:

```
float miles;

int count, num;

double dist, temp;
```

2.5 Integer Qualifiers

Integer numbers are generally used in programs as counters to keep track of the number of times that something has occurred. For most applications, the counts needed are less than 32,767, which is the maximum signed integer value that can be stored in two bytes. Since most computers allocate at least two bytes for integers, there is usually no problem.

Cases do arise, however, where larger integer numbers are needed. In financial applications, for example, dates such as 7/12/89 are typically converted to the number of days from the turn of the century. This conversion makes it possible to store and sort dates using a single number for each date. Unfortunately, for dates after 1987, the number of days from the turn of the century is larger than the maximum value of 32,767 allowed when only two bytes are allocated for each integer variable. For financial programs dealing with mortgages and bonds maturing after 1987 that are run on computers allocating only two bytes per integer (PCs, for example), the limitation on the maximum integer value must be overcome.

To accommodate real application requirements such as this, C++ provides long integer, short integer, and unsigned integer data types. These three additional integer data types are obtained by adding the qualifiers long, short, or unsigned, respectively, to the normal integer declaration statements. For example, the declaration statement

```
long int days;
```

declares the variable `days` to be a long integer. The word `int` in a long integer declaration statement is optional, so the previous declaration statement can also be written as `long days;`. The amount of storage allocated for a long integer depends on the computer being used. Although you would expect that a long integer variable would be allocated more space than a standard integer, this may not be the case. About all that can be said is that long integers will provide no less space than regular integers. The actual amount of storage allocated by your computer should be checked using the `sizeof` operator described at the end of this section.

Once a variable is declared as a long integer, integer values may be assigned as usual for standard integers, or an optional letter `L` (either uppercase or lowercase, with no space between the number and letter) may be appended to the integer. For example, the declaration statement

```
long days = 38276L;
```

declares `days` to be of type long integer and assigns the long integer constant `38276` to the variable `days`.

In addition to the long qualifier, C++ also provides for a short qualifier. Although you would expect a short integer to conserve computer storage by reserving fewer bytes than used for an integer, this is not always the case. Some computers use the same amount of storage for both integers and short integers. Again, the amount of memory space allocated for a short integer data type depends on your computer, and can be checked using the `sizeof` operator (described at the end of this section). As with long integers, short integers may be declared using the terms `short` or `short int` in a declaration statement. Once a variable is declared as a short integer, values are assigned as normally done with integers.

The final integer data type is the unsigned integer. This data type is obtained by prefixing the reserved word `int` with the qualifier `unsigned`. For example, the declaration statement

```
unsigned int days;
```

declares the variable `days` to be of type `unsigned`. Unsigned integers are generally only used for positive integers and effectively double the positive value that can be stored without increasing the number of bytes allocated to an integer. This is accomplished by effectively treating all unsigned integers as positive numbers, as illustrated in Figure 2–8.

Figure 2–9 illustrates all of C++'s fundamental data types and their relationship to each other.

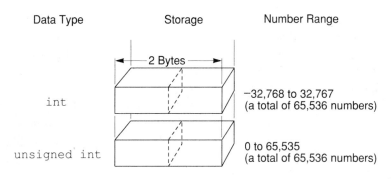

FIGURE 2–8 Unsigned Integer Storage Using Two Bytes

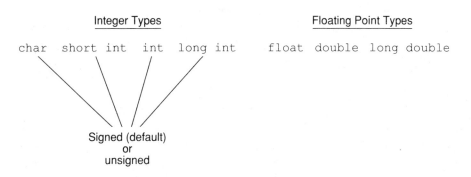

FIGURE 2–9 C++s Fundamental Data Types

Data Type Conversions

The general rules for converting integer and floating point operands in mixed-mode arithmetic expressions were presented in Section 2.2. A more complete set of conversion rules for arithmetic operators, which includes character, short, and long integer operands, is provided in Table 2–10, where the rules are applied in order, starting with Rule 1.

TABLE 2–10   Conversion Rules for Arithmetic Operators

---

1. If both operands are either character or integer operands, then:
  a. when both operands are character, short, or integer data types the result of the expression is an integer value.
  b. when one of operands is a long integer the result is a long integer, unless one of the operands is an unsigned integer. In this case the other operand is converted to an unsigned integer value and the resulting value of the expression is an unsigned value.

---

2. If any one operand is a floating point value, then:
  a. when one or both operands are floats the result of the operation is a float value.
  b. when one or both operands are doubles the result of the operation is a double value.
  c. when one or both operands are long doubles the result is a long double value.

Note that the rules in Table 2–10 apply to each individual arithmetic operation in their correct order of evaluation. For example, in the expression 14.78F − 4 * 3L, the multiplication, which has a higher precedence than the subtraction, is performed first. For this multiplication of two integer operands, the integer 4 is converted to a long integer value, and the result of the expression is 12L (Rule 1b). The result of the next operation, 14.78F − 12L, is the single precision (float) value 2.78 (Rule 2a).

Determining Storage Size[7]

C++ provides an operator for determining the amount of storage your compiler allocates for each data type. This operator, called the sizeof() operator, returns the number of bytes of the variable or data type included in the parentheses. Unlike a function, which itself is made of C++ statements, the sizeof() operator is an integral part of the C++ language itself. Examples using the sizeof() operator are:

```
sizeof(num1)      sizeof(int)      sizeof(float)
```

If the item in parentheses is a variable, as in the example sizeof(num1), sizeof() returns the number of bytes of storage that the computer reserved for the variable. If the item following the word sizeof is a data type, such as int or char, sizeof will return the number of bytes of storage that the computer uses for the given data type. Using either approach, we can use sizeof() to determine the amount of storage used by different data types. Consider Program 2-10.

 Program 2-10

```
#include <iostream.h>
void main(void)
{
  char ch;
  int num1;

  cout << "\nBytes of storage used by a character: "
       << sizeof(ch)
       << "\nBytes of storage used by an integer: "
       << sizeof(num1);
}
```

---

[7] This section assumes a basic understanding of computer storage concepts and terms. If you are unfamiliar with these concepts, please read the supplement at the end of this chapter.

Program 2-10 declares that the variable `ch` is used to store a character and that the variable `num1` is used to store an integer. From our discussion in the last section, we know that each of these declaration statements is also a definition statement. As such, the first declaration statement instructs the compiler to reserve enough storage for a character, and the second declaration statement instructs the compiler to reserve enough storage for an integer. The `sizeof()` operator is then used to tell us how much room the computer really set aside for these two variables. The `sizeof()` operator itself is used as an argument to the `cout` object. When Program 2-10 is run on an IBM personal computer the following output is obtained:

```
Bytes of storage used by a character: 1
Bytes of storage used by an integer: 2
```

Exercises 2.5

1. *a.* Run Program 2-10 to determine how many bytes your computer uses to store character and integer data types.

b. Expand Program 2-10 to determine how many bytes your computer uses for short integers, long integers, and unsigned integers.

2. After running the program written for Exercise 1, use Table 2–1 (see Section 2.1) to determine the maximum and minimum numbers that can be stored in integer, short integer, and long integer variables for your computer.

3. Program 2-10 did not actually store any values into the variables `ch` and `num1`. Why was this not necessary?

4. *a.* Expand Program 2-10 to determine how many bytes your computer uses to store floating point and double precision numbers.

b. Although there is no long float data class, double precision numbers are sometimes considered as the equivalent long form for floating point numbers. Why is this so? Does the output of the program written for Exercise 4a support this statement?

2.6 Common Programming Errors

The common programming errors associated with the material presented in this chapter are:

1. Forgetting to declare all the variables used in a program. This error is detected by the compiler and an error message is generated for all undeclared variables.

2. Attempting to store one data type in a variable declared for a different type. This error is not detected by the compiler. Here, the value is converted to the data type of the variable it is assigned to.

3. Using a variable in an expression before a value has been assigned to the variable. Here, whatever value happens to be in the variable will be used when the expression is evaluated, and the result will be meaningless.

4. Dividing integer values incorrectly. This error is usually disguised within a larger expression and can be a troublesome error to detect. For example, the expression

$$3.425 + 2/3 + 7.9$$

yields the same result as the expression

$$3.425 + 7.9$$

because the integer division of 2/3 is 0.

5. Mixing data types in the same expression without clearly understanding the effect produced. Since C++ allows mixed-mode expressions, it is important to be clear about the order of evaluation and the data type of all intermediate calculations. The rules for evaluating the result of a numeric expression are:

   a. If all operands are integers, the result is an integer.

   b. If any operand is a floating point value, the result is a floating point value.

   As a general rule it is better not to mix data types in an expression unless a specific effect is desired.

6. Forgetting to separate individual data streams passed to cout with an insertion ("put-to") symbol, <<.

2.7 Chapter Summary

1. The three basic types of data recognized by C++ are integer, floating point, and character data. Each of these types of data is typically stored in a computer using different amounts of memory.

2. The cout object can be used to display all of C++'s data types.

3. Every variable in a C++ program must be declared as to the type of value it can store. Declarations within a function may be placed anywhere within the function, although a variable can only be used after it is declared. Variables may also be initialized when they are declared. Additionally, variables of the same type may be declared using a single declaration statement. Variable declaration statements have the general form:

```
data-type variable-name(s);
```

4. Reference variables can be declared that associate a second name to an existing variable. The reference variable, which is also called an alias, is simply another name for the existing variable. Reference declarations have the form:

```
data_type &reference_name = existing_name;
```

5. A simple C++ program containing declaration statements has the typical form:

```
#include <iostream.h>
void main(void)
{
   declaration statements;

   other statements;
}
```

Although declaration statements may be placed anywhere within the function's body, a variable may only be used after it is declared.

6. Declaration statements always play a software role of informing the compiler of a function's valid variable names. When a variable declaration also causes the computer to set aside memory locations for the variable, the declaration statement is also called a definition statement. (All the declarations we have used in this chapter have also been definition statements.)

7. The `sizeof()` operator can be used to determine the amount of storage reserved for variables.

2.8 Chapter Supplement—Bits, Bytes, Addresses, and Number Codes

It would be convenient if computers stored numbers and letters the way that people do. The number 126, for example, would then be stored as 126, and the letter A stored as the letter A. Unfortunately, due to the physical components used in building a computer, this is not the case.

The smallest and most basic storage unit in a computer is called a *bit*. Physically, a bit is really a switch that can be either open or closed. By convention, the open and closed positions of each switch are represented as 0 and 1, respectively.

A single bit that can represent the values 0 and 1, by itself, has limited usefulness. All computers, therefore, group a fixed number of bits together. The grouping of eight bits to form a larger unit is an almost universal computer standard. Such groups are commonly referred to as *bytes*. A single byte consisting of eight bits, where each bit can be 0 or 1, can represent any one of 256 different bit patterns. These consist of the pattern 00000000 (all eight switches open) to the pattern 11111111 (all eight switches closed), and all possible combinations of 0s and 1s in between. Each of these patterns can be used to represent either a letter of the alphabet, other single characters, such as a dollar sign, comma, etc., a single digit, or numbers containing more than one digit. The patterns of 0s and 1s used to represent letters, single digits, and other single characters are called character codes (one such code, called the ASCII code, is presented in Section 2.1). The patterns used to store numbers are called number codes (one such code, called two's complement, is presented at the end of this section).

Words and Addresses

One or more bytes may themselves be grouped into larger units called words. The advantage of combining bytes into words is that multiple bytes are stored or retrieved by the computer for each word access. For example, retrieving a word consisting of four bytes yields more information than that obtained by retrieving a word consisting of a single byte. Such a retrieval is also considerably faster than individual retrievals of four single bytes. The increase in speed, however, is achieved by an increase in cost and complexity of the computer.

Early personal computers, such as the Apple II and Commodore machines, had words consisting of a single byte. The first IBM personal computers, as well as Digital Equipment, Data General, and Prime minicomputers, had words consisting of two bytes each. Most mainframe computers as well as current Intel 386, Intel 486, and Motorola M680x0-based personal computers currently have four-byte words.

The arrangement of words in a computer's memory can be compared to the arrangement of suites in a large hotel, where each suite is made up of rooms of the same size. Just as each suite has a unique room number to locate and identify it, each word has a unique numeric address. In computers that allow each byte to be individually accessed, each byte has its own address. Like room numbers, word and byte addresses are always unsigned whole numbers that are used for location and identification purposes. Also, like hotel rooms with connecting doors for forming larger suites, words can be combined to form larger units for the accommodation of different-size data types.

Two's Complement Numbers

The most common integer code using bit patterns is called the *two's complement* representation. Using this code, the integer equivalent of any bit pattern, such as 10001101, is easy to determine and can be found for either positive or negative numbers with no change in the conversion method. For convenience we will assume words consisting of a single byte, although the procedure carries directly over to larger size words.

The easiest way to determine the integer represented by each bit pattern is to first construct a simple device called a value box. Figure 2–10 illustrates such a box for a single byte.

$-(2^7)$	(2^6)	(2^5)	(2^4)	(2^3)	(2^2)	(2^1)	(2^0)
-128	64	32	16	8	4	2	1

FIGURE 2–10 An Eight-Bit Value Box for Two's Complement Conversion

Mathematically, each value in the box illustrated in Figure 2–10 represents an increasing power of two. Since two's complement numbers must be capable of representing both positive and negative integers, the leftmost position, in addition to having the largest absolute magnitude, also has a negative sign.

Conversion of any binary number, for example 10001101, to decimal form simply requires inserting the bit pattern in the value box and adding the values having ones under them. Thus, as illustrated in Figure 2–11, the bit pattern 10001101 represents the integer number –115.

In reviewing the value box, it is evident that any binary number with a leading 1 represents a negative number, and any bit pattern with a leading 0 represents a non-negative number. The value box can also be used in reverse, to convert a base 10 integer number into its equivalent binary bit pattern. Some conversions, in fact, can be made by inspection. For example, the base 10 number –125 is obtained by adding 3 to –128. Thus, the binary representation of –125 is 10000011, which equals –128 + 2 + 1. Similarly, the two's complement representation of the number 40 is 00101000, which is 32 plus 8.

Although the value box conversion method is deceptively simple, the method is directly related to the mathematical basis of two's complement binary numbers. The original name of the two's complement binary code was the weighted-sign binary code, which correlates directly to the value box. As the name weighted sign implies, each bit position has a weight, or value, of two raised to a power and a sign. The signs of all bits except the leftmost bit are positive and the sign of the leftmost or most significant bit is negative.

FIGURE 2–11 Converting 10001101 to a Base 10 Number

-128	64	32	16	8	4	2	1
1	0	0	0	1	1	0	1

$$-128 + 0 + 0 + 0 + 8 + 4 + 0 + 1 = -115$$

Assignment and Interactive Input

Chapter Three

Chapter 2 introduced the concept of data storage, variables and their associated declaration statements. Additionally, the use of `cout` for formatted output was presented. This chapter completes our introduction to C++ by discussing the proper use of both constants and variables in constructing expressions and statements, and using the `cin` object for entering data interactively while a program is running.

3.1 Assignment Statements

We have already encountered simple assignment statements in Chapter 2. Assignment statements are the most basic C++ statements for both assigning values to variables and performing computations. This statement has the general form:

variable = operand;

The simplest operand in C++ is a single constant. In each of the following assignment statements, the operand to the right of the equal sign is a constant:

```
length = 25;
```

```
width = 17.5;
```

In each of these assignment statements the value of the constant to the right of the equal sign is assigned to the variable on the left of the equal sign. It is important to note that the equal sign in C++ does not have the same meaning as an equal sign in algebra. The equal sign in an assignment statement tells the computer first to determine the value of the operand to the right of the equal sign and then to store (or assign) that value in the locations associated with the variable to the left of the equal sign. In this regard, the C++ statement `length = 25;` is read "length is assigned the value 25." The blank spaces in the assignment statement are inserted for readability only.

Recall that a variable can be initialized when it is declared. If an initialization is not done within the declaration statement, the variable should be assigned a value with an assignment statement before it is used in any computation. Subsequent assignment statements can, of course, be used to change the value assigned to a variable. For example, assume the following statements are executed one after another and that `total` was not initialized when it was declared:

```
total = 3.7;
total = 6.28;
```

The first assignment statement assigns the value of 3.7 to the variable named `total`.[1] The next assignment statement causes the computer to assign a value of 6.28 to `total`. The 3.7 that was in `total` is overwritten with the new value of 6.28, because a variable can store only one value at a time. It is sometimes useful to think of the variable to the left of the equal sign as a temporary parking spot in a huge parking lot. Just as an individual parking spot can be used only by one car at a time, each variable can store only one value at a time. The "parking" of a new value in a variable automatically causes the computer to remove any value previously parked there.

In addition to being a constant, the operand to the right of the equal sign in an assignment statement can be a variable or any other valid C++ expression. An *expression* is any combination of constants and variables that can be evaluated to yield a result. Thus, the expression in an assignment statement can be used to perform calculations using the arithmetic operators introduced in Section 2.2. Examples of assignment statements using expressions containing these operators are:

```
sum = 3 + 7;
diff = 15 - 6;
product = .05 * 14.6;
tally = count + 1;
newtotal = 18.3 + total;
taxes = .06 * amount;
total_weight = factor * weight;
average = sum / items;
slope = (y2 - y1) / (x2 - x1);
```

As always in an assignment statement, the computer first calculates the value of the expression to the right of the equal sign and then stores this value in the variable to the left of the equal sign. For example, in the assignment statement `total_weight = factor * weight;` the arithmetic expression `factor * weight` is first evaluated to yield a result. This result, which is a number, is then stored in the variable `total_weight`.

In writing assignment expressions, you must be aware of two important considerations. Since the expression to the right of the equal sign is evaluated first, all variables used in the expression must previously have been given valid values if the result is to make sense. For example, the assignment statement `total_weight = factor * weight;` causes a valid number to be stored in

---

[1] Since this is the first time a value is explicitly assigned to this variable it is frequently referred to as an initialization. This stems from historical usage that said a variable was initialized the first time a value was assigned to it. Under this usage it is correct to say that "`total` is initialized to 3.7." From an implementation viewpoint, however, this later statement is incorrect. This is because the assignment operation is handled differently by the C++ compiler than an initialization performed when a variable is created by a declaration statement. This difference is only important when using C++'s class features and is explained in detail in Section 12.1.

`total_weight` only if the programmer first takes care to assign valid numbers to `factor` and `weight`. Thus the sequence of statements:

```
factor = 1.06;
weight = 155.0;
total_weight = factor * weight;
```

ensures that we know the values being used to obtain the result that will be stored in `total_weight`.

The second consideration to keep in mind is that since the value of an expression is stored in the variable to the left of the equal sign, there must be a variable listed immediately to the left of the equal sign. For example, the assignment statement

```
amount + 1892 = 1000 + 10 * 5
```

is invalid. The right-side expression evaluates to the integer 1050, which can only be stored in a variable. Since `amount + 1892` is not a valid variable name, the computer does not know where to store the calculated value. Program 3-1 illustrates the use of assignment statements in calculating the area of a rectangle.

 Program 3-1

```
#include <iostream.h>
void main(void)
{
    float length, width, area;

    length = 27.2;
    width = 13.6;
    area = length * width;
    cout << "The length of the rectangle is " << length;
    cout << "\nThe width of the rectangle is " << width;
    cout << "\nThe area of the rectangle is " << area;
}
```

When Program 3-1 is run, the output obtained is:

```
The length of the rectangle is 27.2
The width of the rectangle is 13.6
The area of the rectangle is 369.92
```

Consider the flow of control that the computer uses in executing Program 3-1. Program execution begins with the first statement and continues sequentially, statement by statement, until the closing brace of `main` is encountered. This flow of control is true for all programs. The computer works on one statement at a time, executing that statement with no knowledge of what the next statement will be. This explains why all operands used in an expression must have values assigned to them before the expression is evaluated.

When the computer executes the statement `area = length * width;` in Program 3-1, it uses whatever value is stored in the variables `length` and `width` at the time the assignment is executed. If no values have been specifically assigned to these variables before they are used in the expression `length * width`, the computer uses whatever values happen to occupy these variables when they are referenced. The computer does not "look ahead" to see that you might assign values to these variables later in the program.

It is important to realize that in C++, the equal sign, =, used in assignment statements is itself an operator, *which differs from the way most other high-level languages process this symbol*. In C++ (as in C), the = symbol is called the *assignment operator*, and an expression using this operator, such as `interest = principal * rate`, is an assignment expression. Since the assignment operator has a lower precedence than any other arithmetic operator, the value of any expression to the right of the equal sign will be evaluated first, prior to assignment.

Like all expressions, assignment expressions themselves have a value. The value of the complete assignment expression is the value assigned to the variable on the left of the assignment operator. For example, the expression `a = 5` both assigns a value of 5 to the variable `a` and results in the expression itself having a value of 5. The value of the expression can always be verified using a statement such as

```
cout << "The value of the expression is " << (a = 5);
```

Here, the value of the expression itself is displayed and not the contents of the variable `a`. Although both the contents of the variable and the expression have the same value, it is worthwhile realizing that we are dealing with two distinct entities.

From a programming perspective, it is the actual assignment of a value to a variable that is significant in an assignment expression; the final value of the assignment expression itself is of little consequence. However, the fact that assignment expressions have a value has implications that must be considered when C++'s relational operators are presented.

Any expression that is terminated by a semicolon becomes a C++ statement. The most common example of this is the assignment statement, which is simply an assignment expression terminated with a semicolon. For example, terminating the assignment expression `a = 33` with a semicolon results in the assignment statement `a = 33;` , which can be used in a program on a line by itself.

Since the equal sign is an operator in C++, multiple assignments are possible in the same expression or its equivalent statement. For example, in the expression `a = b = c = 25` all the assignment operators have the same precedence. Since the assignment operator has a right-to-left associativity, the final evaluation proceeds in the sequence

$$c = 25$$
$$b = c$$
$$a = b$$

In this case, this has the effect of assigning the number 25 to each of the variables individually, and can be represented as

$$a = (b = (c = 25))$$

Appending a semicolon to the original expression results in the multiple assignment statement

$$a = b = c = 25;$$

This latter statement assigns the value 25 to the three individual variables, equivalent to the following order:

$$c = 25;$$
$$b = 25;$$
$$a = 25;$$

Note that data type conversions can take place across assignment operators; that is, the value of the expression on the right side of the assignment operator is converted to the data type of the variable to the left of the assignment operator. Thus, assigning an integer value to a real variable causes the integer to be converted to a real value. Similarly, assigning a real value to an integer variable forces conversion of the real value to an integer, which always results in the loss of the fractional part of the number due to truncation. For example, if `temp` is an integer variable, the assignment `temp = 25.89` causes the integer value 25 to be stored in the integer variable `temp`.[2]

A more complete example of data type conversions, which includes both mixed-mode and assignment conversion is the evaluation of the expression

$$a = b * d$$

where `a` and `b` are integer variables and `d` is a floating point variable. When the mixed-mode expression `b * d` is evaluated,[3] the value of `b` used in the expression is converted to a floating point number for purposes of computation

---

[2] The correct integer portion, clearly, is retained only when it is within the range of integers allowed by the compiler.

[3] Review the rules in Table 2–10 in Section 2.5 for the evaluation of mixed-mode expressions, if necessary.

(it is important to note that the value stored in b remains an integer number), and the resulting value of the expression b * d is a floating point number. Finally, data type conversion across the assignment operator comes into play. Since the left side of the assignment operator is an integer variable, the floating point value of the expression (b * d) is truncated to an integer value and stored in the variable a.

Assignment Variations

Although only one variable is allowed immediately to the left of the equal sign in an assignment expression, the variable on the left of the equal sign can also be used on the right of the equal sign. For example, the assignment expression sum = sum + 10 is valid. Clearly, as an algebra equation sum could never be equal to itself plus 10. But in C++, the expression sum = sum + 10 is not an equation—it is an expression that is evaluated in two major steps. The first step is to calculate the value of sum + 10. The second step is to store the computed value in sum. See if you can determine the output of Program 3-2.

 Program 3-2

```
#include <iostream.h>
void main(void)
{
  int sum;

  sum = 25;
  cout << "\nThe number stored in sum is " << sum;
  sum = sum + 10;
  cout << "\nThe number now stored in sum is " << sum;
}
```

The assignment statement sum = 25; tells the computer to store the number 25 in sum, as shown in Figure 3–1.

The first activation of cout causes the value stored in sum to be displayed by the message The number stored in sum is 25. The second assignment statement in Program 3-2, sum = sum + 10; causes the computer to retrieve

FIGURE 3–1 The Integer 25 Is Stored in sum

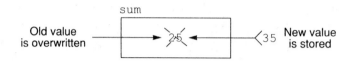

FIGURE 3–2 sum = sum + 10; Causes a New Value to be Stored in sum

the 25 stored in sum and add 10 to this number, yielding the number 35. The number 35 is then stored in the variable on the left side of the equal sign, which is the variable sum. The 25 that was in sum is simply overwritten with the new value of 35, as shown in Figure 3–2.

Assignment expressions like sum = sum + 25, which use the same variable on both sides of the assignment operator, can be written using the following shortcut assignment operators:

$$+=\qquad-=\qquad*=\qquad/=\qquad\%=$$

For example, the expression sum = sum + 10 can be written as sum += 10. Similarly, the expression price *= rate is equivalent to the expression price = price * rate.

In using these new assignment operators it is important to note that the variable to the left of the assignment operator is applied to the *complete* expression on the right. For example, the expression price *= rate + 1 is equivalent to the expression price = price * (rate + 1), not price = price * rate + 1.

Accumulating

Assignment expressions like sum += 10 or its equivalent, sum = sum + 10, are common in programming. These expressions are required in accumulating sub-totals when data is entered one number at a time. For example, if we want to add the numbers 96, 70, 85, and 60 in calculator fashion, the following statements could be used:

Statement	Value in sum
sum = 0;	0
sum = sum + 96;	96
sum = sum + 70;	166
sum = sum + 85;	251
sum = sum + 60;	311

The first statement sets sum to 0. This removes any number ("garbage value") stored in sum that would invalidate the final total. As each number is added, the value stored in sum is increased accordingly. After completion of the last statement, sum contains the total of all the added numbers.

Program 3-3 illustrates the effect of these statements by displaying sum's contents after each addition is made.

Program 3-3

```
#include <iostream.h>
void main(void)
{
  int sum;

  sum = 0;
  cout << "\nThe value of sum is initially set to " << sum;
  sum = sum + 96;
  cout << "\n  sum is now " << sum;
  sum = sum + 70;
  cout << "\n  sum is now " << sum;
  sum = sum + 85;
  cout << "\n  sum is now " << sum;
  sum = sum + 60;
  cout << "\n  The final sum is " << sum;
}
```

The output displayed by Program 3-3 is:

```
The value of sum is initially set to 0
  sum is now 96
  sum is now 166
  sum is now 251
  The final sum is 311
```

Although Program 3-3 is not a practical program (it is easier to add the numbers by hand), it does illustrate the subtotaling effect of repeated use of statements having the form

$$variable = variable + new\_value;$$

We will find many uses for this type of statement when we become more familiar with the repetition statements introduced in Chapter 5.

Counting

An assignment statement that is very similar to the accumulating statement is the counting statement. Counting statements have the form:

$$variable = variable + fixed\_number;$$

Examples of counting statements are:

```
i = i + 1;
n = n + 1;
count = count + 1;
j = j + 2;
m = m + 2;
kk = kk + 3;
```

In each of these examples the same variable is used on both sides of the equal sign. After the statement is executed the value of the respective variable is increased by a fixed amount. In the first three examples the variables i, n, and count have all been increased by one. In the next two examples the respective variables have been increased by two, and in the final example the variable kk has been increased by three.

For the special case in which a variable is either increased or decreased by one, C++ provides two unary operators. Using the *increment operator*,[4] ++, the expression variable = variable + 1 can be replaced by either the expression variable++ or ++variable. Examples of the increment operator are:

Expression	Alternative
i = i + 1	i++ or ++i
n = n + 1	n++ or ++n
count = count + 1	count++ or ++count

Program 3-4 illustrates the use of the increment operator.

Program 3-4

```
#include <iostream.h>
void main(void)
{
  int count;

  count = 0;
  cout << "\nThe initial value of count is " << count;
  count++;
  cout << "\n    count is now " << count;
  count++;
  cout << "\n    count is now " << count;
  count++;
  cout << "\n    count is now " << count;
  count++;
  cout << "\n    count is now " << count;
}
```

---

[4] As a historical note, the ++ in C++ was inspired by the increment operator symbol. It was used to indicate that C++ was the next increment to the C language.

The output displayed by Program 3-4 is:

```
The initial value of count is 0
     count is now 1
     count is now 2
     count is now 3
     count is now 4
```

When the ++ operator appears before a variable it is called a *prefix increment operator;* when it appears after a variable it is called a *postfix increment operator.* The distinction between a prefix and postfix increment operator is important when the variable being incremented is used in an assignment expression. For example, the expression k = ++n does two things in one expression. Initially the value of n is incremented by one and then the new value of n is assigned to the variable k. Thus, the statement k = ++n; is equivalent to the two statements

```
n = n + 1;    // increment n first
k = n;        // assign n's value to k
```

The assignment expression k = n++, which uses a postfix increment operator, reverses this procedure. A postfix increment operates after the assignment is completed. Thus, the statement k = n++; first assigns the current value of n to k and then increments the value of n by one. This is equivalent to the two statements

```
k = n;        // assign n's value to k
n = n + 1;    // and then increment n
```

In addition to the increment operator, C++ also provides a *decrement operator,* --. As you might expect, the expressions variable-- and --variable are both equivalent to the expression variable = variable - 1.

Examples of the decrement operator are:

Expression	Alternative
i = i - 1	i-- or --i
n = n - 1	n-- or --n
count = count - 1	count-- or --count

When the -- operator appears before a variable it is called a *prefix decrement operator.* When the decrement appears after a variable it is called a *postfix decrement operator.* For example, both of the expressions n-- and --n reduce the value of n by one. These expressions are equivalent to the longer expression n = n - 1. As with the increment operator, however, the prefix and postfix decrement operators produce different results when used in assignment expressions. For example, the expression k = --n first decrements the value of n by one before assigning the value of n to k, while the expression k = n-- first assigns the current value of n to k and then reduces the value of n by one.

The increment and decrement operators can often be used advantageously to significantly reduce program storage requirements and increase execution speed. For example, consider the following three statements:

```
count = count + 1;
count += 1;
count++;
```

All perform the same function; however, when these instructions are compiled for execution on an IBM personal computer the storage requirements for the instructions are 9, 4, and 3 bytes, respectively.[5] Using the assignment operator, =, instead of the increment operator results in using three times the storage space for the instruction, with an accompanying decrease in execution speed.

Exercises 3.1

1. Determine and correct the errors in the following programs:

a.
```
#include <iostream.h>
void main(void)
{
  width = 15
  area = length * width;
  cout << "The area is " << area
}
```

b.
```
#include <iostream.h>
void main(void)
{
  int length, width, area;
  area = length * width;
  length = 20;
  width = 15;
  cout << "The area is " << area;
```

c.
```
#include <iostream.h>
void main(void)
{
  int length = 20; width = 15, area;
  length * width = area;
  cout << "The area is " , area;
}
```

---

[5] This is clearly a compiler-dependent result.

2. *a.* Write a C++ program to calculate and display the average of the numbers 32.6, 55.2, 67.9, and 48.6.
   b. Run the program written for Exercise 2a on a computer.

3. *a.* Write a C++ program to calculate the circumference of a circle. The equation for determining the circumference of a circle is *circumference = 2 * 3.1416 * radius*. Assume that the circle has a radius of 3.3 inches.
   b. Run the program written for Exercise 3a on a computer.

4. *a.* Write a C++ program to calculate the area of a circle. The equation for determining the area of a circle is *area = 3.1416 * radius * radius*. Assume that the circle has a radius of 5 inches.
   b. Run the program written for Exercise 4a on a computer.

5. *a.* Write a C++ program to calculate the volume of a pool. The equation for determining the volume is *volume = length * width * depth*. Assume that the pool has a length of 25 feet, a width of 10 feet, and a depth of 6 feet.
   b. Run the program written for Exercise 5a on a computer.

6. *a.* Write a C++ program to convert temperature in degrees Fahrenheit to degrees Celsius. The equation for this conversion is *Celsius = 5.0/9.0 * (Fahrenheit – 32.0)*. Have your program convert and display the Celsius temperature corresponding to 98.6 degrees Fahrenheit.
   b. Run the program written for Exercise 6a on a computer.

7. *a.* Write a C++ program to calculate the dollar amount contained in a piggy bank. The bank currently contains 12 half-dollars, 20 quarters, 32 dimes, 45 nickels, and 27 pennies.
   b. Run the program written for Exercise 7a on a computer.

8. *a.* Write a C++ program to calculate the distance, in feet, of a trip that is 2.36 miles long. One mile is equal to 5,280 feet.
   b. Run the program written for Exercise 8a on a computer.

9. *a.* Write a C++ program to calculate the elapsed time it took to make a 183.67-mile trip. The equation for computing elapsed time is *elapsed time = total distance / average speed*. Assume that the average speed during the trip was 58 miles per hour.
   b. Run the program written for Exercise 9a on a computer.

10. *a.* Write a C++ program to calculate the sum of the numbers from 1 to 100. The formula for calculating this sum is *sum = (n/2) * (2*a + (n–1)*d)*, where *n* = number of terms to be added, *a* = the first number, and *d* = the difference between each number.
   b. Run the program written for Exercise 10a on a computer.

11. Determine why the expression a – b = 25 is invalid but the expression a – (b = 25) is valid.

3.2 Mathematical Library Functions

As we have seen, assignment statements can be used to perform arithmetic computations. For example, the assignment statement

```
total_price = unit_price * amount;
```

multiplies the value in `unit_price` times the value in `amount` and assigns the resulting value to `total_price`. Although addition, subtraction, multiplication, and division are easily accomplished using C++'s arithmetic operators, no such operators exist for raising a number to a power, finding the square root of a number, or determining trigonometric values. To facilitate such calculations, C++ provides standard preprogrammed functions that can be included in a program.

Before using one of C++'s mathematical functions, you need to know:

- The name of the desired mathematical function
- What the mathematical function does
- The type of data required by the mathematical function
- The data type of the result returned by the mathematical function

To illustrate the use of C++'s mathematical functions, consider the mathematical function named `sqrt`, which calculates the square root of a number. The square root of a number is computed using the expression

$$sqrt(number)$$

where the function's name, in this case `sqrt`, is followed by parentheses containing the number for which the square root is desired. The purpose of the parentheses following the function name is to provide a funnel through which data can be passed to the function (see Figure 3–3). The items that are passed to the function through the parentheses are called *arguments* of the function and constitute its input data. For example, the following expressions are used to compute the square root of the arguments 4, 17.0, 25, 1043.29, and 6.4516:

```
sqrt(4)
sqrt(17.0)
sqrt(25)
sqrt(1043.29)
sqrt(6.4516)
```

FIGURE 3–3 Passing Data to the `sqrt()` Function

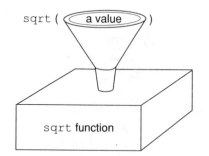

86

Notice that the argument to the `sqrt` function can be either an integer or a real value. This is another example of C++'s overloading capabilities. Function overloading permits the same function name to be defined for different argument data types. In this case there are really five square root functions named `sqrt`—one defined for `integer`, `long integer`, `float`, `double`, and `long double` arguments. The correct `sqrt` function is called depending on the type of value given it. The `sqrt` function determines the square root of its argument and returns the result as a double. The values returned by the previous expressions are:

Expression	Value Returned
`sqrt(4)`	2.0
`sqrt(17.0)`	4.123106
`sqrt(25)`	5.0
`sqrt(1043.29)`	32.3
`sqrt(6.4516)`	2.54

In addition to the `sqrt` function, Table 3–1 lists the more commonly used mathematical functions provided in C++. To access these functions in a program requires that the header file named `math.h`, which contains appropriate declarations for the mathematical function, be included with the function. This is done by placing the following preprocessor statement at the top of any program using a mathematical function:

$$\texttt{\#include <math.h>} \longleftarrow \text{no semicolon}$$

Although some of the mathematical functions listed require more than one argument, all functions, by definition, can directly return at most one value. Additionally, all of the functions listed are overloaded: This means the same function name can be used with integer and real arguments. Table 3–2 illustrates the value returned by selected functions using example arguments.

TABLE 3–1 Common C++ Functions

Function Name	Description	Returned Value
`abs(a)`	absolute value	same data type as argument
`pow(a1,a2)`	a1 raised to the a2 power	data type of argument a1
`sqrt(a)`	square root of a	same data type as argument
`sin(a)`	sine of a (a in radians)	double
`cos(a)`	cosine of a (a in radians)	double
`tan(a)`	tangent of a (a in radians)	double
`log(a)`	natural logarithm of a	double
`log10(a)`	common log (base 10) of a	double
`exp(a)`	e raised to the a power	double

TABLE 3–2 Selected Function Examples

Example	Returned Value
abs(-7.362)	7.362000
abs(-3)	3
pow(2.0,5.0)	32.000000
pow(10,3)	1000
log(18.697)	2.928363
log10(18.697)	1.271772
exp(-3.2)	0.040762

Each time a mathematical function is used it is called into action by giving the name of the function and passing any data to it within the parentheses following the function's name (see Figure 3–4).

The arguments that are passed to a function need not be single constants. An expression can also be an argument, provided that the expression can be computed to yield a value of the required data type. For example, the following arguments are valid for the given functions:

```
sqrt(4.0 + 5.3 * 4.0)        abs(2.3 * 4.6)
sqrt(16.0 * 2.0 - 6.7)       sin(theta - phi)
sqrt(x * y - z/3.2)          cos(2.0 * omega)
```

The expressions in parentheses are first evaluated to yield a specific value. Thus, values would have to be assigned to the variables theta, phi, x, y, z, and omega before their use in the above expressions. After the value of the argument is calculated, it is passed to the function.

Functions may be included as part of larger expressions. For example:

```
4 * sqrt(4.5 * 10.0 - 9.0) - 2.0 =
        4 * sqrt(36.0) - 2.0 =
              4 * 6.0 - 2.0 =
                  24.0 - 2.0 = 22.0
```

FIGURE 3–4 Using and Passing Data to a Function

```
function_name (data passed to function);
```

This indentifies
the called
function

This passes data to
the function

The step-by-step evaluation of an expression such as

```
3.0 * sqrt(5 * 33 - 13.71) / 5
```

is:

Step	Result
1. Perform multiplication in argument	`3.0 * sqrt(165 - 13.71) / 5`
2. Complete argument calculation	`3.0 * sqrt(151.29) / 5`
3. Return a function value	`3.0 * 12.3 /5`
4. Perform the multiplication	`36.9 / 5`
5. Perform the division	`7.38`

Program 3-5 illustrates the use of the `sqrt` function to determine the time it takes a ball to hit the ground after it has been dropped from an 800-foot tower. The mathematical formula used to calculate the time, in seconds, that it takes to fall a given distance, in feet, is:

$$time = sqrt(2 * distance / g)$$

where g is the gravitational constant equal to 32.2 ft/sec^2.

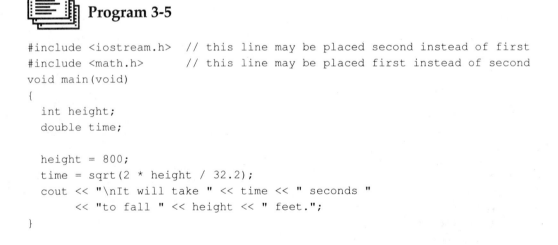 **Program 3-5**

```cpp
#include <iostream.h>   // this line may be placed second instead of first
#include <math.h>       // this line may be placed first instead of second
void main(void)
{
  int height;
  double time;

  height = 800;
  time = sqrt(2 * height / 32.2);
  cout << "\nIt will take " << time << " seconds "
       << "to fall " << height << " feet.";
}
```

The output produced by Program 3-5 is:

```
It will take 7.049074 seconds to fall 800 feet.
```

As used in Program 3-5, the value returned by the `sqrt` function is assigned to the variable `time`. In addition to assigning a function's returned value to a variable, the returned value may be included within a larger expression, or even used as an argument to another function. For example, the expression

```
sqrt ( pow ( abs (num1), num2 ) )
```

is valid. Since parentheses are present the computation proceeds from the inner to the outer pairs of parentheses. Thus, the absolute value of num1 is computed first and used as an argument to the pow function. The value returned by the pow function is then used as an argument to the sqrt function.

Casts

We have already seen the conversion of an operand's data type within mixed-mode arithmetic expressions (Sections 2.2 and 2.5) and across assignment operators (Section 3.1). In addition to these implicit data type conversions that are automatically made in mixed-mode arithmetic and assignment expressions, C++ also provides for explicit user-specified type conversions. The operator used to force the conversion of a value to another type is the cast operator. This is a unary operator having the form *data_type (expression)*, where data type is the desired data type of the expression following the cast. For example, the expression

```
int (a * b)
```

ensures that the value of the expression a * b is converted to an integer value.

Exercises 3.2

1. Write function calls to determine:
  a. The square root of 6.37.
  b. The square root of $x - y$.
  c. The sine of 30 degrees.
  d. The sine of 60 degrees.
  e. The absolute value of $a^2 - b^2$.
  f. The value of e raised to the 3rd power.

2. For $a = 10.6$, $b = 13.9$, $c = -3.42$, determine the value of:

  a. `int (a)`   *g.* `int (a + b + c)`
  b. `int (b)`   *h.* `float (int (a)) + b`
  c. `int (c)`   *i.* `float (int (a + b))`
  d. `int (a + b)`   *j.* `abs (a) + abs (b)`
  e. `int (a) + b + c`   *k.* `sqrt (abs (a - b))`
  f. `int (a + b) + c`

3. Write C++ statements for the following:

a. $c = \sqrt{a^2 + b^2}$

b. $p = \sqrt{|m - n|}$

c. $\text{sum} = \dfrac{a(r^n - 1)}{r - 1}$

4. Write, compile, and execute a C++ program that calculates and returns the 4th root of the number 81, which is 3. When you have verified that your program works correctly, use it to determine the fourth root of 1,728.896400. Your program should make use of the `sqrt` function.

5. Write, compile, and execute a C++ program that calculates the distance between two points whose coordinates are (7,12) and (3,9). Use the fact that the distance between two points having coordinates $(x1,y1)$ and $(x2,y2)$ is $distance = sqrt([x1 - x2]^2 + [y1 - y2]^2)$. When you have verified that your program works correctly, by calculating the distance between the two points manually, use your program to determine the distance between the points (–12,–15) and (22,5).

6. A model of worldwide population, in billions of people, after 1990 is given by the equation

$$\text{Population} = 5.5 \, e^{.02 [\text{Year} - 1990]}$$

Using this formula, write, compile, and execute a C++ program to estimate the worldwide population in the year 1995. Verify the result displayed by your program by calculating the answer manually. After you have verified your program is working correctly, use it to estimate the world's population in the year 2012.

7. Although we have been concentrating on integer and real arithmetic, C++ allows characters and integers to be added or subtracted. This can be done because C++ always converts a character to an equivalent integer value whenever a character is used in an arithmetic expression (the decimal value of each character can be found in Appendix B). Thus, characters and integers can be freely mixed in arithmetic expressions. For example, if your computer uses the ASCII code, the expression `'a' + 1` equals 98, and `'z' - 1` equals 121. These values can be converted back into characters using the cast operator. Thus, `char ('a' + 1) = 'b'` and `char ('z' - 1) = 'y'`. Similarly, `char ('A' + 1)` is `'B'`, and `char ('Z' - 1)` is `'Y'`. With this as background, determine the character results of the following expressions (assume that all characters are stored using the ASCII code):

a. `char ('m' - 5)`

b. `char ('m' + 5)`

c. `char ('G' + 6)`

d. `char ('G' - 6)`

e. `('b' - 'a')`

f. `('g' - 'a' + 1)`

g. `('G' - 'A' + 1)`

8. a. The table in Appendix B lists the integer values corresponding to each letter stored using the ASCII code. Using this table, notice that the uppercase letters consist of contiguous codes starting with an integer value of 65 for A and ending with 90 for the letter Z. Similarly, the lowercase letters begin with the integer value of 97 for the letter a and end with 122 for the letter z. With this as background, determine the character value of the expressions `char ('A' + 32)` and `char ('Z' + 32)`.

b. Using Appendix B, determine the integer value of the expression `'a' - 'A'`.

c. Using the results of Exercises 8a and 8b, determine the character value of the following expression, where *uppercase letter* can be any uppercase letter from A to Z:

`char (uppercase letter + 'a' - 'A')`

3.3 The cin object

Data for programs that are only going to be executed once may be included directly in the program. For example, if we wanted to multiply the numbers 30.0 and 0.05, we could use Program 3-6.

 Program 3-6

```
#include <iostream.h>
void main(void)
{
    float num1, num2, product;

    num1 = 30.0;
    num2 = 0.05;
    product = num1 * num2;
    cout << "30.0 times 0.05 is " << product;
}
```

The output displayed by Program 3-6 is:

```
30.0 times 0.05 is 1.5
```

Program 3-6 can be shortened, as illustrated in Program 3-7. Both programs, however, suffer from the same basic problem in that they must be rewritten in order to multiply different numbers. Both programs lack the facility for entering different numbers to be operated on.

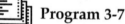 **Program 3-7**

```
#include <iostream.h>
void main(void)
{
    cout << "30.0 times 0.05 is " << 30.0 * 0.05;
}
```

Except for the practice provided to the programmer of writing, entering, and running the program, programs that do the same calculation only once, on the same set of numbers, are clearly not very useful. After all, it is simpler to use a calculator to multiply two numbers than to enter and run either Program 3-6 or 3-7.

This section presents the cin object, which is used to enter data into a program while it is executing. Just as the cout object displays a copy of the value stored inside a variable, the cin object allows the user to enter a value at the terminal (see Figure 3–5). The value is then stored directly in a variable.

When a statement such as cin >> num1; is encountered, the computer stops program execution and accepts data from the keyboard. When a data item is typed, the cin object stores the item in the variable listed after the extraction ("get from") operator, >>. The program then continues execution with the next statement after the call to cin. To see this, consider Program 3-8.

 Program 3-8

```cpp
#include <iostream.h>
void main(void)
{
    float num1, num2, product;

    cout << "Please type in a number: ";
    cin >> num1;
    cout << "Please type in another number: ";
    cin >> num2;
    product = num1 * num2;
    cout << num1 << " times " << num2 << " is " << product;
}
```

The first call to cout in Program 3-8 prints a string that tells the person at the terminal what should be typed. When an output string is used in this manner it is called a *prompt*. In this case the prompt tells the used to type a number. The computer then executes the next statement, which is a call to cin.

FIGURE 3–5 cin Is Used to Enter Data; cout Is Used to Display Data

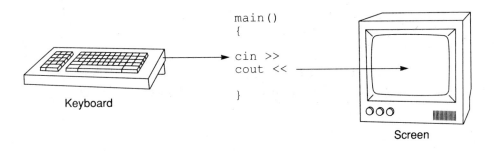

The cin object puts the computer into a temporary pause (or wait) state for as long as it takes the user to type a value. Then the user signals the cin object that the data entry is finished by pressing the return key after the value has been typed. The entered value is stored in the variable to the right of the extraction symbol, and the computer is taken out of its paused state. Program execution then proceeds with the next statement, which in Program 3-8 is another cout activation. This call causes the next message to be displayed. The second cin statement again puts the computer into a temporary wait state while the user types a second value. This second number is stored in the variable num2.

The following sample run was made using Program 3-8.

```
Please type in a number: 30
Please type in another number: 0.05
30 times 0.05 is 1.5
```

In Program 3-8, each time cin is invoked it is used to store one value into a variable. The cin object, however, can be used to enter and store as many values as there are extraction symbols, >>, and variables to hold the entered data. For example, the statement

```
cin >> num1 >> num2;
```

results in two values being read from the terminal and assigned to the variables num1 and num2. If the data entered at the terminal was

```
0.052 245.79
```

the variables num1 and num2 would contain the values 0.052 and 245.79, respectively. Notice that when actually entering numbers such as 0.052 and 245.79, there must be at least one space between the numbers. The space between the entered numbers clearly indicates where one number ends and the next begins. Inserting more than one space between numbers has no effect on cin.

The same spacing also is applicable to entering character data; that is, the extraction operator, >>, will skip blank spaces and store the next nonblank character in a character variable. For example, in response to the statements

```
char ch1, ch2, ch3;   // declare three character variables
cin >> ch1 >> ch2 >> ch3;   // accept three characters
```

the input

```
a          b  c
```

causes the letter a to be stored in the variable ch1, the letter b to be stored in the variable ch2, and the variable c to be stored in the variable ch3. Since a character variable can only be used to store one character, the input

```
abc
```

can also be used.

Any number of statements using the cin object may be made in a program, and any number of values may be input using a single cin statement. Program 3-9 illustrates using the cin object to input three numbers from the keyboard. The program then calculates and displays the average of the numbers entered.

 Program 3-9

```
#include <iostream.h>
void main(void)
{
    int num1, num2, num3;
    float average;

    cout << "Enter three integer numbers: ";
    cin >> num1 >> num2 >> num3;
    average = (num1 + num2 + num3) / 3.0;
    cout << "The average of the numbers is " << average;
}
```

The following sample run was made using Program 3-9:

```
Enter three integer numbers: 22 56 73
The average of the numbers is 50.333333
```

Note that the data typed at the keyboard for this sample run consists of the input:

```
22 56 73
```

In response to this stream of input, Program 3-9 stores the value 22 in the variable num1, the value 56 in the variable num2, and the value 73 in the variable num3 (see Figure 3–6). Since the average of three integer numbers can be a floating point number, the variable average, which is used to store the average, is declared as a floating point variable. Note also that the parentheses are needed in the assignment statement average = (num1 + num2 + num3) / 3.0;. Without these parentheses, the only value that would be divided by three would be the integer in num3 (because division has a higher precedence than addition).

The cin extraction operation, like the cout insertion operation, is "clever" enough to make a few data type conversions. For example, if an integer is entered in place of a floating point or double precision number, the integer will

95

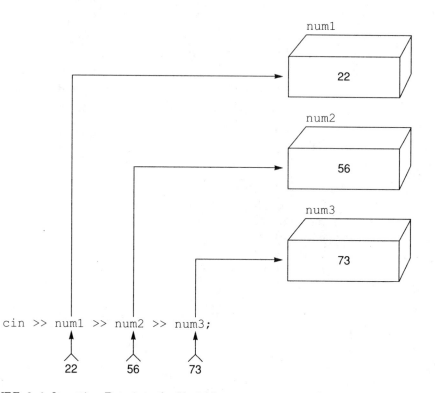

FIGURE 3–6 Inputting Data into the Variables num1, num2, and num3

be converted to the correct data type.[6] Similarly, if a floating point or double precision number is entered when an integer is expected, only the integer part of the number will be used. For example, assume the following numbers are typed in response to the statement cin >> num1 >> num2 >> num3;, where num1 and num3 have been declared as floating point variables and num2 is an integer variable

56   22.879   33.923

The 56 will be converted to 56.0 and stored in the variable num1. The extraction operation continues extracting data from the input stream sent to it, expecting an integer value. As far as cin is concerned, the decimal point after the 22 in the number 22.879 indicates the end of an integer and the start of a decimal number. Thus, the number 22 is assigned to num2. Continuing to process its input stream, cin takes the .879 as the next floating point number and assigns it to num3. As far as cin is concerned, 33.923 is extra input and is ignored. If, though, you do not initially type enough data, the cin object will continue to make the computer pause until sufficient data has been entered.

---

[6] Strictly speaking, what comes in from the keyboard is not any data type, such as an int or float, but is simply a sequence of characters. The extraction operation handles the conversion from the character sequence to a defined data type.

Exercises 3.3

1. For the following declaration statements, write a statement using the `cin` object that will cause the computer to pause while the appropriate data is typed by the user:

   a. `int firstnum;`
   b. `float grade;`
   c. `double secnum;`
   d. `char keyval;`
   e. `int month, years;`
     `float average;`
   f. `char ch;`
     `int num1,num2;`
     `double grade1,grade2;`
   g. `float interest, principal, capital;`
     `double price,yield;`
   h. `char ch,letter1,letter2;`
     `int num1,num2,num3;`
   i. `float temp1,temp2,temp3;`
     `double volts1,volts2;`

2. a. Write a C++ program that displays the following prompt:

```
Enter the radius of a circle:
```

After accepting a value for the radius, your program should calculate and display the circumference of the circle. (**Note:** *circumference = 2 * 3.1416 * radius.*)
b. Check the value displayed by the program written for Exercise 2a by calculating the result manually.

3. a. Write a C++ program that first displays the following prompt:

```
Enter the temperature in degrees Fahrenheit:
```

Have your program accept a value entered from the keyboard and convert the temperature entered to degrees Celsius, using the equation *Celsius = (5.0 / 9.0) * (Fahrenheit – 32.0)*. Your program should then display the temperature in degrees Celsius, using an appropriate output message.
b. Check the value displayed by the program written for Exercise 3a by calculating the result manually.

4. a. Write a C++ program that displays the following prompts:

```
Enter the length of the room:
Enter the width of the room:
```

After each prompt is displayed, your program should use a `cin` object call to accept data from the keyboard for the displayed prompt. After the width of the room is entered, your program should calculate and display the area of the room. The area displayed should be included in an appropriate message and calculated using the equation *area = length * width.*
b. Check the area displayed by the program written for Exercise 4a by calculating the result manually.

5. *a.* Write a C++ program that displays the following prompts:

```
Enter the miles driven:
Enter the gallons of gas used:
```

After each prompt is displayed, your program should use a `cin` object call to accept data from the keyboard for the displayed prompt. After the gallons of gas used has been entered, your program should calculate and display miles per gallon obtained. This value should be included in an appropriate message and calculated using the equation *miles per gallon = miles / gallons used.*

b. Check the value displayed by the program written for Exercise 5a by calculating the result manually.

6. *a.* Write a C++ program that displays the following prompts:

```
Enter the length of the swimming pool:
Enter the width of the swimming pool:
Enter the average depth of the swimming pool:
```

After each prompt is displayed, your program should use a `cin` object call to accept data from the keyboard for the displayed prompt. After the depth of the swimming pool is entered, your program should calculate and display the volume of the pool. The volume should be included in an appropriate message and calculated using the equation *volume = length * width * average depth.*

b. Check the volume displayed by the program written for Exercise 6a by calculating the result manually.

7. *a.* Write a C++ program that displays the following prompts:

```
Enter a number:
Enter a second number:
Enter a third number:
Enter a fourth number:
```

After each prompt is displayed, your program should use a `cin` object call to accept a number from the keyboard for the displayed prompt. After the fourth number has been entered, your program should calculate and display the average of the numbers. The average should be included in an appropriate message.

b. Check the average displayed for the program written in Exercise 7a by calculating the result manually.

c. Repeat Exercise 7a, making sure that you use the same variable name, `number`, for each number input. Also use the variable `sum` for the sum of the numbers. (*Hint:* To do this, you must use the statement `sum = sum + number;` after each number is accepted. Review the material on accumulating presented in Section 3.1.)

8. Write a C++ program that prompts the user to type in a number. Have your program accept the number as an integer and immediately display the integer using a `cout` object call. Run your program three times. The first time you run the program enter a valid integer number, the second time enter a floating point number, and the third time enter a character. Using the output display, see what number your program actually accepted from the data you entered.

9. Repeat Exercise 8 but have your program declare the variable used to store the number as a floating point variable. Run the program four times. The first time enter an integer, the second time enter a decimal number with less than six decimal places, the third time enter a number having more than six decimal places, and the fourth time enter a character. Using the output display, keep track of what number your program actually accepted from the data you typed in. What happened, if anything, and why?

10. Repeat Exercise 8 but have your program declare the variable used to store the number as a double precision variable. Run the program four times. The first time enter an integer, the second time enter a decimal number with less than six decimal places, the third time enter a number having more than six decimal places, and the fourth time enter a character. Using the output display, keep track of what number your program actually accepted from the data you typed in. What happened, if anything, and why?

11. a. Why do you think that successful application programs contain extensive data input validity checks? (*Hint:* Review Exercises 8, 9, and 10.)
   b. What do you think is the difference between a data type check and a data reasonableness check?
   c. Assume that a program requests that a month, day, and year be entered by the user. What are some checks that could be made on the data entered?

12. Program 3-8 prompts the user to input two numbers, where the first value entered is stored in num1 and the second value is stored in num2. Using this program as a starting point, write a program that swaps the values stored in the two variables.

3.4 The const Qualifier

Literal data is any data within a program that explicitly identifies itself. For example, the constants 2 and 3.1416 in the assignment statement

```
circum = 2 * 3.1416 * radius;
```

are also called literals because they are literally included directly in the statement. Additional examples of literals are contained in the following C++ assignment statements. See if you can identify them.

```
perimeter = 2 * length * width;
        y = (5 * p) / 7.2;
  salestax = 0.05 * purchase;
```

The literals are the numbers 2, 5 and 7.2, and 0.05 in the first, second, and third statements, respectively.

Quite frequently, literal data used within a program have a more general meaning that is recognized outside the context of the program. Examples of these types of constants include the number 3.1416, which is π accurate to four decimal places; 32.2 ft/sec^2, which is the gravitational constant; and the number 2.71828, which is Euler's number accurate to five decimal places.

The meaning of certain other constants appearing in a program are defined strictly within the context of the application being programmed. For example, in a program used to determine bank interest charges, the interest rate would typically appear in a number of different places throughout the program. Similarly, in a program used to calculate taxes, the tax rate might appear in many individual instructions. Numbers such as these are referred to by programmers as *magic numbers*. By themselves the numbers are ordinary, but in the context of a particular application they have a special ("magical") meaning. Frequently, the same magic number appears repeatedly within the same program. This recurrence of the same constant throughout a program is a potential source of error should the constant have to be changed. For example, if either the interest rate or sales tax rate change, as rates are prone to do, the programmer would have the cumbersome task of changing the value everywhere it appears in the program. Multiple changes, however, are subject to error—if just one rate value is overlooked and not changed, the result obtained when the program is run will be incorrect and the source of the error difficult to locate.

To avoid the problem of having a magic number spread throughout a program in many places and to permit clear identification of more universal constants, such as π, C++ allows the programmer to give these constants their own symbolic names. Then, instead of using the number throughout the program, the symbolic name is used instead. If the number ever has to be changed, the change need only be made once at the point where the symbolic name is equated to the actual number value. Equating numbers to symbolic names is accomplished using a const variable declaration qualifier. The const qualifier specifies that the declared variable can only be read after it is initialized; it cannot be changed. Three examples using this qualifier are:

```
const float PI = 3.1416;
const double SALESTAX = 0.05;
const int MAXNUM = 100;
```

The first declaration statement creates a floating point variable named PI and initializes it with the value 3.1416, while the second declaration statement creates the double precision variable named SALESTAX and initializes it to 0.05. Finally, the third declaration creates an integer variable named MAXNUM and initializes it with the value 100.

Once a const variable is created and initialized, *the value stored in the variable cannot be changed.* Thus, for all practical purposes the name of the variable and its value are linked together for the duration of the program that declares them.

Although we have typed the const variables in uppercase letters, lowercase letters could have been used. It is common in C++, however, to use uppercase letters for const variables to easily identify them as such. Then, whenever a programmer sees uppercase letters in a program, he or she will know the value of the variable cannot be changed within the program.

Once declared, a const variable can be used in any C++ statement in place of the number it represents. For example, the assignment statements

```
circum = 2 * PI * radius;
amount = SALESTAX * purchase;
```

are both valid. These statements must, of course, appear after the declarations for all their variables. Since a const declaration effectively equates a constant value to a variable, and the variable name can be used as a direct replacement for its initializing constant, such variables are commonly referred to as *symbolic constants* or *named constants*. We shall use these terms interchangeably. Program 3-10 illustrates the use of a symbolic constant.

Program 3-10

```cpp
#include <iostream.h>
#include <iomanip.h>
void main(void)
{
  float amount, taxes, total;
  const float SALESTAX = 0.05;

  cout << "\nEnter the amount purchased: ";
  cin >> amount;
  taxes = SALESTAX * amount;
  total = amount + taxes;
  cout << "The sales tax is " << setiosflags(ios::showpoint)
       << setw(4) << setprecision(2) << taxes;
  cout << "\nThe total bill is " << setiosflags(ios::showpoint)
       << setw(5) << setprecision(2) << total;
}
```

The following sample run was made using Program 3-10:

```
Enter the amount purchased: 36.00
The sales tax is 1.80
The total bill is 37.80
```

Although we have used the const qualifier to construct symbolic constants, we will encounter this data type once again in Chapter 12, where we will show that it is useful as a function argument in ensuring that the argument is not modified within the function.

Exercises 3.4

Determine the purpose of the programs given in Exercises 1 through 3. Then rewrite each program using a symbolic constant for the appropriate literals.

1.
```cpp
#include <iostream.h>
void main(void)
{
    float radius, circum;
    cout << "Enter a radius: ";
    cin >> radius;
    circum = 2.0 * 3.1416 * radius;
    cout << "\nThe circumference of the circle is " << circum;
}
```

2.
```cpp
#include <iostream.h>
void main(void)
{
    float prime, amount, interest;
    prime = .08;        // prime interest rate
    cout << "Enter the amount: ";
    cin >> amount;
    interest = prime * amount;
    cout << "\nThe interest earned is  dollars" << interest;
}
```

3.
```cpp
#include <iostream.h>
void main(void)
{
    float fahren, celsius;
    cout << "Enter a temperature in degrees Fahrenheit: ";
    cin >> fahren;
    celsius = (5.0/9.0) * (fahren - 32.0);
    cout << "\nThe equivalent Celsius temperature is "
         << celsius;
}
```

3.5 Common Programming Errors

In using the material presented in this chapter, be aware of the following possible errors:

1. Forgetting to assign or initialize values for all variables before the variables are used in an expression. Such values can be assigned by assignment statements, initialized within a declaration statement, or assigned interactively by entering values using the cin object.

2. Applying either the increment or decrement operator to an expression. For example, the expression

```
(count + n)++
```

is incorrect. The increment and decrement operators can only be applied to individual variables.

3. Forgetting to separate all variables passed to cin with an extraction symbol, >>.

A more exotic and less common error occurs when the increment and decrement operators are used with variables that appear more than once in the same expression. This error occurs because C++ does not specify the order in which operands are accessed within an expression. For example, the value assigned to result in the statement

```
result = i + i++;
```

is computer dependent. If your computer accesses the first operand, i, first, the above statement is equivalent to

```
result = 2 * i;
i++;
```

However, if your computer accesses the second operand, i++, first, the value of the first operand will be altered before it is used the second time and the value $2i + 1$ is assigned to result. As a general rule, therefore, do not use either the increment or decrement operator in an expression when the variable it operates on appears more than once in the expression.

3.6 Chapter Summary

1. An *expression* is a sequence of one or more operands separated by operators. An operand is a constant, a variable, or another expression. A value is associated with an expression.

2. Expressions are evaluated according to the precedence and associativity of the operators used in the expression.

3. The assignment symbol, =, is an operator. Expressions using this operator assign a value to a variable; additionally, the expression itself takes on a value. Since assignment is an operation in C++, multiple uses of the assignment operator are possible in the same expression.

4. The increment operator, ++, adds one to a variable, while the decrement operator, --, subtracts one from a variable. Both of these operators can be used as prefixes or postfixes. In prefix operation the variable is incremented (or decremented) before its value is used. In postfix operation the variable is incremented (or decremented) after its value is used.

5. The `cin` object is used for data input. This object accepts a stream of data from the keyboard and assigns the data to variables. The general form of a statement using `cin` is:

```
cin >> var1 >> var2 . . . >> varn;
```

The extraction symbol, >>, must be used to separate the variable names.

6. Values can be equated to a single variable, using the `const` variable qualifier when the variable is declared. This makes the variable read-only after it is initialized within the declaration statement. This declaration has the form

```
const data-type variable-name = initial value;
```

and permits the variable to be used instead of the initial value anywhere in the program after the command. Generally, such declarations are placed at the top of a C++ program.

Selection

Chapter Four

The term *flow of control* refers to the order in which a program's statements are executed. Unless directed otherwise, the normal flow of control for all programs is sequential. This means that each statement is executed in sequence, one after another, in the order in which they are placed within the program.

Both selection and repetition statements allow the programmer to alter the normal sequential flow of control. As their names imply, selection statements provide the ability to select which statement, from a well-defined set, will be executed next, while repetition statements provide the ability to go back and repeat a set of statements. In this chapter we present C++'s selection statements. Since selection requires choosing between alternatives, we begin this chapter with a description of C++'s selection criteria.

4.1 Relational Expressions

Besides providing addition, subtraction, multiplication, and division capabilities, all computers have the ability to compare numbers. Because many seemingly "intelligent" decision-making situations can be reduced to the level of choosing between two values, a computer's comparison capability can be used to create a remarkable intelligence-like facility.

The expressions used to compare operands are called *relational expressions*. A *simple relational expression* consists of a relational operator connecting two variable and/or constant operands, as shown in Figure 4–1. The relational operators available in C++ are given in Table 4–1. These relational operators may be used with integer, float, double, or character data, but must be typed exactly as given in Table 4–1. Thus, while the following examples are all valid:

```
age > 40        length <= 50           temp > 98.6
   3 < 4          flag == done      id_num == 682
day != 5          2.0 > 3.3          hours > 40
```

the following are invalid:

```
length =< 50      // incorrect symbol
2.0 >> 3.3        // invalid relational operator
flag = = done     // spaces are not allowed
```

FIGURE 4–1 Anatomy of a Simple Relational Expression

```
        Operand   Relational  Operand
                    operator
            \          |          /
             ↓         ↓         ↓
             price  <   12.5
             _____/
                       
                  Expression
```

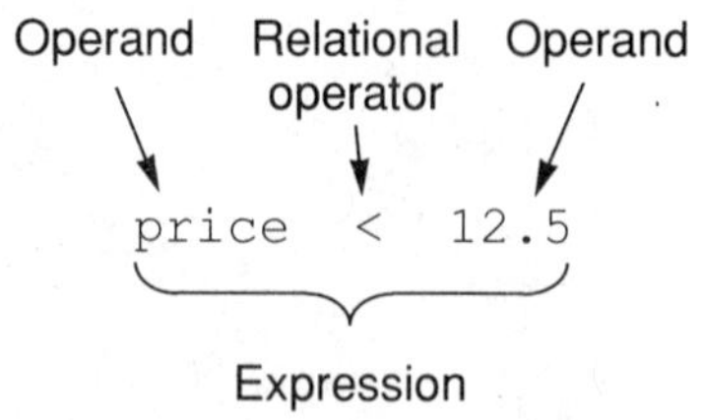

TABLE 4-1   Relational Operators in C++

Relational Operator	Meaning	Example
<	less than	age < 30
>	greater than	height > 6.2
<=	less than or equal to	taxable <= 20000
>=	greater than or equal to	temp >= 98.6
==	equal to	grade == 100
!=	not equal to	number != 250

Relational expressions are sometimes called conditions, and we will use both terms to refer to these expressions. Like all C++ expressions, relational expressions are evaluated to yield a numerical result.[1] *A condition that we would interpret as true evaluates to an integer value of 1, and a false condition results in an integer value of 0.* For example, because the relationship 3 < 4 is always true, this expression has a value of 1, and because the relationship 2.0 > 3.3 is always false, the value of the expression itself is 0. This can be verified using the statements

```
cout << "The value of 3 < 4 is " << (3 < 4);
cout << "\nThe value of 2.0 > 3.0 is " << (2.0 > 3.3);
```

which results in the display

```
The value of 3 < 4 is 1
The value of 2.0 > 3.0 is 0
```

The value of a relational expression such as hours > 40 depends on the value stored in the variable hours.

In a C++ program, a relational expression's value is not as important as the interpretation C++ places on the value when the expression is used as part of a selection statement. In these statements, which are presented in the next section, we will see that a zero value is used by C++ to represent a false condition and any nonzero value is used to represent a true condition. The selection of which statement to execute next is then based on the value obtained.

In addition to numerical operands, character data can also be compared using relational operators. For example, in the ASCII code the letter 'A' is stored using a code having a lower numerical value than the letter 'B', the code for a 'B' is lower in value than the code for a 'C', and so on. For character sets coded in this manner, the following conditions are evaluated as listed.

---

[1] In this regard, both C and C++ differ from other high-level programming languages that yield a Boolean (true, false) result.

Expression	Value	Interpretation
'A' > 'C'	0	False
'D' <= 'Z'	1	True
'E' == 'F'	0	False
'G' >='M'	0	False
'B' != 'C'	1	True

Comparing letters is essential in alphabetizing names or using characters to select a particular choice in decision-making situations.

Logical Operators

In addition to using simple relational expressions as conditions, more complex conditions can be created using the logical operators AND, OR, and NOT. These operators are represented by the symbols &&, ||, and !, respectively.

When the AND operator, &&, is used with two simple expressions, the condition is true only if both individual expressions are true by themselves. Thus, the compound condition

$$(age > 40) \&\& (term < 10)$$

is true (has a value of 1) only if age is greater than 40 and term is less than 10. Since relational operators have a higher precedence than logical operators, the parentheses in this logical expression could have been omitted.

The logical OR operator, ||, is also applied between two expressions. When using the OR operator, the condition is satisfied if either one or both of the two expressions is true. Thus, the compound condition

$$(age > 40) || (term < 10)$$

will be true if either age is greater than 40, term is less than 10, or both conditions are true. Again, the parentheses surrounding the relational expressions are included to make the expression easier to read. Because of the higher precedence of relational operators with respect to logical operators the same evaluation would be made even if the parentheses were omitted.

For the declarations

```
int i,j;
float a,b,complete;
```

the following represent valid conditions:

```
a > b
(i == j) || (a < b) || complete
(a/b > 5) && (i <= 20)
```

Before these conditions can be evaluated, the values of a, b, i, j, and complete must be known. Assuming the assignments

$$
\begin{aligned}
a &= 12.0; \\
b &= 2.0; \\
i &= 15; \\
j &= 30; \\
complete &= 0.0;
\end{aligned}
$$

the previous expressions yield the following results:

Expression	Value	Interpretation
a > b	1	True
(i == j) || (a < b) || complete	0	False
(a/b > 5) && (i <= 20)	1	True

The NOT operator is used to change an expression to its opposite state; that is, if the expression has any nonzero value (true), !expression produces a zero value (false). If an expression is false to begin with (has a zero value), !expression is true and evaluates to 1. For example, assuming the number 26 is stored in the variable age, the expression (age > 40) has a value of zero (it is false), while the expression !(age > 40) has a value of 1. Since the NOT operator is used with only one operand, it is a unary operator.

The relational and logical operators have a hierarchy of execution similar to the arithmetic operators. Table 4–2 lists the precedence of these operators in relation to the other operators we have used.

TABLE 4–2   Precedence of Relational
and Logical Operators

Operator	Associativity
! unary - ++ --	right to left
* / %	left to right
+ -	left to right
< <= > >=	left to right
== !=	left to right
&&	left to right
||	left to right
= += -= *= /=	right to left

The following example illustrates the use of an operator's precedence and associativity to evaluate relational expressions, assuming the following declarations:

```
char key = 'm';
int i = 5, j = 7, k = 12;
double x = 22.5;
```

Expression	Equivalent Expression	Value	Interpretation
i + 2 == k - 1	(i + 2) == (k - 1)	0	False
3 * i - j < 22	((3 * i) - j) < 22	1	True
i + 2 * j > k	(i + (2 * j)) > k	1	True
k + 3 <= -j + 3 * i	(k + 3) <= ((-j) + (3*i))	0	False
'a' + 1 == 'b'	('a' + 1) == 'b'	1	True
key - 1 > 'p'	(key - 1) > 'p'	0	False
key + 1 == 'n'	(key + 1) == 'n'	1	True
25 >= x + 1.0	25 >= (x + 1.0)	0	False

As with all expressions, parentheses can be used to alter the assigned operator priority and improve the readability of relational expressions. By evaluating the expressions within parentheses first, the following compound condition is evaluated as:

```
(6 * 3 == 36 / 2)  || (13 < 3 * 3 + 4)   && !(6 - 2 < 5)
       (18 == 18)  ||    (13 < 9 + 4)    && !(4 < 5)
                1  ||    (13 < 13)        && !1
                1  ||          0          && 0
                1  ||          0
                1
```

A Numerical Accuracy Problem

A problem that can occur with C++'s relational expressions is a subtle numerical accuracy problem relating to floating point and double precision numbers. Because of the way computers store these numbers, tests for equality of floating point and double precision values and variables using the relational operator == should be avoided.

The reason for this is that many decimal numbers, such as 0.1, for example, cannot be represented exactly in binary using a finite number of bits. Thus, testing for exact equality for such numbers can fail. When equality of noninteger values is desired it is better to require that the absolute value of the difference between operands be less than some extremely small value. Thus, for real operands the general expression

$$operand\_1 == operand\_2$$

should be replaced by the condition

$$fabs(operand\_1 - operand\_2) < epsilon$$

where `epsilon` can be a `const` set to any acceptably small value, such as 0.0000001.[2] Thus, if the difference between the two operands is less than the value of `epsilon`, the two operands are considered essentially equal. For example, if x and y are floating point variables, a condition such as

$$x/y == 0.35$$

should be programmed as

$$abs(x/y - 0.35) < epsilon$$

This latter condition ensures that slight inaccuracies in representing non-integer numbers in binary do not affect evaluation of the tested condition.

Exercises 4.1

1. Determine the value of the following expressions. Assume a = 5, b = 2, c = 4, d = 6, and e = 3.

a. a > b	***f.*** a * b
b. a != b	***g.*** a % b * c
c. d % b == c % b	***h.*** c % b * a
d. a * c != d * b	***i.*** b % c * a
e. d * b == c * e	

2. Using parentheses, rewrite the following expressions to correctly indicate their order of evaluation. Then evaluate each expression assuming a = 5, b = 2, and c = 4.

a. a % b * c && c % b * a

b. a % b * c || c % b * a

c. b % c * a && a % c * b

d. b % c * a || a % c * b

---

[2] Using the `abs()` function requires inclusion of the `math.h` header file. This is done by placing the preprocessor statement `#include <math.h>` either immediately before or after the `#include <iostream.h>` preprocessor statement.

3. Write relational expressions to express the following conditions (use variable names of your own choosing):

   a. a person's age is equal to 30
   b. a person's temperature is greater than 98.6
   c. a person's height is less than 6 feet
   d. the current month is 12 (December)
   e. the letter input is m
   f. a person's age is equal to 30 and the person is taller than 6 feet
   g. the current day is the 15th day of the 1st month
   h. a person is older than 50 or has been employed at the company for at least 5 years
   i. a person's identification number is less than 500 and the person is older than 55
   j. a length is greater than 2 feet and less than 3 feet

4. Determine the value of the following expressions, assuming a = 5, b = 2, c = 4, and d = 5.

   a. `a == 5`
   b. `b * d == c * c`
   c. `d % b * c > 5 || c % b * d < 7`

4.2 The `if-else` Statement

The `if-else` statement directs the computer to select a sequence of one or more instructions based on the result of a comparison. For example, if a New Jersey resident's income is less than $20,000, the applicable state tax rate is 2 percent. If the person's income is greater than $20,000, a different rate is applied to the amount over $20,000. The `if-else` statement can be used in this situation to determine the actual tax based on whether the gross income is less than or equal to $20,000. The general form of the `if-else` statement is:

```
if (expression) statement1;
else statement2;
```

The expression is evaluated first. If the value of the expression is nonzero, `statement1` is executed. If the value is zero the statement after the keyword `else` is executed. Thus, one of the two statements (either `statement1` or `statement2`) is always executed depending on the value of the expression. Notice that the tested expression must be put in parentheses and a semicolon is placed after each statement.

   For clarity, the `if-else` statement may also be written on four lines using the form

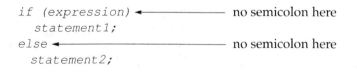

```
if (expression) ◄─────────── no semicolon here
    statement1;
else ◄─────────── no semicolon here
    statement2;
```

The form of the `if-else` statement that is selected generally depends on the length of statements 1 and 2. However, when using the second form do not put a semicolon after the parentheses or the keyword `else`. The semicolons are placed only at the end of each statement.

As an example, let us write an income tax computation program containing an `if-else` statement. As previously described, a New Jersey state income tax is assessed at 2 percent of taxable income for incomes less than or equal to $20,000. For taxable income greater than $20,000, state taxes are 2.5 percent of the income that exceeds $20,000 plus a fixed amount of $400. The expression to be tested is whether taxable income is less than or equal to $20,000. An appropriate `if-else` statement for this situation is:[3]

```
if (taxable <= 20000.0)
   taxes = 0.02 * taxable;
else
   taxes = 0.025 * (taxable - 20000.0) + 400.0;
```

Here we have used the relational operator `<=` to represent the relation "less than or equal to." If the value of `taxable` is less than or equal to 20000.0, the condition is true (has a value of 1) and the statement `taxes = 0.02 * taxable;` is executed. If the condition is not true, the value of the expression is zero, and the statement after the keyword `else` is executed. Program 4-1 illustrates the use of this statement in a complete program.

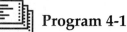 **Program 4-1**

```
#include <iostream.h>
#include <iomanip.h>
void main(void)
{
   float taxable, taxes;

   cout << "Please type in the taxable income: ";
   cin >> taxable;

   if (taxable <= 20000.0)
      taxes = 0.02 * taxable;
   else
      taxes = 0.025 * (taxable - 20000.0) + 400.0;

   cout << setiosflags(ios::showpoint)
        << setprecision(2)
        << "Taxes are $ " << taxes;
}
```

[3] Note that in actual practice the numerical values in this statement would be defined as constants.

A blank line was inserted before and after the `if-else` statement to highlight it in the complete program. We will continue to do this throughout the text to emphasize the statement being presented.

To illustrate selection in action, Program 4-1 was run twice with different input data. The results are:

```
Please type in the taxable income: 10000.
Taxes are $ 200.00
```

and

```
Please type in the taxable income: 30000.
Taxes are $ 650.00
```

Observe that the taxable income input in the first run of the program was less than $20,000, and the tax was correctly calculated as 2 percent of the number entered. In the second run, the taxable income was more than $20,000, and the `else` part of the `if-else` statement was used to yield a correct tax computation of

$$0.025 * (\$30,000. - \$20,000.) + \$400. = \$650.$$

Although any expression can be tested by an `if-else` statement, generally only relational expressions are used. However, statements such as

```
if (num)
    cout << "Bingo!";
else
    cout << "You lose!";
```

are valid. Since `num`, by itself, is a valid expression, the message `Bingo!` is displayed if `num` has any nonzero value and the message `You lose!` is displayed if `num` has a value of zero.

Compound Statements

Although only a single statement is permitted in both the `if` and `else` parts of the `if-else` statement, this statement can be a single compound statement. A *compound statement* is any number of single statements contained between braces, as shown in Figure 4-2.

FIGURE 4-2 A Compound Statement Consists of Individual Statements Enclosed Within Braces

```
{
    statement1;
    statement2;
    statement3;
         .
         .
         .
    last statement;
}
```

The use of braces to enclose a set of individual statements creates a single block of statements, which may be used anywhere in a C++ program in place of a single statement. The next example illustrates the use of a compound statement within the general form of an if-else statement.

```
if (expression)
{
   statement1;     // as many statements as necessary
   statement2;     // can be put within the braces
   statement3;     // each statement must end with a ;
}
else
{
   statement4;
   statement5;
         .
         .
         .
   statementn;
}
```

Program 4-2 illustrates the use of a compound statement in an actual program.

Program 4-2

```cpp
#include <iostream.h>
#include <iomanip.h>
void main(void)
{
  char temp_type;
  float temp, fahren, celsius;

  cout << "Enter the temperature to be converted: ";
  cin >> temp;
  cout << "Enter an f if the temperature is in Fahrenheit";
  cout << "\n or a c if the temperature is in Celsius: ";
  cin >> temp_type;

  if (temp_type == 'f')
  {
    celsius = (5.0 / 9.0) * (temp - 32.0);
    cout << setiosflags(ios::showpoint)
         << setprecision(2)
         << "\nThe equivalent Celsius temperature is " << celsius;
  }
  else
  {
    fahren = (9.0 / 5.0) * temp + 32.0;
    cout << "\nThe equivalent Fahrenheit temperature is " << fahren;
  }

}
```

Program 4-2 checks whether the value in `temp_type` is f. If the value is f, the compound statement corresponding to the `if` part of the `if-else` statement is executed. Any other letter results in execution of the compound statement corresponding to the `else` part. Following is a sample run of Program 4-2:

```
Enter the temperature to be converted: 212
Enter an f if the temperature is in Fahrenheit
or a c if the temperature is in Celsius: f

The equivalent Celsius temperature is 100.00
```

Block Scope

All statements contained within a compound statement constitute a single block of code and any variable declared within such a block only has meaning between its declaration and the closing braces defining the block. For example, consider the following section of code, which consists of two blocks of code:

```
{   // start of outer block
    int a = 25;
    int b = 17;

    cout << "The value of a is " << a << " and b is " << b << "\n";
    {    // start of inner block
      float a = 46.25;
      int c = 10;

      cout << "a is now " << a
           << " b is now " << b
           << " and c is " << c << "\n";
    }   // end of inner block

    cout << "a is now " << a << " and b is "<< b << "\n";
}   // end of outer block
```

The output that is produced by this section of code is:

```
The value of a is 25 and b is 17
a is now 46.25 b is now 17 and c is 10
a is now 25 and b is 17
```

This output is produced as follows.

The first block of code defines two variables named a and b, which may be used anywhere within this block after their declaration, including any block contained inside of it. Within the inner block, two new variables have been declared, named a and c. At this stage, then, we have created four different variables, two of which have the same name. Any referenced variable first results in an attempt to access a variable correctly declared within the block containing the reference. If no variable is defined within the block, an attempt is made to access a variable in the next immediate outside block until a valid access results.

Thus, the values of the variables a and c referenced within the inner block use the values of the variables a and c declared in that block. Since no variable named b was declared inside the inner block, the value of b displayed from within the inner block is obtained from the outer block. Finally, the last cout object, which is outside of the inner block, displays the value of the variable a declared in the outer block. If an attempt was made to display the value of c anywhere in the outer block, the compiler would issue an error message stating that c is an undefined symbol.

The location within a program where a variable can be used is formally referred to as the *scope* of the variable, and we will have much more to say on this subject in Chapter 6.

One-Way Selection

A useful modification of the if-else statement involves omitting the else part of the statement altogether. In this case, the if statement takes the shortened and frequently useful form:

> *if (expression)*
> *statement;*

The statement following the *if (expression)* is only executed if the expression has a nonzero value (a true condition). As before, the statement may be a compound statement.

This modified form of the if statement is called a one-way if statement. It is illustrated in Program 4-3, which checks a car's mileage and prints a message if the car has been driven more than 3000.0 miles.

 Program 4-3

```cpp
#include <iostream.h>
void main(void)
{
    int id_num;
    float miles;
    const float LIMIT = 3000.0;

    cout << "Please type in car number and mileage: ";
    cin >> id_num >> miles;

    if(miles > LIMIT)
        cout << " Car " << id_num << " is over the limit.\n";

    cout << "End of program output.\n";
}
```

To illustrate the one-way selection criteria in action, Program 4-3 was run twice, each time with different input data. Only the input data for the first run causes the message Car 256 is over the limit to be displayed.

```
Please type in car number and mileage: 256 3562.8
  Car 256 is over the limit.
End of program output.
```

and

```
Please type in car number and mileage: 23 2562.3
End of program output.
```

Problems Associated with the if-else Statement

Two of the most common problems encountered in initially using C++'s if-else statement are:

1. Misunderstanding the full implications of what an expression is
2. Using the assignment operator, =, in place of the relational operator, ==

Recall that an expression is any combination of operands and operators that yields a result. This definition is extremely broad and more encompassing than is initially apparent. For example, all of the following are valid C++ expressions:

```
age + 5
age = 30
age == 40
```

Assuming that the variables are suitably declared, each of the above expressions yields a result. The following section of code uses the cout object to display the value of these expressions when age is initially assigned the value 18:

```
age = 18;
cout << "\nThe value of the first expression is " << (age + 5)
     << "\nThe value of the second expression is " << (age = 30)
     << "\nThe value of the third expression is " << (age == 40);
```

The display produced by this section of code is:

```
The value of the first expression is 23
The value of the second expression is 30
The value of the third expression is 0
```

As this output illustrates, each expression, by itself, has a value associated with it. The value of the first expression is the sum of the variable age plus 5, which is 23. The value of the second expression is 30, which is also assigned to the variable `age`. The value of the third expression is zero, since `age` is not equal to 40, and a false condition is represented in C++ with a value of zero. If the value in `age` had been 40, the relational expression a == 40 would be true and would have a value of 1.

Now assume that the relational expression age == 40 was intended to be used in the `if` statement

```
if (age == 40)
   cout << "Happy Birthday!";
```

but was mistyped as age = 40, resulting in

```
if (age = 40)
   cout << "Happy Birthday!";
```

Since the mistake results in a valid C++ expression, and any C++ expression can be tested by an `if` statement, the resulting `if` statement is valid and will cause the message `Happy Birthday!` to be printed regardless of what value was previously assigned to `age`. Can you see why?

The condition tested by the `if` statement does not compare the value in `age` to the number 40, but assigns the number 40 to `age`. That is, the expression age = 40 is not a relational expression at all, but an assignment expression. At the completion of the assignment the expression itself has a value of 40. Since C++ treats any nonzero value as true, the call to `cout` is made. Another way of looking at this is to realize that the `if` statement is equivalent to the following two statements:

```
age = 40;      // assign 40 to age
if (age)       // test the value of age
cout << "Happy Birthday!";
```

Since a C++ compiler has no means of knowing that the expression being tested is not the desired one, you must be especially careful when writing conditions.

Exercises 4.2

1. Rewrite Program 4-1 using the following statements:

```
const float LIMIT = 20000.0;
const float REGRATE = 0.02;
const float HIGHRATE = 0.025;
const float FIXED = 400.0;
```

(If necessary, review Section 3.4 for the use of symbolic constants.)

2. *a.* If money is left in a particular bank for more than 5 years, the interest rate given by the bank is 9.5 percent, else the interest rate is 5.4 percent. Write a C++ program that uses the `cin` object to accept the number of years into the variable `num_yrs` and display the appropriate interest rate depending on the value input into `num_yrs`.

b. How many runs should you make for the program written in Exercise 2a to verify that it is operating correctly? What data should you input in each of the program runs?

3. *a.* In a pass/fail course, a student passes if the grade is greater than or equal to 70 and fails if the grade is lower. Write a C++ program that accepts a grade and prints the message `A passing grade` or `A failing grade`, as appropriate.

b. How many runs should you make for the program written in Exercise 3a to verify that it is operating correctly? What data should you input in each of the program runs?

4. *a.* Write a C++ program to compute and display a person's weekly salary as determined by the following expressions:

If the hours worked are less than or equal to 40, the person receives $8.00 per hour, otherwise the person receives $320.00 plus $12.00 for each hour worked over 40 hours.

The program should request the hours worked as input and should display the salary as output.

b. How many runs should you make for the program written in Exercise 4a to verify that it is operating correctly? What data should you input in each of the program runs?

5. *a.* A senior salesperson is paid $400 a week and a junior salesperson $275 a week. Write a C++ program that accepts as input a salesperson's status in the character variable `status`. If status equals `'s'`, the senior person's salary should be displayed, otherwise the junior person's salary should be output.

b. How many runs should you make for the program written in Exercise 5a to verify that it is operating correctly? What data should you input in each of the program runs?

6. *a.* Write a C++ program that displays either the message `I feel great today!` or `I feel down today #$*!` depending on the input. If the character u is entered in the variable `ch`, the first message should be displayed, else the second message should be displayed.

b. How many runs should you make for the program written in Exercise 6a to verify that it is operating correctly? What data should you input in each of the program runs?

7. *a.* Write a program to display the following two prompts:

```
Enter a month: (use a 1 for Jan, etc.)
Enter a day of the month:
```

Have your program accept and store a number in the variable `month` in response to the first prompt, and accept and store a number in the variable `day` in response to the second prompt. If the month entered is not between 1 and 12 inclusive, print a message informing the user that an invalid month has been entered. If the day entered is not between 1 and 31, print a message informing the user that an invalid day has been entered.

b. What will your program do if the user types a number with a decimal point for the month? How can you ensure that your `if` statements check for an integer number?

8. Write a C++ program that accepts a character using the `cin` object and determines if the character is a lowercase letter. A lowercase letter is any character that is greater than or equal to `'a'` and less than or equal to `'z'`. If the entered character is a lowercase letter, display the message `The character just entered is a lowercase letter`. If the entered letter is not lowercase, display the message `The character just entered is not a lowercase letter.`

9. Write a C++ program that first determines if an entered character is a lowercase letter (see Exercise 8). If the letter is lowercase, determine and print out its position in the alphabet. For example, if the entered letter is c, the program should print out 3, since c is the third letter in the alphabet. (*Hint:* If the entered character is in lowercase, its position can be determined by subtracting `'a'` from the letter and adding 1.)

10. Repeat Exercise 8 to determine if the character entered is an uppercase letter. An uppercase letter is any character greater than or equal to `'A'` and less than or equal to `'Z'`.

11. Write a C++ program that first determines if an entered character is an uppercase letter (see Exercise 10). If the letter is uppercase, determine and print its position in the alphabet. For example, if the entered letter is g, the program should print out 7, since g is the seventh letter in the alphabet. (*Hint:* If the entered character is in uppercase, its position can be determined by subtracting `'A'` from the letter and adding 1.)

12. Write a C++ program that accepts a character using the `cin` object. If the character is a lowercase letter (see Exercise 8), convert the letter to uppercase and display the letter in its uppercase form. (*Hint:* Subtracting the integer value 32 from a lowercase letter yields the code for the equivalent uppercase letter. Thus, `'A' = (char) ('a' - 32)`.)

13. The following program displays the message `Hello there!` regardless of the letter input. Determine where the error is and, if possible, why the program always causes the message to be displayed.

```
#include <iostream.h>
void main(void)
{
  char letter;

  cout << "Enter a letter: ";
  cin >> letter;
  if (letter = 'm')
    cout << "Hello there!";
}
```

14. Write a C++ program that asks the user to input two numbers. After your program accepts these numbers using one or more `cin` object calls, have your program check the numbers. If the first number entered is greater than the second number, print the message `The first number is greater,` else print the message `The first number is not greater than the second.` Test your program by entering the numbers 5 and 8 and then using the numbers 11 and 2. What will your program display if the two numbers entered are equal?

4.3 Nested `if` Statements

As we have seen, an `if-else` statement can contain simple or compound statements. Any valid C++ statement can be used, including another `if-else` statement. Thus, one or more `if-else` statements can be included within either part of an `if-else` statement. For example, substituting the one-way `if` statement

```
if (hours > 6)
   cout << "snap";
```

for `statement1` in the following `if` statement

```
if (hours < 9)
    statement1;
else
    cout << "pop";
```

results in the nested `if` statement

```
if (hours < 9)
{
   if (hours > 6)
     cout << "snap";
}
else
    cout << "pop";
```

The braces around the inner one-way `if` are essential, because in their absence C++ associates an `else` with the closest unpaired `if`. Thus, without the braces, the above statement is equivalent to

```
if (hours < 9)
   if (hours > 6)
     cout << "snap";
   else
     cout << "pop";
```

Here the `else` is paired with the inner `if`, which destroys the meaning of the original `if-else` statement. Notice also that the indentation is irrelevant as far as the compiler is concerned. Whether the indentation exists or not, the statement is compiled by associating the last `else` with the closest unpaired `if`, unless braces are used to alter the default pairing.

The process of nesting `if` statements can be extended indefinitely, so that the `cout << "snap";` statement could itself be replaced by either a complete `if-else` statement or another one-way `if` statement.

The **if-else** Chain

Generally, the case in which the statement in the `if` part of an `if-else` statement is another `if` statement tends to be confusing and is best avoided.

However, an extremely useful construction occurs when the else part of an if statement contains another if-else statement. This takes the form:

```
if (expression_1)
   statement1;
else
   if (expression_2)
     statement2;
   else
     statement3;
```

As with all C++ programs, the indentation we have used is not required. In fact, the above construction is so common that it is typically written using the following arrangement:

```
if (expression_1)
   statement1;
else if (expression_2)
   statement2;
else
   statement3;
```

This construction is called an if-else chain and is used extensively in programming applications. Each condition is evaluated in order, and if any condition is true the corresponding statement is executed and the remainder of the chain is terminated. The final else statement is only executed if none of the previous conditions are satisfied. This serves as a default or catch-all case that is useful for detecting an impossible or error condition.

The chain can be continued indefinitely by repeatedly making the last statement another if-else statement. Thus, the general form of an if-else chain is:

```
if (expression_1)
   statement1;
else if (expression_2)
   statement2;
else if (expression_3)
   statement3;
        .
        .
        .
else if (expression_n)
   statement_n;
else
   last_statement;
```

As with all C++ statements, each individual statement can be a compound statement bounded by the braces { and }. To illustrate the if-else chain, Program 4-4 displays a person's marital status corresponding to a letter input. The following letter codes are used:

Marital Status	Input Code
Married	M
Single	S
Divorced	D
Widowed	W

Program 4-4

```cpp
#include <iostream.h>
void main(void)
{
  char marcode;

  cout << "Enter a marital code: ";
  cin >> marcode;

  if (marcode == 'M')
    cout << "\nIndividual is married.";
  else if (marcode == 'S')
    cout << "\nIndividual is single.";
  else if (marcode == 'D')
    cout << "\nIndividual is divorced.";
  else if (marcode == 'W')
    cout << "\nIndividual is widowed.";
  else
    cout << "\nAn invalid code was entered.";
}
```

As a final example illustrating the if-else chain, let us calculate the monthly income of a salesperson using the following commission schedule:

Monthly Sales	Income
greater than or equal to $50,000	$375 plus 16% of sales
less than $50,000 but greater than or equal to $40,000	$350 plus 14% of sales
less than $40,000 but greater than or equal to $30,000	$325 plus 12% of sales
less than $30,000 but greater than or equal to $20,000	$300 plus 9% of sales
less than $20,000 but greater than or equal to $10,000	$250 plus 5% of sales
less than $10,000	$200 plus 3% of sales

The following if-else chain can be used to determine the correct monthly income, where the variable mon_sales is used to store the salesperson's current monthly sales:

```
if (mon_sales >= 50000.00)
  income = 375.00 + .16 * mon_sales;
else if (mon_sales >= 40000.00)
  income = 350.00 + .14 * mon_sales;
else if (mon_sales >= 30000.00)
  income = 325.00 + .12 * mon_sales;
else if (mon_sales >= 20000.00)
  income = 300.00 + .09 * mon_sales;
else if (mon_sales >= 10000.00)
  income = 250.00 + .05 * mon_sales;
else
  income = 200.000 + .03 * mon_sales;
```

Notice that this example makes use of the fact that the chain is stopped once a true condition is found. This is accomplished by checking for the highest monthly sales first. If the salesperson's monthly sales are less than $50,000, the if-else chain continues checking for the next highest sales amount until the correct category is obtained.

Program 4-5 uses this if-else chain to calculate and display the income corresponding to the value of monthly sales input to the cin object.

 Program 4-5

```
#include <iostream.h>
#include <iomanip.h>
void main(void)
{
  float mon_sales, income;

  cout << "Enter the value of monthly sales: ";
  cin >> mon_sales;

  if (mon_sales >= 50000.00)
    income = 375.00 + .16 * mon_sales;
  else if (mon_sales >= 40000.00)
    income = 350.00 + .14 * mon_sales;
  else if (mon_sales >= 30000.00)
    income = 325.00 + .12 * mon_sales;
  else if (mon_sales >= 20000.00)
    income = 300.00 + .09 * mon_sales;
  else if (mon_sales >= 10000.00)
    income = 250.00 + .05 * mon_sales;
  else
    income = 200.00 + .03 * mon_sales;

  cout << setiosflags(ios::showpoint)
       << setiosflags(ios:: fixed)
       << setprecision(2)
       << "The income is $" << income;
}
```

A sample run using Program 4-5 is illustrated below:

```
Enter the value of monthly sales: 36243.89
The income is $4674.27
```

Exercises 4.3

1. A student's letter grade is calculated according to the following schedule:

Numerical Grade	Letter Grade
greater than or equal to 90	A
less than 90 but greater than or equal to 80	B
less than 80 but greater than or equal to 70	C
less than 70 but greater than or equal to 60	D
less than 60	F

Write a C++ program that accepts a student's numerical grade, converts the numerical grade to an equivalent letter grade, and displays the letter grade.

2. The interest rate used on funds deposited in a bank is determined by the amount of time the money is left on deposit. For a particular bank, the following schedule is used:

Time on Deposit	Interest Rate
greater than or equal to 5 years	.095
less than 5 years but greater than or equal to 4 years	.09
less than 4 years but greater than or equal to 3 years	.085
less than 3 years but greater than or equal to 2 years	.075
less than 2 years but greater than or equal to 1 year	.065
less than 1 year	.058

Write a C++ program that accepts the time that funds are left on deposit and displays the interest rate corresponding to the time entered.

3. Write a C++ program that accepts a number followed by one space and then a letter. If the letter following the number is f, the program is to treat the number entered as a temperature in degrees Fahrenheit, convert the number to the equivalent degrees Celsius, and print a suitable display message. If the letter following the number is c, the program is to consider the number entered as a Celsius temperature, convert the number to the equivalent degrees Fahrenheit, and print a suitable display message. If the letter is neither f nor c the program is to print a message that the data entered is incorrect and terminate. Use an if-else chain in your program and make use of the conversion formulas:

$$\text{Celsius} = (5.0 / 9.0) * (\text{Fahrenheit} - 32.0)$$
$$\text{Fahrenheit} = (9.0 / 5.0) * \text{Celsius} + 32.0$$

4. Using the commission schedule from Program 4-5, the following program calculates monthly income:

```cpp
#include <iostream.h>
#include <iomanip.h>
void main(void)
{
  float mon_sales, income;


  cout << "Enter the value of monthly sales: ";
  cin >> mon_sales;


  if (mon_sales >= 50000.00)
    income = 375.00 + .16 * mon_sales;
  if (mon_sales >= 40000.00 && mon_sales < 50000.00)
    income = 350.00 + .14 * mon_sales;
  if (mon_sales >= 30000.00 && mon_sales < 40000.00)
    income = 325.00 + .12 * mon_sales;
  if (mon_sales >= 20000.00 && mon_sales < 30000.00)
    income = 300.00 + .09 * mon_sales;
  if (mon_sales >= 10000.00 && mon_sales < 20000.00)
    income = 250.00 + .05 * mon_sales;
  if (mon_sales < 10000.00)
    income = 200.00 + .03 * mon_sales;


  cout << setiosflags(ios::showpoint)
       << setiosflags(ios:: fixed)
       << setprecision(2)
       << "\n\nThe income is $" << income;
}
```

a. Will this program produce the same output as Program 4-5?

b. Which program is better and why?

5. The following program was written to produce the same result as Program 4-5:

```cpp
#include <iostream.h>
#include <iomanip.h>
void main(void)
{
   float mon_sales, income;

   cout << "Enter the value of monthly sales: ";
   cin >> mon_sales;

   if (mon_sales < 10000.00)
      income = 200.00 + .03 * mon_sales;
   else if (mon_sales >= 10000.00)
      income = 250.00 + .05 * mon_sales;
   else if (mon_sales >= 20000.00)
      income = 300.00 + .09 * mon_sales;
   else if (mon_sales >= 30000.00)
      income = 325.00 + .12 * mon_sales;
   else if (mon_sales >= 40000.00)
      income = 350.00 + .14 * mon_sales;
   else if (mon_sales >= 50000.00)
      income = 375.00 + .16 * mon_sales;

   cout << setiosflags(ios::showpoint)
        << setiosflags(ios:: fixed)
        << setprecision(2)
        << "\n\nThe income is $" << income;
}
```

a. Will this program run?

b. What does this program do?

c. For what values of monthly sales does this program calculate the correct income?

4.4 The **switch** Statement

The `if-else` chain is used in programming applications where one set of instructions must be selected from many possible alternatives. The `switch` statement provides an alternative to the `if-else` chain for cases that compare the value of an integer expression to a specific value. The general form of a `switch` statement is:

```
switch (expression)
{                              // start of compound statement
    case value_1: ◄─────────────── terminated with a colon
        statement1;
        statement2;
            .
            .
            .
        break;
    case value_2: ◄─────────────── terminated with a colon
        statementm;
        statementn;
            .
            .
            .
        break;
            .
            .
            .
    case value_n: ◄─────────────── terminated with a colon
        statementw;
        statementx;
            .
            .
            .
        break;
    default: ◄─────────────── terminated with a colon
        statement_aa;
        statement_bb;
}                              // end of switch and compound statement
```

The `switch` statement uses four new keywords: `switch`, `case`, `default`, and `break`. Let's see what each of these words does.

The keyword `switch` identifies the start of the `switch` statement. The expression in parentheses following this word is evaluated and the result of the expression compared to various alternative values contained within the compound statement. The expression in the `switch` statement must evaluate to an integer result or a compilation error results.

Internal to the `switch` statement, the keyword `case` is used to identify or label individual values that are compared to the value of the `switch` expression. The `switch` expression's value is compared to each of these `case` values in the order that these values are listed until a match is found. When a match occurs, execution begins with the statement immediately following the match. Thus, as illustrated in Figure 4–3, the value of the expression determines where in the `switch` statement execution actually begins.

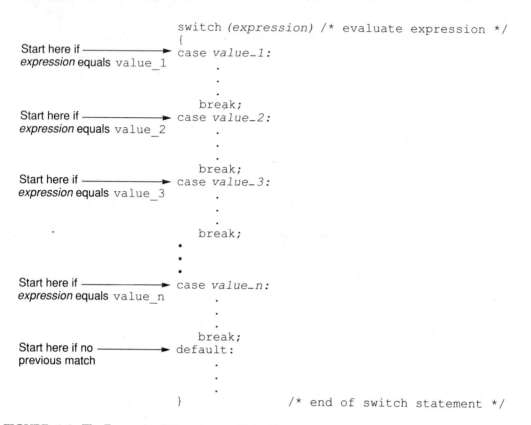

FIGURE 4–3 The Expression Determines an Entry Point

Any number of `case` labels may be contained within a `switch` statement, in any order. If the value of the expression does not match any of the `case` values, however, no statement is executed unless the keyword `default` is encountered. The keyword `default` is optional and operates the same as the last `else` in an `if-else` chain. If the value of the expression does not match any of the `case` values, program execution begins with the statement following the word `default`.

Once an entry point has been located by the `switch` statement, all further `case` evaluations are ignored and execution continues through the end of the compound statement unless a `break` statement is encountered. This is the reason for the `break` statement, which identifies the end of a particular `case` and causes an immediate exit from the `switch` statement. Thus, just as the word `case` identifies possible starting points in the compound statement, the `break` statement determines terminating points. If the `break` statements are omitted, all `cases` following the matching `case` value, including the `default` case, are executed.

In writing a `switch` statement, multiple `case` values can be used to refer to the same set of statements; the `default` label is optional. For example, consider the following:

```
            switch (number)
            {
              case 1:
                cout << "Have a Good Morning";
                break;
              case 2:
                cout << "Have a Happy Day";
                break;
              case 3: case 4: case 5:
                cout << "Have a Nice Evening";
            }
```

If the value stored in the variable number is 1, the message Have a Good Morning is displayed. Similarly, if the value of number is 2, the second message is displayed. Finally, if the value of number is 3 or 4 or 5, the last message is displayed. Since the statement to be executed for these last three cases is the same, the cases for these values can be "stacked together" as shown in the example. Also, since there is no default, no message is printed if the value of number is not one of the listed case values. Although it is good programming practice to list case values in increasing order, this is not required by the switch statement. A switch statement may have any number of case values, in any order; only the values being tested for need be listed.

Program 4-6 uses a switch statement to select the arithmetic operation (addition, multiplication, or division) to be performed on two numbers depending on the value of the variable opselect.

Program 4-6

```
#include <iostream.h>
void main(void)
{
  int opselect;
  double fnum, snum;

  cout << "Please type in two numbers: ";
  cin >> fnum >> snum;
  cout << "Enter a select code: ";
  cout << "\n        1 for addition";
  cout << "\n        2 for multiplication";
  cout << "\n        3 for division : ";
  cin >> opselect;

  switch (opselect)
  {
    case 1:
      cout << "The sum of the numbers entered is " << fnum+snum;
      break;
```

(continued on next page)

(continued from previous page)

```
     case 2:
       cout << "The product of the numbers entered is " << fnum*snum;
       break;
     case 3:
       cout << "The first number divided by the second is " << fnum/snum;
       break;
 }       /* end of switch */

}    /* end of main() */
```

Program 4-6 was run twice. The resulting display clearly identifies the case selected. The results are:

```
          Please type in two numbers: 12 3
          Enter a select code:
                 1 for addition
                 2 for multiplication
                 3 for division : 2
          The product of the numbers entered is 36
```

and

```
          Please type in two numbers: 12 3
          Enter a select code:
                 1 for addition
                 2 for multiplication
                 3 for division : 3

          The first number divided by the second is 4
```

In reviewing Program 4-6 notice the break statement in the last case. Although this break is not necessary, it is a good practice to terminate the last case in a switch statement with a break. This prevents a possible program error later, if an additional case is subsequently added to the switch statement. With the addition of a new case, the break between cases becomes necessary; having the break in place ensures you will not forget to include it at the time of the modification.

Since character data types are always converted to integers in an expression, a switch statement can also be used to "switch" based on the value of a character expression. For example, assuming that choice is a character variable, the following switch statement is valid:

```
switch (choice)
{
   case 'a': case 'e': case 'i': case 'o': case 'u':
     cout << "\nThe character in choice is a vowel";
     break;
   default:
      cout << "\nThe character in choice is not a vowel";
      break;   // this break is optional
 }    // end of switch statement
```

Exercises 4.4

1. Rewrite the following if-else chain using a switch statement:

```
if (let_grad == 'A')
  cout << "The numerical grade is between 90 and 100";
else if (let_grad == 'B')
  cout << "The numerical grade is between 80 and 89.9";
else if (let_grad == 'C')
  cout << "The numerical grade is between 70 and 79.9";
else if (let_grad == 'D';
  cout << "How are you going to explain this one";
else
{
  cout << "Of course I had nothing to do with my grade.";
  cout << "\nThe professor was really off the wall.";
}
```

2. Rewrite the following if-else chain using a switch statement:

```
if (bond_typ == 1)
{
  in_data();
  check();
}
else if (bond_typ == 2)
{
  dates();
  leap_yr();
}
else if (bond_typ == 3)
{
  yield();
  maturity();
}
else if (bond_typ == 4)
{
  price();
  roi();
}
else if (bond_typ == 5)
{
  files();
  save();
}
else if (bond_typ == 6)
{
  retrieve();
  screen();
}
```

3. Rewrite Program 4-4 in Section 4.3 using a switch statement.

4. Determine why the `if-else` chain in Program 4-5 cannot be replaced with a `switch` statement.

5. Repeat Exercise 3 in Section 4.3 using a `switch` statement instead of an `if-else` chain.

6. Rewrite Program 4-6 using a character variable for the select code.

4.5 Common Programming Errors

There are three programming errors common to C++'s selection statements. These are:

1. Using the assignment operator, =, in place of the relational operator, ==. This can cause an enormous amount of frustration because any expression can be tested by an `if-else` statement. For example, the statement

```
if (opselect = 2)
   cout << "Happy Birthday";
else
   cout << "Good Day";
```

always results in the message Happy Birthday being printed, regardless of the initial value in the variable opselect. The reason for this is that the assignment expression opselect = 2 has a value of 2, which is considered a true value in C++. The correct expression to determine the value in opselect is opselect == 2.

2. Assuming the `if-else` statement is selecting an incorrect choice when the problem is really the values being tested. This is a typical debugging problem in which the programmer mistakenly concentrates on the tested condition as the source of the problem rather than the values being tested. For example, assume that the following correct `if-else` statement is part of your program:

```
if (key == 'F')
{
  contemp = (5.0/9.0) * (intemp - 32.0);
  cout << "Conversion to Celsius was done";
}
else
{
  contemp = (9.0/5.0) * intemp + 32.0;
  cout << "Conversion to Fahrenheit was done";
}
```

This statement will always display `Conversion to Celsius was done` when the variable `key` contains an `F`. Therefore, if this message is displayed when you believe `key` does not contain `F`, investigation of `key`'s value is called for. As a general rule, whenever a selection statement does not act as you think it should, make sure to test your assumptions about the values assigned to the tested variables by displaying their values. If an unanticipated value is displayed, you have at least isolated the source of the problem to the variables themselves, rather than the structure of the `if-else` statement. From there you will have to determine where and how the incorrect value was obtained.

3. Using nested `if` statements without including braces to clearly indicate the desired structure. Without braces the compiler defaults to pairing `else`s with the closest unpaired `if`s, which sometimes destroys the original intent of the selection statement. To avoid this problem and to create code that is readily adaptable to change it is useful to write all `if-else` statements as compound statements in the form

```
if (expression)
{
   one or more statements in here
}
else
{
   one or more statements in here
}
```

By using this form, no matter how many statements are added later, the original integrity and intent of the `if` statement is maintained.

4.6 Chapter Summary

1. Relational expressions, which are also called simple conditions, are used to compare operands. If a relational expression is true, the value of the expression is the integer 1. If the relational expression is false, it has an integer value of 0. Relational expressions are created using the following relational operators:

Relational Operator	Meaning	Example
<	less than	age < 30
>	greater than	height > 6.2
<=	less than or equal to	taxable <= 20000
>=	greater than or equal to	temp >= 98.6
==	equal to	grade == 100
!=	not equal to	number != 250

2. More complex conditions can be constructed from relational expressions using C++'s logical operators, && (AND), || (OR), and ! (NOT).

3. if-else statements are used to select between two alternative statements based on the value of an expression. Although relational expressions are usually used for the tested expression, any valid expression can be used. In testing an expression, if-else statements interpret a nonzero value as true and a zero value as false. The most common form of an if-else statement is:

```
if (expression)
    statement1;
else
    statement2;
```

This is a two-way selection statement. If the expression has a nonzero value it is considered as true, and statement1 is executed; otherwise statement2 is executed.

4. if-else statements can contain other if-else statements. In the absence of braces, each else is associated with the closest unpaired if.

5. The if-else chain is a multiway selection statement having the general form:

```
if (expression_1)
    statement_1;
else if (expression_2)
    statement_2;
else if (expression_3)
    statement_3;
            .
            .
            .
else if (expression_m)
    statement_m;
else
    statement_n;
```

Each expression is evaluated in the order it appears in the chain. Once an expression is true (has a nonzero value), only the statement between that expression and the next `else if` or `else` is executed, and no further expressions are tested. The final `else` is optional, and the statement corresponding to the final `else` is only executed if none of the previous expressions were true.

6. A compound statement consists of any number of individual statements enclosed within the brace pair { and }. Compound statements are treated as a single block and can be used anywhere a single statement is called for.

7. Variables only have meaning within the block they are declared, which includes any inner blocks contained within the declaring block.

8. The `switch` statement is a multiway selection statement. The general form of a `switch` statement is:

```
switch (expression)
{                                     // start of compound statement
    case value_1: ◄─────────────────── terminated with a colon
        statement1;
        statement2;
          .
          .
          .
        break;
    case value_2: ◄─────────────────── terminated with a colon
        statementm;
        statementn;
          .
          .
          .
        break;
          .
          .
          .
    case value_n: ◄─────────────────── terminated with a colon
        statementw;
        statementx;
          .
          .
          .
        break;
    default: ◄─────────────────────── terminated with a colon
        statement_aa;
        statement_bb;
          .
          .
          .
}                        // end of switch and compound statement
```

For this statement the value of an integer expression is compared to a number of integer or character constants or constant expressions. Program execution is transferred to the first matching `case` and continues through the end of the `switch` statement unless an optional `break` statement is encountered. `cases` in a `switch` statement can appear in any order and an optional `default case` can be included. The `default case` is executed if none of the other `cases` is matched.

4.7   Chapter Supplement: Errors, Testing, and Debugging

The ideal in programming is to efficiently produce readable, error-free programs that work correctly and can be modified or changed with a minimum of testing required for reverification. In this regard it is useful to know the different types of errors that can occur, when they are detected, and how to correct them.

Compile-Time and Run-Time Errors

A program error can be detected in a variety of ways:

1. Before a program is compiled
2. While the program is being compiled
3. While the program is being run
4. After the program has been executed and the output is being examined
5. Not at all

Errors detected by the compiler are formally referred to as *compile-time errors* and errors that occur while the program is being run are formally referred to as *run-time errors*.

There are methods for detecting errors both before a program is compiled and after it has been executed. The method for detecting errors after a program has been executed is called *program verification and testing*. The method for detecting errors before a program is compiled is called desk checking. *Desk checking* refers to the procedure of checking a program, by hand, at a desk or table for syntax and logic errors, which are described next.

Syntax and Logic Errors

Computer literature distinguishes between two primary types of errors, called syntax errors and logic errors. A *syntax error* is an error in the structure or spelling of a statement. For example the statement

```
if ( a lt b
{
  out << "There are five syntax errors here\n"
  cout << " Can you find tem;
}
```

contains five syntax errors. These errors are:

1. The relational operator in the first line is incorrect, and should be the symbol <

2. The closing parenthesis is missing in the first line

3. The object name `cout` is misspelled in the third line

4. The third line is missing the terminating semicolon (;)

5. The string in the fourth line is not terminated with quotes

All of these errors will be detected by the compiler when the program is compiled. This is true of all syntax errors—since they violate the basic rules of C++, if they are not discovered by desk checking, the compiler will detect them and display an error message indicating that a syntax error exists.[4] In some cases the error message is clear and the error is obvious; in other cases it takes a little detective work to understand the error message displayed by the compiler. Since all syntax errors are detected at compile time, the terms compile-time and syntax errors are frequently used interchangeably. Strictly speaking, however, compile-time refers to when the error was detected and syntax refers to the type of error detected. Note that the misspelling of the word `tem` in the second `cout` stream is not a syntax error. Although this spelling error will result in an undesirable output line being displayed, it is not a violation of C++'s syntactical rules. It is a simple case of a typographical error, commonly referred to as a "typo."

Logic errors are characterized by erroneous, unexpected, or unintentional errors that are a direct result of some flaw in the program's logic. These errors, which are never caught by the compiler, may be detected by desk checking, by program testing, by accident when a user obtains an obviously erroneous output, or while the program is executing. In the latter case a run-time error occurs that results in an error message being generated and/or abnormal and premature program termination.

Since logic errors may not be detected by the compiler, they are always more difficult to detect than syntax errors. If not detected by desk checking, a logic error will reveal itself in two predominant ways. In one instance the program executes to completion but produces incorrect results. Logic errors of this type include:

No output: This is either caused by an omission of a `cout` statement or a sequence of statements that inadvertently bypasses a `cout` statement.

Unappealing or misaligned output: This is always caused by an error in a `cout` statement.

Incorrect numerical results: This is always caused by either incorrect values assigned to the variables used in an expression, the use of an incorrect arithmetic expression, an omission of a statement, roundoff error, or the use of an improper sequence of statements.

---

[4] They may not, however, all be detected at the same time. Frequently, one syntax error "masks" another error and the second error is only detected after the first error is corrected.

See if you can detect the logic error in Program 4-7.

Program 4-7

```cpp
#include <iostream.h>
#include <iomanip.h>
#include <math.h>
void main(void)  // a compound interest program
{
  int nyears;
  float capital, amount, rate;

  // display a program message
  cout << "This program calculates the amount of money\n";
  cout << "in a bank account for an initial deposit\n";
  cout << "invested for n years at an interest rate r.\n\n";

  // get the input data
  cout << "Enter the initial amount in the account: ";
  cin >> amount;
  cout << "Enter the interest rate (ex 5 for 5%): ";
  cin >> rate;

  // compute the capital and display the result
  capital = amount * pow( (1.0 + rate/100.0), nyears);
  cout << setiosflags(ios::showpoint)
       << setiosflags(ios::fixed) << setprecision(2)
       << "\nThe final amount of money is $ " << capital;
}
```

Following is a sample run of Program 4-7:

```
This program calculates the amount of money
in a bank account for an initial deposit
invested for n years at an interest rate r.

Enter the initial amount in the account: 1000.
Enter the interest rate (ex. 5 for 5%): 5

The final amount of money is $ 1000.00
```

As indicated in the output, the final amount of money is identical to the initial amount input. Did you spot the error in Program 4-7 that produced this apparently erroneous output?

Unlike a misspelled output message, the error in Program 4-7 causes a mistake in a computation. Here the error is that the program does not initialize the variable nyears before this variable is used in the calculation of capital. When the assignment statement that calculates capital is executed the computer uses whatever value is stored in nyears. On those systems that initialize all variables to zero, the value zero will be used for nyears. However, on those systems that do not initialize all variables to zero, whatever "garbage" value that happens to occupy the storage locations corresponding to the variable nyears will be used (the manuals supplied with your compiler will indicate which of these two actions your compiler takes). In either case an error is produced. For predictable results and to ensure that the code you write will work correctly on any computer, it is always best to assume that uninitialized variables contain "garbage" values.

The second major type of logic error is one that causes the program to prematurely terminate execution, and almost always results in a system error message being displayed. Examples of this type of error are attempts to divide by zero or take the square root of a negative number. When this type of logic error occurs, it becomes a run-time error.

Testing and Debugging

In theory, a comprehensive set of test runs would reveal all logic errors and ensure that a program will work correctly for any and all combinations of input and computed data. In practice this requires checking all possible combinations of statement executions. Due to the time and effort required, this is an impossible goal except for extremely simple programs. Let us see why this is so. Consider Program 4-8.

 Program 4-8

```cpp
#include <iostream.h>
void main(void)
{
  int num;

  cout << "Enter a number: ";
  cin >> num;

  if (num == 5)
    cout << "Bingo!";
  else
    cout << "Bongo!";
}
```

Program 4-8 has two paths that can be traversed from when the program is run to when the program reaches its closing brace. The first path, which is executed when the input number is 5, is in the sequence:

```
cout << "Enter a number: ";
cin >> num;
cout << "Bingo!";
```

The second path, which is executed whenever any number except 5 is input, includes the sequence of instructions:

```
cout << "Enter a number: ";
cin >> num;
cout << "Bongo!";
```

To test each possible path through Program 4-8 requires two runs of the program, with a judicious selection of test input data to ensure that both paths of the `if` statement are exercised. The addition of one more `if` statement in the program increases the number of possible execution paths by a factor of two and requires four (2^2) runs of the program for complete testing. Similarly, two additional `if` statements increase the number of paths by a factor of four and require eight (2^3) runs for complete testing and three additional `if` statements would produce a program that required sixteen (2^4) test runs.

Now consider a modestly sized application program consisting of only ten modules, each module containing five `if` statements. Assuming the modules are always called in the same sequence, there are 32 possible paths through each module (2 raised to the fifth power) and more than 1,000,000,000,000,000 (2 raised to the fiftieth power) possible paths through the complete program (all modules executed in sequence). The time needed to create individual test data to exercise each path and the actual computer run time required to check each path make the complete testing of such a program impossible to achieve.

The inability to fully test all combinations of statement execution sequences has led to the programming proverb, "There is no error-free program." It has also led to the realization that any testing that is done should be well thought out to maximize the possibility of locating errors. An important corollary is the realization that although a single test can reveal the presence of an error, it does not verify the absence of one. The fact that one error is revealed by testing does not indicate that another error is not lurking somewhere else in the program; the fact that one test revealed no errors does not indicate that there are no errors.

Once an error is discovered, however, the programmer must locate where the error occurs and then fix it. In computer jargon, a program error is referred to as a *bug* and the process of isolating, correcting, and verifying the correction is called *debugging*.[5]

---

[5] The derivation of this term is rather interesting. When a program stopped running on one of the first computers, the error was traced to a dead insect that had gotten into the electrical circuits and caused a malfunction.

Although there are no hard and fast rules for isolating the cause of an error, some useful techniques can be applied. The first of these is a preventive technique. Frequently many errors are introduced by the programmer in the rush to code and run a program before fully understanding what is required and how the result is to be achieved. A symptom of this haste to get a program entered into the computer is the lack of an outline of the proposed program (pseudocode or flowcharts) or a handwritten program itself. Many errors can be eliminated simply by checking a copy of the program before it is ever entered or compiled, by desk checking the program. A second useful technique is to mimic the computer and execute each statement by hand, as the computer would. This means writing down each variable as it is encountered in the program and listing the value that should be stored in the variable as each input and assignment statement is encountered. Doing this also sharpens your programming skills, because it requires that you fully understand what each statement in your program causes to happen. Such a check is called *program tracing*.

A third and very powerful debugging technique is to use the cout object stream to display the values of selected variables. For example, again consider Program 4-7. Since this program produced an incorrect value for capital, it is worthwhile placing a cout statement immediately before the assignment statement for capital to display the value of all variables used in the computation. If the displayed values are correct then the problem is in the assignment statement; if the values are incorrect we must determine where the incorrect values were actually obtained.

In the same manner, another use of the cout object stream in debugging is to immediately display the values of all input data. This technique is referred to as *echo printing*, and is useful in establishing that the computer is correctly receiving and interpreting the input data.

The most powerful of all debugging and tracing techniques is to use a program called a debugger. The debugger program controls the execution of a C++ program, can interrupt the C++ program at any point in its execution, and can display the values of all variables at the point of interruption.

Finally, no discussion of debugging is complete without mentioning the primary ingredient needed for successful isolation and correction of errors. This is the attitude and spirit you bring to the task. Since you wrote the program your natural assumption is that it is correct or you would have changed it before it was compiled. It is extremely difficult to back away and honestly test and find errors in your own software. As a programmer you must constantly remind yourself that just because you think your program is correct does not make it so. Finding errors in your own programs is a sobering experience, but one that will help you become a master programmer. It can also be exciting and fun if approached as a detection problem with you as the master detective.

Repetition

The programs examined so far have been useful in illustrating the correct structure of C++ programs and in introducing fundamental C++ input, output, assignment, and selection capabilities. By this time you should have gained enough experience to be comfortable with the concepts and mechanics of the C++ programming process. It is now time to move up a level in our knowledge and abilities.

The real power of most computer programs resides in their ability to repeat the same calculation or sequence of instructions many times over, each time using different data, without the necessity of rerunning the program for each new set of data values. In this chapter we explore the C++ statements that permit this. These statements are the while, for, and do-while statements.

5.1 The while Statement

The while statement is a general repetition statement that can be used in a variety of programming situations. The general form of the while statement is:

```
while (expression)
    statement;
```

The expression contained within the parentheses is evaluated in exactly the same manner as an expression contained in an if-else statement; the difference is how the expression is used. As we have seen, when the expression is true (has a nonzero value) in an if-else statement, the statement following the expression is executed once. In a while statement the statement following the expression is executed repeatedly as long as the expression retains a nonzero value. This naturally means that somewhere in the while statement there must be a statement that alters the value of the tested expression. As we will see, this is indeed the case. For now, however, considering just the expression and the statement following the parentheses, the process used by the computer in evaluating a while statement is:

1. test the expression
2. if the expression has a nonzero (true) value
     a. execute the statement following the parentheses
     b. go back to step 1
   else
     exit the while statement

Notice that step 2b forces program control to be transferred back to step 1. The transfer of control back to the start of a while statement in order to reevaluate the expression is called a program loop. The while statement literally loops back on itself to recheck the expression until it evaluates to zero (becomes false).

This looping process is illustrated in Figure 5–1. A diamond shape is used to show the two entry and two exit points required in the decision part of the while statement.

To make this a little more tangible, consider the relational expression count <= 10 and the statement cout << count;. Using these, we can write the following valid while statement:

```
while (count <= 10)
    cout << count;
```

Although the above statement is valid, the alert reader will realize that we have created a situation in which the cout object either is called forever (or until we stop the program) or is not called at all. Let us see why this happens.

If count has a value less than or equal to 10 when the expression is first evaluated, the cout object is activated. The while statement then automatically

FIGURE 5–1 Anatomy of a while Loop

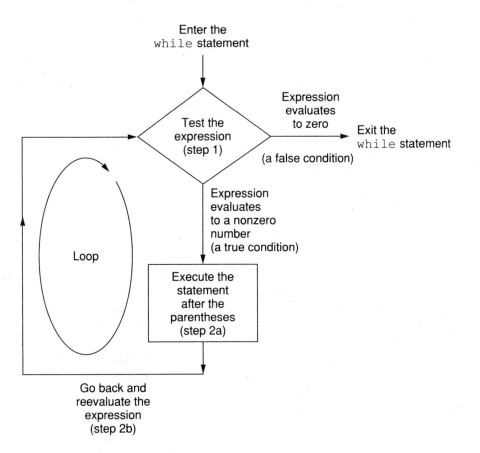

loops back on itself and retests the expression. Since we have not changed the value stored in count, the expression is still true and another call to cout is made. This process continues forever, or until the program containing this statement is prematurely stopped by the user. However, if count starts with a value greater than 10, the expression is false to begin with and the cout object call is never made.

How do we set an initial value in count to control what the while statement does the first time the expression is evaluated? The answer, of course, is to assign values to each variable in the tested expression before the while statement is encountered. For example, the following sequence of instructions is valid:

```
count = 1;
while (count <= 10)
   cout << count;
```

Using this sequence of instructions, we have ensured that count starts with a value of 1. We could assign any value to count in the assignment statement—the important thing is to assign some value. In practice, the assigned value depends on the application.

We must still change the value of count so that we can finally exit the while statement. To do this requires an expression such as count++ to increment the value of count each time the while statement is executed. The fact that a while statement provides for the repetition of a single statement does not prevent us from including an additional statement to change the value of count. All we have to do is replace the single statement with a compound statement. For example:

```
count = 1;                  // initialize count
while (count <= 10)
{
   cout << count;
   count++;                 // increment count
}
```

Note that, for clarity, we have placed each statement in the compound statement on a different line. This is consistent with the convention adopted for compound statements in the last chapter. Let us now analyze the above sequence of instructions.

The first assignment statement sets count equal to 1. The while statement is then entered and the expression is evaluated for the first time. Since the value of count is less than or equal to 10, the expression is true and the compound statement is executed. The first statement in the compound statement is a call to the cout object to display the value of count. The next statement adds 1 to the value currently stored in count, making this value equal to 2. The while statement now loops back to retest the expression. Since count is still less than or equal to 10, the compound statement is again executed. This process continues until the value of count reaches 11. Program 5-1 illustrates these statements in an actual program, with the addition of two blank spaces placed between each output value for readability.

 Program 5-1

```
#include <iostream.h>
void main(void)
{
  int count;

  count = 1;                    // initialize count
  while (count <= 10)
  {
    cout << count << "  ";
    count++;                    // increment count
  }
}
```

The output for Program 5-1 is:

        1 2 3 4 5 6 7 8 9 10

There is nothing special about the name count used in Program 5-1. Any valid integer variable could have been used.

Before we consider other examples of the while statement two comments concerning Program 5-1 are in order. First, the statement count++ can be replaced with any statement that changes the value of count. A statement such as count = count + 2, for example, would cause every second integer to be displayed. Second, it is the programmer's responsibility to ensure that count is changed in a way that ultimately leads to a normal exit from the while. For example, if we replace the expression count++ with the expression count--, the value of count will never reach 11 and an infinite loop will be created. An infinite loop is a loop that never ends. The computer will not reach out, touch you, and say, "Excuse me, you have created an infinite loop." It just keeps displaying numbers until you realize that the program is not working as you expected.

Now that you have some familiarity with the while statement, see if you can read and determine the output of Program 5-2.

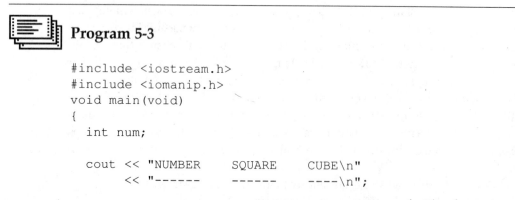

Program 5-2

```cpp
#include <iostream.h>
void main(void)
{
  int i;

  i = 10;
  while (i >= 1)
  {
    cout << i << "  ";
    i--;                    // subtract 1 from i
  }
}
```

The assignment statement in Program 5-2 initially sets the int variable i to 10. The while statement then checks to see if the value of i is greater than or equal to 1. While the expression is true, the value of i is displayed by the cout object and the value of i is decremented by 1. When i finally reaches zero, the expression is false and the program exits the while statement. Thus, the following display is obtained when Program 5-2 is run:

10   9   8   7   6   5   4   3   2   1

To illustrate the power of the while statement, consider the task of printing a table of numbers from 1 to 10 with their squares and cubes. This can be done with a simple while statement as illustrated by Program 5-3.

Program 5-3

```cpp
#include <iostream.h>
#include <iomanip.h>
void main(void)
{
  int num;

  cout << "NUMBER     SQUARE     CUBE\n"
       << "------     ------     ----\n";
```

(continued on next page)

(continued from previous page)

```
            num = 1;
            while (num < 11)
            {
              cout << setw(3) << num << "        "
                      << setw(3) << num * num        << "        "
                      << setw(4) << num * num * num <<"\n";
              num++;            // increment num
            }
          }
```

When Program 5-3 is run, the following display is produced:

NUMBER	SQUARE	CUBE
1	1	1
2	4	8
3	9	27
4	16	64
5	25	125
6	36	216
7	49	343
8	64	512
9	81	729
10	100	1000

Note that the expression used in Program 5-3 is num < 11. For the integer variable num, this expression is exactly equivalent to the expression num <= 10. The choice of which to use is entirely up to you.

If we want to use Program 5-3 to produce a table of 100 numbers, all we do is change the expression in the while statement from i < 11 to i < 101. Changing the 11 to 101 produces a table of 100 lines—not bad for a simple five-line while statement.

All the program examples illustrating the while statement have checked for a fixed-count condition. Since any valid expression can be evaluated by a while statement we are not restricted to constructing such loops. For example, consider the task of producing a Celsius to Fahrenheit temperature conversion table. Assume that Fahrenheit temperatures corresponding to Celsius temperatures ranging from 5 to 50 degrees are to be displayed in increments of five degrees. The desired display can be obtained with the series of statements:

```
          celsius = 5;      // starting Celsius value
          while (celsius <= 50)
          {
            fahren = (9.0/5.0) * celsius + 32.0;
            cout << celsius
                  << fahren;
            celsius = celsius + 5;
          }
```

As before, the `while` statement consists of everything from the word `while` through the closing brace of the compound statement. Prior to entering the `while` loop we have made sure to assign a value to the operand being evaluated, and there is a statement to alter the value of Celsius to ensure an exit from the `while` loop. Program 5-4 illustrates the use of this code, with additional format manipulators included, in a complete program.

 Program 5-4

```
#include <iostream.h>
#include <iomanip.h>
void main(void) // program to convert Celsius to Fahrenheit
{
  int celsius;
  float fahren;

  cout << "DEGREES   DEGREES\n"
       << "CELSIUS   FAHRENHEIT\n"
       << "-------   ----------\n";

  celsius = 5;    // starting Celsius value
  while (celsius <= 50)
  {
    fahren = (9.0/5.0) * celsius + 32.0;
    cout << setw(4) << celsius
         << setiosflags(ios::showpoint) << setw(13)
         << setprecision(2) << fahren << '\n';
    celsius = celsius + 5;
  }
}
```

The display obtained when Program 5-4 is executed is:

```
DEGREES   DEGREES
CELSIUS   FAHRENHEIT
-------   ----------
      5       41.00
     10       50.00
     15       59.00
     20       68.00
     25       77.00
     30       86.00
     35       95.00
     40      104.00
     45      113.00
     50      122.00
```

Exercises 5.1

1. Rewrite Program 5-1 to print the numbers 2 to 10 in increments of two. The output of your program should be:

```
2   4   6   8   10
```

2. Rewrite Program 5-4 to produce a table that starts at a Celsius value of –10 and ends with a Celsius value of 60, in increments of ten degrees.

3. a. For the following program determine the total number of items displayed. Also determine the first and last numbers printed.

```
#include <iostream.h>
void main(void)
{
   int num = 0;

   while (num <= 20)
   {
     num++;
     cout << num << "   ";
   }
}
```

b. Enter and run the program from Exercise 3a on a computer to verify your answers to the exercise.
c. How would the output be affected if the two statements within the compound statement were reversed (that is, if the cout call were made before the num++ statement)?

4. Write a C++ program that converts gallons to liters. The program should display gallons from 10 to 20 in one-gallon increments and the corresponding liter equivalents. Use the relationship that one gallon of liquid contains 3.785 liters.

5. Write a C++ program that converts feet to meters. The program should display feet from 3 to 30 in three-foot increments and the corresponding meter equivalents. Use the relationship: meters = feet / 3.28.

6. A machine purchased for $28,000 is depreciated at a rate of $4,000 a year for seven years. Write and run a C++ program that computes and displays a depreciation table for seven years. The table should have the form:

YEAR	DEPRECIATION	END-OF-YEAR VALUE	ACCUMULATED DEPRECIATION
1	4000	24000	4000
2	4000	20000	8000
3	4000	16000	12000
4	4000	12000	16000
5	4000	8000	20000
6	4000	4000	24000
7	4000	0	28000

7. An automobile travels at an average speed of 55 miles per hour for four hours. Write a C++ program that displays the distance driven, in miles, that the car has traveled after .5, 1, 1.5, etc., hours until the end of the trip.

5.2 cin Within a while Loop

Combining the cin object with the repetition capabilities of the while statement produces very adaptable and powerful programs. To understand the
concept involved, consider Program 5-5, in which a while statement is used
to accept and then display four user-entered numbers, one at a time. Although
it uses a very simple idea, the program highlights the flow of control concepts
needed to produce more useful programs.

 Program 5-5

```
#include <iostream.h>
#include <iomanip.h>
void main(void)
{
   int count;
   float num;

   cout << "\nThis program will ask you to enter some numbers.\n";
   count = 1;

   while (count <= 4)
   {
     cout << "\nEnter a number: ";
     cin >> num;
     cout << "The number entered is " << num;
     count++;
   }
}
```

Following is a sample run of Program 5-5. The underlined items were input
in response to the appropriate prompts.

```
This program will ask you to enter some numbers.

Enter a number: 26.2
The number entered is 26.2
Enter a number: 5
The number entered is 5
Enter a number: 103.456
The number entered is 103.456
Enter a number: 1267.89
The number entered is 1267.89
```

Let us review the program to clearly understand how the output was produced. The first message displayed is caused by execution of the first cout object call. This call is outside and before the while statement, so it is executed once before any statement in the while loop.

Once the while loop is entered, the statements within the compound statement are executed while the tested condition is true. The first time through the compound statement, the message Enter a number: is displayed. The program then activates cin, which forces the computer to wait for a number to be entered at the keyboard. Once a number is typed and the RETURN key is pressed, the call to cout displaying the number is executed. The variable count is then incremented by one. This process continues until four passes through the loop have been made and the value of count is 5. Each pass causes the message Enter a number: to be displayed, causes one call to cin to be made, and causes the message The number entered is to be displayed. Figure 5–2 illustrates this flow of control.

Rather than simply displaying the entered numbers, Program 5-5 can be modified to use the entered data. For example, let us add the numbers entered and display the total. To do this, we must be very careful in how we add the numbers, since the same variable, num, is used for each number entered. Because of this the entry of a new number in Program 5-5 automatically causes the previous number stored in num to be overwritten. Thus, each number entered must be added to the total before another number is entered. The required sequence is:

```
Enter a number
Add the number to the total
```

How do we add a single number to a total? A statement such as total = total + num; does the job perfectly. This is the accumulating statement introduced in Section 3.1. After each number is entered, the accumulating statement adds the number into the total, as illustrated in Figure 5–3. The complete flow of control required for adding the numbers is illustrated in Figure 5–4.

In reviewing Figure 5–4, observe that we have made a provision for initially setting the total to zero before the while loop is entered. If we were to clear the total inside the while loop, it would be set to zero each time the loop was executed and any value previously stored would be erased.

Program 5-6 incorporates the necessary modifications to Program 5-5 to total the numbers entered. As indicated in the flow diagram shown in Figure 5–4, the statement total = total + num; is placed immediately after the cin object call. Putting the accumulating statement at this point in the program ensures that the entered number is immediately "captured" into the total.

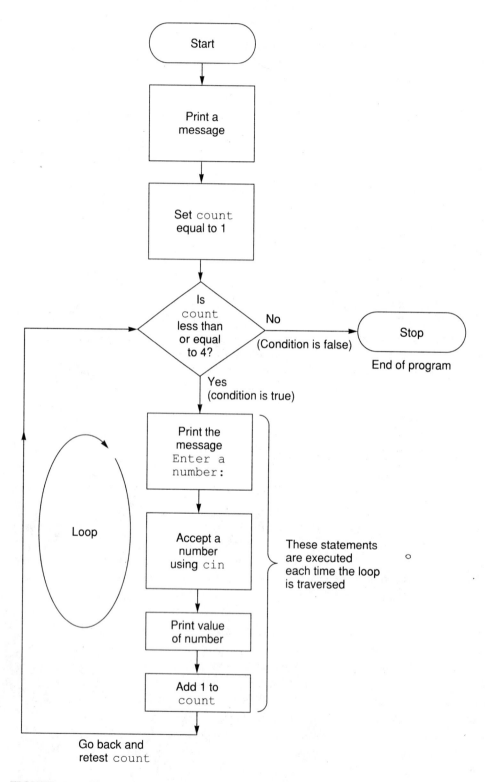

FIGURE 5–2 Flow of Control Diagram for Program 5-5

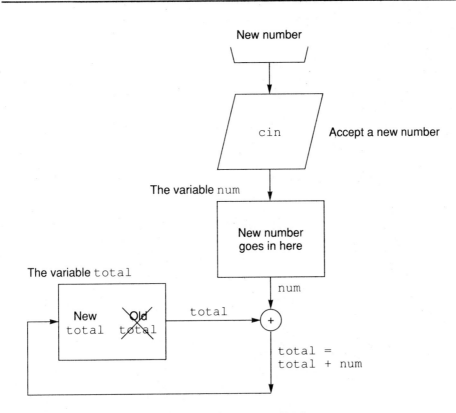

FIGURE 5-3 Accepting and Adding a Number to a Total

Program 5-6

```cpp
#include <iostream.h>
#include <iomanip.h>
void main(void)
{
  int count;
  float num, total;

  cout << "\nthis program will ask you to enter some numbers.\n";
  count = 1;
  total = 0;

  while (count <= 4)
  {
    cout << "\nenter a number: ";
    cin >> num;
    total = total + num;
    cout << "The total is now " << total;
    count++;
  }
  cout << "\n\nthe final total is " << total;
}
```

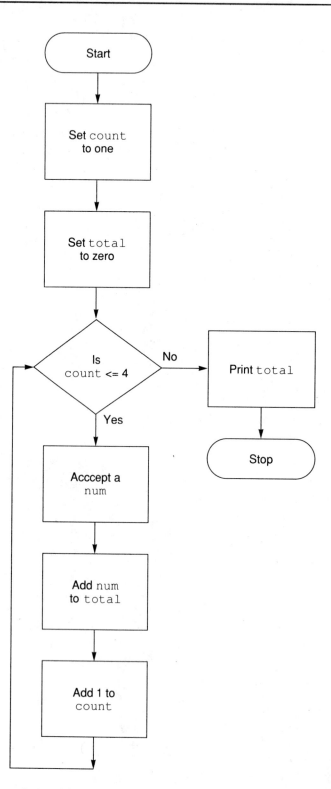

FIGURE 5–4 Accumulation Flow of Control

Let us review Program 5-6. The variable total was created to store the total of the numbers entered. Prior to entering the while statement the value of total is set to zero. This ensures that any previous value present in the storage location(s) assigned to the variable total are erased. When the while loop is entered, the statement total = total + num; is used to add the value of the entered number into total. As each value is entered, it is added into the existing total to create a new total. Thus, total becomes a running subtotal of all the values entered. Only when all numbers are entered does total contain the final sum of all the numbers. After the while loop is finished, the last cout object call is used to display this sum.

Using the same data that was entered in the sample run for Program 5-5, the following sample run of Program 5-6 was made (again, the underlined items represent user input data):

```
This program will ask you to enter some numbers.

Enter a number: 26.2
The total is now 26.2
Enter a number: 5
The total is now 31.2
Enter a number: 103.456
The total is now 134.656
Enter a number: 1267.89
The total is now 1402.546

The final total is 1402.546
```

Having used an accumulating assignment statement to add the numbers entered, we can now go further and calculate the average of the numbers. Where do we calculate the average—within the while loop or outside it?

In the case at hand, calculating an average requires that both a final sum and the number of items in that sum be available. The average is then computed by dividing the final sum by the number of items. At this point, we must ask, "At what point in the program is the correct sum available, and at what point is the number of items available?" In reviewing Program 5-6 we see that the correct sum needed for calculating the average is available after the while loop is finished. In fact, the whole purpose of the while loop is to ensure that the numbers are entered and added correctly to produce a correct sum. After the loop is finished, we also have a count of the number of items used in the sum. However, because of the way the while loop was constructed, the number in count (5) when the loop is finished is one more than the number of items (4) used to obtain the total. Knowing this, we simply subtract one from count before using it to determine the average. With this as background, see if you can read and understand Program 5-7.

Program 5-7

```cpp
#include <iostream.h>
#include <iomanip.h>
void main(void)
{
  int count;
  float num, total, average;

  cout << "\nthis program will ask you to enter some numbers.\n";
  count = 1;
  total = 0;

  while (count <= 4)
  {
    cout << "Enter a number: ";
    cin >> num;
    total = total + num;
    count++;
  }
  count--;
  average = total / count;
  cout << "\nThe average of the numbers is " << average;
}
```

Program 5-7 is almost identical to Program 5-6, except for the calculation of the average. We have also removed the constant display of the total within and after the while loop. The loop in Program 5-7 is used to enter and add four numbers. Immediately after the loop is exited, the average is computed and displayed. Following is a sample run using Program 5-7:

```
This program will ask you to enter some numbers.

Enter a number: 26.2
Enter a number: 5
Enter a number: 103.456
Enter a number: 1267.89

The average of the numbers is 350.6365
```

Sentinels

In many situations the exact number of items to be entered is not known in advance or the items are too numerous to count beforehand. For example, when entering a large amount of market research data we might not want to take the time to count the number of actual data items to be entered. In cases like this we want to be able to enter data continuously and, at the end, type in a special data value to signal the end of data input.

In computer programming, data values used to signal either the start or end of a data series are called sentinels. The sentinel values must, of course, be selected so as not to conflict with legitimate data values. For example, if we were constructing a program that accepts a student's grades, and assuming that no extra credit is given that could produce a grade higher than 100, we could use any grade higher than 100 as a sentinel value. Program 5-8 illustrates this concept. In Program 5-8 data is continuously requested and accepted until a number larger than 100 is entered. Entry of a number higher than 100 alerts the program to exit the while loop and display the sum of the numbers entered.

 Program 5-8

```cpp
#include <iostream.h>
void main(void)
{
  float grade, total;

  grade = 0;
  total = 0;
  cout << "\nTo stop entering grades, type in any number";
  cout << "\n greater than 100.\n\n";

  while (grade <= 100)
  {
    total = total + grade;
    cout << "Enter a grade: ";
    cin >> grade;
  }

  cout << "\nThe total of the grades is " << total;
}
```

Following is a sample run using Program 5-8 (as before, the date entered has been underlined). As long as grades less than or equal to 100 are entered, the program continues to request and accept additional data. When a number less than or equal to 100 is entered the program adds this number to the total. When a number greater than 100 is entered the while loop is exited and the sum of the grades that were entered is displayed.

```
To stop entering grades, type in any number
   greater than 100.

Enter a grade: 95
Enter a grade: 100
Enter a grade: 82
Enter a grade: 101

The total of the grades is 277
```

break and continue Statements

Two useful statements in connection with repetition statements are the break and continue statements. We have previously encountered the break statement in relation to the switch statement. The general form of this statement is:

break;

A break statement, as its name implies, forces an immediate break, or exit, from the nearest enclosing switch, while, for, or do-while statement.

For example, execution of the following while loop is immediately terminated if a number greater than 76 is entered:

```
while(count <= 10)
{
   cout << "Enter a number: ";
   cin >> num;
   if (num > 76)
   {
     cout << "You lose!";
     break;          // break out of the loop
   }
   else
     cout << "Keep on truckin!";
   count++;
}
// break jumps to here
```

The break statement is extremely useful and valuable for breaking out of loops when an unusual condition is detected. The break statement is also used to exit from a switch statement, but this is because the desired case has been detected and processed.

The continue statement is similar to the break statement but applies only to loops (not to switch statements). The general format of a continue statement is:

continue;

When `continue` is encountered in a loop, the rest of the loop is skipped and control is transferred to the testing expression. For `while` loops this means that execution is automatically transferred to the top of the loop and reevaluation of the tested expression is initiated. Although the `continue` statement has no direct effect on a `switch` statement, it can be included within a `switch` statement that itself is contained in a loop. Here the effect of `continue` is the same: the next loop iteration is begun.

As a general rule the `continue` statement is less useful than the `break` statement, but it is convenient for skipping over data that should not be processed while remaining in a loop. For example, invalid grades are simply ignored in the following section of code and only valid grades are added into the total:[1]

```
while (count < 30)
{
  cout << "Enter a grade: ";
  cin >> grade;
  if(grade < 0 || grade > 100)
    continue;
  total = total + grade;
  count++;
}
```

The Null Statement

Statements are always terminated by a semicolon. A semicolon with nothing preceding it is also a valid statement, called the null statement. Thus, the statement

```
;
```

is a null statement. This is a do-nothing statement that is used where a statement is syntactically required, but no action is called for. Null statements typically are used with either `while` or `for` statements. An example of a `for` statement using a null statement is found in Program 5-9c in the next section.

---

[1] While this section of code is useful in illustrating the flow of control provided by the `continue` statement it is not the preferred way of achieving the desired result. Rather than using an `if` and `continue` statement to *exclude* invalid data, a better method is to *include* valid data using the statement:

```
if(grade >= 0 && grade <= 100)
  total = total + grade;
```

Exercises 5.2

1. Rewrite Program 5-6 to compute the total of eight numbers.

2. Rewrite Program 5-6 to display the prompt:

```
Please type in the total number of data values to be added:
```

In response to this prompt, the program should accept a user-entered number and then use this number to control the number of times the while loop is executed. Thus, if the user enters 5 in response to the prompt, the program should request the input of five numbers and display the total after five numbers have been entered.

3. a. Write a C++ program to convert Celsius degrees to Fahrenheit. The program should request the starting Celsius value, the number of conversions to be made, and the increment between Celsius values. The display should have appropriate headings and list the Celsius value and the corresponding Fahrenheit value. Use the relationship Fahrenheit = (9.0 / 5.0) * Celsius + 32.0.
  b. Run the program written in Exercise 3a on a computer. Verify that your program starts at the correct starting Celsius value and contains the exact number of conversions specified in your input data.

4. a. Modify the program written in Exercise 3 to request the starting Celsius value, the ending Celsius value, and the increment. Thus, instead of the condition checking for a fixed count, the condition will check for the ending Celsius value.
  b. Run the program written in Exercise 4a on a computer. Verify that your output starts at the correct beginning value and ends at the correct ending value.

5. Rewrite Program 5-7 to compute the average of ten numbers.

6. Rewrite Program 5-7 to display the prompt:

```
Please type in the total number of data values to be averaged:
```

In response to this prompt, the program should accept a user-entered number and then use this number to control the number of times the while loop is executed. Thus, if the user enters 6 in response to the prompt, the program should request the input of six numbers and display the average of the next six numbers entered.

7. By mistake, a programmer put the statement average = total / count; within the while loop immediately after the statement total = total + num; in Program 5-7. Thus, the while loop becomes:

```
while (count <=4)
{
  cout << "\nEnter a number: ";
  cin >> num;
  total = total + num;
  average = total / count;
  count++;
}
```

Will the program yield the correct result with this while loop? From a programming perspective, which while loop is better to use, and why?

8. a. Modify Program 5-8 to compute the average of the grades entered.
  b. Run the program written in Exercise 8a on a computer and verify the results.

9. a. A bookstore summarizes its monthly transactions by keeping the following information for each book in stock:

Book identification number
Inventory balance at the beginning of the month
Number of copies received during the month
Number of copies sold during the month

Write a C++ program that accepts this data for each book and then displays the book identification number and an updated book inventory balance using the relationship:

> New Balance = Inventory balance at the beginning of the month
>   + Number of copies received during the month
>   – Number of copies sold during the month

Your program should use a `while` statement with a fixed-count condition so that information on only three books is requested.
  b. Run the program written in Exercise 9a on a computer. Review the display produced by your program and verify that the output produced is correct.

10. Modify the program you wrote for Exercise 9 to keep requesting and displaying results until a sentinel identification value of 999 is entered. Run the program on a computer.

5.3 The **for** Statement

The `for` statement performs the same functions as the `while` statement, but uses a different form. In many situations, especially those that use a fixed-count condition, the `for` statement format is easier to use than its `while` statement equivalent. The general form of the `for` statement is:

```
for (initializing list; expression; altering list)
    statement;
```

Although the `for` statement looks a little complicated, it is really quite simple if we consider each of its parts separately. Within the parentheses of the `for` statement are three items, separated by semicolons. Each of these items is optional and can be described individually, but the semicolons must be present. As we shall see, the items in parentheses correspond to the initialization, expression evaluation, and altering of expression values that we have already used with the `while` statement.

The middle item in the parentheses, the expression, is any valid C++ expression, and there is no difference in the way `for` and `while` statements use this expression. In both statements, as long as the expression has a nonzero (true) value, the statement following the parentheses is executed. This means that prior to the first check of the expression, initial values for the tested expression's variables must be assigned. It also means that before the expression is reevaluated, there must be one or more statements that alter these values. Recall that the general placement of these statements using a `while` statement follows the pattern:

```
initializing statements;
while (expression)
{
    loop statements;
                   .

                   .

                   .

    expression-altering statements;
}
```

The need to initialize variables or make some other evaluations prior to entering a repetition loop is so common that the `for` statement allows all the initializing statements to be grouped together as the first set of items within the `for`'s parentheses. The items in this initializing list are executed only once, before the expression is evaluated for the first time.

The `for` statement also provides a single place for all expression-altering statements. These items can be placed in the altering list, which is the last list contained within the `for`'s parentheses. All items in the altering list are executed by the `for` statement at the end of the loop, just before the expression is reevaluated. Figure 5–5 illustrates the `for` statement's flow of control diagram.

The following section of code illustrates the correspondence between the `for` and `while` statements:

```
count = 1;
while (count <= 10)
{
    cout << count;
    count++;
}
```

The `for` statement corresponding to this section of code is:

```
for (count = 1; count <= 10; count++)
    cout << count;
```

As seen in this example, the only difference between the `for` statement and the `while` statement is the placement of equivalent expressions. The grouping together of the initialization, expression test, and altering list in the `for`

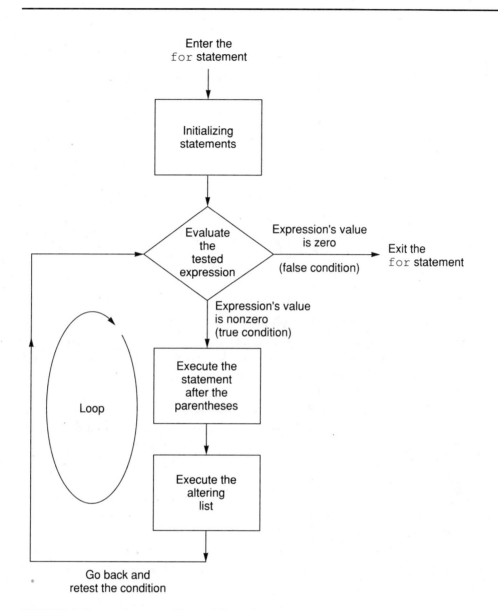

FIGURE 5–5   for Statement Flow of Control

statement is very convenient, especially when they are used to create fixed-count loops. Consider the following for statement:

```
for (count = 2; count <= 20; count = count + 2)
    cout << count;
```

In this statement all the loop control information is contained within the parentheses. The loop starts with a count of 2, stops when the count exceeds 20, and increments the loop counter in steps of 2. Program 5-9 illustrates this for statement in an actual program. Two blanks are placed between each output value for readability.

Program 5-9

```
#include <iostream.h>
void main(void)
{
  int count;

  for (count = 2; count <= 20; count = count + 2)
    cout << count << "   ";
}
```

The output of Program 5-9 is:

2   4   6   8   10   12   14   16   18   20

The for statement does not require that any of the items in parentheses be present or that they be used for initializing or altering the values in the expression statements. However, the two semicolons must be present within the for's parentheses. For example, the construction for (; count <= 20 ;) is valid.

If the initializing list is missing, the initialization step is omitted when the for statement is executed. This, of course, means that the programmer must provide the required initializations before the for statement is encountered. Similarly, if the altering list is missing, any expressions needed to alter the evaluation of the tested expression must be included directly within the statement part of the loop. The for statement only ensures that all expressions in the initializing list are executed once, before evaluation of the tested expression, and that all expressions in the altering list are executed at the end of the loop before the tested expression is rechecked. Thus, Program 5-9 can be rewritten in any of the three ways shown in Programs 5-9a, 5-9b, and 5-9c.

Program 5-9a

```
#include <iostream.h>
void main(void)
{
  int count;

  count = 2;     // initializer outside for statement
  for ( ; count <= 20; count = count + 2)
    cout << count << "   ";
}
```

Program 5-9b

```
#include <iostream.h>
void main(void)
{
  int count;

  count = 2;     // initializer outside for loop
  for( ; count <= 20; )
  {
    cout << count << "   ";
    count = count + 2;      // alteration statement
  }
}
```

Program 5-9c

```
#include <iostream.h>
void main(void)    // all expressions within the for's parentheses
{
  int count;

  for (count = 2; count <= 20; cout << count << "   ", count = count + 2);
}
```

In Program 5-9a count is initialized outside the for statement and the first list inside the parentheses is left blank. In Program 5-9b, both the initializing list and the altering list are removed from within the parentheses. Program 5-9b also uses a compound statement within the for loop, with the expression-altering statement included in the compound statement. Finally, Program 5-9c has included all items within the parentheses, so there is no need for any useful statement following the parentheses. Here the null statement satisfies the syntactical requirement of one statement to follow the for's parentheses. Observe also in Program 5-9c that the altering list (last set of items in parentheses) consists of two items, and that a comma has been used to separate these items. The use of commas to separate items in both the initializing and altering lists is required if either of these two lists contains more than one item. Last, note the fact that Programs 5-9a, 5-9b, and 5-9c are all inferior to Program 5-9. The for statement in Program 5-9 is much clearer since all the expressions pertaining to the tested expression are grouped together within the parentheses.

Although the initializing and altering lists can be omitted from a `for` statement, omitting the tested expression results in an infinite loop. For example, such a loop is created by the statement

```
for (count = 2; ; count++)
    cout << count;
```

As with the `while` statement, both `break` and `continue` statements can be used within a `for` loop. The `break` forces an immediate exit from the `for` loop, as it does in the `while` loop. The `continue`, however, forces control to be passed to the altering list in a `for` statement, after which the tested expression is reevaluated. This differs from the action of `continue` in a `while` statement, where control is passed directly to the reevaluation of the tested expression.

Finally, many programmers use the initializing list of a `for` statement to both declare and initialize the counter variable and any other variables used primarily within the `for` loop. For example, in the following `for` statement:

```
for(int count = 0; count < 10; count++)
    cout << count << '\n';
```

the variable `count` is both declared and initialized from within the `for` statement. As always, having been declared, the variable `count` can now be used anywhere following its declaration within the body of the function containing the declaration.

To understand the enormous power of the `for` statement, consider the task of printing a table of numbers from 1 to 10, including their squares and cubes, using this statement. Such a table was previously produced using a `while` statement in Program 5-3. You may wish to review Program 5-3 and compare it to Program 5-10 to get a further sense of the equivalence between the `for` and `while` statements.

 Program 5-10

```
#include <iostream.h>
#include <iomanip.h>
void main(void)
{
    int num;

    cout << "NUMBER     SQUARE     CUBE\n"
         << "------     ------     ----\n";

    for (num = 1; num <= 10; num++)
        cout << setw(3) << num << "          "
             << setw(3) << num * num << "        "
             << setw(4) << num * num * num << '\n';
}
```

When Program 5-10 is run, the display produced is:

NUMBER	SQUARE	CUBE
1	1	1
2	4	8
3	9	27
4	16	64
5	25	125
6	36	216
7	49	343
8	64	512
9	81	729
10	100	100

Simply changing the number 10 in the `for` statement of Program 5-10 to 100 creates a loop that is executed 100 times and produces a table of numbers from 1 to 100. As with the `while` statement this small change produces an immense increase in the processing and output provided by the program.

cin Within a for Loop

Using the `cin` object inside a `for` loop produces the same effect as when this object is called inside a `while` loop. For example, in Program 5-11 a `cin` object call is used to input a set of numbers. As each number is input, it is added to a total. When the `for` loop is exited, the average is calculated and displayed.

Program 5-11

```cpp
#include <iostream.h>
void main(void)
// This program calculates the average
// of five user-entered numbers.
{
  int count;
  float num, total, average;

  total = 0.0;

  for (count = 0; count < 5; count++)
  {
    cout << "Enter a number: ";
    cin >> num;
    total = total + num;
  }

  average = total / count;
  cout << "\nThe average of the data entered is " << average;
}
```

The `for` statement in Program 5-11 creates a loop that is executed five times. The user is prompted to enter a number each time through the loop. After each number is entered, it is immediately added to the total. Although total was initialized to zero before the `for` statement, this initialization could have been included with the initialization of count, as follows:

```
for (total = 0.0, count = 0; count < 5; count++)
```

Additionally, the declarations for both `total` and `count` could have been included with their initializations from within the initializing list, as follows:

```
for (float total = 0.0, int count = 0; count < 5; count++)
```

Any one of these `for` constructs represent good programming practice; which one you choose is simply a matter of your own programming style.

Nested Loops

In many situations it is very convenient to have a loop contained within another loop. Such loops are called nested loops. A simple example of a nested loop is:

```
for(i = 1; i <= 5; i++)              // start of outer loop <-------+
{                                    //                            |
   cout << "\ni is now " << i << '\n';  //                         |
                                     //                            |
   for(j = 1; j <= 4; j++)           // start of inner loop        |
      cout << "  j = " << j;         // end of inner loop          |
}                                    // end of outer loop   <------+
```

The first loop, controlled by the value of `i`, is called the outer loop. The second loop, controlled by the value of `j`, is called the inner loop. Notice that all statements in the inner loop are contained within the boundaries of the outer loop and that we have used a different variable to control each loop. For each single trip through the outer loop, the inner loop runs through its entire sequence. Thus, each time the `i` counter increases by 1, the inner `for` loop executes completely. This situation is illustrated in Figure 5–6.

Program 5-12 includes the above code in a working program.

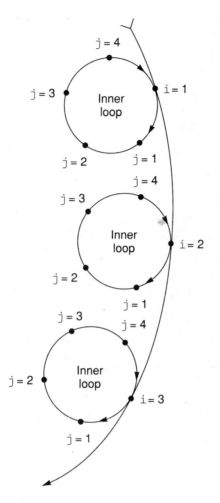

FIGURE 5–6 For Each i, j Loops

Program 5-12

```cpp
#include <iostream.h>
void main(void)
{
  int i,j;
  for(i = 1; i <= 5; i++)          // start of outer loop <-------+
  {                                //                             |
    cout << "\ni is now " << i << '\n';  //                       |
                                   //                             |
    for(j = 1; j <= 4; j++)        // start of inner loop         |
      cout << "  j = " << j;       // end of inner loop           |
  }                                // end of outer loop    <-------+
}
```

Following is the output of a sample run of Program 5-12:

```
i is now 1
    j = 1   j = 2   j = 3   j = 4
i is now 2
    j = 1   j = 2   j = 3   j = 4
i is now 3
    j = 1   j = 2   j = 3   j = 4
i is now 4
    j = 1   j = 2   j = 3   j = 4
i is now 5
    j = 1   j = 2   j = 3   j = 4
```

Let us use a nested loop to compute the average grade for each student in a class of 20 students. Each student has taken four exams during the course of the semester. The final grade is calculated as the average of these examination grades.

The outer loop in our program will consist of 20 passes. Each pass through the outer loop is used to compute the average for one student. The inner loop will consist of 4 passes. One examination grade is entered in each inner loop pass. As each grade is entered it is added to the total for the student, and at the end of the loop the average is calculated and displayed. Program 5-13 uses a nested loop to make the required calculations.

Program 5-13

```cpp
#include <iostream.h>
void main(void)
{
  int i,j;
  float grade, total, average;

  for (i = 1; i <= 20; i++)      // start of outer loop
  {
    total = 0;                   // clear the total for this student
    for (j = 1; j <= 4; j++)     // start of inner loop
    {
      cout << "Enter an examination grade for this student: ";
      cin >> grade;
      total = total + grade;     // add the grade into the total
    }                            // end of the inner for loop
    average = total / 4;         // calculate the average
    cout << "\nThe average for student " << i
         << " is " << average << "\n\n";
  }                              // end of the outer for loop
}
```

In reviewing Program 5-13, pay particular attention to the initialization of `total` within the outer loop, before the inner loop is entered. `total` is initialized 20 times, once for each student. Also notice that the average is calculated and displayed immediately after the inner loop is finished. Since the statements that compute and print the average are also contained within the outer loop, 20 averages are calculated and displayed. The entry and addition of each grade within the inner loop use techniques we have seen before, which should now be familiar to you.

Exercises 5.3

1. Determine the output of the following program:

```
#include <iostream.h>
void main(void)
{
    int i;

    for (i = 20; i >= 0; i -= 4)
        cout << i;
}
```

2. Modify Program 5-10 to produce a table of the numbers 0 through 20 in increments of 2, with their squares and cubes.

3. Modify Program 5-10 to produce a table of numbers from 10 to 1, instead of 1 to 10 as it currently does.

4. Write and run a C++ program that displays a table of 20 temperature conversions from Fahrenheit to Celsius. The table should start with a Fahrenheit value of 20 degrees and be incremented in values of 4 degrees. Recall that Celsius = (5.0/9.0) * (Fahrenheit − 32).

5. Modify the program written for Exercise 4 to initially request the number of conversions to be displayed.

6. Write a C++ program that converts Fahrenheit to Celsius temperature in increments of 5 degrees. The initial value of Fahrenheit temperature and the total conversions to be made are to be requested as user input during program execution. Recall that Celsius = (5.0/9.0) * (Fahrenheit − 32.0).

7. Write and run a C++ program that accepts six Fahrenheit temperatures, one at a time, and converts each value entered to its Celsius equivalent before the next value is requested. Use a `for` loop in your program. The conversion required is Celsius = (5.0/9.0) * (Fahrenheit − 32).

8. Write and run a C++ program that accepts ten individual values of gallons, one at a time, and converts each value entered to its liter equivalent before the next value is requested. Use a `for` loop in your program. There are 3.785 liters in one gallon of liquid.

9. Modify the program written for Exercise 7 to initially request the number of data items that will be entered and converted.

10. Is the following program correct? If it is, determine its output. If it is not, determine and correct the error so the program will run.

```
#include <iostream.h>
void main(void)
{

  for(int i = 1; i < 10; i++)
    cout << i << '\n';

  for (int i = 1; i < 5; i++)
    cout << i << '\n';

}
```

11. Write and run a C++ program that calculates and displays the amount of money available in a bank account that initially has $1,000 deposited in it and that earns 8 percent interest a year. Your program should display the amount available at the end of each year for a period of ten years. Use the relationship that the money available at the end of each year equals the amount of money in the account at the start of the year plus .08 times the amount available at the start of the year.

12. a. Modify the program written for Exercise 11 to initially prompt the user for the amount of money initially deposited in the account.
b. Modify the program written for Exercise 11 to initially prompt the user for both the amount of money initially deposited and the number of years that should be displayed.
c. Modify the program written for Exercise 11 to initially prompt for the amount of money initially deposited, the interest rate to be used, and the number of years to be displayed.

13. A machine purchased for $28,000 is depreciated at a rate of $4,000 a year for seven years. Write and run a C++ program that computes and displays a depreciation table for seven years. The table should have the form:

```
                   DEPRECIATION SCHEDULE
                   ---------------------


                            END-OF-YEAR        ACCUMULATED
    YEAR     DEPRECIATION       VALUE          DEPRECIATION
    ----     ------------    ------------      ------------
     1           4000           24000             4000
     2           4000           20000             8000
     3           4000           16000            12000
     4           4000           12000            16000
     5           4000            8000            20000
     6           4000            4000            24000
     7           4000               0            28000
```

14. A well-regarded manufacturer of widgets has been losing 4 percent of its sales each year. The annual profit for the firm is 10 percent of sales. This year the firm has had $10 million in sales and a profit of $1 million. Determine the expected sales and profit for the next 10 years. Your program should complete and produce a display as follows:

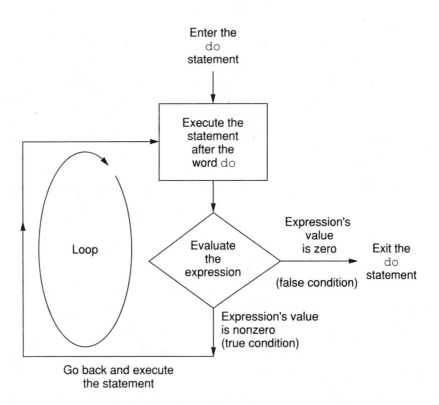

Go back and execute
the statement

FIGURE 5–7 The do Statement's Flow of Control

Observe that only one prompt and cin statement are used here because the tested expression is evaluated at the end of the loop.

As with all repetition statements, the do statement can always replace or be replaced by an equivalent while or for statement. The choice of which statement to use depends on the application and the style preferred by the programmer. In general, the while and for statements are preferred because they clearly let anyone reading the program know what is being tested "right up front" at the top of the program loop.

Validity Checks

The do statement is particularly useful in filtering user-entered input and providing data validity checks. For example, assume that an operator is required to enter a valid customer identification number between the numbers 100 and 1999. A number outside this range is to be rejected and a new request for a valid number made. The following section of code provides the necessary data filter to verify the entry of a valid identification number:

```
   do
   {
      cout << "\nEnter an identification number: ";
      cin >> id_num;
   }
   while (id_num < 100 || id_num > 1999);
```

Here, a request for an identification number is repeated until a valid number is entered. This section of code is "bare bones" in that it neither alerts the operator to the cause of the new request for data nor allows premature exit from the loop if a valid identification number cannot be found. An alternative removing the first drawback is:

```
do
{
   cout << "\nEnter an identification number: ";
   cin >> id_num;
   if (id_num < 100 || id_num > 1999)
   {
      cout << "\n An invalid number was just entered"
           << "\nPlease check the ID number and re-enter";
   }
   else
      break;      // break if a valid id num was entered
} while(1);       // this expression is always true
```

Here we have used a break statement to exit from the loop. Since the expression being evaluated by the do statement is always 1 (true), an infinite loop has been created that is only exited when the break statement is encountered.

Exercises 5.4

1. a. Using a do statement, write a C++ program to accept a grade. The program should request a grade continuously as long as an invalid grade is entered. An invalid grade is any grade less than 0 or greater than 100. After a valid grade has been entered, your program should display the value of the grade entered.
b. Modify the program written for Exercise 1a so that the user is alerted when an invalid grade has been entered.
c. Modify the program written for Exercise 1b so that it allows the user to exit the program by entering the number 999.
d. Modify the program written for Exercise 1b so that it automatically terminates after five invalid grades are entered.

2. a. Write a C++ program that continuously requests a grade to be entered. If the grade is less than 0 or greater than 100, your program should print an appropriate message informing the user that an invalid grade has been entered, else the grade should be added to a total. When a grade of 999 is entered the program should exit the repetition loop and compute and display the average of the valid grades entered.

b. Run the program written in Exercise 2a on a computer and verify the program using appropriate test data.

3. *a.* Write a C++ program to reverse the digits of a positive integer number. For example, if the number 8735 is entered, the number displayed should be 5378. (*Hint:* Use a do statement and continuously strip off and display the units digit of the number. If the variable num initially contains the number entered, the units digit is obtained as (num % 10). After a units digit is displayed, dividing the number by 10 sets up the number for the next iteration. Thus, (8735 % 10) is 5 and (8735 / 10) is 873. The do statement should continue as long as the remaining number is not zero.)

b. Run the program written in Exercise 3a on a computer and verify the program using appropriate test data.

4. Repeat any of the exercises in Section 5.3 using a do statement rather than a for statement.

5.5 Common Programming Errors

Five errors are commonly made by beginning C++ programmers when using repetition statements. Two of these pertain to the tested expression and have already been encountered with the if and switch statements. The first is the inadvertent use of the assignment operator, =, for the equality operator, ==, in the tested expression. An example of this error is typing the assignment expression a = 5 instead of the desired relational expression a == 5. Since the tested expression can be any valid C++ expression, including arithmetic and assignment expressions, this error is not detected by the compiler.

As with the if statement, repetition statements should not use the equality operator, ==, when testing real valued operands. For example, the expression fnum == .01 should be replaced by an equivalent test requiring that the absolute value of fnum - .01 be less than an acceptable amount. The reason for this is that all numbers are stored in binary form and using a finite number of bits, decimal numbers such as .01 have no exact binary equivalent, so that tests requiring equality with such numbers can fail.

The next two errors are particular to the for statement. The most common is to place a semicolon at the end of the for's parentheses, which frequently produces a do-nothing loop. For example, consider the statements

```
for(count = 0; count < 10; count++);
    total = total + num;
```

Here the semicolon at the end of the first line of code is a null statement. This has the effect of creating a loop that is traversed 10 times with nothing done except the incrementing and testing of count. This error tends to occur because C++ programmers are used to ending most lines with a semicolon.

The next error occurs when commas are used to separate the items in a `for` statement instead of the required semicolons. An example of this is the statement

```
for (count = 1, count < 10, count++)
```

Commas must be used to separate items within the initializing and altering lists, and semicolons must be used to separate these lists from the tested expression.

The last error occurs when the final semicolon is omitted from the `do` statement. This error is usually made by programmers who have learned to omit the semicolon after the parentheses of a `while` statement and carry over this habit when the keyword `while` is encountered at the end of a `do` statement.

5.6 Chapter Summary

1. The `while`, `for`, and `do` repetition statements create program loops. These statements evaluate an expression and, based on the resulting expression value, either terminate the loop or continue with it.

2. The `while` statement checks its expression before any other statement in the loop. This requires that any variables in the tested expression have values assigned before the `while` is encountered. Within a `while` loop there must be a statement that either alters the tested expression's value or forces a break from the loop. The general form of a `while` statement is:

   ```
   while (expression)
       statement;
   ```

   If the statement contained within a `while` statement is a compound statement, the `while` statement takes the form:

   ```
   while(expression)
   {
       any number of statements in here;
   }
   ```

3. The `for` statement is extremely useful in creating loops that must be executed a fixed number of times. Initializing expressions (including declarations), the tested expression, and expressions affecting the tested expression can all be included in parentheses at the top of a `for` loop. Additionally, any other loop statement can be included within the `for`'s parentheses as part of its altering list. The general form of a `for` statement is:

```
for(initialization; expression; altering-statements)
   statement;
```

If the statement contained within a `for` statement is a compound statement, the `for` statement takes the form:

```
for(initialization; expression; altering-statements)
{
   any number of statements in here;
}
```

4. The do statement checks its expression at the end of the loop. This ensures that the body of a do loop is executed at least once. Within a do loop there must be at least one statement that either alters the tested expression's value or forces a break from the loop. The general form of a do statement is:

```
do
   statement;
while (expression);
```

If the statement contained within a do statement is a compound statement, the do statement takes the form:

```
do
{
   any number of statements in here;
}
while(expression);
```

Writing Your Own Functions

Chapter Six

In the programs we have written so far, the only functions we have had to call have been the mathematical functions introduced in Section 3.2. It is now time to create our own, user-written functions, in addition to the `main()` function required in all programs. In this chapter we learn how to write these functions, pass data to them, process the passed data, and return a result to the calling function.

6.1 Function and Argument Declarations

In creating C++ functions we must be concerned with both the function itself and how it interfaces with other functions, such as `main()`. This includes correctly passing data into a function when it is called and returning a value back from a function. In this section we describe the first part of the interface, passing data to a function and having the function correctly receive, store, and process the transmitted data.

As we have already seen with mathematical functions, a function is called, or used, by giving the function's name and passing any data to it in the parentheses following the function name (see Figure 6–1).

The called function must be able to accept the data passed to it by the function doing the calling. Only after the called function successfully receives the data can the data be manipulated to produce a useful result.

To clarify the process of sending and receiving data, consider Program 6-1, which calls a function named `find_max()`.* The program, as shown, is not yet complete. Once the function `find_max()` is written and included in Program 6-1, the completed program, consisting of the functions `main()` and `find_max()`, can be run.

 Program 6-1

```
#include <iostream.h>
void main(void)
{
  int firstnum, secnum;
  void find_max(int, int);  // the function declaration (prototype)

  cout << "\nEnter a number: ";
  cin >> firstnum;
  cout << "Great! Please enter a second number: ";
  cin >> secnum;

  find_max(firstnum, secnum); // the function is called here
}
```

---

* To clearly distinguish between identifiers used as variable names and those used as function names, all names that refer to functions will be followed by parentheses.

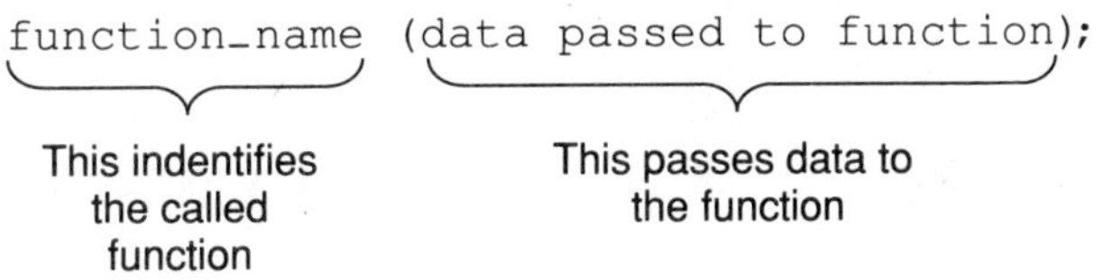

```
function_name (data passed to function);
```

This indentifies
the called
function

This passes data to
the function

FIGURE 6–1 Calling and Passing Data to a Function

Let us examine declaring and calling the function `find_max()` from the `main()` function. We will then write `find_max()` to accept the data passed to it and determine the largest or maximum value of the two passed values.

The function `find_max()` is referred to as the *called function*, since it is called or summoned into action by its reference in `main()`. The function that does the calling, in this case `main()`, is referred to as the *calling function*. The terms called and calling come from standard telephone usage, where one party calls the other on a telephone. The party initiating the call is referred to as the calling party, and the party receiving the call is referred to as the called party. The same terms describe function calls. Within `main()`, the called function, in this case `find_max()`, is declared as a function that expects to receive two integer numbers and return no value (a void) back to `main()`. This declaration is formally referred to as a function prototype. The function is then called by the last statement in the program.

Function Prototypes

Before a function can be called, it must be declared to the function that will do the calling. The declaration statement for a function is referred to as a *function prototype*. The function prototype tells the calling function the type of value that will be formally returned, if any, and the data type of the values that the calling function should transmit to the called function. For example, the function prototype previously used in Program 6-1:

```
void find_max(int, int);
```

declares that the function `find_max()` expects two integer values to be sent to it, and that this particular function formally returns no value (`void`). Function prototypes may be placed with the variable declaration statements of the calling function, as in Program 6-1, or above the calling function name. Thus, the function prototype for `find_max()` could have been placed either before or after the statement `#include <iostream.h>`, prior to `main()`, or within `main()`, as in Program 6-1. (The reasons for the choice of placement are presented in Section 6.4.) The general form of function prototype statements is:

```
return-data-type  function-name(list of argument data types);
```

The data-type refers to the data type of the value that will be formally returned by the function. Examples of function prototypes are:

```
int fmax(int, int);

float swap(int, char, char, double);

void display(double, double);
```

The function prototype for `fmax()` declares that this function expects to receive two integer arguments and will formally return an integer value. The function prototype for `swap()` declares that this function requires four arguments consisting of an integer, two characters, and a double precision argument, in this order, and will formally return a floating point number. Finally, the function prototype for `display()` declares that this function requires two double precision arguments and does not return any value. Such a function might be used to display the results of a computation directly, without returning any value to the called function.

The use of function prototypes permits error checking of data types by the compiler. If the function prototype does not agree with data types defined when the function is written, an error message (typically `TYPE MISMATCH`) will occur. The prototype also serves another task: It ensures conversion of all arguments passed to the function to the declared argument data type when the function is called.

Calling a Function

Calling a function is rather trivial. All that is required is that the name of the function be used and that any data passed to the function be enclosed within the parentheses following the function name. The items enclosed within the parentheses are called *actual arguments* of the called function (see Figure 6–2).

If a variable is one of the actual arguments in a function call, the called function receives a copy of the value stored in the variable.* For example, the statement `find_max(firstnum,secnum);` calls the function `find_max()` and causes the values currently residing in the variables `firstnum` and `secnum` to be passed to `find_max()`. The variable names in parentheses are actual arguments that provide values to the called function. After the values are passed, control is transferred to the called function.

FIGURE 6–2 Calling and Passing Two Values to `find_max()`

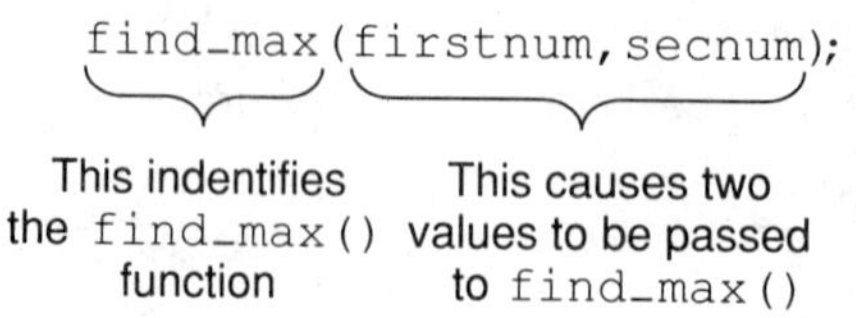

```
find_max(firstnum,secnum);
```

This indentifies	This causes two
the `find_max()`	values to be passed
function	to `find_max()`

---

* Except for arrays, which is the topic of Chapter 7.

As illustrated in Figure 6–3, the function `find_max()` *does not receive the variable names* `firstnum` *and* `secnum` *and has no knowledge of these variable names.*[1] The function simply receives the values in these variables and must itself determine where to store these values before it does anything else. Although this procedure for passing data to a function, which is referred to as pass by value, may seem surprising, it is really a safety procedure for ensuring that a called function does not inadvertently change data stored in a variable. The function gets a copy of the data to use. It may change its copy and, of course, change any variables or arguments declared inside itself. However, unless specific steps are taken to do so, a function is not allowed to change the contents of variables declared in other functions.

Let us now begin writing the function `find_max()` to process the values passed to it.

Defining a Function

A function is defined when it is written. Each function is defined once (that is, written once) in a program and can then be used by any other function in the program that suitably declares it.

FIGURE 6–3 `find_max()` Receives Actual Values

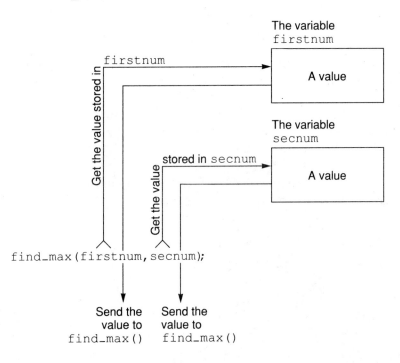

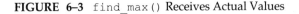

---

[1] This is significantly different from computer languages such as FORTRAN, where functions and subroutines receive access to the variables and can pass data back through them. In Section 6.3 we will see how, using reference variables, C++ also permits direct access to the calling function's variables.

Like the `main()` function, every C++ function definition consists of two parts, a *function header* and a *function body*, as illustrated in Figure 6–4. The purpose of the function header is to identify the data type of the value returned by the function, provide the function with a name, and specify the number, order, and type of arguments expected by the function. The purpose of the function body is to operate on the passed data and directly return, at most, one value back to the calling function. (We will see, in Section 6.3, how a function can be made to return multiple values through the argument list.)

The function header is always the first line of a function and contains the function's returned value type, its name, and the names and data types of its arguments. Since `find_max()` will not formally return any value and is to receive two integer arguments, the following header line can be used:

$$\text{void find\_max(int x, int y)} \longleftarrow \text{no semicolon}$$

The argument names in the header line are formally referred to as *parameters* or *formal arguments*, and we shall use the these terms interchangeably.[2] Thus, the argument x will be used to store the first value passed to `find_max()` and the argument y will be used to store the second value passed at the time of the function call. The function does not know where the values come from when the call is made from `main()`. The first part of the call procedure executed by the computer involves going to the variables `firstnum` and `secnum` and retrieving the stored values. These values are then passed to `find_max()` and ultimately stored in the formal arguments x and y (see Figure 6–5).

The function name and all parameter names in the header line, in this case `find_max`, x, and y, are chosen by the programmer. Any names selected according to the rules used to choose variable names can be used. All parameters listed in the function header line must be separated by commas and must have their individual data types declared separately.

Now that we have written the function header for the `find_max()` function, we can construct the body of this function. Let us assume that the `find_max()` function selects and displays the larger of the two numbers passed to it.

FIGURE 6–4 General Format of a Function

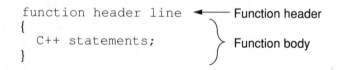

```
function header line        ← Function header
{
    C++ statements;         } Function body
}
```

----

[2] The portion of the function header that contains the function name and parameters is formally referred to as a function declarator, which should not be confused with a function declaration (prototype).

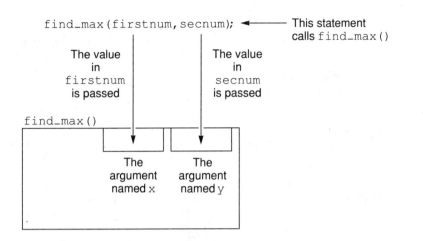

FIGURE 6-5 Storing Values into Arguments

As illustrated in Figure 6–6, a function body begins with an opening brace, {, contains any necessary variable declarations and other C++ statements, and ends with a closing brace, }. This should be familiar to you because it is the same structure used in all the main() functions we have written. This should not be a surprise, since main() is itself a function and must adhere to the rules required for constructing all legitimate functions.

In the body of the function find_max(), we will declare one variable to store the maximum of the two numbers passed to it. We will then use an if-else statement to find the maximum of the two numbers. Finally, a cout object stream will be used to display the maximum. The complete function definition for the find_max() function is:

```cpp
void find_max(int x, int y)
{                       // start of function body
  int maxnum;           // variable declaration

  if (x >= y)           // find the maximum number
    maxnum = x;
  else
    maxnum = y;

  cout << "\nThe maximum of the two numbers is " << maxnum;

}   // end of function body and end of function
```

FIGURE 6-6 Structure of a Function Body

```
{
    variable declarations and
    other C++ statements
}
```

Notice that the argument declarations are made within the header line and the variable declaration is made immediately after the opening brace of the function's body. This is in keeping with the concept that argument values are passed to a function from outside the function, and that variables are declared and assigned values from within the function body.

Program 6-2 includes the find_max() function within the program code previously listed in Program 6-1.

 **Program 6-2**

```
#include <iostream.h>
void main(void)
{
  int firstnum, secnum;
  void find_max(int, int);   // the function prototype

  cout << "\nEnter a number: ";
  cin >> firstnum;
  cout << "Great! Please enter a second number: ";
  cin >> secnum;

  find_max(firstnum, secnum); // the function is called here

}

// following is the function find_max()

void find_max(int x, int y)
{                       // start of function body
  int maxnum;           // variable declaration

  if (x >= y)           // find the maximum number
    maxnum = x;
  else
    maxnum = y;

  cout << "\nThe maximum of the two numbers is " << maxnum;

}   // end of function body and end of function
```

Program 6-2 can be used to select and print the maximum of any two integer numbers entered by the user. Following is a sample run using Program 6-2:

```
Enter a number: 25
Great! Please enter a second number: 5
The maximum of the two numbers is 25
```

The placement of the `find_max()` function definition after the `main()` function in Program 6-2 is a matter of choice. Some programmers prefer to put all called functions at the top of a program and make `main()` the last function listed. In the case where a function is defined before it is called no function prototype is required. We prefer to list `main()` first because it is the driver function that should give anyone reading the program an idea of what the complete program is about before encountering the details of each function. Either placement approach is acceptable and you will encounter both styles in your programming work. In no case, however, can `find_max()` be placed inside `main()`. This is true for all C++ functions, which must be defined by themselves outside any other function. Each C++ function is a separate and independent entity with its own arguments and variables; nesting of functions is never permitted.

Default Arguments

A convenient feature of C++ is the flexibility of providing default arguments in a function call. The default argument values are listed in the function prototype and are automatically transmitted to the called function when the corresponding arguments are omitted from the function call. For example, the function prototype

```
void example(int, int = 5, float = 6.78);
```

provides default values for the last two arguments. If any of these arguments are omitted when the function is actually called, the C++ compiler will supply these default values. Thus, all of the following function calls are valid:

```
example(7, 2, 9.3)   // no defaults used
example(7, 2)        // same as example(7, 2, 6.78)
example(7)           // same as example(7, 5, 6.78)
```

Three rules must be followed when using default parameters. The first is that if any parameter is given a default value in the function prototype, all parameters following it must also be supplied with default values. The second rule is that if one argument is omitted in the actual function call, then all arguments to its right must also be omitted. These two rules make it clear to the C++ compiler which arguments are being omitted and permits the compiler to supply correct default values for the missing arguments, starting with the rightmost argument and working in toward the left. The last rule specifies that the default value used in the function prototype may be an expression consisting of both constants and previously declared variables. If such an expression is used, it must pass the compiler's check for validly declared variables, even though the actual value of the expression is evaluated and assigned at run time.

Default arguments are extremely useful when extending an existing function to include more features that require additional arguments. Adding the new arguments to the right of the existing arguments and providing each new argument with a default value permits all existing function calls to remain as they are. Thus, the effect of the new changes is conveniently isolated from existing code in the program.

Reusing Function Names (Function Overloading)

In most high-level languages, including C++'s immediate predecessor, C, each function requires its own unique name. In theory this makes sense, but in practice it can lead to a profusion of function names, even for functions that perform essentially the same operations. For example, consider determining and displaying the absolute value of a number. If the number passed into the function can be either an integer, a long integer, or a double precision value, three distinct functions must be written to handle each case correctly. As was done in C, we could give each of these functions a unique name, such as abs(), labs(), and fabs(), respectively, having the function prototypes:

```
void abs(int);
void labs(long);
void fabs(double);
```

Clearly, each of these three functions perform essentially the same operation, but on different argument data types. In C++, as long as the compiler can determine which function to use based on the data types of the arguments (not the data type of the return value, if any), the same function name can be used for more than one function. Using the same function name for more than one function is referred to as *function overloading*.

Applying function overloading to our absolute value functions permits us to write three C++ functions that all have the same name. Using the function name abs for our functions, they can be written as follows:

```
void abs(int x)   // take the absolute value of an integer
{
  if ( x < 0 )
    x = -x;
  cout << "The absolute value of the integer is  " << x << '\n';
}
void abs(long x)   // take the absolute value of a long integer
{
  if ( x < 0 )
    x = -x;
  cout << "The absolute value of the long integer is  " << x << '\n';
}

void abs(double x)   // take the absolute value of a double
{
  if ( x < 0 )
    x = -x;
  cout << "The absolute value of the double is  " << x << '\n';
}
```

Which of the three functions named abs() is actually called depends on the argument types supplied at the time of the call. Thus, the function call abs(10); would cause the compiler to use the function named abs that expects an integer argument, and the function call abs(6.28); would cause the compiler to use the function named abs that expects an argument whose value is of type double.[3]

Notice that overloading a function's name simply means using the same name for more than one function. Each function that uses the name must still be written and exists as a separate entity. The use of the same function name does not require that the code within the functions be similar, although good programming practice dictates that functions with the same name should perform essentially the same operations. All that is formally required in using the same function name is that the compiler can distinguish which function to select based on the data types of the arguments when the function is called.

Exercises 6.1

1. For the following function headers, determine the number, type, and order (sequence) of the values that must be passed to the function:
  a. void factorial(int n)
  b. void price(int type, double yield, double maturity)
  c. void yield(int type, double price, double maturity)
  d. void interest(char flag, float price, float time)
  e. void total(float amount, float rate)
  f. void roi(int a, int b, char c, char d, float e, float f)
  g. void get_val(int item, int iter, char decflag, char delim)

2. a. Write a function named check, which has three arguments. The first argument should accept an integer number, the second argument a floating point number, and the third argument a double precision number. The body of the function should just display the values of the data passed to the function when it is called.

  (*Note:* When tracing errors in functions, it is helpful to have the function display the values it has been passed. Quite frequently, the error is not in what the body of the function does with the data, but in the data received and stored.)

  b. Include the function written in Exercise 2a in a working program. Make sure your function is called from main(). Test the function by passing various data to it.

3. a. Write a function named find_abs() that accepts a double precision number passed to it, computes its absolute value, and displays the absolute value. The absolute value of a number is the number itself if the number is positive, and the negative of the number if the number is negative.

---

[3] This is accomplished by *name mangling*, a process whereby the function name generated by the C++ compiler differs from the function name used in the source code. The compiler appends information to the source code function name depending on the type of data being passed, and the resulting name is said to be a mangled version of the source code name.

b. Include the function written in Exercise 3a in a working program. Make sure your function is called from `main()`. Test the function by passing various data to it.

4. *a.* Write a function called `mult()` that accepts two floating point numbers as arguments, multiplies these two numbers, and displays the result.
b. Include the function written in Exercise 4a in a working program. Make sure your function is called from `main()`. Test the function by passing various data to it.

5. *a.* Write a function named `sqr_it()` that computes the square of the value passed to it and displays the result. The function should be capable of squaring numbers with decimal points.
b. Include the function written in Exercise 5a in a working program. Make sure your function is called from `main()`. Test the function by passing various data to it.

6. *a.* Write a function named `powfun()` that raises an integer number passed to it to a positive integer power and displays the result. The positive integer should be the second value passed to the function. Declare the variable used to store the result as a long integer data type to ensure sufficient storage for the result.
b. Include the function written in Exercise 6a in a working program. Make sure your function is called from `main()`. Test the function by passing various data to it.

7. *a.* Write a function that produces a table of the numbers from 1 to 10, their squares, and their cubes. The function should produce the same display as that produced by Program 5-10.
b. Include the function written in Exercise 7a in a working program. Make sure your function is called from `main()`. Test the function by passing various data to it.

8. *a.* Modify the function written for Exercise 7 to accept the starting value of the table, the number of values to be displayed, and the increment between values. If the increment is not explicitly sent, the function should use a default value of 1. Name your function `sel_tab()`. A call to `sel_tab(6,5,2);` should produce a table of five lines, the first line starting with the number 6 and each succeeding number increasing by 2.
b. Include the function written in Exercise 8a in a working program. Make sure your function is called from `main()`. Test the function by passing various data to it.

6.2 Returning Values

Using the method of passing data into a function presented in Section 6.1, the called function only receives copies of the values contained in the arguments at the time of the call (review Figure 6–3 if this is unclear to you). This method of calling a function and passing values to it is referred to as a function *call by value*, and is a distinct advantage of C++. Since the called function does not have direct access to any of the calling function's variables, it cannot inadvertently alter the value stored in one of these variables.

When a function is called by value it may process the data sent to it in any fashion desired and directly return at most one, and only one, "legitimate" value to the calling function (see Figure 6–7). In this section we see how such a value

A function can receive many values

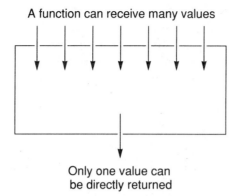
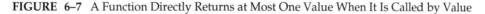

Only one value can
be directly returned

FIGURE 6–7 A Function Directly Returns at Most One Value When It Is Called by Value

is returned to the calling function. As you might expect, given C++'s flexibility, there is a way of returning more than a single value, but that is the topic of the next section.

As with the calling of a function, directly returning a value requires that the interface between the called and calling functions be handled correctly. From its side of the return transaction, the called function must provide the following items:

- the data type of the returned value
- the actual value being returned

A function returning a value must specify, in its header line, the data type of the value that will be returned. Recall that the function header line is the first line of the function, which includes both the function's name and a list of argument names. As an example, consider the find_max() function written in the last section. It determined the maximum value of two numbers passed to the function. For convenience, the original code of find_max() is listed below:

```
void find_max(int x, int y)
{                       // start of function body
  int maxnum;           // variable declaration

  if (x >= y)           // find the maximum number
    maxnum = x;
  else
    maxnum = y;

  cout << "\nThe maximum of the two numbers is " << maxnum;

}  // end of function body and end of function
```

As written, the function's header line is `void find_max(int x, int y)`, where `x` and `y` are the names chosen for the function's formal arguments.

If `find_max()` is now to return a value, the function's header line must be amended to include the data type of the value being returned. For example, if an integer value is to be returned, the proper function header line is:

```
int find_max(int x, int y)
```

Similarly, if the function is to return a floating point value, the correct function header line is:

```
float find_max(int x, int y)
```

and if the function is to return a double precision value the header line would be:

```
double find_max(int x, int y)
```

Let us now modify the function `find_max()` to return the maximum value of the two numbers passed to it. To do this, we must first determine the data type of the value that is to be returned and include this data type in the function's header line.

Since the maximum value determined by `find_max()` is stored in the integer variable `maxnum`, it is the value of this variable that the function should return. Returning an integer value from `find_max()` requires that the function declaration be `int find_max(int x, int y)`. Observe that this is the same as the original function header line for `find_max()` with the substitution of the keyword `int` for the keyword `void`.

Having declared the data type that `find_max()` will return, all that remains is to include a statement within the function to cause the return of the correct value. To return a value, a function must use a `return` statement, which has the form:

```
return expression;
```

When the `return` statement is encountered, the expression is evaluated first. The value of the expression is then automatically converted to the data type declared in the function header before being sent back to the calling function. After the value is returned, program control reverts to the calling function. Thus, to return the value stored in `maxnum`, all we need to do is add the statement `return(maxnum);` before the closing brace of the `find_max()` function. The complete function code is:

These
should be
the same
data type

```
int find_max(int x, int y)    // function header line
{                             // start of function body
    int maxnum;              // variable declaration

    if (x >= y)
        maxnum = x;
    else
        maxnum = y;

    return maxnum;            // return statement
}
```

In the new code for the function `find_max()`, note that the data type of the expression contained within the parentheses of the `return` statement correctly matches the data type in the function's header line. It is up to the programmer to ensure that this is so for every function returning a value. Failure to exactly match the `return` value with the function's declared data type may not result in an error when your program is compiled, but it may lead to undesired results since the `return` value is always converted to the data type declared in the function declaration. Usually this is a problem only when the fractional part of a returned floating point or double precision number is truncated because the function was declared to return an integer value.

Having taken care of the sending side of the `return` transaction, we must now prepare the calling function to receive the value sent by the called function. On the calling (receiving) side, the calling function must:

- be alerted to the type of value to expect
- properly use the returned value

Alerting the calling function as to the type of `return` value to expect is properly taken care of by the function prototype. For example, including the function prototype

```
int find_max(int, int);
```

with `main()`'s variable declarations is sufficient to alert `main()` that `find_max()` is a function that will return an integer value.

To actually use a returned value we must either provide a variable to store the value or use the value directly in an expression. Storing the returned value in a variable is accomplished using a standard assignment statement. For example, the assignment statement

```
max = find_max(firstnum,secnum);
```

can be used to store the value returned by `find_max()` in the variable named `max`. This assignment statement does two things. First the right-hand side of the assignment statement calls find_max(), then the result returned by find_max is stored in the variable max. Since the value returned by find_max() is an integer, the variable max must also be declared as an integer variable within the calling function's variable declarations.

The value returned by a function need not be stored directly in a variable, but can be used wherever an expression is valid. For example, the expression 2 * find_max(firstnum, secnum) multiplies the value returned by find_max() by two, and the statement cout << find_max(firstnum, secnum); displays the returned value.

Program 6-3 illustrates the inclusion of both prototype and assignment statements for main() to correctly declare, call, and store a returned value from find_max(). As before, and in keeping with our convention of placing the main() function first, we have placed the find_max() function after main().

Program 6-3

```
#include <iostream.h>
void main(void)
{
  int firstnum, secnum, max;
  int find_max(int, int);   // the function prototype

  cout << "\nEnter a number: ";
  cin >> firstnum;
  cout << "Great! Please enter a second number: ";
  cin >> secnum;

  max = find_max(firstnum, secnum); // the function is called here

  cout << "\nThe maximum of the two numbers is " << max;

}

int find_max(int x, int y)
{                       // start of function body
  int maxnum;           // variable declaration

  if (x >= y)           // find the maximum number
    maxnum = x;
  else
    maxnum = y;

  return maxnum;        // return statement
}
```

In reviewing Program 6-3 it is important to note the four items we have introduced in this section. The first item is the prototype for `find_max()` within `main()`. This statement, which ends with a semicolon as all declaration statements do, alerts `main()` to the data type that `find_max()` will be returning. The parentheses after the name `find_max` inform `main()` that `find_max` is a function rather than a variable. The second item to notice in `main()` is the use of an assignment statement to store the returned value from the `find_max()` call into the variable `max`. We have also made sure to correctly declare `max` as an integer within `main()`'s variable declarations so that it matches the data type of the returned value.

The last two items of note concern the coding of the `find_max()` function. The first line of `find_max()` declares that the function will return an integer value, and the expression in the `return` statement evaluates to a matching data type. Thus, `find_max()` is internally consistent in sending an integer value back to `main()`, and `main()` has been correctly alerted to receive and use the returned integer.

In writing your own functions you must always keep these four items in mind. For another example, see if you can identify these four items in Program 6-4.

Program 6-4

```
#include <iostream.h>
void main(void)
{
   int count;                  // start of declarations
   double fahren;
   double tempvert(double);    // function prototype

   for(count = 1; count <= 4; count++)
   {
     cout << "\nEnter a Fahrenheit temperature: ";
     cin >> fahren;
     cout << "The Celsius equivalent is " << tempvert(fahren);
   }
}

// convert fahrenheit to celsius
double tempvert(double in_temp)
{
   return( (5.0/9.0) * (in_temp - 32.0) );
}
```

In reviewing Program 6-4 let us first analyze the function `tempvert()`. The complete definition of the function begins with the function's header line and ends with the closing brace after the return statement. The function is declared as returning a value of type double; this means the expression in the function's `return` statement must evaluate to a double precision number, which it does. Since a function header line is not a statement but the start of the code defining the function, the function header line does not end with a semicolon.

On the receiving side, `main()` has a prototype for the function `tempvert()` that agrees with `tempvert()`'s function definition. As with all declaration statements, multiple declarations of the same type may be made within the same statement. Thus, we could have used the same declaration statement to declare both the variable `fahren` and the function `tempvert()` as double precision data types. If we had done so, the single declaration statement `double fahren, tempvert(double);` could have been used to replace the two individual declarations for `fahren` and `tempvert()`. For clarity, however, we will always keep function prototype statements apart from variable declaration statements. No additional variable is declared in `main()` to store the returned value from `tempvert()` because the returned value is immediately passed to `cout` for display.

One further point is worth mentioning here. One of the purposes of declarations, as we learned in Chapter 2, is to alert the computer to the amount of internal storage reserved for the data. The prototype within `main()` for `tempvert()` performs this task and tells the computer how much storage must be accessed by `main()` when the returned value is retrieved. Had we placed the `tempvert()` function before `main()`, however, the function header line for `tempvert()` would suffice to alert the computer to the type of storage needed for the returned value. In this case, the function prototype for `tempvert()`, within `main()`, could be eliminated. Since we have chosen always to list `main()` as the first function in a file, we must include function prototypes for all functions called by `main()`. This style also serves to document what functions will be accessed by `main()`.

Inline Functions[4]

Calling a function places a certain amount of overhead on a computer. This consists of placing argument values in a reserved memory region that the function has access to (this memory region is referred to as the *stack*), passing control to the function, providing a reserved memory location for any returned value (again, the stack region of memory is used), and finally returning to the proper point in the calling program. Paying this overhead is well justified when a function is called many times, because it can significantly reduce the size of a program. Rather than repeating the same code within a function each time it is needed, the code is written once, as a function, and called whenever it is needed.

---

[4] This section is optional and may be omitted on first reading without loss of subject continuity.

For small functions that are not called many times, however, paying the overhead for passing and returning values may not be warranted. It still would be convenient, though, to group repeating lines of code together under a common function name and have the compiler place this code directly into the program wherever the function is called. This capability is provided by inline functions.

Telling the C++ compiler that a function is *inline* causes a copy of the function code to be placed in the program at the point where the function is called. For example, consider the function tempvert() defined in Program 6-4. Since this is a relatively short function it is an ideal candidate to be an inline function.

To make this, or any other function, an inline one, simply requires placing the reserved word inline before the function name and defining the function before any calls are made to it. This is done for the tempvert() function in Program 6-5.

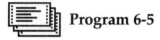 **Program 6-5**

```
#include <iostream.h>

inline double tempvert(double in_temp)   // an inline function
{
  return( (5.0/9.0) * (in_temp - 32.0) );
}

void main(void)
{
  int count;                     // start of declarations
  double fahren;

  for(count = 1; count <= 4; count++)
  {
    cout << "\nEnter a Fahrenheit temperature: ";
    cin >> fahren;
    cout << "The Celsius equivalent is " << tempvert(fahren);
  }
}
```

Observe in Program 6-5 that the inline function is placed ahead of any calls to it. This is a requirement of all inline functions and obviates the need for a function prototype within any subsequent function calling it. Since the function is now an inline one, its code will be expanded directly into the program wherever it is called.

The advantage of using an `inline` function is an increase in execution speed. Since the `inline` function is directly expanded and included in every expression or statement calling it, there is no execution time loss due to the call and return overhead required by a non-`inline` function. The disadvantage is the increase in program size when an `inline` function is called repeatedly. Each time an `inline` function is referenced the complete function code is reproduced and stored as an integral part of the program. A non-`inline` function, however, is stored in memory only once. No matter how many times the function is called, the same code is used. Therefore, `inline` functions should only be used for small functions that are not extensively called in the program.

Exercises 6.2

1. Rewrite Program 6-3 to have the function `find_max()` accept two floating point arguments and return a floating point value to `main()`. Make sure to modify `main()` in order to pass two floating point values to `find_max()` and accept and store the floating point value returned by `find_max()`.

2. For the following function headers, determine the number, type, and order (sequence) of values that should be passed to the function when it is called and the data type of the value returned by the function.

   a. `int factorial(int n)`
   b. `double price(int type, double yield, double maturity)`
   c. `double yield(int type, double price, double maturity)`
   d. `char interest(char flag, float price, float time)`
   e. `int total(float amount, float rate)`
   f. `float roi(int a, int b, char c, char d, float e, float f)`
   g. `void get_val(int item, int iter, char decflag)`

  3. Write function headers for the following:

   a. A function named `check()`, which has three arguments. The first argument should accept an integer number, the second argument a floating point number, and the third argument a double precision number. The function returns no value.
   b. A function named `find_abs()` that accepts a double-precision number passed to it and returns its absolute value.
   c. A function named `mult()` that accepts two floating point numbers as arguments, multiplies these two numbers, and returns the result.
   d. A function named `sqr_it()` that computes and returns the square of the integer value passed to it.
   e. A function named `powfun()` that raises an integer number passed to it to a positive integer power and returns the result as a long integer.
   f. A function named `table()` that produces a table of the numbers from 1 to 10, their squares, and their cubes. No arguments are to be passed to the function and the function returns no value.

  4. a. Write a C++ function named `find_abs()` that accepts a double precision number passed to it, computes its absolute value, and returns the absolute value to the calling function. The absolute value of a number is the number itself if the number is positive or zero, and the negative of the number if the number is negative.

b. Include the function written in Exercise 4a in a working program. Make sure your function is called from `main()` and correctly returns a value to `main()`. Have `main()` use `cout` to display the value returned. Test the function by passing various data to it.

5. a. Write a C++ function called `mult()` that accepts two double precision numbers as arguments, multiplies these two numbers, and returns the result to the calling function.

b. Include the function written in Exercise 5a in a working program. Make sure your function is called from `main()` and correctly returns a value to `main()`. Have `main()` use `cout` to display the value returned. Test the function by passing various data to it.

6. a. Write a C++ function named `powfun()` that raises an integer number passed to it to a positive integer power and returns the result to the calling function. Declare the variable used to return the result as a long integer data type to ensure sufficient storage for the result.

b. Include the function written in Exercise 6a in a working program. Make sure your function is called from `main()` and correctly returns a value to `main()`. Have `main()` use `cout` to display the value returned. Test the function by passing various data to it.

7. A second-degree polynomial in x is given by the expression $ax^2 + bx + c$, where a, b, and c are known numbers and a is not equal to zero. Write a C++ function named `poly_two(a,b,c,x)` that computes and returns the value of a second-degree polynomial for any passed values of a, b, c, and x.

8. a. Rewrite the function `tempvert()` in Program 6-4 to accept a temperature and a character as arguments. If the character passed to the function is the letter `f`, the function should convert the passed temperature from Fahrenheit to Celsius, else the function should convert the passed temperature from Celsius to Fahrenheit.

b. Modify the `main()` function in Program 6-4 to call the function written for Exercise 8a. Your `main()` function should ask the user for the type of temperature being entered and pass the type (`f` or `c`) into `tempvert()`.

9. a. An extremely useful programming algorithm for rounding a real number to n decimal places is:

Step 1. Multiply the number by 10^n
Step 2. Add .5
Step 3. Delete the fractional part of the result
Step 4. Divide by 10^n

For example, using this algorithm to round the number 78.374625 to three decimal places yields:

Step 1: $78.374625 \times 10^3 = 78374.625$
Step 2: $78374.625 + .5 = 78375.125$
Step 3: Retaining the integer part = 78375
Step 4: 78375 divided by $10^3 = 78.375$

Using this algorithm, write a C++ program that accepts a user-entered value of money, multiplies the entered amount by an 8.675% interest rate, and displays the result rounded to two decimal places.

b. Enter, compile, and execute the program written for Exercise 9a.

10. a. Write a C++ function named `whole()` that returns the integer part of any number passed to the function. (*Hint:* Assign the passed argument to an integer variable.)

b. Include the function written in Exercise 10a in a working program. Make sure your function is called from `main()` and correctly returns a value to `main()`. Have `main()` use `cout` to display the value returned. Test the function by passing various data to it.

11. a. Write a C++ function named `fracpart()` that returns the fractional part of any number passed to the function. For example, if the number 256.879 is passed to `fracpart()`, the number .879 should be returned. Have the function `fracpart()` call the function `whole()` that you wrote in Exercise 10. The number returned can then be determined as the number passed to `fracpart()` less the returned value when the same argument is passed to `whole()`. The completed program should consist of `main()` followed by `fracpart()` followed by `whole()`.

b. Include the function written in Exercise 11a in a working program. Make sure your function is called from `main()` and correctly returns a value to `main()`. Have `main()` use `cout` to display the value returned. Test the function by passing various data to it.

6.3 Call by Reference

In the normal course of operation a called function receives values from its calling function, stores and manipulates the passed values, and possibly returns a single value. As we have seen, this method of calling a function and passing values to it is referred to as a function call by value.

Calling a function by value is a distinct advantage of C++. It allows functions to be written as independent entities without concern that altering an argument or variable in one function may inadvertently alter the value of a variable in another function. Under this approach, formal (receiving) arguments can be considered as either initialized variables or variables that will be assigned values when the function is called. At no time, however, does the called function have direct access to any variable contained in the calling function.

There are situations, however, when it is convenient to alter this approach and give a function direct access to variables of its calling function. To do this requires that both the actual (sending) and formal (receiving) arguments reference the same storage locations in memory. Once the called function can reference the storage locations of a passed argument it can directly access and change the value stored there. When a reference is passed to a function, it is referred to as a *call by reference*. In this section we describe the techniques required to pass a reference to a function and have the function accept and use the reference.

Passing and Using References

As always, in exchanging data between two functions we must be concerned with both the sending and receiving sides of the data exchange. From the sending side, however, calling a function and passing a reference is exactly the same as calling a function and passing a value: The called function is summoned into action by giving its name and a list of arguments. For example, the statement `newval(firstnum, secnum);` both calls the function named `newval` and passes two arguments to it. Let us now write the `newval` function so that it receives direct access to the variables `firstnum` and `secnum`, which we assume to be floating point variables, rather than their values.

One of the first requirements in writing `newval()` is to declare two arguments that can store references. The argument declarations `float &num1;` `float &num2` can be used for this purpose. Here `num1` is declared as a reference variable to a floating point number, as is `num2` (review Section 2.4 for the declaration of reference variables). The choice of the argument names `num1` and `num2` is, as with all argument names, up to the programmer. Including these declarations within the argument list for `newval()`, and assuming that the function returns no value (`void`), the function header for `newval()` becomes:

```
void newval(float &num1, float &num2)
```

For this function header line, an appropriate function prototype is:

```
void newval(float &, float &);
```

This prototype and header line are included in Program 6-6, which includes a completed `newval()` function body that both displays and directly alters the values stored in these reference variables from within the called function.

Program 6-6

```cpp
#include <iostream.h>
void main(void)
{
  float firstnum, secnum;
  void newval(float &, float &);  // prototype - accept two references

  cout << "Enter two numbers: ";
  cin >> firstnum >> secnum;
  cout << "\nThe value in firstnum is: " << firstnum << '\n';
  cout << "The value in secnum is: " << secnum << "\n\n";

  newval(firstnum, secnum);   // call the function

  cout << "The value in firstnum is now: " << firstnum << '\n';
  cout << "The value in secnum is now: " << secnum << '\n';
}

void newval(float &xnum, float &ynum)
{
  cout << "The value in xnum is: " << xnum << '\n';
  cout << "The value in ynum is: " << ynum << "\n\n";
  xnum = 89.5;
  ynum = 99.5;
  return;
}
```

In calling the `newval()` function in Program 6-6 it is important to understand the connection between the actual arguments, `firstnum` and `secnum`, used in the function call and the formal arguments, `xnum` and `ynum`, used in the function header. *Both reference the same data items.* The significance of this is that the values in the actual arguments (`firstnum` and `secnum`) can now be altered from within `newval()` by using the formal argument names (`xnum` and `ynum`). Thus, the formal arguments `xnum` and `ynum` do not store copies of the values in `firstnum` and `secnum`, but directly access the locations in memory set aside for these two arguments. The equivalence of argument names in Program 6-6, which is the essence of a call by reference, is illustrated in Figure 6–8. As illustrated in this figure, both actual and formal argument names are simply different names referring to the same memory storage areas. In `main()` these memory locations are referenced by the names `firstnum` and `secnum`, respectively, while in `newval()` the same locations are referenced by the formal argument names `xnum` and `ynum`, respectively.

The following sample run was obtained using Program 6-6:

```
Enter two numbers: 22.5 33.0

The value in firstnum is: 22.5
The value in secnum is:    33

The value in xnum is: 22.5
The value in ynum is: 33

The value in firstnum is now: 89.5
The value in secnum is now: 99.5
```

In reviewing this output notice that the values initially displayed for the formal arguments `xnum` and `ynum` are the same as those displayed for the actual arguments `firstnum` and `secnum`. Since `xnum` and `ynum` are reference variables, however, `newval()` now has direct access to the arguments `firstnum`

FIGURE 6–8 The Equivalence of Actual and Formal Arguments in Program 6-6

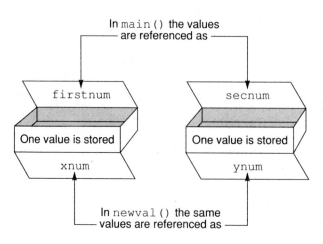

and `secnum`. Thus, any change to `xnum` within `newval()` directly alters the value of `firstnum` in `main()` and any change to `ynum` directly changes `secnum`'s value. As illustrated by the final displayed values, the assignment of values to `xnum` and `ynum` within `newval()` is reflected in `main()` as the altering of `firstnum`'s and `secnum`'s values.

The equivalence between actual calling arguments and formal function arguments illustrated in Program 6-6 provides the basis for returning multiple values from within a function. For example, assume that a function is required to accept three values, compute these values' sum and product, and return these computed results to the calling routine. Naming the function `calc()` and providing five formal arguments (three for the input data and two references for the returned values), the following function can be used:

```
void calc(float num1, float num2, float num3, float &total, float &product)
{
  total = num1 + num2 + num3;
  product = num1 * num2 * num3;
}
```

This function has five formal arguments named `num1`, `num2`, `num3`, `total`, and `product`, of which only the last two are declared as references. Within the function only the last two arguments are altered. The value of the fourth argument, `total`, is calculated as the sum of the first three arguments and the last argument, `product`, is computed as the product of the arguments `num1`, `num2`, and `num3`. Program 6-7 includes this function in a complete program.

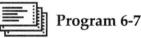 **Program 6-7**

```
#include <iostream.h>
void main(void)
{
  float firstnum, secnum, thirdnum, sum, product;
  void calc(float, float, float, float &, float &);  // prototype

  cout << "Enter three numbers: ";
  cin >> firstnum >> secnum >> thirdnum;

  calc(firstnum, secnum, thirdnum, sum, product);  // function call

  cout << "\nThe sum of the numbers is: " << sum;
  cout << "\nThe product of the numbers is: " << product;
}

void calc(float num1, float num2, float num3, float &total, float &product)
{
  total = num1 + num2 + num3;
  product = num1 * num2 * num3;
}
```

Within main(), the function calc() is called using the five actual arguments firstnum, secnum, thirdnum, sum, and product. As required, these arguments agree in number and data type with the formal arguments declared by calc(). Of the five actual arguments passed, only firstnum, secnum, and thirdnum have been assigned values when the call to calc() is made. The remaining two arguments have not been initialized and will be used to receive values back from calc(). Depending on the compiler used in compiling the program, these arguments will initially contain either zeros or "garbage" values. For safety, it is best to assume that these values are unknown (never assumed). Figure 6–9 illustrates the relationship between actual and formal argument names and the values they contain after the return from calc().

Once calc() is called, it uses its first three arguments to calculate values for total and product and then returns control to main(). Because of the order of its actual calling arguments, main() knows the values calculated by calc() as sum and product, which are then displayed. Following is a sample run using Program 6-7:

```
Enter three numbers: 2.5 6.0 10.0

The sum of the entered numbers is: 18.5
The product of the entered numbers is: 150
```

FIGURE 6–9 Relationship Between Actual and Formal Arguments

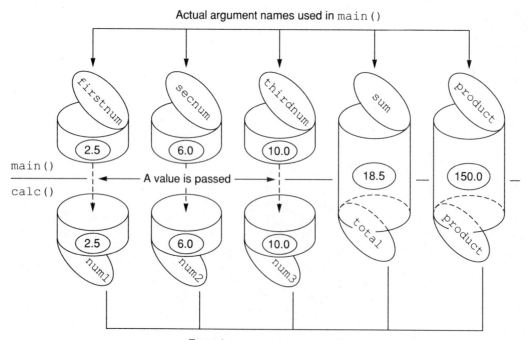

As a final example illustrating the usefulness of passing references to a called function, we will construct a function named swap() that exchanges the values of two of main()'s floating point variables. Such a function is useful when sorting a list of numbers and will be used again in Section 7.7 and 8.4 for just such an application.

Since the value of more than a single variable is affected, swap() cannot be written as a call by value function that returns a single value. The desired exchange of main()'s variables by swap() can only be obtained by giving swap() access to main()'s variables. One way of doing this is by using reference variables.

We have already seen how to pass references to two variables in Program 6-6. We will now construct a function to exchange the values in the passed reference arguments. Exchanging values in two variables is accomplished using the three-step exchange algorithm:

1. Store the first argument's value in a temporary location (see Figure 6–10a)
2. Store the second argument's value in the first variable (see Figure 6–10b)
3. Store the temporary value in the second argument (see Figure 6–10c)

FIGURE 6–10a Save the First Value

FIGURE 6–10b Replace the First Value with the Second Value

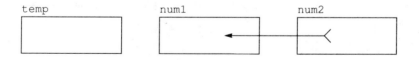

FIGURE 6–10c Change the Second Value

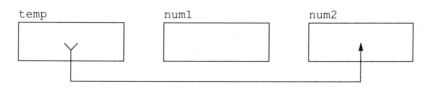

Following is the function `swap` written according to these specifications:

```
void swap(float &num1, float &num2)
{
  float temp;

  temp = num1;      // save num1's value
  num1 = num2;      // store num2's value in num1
  num2 = temp;      // change num2's value

}
```

Notice that the use of references in `swap()`'s header line gives `swap()` access to the equivalent arguments in the calling function. Thus, any changes to the two reference arguments in `swap()` automatically changes the values in the calling function's arguments. Program 6-8 contains `swap()` in a complete program.

Program 6-8

```
#include <iostream.h>
void main(void)
{
  float firstnum = 20.5, secnum = 6.25;
  void swap(float &, float &);   // function receives 2 references

  cout << "The value stored in firstnum is: " << firstnum << '\n';
  cout << "The value stored in secnum is: "<< secnum << "\n\n";

  swap(firstnum, secnum);   // call the function with references

  cout << "The value stored in firstnum is now: " << firstnum << '\n';
  cout << "The value stored in secnum is now: "<< secnum << '\n';
}

void swap(float &num1, float &num2)
{
  float temp;

  temp = num1;      // save num1's value
  num1 = num2;      // store num2's value in num1
  num2 = temp;      // change num2's value

}
```

The following sample run was obtained using Program 6-8:

```
The value stored in firstnum is: 20.5
The value stored in secnum is: 6.25

The value stored in firstnum is now: 6.25
The value stored in secnum is now: 20.5
```

As illustrated in this output, the values stored in main()'s variables have been modified from within swap(), which was made possible by the use of reference arguments. If a call by value had been used instead, the exchange within swap() would only affect swap()'s arguments and would accomplish nothing with respect to main()'s variables. Thus, a function such as swap() can only be written using references or some other means that provides access to main()'s variables (this other means is by pointers, the topic of Chapter 8).

In using reference arguments two cautions need to be mentioned. The first is that reference arguments *cannot* be used to change constants. For example, calling swap() with two constants, such as in the call swap(20.5, 6.5), passes two constants to the function. Although swap() may execute, it will not change the values of these constants.[5]

The second caution is that a function call itself gives no indication that the called function will be using reference arguments. The convention in C++ is to make calls by value rather than calls by reference, precisely to limit a called function's ability to alter variables in the calling function. This convention should be adhered to whenever possible, which means that reference arguments should only be used in restricted situations that actually require multiple return values, such as in the swap() function illustrated in Program 6-8. The calc() function, included in Program 6-7, while useful for illustrative purposes, could also be written as two separate functions, each returning a single value.

Exercises 6.3

1. Write argument declarations for:
   a. a formal argument named amount that will be a reference to a floating point value
   b. a formal argument named price that will be a reference to a double precision number
   c. a formal argument named minutes that will be a reference to an integer number
   d. a formal argument named key that will be a reference to a character
   e. a formal argument named yield that will be a reference to a double precision number

2. Three integer arguments are to be used in a call to a function named time(). Write a suitable function header for time(), assuming that time() accepts these variables as the reference arguments sec, min, and hours, and returns no value to its calling function.

---

[5] Most compilers will catch this error.

3. Rewrite the `find_max()` function in Program 6-3 so that the variable `max`, declared in `main()`, is used to store the maximum value of the two passed numbers. The value of `max` should be set directly from within `find_max()`. (*Hint:* A reference to `max` will have to be accepted by `find_max()`.)

4. Write a function named `change()` that has a floating point argument and four integer reference arguments named `quarters`, `dimes`, `nickels`, and `pennies`, respectively. The function is to consider the floating point passed value as a dollar amount and convert the value into an equivalent number of quarters, dimes, nickels, and pennies. Using the references the function should directly alter the respective actual arguments in the calling function.

5. Write a function named `time()` that has an integer argument named `seconds` and three integer reference arguments named `hours`, `min`, and `sec`. The function is to convert the passed number of seconds into an equivalent number of hours, minutes, and seconds. Using the references the function should directly alter the respective actual arguments in the calling function.

6. Write a function named `yr_calc()` that has a long integer argument representing the total number of days from the turn of the century and reference arguments named `year`, `month`, and `day`. The function is to calculate the current year, month, and day for the given number of days passed to it. Using the references the function should directly alter the respective actual arguments in the calling function. For this problem assume that each year has 365 days and each month has 30 days.

7. Write a function named `liquid()` that has an integer number argument and reference arguments named `gallons`, `quarts`, `pints`, and `cups`. The passed integer represents the total number of cups and the function is to determine the number of gallons, quarts, pints, and cups in the passed value. Using the references the function should directly alter the respective actual arguments in the calling function. Use the relationships of two cups to a pint, four cups to a quart, and 16 cups to a gallon.

8. The following program uses the same argument names in both the calling and called function. Determine if this causes any problem for the computer.

```cpp
#include <iostream.h>
void main(void)
{
   int min, hour;
   void time(int &, int &);   // function prototype

   cout << "Enter two numbers :";
   cin >> min >> hour;
   time(min, hour);
}

void time(int &min, int &hour)    // accept two references
{
   int sec;

   sec = (hour * 60 + min) * 60;
   cout << "The total number of seconds is " << sec;
}
```

6.4 Variable Scope

Now that we have begun to write programs containing more than one function, we can look more closely at the variables declared within each function and their relationship to variables in other functions.

By their very nature, C++ functions are constructed to be independent modules. As we have seen, values are passed to a function using the function's argument list and a value is returned from a function using a `return` statement. Seen in this light, a function can be thought of as a closed box, with slots at the top to receive values and a single slot at the bottom of the box to return a value (see Figure 6–11).

The metaphor of a closed box is useful because it emphasizes the fact that what goes on inside the function, including all variable declarations within the function's body, are hidden from the view of all other functions. Since the variables created inside a function are conventionally available only to the function itself, they are said to be *local* to the function, or *local variables*. This term refers to the *scope* of a variable, where scope is defined as the section of the program where the variable is valid or "known." This section of the program is also referred to as where the variable is visible. A variable can have either a local scope or a global scope. A variable with a local scope is simply one that has had storage locations set aside for it by a declaration statement made within a function body. Local variables are meaningful only when used in expressions or statements inside the function that declared them. This means that the same variable name can be declared and used in more than one function. For each function that declares the variable, a separate and distinct variable is created.

All the variables we have used until now have been local variables. This is a direct result of placing our declaration statements inside functions and using them as definition statements that cause the computer to reserve storage for the

FIGURE 6–11 A Function Can Be Considered a Closed Box

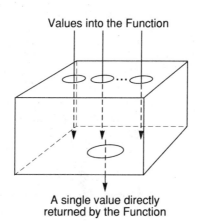

Values into the Function

A single value directly
returned by the Function

declared variable. As we shall see, declaration statements can be placed outside functions and need not act as definitions that cause new storage areas to be reserved for the declared variable.

A variable with *global scope*, more commonly termed a *global variable*, is one whose storage has been created for it by a declaration statement located outside any function. These variables can be used by all functions that are physically placed after the global variable declaration. This is shown in Program 6-9, where we have purposely used the same variable name inside both functions contained in the program.

Program 6-9

```cpp
#include <iostream.h>
int firstnum;      // create a global variable named firstnum
void main(void)
{
  int secnum;           // create a local variable named secnum
  void valfun(void);    // function prototype (declaration)

  firstnum = 10; // store a value into the global variable
  secnum = 20;   // store a value into the local variable

  cout << "\nFrom main(): firstnum = " << firstnum;
  cout << "\nFrom main(): secnum =  " << secnum;

  valfun();        // call the function valfun

  cout << "\n\nFrom main() again: firstnum = " << firstnum;
  cout << "\nFrom main() again: secnum = " << secnum;
}

void valfun(void)    // no values are passed to this function
{
  int secnum;   // create a second local variable named secnum

  secnum = 30; // this only affects this local variable's value

  cout << "\n\nFrom valfun(): firstnum = " << firstnum;
  cout << "\nFrom valfun(): secnum = " << secnum;

  firstnum = 40;    // this changes firstnum for both functions
}
```

The variable `firstnum` in Program 6-9 is a global variable because its storage is created by a definition statement located outside a function. Since both functions, main() and valfun(), follow the definition of firstnum, both of these functions can use this global variable with no further declaration needed.

Program 6-9 also contains two separate local variables, both named secnum. Storage for the secnum variable named in main() is created by the definition statement located in main(). A different storage area for the secnum variable in valfun() is created by the definition statement located in the valfun() function. Figure 6–12 illustrates the three distinct storage areas reserved by the three definition statements found in Program 6-9.

Each of the variables named secnum are local to the function in which their storage is created, and each of these variables can only be used from within the appropriate function. Thus, when secnum is used in main(), the storage area reserved by main() for its secnum variable is accessed, and when secnum is used in valfun(), the storage area reserved by valfun() for its secnum variable is accessed. The following output is produced when Program 6-9 is run:

```
From main():  firstnum = 10
From main():  secnum = 20

From valfun():  firstnum = 10
From valfun():  secnum = 30

From main() again:  firstnum = 40
From main() again:  secnum = 20
```

FIGURE 6–12 The Three Storage Areas Created by Program 6-9

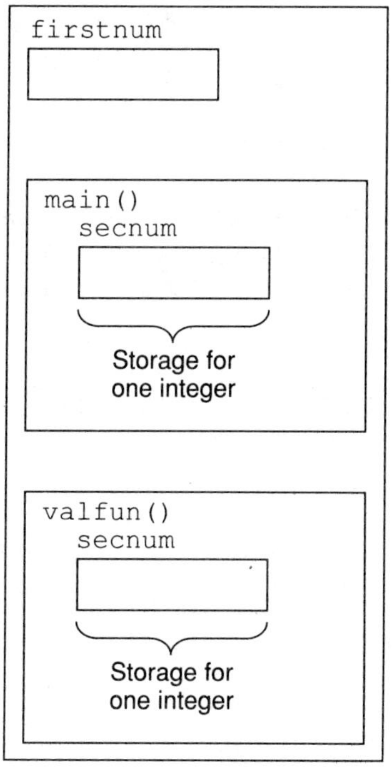

Let us analyze the output produced by Program 6-9. Since firstnum is a global variable, both the main() and valfun() functions can use and change its value. Initially, both functions print the value of 10 that main() stored in firstnum. Before returning, valfun() changes the value of firstnum to 40, which is the value displayed when the variable firstnum is next displayed from within main().

Since each function only "knows" its own local variables, main() can only send the value of its secnum to the cout object, and valfun() can only send the value of its secnum to the cout object. Thus, whenever secnum is obtained from main() the value of 20 is displayed, and whenever secnum is obtained from valfun() the value 30 is displayed.

C++ does not confuse the two secnum variables because only one function can execute at a given moment. Only the storage area for the variables created by the function currently being executed are accessed. If a variable that is not local to the function is used by the function, the program searches the global storage areas for the correct name.

The scope of a variable in no way influences or restricts the data type of the variable. Just as a local variable can be a character, integer, float, double, or any of the other data types (long/short) we have introduced, so can global variables be of these data types, as illustrated in Figure 6–13. The scope of a variable is determined by the placement of the definition statement that reserves storage for it and optionally by a declaration statement that makes it visible, while the data type of the variable is determined by using the appropriate keyword (char, int, float, double, etc.) before the variable's name in a declaration statement.

Global Scope Resolution Operator

When a local variable has the same name as a global variable, all references to the variable name made within the scope of the local variable refer to the local variable. This situation is illustrated in Program 6-10, where the variable name number is defined as both a global and local variable.

FIGURE 6–13 Relating the Scope and Type of a Variable

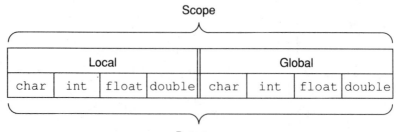

Program 6-10

```
#include <iostream.h>
float number = 42.8;        // a global variable named number
void main(void)
{
  float number = 26.4;      // a local variable named number

  cout << "The value of number is " << number << '\n';
}
```

When Program 6-10 is executed, the following output is displayed:

```
The value of number is 26.4
```

As shown by this output, the local variable name takes precedence over the global variable. In such cases, we can still access the global variable by using C++'s global resolution operator. This operator, which has the symbol ::, must be placed immediately before the variable name, as in ::number. When used in this manner the :: tells the compiler to use the global variable. As an example, the global resolution operator is used in Program 6-10a.

Program 6-10a

```
#include <iostream.h>
float number = 42.5;        // a global variable named number
void main(void)
{
  float number = 26.4;      // a local variable named number

  cout << "The value of number is " << ::number << '\n';
}
```

The output produced by Program 6-10a is:

```
The value of number is 42.5
```

As indicated by this output, the global resolution operator causes the global rather than the local variable to be accessed.

Misuse of Globals

Global variables allow the programmer to "jump around" the normal safeguards provided by functions. Rather than passing variables to a function, it is possible to make all variables global ones. **Do not do this**. By indiscriminately making all variables global you instantly destroy the safeguards C++ provides to make functions independent and insulated from each other, including the necessity of carefully designating the type of arguments needed by a function, the variables used in the function, and the value returned.

Using only global variables can be especially disastrous in larger programs that have many user-created functions. Since all variables in a function must be declared, creating functions that use global variables requires that you remember to write the appropriate global declarations at the top of each program using the function—they no longer come along with the function. More devastating than this, however, is the horror of trying to track down an error in a large program using global variables. Since a global variable can be accessed and changed by any function following the global declaration, it is a time-consuming and frustrating task to locate the origin of an erroneous value.

Global variables, however, are sometimes useful in creating variables that must be shared between many functions. Rather than passing the same variable to each function, it is easier to define the variable once as a global. Doing so also alerts anyone reading the program that many functions use the variable. Most large programs almost always use a few global variables. Smaller programs containing a few functions, however, should almost never contain globals.

Exercises 6.4

1. a. For the following section of code, determine the data type and scope of all declared variables. To do this use a separate sheet of paper and list the three column headings that follow (we have filled in the entries for the first variable):

Variable Name	Data Type	Scope
price	integer	global to `main()`, `roi()`, and `step()`

```
#include <iostream.h>
int price;
long int years;
double yield;
void main(void)
{
   int bondtype;
   double interest, coupon;
      .
      .
      .
}
```

(continued on next page)

(continued from previous page)

```
double roi(int mat1, int mat2)
{
   int count;
   double eff_int;
          .
          .
   return(eff_int);
}
int step(float first, float last)
{
   int numofyrs;
   float fracpart;
          .
          .
   return(10*numofyrs);
}
```

b. Draw boxes around the appropriate section of the above code to enclose the scope of each variable.

c. Determine the data type of the arguments that the functions `roi()` and `step()` expect, and the data type of the value returned by these functions.

2. a. For the following section of code, determine the data type and scope of all declaredvariables. To do this use a separate sheet of paper and list the three column headings that follow (we have filled in the entries for the first variable):

Variable Name	Data Type	Scope
key	char	**global to** `main()`, `func1()`, **and** `func2()`

```
#include <iostream.h>
char key;
long int number;
void main(void)
{
   int a,b,c;
   double x,y;
        .
        .
}
double secnum;
int func1(int num1, int num2)
{
   int o,p;
   float q;
        .
        .
   return(p);
}
```

(continued on next page)

(continued from previous page)

```
double func2(float first, float last)
{
  int a,b,c,o,p;
  float r;
  double s,t,x;
       .
       .
  return(s * t);
}
```

b. Draw a box around the appropriate section of the above code to enclose the scope of the variables key, secnum, y, and r.

c. Determine the data type of the arguments that the functions func1() and func2() expect, and the data type of the value returned by these functions.

3. Besides speaking about the scope of a variable, we can also apply the term to the arguments declared inside a function. What do you think is the scope of all function arguments?

4. Determine the values displayed by each call to cout in the following program:

```
#include <iostream.h>
int firstnum = 10;   // declare and initialize a global variable
void main(void)
{
  int firstnum = 20;    // declare and initialize a local variable

  void display(void);   // function prototype
  cout << "\nThe value of firstnum is " << firstnum;
  display();
}
void display(void)
{
  cout << "\nThe value of firstnum is now " << firstnum;
}
```

6.5 Variable Storage Class

The scope of a variable defines the location within a program where that variable can be used. Given a program, you could take a pencil and draw a box around the section of the program where each variable is valid. The space inside the box would represent the scope of a variable. From this viewpoint, the scope of a variable can be thought of as the space within the program where the variable is valid.

In addition to the space dimension represented by its scope, variables also have a time dimension. The time dimension refers to the length of time that storage locations are reserved for a variable. This time dimension is referred to as the variable's "lifetime" or "persistence." For example, all variable storage locations are released back to the computer when a program is finished running. However, while a program is still executing, interim variable storage areas are reserved and subsequently released back to the computer. Where and how long a variable's storage locations are kept before they are released can be determined by the storage class of the variable.

Besides having a data type and scope, every variable also has a storage class. The four available storage classes are called `auto`, `static`, `extern`, and `register`. If one of these class names is used, it must be placed before the variable's data type in a declaration statement. Examples of declaration statements that include a storage class designation are:

```
auto int num;       // auto storage class and int data type
static int miles;   // static storage class and int data type
register int dist;  // register storage class and int data type
extern int price;   // extern storage class and int data type
auto float coupon;  // auto storage class and float data type
static double yrs;  // static storage class and double data type
extern float yld;   // extern storage class and float data type
auto char in_key;   // auto storage class and char variable
```

To understand what the storage class of a variable means, we will first consider local variables (those variables created inside a function) and then global variables (those variables created outside a function).

Local Variable Storage Classes

Local variables can only be members of the `auto`, `static`, or `register` storage classes. If no storage class description is included in the declaration statement, the variable is automatically assigned to the `auto` class. Thus, `auto` is the default class used by C++. All the local variables we have used, since the storage class designation was omitted, have been `auto` variables.

The term `auto` is short for *automatic*. Storage for automatic local variables is automatically reserved or created each time a function declaring automatic variables is called. As long as the function has not returned control to its calling function, all automatic variables local to the function are "alive"—that is, storage for the variables is available. When the function returns control to its calling function, its local automatic variables "die"—that is, the storage for the variables is released back to the computer. This process repeats itself each time a function is called. For example, consider Program 6-11, where the function `testauto()` is called three times from `main()`.

Program 6-11

```cpp
#include <iostream.h>
void main(void)
{
  int count;                // count is a local auto variable
  void testauto(void);      // function prototype
  for(count = 1; count <= 3; count++)
    testauto();
}
void testauto(void)
{
  int num = 0;        // num is a local auto variable
                      // and initialize to zero
  cout << "\nThe value of the automatic variable num is " << num;
  num++;
}
```

The output produced by Program 6-11 is:

```
The value of the automatic variable num is 0
The value of the automatic variable num is 0
The value of the automatic variable num is 0
```

Each time testauto() is called, the automatic variable num is created and initialized to zero. When the function returns control to main() the variable num is destroyed along with any value stored in num. Thus, the effect of incrementing num in testauto(), before the function's return statement, is lost when control is returned to main().

For most applications, the use of automatic variables works just fine. In some cases, however, we would like a function to remember values between function calls. This is the purpose of the static storage class. A local variable that is declared as static causes the program to keep the variable and its latest value even when the function that declared it is through executing. Examples of static variable declarations are:

```
static int rate;
static float taxes;
static double amount;
static char in_key;
static long years;
```

A local static variable is not created and destroyed each time the function declaring the static variable is called. Once created, local static variables remain in existence for the life of the program. This means that the last value stored in the variable when the function is finished executing is available to the function the next time it is called.

Since local static variables retain their values, they are not initialized within a declaration statement in the same way as automatic variables. To see why, consider the automatic declaration int num = 0;, which causes the automatic variable num to be created and set to zero each time the declaration is encountered. This is called a *run-time initialization* because initialization occurs each time the declaration statement is encountered. This type of initialization would be disastrous for a static variable, because resetting the variable's value to zero each time the function is called would destroy the very value we are trying to save.

The initialization of static variables (both local and global) is done only once, when the program is first compiled. At compilation time the variable is created and any initialization value is placed in it.[6] Thereafter, the value in the variable is kept without further initialization each time the function is called. To see how this works, consider Program 6-12.

Program 6-12

```
#include <iostream.h>
void main(void)
{
  int count;              // count is a local auto variable
  void teststat(void);    // function prototype
  for(count = 1; count <= 3; count++)
    teststat();
}
void teststat(void)
{
  static int num = 0;     // num is a local static variable
  cout << "\nThe value of the static variable num is now " << num;
  num++;
}
```

The output produced by Program 6-12 is:

```
The value of the static variable num is now 0
The value of the static variable num is now 1
The value of the static variable num is now 2
```

---

[6] Some compilers initialize static local variables the first time the definition statement is executed rather than when the program is compiled.

As illustrated by the output of Program 6-12, the `static` variable `num` is set to zero only once. The function `teststat()` then increments this variable just before returning control to `main()`. The value that `num` has when leaving the function `teststat()` is retained and displayed when the function is next called.

Unlike automatic variables that can be initialized by either constants or expressions using both constants and previously initialized variables, `static` variables can only be initialized using constants or constant expressions, such as `3.2 + 8.0`. Also, unlike automatic variables, all `static` variables are set to zero when no explicit initialization is given. Thus, the specific initialization of `num` to zero in Program 6-12 is not required, but is recommended for clarity.

The remaining storage class available to local variables, the `register` class, is not used as extensively as either `automatic` or `static` variables. Examples of `register` variable declarations are:

```
register int time;
register double diffren;
register float coupon;
```

`Register` variables have the same time duration as automatic variables; that is, a local `register` variable is created when the function declaring it is entered, and is destroyed when the function completes execution. The only difference between `register` and automatic variables is where the storage for the variable is located.

Storage for all variables (local and global), except `register` variables, is reserved in the computer's memory area. Most computers have a few additional high-speed storage areas located directly in the processing unit that can also be used for variable storage. These special high-speed storage areas are called registers. Since registers are physically located in the computer's processing unit, they can be accessed faster than the normal memory storage areas located in the computer's memory unit. Also, computer instructions that reference registers typically require less space than instructions that reference memory locations because there are fewer registers that can be accessed than there are memory locations.

For example, although the AT&T WE 32100 Central Processing Unit has nine registers that can be used for local C++ program variables, it can be connected to memories that have more than four billion bytes. Most other computers have a similar set of user-accessible registers but millions of memory locations. When the compiler substitutes the location of a register for a variable during program compilation, less space in the instruction is needed than is required to address a memory having millions of locations.

Besides decreasing the size of a compiled C++ program, using `register` variables can also increase the execution speed of a C++ program, if the computer you are using supports this data type. Variables declared with the `register` storage class are automatically switched to the `auto` storage class if your computer does not support `register` variables or if the declared `register` variables exceed the computer's register capacity.

The only restriction in using the `register` storage class is that the address of a `register` variable, using the address operator `&`, cannot be taken. This is easily understood when you realize that registers do not have standard memory addresses.

Global Variable Classes

Global variables, also referred to as external variables, are created by definition statements external to a function. By their nature, these externally defined variables do not come and go with the calling of any function. Once an external (global) variable is created, it exists until the program in which it is declared is finished executing. Thus, external variables cannot be declared as either `auto` or `register` variables that are created and destroyed as the program is executing. Global variables may, however, be declared as members of the `static` or `extern` storage classes. Examples of declaration statements including these two storage class descriptions are:

```
extern int sum;
extern double price;
static double yield;
```

The `static` and `extern` classes affect only the scope, not the time duration, of global variables. As with `static` local variables, all global variables are initialized to zero at compile time.

The purpose of the `extern` storage class is to extend the scope of a global variable beyond its normal boundaries. To understand this, we must first note that all of the programs we have written so far have always been contained in one file. Thus, when you have saved or retrieved programs you have only needed to give the computer a single name for your program. This is not required by C++.

Larger programs typically consist of many functions that are stored in multiple files. An example of this is shown in Figure 6–14, where the three functions `main()`, `func1()`, and `func2()` are stored in one file and the two functions `func3()` and `func4()` are stored in a second file.

For the files illustrated in Figure 6–14, the global variables `price`, `yield`, and `coupon` declared in `file1` can only be used by the functions `main()`, `func1()`, and `func2()` in this file. The single global variable `interest` declared in `file2` can only be used by the functions `func3()` and `func4()` in `file2`.

Although the variable `price` has been created in `file1`, we may want to use it in `file2`. Placing the declaration statement `extern int price;` in `file2`, as shown in Figure 6–15, allows us to do this. Putting this statement at the top of `file2` extends the scope of the variable `price` into `file2` so that it may be used by both `func3()` and `func4()`.

```
file1                              file2
┌─────────────────────────────┐   ┌─────────────────────────────┐
│ int price;                  │   │ double interest;            │
│ float yield;                │   │ func3()                     │
│ static double coupon;       │   │ {                           │
│ main()                      │   │      .                      │
│ {                           │   │      .                      │
│    func1();                 │   │      .                      │
│    func2();                 │   │ }                           │
│    func3();                 │   │ func4()                     │
│    func4();                 │   │ {                           │
│ }                           │   │      .   .                  │
│ func1()                     │   │      .                      │
│ {                           │   │      .                      │
│      .                      │   │                             │
│      .                      │   │ }                           │
│      .                      │   │                             │
│                             │   │                             │
│ }                           │   │                             │
│ func2()                     │   │                             │
│ {                           │   │                             │
│      .                      │   │                             │
│      .                      │   │                             │
│      .                      │   │                             │
│                             │   │                             │
│ }                           │   │                             │
└─────────────────────────────┘   └─────────────────────────────┘
```

FIGURE 6–14 A Program May Extend Beyond One File

```
file1                              file2
┌─────────────────────────────┐   ┌─────────────────────────────┐
│ int price;                  │   │ double interest;            │
│ float yield;                │   │ extern int price;           │
│ static double coupon;       │   │ func3()                     │
│ main()                      │   │ {                           │
│ {                           │   │      .                      │
│    func1();                 │   │      .                      │
│    func2();                 │   │      .                      │
│    func3();                 │   │ }                           │
│    func4();                 │   │ func4()                     │
│ }                           │   │ {                           │
│ extern double interest;     │   │    extern float yield;      │
│ func1()                     │   │      .                      │
│ {                           │   │      .                      │
│      .                      │   │      .                      │
│      .                      │   │                             │
│      .                      │   │ }                           │
│                             │   │                             │
│ }                           │   │                             │
│ func2()                     │   │                             │
│ {                           │   │                             │
│      .                      │   │                             │
│      .                      │   │                             │
│      .                      │   │                             │
│                             │   │                             │
│ }                           │   │                             │
└─────────────────────────────┘   └─────────────────────────────┘
```

FIGURE 6–15 Extending the Scope of a Global Variable

Similarly, placing the statement `extern float yield;` in `func4()` extends the scope of this global variable, created in `file1`, into `func4()`, and the scope of the global variable `interest`, created in `file2`, is extended into `func1()` and `func2()` by the declaration statement `extern double interest;` placed before `func1()`. Notice that interest is not available to `main()`.

An `extern` declaration statement simply informs the compiler that the variable already exists and can now be used. The actual storage for the variable must be created somewhere else in the program using one, and only one, definition statement. Initialization within an `extern` declaration statement is also allowed, but any subsequent initialization attempt will cause a compilation error.

The existence of the `extern` storage class is the reason we have been so careful to distinguish between the creation and declaration of a variable. Declaration statements containing the word `extern` do not create new storage areas; they only extend the scope of existing global variables.

The last global class, `static` global variables, is used to prevent the extension of a global variable defined in one file into any other file. Global `static` variables are declared in the same way as local `static` variables, except that the declaration statement is placed outside any function.

The scope of a global `static` variable cannot be extended beyond the file in which it is declared. This provides a degree of privacy for `static` global variables. Since they are only "known" and can only be used in the file in which they are declared, other files cannot access or change their values. `Static` global variables cannot be subsequently extended to a second file using an `extern` declaration statement. Trying to do so will result in a compilation error.

Exercises 6.5

---

1. a. List the storage classes available to local variables.

   b. List the storage classes available to global variables.

2. Describe the difference between a local `auto` variable and a local `static` variable.

3. What is the difference between the following functions:

```
void init1(void)
{
  static int yrs = 1;
  cout << "\nThe value of yrs is " << yrs;
  yrs = yrs + 2;
}

void init2(void)
{
  static int yrs;
  yrs = 1;
  cout << "\nThe value of yrs is " << yrs;
  yrs = yrs + 2;
}
```

```
file1                              file2
┌─────────────────────────┐      ┌─────────────────────────┐
│ char choice;            │      │ char b_type;            │
│ int flag;               │      │ double maturity;        │
│ long date, time;        │      │ roi()                   │
│ main()                  │      │ {                       │
│ {                       │      │      .                  │
│      .                  │      │      .                  │
│      .                  │      │      .                  │
│      .                  │      │                         │
│                         │      │ }                       │
│ }                       │      │ pduction()              │
│ double coupon;          │      │ {                       │
│ price()                 │      │      .                  │
│ {                       │      │      .                  │
│      .                  │      │      .                  │
│      .                  │      │                         │
│      .                  │      │ }                       │
│                         │      │ bid()                   │
│ }                       │      │ {                       │
│ yield()                 │      │      .                  │
│ {                       │      │      .                  │
│      .                  │      │      .                  │
│      .                  │      │                         │
│      .                  │      │ }                       │
│                         │      │                         │
│ }                       │      └─────────────────────────┘
└─────────────────────────┘
```

FIGURE 6–16 Files for Exercise 6

4. a. Describe the difference between a `static` global variable and an `extern` global variable.

    b. If a variable is declared with an `extern` storage class, what other declaration statement must be present somewhere in the program?

5. The declaration statement `static double years;` can be used to create either a local or global `static` variable. What determines the scope of the variable `years`?

6. For the function and variable declarations illustrated in Figure 6–16, place an `extern` declaration to individually accomplish the following:

    a. Extend the scope of the global variable `choice` into all of `file2`.

    b. Extend the scope of the global variable `flag` into function `pduction()` only.

    c. Extend the scope of the global variable `date` into `pduction()` and `bid()`.

    d. Extend the scope of the global variable `date` into `roi()` only.

    e. Extend the scope of the global variable `coupon` into `roi()` only.

    f. Extend the scope of the global variable `b_type` into all of `file1`.

    g. Extend the scope of the global variable `maturity` into both `price()` and `yield()`.

6.6 Common Programming Errors

An extremely common programming error related to functions is passing incorrect data types. The values passed to a function must correspond to the data types of the arguments declared for the function. One way to verify that correct values have been received is to display all passed values within a function's body before any calculations are made. Once this verification has taken place, the display should be dispensed with.[7]

Another common error can occur when the same variable is declared locally within both the calling and called functions. Even though the variable name is the same, a change to one local variable *does not* alter the value in the other local variable.

Related to this error is the error that can occur when a local variable has the same name as a global variable. Within the function declaring it, the use of the local variable name only affects the local variable's contents unless the global resolution operator, : :, is used.

Another common error is omitting the called function's prototype within the calling function. The called function must be alerted to the type of value that will be returned, and this information is provided by the function prototype. The prototype within the calling function can be omitted if the called function is physically placed in a program before its calling function or if the prototype appears as an external global declaration placed physically before the function. Although it is also permissible to omit the prototype and return type for functions returning an integer, it is poor documenting practice to do so. The actual value returned by a function can be verified by displaying it both before and after it is returned.

The last two common errors are terminating a function's header line with a semicolon and forgetting to include the data type of a function's parameters.

6.7 Chapter Summary

1. A function is called by giving its name and passing any data to it in the parentheses following the name. If a variable is one of the arguments in a function call, the called function receives a copy of the variable's value.

2. The commonly used form of a user-written function is:

```
return-type function-name(argument declarations)
{
    declarations and other C++ statements;
    return(expression);
}
```

The first line of the function is called the *function header*. The opening and closing braces of the function and all statements in between these braces constitute the function's *body*.

---

[7] In practice a good debugger program should be used. The use of debuggers is beyond the scope of this text.

The storage class of the function specified in the header is optional and can be either `static` or `extern`. If no storage class is specified it defaults to `extern`. The returned data type is, by default, an integer when no returned data type is specified. The function declarator must be included for each function and is of the form:

function-name(parameter list)

The parameter list must include the names of all parameters and their data types.

3. A function's return type is the data type of the value returned by the function. If no type is declared the function is assumed to return an integer value. If the function does not return a value it should be declared as a `void` type.

4. Functions can directly return at most a single data type value to their calling functions. This value is the value of the expression in the `return` statement.

5. Functions can be declared to all calling functions by means of a *function prototype*. The prototype provides a declaration for a function that specifies the data type returned by the function, its name, and the data types of the parameters expected by the function. As with all declarations, a function prototype is terminated with a semicolon and may be included within local variable declarations or as a global declaration. The most common form of a function prototype is:

data-type function-name(parameter data types);

If the called function is placed physically above the calling function no further declaration is required, since the function's definition serves as a global declaration to all following functions.

6. Every variable used in a program has a scope, which determines where in the program the variable can be used. The scope of a variable is either local or global and is determined by where the variable's definition statement is placed. A local variable is defined within a function and can only be used within its defining function or block. A global variable is defined outside a function and can be used in any function following the variable's definition. All global variables that are not specifically initialized by the user are initialized to zero by the compiler and can be shared between files using the keyword `extern`.

7. Every variable has a class. The class of a variable determines how long the value in the variable will be retained. `Auto` variables are local variables that exist only while their defining function is executing. `Register` variables are similar to automatic variables but are stored in a computer's internal registers rather than in memory. `Static` variables can be either global or local and retain their values for the duration of a program's execution. `Static` variables are also set to zero when they are defined if they are not explicitly initialized by the user.

Arrays

The variables used so far have all had a common characteristic: Each variable could only be used to store a single value at a time. For example, although the variables key, count, and grade declared in the statements

```
char key;

int count;

int grade;
```

are of different data types, each variable can only store one value of the declared data type. These types of variables are called scalar variables. A *scalar* variable is a single variable that cannot be further subdivided or separated into a legitimate data type.

Frequently we may have a set of values, all of the same data type, that form a logical group. For example, Figure 7–1 illustrates three groups of items. The first group is a list of five integer grades, the second group is a list of four character codes, and the last group is a list of six floating point prices.

A simple list containing individual items of the same scalar data type is called a *one-dimensional array*. In this chapter we describe how one-dimensional arrays are declared, initialized, stored inside a computer, and used. Additionally, we explore the use of one-dimensional arrays with example programs and present the procedures for declaring and using multidimensional arrays.

7.1 One-Dimensional Arrays

A one-dimensional array, which is also referred to as either a single-dimensional array, a list, or a vector, is a group of related values with the same data type that is stored using a single group name. In C++, as in other computer languages, the group name is referred to as the array name. For example, consider the list of grades illustrated in Figure 7–2.

All the grades in the list are integer numbers and must be declared as such. However, the individual items in the list do not have to be declared separately.

FIGURE 7–1 Three Lists of Items

Grades	Codes	Prices
98	x	10.96
87	a	6.43
92	m	2.58
79	n	.86
85		12.27
		6.39

Grade
98
87
92
79
85

FIGURE 7–2 A List of Grades

The items in the list can be declared as a single unit and stored under a common variable name called the array name. For convenience, we will choose grade as the name for the list shown in Figure 7–2. To specify that grade is to store five individual integer values requires the declaration statement int grade[5];. Notice that this declaration statement gives the data type of the items in the array, the array (or list) name, and the number of items in the array. Further examples of array declarations are:

```
char code[4];        // an array of four character values
float prices[6];     // an array of six floating point values
double amount[100];   // an array of 100 double precision values
```

Each array has sufficient memory reserved for it to hold the number of data items given in the declaration statement. Thus, the array named code has storage reserved for four characters, the array named prices has storage reserved for six floating point numbers, and the array named amount has storage reserved for 100 double precision numbers. Figure 7–3 illustrates the storage reserved for the grade and code arrays.

FIGURE 7–3 The grade and code Arrays in Memory

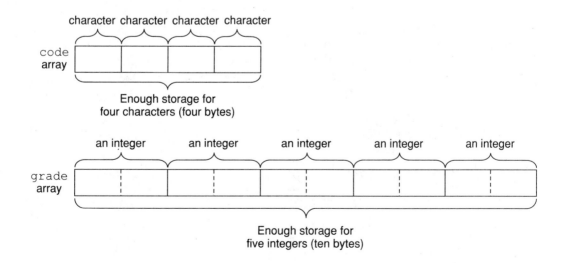

Each item in an array is called an *element* or *component* of the array. The individual elements stored in the arrays illustrated in Figure 7–3 are stored sequentially, with the first array element stored in the first reserved location, the second element stored in the second reserved location, and so on until the last element is stored in the last reserved location.

To access individual elements in an array requires some unique means of identifying each element. Since elements in the array are stored sequentially, any individual element can be accessed by giving the name of the array and the element's position. This position is called the element's subscript or index value (the two terms are synonymous). For a single-dimensioned array the first element has a subscript of 0, the second element has a subscript of 1, and so on. In C++, the array name and subscript of the desired element are combined by listing the subscript in braces after the array name. For example, given the declaration `int grade[5];`,

`grade[0]` refers to the first grade stored in the `grade` array
`grade[1]` refers to the second grade stored in the `grade` array
`grade[2]` refers to the third grade stored in the `grade` array
`grade[3]` refers to the fourth grade stored in the `grade` array
`grade[4]` refers to the fifth grade stored in the `grade` array

Figure 7–4 illustrates the `grade` array in memory with the correct designation for each array element. Each individual element is called a *subscripted variable* or an *indexed variable* (the two terms are synonymous), since both a variable name and a subscript or index value must be used to reference the element. Remember that the subscript or index value gives the position of the element in the array.

The subscripted variable, `grade[0]`, is read as "grade sub zero." This is a shortened way of saying "the grade array subscripted by zero," and distinguishes the first element in an array from a scalar variable that could be declared as `grade0`. Similarly, `grade[1]` is read as "grade sub one," `grade[2]` as "grade sub two," `grade[3]` as "grade sub three," and `grade[4]` as "grade sub four."

Although it may seem unusual to reference the first element with an index of zero, it makes sense when you understand how the compiler accesses array elements. Internally, unseen by the programmer, the computer uses the index as an offset from the array's starting position. As illustrated in Figure 7–5, the

FIGURE 7–4 Identifying Individual Array Elements

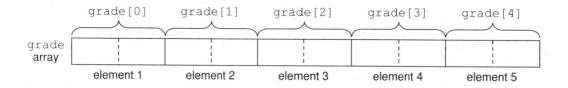

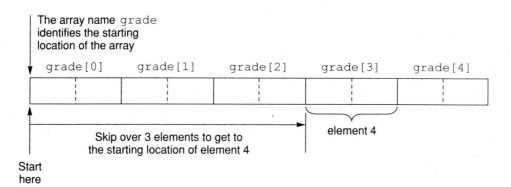

FIGURE 7–5 Accessing an Individual Array Element—Element 3

index tells the computer how many elements to skip over, starting from the beginning of the array, to get to the desired element.

Subscripted variables can be used anywhere scalar variables are valid. Examples using the elements of the grade array are:

```
grade[0] = 98;
grade[1] = grade[0] - 11;
grade[2] = 5 * grade[0];
grade[3] = 79;
grade[4] = (grade[1] + grade[2] - 3) / 2;
sum = grade[0] + grade[1] + grade[2] + grade[3] + grade[4];
```

The subscript contained within braces need not be an integer constant; any expression that evaluates to an integer may be used as a subscript.[1] In each case, of course, the value of the expression must be within the valid subscript range defined when the array is declared. For example, assuming that i and j are int variables, the following subscripted variables are valid:

```
grade[i]
grade[2*i]
grade[j-i]
```

One extremely important advantage of using integer expressions as subscripts is that it allows sequencing through an array by using a loop. This makes statements like the following unnecessary:

```
sum = grade[0] + grade[1] + grade[2] + grade[3] + grade[4];
```

---

[1] Some compilers permit floating point variables as subscripts; in these cases the floating point value is truncated to an integer value.

The subscript values in this statement can be replaced by a `for` loop counter to access each element in the array sequentially. For example, the code

```
sum = 0;                        // initialize the sum to zero
for (int i = 0; i <= 4; i++)
   sum = sum + grade[i];        // add in a grade
```

sequentially retrieves each array element and adds the element to `sum`. Here the variable `i` is used both as the counter in the `for` loop and as a subscript. As `i` increases by one each time through the loop, the next element in the array is referenced. This procedure for adding the array elements within the `for` loop is similar to the accumulation procedure we have used many times before.

The advantage of using a `for` loop to sequence through an array becomes apparent when working with larger arrays. For example, if the `grade` array contained 100 values rather than just 5, simply changing the number 4 to 99 in the `for` statement is sufficient to sequence through the 100 elements and add each grade to the sum.

As another example of using a `for` loop to sequence through an array, assume that we want to locate the maximum value in an array of 1000 elements named `prices`. The procedure we will use to locate the maximum value is to assume initially that the first element in the array is the largest number. Then, as we sequence through the array, the maximum is compared to each element. When an element with a higher value is located, that element becomes the new maximum. The following code does the job:

```
maximum = prices[0];         // set the maximum to element zero
for (int i = 1; i <= 999; i++)  // cycle through the rest of the array
   if (prices[i] > maximum)   // compare each element to the maximum
      maximum = prices[i];    // capture the new high value
```

In this code the `for` statement consists of one `if` statement. The search for a new maximum value starts with the element 1 of the array and continues through the last element. In a 1000-element array, the last element is 999. Each element is compared to the current maximum, and when a higher value is encountered it becomes the new maximum.

Input and Output of Array Values

Individual array elements can be assigned values interactively using the `cin` object. Examples of individual data entry statements are:

```
cin >> grade[0];
cin >> grade[1] >> grade[2] >> grade[3];
cin >> grade[4] >> prices[6];
```

In the first statement a single value will be read and stored in the variable named `grade[0]`. The second statement causes three values to be read and stored in the variables `grade[1]`, `grade[2]`, and `grade[3]`, respectively. Finally, the last `cin` statement can be used to read values into the variables `grade[4]` and `prices[6]`.

Alternatively, a `for` loop can be used to cycle through the array for interactive data input. For example, the code

```
for (int i = 0; i <= 4; i++)
{
  cout << "Enter a grade: ";
  cin >> grade[i];
}
```

prompts the user for five grades. The first grade entered is stored in `grade[0]`, the second grade entered in `grade[1]`, and so on until five grades have been input.

One caution should be mentioned about storing data or accessing in an array. Most implementations of C++ do not check the value of the index being used (called a *bounds check*). If an array has been declared as consisting of 10 elements, for example, and you use an index of 12, which is outside the bounds of the array, C++ will not notify you of the error when the program is compiled. The program will attempt to access element 12 by skipping over the appropriate number of bytes from the start of the array. Usually this results in a program crash—but not always. If the referenced location itself contains a data value, the program will simply access the value in the referenced memory locations. This leads to more errors, which are particularly troublesome to locate when the variable legitimately assigned to the storage location is used at a different point in the program.

During output, individual array elements can be displayed using the `cout` object or complete sections of the array can be displayed by including a `cout` object call within a `for` loop. Examples using `cout` to display subscripted variables are:

```
cout << prices[5];
cout << "The value of element " << i << " is " << grade[i];
for (int n = 5; n <= 20; n++)
  cout << n << " " << amount[n];
```

The first `cout` statement displays the value of the subscripted variable `prices[5]`. The second `cout` statement displays the value of the subscript `i` and the value of `grade[i]`. Before this statement can be executed, `i` would have to have an assigned value. Finally, the last example includes a `cout` statement within a `for` loop. Both the value of the index and the value of the elements from 5 to 20 are displayed.

Program 7-1 illustrates these input and output techniques using an array named `grade` that is defined to store five integer numbers. Included in the program are two `for` loops. The first `for` loop is used to cycle through each array element and allows the user to input individual array values. After five values have been entered, the second `for` loop is used to display the stored values.

Program 7-1

```
#include <iostream.h>
void main(void)
{
   int grade[5];

   for (int i = 0; i <= 4; ++i)          // Enter five grades
   {
     cout << "Enter a grade: ";
     cin >> grade[i];
   }
   for (i = 0; i <= 4; i++)              // Print five grades
     cout << "\ngrade[" << i << "] is " << grade[i];
}
```

Following is a sample run using Program 7-1:

```
Enter a grade: 85
Enter a grade: 90
Enter a grade: 78
Enter a grade: 75
Enter a grade: 92

grade[0] is 85
grade[1] is 90
grade[2] is 78
grade[3] is 75
grade[4] is 92
```

In reviewing the output produced by Program 7-1, pay particular attention to the difference between the subscript value displayed and the numerical value stored in the corresponding array element. The subscript value refers to the location of the element in the array, while the subscripted variable refers to the value stored in the designated location.

In addition to simply displaying the values stored in each array element, the elements can also be processed by appropriately referencing the desired element. For example, in Program 7-2, the value of each element is accumulated in a total, which is displayed upon completion of the individual display of each array element.

Program 7-2

```cpp
#include <iostream.h>
void main(void)
{
   int grade[5], total = 0;

   for (int i = 0; i <= 4; ++i)          // Enter five grades
   {
     cout << "Enter a grade: ";
     cin >> grade[i];
   }

   cout << "\nThe total of the grades ";

   for (i = 0; i <= 4; i++)              // Print five grades
   {
     cout << grade[i] << "   ";
     total = total + grade[i];
   }

   cout << "is   " << total;
}
```

Following is a sample run using Program 7-2:

```
Enter a grade: 85
Enter a grade: 90
Enter a grade: 78
Enter a grade: 75
Enter a grade: 92

The total of the grades  85  90  78  75  92  is  420
```

Notice that in Program 7-2, unlike Program 7-1, only the values stored in each array element are displayed. Although the second `for` loop was used to accumulate the total of each element, the accumulation could also have been accomplished in the first loop by placing the statement `total = total + grade[i];` after the `cin` call used to enter a value. Also notice that the `cout` call used to display the total is made outside the second `for` loop, so that the total is displayed only once, after all values have been added to the total. If this `cout` call were placed inside the `for` loop five totals would be displayed, with only the last displayed total containing the sum of all of the array values.

Exercises 7.1

1. Write array declarations for the following:
   a. a list of 100 integer grades
   b. a list of 50 floating point temperatures
   c. a list of 30 characters, each representing a code
   d. a list of 100 integer years
   e. a list of 32 floating point velocities
   f. a list of 1000 floating point distances
   g. a list of 6 integer code numbers

2. Write appropriate notation for the first, third, and seventh elements of the following arrays:
   a. `int grades[20]`
   b. `float prices[10]`
   c. `float amps[16]`
   d. `int dist[15]`
   e. `float velocity[25]`
   f. `float time[100]`

3. a. Using the `cin` object, write individual statements that can be used to enter values into the first, third, and seventh elements of each of the arrays declared in Exercises 2a through 2f.
   b. Write a `for` loop that can be used to enter values for the complete array declared in Exercise 2a.

4. a. Write individual statements that can be used to display the values from the first, third, and seventh elements of each of the arrays declared in Exercises 2a through 2f.
   b. Write a `for` loop that can be used to display values for the complete array declared in Exercise 2a.

5. List the elements that will be displayed by the following sections of code:
```
a. for (m = 1; m <= 5; m++)
       cout << a[m] << " ";
b. for (k = 1; k <= 5; k = k + 2)
       cout << a[k] << " ";
c. for (j = 3; j <= 10; j++)
       cout << b[j] << " ";
d. for (k = 3; k <= 12; k = k + 3)
       cout << b[k] << " ";
e. for (i = 2; i < 11; i = i + 2)
       cout << c[i] << " ";
```

6. a. Write a program to input the following values into an array named `prices`: 10.95, 16.32, 12.15, 8.22, 15.98, 26.22, 13.54, 6.45, 17.59. After the data have been entered, have your program output the values.
   b. Repeat Exercise 6a, but after the data have been entered, have your program display them in the following form:

$$
\begin{array}{ccc}
10.95 & 16.32 & 12.15 \\
8.22 & 15.98 & 26.22 \\
13.54 & 6.45 & 17.59
\end{array}
$$

7. Write a C++ program to input eight integer numbers into an array named `grade`. As each number is input, add the numbers into a total. After all numbers are input, display the numbers and their average.

8. a. Write a C++ program to input 10 integer numbers into an array named `fmax` and determine the maximum value entered. Your program should contain only one loop and the maximum should be determined as array element values are being input. (*Hint:* Set the maximum equal to the first array element, which should be input before the loop used to input the remaining array values.)
b. Repeat Exercise 8a, keeping track of both the maximum element in the array and the index number for the maximum. After displaying the numbers, display these two messages:

```
The maximum value is: ____
This is element number ____ in the list of numbers
```

Have your program display the correct values in place of the underlines in the messages.
c. Repeat Exercise 8b, but have your program locate the minimum value of the data entered.

9. a. Write a C++ program to input the following integer numbers into an array named `grades`: 89, 95, 72, 83, 99, 54, 86, 75, 92, 73, 79, 75, 82, 73. As each number is input, add the numbers to a total. After all numbers are input and the total is obtained, calculate the average of the numbers and use the average to determine the deviation of each value from the average. Store each deviation in an array named `deviation`. Each deviation is obtained as the element value less the average of all the data. Have your program display each deviation alongside its corresponding element from the `grades` array.
b. Calculate the variance of the data used in Exercise 9a. The variance is obtained by squaring each individual deviation and dividing the sum of the squared deviations by the number of deviations.

10. Write a C++ program that specifies three one-dimensional arrays named `price`, `amount`, and `total`. Each array should be capable of holding ten elements. Using a `for` loop, input values for the `price` and `amount` arrays. The entries in the `total` array should be the product of the corresponding values in the `price` and `amount` arrays (thus, `total[i] = price[i] * amount[i]`). After all the data have been entered, display the following output:

```
total          price          amount
-----          -----          ------
```

Under each column heading display the appropriate value.

11. a. Write a program that inputs ten floating point numbers into an array named `raw`. After ten user-input numbers are entered into the array, your program should cycle through `raw` ten times. During each pass through the array, your program should select the lowest value in `raw` and place the selected value in the next available slot in an array named `sorted`. Thus, when your program is complete, the `sorted` array should contain the numbers in `raw` in sorted order from lowest to highest. (*Hint:* Make sure to reset the lowest value selected during each pass to a very high number so that it is not selected again. You will need a second `for` loop within the first `for` loop to locate the minimum value for each pass.)

b. The method used in Exercise 11a to sort the values in the array is very inefficient. Can you determine why? What might be a better method of sorting the numbers in an array?

7.2 Array Initialization

Array elements can be initialized within their declaration statements in the same manner as scalar variables, except that the initializing elements must be included in braces. Examples of such initializations are:

```
int grade[5] = {98, 87, 92, 79, 85};
char code[6] = {'s', 'a', 'm', 'p', 'l', 'e'};
double width[7] = {10.96, 6.43, 2.58, .86, 5.89, 7.56, 8.22};
```

Initializers are applied in the order they are written, with the first value used to initialize element 0, the second value used to initialize element 1, and so on, until all values have been used. Thus, in the declaration

```
int grade[5] = {98, 87, 92, 79, 85};
```

grade[0] is initialized to 98, grade[1] is initialized to 87, grade[2] is initialized to 92, grade[3] is initialized to 79, and grade[4] is initialized to 85.

Since whitespace is ignored in C++, initializations may be continued across multiple lines. For example, the declaration

```
int gallons[20] = {19, 16, 14, 19, 20, 18,   // initializing values
                   12, 10, 22, 15, 18, 17,   // may extend across
                   16, 14, 23, 19, 15, 18,   // multiple lines
                   21, 5};
```

uses four lines to initialize all of the array elements.

If the number of initializers is less than the declared number of elements listed in square brackets, the initializers are applied starting with array element zero. Thus, in the declaration

```
float length[7] = {7.8, 6.4, 4.9, 11.2};
```

only length[0], length[1], length[2], and length[3] are initialized with the listed values. The other array elements will be initialized to zero.

Unfortunately, there is no method of either indicating repetition of an initialization value or initializing later array elements without first specifying values for earlier elements.

A unique feature of initializers is that the size of an array may be omitted when initializing values are included in the declaration statement. For example, the declaration

```
int gallons[] = {16, 12, 10, 14, 11};
```

reserves enough storage room for five elements. Similarly, the following two declarations are equivalent:

```
char code[6] = {'s', 'a', 'm', 'p', 'l', 'e'};
char code[] = {'s', 'a', 'm', 'p', 'l', 'e'};
```

Both of these declarations set aside six character locations for an array named code. An interesting and useful simplification can also be used when initializing character arrays. For example, the declaration

```
char code[] = "sample";    // no braces or commas
```

uses the string "sample" to initialize the code array. Recall that a string is any sequence of characters enclosed in double quotes. This last declaration creates an array named code having seven elements and fills the array with the seven characters illustrated in Figure 7–6. The first six characters, as expected, consist of the letters s, a, m, p, l, and e. The last character, which is the escape sequence \0, is called the *null character*. The null character is automatically appended to all strings by the C++ compiler. This character has an internal storage code that is numerically equal to zero (the storage code for the zero character has a numerical value of decimal 48, so the two cannot be confused by the computer), and is used as a marker, or sentinel, to mark the end of a string. As we shall see in Chapter 9, this marker is invaluable when manipulating strings of characters.

Once values have been assigned to array elements, either through initialization within the declaration statement or using interactive input, the array elements can be processed as described in the previous section. For example, Program 7-3 illustrates element initialization within the declaration of the array and then uses a for loop to locate the maximum value stored in the array.

FIGURE 7–6 A String Is Terminated with a Special Sentinel

code[0]	code[1]	code[2]	code[3]	code[4]	code[5]	code[6]
s	a	m	p	l	e	\0

Program 7-3

```
#include <iostream.h>
void main(void)
{
    int max, nums[5] = {2, 18, 1, 27, 16};

    max = nums[0];
    for (int i = 1; i <= 4; i++)
        if (max < nums[i])
            max = nums[i];

    cout << "\nThe maximum value is " << max;
}
```

The output produced by Program 7-3 is:

```
The maximum value is 27
```

Exercises 7.2

1. Write array declarations, including initializers, for the following:
    a. a list of ten integer grades: 89, 75, 82, 93, 78, 95, 81, 88, 77, 82
    b. a list of five double precision amounts: 10.62, 13.98, 18.45, 12.68, 14.76
    c. a list of 100 double precision interest rates; the first six rates are 6.29, 6.95, 7.25, 7.35, 7.40, 7.42
    d. a list of 64 floating point temperatures; the first ten temperatures are 78.2, 69.6, 68.5, 83.9, 55.4, 67.0, 49.8, 58.3, 62.5, 71.6
    e. a list of 15 character codes; the first seven codes are f, j, m, q, t, w, z

2. Write an array declaration statement that stores the following values in an array named `prices`: 16.24, 18.98, 23.75, 16.29, 19.54, 14.22, 11.13, 15.39. Include these statements in a program that displays the values in the array.

3. Write a program that uses an array declaration statement to initialize the following numbers in an array named `slopes`: 17.24, 25.63, 5.94, 33.92, 3.71, 32.84, 35.93, 18.24, 6.92. Your program should locate and display both the maximum and minimum values in the array.

4. Write a program that stores the following numbers in an array named `prices`: 9.92, 6.32, 12.63, 5.95, 10.29. Your program should also create two arrays named `units` and `amounts`, each capable of storing five double precision numbers. Using a `for` loop and a `cin` object call, have your program accept five user-input numbers into the `units` array when the program is run. Your program should store the product of the corresponding values in the `prices` and `units` arrays in the `amounts` array (for example, `amounts[1] = prices[1] * units[1]`) and display the following output (fill in the table appropriately):

```
        Price           Units        Amount
        -----           -----        ------
         9.92             .             .
         6.32             .             .
        12.63             .             .
         5.95             .             .
        10.29             .             .
                                      ------
        Total:                          .
```

5. The string of characters `"Good Morning"` is to be stored in a character array named `goodstr1`. Write the declaration for this array in three different ways.

6. *a*. Write declaration statements to store the string of characters `"Input the Following Data"` in a character array named `messag1`, the string `"-----------------------"` in the array named `messag2`, the string `"Enter the Date: "` in the array named `messag3`, and the string `"Enter the Account Number: "` in the array named `messag4`.

b. Include the array declarations written in Exercise 6a in a program that uses the `cout` object to display the messages. For example, the statement `cout << messag1;` causes the string stored in the `messag1` array to be displayed. Your program will require four such statements to display the four individual messages. Using the `cout` object to display a string requires that the end-of-string marker `\0` be present in the character array used to store the string.

7. *a*. Write a declaration to store the string `"This is a test"` into an array named `strtest`. Include the declaration in a program to display the message using the following loop:

```
for (int i = 0; i <= 14; i++)
  cout << strtest[i];
```

b. Modify the `for` statement in Exercise 7a to display only the array characters t, e, s, and t.

c. Include the array declaration written in Exercise 7a in a program that uses the `cout` object to display characters in the array. For example, the statement `cout << strtest;` will cause the string stored in the `strtest` array to be displayed. Using this statement requires that the last character in the array be the end-of-string marker `\0`.

d. Repeat Exercise 7a using a `while` loop. (*Hint:* Stop the loop when the `\0` escape sequence is detected. The expression `while (strtest[i] != '\0')` can be used.)

7.3 Arrays as Arguments

Individual array elements are passed to a called function in the same manner as individual scalar variables; they are simply included as subscripted variables when the function call is made. For example, the function call find_min(grades[2], grades[6]); passes the values of the elements grades[2] and grades[6] to the function find_min().

Passing a complete array of values to a function is in many respects an easier operation than passing individual elements. The called function receives access to the actual array, rather than a copy of the values in the array. For example, if grades is an array, the function call find_max(grades); makes the complete grades array available to the find_max() function. This is different from passing a single variable to a function.

Recall that when a single scalar argument is passed to a function, the called function only receives *a copy* of the passed value, which is stored in one of the function's parameters. If arrays were passed in this manner, a copy of the complete array would have to be created. For large arrays, making duplicate copies of the array for each function call would be wasteful of computer storage and would frustrate the effort to return multiple element changes made by the called program (recall that a function directly returns at most one value). To avoid these problems, the called function is given direct access to the original array. Thus, any changes made by the called function are made directly to the array itself. For the following specific examples of function calls, assume that the arrays nums, keys, units, and grades are declared as:

```
int nums[5];                        // an array of five integers
char keys[256];                     // an array of 256 characters
double units[500], grades[500];     // two arrays of 500 doubles
```

For these arrays, the following function calls can be made:

```
find_max(nums);
find_ch(keys);
calc_tot(nums, units, grades);
```

In each case, the called function receives direct access to the named array.

On the receiving side, the called function must be alerted that an array is being made available. For example, suitable function header lines for the previous functions are:

```
int find_max(int vals[5])
char find_ch(char in_keys[256])
void calc_tot(int arr1[5], double arr2[500], double arr3[500])
```

In each of these function header lines, the names in the parameter list are chosen by the programmer. However, the parameter names used by the functions still refer to the original array created outside the function. This is made clear in Program 7-4.

Program 7-4

```
#include <iostream.h>
void main(void)
{
  int nums[5] = {2, 18, 1, 27, 16};
  int find_max(int [5]);        // function prototype

  cout << "\nThe maximum value is " << find_max(nums);
}
int find_max(int vals[5])       // find the maximum value
{
  int i, max = vals[0];

  for (i = 1; i <= 4; i++)
    if (max < vals[i]) max = vals[i];

  return max;
}
```

Notice that the function prototype for find_max() within main() declares that find_max() will return an integer and expects an array of five integers as an actual argument. It is also important to know that only one array is created in Program 7-4. In main() this array is known as nums, and in find_max() the array is known as vals. As illustrated in Figure 7–7, both names refer to the same array. Thus, in Figure 7–7 vals[3] is the same element as nums[3].

The parameter declaration in the find_max() header line actually contains extra information that is not required by the function. All that find_max() must know is that the argument vals references an array of integers. Since the array has been created in main() and no additional storage space is needed in find_max(), the declaration for vals can omit the size of the array. Thus, an alternative function header line is:

```
int find_max(int vals[])
```

This form of the function header makes more sense when you realize that only one item is actually passed to find_max() when the function is called, which is the starting address of the num array. This is illustrated in Figure 7–8.

Since only the starting address of nums is passed to find_max(), the number of elements in the array need not be included in the declaration for vals.[2] In fact, it is generally advisable to omit the size of the array in the function header line. For example, consider the more general form of find_max(), which can be used to find the maximum value of an integer array of arbitrary size:

---

[2] An important consequence of this is that find_max() has direct access to the passed array. This means that any change to an element of the vals array actually is a change to the nums array. This is significantly different from the situation with scalar variables, where the called function does not receie direct access to the passed variable.

```
int find_max(int vals[], int num_els)    // find the maximum value
{
  int i, max = vals[0];

  for (i = 1; i < num_els; i++)
   if (max < vals[i])
     max = vals[i];
  return max;
}
```

FIGURE 7–7 Only One Array Is Created

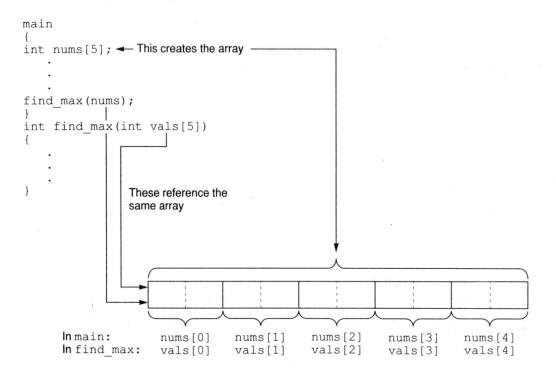

```
main
{
int nums[5];  ◀— This creates the array

     .
     .
     .
find_max(nums);
}
int find_max(int vals[5])
{
  .
  .
  .
}
```

These reference the same array

In `main`:   `nums[0]`   `nums[1]`   `nums[2]`   `nums[3]`   `nums[4]`
In `find_max`: `vals[0]`   `vals[1]`   `vals[2]`   `vals[3]`   `vals[4]`

FIGURE 7–8 The Starting Address of the Array Is Passed

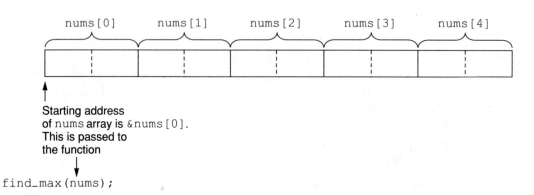

`nums[0]`   `nums[1]`   `nums[2]`   `nums[3]`   `nums[4]`

Starting address
of `nums` array is `&nums[0]`.
This is passed to
the function

```
find_max(nums);
```

The more general form of find_max() declares that the function returns an integer value. The function expects the starting address of an integer array and the number of elements in the array as arguments. Then, using the number of elements as the boundary for its search, the function's for loop causes each array element to be examined in sequential order to locate the maximum value. Program 7-5 illustrates the use of find_max() in a complete program.

 Program 7-5

```
#include <iostream.h>
void main(void)
{
  int nums[5] = {2, 18, 1, 27, 16};
  int find_max(int [], int);   // function prototype

  cout << "\nThe maximum value is " << find_max(nums,5);
}

int find_max(int vals[], int num_els)
{
  int i, max = vals[0];

  for (i = 1; i < num_els; i++)
    if (max < vals[i]) max = vals[i];

  return max;
}
```

The output displayed by both Programs 7-4 and 7-5 is:

```
The maximum value is 27
```

Exercises 7.3

1. The following declaration was used to create the grades array:

```
double grades[500];
```

Write two different function header lines for a function named sort_arr() that accepts the grades array as an argument named in_array and returns no value.

2. The following declaration was used to create the keys array:

```
char keys[256];
```

Write two different function header lines for a function named `find_key()` that accepts the `keys` array as an argument named `select` and returns a character.

3. The following declaration was used to create the `rates` array:

```
float rates[256];
```

Write two different function header lines for a function named `prime()` that accepts the `rates` array as an argument named `rates` and returns a floating point number.

4. *a.* Modify the `find_max()` function in Program 7-4 to locate the minimum value of the passed array.

b. Include the function written in Exercise 4a in a complete program and run the program on a computer.

5. Write a program that has a declaration in `main()` to store the following numbers into an array named `rates`: 6.5, 7.2, 7.5, 8.3, 8.6, 9.4, 9.6, 9.8, 10.0. There should be a function call to `show()` that accepts the `rates` array as an argument named `rates` and then displays the numbers in the array.

6. *a.* Write a program that has a declaration in `main()` to store the string `"Vacation is near"` into an array named `message`. There should be a function call to `display()` that accepts `message` in an argument named `strng` and then displays the message.

b. Modify the `display()` function written in Exercise 6a to display the first eight elements of the `message` array.

7. Write a program that declares three single-dimensional arrays named `price`, `quantity`, and `amount`. Each array should be declared in `main()` and should be capable of holding ten double precision numbers. The numbers that should be stored in `price` are 10.62, 14.89, 13.21, 16.55, 18.62, 9.47, 6.58, 18.32, 12.15, 3.98. The numbers that should be stored in `quantity` are 4, 8.5, 6, 7.35, 9, 15.3, 3, 5.4, 2.9, 4.8. Your program should pass these three arrays to a function called `extend()`, which should calculate the elements in the `amount` array as the product of the corresponding elements in the `price` and `quantity` arrays (for example, `amount[1] = price[1] * quantity[1]`). After `extend()` has put values into the amount array, the values in the array should be displayed from within `main()`.

8. Write a program that includes two functions named `calc_avg()` and `variance()`. The `calc_avg()` function should calculate and return the average of the values stored in an array named `testvals`. The array should be declared in `main()` and include the values 89, 95, 72, 83, 99, 54, 86, 75, 92, 73, 79, 75, 82, 73. The `variance()` function should calculate and return the variance of the data. The variance is obtained by subtracting the average from each value in `testvals`, squaring the values obtained, adding them, and dividing by the number of elements in `testvals`. The values returned from `calc_avg()` and `variance()` should be displayed using `cout` object calls in `main()`.

7.4 Two-Dimensional Arrays

A *two-dimensional array*, which is also referred to as a table, consists of both rows and columns of elements. For example, the array of numbers

$$\begin{array}{cccc} 8 & 16 & 9 & 52 \\ 3 & 15 & 27 & 6 \\ 14 & 25 & 2 & 10 \end{array}$$

is called a two-dimensional array of integers. This array consists of three rows and four columns. To reserve storage for this array, both the number of rows and the number of columns must be included in the array's declaration. Calling the array `val`, the correct specification for this two-dimensional array is

```
int val[3][4];
```

Similarly, the declarations

```
float prices[10][5];
```

```
char code[6][26];
```

declare that the array `prices` consists of 10 rows and 5 columns of floating point numbers and that the array `code` consists of 6 rows and 26 columns, with each element capable of holding one character.

In order to locate each element in a two-dimensional array, an element is identified by its position in the array. As illustrated in Figure 7–9, the term `val[1][3]` uniquely identifies the element in row 1, column 3. As with single-dimensional array variables, double-dimensional array variables can be used anywhere scalar variables are valid. Examples using elements of the `val` array are:

```
price = val[2][3];
val[0][0] = 62;
newnum = 4 * (val[1][0] - 5);
sum_row = val[0][0] + val[0][1] + val[0][2] + val[0][3];
```

The last statement causes the values of the four elements in row 0 to be added and the sum to be stored in the scalar variable `sum_row`.

FIGURE 7–9 Each Array Element Is Identified by Its Row and Column Position

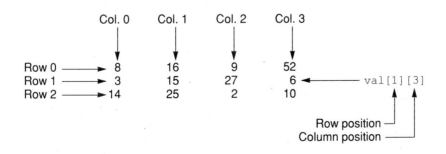

As with single-dimensional arrays, two-dimensional arrays can be initialized from within their declaration statements. This is done by listing the initial values within braces and separating them by commas. Additionally, braces can be used to separate individual rows. For example, the declaration

```
int val[3][4] = {  {8,16,9,52},
                   {3,15,27,6},
                   {14,25,2,10}  };
```

declares val to be an array of integers with three rows and four columns, with the initial values given in the declaration. The first set of internal braces contains the values for row 0 of the array, the second set of internal braces contains the values for row 1, and the third set of braces the values for row 2.

Although the commas in the initialization braces are always required, the inner braces can be omitted. Thus, the initialization for val may be written as

```
int val[3][4] = {8,16,9,52,
                 3,15,27,6,
                 14,25,2,10};
```

The separation of initial values into rows in the declaration statement is not necessary since the compiler assigns values beginning with the [0][0] element and proceeds row by row to fill in the remaining values. Thus, the initialization

```
int val[3][4] = {8,16,9,52,3,15,27,6,14,25,2,10};
```

is equally valid but does not clearly illustrate to another programmer where one row ends and another begins.

As illustrated in Figure 7–10, the initialization of a two-dimensional array is done in row order. First, the elements of the first row are initialized, then the elements of the second row are initialized, and so on, until the initializations are completed. This row ordering is also the same ordering used to store

FIGURE 7–10 Storage and Initialization of the val[] array

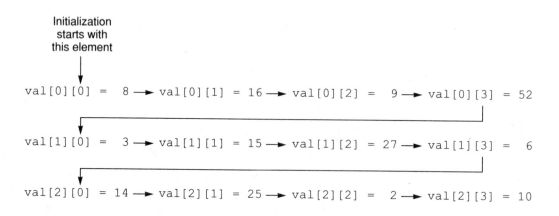

Initialization
starts with
this element

val[0][0] = 8 ⟶ val[0][1] = 16 ⟶ val[0][2] = 9 ⟶ val[0][3] = 52

val[1][0] = 3 ⟶ val[1][1] = 15 ⟶ val[1][2] = 27 ⟶ val[1][3] = 6

val[2][0] = 14 ⟶ val[2][1] = 25 ⟶ val[2][2] = 2 ⟶ val[2][3] = 10

two-dimensional arrays. That is, array element [0][0] is stored first, followed by element [0][1], followed by element [0][2], and so on. Following the first row's elements are the second row's elements, and so on for all the rows in the array.

As with single-dimensional arrays, two-dimensional arrays may be displayed by individual element notation or by using loops (either while or for). This is illustrated by Program 7-6, which displays all the elements of a three-by-four two-dimensional array using two different techniques.

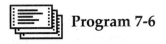 **Program 7-6**

```
#include <iostream.h>
#include <iomanip.h>
void main(void)
{
  int i, j, val[3][4] = {8,16,9,52,3,15,27,6,14,25,2,10};

  cout << "\nDisplay of val array by explicit element"
       << '\n' << setw(4) << val[0][0] << setw(4) << val[0][1]
       << setw(4) << val[0][2] << setw(4) << val[0][3]
       << '\n' << setw(4) << val[1][0] << setw(4) << val[1][1]
       << setw(4) << val[1][2] << setw(4) << val[1][3]
       << '\n' << setw(4) << val[2][0] << setw(4) << val[2][1]
       << setw(4) << val[2][2] << setw(4) << val[2][3];

  cout << "\n\nDisplay of val array using a nested for loop";
  for (i = 0; i < 3; i++)
  {
    cout << '\n';        // print a new line for each row
    for (j = 0; j < 4; j++)
      cout << setw(4) << val[i][j];
  }
}
```

Following is the display produced by Program 7-6.

```
Display of val array by explicit element
   8   16    9   52
   3   15   27    6
  14   25    2   10

Display of val array using a nested for loop
   8   16    9   52
   3   15   27    6
  14   25    2   10
```

255

The first display of the `val` array produced by Program 7-6 is constructed by explicitly designating each array element. The second display of array element values, which is identical to the first, is produced using a nested `for` loop. Nested loops are especially useful when dealing with two-dimensional arrays because they allow the programmer to easily designate and cycle through each element. In Program 7-6, the variable `i` controls the outer loop and the variable `j` controls the inner loop. Each pass through the outer loop corresponds to a single row, with the inner loop supplying the appropriate column elements. After a complete row is printed a new line is started for the next row. The effect is a display of the array in a row-by-row fashion.

Once two-dimensional array elements have been assigned values, array processing can begin. Typically, `for` loops are used to process two-dimensional arrays because, as previously noted, they allow the programmer to easily designate and cycle through each array element. For example, the nested `for` loop illustrated in Program 7-7 is used to multiply each element in the `val` array by the scalar number 10 and display the resulting value.

 Program 7-7

```
#include <iostream.h>
#include <iomanip.h>
void main(void)
{
   int i, j, val[3][4] = {8,16,9,52,
                          3,15,27,6,
                          14,25,2,10};

   // multiply each element by 10 and display it
   cout << "\n\nDisplay of multiplied elements\n";
   for (i = 0; i < 3; i++)
   {
     cout << '\n';          // start a new line
     for (j = 0; j < 4; j++)
     {
       val[i][j] = val[i][j] * 10;
       cout << setw(5) << val[i][j];
     }  // end of inner loop
   }    // end of outer loop
}
```

Following is the output produced by Program 7-7:

```
Display of multiplied elements

   80   160    90   520
   30   150   270    60
  140   250    20   100
```

Passing two-dimensional arrays into functions is a process identical to passing single-dimensional arrays. The called function receives access to the entire array. For example, the function call `display(val);` makes the complete `val` array available to the function named `display()`. Thus, any changes made by `display()` will be made directly to the `val` array. Assuming that the following two-dimensional arrays named `test`, `code`, and `stocks` are declared as:

```
int test[7][9];
char code[26][10];
float stocks[256][52];
```

the following function calls are valid:

```
find_max(test);
obtain(code);
price(stocks);
```

On the receiving side, the called function must be alerted that a two-dimensional array is being made available. For example, suitable function header lines for the previous functions are:

```
int find_max(int nums[7][9])
char obtain(char key[26][10])
void price(float names[256][52])
```

In each of these function header lines, the argument names chosen are local to the function. However, the internal local names used by the function still refer to the original array created outside the function. If the array is a global one, there is no need to pass the array because the function could reference the array by its global name. Program 7-8 illustrates passing a local, two-dimensional array into a function that displays the array's values.

 Program 7-8

```
#include <iostream.h>
#include <iomanip.h>
void main(void)
{
   int val[3][4] = {8,16,9,52,
                    3,15,27,6,
                    14,25,2,10};
   void display(int [3][4]);    // function prototype
   display(val);
}
```

(continued on next page)

```
(continued from previous page)
void display(int nums[3][4])
{
   int row_num, col_num;

   for (row_num = 0; row_num < 3; row_num++)
   {
     cout << '\n';      // start a new line
     for(col_num = 0; col_num < 4; col_num++)
       cout << setw(4) << nums[row_num][col_num];
   }
}
```

Only one array is created in Program 7-8. This array is known as `val` in `main()` and as `nums` in `display()`. Thus, `val[0][2]` refers to the same element as `nums[0][2]`.

Notice the use of the nested `for` loop in Program 7-8. Nested `for` statements are especially useful when dealing with multidimensional arrays because they allow the programmer to cycle through each element. In Program 7-8, the variable `row_num` controls the outer loop and the variable `col_num` controls the inner loop. For each pass through the outer loop, which corresponds to a row, the inner loop makes one pass through the column elements. After a complete row is printed, the `\n` escape sequence causes a new line to be started for the next row. The effect is a display of the array in a row-by-row fashion:

```
 8   16    9   52
 3   15   27    6
14   25    2   10
```

The argument declaration for `nums` in `display()` contains extra information that is not required by the function. The declaration for `nums` can omit the row size of the array. Thus, an alternative function declaration is:

```
display(int nums[][4]);
```

The reason why the column size must be included while the row size is optional becomes obvious when you consider how the array elements are stored in memory. Starting with element `val[0][0]`, each succeeding element is stored consecutively, row by row, as `val[0][0]`, `val[0][1]`, `val[0][2]`, `val[0][3]`, `val[1][0]`, `val[1][1]`, and so on, as illustrated in Figure 7–11.

As with all array accesses, an individual element of the `val` array is obtained by adding an offset to the starting location of the array. For example, the element `val[1][3]` is located at an offset of 14 bytes from the start of the array.

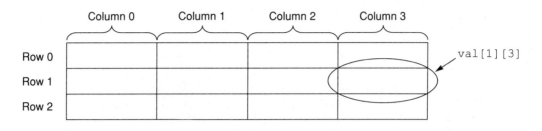

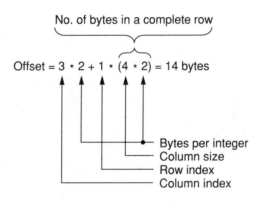

FIGURE 7–11 Storage of the `val` Array

Internally, the computer uses the row index, column index, and column size to determine this offset using the following calculation (again, assuming two bytes for an `int`):

The number of columns is necessary in the offset calculation so that the computer can determine the number of positions to skip over in order to get to the desired row.

Larger-Dimensional Arrays

Although arrays with more than two dimensions are not commonly used, C++ does allow any number of dimensions to be declared. This is done by listing the maximum size of all dimensions for the array. For example, the declaration `int response [4][10][[6];` declares a three-dimensional array. The first element in the array is designated as `response [0][0][0]` and the last element as `response [3][9][5]`.

Conceptually, as illustrated in Figure 7–12, a three-dimensional array can be viewed as a book of data tables. Using this visualization, the first subscript, which is often called the "rank," can be thought of as the page number of the

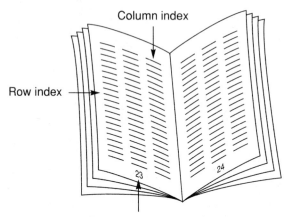

FIGURE 7–12   Representation of a Three Dimensional Array

selected table, the second subscript value as the desired row in the table, and the third subscript value as the desired column.

Similarly, arrays of any dimension can be declared. Conceptually, a four-dimensional array can be represented as a shelf of books, where the first dimension is used to declare a desired book on the shelf, and a five-dimensional array can be viewed as a bookcase filled with books where the first dimension refers to a selected shelf in the bookcase. Using the same analogy, a six-dimensional array can be considered as a single row of bookcases where the first dimension references the desired bookcase in the row; a seven-dimensional array can be considered as multiple rows of bookcases where the first dimension references the desired row, and so on. Alternatively, arrays of three, four, five, six, etc. dimensional arrays can be viewed as mathematical n-tuples of order three, four, five, six, etc., respectively.

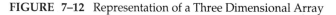

Exercises 7.4

1. Write appropriate specification statements for:
   a. an array of integers with 6 rows and 10 columns
   b. an array of integers with 2 rows and 5 columns
   c. an array of characters with 7 rows and 12 columns
   d. an array of characters with 15 rows and 7 columns
   e. an array of floating point numbers with 10 rows and 25 columns
   f. an array of floating point numbers with 16 rows and 8 columns

2. Determine the output produced by the following program:

```
#include <iostream.h>
void main(void)
{
  int i, j, val[3][4] = {8,16,9,52,3,15,27,6,14,25,2,10};

  for (i = 0; i < 3; i++)
    for (j = 0; j < 4; j++)
      cout << val[i][j] << "   ";
}
```

3. a. Write a C++ program that adds the values of all elements in the `val` array used in Exercise 2 and displays the total.

b. Modify the program written for Exercise 3a to display the total of each row separately.

4. Write a C++ program that adds equivalent elements of the two-dimensional arrays named `first` and `second`. Both arrays should have two rows and three columns. For example, element `[1][2]` of the resulting array should be the sum of `first[1][2]` and `second[1][2]`. The `first` and `second` arrays should be initialized as follows:

First				Second		
16	18	23		24	52	77
54	91	11		16	19	59

5. a. Write a C++ program that finds and displays the maximum value in a two-dimensional array of integers. The array should be declared as a four-by-five array of integers and initialized with these data: 16, 22, 99, 4, 18, –258, 4, 101, 5, 98, 105, 6, 15, 2, 45, 33, 88, 72, 16, 3.

b. Modify the program written in Exercise 5a so that it also displays the maximum value's row and column subscript values.

6. Write a C++ program to select the values in a four-by-five array of integers in increasing order and store the selected values in the single-dimensional array named `sort`. Use the data statement given in Exercise 5a to initialize the two-dimensional array.

7. a. A professor has constructed a two-dimensional array of float numbers having 3 rows and 5 columns. This array currently contains the test grades of the students in the professor's advanced compiler design class. Write a C++ program that reads 15 array values and then determine the total number of grades in the ranges less than 60, greater than or equal to 60 and less than 70, greater than or equal to 70 and less than 80, greater than or equal to 80 and less than 90, and greater than or equal to 90.

b. Entering 15 grades each time the program written for Exercise 7a is run is cumbersome. What method is appropriate for initializing the array during the testing phase?

c. How might the program you wrote for Exercise 7a be modified to include the case of no grade being present? That is, what grade could be used to indicate an invalid grade and how would your program have to be modified to exclude counting such a grade?

8. a. Write a function named `find_max()` that finds and displays the maximum value in a two-dimensional array of integers. The array should be declared as a 10-row by 20-column array of integers in `main()`.

b. Modify the function written in Exercise 8a so that it also displays the row and column number of the element with the maximum value.

c. Can the function you wrote for Exercise 8a be generalized to handle any size two-dimensional array?

9. Write a function that can be used to sort the elements of a 10-by-20 two-dimensional array of integers. (*Hint:* Use the `swap()` function developed for Program 6-8 to exchange array elements.)

7.5 Common Programming Errors

Four common errors associated with using arrays:

1. Forgetting to declare the array. This error results in a compiler error message equivalent to "invalid indirection" each time a subscripted variable is encountered within a program.

2. Using a subscript that references a nonexistent array element; for example, declaring the array to be of size 20 and using a subscript value of 25. This error is not detected by most C++ compilers. It will, however, probably result in a run-time error that results either in a program "crash" or a value that has no relation to the intended element being accessed from memory. In either case this is usually an extremely troublesome error to locate. The only solution to this problem is to make sure, either by specific programming statements or by careful coding, that each subscript references a valid array element.

3. Not using a large enough conditional value in a `for` loop counter to cycle through all the array elements. This error usually occurs when an array is initially specified to be of size n and there is a `for` loop within the program of the form `for (int i = 0; i < n; i++)`. The array size is then expanded but the programmer forgets to change the interior `for` loop parameters. In practice this error is eliminated by using the same `const` declaration for the array size and loop parameter.

4. Forgetting to initialize the array. Although many compilers automatically set all elements of integer and real valued arrays to zero and all elements of character arrays to blanks, it is up to the programmer to ensure that each array is correctly initialized before processing of array elements begins.

7.6 Chapter Summary

1. A single-dimensional array is a data structure that can be used to store a list of values of the same data type. Such arrays must be declared by giving the data type of the values that are stored in the array and the array size. For example, the declaration

```
int num[100];
```

creates an array of 100 integers.

2. Array elements are stored in contiguous locations in memory and referenced using the array name and a subscript, for example, `num[22]`. Any non-negative integer-value expression can be used as a subscript and the subscript 0 always refers to the first element in an array.

3. Two-dimensional arrays are declared by specifying both a row and a column size. For example, the declaration

```
float rates[12][20];
```

reserves memory space for a table of 12-by-20 floating point values. Individual elements in a two-dimensional array are identified by providing both a row and a column subscript. The element in the first row and first column has row and column subscripts of 0.

4. Arrays are passed to a function by passing the name of the array as an argument. The value actually passed is the memory address of the first array storage location. Thus, the called function receives direct access to the original array and not a copy of the array elements. Within the called function a formal argument must be declared to receive the passed array name.

7.7 Chapter Supplement: Sorting Methods

Most programmers encounter the need to sort a list of data items at some time in their programming careers. For example, experimental results might have to be arranged in either increasing (ascending) or decreasing (descending) order for statistical analysis, lists of names may have to be sorted in alphabetical order, or a list of dates may have to be rearranged in ascending date order.

For sorting data, two major categories of sorting techniques exist, called internal and external sorts, respectively. *Internal sorts* are used when the data list is not too large and the complete list can be stored within the computer's memory, usually in an array. *External sorts* are used for much larger data sets that are stored in large external disk or tape files and cannot be accommodated within the computer's memory as a complete unit.

In this section we present two internal sort algorithms, the selection and exchange sorts. Although the exchange sort, also known as a "bubble sort," is the more commonly known of the two, we will see that the selection sort is easier and frequently more efficient.

Initial List	Pass 1	Pass 2	Pass 3	Pass 4
690	32	32	32	32
307	307	155	144	144
32	690	690	307	307
155	155	307	690	426
426	426	426	426	690

FIGURE 7-13 A Sample Selection Sort

Selection Sort

In a selection sort the smallest (or largest) value is initially selected from the complete list of data and exchanged with the first element in the list. After this first selection and exchange, the next smallest (or largest) element in the revised list is selected and exchanged with the second element in the list. Since the smallest element is already in the first position in the list, this second pass need only consider the second through last elements. For a list consisting of *n* elements this process is repeated *n*–1 times, with each pass through the list requiring one less comparison than the previous pass.

For example, consider the list of numbers illustrated in Figure 7–13. The first pass through the initial list results in the number 32 being selected and exchanged with the first element in the list. The second pass, made on the reordered list, results in the number 155 being selected from the second through fifth elements. This value is then exchanged with the second element in the list. The third pass selects the number 307 from the third through fifth elements in the list and exchanges this value with the third element. Finally, the fourth and last pass through the list selects the remaining minimum value and exchanges it with the fourth list element. Although each pass in this example resulted in an exchange, no exchange would have been made in a pass if the smallest value were already in the correct location.

Program 7-9 implements a selection sort for a list of ten numbers that are stored in an array named nums.

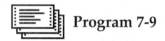 **Program 7-9**

```
#include <iostream.h>
#include <iomanip.h>
void main(void)
{
  int nums[10] = {22,5,67,98,45,32,101,99,73,10};
  int i, j, temp, moves, min, minind;
```

(continued on next page)

(continued from previous page)

```
  moves = 0;
  for (i = 0; i < 9; i++)
  {
    min = nums[i];
    minind = i;
    for (j = i + 1; j < 10; j++)
      if (nums[j] < min)
      {
        min = nums[j];
        minind = j;
      }
    // perform the switch
    if (min < nums[i])
    {
      temp = nums[i];
      nums[i] = min;
      nums[minind] = temp;
      ++moves;
    }
  }
  cout << "\nThe sorted list, in ascending order, is:\n";
  for (i = 0; i < 10; ++i)
    cout << setw(4) << nums[i];
  cout << '\n' << moves << " moves were made to sort this list\n";
}
```

Program 7-9 uses a nested `for` loop to perform the selection sort. The outer `for` loop causes nine passes to be made through the data, which is one less than the total number of data items in the list. For each pass the variable `min` is initially assigned the value `nums[i]`, where `i` is the outer `for` loop's counter variable. Since `i` begins at 0 and ends at 9, each element in the list is successively designated as the next exchange element.

The inner loop is used in Program 7-9 to cycle through the elements below the designated exchange element to select the next smallest value. Thus, this loop begins at the index value `i+1` and continues through the end of the list. When a new minimum is found its value and position in the list are stored in the variables named `min` and `minind`, respectively. Upon completion of the inner loop an exchange is made only if a value less than that in the designated exchange position was found.

Following is the output produced by Program 7-9:

```
The sorted list, in ascending order, is:
   5   10   22   32   45   67   73   98   99  101
8 moves were made to sort this list
```

Clearly the number of moves displayed depends on the initial order of the values in the list. An advantage of the selection sort is that the maximum number of moves that must be made is $n-1$, where n is the number of items in the list. Further, each move is a final move that results in an element residing in its final location in the sorted list.

A disadvantage of the selection sort is that $n(n-1)/2$ comparisons are always required, regardless of the initial arrangement of the data. This number of comparisons is obtained as follows: The last pass always requires one comparison, the next-to-last pass requires two comparisons, and so on to the first pass, which requires $n-1$ comparisons. Thus, the total number of comparisons is:

$$1 + 2 + 3 + \ldots + (n-1) = n(n-1)/2$$

Exchange Sort

In an exchange sort successive values in the list are compared, beginning with the first two elements. If the list is to be sorted in ascending (from smallest to largest) order, the smaller value of the two being compared is always placed before the larger value. For lists sorted in descending (from largest to smallest) order, the smaller of the two values being compared is always placed after the larger value.

For example, assuming that a list of values is to be sorted in ascending order. If the first element in the list is larger than the second, the two elements are interchanged. Then the second and third elements are compared. Again, if the second element is larger than the third, these two elements are interchanged. This process continues until the last two elements have been compared and exchanged, if necessary. If no exchanges were made during this initial pass through the data, the data are in the correct order and the process is finished; otherwise a second pass is made through the data, starting from the first element and stopping at the next-to-last element. The reason for stopping at the next-to-last element on the second pass is that the first pass always results in the most positive value "sinking" to the bottom of the list.

As a specific example of this process, consider the list of numbers illustrated in Figure 7–14. The first comparison results in the interchange of the first two element values, 690 and 307. The next comparison, between elements two and three in the revised list, results in the interchange of values between the second and third elements, 609 and 32. This comparison and possible switching of adjacent values is continued until the last two elements have been compared and possibly switched. This process completes the first pass through the data and results in the largest number moving to the bottom of the list. As the largest value sinks to its resting place at the bottom of the list, the smaller elements slowly rise or "bubble" to the top of the list. This bubbling effect of the smaller elements gave rise to the name "bubble sort" for this sorting algorithm.

As the first pass through the list ensures that the largest value always moves to the bottom of the list, the second pass stops at the next-to-last element. This process continues with each pass stopping at one higher element than the

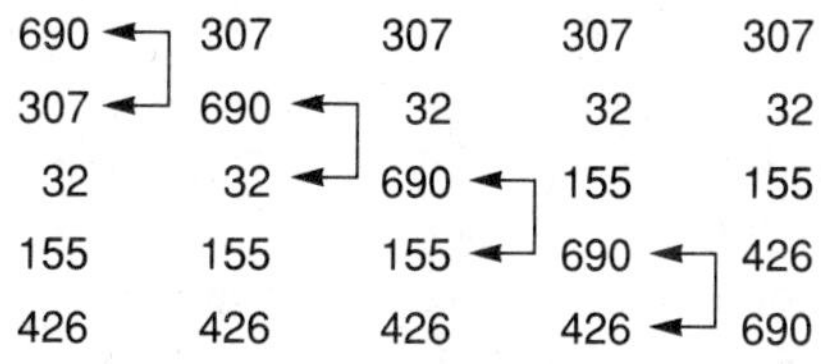

690	307	307	307	307
307	690	32	32	32
32	32	690	155	155
155	155	155	690	426
426	426	426	426	690

FIGURE 7–14 The First Pass of an Exchange Sort

previous pass, until either $n-1$ passes through the list have been completed or no exchanges are necessary in any single pass. In both cases the resulting list is in sorted order.

Program 7-10 implements an exchange sort for the same list of ten numbers used in Program 7-9. For comparison to the earlier selection sort, the number of adjacent moves (exchanges) made by the program are also counted and displayed.

Program 7-10

```cpp
#include <iostream.h>
#include <iomanip.h>
const TRUE = 1;      // the default is an integer type
const FALSE = 0;     // the default is an integer type
void main(void)
{
  int nums[10] = {22,5,67,98,45,32,101,99,73,10};
  int i, temp, moves, npts, outord;

  moves = 0;
  npts = 10;
  outord = TRUE;
  while (outord && npts > 0)
  {
    outord = FALSE;
    for (i = 0; i < npts - 1; i++)
      if (nums[i] > nums[i+1])
      {
        temp = nums[i+1];
        nums[i+1] = nums[i];
        nums[i] = temp;
        outord = TRUE;
        moves++;
      }
    npts--;
  }
  cout << "\nThe sorted list, in ascending order, is:\n";
  for (i = 0; i < 10; ++i)
    cout << setw(4) << nums[i];
  cout << '\n' << moves << " moves were made to sort this list\n";
}
```

As illustrated in Program 7-10, the exchange sort requires a nested loop. The outer loop in Program 7-10 is a while loop that checks if any exchanges were made in the last pass. It is the inner for loop that does the actual comparison and exchanging of adjacent element values.

Immediately before the inner loop's for statement is encountered the value of the variable outord is set to TRUE, to indicate that the list is initially out of order (not sorted) and force the first pass through the list. If the inner loop then detects an element is out of order outord is again set to TRUE, which indicates that the list is still unsorted. The outord variable is then used by the outer loop to determine whether another pass through the data is to be made. Thus, the sort is stopped either because outord is FALSE after at least one pass has been completed or $n-1$ passes through the data have been made. In both cases the resulting list is in sorted order.

Following is the output produced by Program 7-10:

```
The sorted list, in ascending order, is:
    5   10   22   32   45   67   73   98   99  101
18 moves were made to sort this list
```

As with the selection sort, the number of moves required by an exchange sort depends on the initial order of the values in the list.

An advantage of the exchange sort is that processing is terminated whenever a sorted list is encountered. In the best case, when the data is in sorted order to begin with, an exchange sort requires no moves (the same for the selection sort) and only $n-1$ comparisons (the selection sort always requires $n(n-1)/2$ comparisons). In the worst case, when the data is in reverse sorted order, the selection sort does better. Here both sorts require $n(n-1)/2$ comparisons but the selection sort needs only $n-1$ moves while the exchange sort needs $n(n-1)/2$ moves. The additional moves required by the exchange sort result from the intermediate exchanges between adjacent elements to "settle" each element into its final position. In this regard the selection sort is superior because no intermediate moves are necessary. For random data, such as that used in Programs 7-9 and 7-10, the selection sort generally performs as well as or better than the exchange sort. For large numbers of data values there are more efficient sorting routines, such as the quick sort, which is of order $n\log_{10}n$ comparisons.

Pointers

Chapter Eight

A fact generally unknown to most programmers of high-level languages other than C and C++ is that memory addresses of variables are used extensively throughout the executable versions of their programs. These addresses are used by the computer to keep track of where data and instructions are physically located inside of the computer.

One of C++'s advantages is that it provides the programmer access to the addresses of variables used in a program. This access allows a programmer to enter directly into the computer's inner workings and manipulate the computer's basic storage structure. It provides the C++ programmer with capabilities and programming power that is not typically available in other high-level languages.

This chapter presents the basics of declaring variables to store addresses. Such variables are referred to as *pointer variables*, or simply *pointers*. Additionally, we discuss methods of using pointer variables to access and use their stored addresses in meaningful ways.

8.1 Addresses and Pointers

Every variable has three major items associated with it: its data type, the actual value stored in the variable, and the address of the variable. As we have already seen, a variable's data type is declared with a declaration statement and a value is stored in a variable either by initialization when the variable is declared, by assignment, or by input. For the majority of applications the variable's name is a simple and sufficient means of locating the variable's contents, and the translation of a variable's name to actual memory storage location is done by the computer each time the variable is referenced in a program.

Figure 8–1 illustrates the relationship between these three variable attributes (type, contents, location). As seen in this figure, the data type determines the number of memory bytes set aside for the variable and the variable's name is a stand-in for the variable's actual memory address.

FIGURE 8–1 A Typical Variable

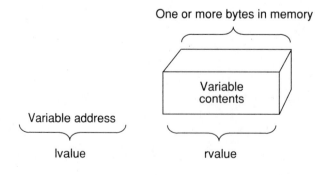

Programmers are usually concerned only with the value assigned to a variable (its contents) and give little attention to where the value is stored (its address).[1] For example, consider Program 8-1.

Program 8-1

```
#include <iostream.h>
void main(void)
{
  int num;

  num = 22;
  cout << "The value stored in num is " << num << '\n';
  cout << sizeof(num) << " bytes are used to store this value" << '\n';
}
```

The output displayed when Program 8-1 is run is:

```
The value stored in num is 22
2 bytes are used to store this value
```

Program 8-1 displays both the number 22, which is the value stored in the integer variable num, and the amount of storage used for this number.[2] The information provided by Program 8-1 is illustrated in Figure 8–2.

FIGURE 8–2 Somewhere in Memory

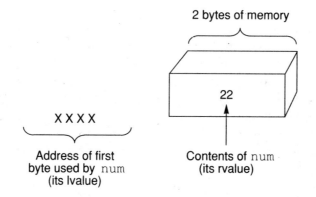

---

[1] In C++, as in C, the content of a memory location is also referred to as an *rvalue*, and the address as an *lvalue*.

[2] The amount of storage allocated for each data type is computer dependent.

We can go further and obtain the address corresponding to the variable num. The address that is displayed corresponds to the address of the first byte set aside in the computer's memory for the variable.

To determine the address of num, we must use the address operator, &. We have seen this symbol before in declaring reference variables. Here it means *the address of* and when placed in front of a variable name is translated as *the address of the variable.*[3] For example, &num means *the address of* num, &total means *the address of* total, and &price means *the address of* price. Program 8-2 uses the address operator to display the address of the variable num.

 Program 8-2

```
#include <iostream.h>
void main(void)
{
   int num;

   num = 22;
   cout << "num = " << num << '\n';
   cout << "The address of num = " << &num << '\n';
}
```

The output of Program 8-2 is:

```
num = 22
The address of num = 0xffe0
```

Figure 8–3 illustrates the additional address information provided by the output of Program 8-2.

Clearly, the address output by Program 8-2 depends on the computer used to run the program. Every time Program 8-2 is executed, however, it displays the address of the first memory location used to store the variable num. As illustrated by the output of Program 8-2, the display of addresses is in hexadecimal notation. This display has no effect on how addresses are used within the program; it merely provides us with a means of displaying addresses that is helpful in understanding them. As we shall see, using addresses as opposed to only displaying them provides the C++ programmer with an extremely powerful programming tool.

---

[3] When used in the declaration of a reference variable the & symbol retains a similar meaning. For example, the declaration int &num = factor; can also be read as "num is the address of an int" (although it is more usually read as "num is a reference to an int"). Since num is a reference variable the compiler automatically assigns the address of factor to the address of num; since both variables have the same memory address, they both refer to the same variable.

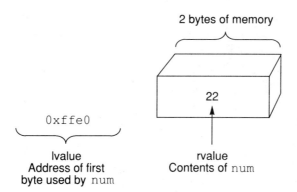

FIGURE 8–3 A More Complete Picture of the Variable num

Storing Addresses

Besides displaying the address of a variable, as was done in Program 8-2, we can also store addresses in suitably declared variables. For example, the statement

```
num_addr = &num;
```

stores the address corresponding to the variable num in the variable num_addr, as illustrated in Figure 8–4. Similarly, the statements

```
d = &m;
tab_point = &list;
chr_point = &ch;
```

store the addresses of the variables m, list, and ch in the variables d, tab_point, and chr_point, respectively, as illustrated in Figure 8–5.

The variables num_addr, d, tab_point, and chr_point are formally called *pointer variables*, or *pointers* for short. Pointers are simply variables that are used to store the addresses of other variables.

Using Addresses

To use a stored address, C++ provides us with an *indirection operator*, *. The * symbol, when followed by a pointer means *the variable whose address is stored in.* Thus, if num_addr is a pointer (remember that a pointer is a variable that stores an address), *num_addr means *the variable whose address is stored in* num_addr.

FIGURE 8–4 Storing num's Address in num_addr

Variable	Contents
num_addr	Address of num

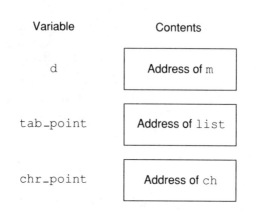

Variable	Contents
d	Address of m
tab_point	Address of list
chr_point	Address of ch

FIGURE 8–5 Storing More Addresses

Similarly, *tab_point means *the variable whose address is stored in* tab_point and *chr_point means *the variable whose address is stored in* chr_point. Figure 8–6 shows the relationship between the address contained in a pointer variable and the variable ultimately addressed.

Although *d literally means *the variable whose address is stored in* d, this is commonly shortened to the statement *the variable pointed to by* d. Similarly, referring to Figure 8–6, *y can be read as *the variable pointed to by* y. The value ultimately obtained, as shown in Figure 8–6, is qqqq.

When using a pointer variable, the value that is finally obtained is always found by first going to the pointer variable (or pointer, for short) for an address. The address contained in the pointer is then used to get the desired contents. Certainly, this is a rather indirect way of getting to the final value and, not unexpectedly, the term *indirect addressing* is used to describe this procedure.

Since using a pointer requires the computer to do a double lookup (first the address is retrieved, then the address is used to retrieve the actual data), a worthwhile question is, why would you want to store an address in the first place? The answer to this question rests on the intimate relationship between pointers and arrays and the ability of pointers to create and delete new variable storage locations dynamically, as a program is running. Both of these topics are presented later in this chapter. For now, however, given that each variable has

FIGURE 8–6 Using a Pointer Variable

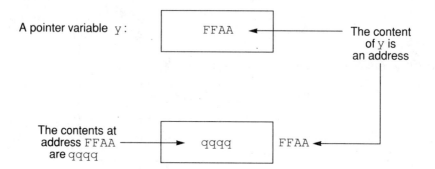

a memory address associated with it, the idea of actually storing an address should not seem overly strange.

Declaring Pointers

Like all variables, pointers must be declared before they can be used to store an address. When we declare a pointer variable, C++ requires that we also specify the type of variable that is pointed to. For example, if the address in the pointer num_addr is the address of an integer, the correct declaration for the pointer is:

```
int *num_addr;
```

This declaration is read as *the variable pointed to by* num_addr (from the *num_addr in the declaration) *is an integer*.

Notice that the declaration int *num_addr; specifies two things: first, that the variable pointed to by num_addr is an integer; second, that num_addr must be a pointer (because it is used with the indirection operator *). Similarly, if the pointer tab_point points to (contains the address of) a floating point number and chr_point points to a character variable, the required declarations for these pointers are:

```
float *tab_point;

char *chr_point;
```

These two declarations can be read, respectively, as *the variable pointed to by* tab_point *is a float* and *the variable pointed to by* chr_point *is a char*. Consider Program 8-3.

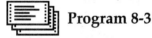 **Program 8-3**

```
#include <iostream.h>
void main(void)
{
  int *num_addr;      // declare a pointer to an int
  int miles, dist;    // declare two integer variables

  dist = 158;         // store the number 158 into dist
  miles = 22;         // store the number 22 into miles
  num_addr = &miles;  // store the 'address of miles' in num_addr

  cout << "The address stored in num_addr is " << num_addr << '\n';
  cout << "The value pointed to by num_addr is " << *num_addr << '\n';

  num_addr = &dist;   // now store the address of dist in num_addr
  cout << "The address now stored in num_addr is " << num_addr << '\n';
  cout << "The value now pointed to by num_addr is " << *num_addr << '\n';
}
```

The output of Program 8-3 is:

```
The address stored in num_addr is 0xffe0
The value pointed to by num_addr is 22

The address now stored in num_addr is 0xffe2
The value now pointed to by num_addr is 158
```

The only value of Program 8-3 is in helping us understand "what gets stored where." Let's review the program to see how the output was produced.

The declaration statement `int *num_addr;` declares `num_addr` to be a pointer variable used to store the address of an integer variable. The statement `num_addr = &miles;` stores the address of the variable `miles` into the pointer `num_addr`. The first activation of `cout` causes this address to be displayed. The second activation of `cout` in Program 8-3 uses the indirection operator to retrieve and print out *the value pointed to by* `num_addr`, which is, of course, the value stored in `miles`.

Since `num_addr` has been declared as a pointer to an integer variable, we can use this pointer to store the address of any integer variable. The statement `num_addr = &dist` illustrates this by storing the address of the variable `dist` in `num_addr`. The last two `cout` activations verify the change in `num_addr`'s value and that the new stored address does point to the variable `dist`. As illustrated in Program 8-3, only addresses should be stored in pointers.

It certainly would have been much simpler if the pointer used in Program 8-3 could have been declared as `pointer num_addr;`. Such a declaration, however, conveys no information as to the storage used by the variable whose address is stored in `num_addr`. This information is essential when the pointer is used with the indirection operator, as it is in the second `cout` activation in Program 8-3. For example, if the address of an integer is stored in `num_addr`, then only two bytes of storage are typically retrieved when the address is used. If the address of a character is stored in `num_addr`, only one byte of storage would be retrieved, and a float typically requires the retrieval of four bytes of storage.[4] The declaration of a pointer must, therefore, include the type of variable being pointed to. Figure 8–7 illustrates this concept.

References and Pointers

At this point you might be asking what the difference is between a pointer and a reference. Essentially, a reference is a pointer with restricted capabilities that has the advantage of hiding a lot of internal pointer manipulations from the programmer. For example, consider these statements:

```
int b;         // b is an integer variable
int &a = b;    // a is a reference variable that stores b's address
a = 10;        // this changes b's value to 10
```

---

[4] The amount of storage used is compiler dependent.

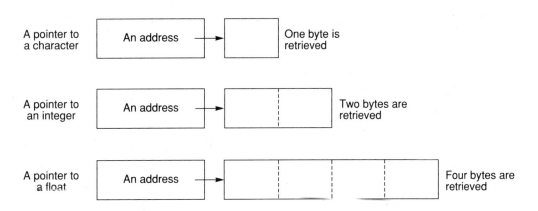

FIGURE 8–7 Addressing Different Data Types Using Pointers

Here, a is declared as a reference variable that contains the address of an integer—the address of b, in particular. Since the compiler knows, from the declaration, that a is a reference variable, it automatically assigns the address of b (rather than the contents of b) in the declaration statement. Finally, in the statement a = 10; the compiler uses the address stored in a to change the value stored in b to 10. The advantage of using the reference is that it automatically performs an indirect access of b's value without the need for explicitly using the indirection operator symbol, *. This type of access is referred to as an automatic *dereference*.

Implementing this same correspondence between a and b using pointers is done by the following sequence of instructions:

```
int b;        // b is an integer variable
int *a = &b;  // a is a pointer - store b's address in a
*a = 10;      // this changes b's value to 10
```

Here a is defined as a pointer that is initialized to store the address of b. Thus, *a, which can be read as either "the variable whose address is in a" or "the variable pointed to by a," is b, and the expression *a = 10 changes b's value to 10. Notice that in the pointer case the stored address can be altered to point to another variable; in the reference case the reference variable cannot be altered to refer to any variable except the one to which it is initialized.

For simple cases, where an alias is required, the use of references over pointers is easier and clearly preferred. The same is true when we consider references to structures, which is the topic of Section 10.3. For other situations, such as dynamically allocating new sections of memory for additional variables as a program is running or using alternatives to array notation (both topics of the next section), pointers are required. In other situations, such as passing addresses to a function, references provide a simpler notational interface and are usually preferred (see Section 8.4). Pointers are described in the remaining sections of this chapter.

Exercises 8.1

1. If `average` is a variable, what does `&average` mean?

2. For the variables and addresses illustrated in Figure 8–8, determine `&temp`, `&dist`, `&date`, and `&miles`.

3. a. Write a C++ program that includes the following declaration statements. Have the program use the address operator and the `cout` object to display the addresses corresponding to each variable.

```
int num, count;
long date;
float yield;
double price;
```

b. After running the program written for Exercise 3a, draw a diagram of how your computer has set aside storage for the variables in the program. On your diagram, fill in the addresses displayed by the program.

c. Modify the program written in Exercise 3a to display the amount of storage your computer reserves for each data type (use the `sizeof()` operator). With this information and the address information provided in Exercise 3b, determine if your computer set aside storage for the variables in the order they were declared.

4. If a variable is declared as a pointer, what must be stored in the variable?

FIGURE 8–8 Memory Bytes for Exercise 2

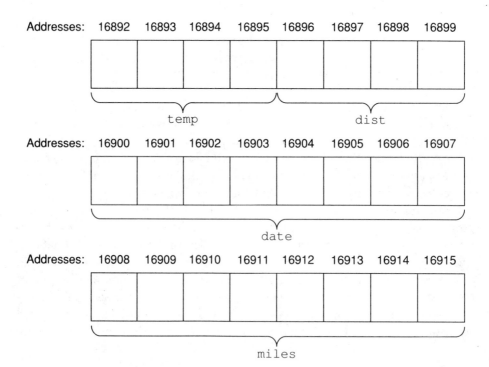

5. Using the indirection operator, write expressions for the following:
   - **a.** The variable pointed to by `x_addr`
   - **b.** The variable whose address is in `y_addr`
   - **c.** The variable pointed to by `pt_yld`
   - **d.** The variable pointed to by `pt_miles`
   - **e.** The variable pointed to by `mptr`
   - **f.** The variable whose address is in `pdate`
   - **g.** The variable pointed to by `dist_ptr`
   - **h.** The variable pointed to by `tab_pt`
   - **i.** The variable whose address is in `hours_pt`

6. Write declaration statements for the following:
   - **a.** The variable pointed to by `y_addr` is an integer.
   - **b.** The variable pointed to by `ch_addr` is a character.
   - **c.** The variable pointed to by `pt_yr` is a long integer.
   - **d.** The variable pointed to by `amt` is a double precision variable.
   - **e.** The variable pointed to by `z` is an integer.
   - **f.** The variable pointed to by `qp` is a floating point variable.
   - **g.** `date_pt` is a pointer to an integer.
   - **h.** `yld_addr` is a pointer to a double precision variable.
   - **i.** `amt_pt` is a pointer to a floating point variable.
   - **j.** `pt_chr` is a pointer to a character.

7. **a.** What are the variables `y_addr`, `ch_addr`, `pt_yr`, `amt`, `z`, `qp`, `date_ptr`, `yld_addr`, `amt_pt`, and `pt_chr`, used in Exercise 6, called?
   b. Why are the variable names `amt`, `z`, and `qp`, used in Exercise 6, not good choices for pointer variable names?

8. Write English sentences that describe what is contained in the following declared variables:

   - **a.** `char *key_addr;`
   - **b.** `int *m;`
   - **c.** `double *yld_addr;`
   - **d.** `long *y_ptr;`
   - **e.** `float *p_cou;`
   - **f.** `int *pt_date;`

9. Which of the following are declarations for pointers?

   - **a.** `long a;`
   - **b.** `char b;`
   - **c.** `char *c;`
   - **d.** `int x;`
   - **e.** `int *p;`
   - **f.** `double w;`
   - **g.** `float *k;`
   - **h.** `float l;`
   - **i.** `double *z;`

10. For the following declarations,

```
int *x_pt, *y_addr;
long *dt_addr, *pt_addr;
double *pt_z;
int a;
long b;
double c;
```

determine which of the following statements is valid:

   - **a.** `y_addr = &a;`
   - **b.** `y_addr = &b;`
   - **c.** `y_addr = &c;`
   - **d.** `y_addr = a;`
   - **e.** `y_addr = b;`
   - **f.** `y_addr = c;`

(continued on next page)

279

g. dt_addr = &a;　　**h.** dt_addr = &b;　　**i.** dt_addr = &c;
j. dt_addr = a;　　**k.** dt_addr = b;　　**l.** dt_addr = c;
m. pt_z = &a;　　**n.** pt_addr = &b;　　**o.** pt_addr = &c;
p. pt_addr = a;　　**q.** pt_addr = b;　　**r.** pt_addr = c;
s. y_addr = x_pt;　　**t.** y_addr = dt_addr;　**u.** y_addr = pt_addr;

11. For the variables and addresses illustrated in Figure 8–9, fill in the appropriate data as determined by the following statements:

a. pt_num = &m;　　　　　　**e.** pt_day = z_addr;
b. amt_addr = &amt;　　　　**f.** *pt_yr = 1987;
c. *z_addr = 25;　　　　　　**g.** *amt_addr = *num_addr;
d. k = *num_addr;

12. Using the sizeof() operator, determine the number of bytes used by your computer to store the address of an integer, character, and double precision number. (*Hint:* sizeof(*int) can be used to determine the number of memory bytes used for a pointer to an integer.) Would you expect the size of each address to be the same? Why or why not?

FIGURE 8–9 Memory Locations for Exercise 11

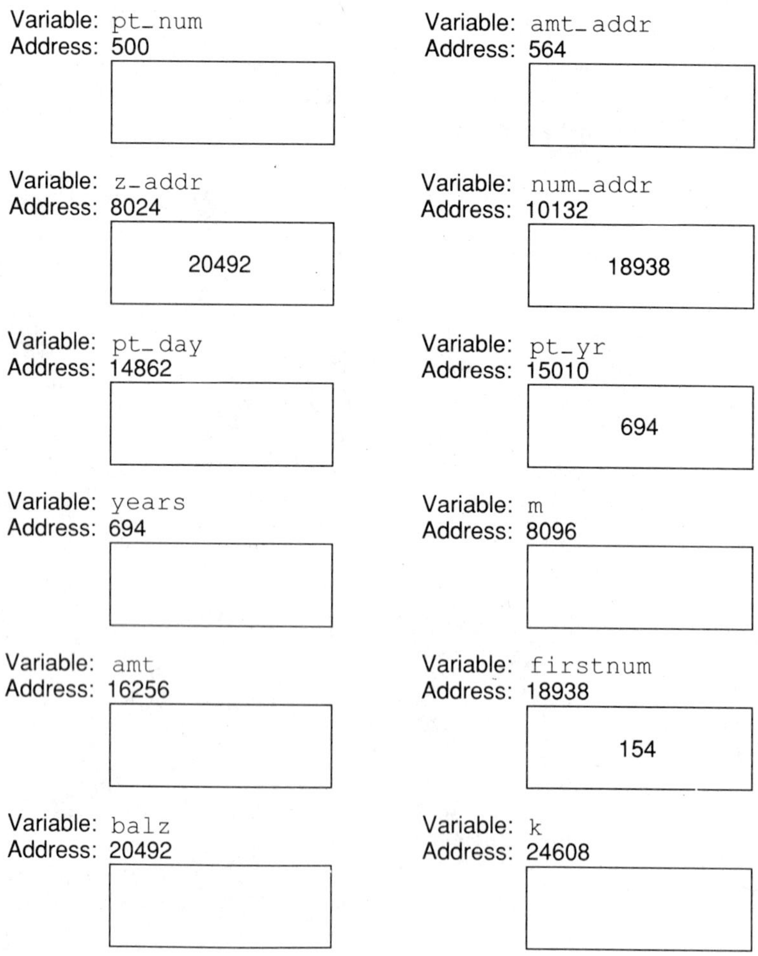

Variable: pt_num
Address: 500

Variable: amt_addr
Address: 564

Variable: z_addr
Address: 8024
> 20492

Variable: num_addr
Address: 10132
> 18938

Variable: pt_day
Address: 14862

Variable: pt_yr
Address: 15010
> 694

Variable: years
Address: 694

Variable: m
Address: 8096

Variable: amt
Address: 16256

Variable: firstnum
Address: 18938
> 154

Variable: balz
Address: 20492

Variable: k
Address: 24608

8.2 Array Names as Pointers

Although pointers are simply, by definition, variables used to store addresses, there is also a direct and intimate relationship between array names and pointers. In this section we describe this relationship in detail.

Figure 8–10 illustrates the storage of a single-dimensional array named grade, which contains five integers. Assume that each integer requires two bytes of storage.

Using subscripts, the fourth element in the grade array is referred to as grade[3]. The use of a subscript, however, conceals the extensive use of addresses by the computer. Internally, the computer immediately uses the subscript to calculate the address of the desired element based on both the starting address of the array and the amount of storage used by each element. Calling the fourth element grade[3] forces the compiler, internally, to make the address computation (assuming two bytes per integer)

$$\&grade[3] = \&grade[0] + (3 * 2)$$

Remembering that the address operator, &, means "the address of," this last statement is read "the address of grade[3] equals the address of grade[0] plus 6." Figure 8–11 illustrates the address computation used to locate grade[3].

FIGURE 8–10 The grade Array in Storage

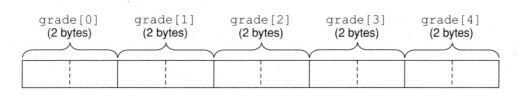

FIGURE 8–11 Using a Subscript to Obtain an Address

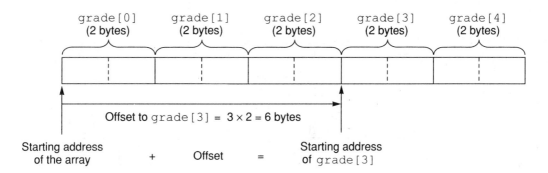

Recall that a pointer is a variable used to store an address. If we create a pointer to store the address of the first element in the grade array, we can mimic the operation used by the computer to access the array elements. Before we do this, let us first consider Program 8-4.

 Program 8-4

```
#include <iostream.h>
void main(void)
{
    const int SIZE = 5;
    int i, grade[SIZE] = {98, 87, 92, 79, 85};

    for (i = 0; i < SIZE; i++)
        cout << "\nElement " << i << " is " << grade[i];
}
```

When Program 8-4 is run, the following display is obtained:

```
Element 0 is 98
Element 1 is 87
Element 2 is 92
Element 3 is 79
Element 4 is 85
```

Program 8-4 displays the values of the array grade using standard subscript notation. Now, let us store the address of array element 0 in a pointer. Then, using the indirection operator, *, we can use the address in the pointer to access each array element. For example, if we store the address of grade[0] in a pointer variable named g_ptr (using the assignment statement g_ptr = &grade[0];), then, as illustrated in Figure 8–12, the expression *g_ptr, which means "the variable pointed to by g_ptr," references grade[0].

One unique feature of pointers is that offsets may be included in expressions using pointers. For example, the 1 in the expression *(g_ptr + 1) is an offset.

FIGURE 8–12 The Variable Pointed to by *g_ptr Is grade[0]

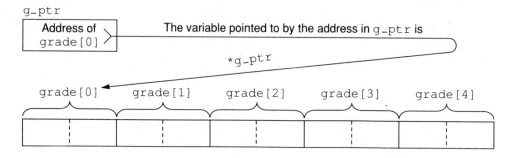

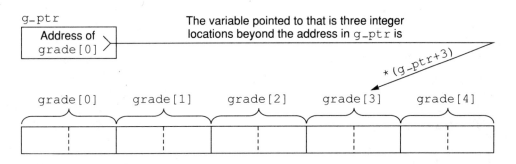

FIGURE 8–13 An Offset of 3 from the Address in g_ptr

The complete expression references the integer that is one beyond the variable pointed to by g_ptr. Similarly, as illustrated in Figure 8–13, the expression *(g_ptr + 3) references the variable that is three integers beyond the variable pointed to by g_ptr. This is the variable grade[3].

Table 8–1 lists the complete correspondence between elements referenced by subscripts and by pointers and offsets. The relationships listed in Table 8–1 are illustrated in Figure 8–14.

TABLE 8–1   Array Elements May Be Referenced in Two Ways

Array Element	Subscript Notation	Pointer Notation
Element 0	grade[0]	*g_ptr
Element 1	grade[1]	*(g_ptr + 1)
Element 2	grade[2]	*(g_ptr + 2)
Element 3	grade[3]	*(g_ptr + 3)
Element 4	grade[4]	*(g_ptr + 4)

FIGURE 8–14 The Relationship Between Array Elements and Pointers

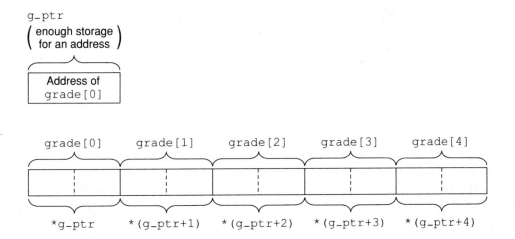

Using the correspondence between pointers and subscripts illustrated in Figure 8–14, the array elements previously accessed in Program 8-4 using subscripts can now be accessed using pointers. This is done in Program 8-5.

Program 8-5

```
#include <iostream.h>
void main(void)
{
  int *g_ptr;           // declare a pointer to an int
  const int SIZE = 5;
  int i, grade[SIZE] = {98, 87, 92, 79, 85};

  g_ptr = &grade[0];    // store the starting array address
  for (i = 0; i < SIZE; i++)
    cout << "\nElement " << i << " is " << *(g_ptr + i);
}
```

The following display is obtained when Program 8-5 is run:

```
Element 0 is 98
Element 1 is 87
Element 2 is 92
Element 3 is 79
Element 4 is 85
```

Notice that this is the same display produced by Program 8-4.

The method used in Program 8-5 to access individual array elements simulates how the compiler internally references all array elements. Any subscript used by a programmer is automatically converted to an equivalent pointer expression by the compiler. In our case, since the declaration of g_ptr included the information that integers are pointed to, any offset added to the address in g_ptr is automatically scaled by the size of an integer. Thus, *(g_ptr + 3), for example, refers to the address of grade[0] plus an offset of six bytes (3 * 2). This is the address of grade[3] illustrated in Figure 8–14.

The parentheses in the expression *(g_ptr + 3) are necessary to correctly reference the desired array element. Omitting the parentheses results in the expression *g_ptr + 3. Due to the precedence of the operators, this expression adds 3 to "the variable pointed to by g_ptr." Since g_ptr points to grade[0], this expression adds the value of grade[0] and 3 together. Note also that the expression *(g_ptr + 3) does not change the address stored in g_ptr. Once the computer uses the offset to locate the correct variable from the starting address in g_ptr, the offset is discarded and the address in g_ptr remains unchanged.

Although the pointer g_ptr used in Program 8-5 was specifically created to store the starting address of the grade array, this was, in fact, unnecessary. When an array is created, the compiler automatically creates an internal pointer constant for it and stores the starting address of the array in this pointer. In almost all respects, a pointer constant is very similar to a pointer variable created by a programmer; but, as we shall see, there are some differences.

For each array created, the name of the array becomes the name of the pointer constant created by the compiler for the array, and the starting address of the first location reserved for the array is stored in this pointer. Thus, declaring the grade array in both Program 8-4 and Program 8-5 actually reserved enough storage for five integers, created an internal pointer named grade, and stored the address of grade[0] in the pointer. This is illustrated in Figure 8–15.

The implication is that every reference to grade using a subscript can be replaced by an equivalent reference using grade as a pointer. Thus, wherever the expression grade[i] is used, the expression *(grade + i) can also be used. This is illustrated in Program 8-6, where grade is used as a pointer to reference all of its elements.

Program 8-6

```cpp
#include <iostream.h>
void main(void)
{
  const int SIZE = 5;
  int i, grade[SIZE] = {98, 87, 92, 79, 85};

  for (i = 0; i < SIZE; i++)
    cout << "\nElement " << i << " is " << *(grade + i);
}
```

FIGURE 8–15   Creating an Array Also Creates a Pointer

grade

&grade[0]

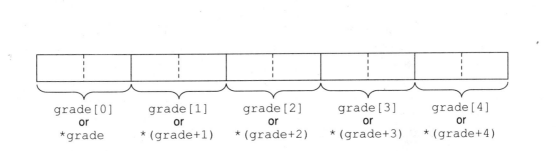

grade[0]	grade[1]	grade[2]	grade[3]	grade[4]
or	or	or	or	or
*grade	*(grade+1)	*(grade+2)	*(grade+3)	*(grade+4)

Executing Program 8-6 produces the same output previously produced by Program 8-4 and Program 8-5. However, using `grade` as a pointer made it unnecessary to declare and initialize the pointer `g_ptr` used in Program 8-5.

In most respects an array name and pointer can be used interchangeably. *A true pointer, however, is a variable and the address stored in it can be changed. An array name is a pointer constant and the address stored in the pointer cannot be changed by an assignment statement.* Thus, a statement such as `grade = &grade[2];` is invalid. This should come as no surprise. Since the whole purpose of an array name is to correctly locate the beginning of the array, allowing a programmer to change the address stored in the array name would defeat this purpose and lead to havoc whenever array elements were referenced. Also, expressions taking the address of an array name are invalid because the pointer created by the compiler is internal to the computer, not stored in memory as are pointer variables. Thus, trying to store the address of `grade` using the expression `&grade` results in a compiler error.

An interesting sidelight to the observation that elements of an array can be referenced using pointers is that a pointer reference can always be replaced with a subscript reference. For example, if `num_ptr` is declared as a pointer variable, the expression `*(num_ptr + i)` can also be written as `num_ptr[i]`. This is true even though `num_ptr` is not created as an array. As before, when the compiler encounters the subscript notation, it replaces it internally with the pointer notation.

Dynamic Array Allocation

As each variable is defined in a program, sufficient storage for it is assigned from a pool of computer memory locations made available to the compiler. Once specific memory locations have been reserved for a variable, these locations are fixed for the life of that variable, whether they are used or not. For example, if a function requests storage for an array of 500 integers, the storage for the array is allocated and fixed from the point of the array's definition. If the application requires less than 500 integers, the unused allocated storage is not released back to the system until the array goes out of existence. On the other hand, if the application requires more than 500 integers, the size of the integer array must be increased and the function defining the array recompiled.

An alternative to this fixed or static allocation of memory storage locations is the dynamic allocation of memory. Under a dynamic allocation scheme, the amount of storage to be allocated is determined and adjusted as the program is run, rather than being fixed at compile time.

The dynamic allocation of memory is extremely useful when dealing with lists, because it allows the list to expand as new items are added and contract as items are deleted. For example, in constructing a list of grades, the exact number of grades ultimately needed may not be known. Rather than creating a fixed array to store the grades, it is extremely useful to have a mechanism whereby the array can be enlarged and shrunk as necessary. Two C++ operators, `new` and `delete`, that provide this capability are described in Table 8-2.

TABLE 8-2 Dynamic Allocation and Deallocation Operators

Operator Name	Description
new	Reserves the number of bytes requested by the declaration. Returns the address of the first reserved location or NULL if sufficient memory is not available.
delete	Releases a block of bytes previously reserved. The address of the first reserved location is passed as an argument to the function.

Explicit dynamic storage requests for scalar variables or arrays are made either as part of a declaration or an assignment statement.[5] For example, the declaration statement int *num = new int; reserves an area sufficient to hold one integer and places the address of this storage area into the pointer num. This same dynamic allocation can be made by first declaring the pointer using the declaration statement int *num; and then subsequently assigning the pointer an address with the assignment statement num = new int;. In either case the allocated storage area comes from the computer's free storage area.[6]

In a similar manner and of more usefulness is the dynamic allocation of arrays. For example, the declaration

```
int *grades = new int[200];
```

reserves an area sufficient to store 200 integers and places the address of the first integer into the pointer grades. Although we have used the constant 200 in this example declaration, a variable dimension can be used. For example, consider the sequence of instructions

```
cout << "Enter the number of grades to be processed: ";
cin >> numgrades;
int *grades = new int[numgrades];
```

In this sequence the actual size of the array that is created depends on the number input by the user. Since pointer and array names are related, each value in the newly created storage area can be accessed using standard array notation, such as grades[i], rather than the equivalent pointer notation *(grades + i). Program 8-7 illustrates this sequence of code in the context of a complete program.

---

[5] Note that the compiler automatically provides this dynamic allocation and deallocation from the stack for all auto variables.

[6] The free storage area of a computer is formally referred to as the *heap*. The heap consists of unallocated memory that can be allocated to a program, as requested, while the program is running.

Program 8-7

```
#include <iostream.h>
void main(void)
{
  int numgrades, i;

  cout << "Enter the number of grades to be processed: ";
  cin >> numgrades;

  int *grade = new int[numgrades];  // create the array

  for(i = 0; i < numgrades; i++)
  {
    cout << "  Enter a grade: ";
    cin >> grade[i];
  }
  cout << "\nAn array was created for " << numgrades << " integers\n";
  cout << " The values stored in the array are:";
  for (i = 0; i < numgrades; i++)
    cout << "\n    " << grade[i];

  delete grade;    // return the storage to the heap
}
```

Notice in Program 8-7 that the delete operator has been used to restore the allocated block of storage back to the operating system while the programming is executing.[7] The only address required by delete is the starting address of the block of storage that was dynamically allocated. Thus, any address returned by new can subsequently be used by delete to restore the reserved memory back to the computer. The delete operator does not alter the address passed to it, but simply removes the storage that the address references. Following is a sample run using Program 8-7:

```
Enter the number of grades to be processed: 4
    Enter a grade: 85
    Enter a grade: 96
    Enter a grade: 77
    Enter a grade: 92

An array was created for 4 integers
 The values stored in the array are:
    85
    96
    77
    92
```

---

[7] The allocated storage would be returned automatically to the heap when the program has completed execution. It is, however, good practice to formally restore the allocated storage back to the heap using delete when the memory is no longer needed. This is especially true for larger programs that make numerous requests for additional storage areas.

Exercises 8.2

1. Replace each of the following references to a subscripted variable with a pointer reference:

a. `prices[5]`   *b.* `grades[2]`   *c.* `yield[10]`

d. `dist[9]`   *e.* `mile[0]`   *f.* `temp[20]`

g. `celsius[16]`   *h.* `num[50]`   *i.* `time[12]`

2. Replace each of the following references using a pointer with a subscript reference:

a. `* (message + 6)`   *b.* `*amount`   *c.* `* (yrs + 10)`

d. `* (stocks + 2)`   *e.* `* (rates + 15)`   *f.* `* (codes + 19)`

3. a. List the three things that the declaration statement `double prices[5];` causes the compiler to do.

b. If each double precision number uses eight bytes of storage, how much storage is set aside for the `prices` array?

c. Draw a diagram similar to Figure 8–15 for the `prices` array.

d. Determine the byte offset relative to the start of the `prices` array, corresponding to the offset in the expression `* (prices + 3)`.

4. a. Write a declaration to store the string `"This is a sample"` into an array named `samtest`. Include the declaration in a program that displays the values in `samtest` using a `for` loop and pointer references to each element in the array.

b. Modify the program written in Exercise 4a to display only array elements 10 through 15 (these are the letters s, a, m, p, l, and e).

5. Write a declaration to store the following values into an array named `rates`: 12.9, 18.6, 11.4, 13.7, 9.5, 15.2, 17.6. Include the declaration in a program that displays the values in the array using pointer notation.

6. Repeat Exercise 6 in Section 7.1, but use pointer references to access all array elements.

7. Repeat Exercise 7 in Section 7.1, but use pointer references to access all array elements.

8. As described in Table 8–2, the new operator returns either the address of the first new storage area allocated, or NULL if insufficient storage is available. Modify Program 8-7 to check that a valid address has been returned before attempting to place values into the `grades` array. Display an appropriate message if sufficient storage is not available.

8.3 Pointer Arithmetic

Pointer variables, like all variables, contain values. The value stored in a pointer is, of course, an address. Thus, by adding and subtracting numbers to pointers we can obtain different addresses. Additionally, the addresses in pointers can be compared using any of the relational operators (==, !=, <, >, etc.) that are valid for comparing other variables. In performing arithmetic on pointers we must be careful to produce addresses that point to something meaningful. In comparing pointers we must also make comparisons that make sense. Consider these declarations:

```
int nums[100];
int *n_pt;
```

To set the address of nums[0] into n_pt, either of the following two assignment statements can be used:

```
n_pt = &nums[0];
n_pt = nums;
```

The two assignment statements produce the same result because nums is a pointer constant that is the address of the first location in the array. This is, of course, the address of nums[0]. Figure 8–16 illustrates the allocation of memory resulting from the previous declaration and assignment statements, assuming that each integer requires two bytes of memory and that the location of the beginning of the nums array is at address 18934.

Once n_pt contains a valid address, values can be added and subtracted from the address to produce new addresses. When adding or subtracting numbers to pointers, the computer automatically adjusts the number to ensure that the result still "points to" a value of the correct type. For example, the statement n_pt = n_pt + 4; forces the computer to scale the 4 by the correct number to ensure that the resulting address is the address of an integer. Assuming that each integer requires two bytes of storage, as illustrated in Figure 8–16, the computer multiplies the 4 by two and then adds eight to the address in n_pt. The resulting address is 18942, which is the correct address of nums[4].

This automatic scaling by the computer ensures that the expression n_pt + i, where i is any positive integer, correctly points to the ith element beyond the one currently being pointed to by n_pt. Thus, if n_pt initially contains the address of nums[0], n_pt + 4 is the address of nums[4], n_pt + 50 is the address of nums[50], and n_pt + i is the address of nums[i]. Although we

FIGURE 8–16 The nums Array in Memory

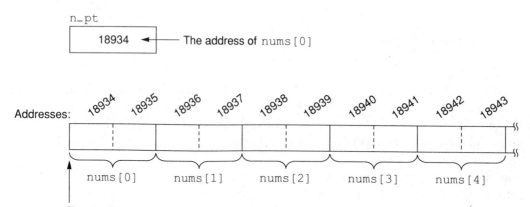

The starting address of the nums array is 18934

have used actual addresses in Figure 8–16 to illustrate the scaling process, the programmer normally does not know or need to know the actual addresses used by the computer. The manipulation of addresses using pointers generally does not require knowledge of the actual address.

Addresses can also be incremented or decremented using both prefix and postfix increment and decrement operators. Adding one to a pointer causes the pointer to point to the next element of the type being pointed to. Decrementing a pointer causes the pointer to point to the previous element. For example, if the pointer variable p is a pointer to an integer, the expression p++ causes the address in the pointer to be incremented to point to the next integer. This is illustrated in Figure 8–17.

In reviewing Figure 8–17, notice that the increment added to the pointer is correctly scaled to account for the fact that the pointer is used to point to integers. It is, of course, up to the programmer to ensure that the correct type of data is stored in the new address contained in the pointer.

The increment and decrement operators can be applied as both prefix and postfix pointer operators. All of the following combinations using pointers are valid:

```
*pt_num++      // use the pointer and then increment it
*++pt_num      // increment the pointer before using it
*pt_num--      // use the pointer and then decrement it
*--pt_num      // decrement the pointer before using it
```

Of the four possible forms, the most commonly used is the form *pt_num++. This is because such an expression allows each element in an array to be accessed as the address is "marched along" from the starting address of the array to the address of the last array element. To see the use of the increment operator, consider Program 8-8. In this program each element in the nums array is retrieved by successively incrementing the address in n_pt.

FIGURE 8–17 Increments Are Scaled When Used with Pointers

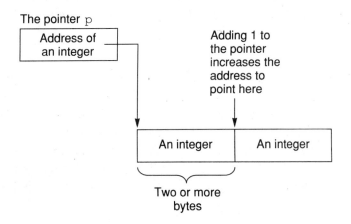

Program 8-8

```cpp
#include <iostream.h>
void main(void)
{
  const int NUMPTS = 5;
  int nums[NUMPTS] = {16, 54, 7, 43, -5};
  int i, total = 0, *n_pt;

  n_pt = nums;     // store address of nums[0] in n_pt
  for (i = 0; i < NUMPTS; i++)
    total = total + *n_pt++;

  cout << "\nThe total of the array elements is " << total;
}
```

The output produced by Program 8-8 is:

```
The total of the array elements is 115
```

The expression `total = total + *n_pt++` used in Program 8-8 is a standard accumulating expression. Within this expression, the term `*n_pt++` first causes the compiler to retrieve the integer pointed to by n_pt. This is done by the `*n_pt` part of the term. The postfix increment, `++`, then adds one to the address in n_pt so that n_pt now contains the address of the next array element. The increment is, of course, scaled by the computer so that the actual address in n_pt is the correct address of the next element.

Pointers may also be compared. This is particularly useful when dealing with pointers that point to elements in the same array. For example, rather than using a counter in a `for` loop to correctly access each element in an array, the address in a pointer can be compared to the starting and ending address of the array itself. The expression

```
n_pt <= &nums[4]
```

is true (nonzero) as long as the address in n_pt is less than or equal to the address of nums[4]. Since nums is a pointer constant that contains the address of nums[0], the term &nums[4] can be replaced by the equivalent term nums + 4. Using either of these forms, Program 8-8 can be rewritten as Program 8-9 to continue adding array elements while the address in n_pt is less than or equal to the address of the last array element.

Program 8-9

```
#include <iostream.h>
void main(void)
{
  const int NUMPTS = 5;
  int nums[NUMPTS] = {16, 54, 7, 43, -5};
  int total = 0, *n_pt;

  n_pt = nums;     // store address of nums[0] in n_pt

  while (n_pt < nums + NUMPTS)
    total += *n_pt++;

  cout << "\nThe total of the array elements is " << total;
}
```

Notice that in Program 8-9 the compact form of the accumulating expression, `total += *n_pt++`, was used in place of the longer form, `total = total + *n_pt++`. Also, the expression `nums + NUMPTS` does not change the address in `nums`. This expression retrieves the address in `nums`, adds 4 to this address (appropriately scaled), and uses the result for comparison purposes. Expressions such as `*nums++`, which attempt to change the address, are invalid because `nums` is an array name and not a pointer variable; as such its value cannot be changed. Expressions such as `*nums` or `*(nums + i)`, which use the address without attempting to alter it, are valid.

Pointer Initialization

Like all variables, pointers can be initialized when they are declared. When initializing pointers, however, you must be careful to set an address in the pointer. For example, an initialization such as

```
int *pt_num = &miles;
```

is only valid if `miles` itself were declared as an integer variable prior to `pt_num`. Here we are creating a pointer to an integer and setting the address in the pointer to the address of an integer variable. Notice that if the variable `miles` is declared subsequently to `pt_num`, as follows,

```
int *pt_num = &miles;
int miles;
```

an error occurs. This is because the address of `miles` is used before `miles` has even been defined. Since the storage area reserved for `miles` has not been allocated when `pt_num` is declared, the address of `miles` does not yet exist.

Pointers to arrays can be initialized within their declaration statements. For example, if `prices` has been declared an array of floating point numbers, either of the following two declarations can be used to initialize the pointer named `zing` to the address of the first element in `prices`:

```
float *zing = &prices[0];
float *zing = prices;
```

The last initialization is correct because `prices` is itself a pointer constant containing an address of the proper type. (The variable name `zing` was selected in this example to reinforce the idea that any variable name can be selected for a pointer.)

Exercises 8.3

1. Replace the `while` statement in Program 8-9 with a `for` statement.

2. a. Write a C++ program that initializes an array named `rates` with the following numbers: 6.25, 6.50, 6.8, 7.2, 7.35, 7.5, 7.65, 7.8, 8.2, 8.4, 8.6, 8.8, 9.0. Display the values in the array by changing the address in a pointer called `disp_pt`. Use a `for` statement in your program.

b. Modify the program written in Exercise 2a to use a `while` statement.

3. a. Write a program that stores the string `Hooray for All of Us` into an array named `strng`. Use the declaration `strng[] = "Hooray for All of Us";`, which ensures that the end-of-string escape sequence `\0` is included in the array. Display the characters in the array by changing the address in a pointer called `mess_pt`. Use a `for` statement in your program.

b. Modify the program written in Exercise 3a to use the `while` statement `while (*mess_pt++ != '\0')`.

c. Modify the program written in Exercise 3a to start the display with the word `All`.

4. Write a C++ program that stores the following numbers in the array named `miles`: 15, 22, 16, 18, 27, 23, 20. Have your program copy the data stored in `miles` to another array named `dist` and then display the values in the `dist` array.

5. Write a C++ program that stores the following letters in the array named `message`: `This is a test`. Have your program copy the data stored in `message` to another array named `mess2` and then display the letters in the `mess2` array.

6. Write a C++ program that declares three single-dimensional arrays named `miles`, `gallons`, and `mpg`. Each array should be capable of holding ten elements. In the `miles` array store the numbers 240.5, 300.0, 189.6, 310.6, 280.7, 216.9, 199.4, 160.3, 177.4, 192.3. In the `gallons` array store the numbers 10.3, 15.6, 8.7, 14, 16.3, 15.7, 14.9, 10.7, 8.3, 8.4. Each element of the `mpg` array should be calculated as the corresponding element of the `miles` array divided by the equivalent element of the `gallons` array; for example, `mpg[0] = miles[0] / gallons[0]`. Use pointers when calculating and displaying the elements of the `mpg` array.

8.4 Passing Addresses

We have already seen one method of passing addresses to a function. This was accomplished using reference variables, as was described in Section 6.3. Although passing reference variables to a function provides the function with the address of the passed variables, it is an implied use of addresses because the function call does not reveal the fact that reference variables are being used. For example, the function call `swap(num1, num2);` does not reveal whether `num1` or `num2` is a reference variable. Only by looking at the declaration for these variables or by examining the function header line for `swap()` are the data types of `firstnum` and `secnum` revealed.

In contrast to implicitly passing addresses using reference variables, addresses can be explicitly passed using pointer variables. Let us see how this is accomplished.

To explicitly pass an address to a function all that needs to be done is to place the address of operator, `&`, in front of the variable being passed. For example, the function call

```
swap(&firstnum, &secnum);
```

passes the addresses of the variables `firstnum` and `secnum` to `swap()`, as illustrated in Figure 8–18. Explicitly passing addresses using the address operator effectively is a *call by reference* because the called function can reference, or access, variables in the calling function using the passed addresses. As we saw in Section 6.3 calls by reference are also accomplished using reference variables. Here we will use the passed addresses and pointers to directly access the variables `firstnum` and `secnum` from within `swap()` and exchange their values—a procedure that was previously accomplished in Program 6-8 using reference variables.

FIGURE 8–18 Explicitly Passing Addresses to `swap()`

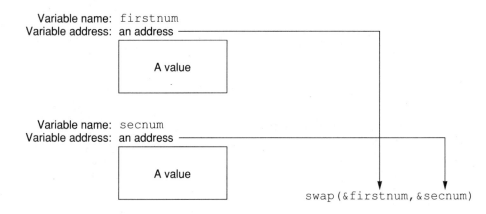

One of the first requirements in writing swap() is to construct a function header line that correctly receives and stores the passed values, which in this case are two addresses. As we saw in Section 8.1, addresses are stored in pointers, which means that the arguments of swap() must be declared as pointers. Assuming that firstnum and secnum are double precision variables and that swap() returns no value, a suitable function header line for swap() is:

```
void swap(double *nm1_addr, double *nm2_addr)
```

The choice of the argument names nm1_addr and nm2_addr is, as with all argument names, up to the programmer. The declaration double *nm1_addr, however, declares that the argument named nm1_addr will be used to store the address of a double precision value. Similarly, the declaration double *nm2_addr declares that nm2_addr will also store the address of a double precision value.

Before writing the body of swap() to exchange the values in firstnum and secnum, let's first check that the values accessed using the addresses in nm1_addr and nm2_addr are correct. This is done in Program 8-10.

 Program 8-10

```
#include <iostream.h>
void main(void)
{
  double firstnum = 20.5, secnum = 6.25;
  void swap(double *, double *);        // function prototype

  swap(&firstnum, &secnum);             // call swap
}

void swap(double *nm1_addr, double *nm2_addr)
{
  cout << "The number whose address is in nm1_addr is "
       << *nm1_addr;
  cout << "\nThe number whose address is in nm2_addr is "
       << *nm2_addr;

}
```

The output displayed when Program 8-10 is run is:

```
The number whose address is in nm1_addr is 20.5
The number whose address is in nm2_addr is 6.25
```

In reviewing Program 8-10, note two things. First, the function prototype for swap(),

```
void swap(double *, double *)
```

declares that swap() returns no value directly and that its arguments are two pointers that "point to" double precision values. As such, when the function is called it will require that two addresses be passed, and that each address is the address of a double precision value.

The second item to notice is that within swap() the indirection operator is used to access the values stored in firstnum and secnum. swap() itself has no knowledge of these variable names, but it does have the address of firstnum stored in nm1_addr and the address of secnum stored in nm2_addr. The expression *nm1_addr used in the first cout activation means "the variable whose address is in nm1_addr." This is of course the variable firstnum. Similarly, the second cout activation obtains the value stored in secnum as "the variable whose address is in nm2_addr." Thus, we have successfully used pointers to allow swap() to access variables in main(). Figure 8–19 illustrates the concept of storing addresses in arguments.

Having verified that swap() can access main()'s local variables firstnum and secnum, we can now expand swap() to exchange the values in these variables. The values in main()'s variables firstnum and secnum can be interchanged from within swap() using the three-step interchange algorithm previously described in Section 6.3, which for convenience is relisted below:

1. Store firstnum's value in a temporary location.
2. Store secnum's value in firstnum.
3. Store the temporary value in secnum.

FIGURE 8–19 Storing Addresses in Arguments

Argument name: nm1_addr   swap(&firstnum,&secnum)

&firstnum

Argument name: nm2_addr

&secnum

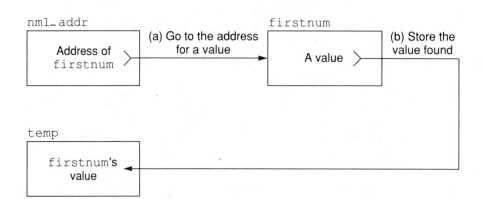

FIGURE 8–20 Indirectly Storing firstnum's value

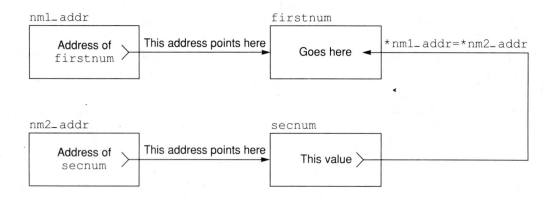

FIGURE 8–21 Indirectly Changing firstnum's Value

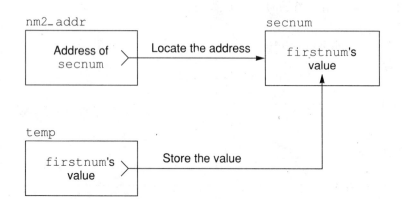

FIGURE 8–22 Indirectly Changing secnum's Value

Using pointers from within `swap()`, this takes the form:

1. Store the value of the variable pointed to by `nm1_addr` in a temporary location. The statement `temp = *nm1_addr;` does this (see Figure 8–20).
2. Store the value of the variable whose address is in `nm2_addr` in the variable whose address is in `nm1_addr`. The statement `*nm1_addr = *nm2_addr;` does this (see Figure 8–21).
3. Move the value in the temporary location into the variable whose address is in `nm2_addr`. The statement `*nm2_addr = temp;` does this (see Figure 8–22).

Program 8-11 contains the final form of `swap()`, written according to our description.

Program 8-11

```
#include <iostream.h>
void main(void)
{
  double firstnum = 20.5, secnum = 6.25;
  void swap(double *, double *);      // function prototype

  cout << "The value stored in firstnum is: " << firstnum <<'\n';
  cout << "The value stored in secnum is: " << secnum << "\n\n";

  swap(&firstnum, &secnum);           // call swap

  cout << "The value stored in firstnum is now: " << firstnum << '\n';
  cout << "The value stored in secnum is now: " << secnum << '\n';
}

void swap(double *nm1_addr, double *nm2_addr)
{
  double temp;

  temp = *nm1_addr;            // save firstnum's value
  *nm1_addr = *nm2_addr;       // move secnum's value in firstnum
  *nm2_addr = temp;            // change secnum's value

}
```

The following sample run was obtained using Program 8-11:

```
The value stored in firstnum is: 20.5
The value stored in secnum is: 6.25

The value stored in firstnum is now: 6.25
The value stored in secnum is now: 20.5
```

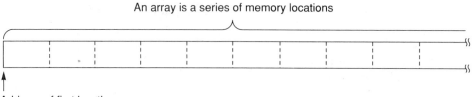

An array is a series of memory locations

Address of first location

FIGURE 8–23 The Address of an Array Is the Address of the First Location Reserved for the Array

As illustrated in this output, the values stored in main()'s variables have been modified from within swap(), which was made possible by the use of pointers. The interested reader should compare this version of swap() with the version using references that was presented in Program 6-8. The advantage of using pointers in preference to references is that the function call itself explicitly designates that addresses are being used, which directly alerts you that the function will most likely alter variables of the calling function. The advantage of using references is that the notation is much simpler.

Generally, for functions such as swap(), the notational convenience wins out and references are used. In passing arrays to functions, however, which is our next topic, the compiler automatically passes an address. This dictates that pointer variables will be used to store the address.

Passing Arrays

When an array is passed to a function, its address is the only item actually passed. By this we mean the address of the first location used to store the array, as illustrated in Figure 8–23. Since the first location reserved for an array corresponds to element 0 of the array, the "address of the array" is also the address of element 0.

For a specific example in which an array is passed to a function, consider Program 8-12. In this program, the nums array is passed to the find_max() function using conventional array notation.

 **Program 8-12**

```
#include <iostream.h>
void main(void)
{
  const int NUMPTS = 5;
  int nums[NUMPTS] = {2, 18, 1, 27, 16};
  int find_max(int [], int);    // function prototype
```

(continued on next page)

(continued from previous page)
```
   cout << "\nThe maximum value is "
        << find_max(nums,NUMPTS) << '\n';
}

int find_max(int vals[], int num_els)  // find the maximum value
{
  int i, max = vals[0];

  for (i = 1; i < num_els; ++i)
   if (max < vals[i]) max = vals[i];

  return max;
}
```

The output displayed when Program 8-12 is executed is:

```
The maximum value is 27
```

The argument named `vals` in the header line declaration for `find_max()` actually receives the address of the array `nums`. As such, `vals` is really a pointer, since pointers are variables (or arguments) used to store addresses. Since the address passed into `find_max()` is the address of an integer, another suitable header line for `find_max()` is:

```
int find_max(int *vals, int num_els) // here vals is declared as
                                     // a pointer to an integer
```

The declaration `int *vals` in the header line declares that `vals` is used to store an address of an integer. The address stored is, of course, the location of the beginning of an array.

The following is a rewritten version of the `find_max()` function that uses a pointer declaration for `vals`, but retains the use of subscripts to refer to individual array elements:

```
int find_max(int *vals, int num_els)    // find the maximum value
{
  int i, max = vals[0];

  for (i = 1; i < num_els; i++)
   if (max < vals[i]) max = vals[i];

  return max;
}
```

Regardless of how `vals` is declared in the function header or how it is used within the function body, it is truly a pointer variable. Thus, the address in vals may be modified. This is not true for the name nums. Since nums is the name of the originally created array, it is a pointer constant. As described in Section 8.2, this means that the address in nums cannot be changed and that the address of nums itself cannot be taken. No such restrictions, however, apply to the pointer variable named vals. All the address arithmetic that we learned in the previous section can be legitimately applied to vals.

We shall write two additional versions of find_max(), both using pointers instead of subscripts. In the first version we simply substitute pointer notation for subscript notation. In the second version we use address arithmetic to change the address in the pointer.

As previously stated, access to an array element using the subscript notation array_name[i] can always be replaced by the pointer notation *(array_name + i). In our first modification to find_max(), we use this correspondence by simply replacing all references to vals[i] with the equivalent expression *(vals + i):

```
int find_max(int *vals, int num_els)    // find the maximum value
{
   int i, max = *vals;

   for (i = 1; i < num_els; i++)
    if (max < *(vals + i) )   max = *(vals + i);

   return max;
}
```

Our next version of find_max() uses the fact that the address stored in vals can be changed. After each array element is retrieved using the address in vals, the address itself is incremented by one in the altering list of the for statement. The expression max = *vals previously used to set max to the value of vals[0] is replaced by the expression max = *vals++, which adjusts the address in vals to point to the second element in the array. The element assigned to max by this expression is the array element pointed to by vals before vals is incremented. The postfix increment, ++, does not change the address in vals until after the address has been used to retrieve the array element.

```
int find_max(int *vals, int num_els)    // find the maximum value
{
   int i, max = *vals++;    // get the first element and increment
   for (i = 1; i < num_els; i++, vals++)
   {
     if (max < *vals)   max = *vals;
   }
   return max;
}
```

Let us review this version of find_max(). Initially the maximum value is set to "the thing pointed to by vals." Since vals initially contains the address of the first element in the array passed to `find_max()`, the value of this first element is stored in `max`. The address in `vals` is then incremented by one. The one that is added to `vals` is automatically scaled by the number of bytes used to store integers. Thus, after the increment, the address stored in `vals` is the address of the next array element. This is illustrated in Figure 8–24. The value of this next element is compared to the maximum and the address is again incremented, this time from within the altering list of the `for` statement. This process continues until all the array elements have been examined.

The version of `find_max()` that appeals to you is a matter of personal style and taste. Generally, beginning programmers feel more at ease using subscripts rather than pointers. Also, if the program uses an array as the natural storage structure for the application and data at hand, an array reference using subscripts is more appropriate to clearly indicate the intent of the program. However, as we learn about strings and data structures, we will see that the use of pointers becomes an increasingly useful and powerful tool in its own right. In these instances there is no simple or easy equivalence using subscripts.

One further "neat trick" can be gleaned from our discussion. Since passing an array to a function really involves passing an address, we can just as well pass any valid address. For example, the function call `find_max(&nums[2],3)` passes the address of `nums[2]` to `find_max()`. Within `find_max()` the pointer `vals` stores the address and the function starts the search for a maximum at the element corresponding to this address. Thus, from `find_max()`'s perspective, it has received an address and proceeds appropriately.

Advanced Pointer Notation[8]

Access to multidimensional arrays can also be made using pointer notation, although the notation becomes more and more cryptic as the array dimensions

FIGURE 8–24 Pointing to Different Elements

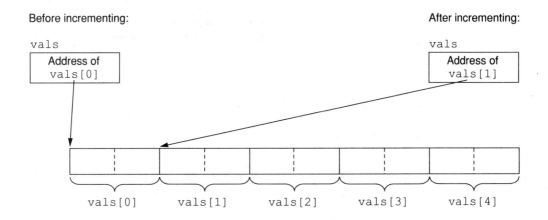

---
[8] This topic may be omitted with no loss of subject continuity.

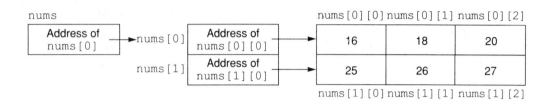

FIGURE 8–25 Storage of the nums Array and Associated Pointer Constants

increase. An extremely useful application of this notation occurs with two-dimensional character arrays, one of the topics of the next chapter. Here we consider pointer notation for two-dimensional numeric arrays. For example, consider the declaration

```
int nums[2][3] = { {16,18,20},
                   {25,26,27} };
```

This declaration creates an array of elements and a set of pointer constants named nums, nums[0], and nums[1]. The relationship between these pointer constants and the elements of the nums array are illustrated in Figure 8–25.

The availability of the pointer constants associated with a two-dimensional array allows us to reference array elements in a variety of ways. One way is to consider the two-dimensional array as an array of rows, where each row is itself an array of three elements. Considered in this light, the address of the first element in the first row is provided by nums[0] and the address of the first element in the second row is provided by nums[1]. Thus, the variable pointed to by nums[0] is num[0][0] and the variable pointed to by nums[1] is num[1][0]. Once the nature of these constants is understood, each element in the array can be accessed by applying an appropriate offset to the appropriate pointer. Thus, the following notations are equivalent:

Pointer Notation	Subscript Notation	Value
*nums[0]	nums[0][0]	16
*(nums[0] + 1)	nums[0][1]	18
*(nums[0] + 2)	nums[0][2]	20
*nums[1]	nums[1][0]	25
*(nums[1] + 1)	nums[1][1]	26
*(nums[1] + 2)	nums[1][2]	27

We can now go even further and replace nums[0] and nums[1] with their respective pointer notations, using the address of nums itself. As illustrated in

Figure 8–25, the variable pointed to by nums is nums[0]. That is, *nums is nums[0]. Similarly, *(nums + 1) is nums[1]. Using these relationships leads to the following equivalences:

Pointer Notation	Subscript Notation	Value
*(*nums)	nums[0][0]	16
*(*nums + 1)	nums[0][1]	18
*(*nums + 2)	nums[0][2]	20
((nums + 1))	nums[1][0]	25
((nums + 1) + 1)	nums[1][1]	26
((nums + 1) + 2)	nums[1][2]	27

The same notation applies when a two-dimensional array is passed to a function. For example, assume that the two-dimensional array nums is passed to the function calc() using the call calc(nums);. Here, as with all array passes, an address is passed. A suitable function header line for the function calc() is:

```
calc(int pt[2][3])
```

As we have already seen, the argument declaration for pt can also be:

```
calc(int pt[][3])
```

Using pointer notation, another suitable declaration is:

```
calc(int (*pt)[3])
```

In this last declaration the inner parentheses are required to create a single pointer to objects of three integers. Each object is, of course, equivalent to a single row of the nums array. By suitably offsetting the pointer, each element in the array can be accessed. Notice that without the parentheses the declaration becomes

```
int *pt[3]
```

which creates an array of three pointers, each one pointing to a single integer.

Once the correct declaration for pt is made (any of the three valid declarations can be used), the following notations within the function calc() are all equivalent:

Pointer Notation	Subscript Notation	Value
*(*pt)	pt[0][0]	16
*(*pt+1)	pt[0][1]	18
*(*pt+2)	pt[0][2]	20
((pt+1))	pt[1][0]	25
((pt+1)+1)	pt[1][1]	26
((pt+1)+2)	pt[1][2]	27

The last two notations using pointers are encountered in more advanced C++ programs. The first of these occurs because functions can return any valid C++ scalar data type, including pointers to any of these data types. If a function returns a pointer, the data type being pointed to must be declared in the function's declaration. For example, the declaration

```
int *calc()
```

declares that calc() returns a pointer to an integer value. This means that an address of an integer variable is returned. Similarly, the declaration

```
float *taxes()
```

declares that taxes() returns a pointer to a floating point value. This means that an address of a floating point variable is returned.

In addition to declaring pointers to integers, floating point numbers, and C++'s other data types, pointers can also be declared that point to (contain the address of) a function. Pointers to functions are possible because function names, like array names, are themselves pointer constants. For example, the declaration

```
int (*calc)()
```

declares calc() to be a pointer to a function that returns an integer. This means that calc will contain the address of a function, and the function whose address is in the variable calc returns an integer value. If, for example, the function sum() returns an integer, the assignment calc = sum; is valid.

Exercises 8.4

1. The following declaration was used to create the prices array:

```
double prices[500];
```

Write three different header lines for a function named `sort_arr()` that accepts the `prices` array as an argument named `in_array` and returns no value.

2. The following declaration was used to create the `keys` array:

```
char keys[256];
```

Write three different header lines for a function named `find_key()` that accepts the `keys` array as an argument named `select` and returns no value.

3. The following declaration was used to create the `rates` array:

```
float rates[256];
```

Write three different header lines for a function named `prime()` that accepts the `rates` array as an argument named `rates` and returns a floating point value.

4. Modify the `find_max()` function to locate the minimum value of the `passed` array. Write the function using only pointers.

5. In the last version of `find_max()` presented, `vals` was incremented inside the altering list of the `for` statement. Instead, suppose that the incrementing was done within the condition expression of the `if` statement, as follows:

```
int find_max(int *vals, int num_els)     // incorrect version
{
  int i, max = *vals++;    // get the first element and increment
  for (i = 1; i < num_els; i++)
  {
    if (max < *vals++)   max = *vals;
  }
  return max;
}
```

This version produces an incorrect result. Determine why.

6. *a.* Write a program that has a declaration in `main()` to store the following numbers into an array named `rates`: 6.5, 7.2, 7.5, 8.3, 8.6, 9.4, 9.6, 9.8, 10.0. There should be a function call to `show()` that accepts `rates` in an argument named `rates` and then displays the numbers using the pointer notation `*(rates + i)`.
b. Modify the `show()` function written in Exercise 6a to alter the address in `rates`. Always use the expression `*rates` rather than `*(rates + i)` to retrieve the correct element.

7. *a.* Write a program that has a declaration in `main()` to store the string `Vacation is near` into an array named `message`.
There should be a function call to `display()` that accepts `message` in an argument named `strng` and then displays the message using the pointer notation `*(strng + i)`.
b. Modify the `display()` function written in Exercise 7a to alter the address in `message`. Always use the expression `*strng` rather than `*(strng + i)` to retrieve the correct element.

8. Write a program that declares three single-dimensional arrays named `price`, `quantity`, and `amount`. Each array should be declared in `main()` and be capable of holding ten double precision numbers. The numbers to be stored in `price` are 10.62, 14.89, 13.21,

16.55, 18.62, 9.47, 6.58, 18.32, 12.15, 3.98. The numbers to be stored in `quantity` are 4, 8.5, 6, 7.35, 9, 15.3, 3, 5.4, 2.9, 4.8. Have your program pass these three arrays to a function called `extend()`, which calculates the elements in the `amount` array as the product of the equivalent elements in the `price` and `quantity` arrays (for example, `amount[1]` `= price[1] * quantity[1]`).

   After `extend()` has put values into the `amount` array, display the values in the array from within `main()`. Write the `extend()` function using pointers.

9. a. Determine the output of the following program:

```
#include <iostream.h>
void main(void)
{
   void arr(int [][3]);
   int nums[2][3] = {  {33,16,29},
                       {54,67,99}};
   arr(nums);
}

void arr(int (*val)[3])
{
    cout << '\n' << *(*val);
    cout << '\n' << *(*val + 1);
    cout << '\n' << *(*(val + 1) + 2);
    cout << '\n' << *(*val) + 1;
}
```

b. Given the declaration for `val` in the `arr()` function, would the reference `val[1][2]` be valid within the function?

8.5 Common Programming Errors

In using the material presented in this chapter, be aware of the following possible errors:

1. Attempting to store an address in a variable that has not been declared as a pointer.

2. Using a pointer to access nonexistent array elements. For example, if `nums` is an array of ten integers, the expression `*(nums + 10)` points one integer location beyond the last element of the array. As most C++ compilers do not do any bounds checking on array accesses, this type of error is not caught by the compiler. This is the same error, disguised in pointer notation form, as using a subscript to access an out-of-bounds array element.

3. Incorrectly applying the address and indirection operators. For example, if `pt` is a pointer variable, the expressions

```
pt = &45

pt = &(miles + 10)
```

are both invalid because they attempt to take the address of a value. Notice that the expression `pt = &miles + 10`, however, is valid. Here, 10 is added to the address of `miles`. Again, it is the programmer's responsibility to ensure that the final address "points to" a valid data element.

4. Taking addresses of a register variable. Thus, for the declarations

```
register int total;

int *pt_tot;
```

the assignment

```
pt_tot = &total;     // INVALID
```

is invalid. The reason is that register variables are stored in a computer's internal registers, and these storage areas do not have standard memory addresses.

5. Taking addresses of pointer constants. For example, given the declarations

```
int nums[25];

int *pt;
```

the assignment

```
pt = &nums;
```

is invalid. `nums` is a pointer constant that is itself equivalent to an address. The correct assignment is `pt = nums`.

6. Initializing pointer variables incorrectly. For example, the initialization

```
int *pt = 5;
```

is invalid. Since `pt` is a pointer to an integer, it must be initialized with a valid address.

7. Becoming confused about whether a variable *contains* an address or *is* an address. Pointer variables and pointer arguments contain addresses. Although a pointer constant is synonymous with an address, it is useful to treat pointer constants as pointer variables with two restrictions:

- The address of a pointer constant cannot be taken.
- The address "contained in" the pointer constant cannot be altered.

Except for these two restrictions, pointer constants and variables can be used almost interchangeably. Therefore, when an address is required any of the following can be used:

- a pointer variable name
- a pointer argument name
- a pointer constant name
- a nonpointer variable name preceded by the address operator (e.g., `&variable`)
- a nonpointer argument name preceded by the address operator (e.g., `&argument`)

Some of the confusion surrounding pointers is caused by the cavalier use of the word *pointer*. For example, the phrase "a function requires a pointer argument" is more clearly understood when it is realized that the phrase really means "a function requires an address as an argument." Similarly, the phrase "a function returns a pointer" really means "a function returns an address."

If you are ever in doubt as to what is really contained in a variable or how it should be treated, use the `cout` object to display the contents of the variable, the "thing pointed to," or "the address of the variable." Seeing what is displayed frequently helps sort out what is really in the variable.

8.6 Chapter Summary

1. All variables, except register variables, have an address (lvalue). Each variable also has a data type and a content, which is the current value stored in the variable (its rvalue). Although programmers typically use a variable's name to access the variable's contents, the compiler typically uses a variable's name to reference its address. The address operator, `&`, can be used to obtain a variable's address.

2. A pointer is a variable that is used to store the address of another variable. Pointers, like all C++ variables, must be declared. The indirection operator, `*`, is used both to declare a pointer variable and to access the variable whose address is stored in a pointer.

3. An array name is a pointer constant. The value of the pointer constant is the address of the first element in the array. Thus, if `val` is the name of an array, `val` and `&val[0]` can be used interchangeably.

4. Any access to an array element using subscript notation can always be replaced using pointer notation. That is, the notation `a[i]` can always be replaced by the notation `*(a + i)`. This is true whether `a` was initially declared explicitly as an array or as a pointer.

5. Arrays can be dynamically created as a program is executing. For example, the sequence of statements

```
cout << "Enter the array size: ";
cin >> num;
int *grades = new int[num];
```

creates an array named `grades` of size `num`. The area allocated for the array can be dynamically destroyed using the `delete` operator. For example, the statement `delete grades;` will return the allocated area for the `grades` array back to the computer.

6. Arrays are passed to functions as addresses. The called function always receives direct access to the originally declared array elements.

7. When a single-dimensional array is passed to a function, the argument declaration for the function can be either an array declaration or a pointer declaration. Thus, the following argument declarations are equivalent:

```
float a[];
float *a;
```

8. Pointers can be incremented, decremented, compared, and assigned. Numbers added to or subtracted from a pointer are automatically scaled. The scale factor used is the number of bytes required to store the data type originally pointed to.

Character Strings

Chapter Nine

On a fundamental level, strings are simply arrays of characters. As such, they can be manipulated using standard element-by-element array-processing techniques. On a higher level, string library functions are available for handling strings as complete entities. This chapter explores the input, manipulation, and output of strings using all of these approaches. We also examine the particularly close connection between string-handling functions and pointers.

9.1 String Fundamentals

A string constant, informally referred to as a string, is any sequence of characters enclosed in double quotes. For example, `"This is a string"`, `"Hello World!"`, and `"xyz 123 *!#@&"` are all strings.

A string is stored as an array of characters terminated by a special end-of-string marker called the null character. The null character, represented by the escape sequence `\0`, is the sentinel marking the end of the string. For example, Figure 9–1 illustrates how the string `"Good Morning!"` is stored in memory. The string uses fourteen storage locations, with the last character in the string being the end-of-string marker `\0`. The double quotes are not stored as part of the string.

Since a string is stored as an array of characters, the individual characters in the array can be input, manipulated, or output using standard array-handling techniques utilizing either subscript or pointer notations. The end-of-string null character is useful for detecting the end of the string when handling strings in this fashion.

String Input and Output

Although you have a choice of using either library or user-written functions for processing a string already in memory, inputting a string from a keyboard or displaying a string always requires some reliance on standard library routines. Table 9–1 lists the commonly available library routines for both character-by-character and complete string input/output.

As listed in Table 9–1, in addition to the `cout` and `cin` streams, C++ provides two routines, `cin.getline()` and `cin.get()`, which are especially designed for string and character input. Earlier C functions that provide similar

FIGURE 9–1 Storing a String in Memory

G	o	o	d		M	o	r	n	i	n	g	!	\0

TABLE 9–1   String and Character Library Routines[1]

C++ Routine	Description	C Routine
cout	General-purpose screen output	printf()
cout	String output to screen	puts()
cout	Character output to screen	putchar()
cin	General-purpose screen input	scanf()
cin.getline()	String input from terminal	gets()
cin.get()	Character input from terminal	getchar()

features to these C++ routines, and are still available in C++, are gets() and getchar(). For output C provided the puts() and putchar() functions; the features of these two functions are essentially provided in C++ by cout. Programs that use the newer C++ routines must include the iostream.h header, while the older C functions require the stdio.h header.

Program 9-1 illustrates the use of the cin.getline() and cout routines to input and output a string entered at the user's terminal.

 Program 9-1

```cpp
#include <iostream.h>
void main(void)
{
    char message[80];    // enough storage for a complete line

    cout << "Enter a string:\n";
    cin.getline(message,80);
    cout << "The string just entered is:\n";
    cout << message << '\n';
}
```

The following is a sample run of Program 9-1:

```
Enter a string:
This is a test input of a string of characters.
The string just entered is:
This is a test input of a string of characters.
```

---

[1] Additionally, the functions getche() and putch() are available in C++. These are character input and output functions that provide features identical to getchar() and putchar(), but are specifically written for IBM-compatible PCs.

The `cin.getline()` (the reason for the period in `cin.getline()` is discussed in Chapter 11) function used in Program 9-1 continuously accepts and stores characters typed at the terminal into the character array named `message` until either 79 characters are entered (the 80th character is then used to store the end-of-string Null character, \0), or the ENTER key is detected. Pressing the ENTER key at the terminal generates a newline character, \n, which is interpreted by `cin.getline()` as the end-of-line entry. All the characters encountered by `cin.getline()`, except the newline character, are stored in the `message` array. Before returning, the `cin.getline()` function appends the null character to the stored set of characters, as illustrated in Figure 9–2. The `cout` routine is then used to display the string.

Although the `cout` object is used in Program 9-1 for string output, `cin` could not be used in place of `cin.getline()` for string input. This is because the `cin` object reads a set of characters up to either a blank space or a newline character. Thus, attempting to enter the characters This is a string using the statement `cin >> message;` only results in the word This being assigned to the `message` array. Entering the complete line using a `cin` object call requires a statement such as:

```
cin >> message1 >> message2 >> message3 >> message4;
```

Here, the word This is assigned to the string `message1`, the word is is assigned to the string `message2`, and so on. The fact that a blank is `cin`'s default delimiter restricts this object's usefulness for entering string data and is the reason for using `cin.getline()`.

In its most general form, the `cin.getline()` function has the syntax

```
cin.getline(str, length, char)
```

where `str` is a string or character pointer variable, `length` is an integer constant or variable indicating the maximum number of input characters, and `char` is an optional character constant or variable specifying the terminating character. If this optional third argument is omitted, the default terminating character is the newline (`'\n'`) character. Thus, the statement `cin.getline(message, 80, '\n');` can be used in place of the statement `cin.getline(message, 80);` in Program 9-1. Both of these functions stop reading characters when the return key is pressed or until 80 characters have

FIGURE 9–2 Inputting a String with `cin.getline()`

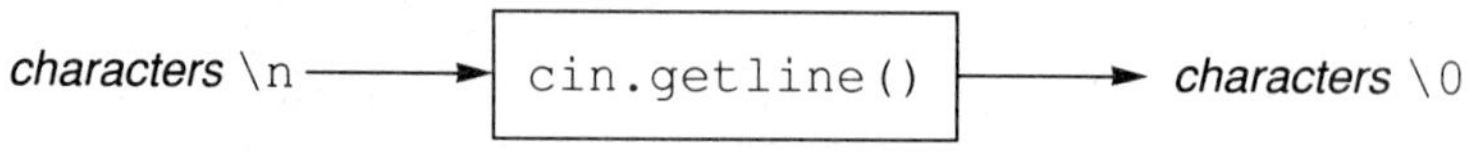

characters \n ⟶ `cin.getline()` ⟶ *characters* \0

been read, whichever comes first. Since `cin.getline()` permits specification of any terminating character for the input stream, a statement such as `cin.getline(message,80,'x');` is also valid. This particular statement will stop accepting characters whenever the X key is pressed.

String Processing

Strings can be manipulated using either standard library functions or standard array-processing techniques. The library functions typically available for use are presented in the next section. For now we will concentrate on processing a string in a character-by-character fashion. This will allow us to understand how the standard library functions are constructed and to create our own library functions. For a specific example, consider the function `strcopy()` that copies the contents of `string2` to `string1`.

```
// copy string2 to string 1
void strcopy(char string1[], char string2[])
{
  int i = 0;                        // i will be used as a subscript

  while ( string2[i] != '\0')   // check for the end-of-string
  {
    string1[i] = string2[i];    // copy the element to string1
    i++;
  }
  string1[i] = '\0';            // terminate the first string
  return;
}
```

Although this string copy function can be shortened considerably and written more compactly, which is done in Section 9.2, the function illustrates the main features of string manipulation. The two strings are passed to `strcopy` as arrays. Each element of `string2` is then assigned to the equivalent element of `string1` until the end-of-string marker is encountered. The detection of the null character forces the termination of the `while` loop controlling the copying of elements. Since the null character is not copied from `string2` to `string1`, the last statement in `strcopy()` appends an end-of-string character to `string1`. Prior to calling `strcopy()`, the programmer must ensure that sufficient space has been allocated for the `string1` array to be able to store the elements of the `string2` array. Program 9-2 includes the `strcopy()` function in a complete program. Notice that the function prototype for `strcopy()` in `main()` declares that the function expects to receive the addresses of the beginnings of the two character arrays.

Program 9-2

```cpp
#include <iostream.h>
void main(void)
{
  char message[80];       // enough storage for a complete line
  char new_message[80];   // enough storage for a copy of message
  int i;
  void strcopy(char [], char []); // function prototype

  cout << "Enter a sentence: ";
  cin.getline(message,80);        // get the string
  strcopy(new_message,message);   // pass two array addresses
  cout << new_message << '\n';

}

void strcopy(char string1[], char string2[])   // copy string2 to string1
{
  int i = 0;                      // i will be used as a subscript

  while (string2[i] != '\0')      // check for the end-of-string
  {
    string1[i] = string2[i];      // copy the element to string1
    i++;
  }
  string1[i] = '\0';              // terminate the first string
  return;
}
```

The following is a sample run of Program 9-2:

```
Enter a sentence: How much wood could a woodchuck chuck.
How much wood could a woodchuck chuck.
```

Character-by-Character Input

Just as strings can be processed using character-by-character techniques, they can also be entered and displayed in this manner. For example, consider Program 9-3, which uses the character-input function cin.get() to accept a string one character at a time. The shaded portion of Program 9-3 essentially replaces the cin.getline() function previously used in Program 9-1.

Program 9-3

```cpp
#include <iostream.h>
void main(void)
{
  char message[80], c;

  cout << "Enter a sentence:\n";

  int i = 0;
  while(i < 80 && (c = cin.get()) != '\n')
  {
    message[i] = c;          // store the character entered
    i++;
  }
  message[i] = '\0';         // terminate the string a

  cout << "The sentence just entered is:\n";
  cout << message << '\n';
}
```

The following is a sample run of Program 9-3:

```
Enter a sentence:
This is a test input of a string of characters.
The sentence just entered is:
This is a test input of a string of characters.
```

The while statement in Program 9-3 causes characters to be read providing the number of characters entered is less than 80 and the character returned by cin.get() is not the newline character. The parentheses surrounding the expression c = cin.get() are necessary to assign the character returned by cin.get() to the variable c prior to comparing it to the newline escape sequence. Without the surrounding parentheses, the comparison operator, !=, which takes precedence over the assignment operator, causes the entire expression to be equivalent to

$$c = (cin.get() != '\n')$$

which is an invalid application of cin.get().[2]

---

[2] The equivalent statement in C is c= (getchar() != '\n'), which is a valid expression that produces an unexpected result for most beginning programmers. Here the character returned by getchar() is compared to '\n', and the value of the comparison is either 0 or 1, depending on whether or not getchar() received the newline character. This value, either 0 or 1, is then assigned to c.

Program 9-3 also illustrates a useful technique for developing functions. The shaded statements constitute a self-contained unit for entering a complete line of characters from a terminal. These statements can be removed from main() and placed together as a new function. Program 9-4 illustrates placing the shaded statements from Program 9-3 in a separate function named getaline().

Program 9-4

```
#include <iostream.h>
void main(void)
{
  char message[80];    // enough storage for a complete line
  int i;
  void getaline(char []);   // function prototype


  cout << "Enter a sentence:\n";
  getaline(message);
  cout << "The sentence just entered is:\n";
  cout << message << '\n';
}


void getaline(char strng[])
{
  int i = 0;
  char c;
  while(i < 80 && (c = cin.get()) != '\n')
  {
    strng[i] = c;        // store the character entered
    i++;
  }
  strng[i] = '\0';       // terminate the string
  return;
}
```

Exercises 9.1

1. a. The following function can be used to select and display all vowels contained within a user-input string:

```
void vowels(char strng[])
{
  int i = 0;
  char c;
  while ((c = strng[i++]) != '\0')
    switch(c)
    {
      case 'a':
      case 'e':
      case 'i':
      case 'o':
      case 'u':
        cout << c;
    } // end of switch
    cout << '\n';
}
```

Notice that the `switch` statement in `vowels()` uses the fact that selected cases "drop through" in the absence of `break` statements. Thus, all selected cases result in a `cout` object call. Include `vowels()` in a working program that accepts a user-input string and then displays all vowels in the string. In response to the input `How much is the little worth worth?`, your program should display `ouieieoo`.

b. Modify `vowels()` to count and display the total number of vowels contained in the string passed to it.

2. Modify the `vowels()` function given in Exercise 1a to count and display the individual numbers of each vowel contained in the string.

3. *a.* Write a C++ function to count the total number of characters, including blanks, contained in a string. Do not include the end-of-string marker in the count.

b. Include the function written for Exercise 3a in a complete working program.

4. Write a program that accepts a string of characters from a terminal and displays the hexadecimal equivalent of each character.

5. Write a C++ program that accepts a string of characters from a terminal and displays the string one word per line.

6. Write a function that reverses the characters in a string. (*Hint:* This can be considered as a string copy starting from the back end of the first string.)

7. Write a function called `del_char()` that can be used to delete characters from a string. The function should take three arguments: the string name, the number of characters to delete, and the starting position in the string where characters should be deleted. For example, the function call `del_char(strng,13,5)`, when applied to the string `all enthusiastic people`, should result in the string `all people`.

8. Write a function call `add_char()` to insert one string of characters into another string. The function should take three arguments: the string to be inserted, the original string, and the position in the original string where the insertion should begin. For example, the call `add_char("for all",message,6)` should insert the characters `for all` in `message` starting at `message[5]`.

9. *a.* Write a C++ function named `to_upper()` that converts lowercase letters into uppercase letters. The expression `c - 'a' + 'A'` can be used to make the conversion for any lowercase character stored in `c`.

b. Add a data input check to the function written in Exercise 9a to verify that a valid lowercase letter is passed to the function. A character in ASCII is lowercase if it is greater than or equal to a and less than or equal to z. If the character is not a valid lowercase letter, have the function `to_upper()` return the passed character unaltered.

c. Write a C++ program that accepts a string from a terminal and converts all lowercase letters in the string to uppercase letters.

10. Write a C++ program that accepts a string from a terminal and converts all uppercase letters in the string to lowercase letters.

11. Write a C++ program that counts the number of words in a string. A word is encountered whenever a transition from a blank space to a nonblank character is encountered. Assume the string contains only words separated by blank spaces.

9.2 Pointers and Library Functions

Pointers are exceptionally useful in constructing string-handling functions. When pointer notation is used in place of subscripts to access individual characters in a string, the resulting statements are both more compact and more efficient. In this section we describe the equivalence between subscripts and pointers when accessing individual characters in a string.

Consider the `strcopy()` function introduced in the previous section. This function was used to copy the characters of one string to a second string. For convenience, this function is repeated below:

```
void strcopy(char string1[], char string2[])    // copy string2 to string1
{
  int i = 0;

  while (string2[i] != '\0')     // check for the end-of-string
  {
    string1[i] = string2[i];     // copy the element to string1
    i++;
  }
  string1[i] = '\0';             // terminate the first string
  return;
}
```

The function `strcopy()` is used to copy the characters from one array to another array, one character at a time. As currently written, the subscript i in the function is used successively to reference each character in the array named `string1` by "marching along" the string one character at a time. Before we write a pointer version of `strcopy()`, we will make two modifications to the function to make it more efficient.

The `while` statement in `strcopy()` tests each character to ensure that the end of the string has not been reached. As with all relational expressions, the tested expression, string2[i] != '\0', is either true or false. Using the string this is a string illustrated in Figure 9–3 as an example, as long as string2[i] does not reference the end-of-string character the value of the expression is nonzero and is considered to be true. The expression is only false when the value of the expression is zero. This occurs when the last element in the string is accessed.

Recall that C++ defines false as zero and true as anything else. Thus, the expression string2[i] != '\0' becomes zero, or false, when the end of the string is reached. It is nonzero, or true, everywhere else. Since the null character has an internal value of zero by itself, the comparison to '\0' is not necessary.

FIGURE 9–3 The while Test Becomes False at the End of the String

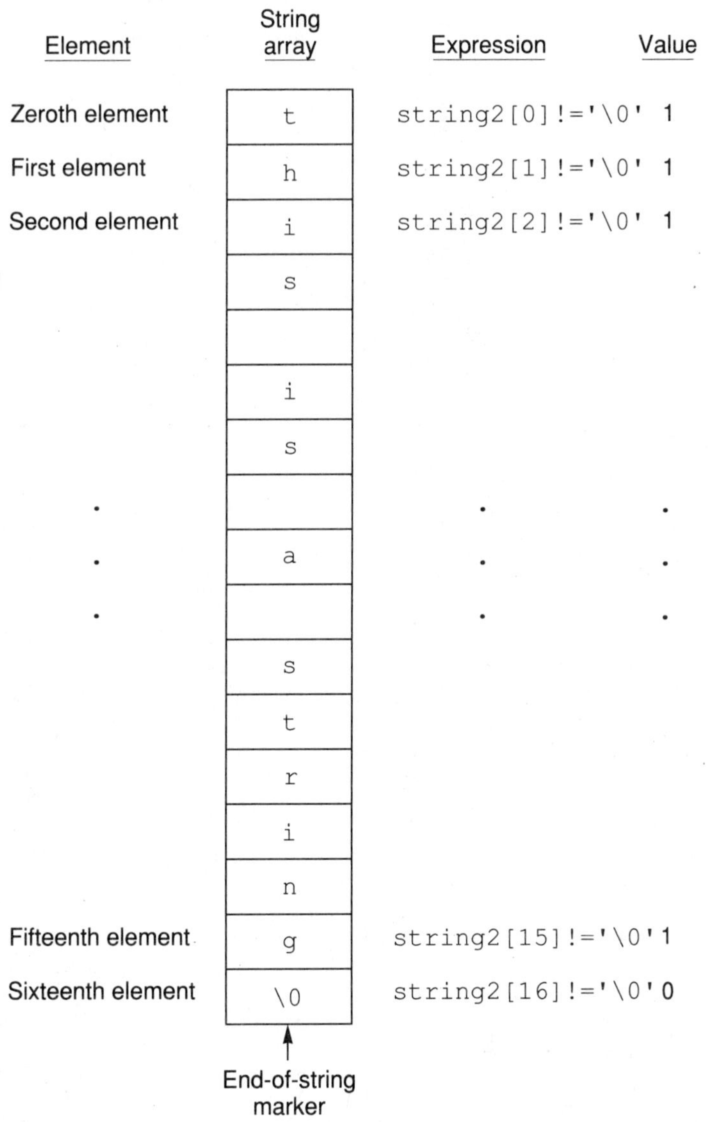

Element	String array	Expression	Value
Zeroth element	t	string2[0]!='\0'	1
First element	h	string2[1]!='\0'	1
Second element	i	string2[2]!='\0'	1
	s		
	i		
	s		
.		.	.
.	a	.	.
.		.	.
	s		
	t		
	r		
	i		
	n		
Fifteenth element	g	string2[15]!='\0'	1
Sixteenth element	\0	string2[16]!='\0'	0

End-of-string
marker

When `string2[i]` references the end-of-string character, the value of `string2[i]` is zero. When `string2[i]` references any other character, the value of `string2[i]` is the value of the code used to store the character and is nonzero. Figure 9–4 lists the ASCII codes for the string `this is a string`. As seen in the figure, each element has a nonzero value except for the null character.

Since the expression `string2[i]` is only zero at the end of a string and nonzero for every other character, the expression `while (string2[i] != '\0')` can be replaced by the simpler expression `while (string2[i])`. Although this may appear confusing at first, the revised test expression is certainly more compact than the longer version. Since end-of-string tests are frequently written by advanced C++ programmers in this shorter form, it is

FIGURE 9–4 The ASCII Codes Used to Store `this is a string`

String array	Stored codes	Expression	Value
t	116	`string2[0]`	116
h	104	`string2[1]`	104
i	105	`string2[2]`	105
s	115		
	32		
i	105		
s	115		
	32	.	.
a	97	.	.
	32	.	.
s	115		
t	116		
r	114		
i	105		
n	110		
g	103	`string2[15]`	113
\0	0	`string2[16]`	0

worthwhile being familiar with this expression. Including this expression in strcopy() results in the following version of strcopy():

```
void strcopy(char string1[], char string2[])    // copy string2 to string1
{
  int i = 0;

  while (string2[i])
  {
    string1[i] = string2[i];    // copy the element to string1
    i++;
  }
  string1[i] = '\0';            // terminate the first string
  return;
}
```

The second modification that can be made to this string copy function is to include the assignment inside the test portion of the while statement. Our new version of the string copy function is:

```
void strcopy(char string1[], char string2[])    // copy string2 to string1
{
  int i = 0;

  while (string1[i] = string2[i])
    i++;
  return;
}
```

Notice that including the assignment statement within the test part of the while statement eliminates the necessity of separately terminating the copied string with the null character. The assignment within the parentheses ensures that the null character is copied from string2 to string1. The value of the assignment expression only becomes zero after the null character is assigned to string1, at which point the while loop is terminated.

The conversion of strcopy() from subscript notation to pointer notation is now straightforward. Although each subscript version of strcopy() can be rewritten using pointer notation, the following is the equivalent of our last subscript version:

```
void strcopy(char *string1, char *string2)    // copy string2 to string1
{
  while (*string1 = *string2)
  {
    string1++;
    string2++;
  }
  return;
}
```

In both subscript and pointer versions of strcopy(), the function receives the name of the array being passed. Recall that passing an array name to a function actually passes the address of the first location of the array. In our pointer version of strcopy() the two passed addresses are stored in the pointer arguments string1 and string2, respectively.

The declarations char *string1; and char *string2; used in the pointer version of strcopy() indicate that string1 and string2 are both pointers containing the address of a character, and stress the treatment of the passed addresses as pointer values rather than array names. These declarations are equivalent to the declarations char string1[] and char string2[], respectively.

Internal to strcopy(), the pointer expression *string1, which refers to "the element whose address is in string1," replaces the equivalent subscript expression string1[i]. Similarly, the pointer expression *string2 replaces the equivalent subscript expression string2[i]. The expression *string1 = *string2 causes the element pointed to by string2 to be assigned to the element pointed to by string1. Since the starting addresses of both strings are passed to strcopy() and stored in string1 and string2, respectively, the expression *string1 initially refers to string1[0] and the expression *string2 initially refers to string2[0].

Consecutively incrementing both pointers in strcopy() with the expressions string1++ and string2++ simply causes each pointer to "point to" the next consecutive character in the respective string. As with the subscript version, the pointer version of strcopy() steps along, copying element by element, until the end of the string is copied. One final change to the string copy function can be made by including the pointer increments as postfix operators within the test part of the while statement. The final form of the string copy function is:

```
void strcopy(char *string1, char *string2)     // copy string2 to string1
{
   while (*string1++ = *string2++)
     ;
   return;
}
```

There is no ambiguity in the expression *string1++ = *string2++ even though the indirection operator, *, and the increment operator, ++, have the same precedence. Here the character pointed to is accessed before the pointer is incremented. Only after completion of the assignment *string1 = *string2 are the pointers incremented to correctly point to the next characters in the respective strings.

The string copy function included in the standard library supplied with C++ compilers is typically written exactly like our pointer version of strcopy().

Library Functions

Extensive collections of string-handling functions and routines are included with all C++ compilers. The more common of these are listed in Table 9–2.

TABLE 9–2   String and Character Library Routines

Name	Description	Required Header
strcat(string1,string2)	Concatenates `string2` to `string1`.	string.h
strchr(string,character)	Locates the position of the first occurrence of the character within the string. Returns the address of the character.	string.h
strcmp(string1,string2)	Compares `string1` to `string2`. Returns a negative integer if `string1 < string2`, 0 if `string1 == string2`, and a positive integer if `string1 > string2`.	string.h
strncmp(string1,string2,n)	Compare at most *n* characters of `string1` to `string2`. Returns the same values as `strcmp()` based on the number of characters compared.	string.h
strcpy(string1,string2)	Copies `string2` to `string1`, including the `'\0'`. Returns `string1`.	string.h
strncpy(string1,string2,n)	Copies at most *n* characters of `string2` to `string1`. If `string2` has fewer than *n* characters it will pad `string1` with `'\0'`s. Returns `string1`.	string.h
strlen(string)	Returns the length of the string.	string.h
isalpha(character)	Returns a nonzero number if the character is a letter; otherwise it returns a zero.	ctype.h
isupper(character)	Returns a nonzero number if the character is uppercase; otherwise it returns a zero.	ctype.h
islower(character)	Returns a nonzero number if the character is lowercase; otherwise it returns a zero.	ctype.h
isdigit(character)	Returns a nonzero number if the character is a digit (0 through 9); otherwise it returns a zero.	ctype.h
toupper(character)	Returns the uppercase equivalent if the character is lowercase; otherwise it returns the character unchanged.	ctype.h
tolower(character)	Returns the lowercase equivalent if the character is uppercase; otherwise it returns the character unchanged.	ctype.h
atoi(string)	Converts an ASCII string to an integer.	stdlib.h
atof(string)	Converts an ASCII string to a real.	stdlib.h
itoa(string)	Converts an integer to an ASCII string.	stdlib.h

Library functions and routines are called in the same manner that all C++ functions are called. This means that if a library function returns a value the function must be declared within your program before it is called. For example, if a library function named strngfoo() returns a pointer to a character, the calling function must be alerted that an address is being returned. Thus, the statement char *strngfoo();, which declares that strngfoo() returns the address of a character (pointer to char), must be placed either as an external declaration or directly within the calling function's variable declarations.

Before attempting to use any standard library functions, check that they are included in the C++ compiler available on your computer system. Be careful to check the type of arguments expected by the function, the data type of any returned value, and the standard header files, such as <string.h>, <ctype.h>, or <stdlib.h>, that must be included in your program to access these routines.

Exercises 9.2

1. Determine the value of *text, * (text + 3), and * (text + 10), assuming that text is an array of characters and the following has been stored in the array:

   a. now is the time
   b. rocky raccoon welcomes you
   c. Happy Holidays
   d. The good ship

2. a. The following function, convert(), "marches along" the string passed to it and sends each character in the string one at a time to the to_upper() function until the null character is encountered.

```
void convert(char strng[])      // convert a string to uppercase letters
{
  int i = 0;
  while (strng[i] != '\0')
  {
    strng[i] = to_upper(strng[i]);
    i++;
  }
  return;
}

char to_upper(char letter)  // convert a character to uppercase
{
  if( (letter >= 'a') && (letter <= 'z') )
    return (letter - 'a' + 'A');
  else
    return (letter);
}
```

The to_upper() function takes each character passed to it and first examines it to determine if the character is a lowercase letter (a lowercase letter is any character between a and z, inclusive). Assuming that characters are stored using the standard ASCII character codes, the expression `letter - 'a' + 'A'` converts a lowercase letter to its uppercase equivalent. Rewrite the `convert()` function using pointers.

b. Include the `convert()` and `to_upper()` functions in a working program. The program should prompt the user for a string and echo the string back to the user in uppercase letters.

3. Using pointers, repeat Exercise 1 from Section 9.1.

4. Using pointers, repeat Exercise 2 from Section 9.1.

5. Using pointers, repeat Exercise 3 from Section 9.1.

6. Write a function named `remove()` that returns nothing and deletes all occurrences of a character from a string. The function should take two arguments: the string name and the character to be removed. For example, if `message` contains the string `Happy Holidays`, the function call `remove(message,'H')` should place the string `appy olidays` into `message`.

7. Using pointers, repeat Exercise 6 from Section 9.1.

8. Write a program using the `cin.get()`, `toupper()`, and `cout()` library routines to echo back each entered letter in its uppercase form. The program should terminate when the digit 1 key is pressed.

9. Write a function that uses pointers to add a single character at the end of an existing string. The function should replace the existing `\0` character with the new character and append a new `\0` at the end of the string. The function returns nothing.

10. Write a function that uses pointers to delete a single character from the end of a string. This is effectively achieved by moving the `\0` character one position closer to the start of the string. The function returns nothing.

11. Determine the string-handling functions that are available with your C++ compiler. For each available function list the data types of the arguments expected by the function and the data type of any returned value.

12. Write a function named `trimfrnt()` that deletes all leading blanks from a string. Write the function using pointers. The function returns nothing.

13. Write a function named `trimrear()` that deletes all trailing blanks from a string. Write the function using pointers. The function returns nothing.

14. Write a function named `strlen()` that returns the number of characters in a string. Do not include the `\0` character in the returned count.

9.3 String Definitions and Pointer Arrays

The definition of a string automatically involves a pointer. For example, the definition `char message1[80];` both reserves storage for 80 characters and automatically creates a pointer constant, `message1`, that contains the address of `message1[0]`. As a pointer constant, the address associated with the pointer cannot be changed—it must always "point to" the beginning of the created array.

Instead of creating a string as an array, however, it is also possible to create a string using a pointer. For example, the definition `char *message2;` creates a pointer to a character. In this case, `message2` is a true pointer variable. Once a pointer to a character is defined, assignment statements, such as `message2 = "this is a string";`, can be made. In this assignment, `message2`, which is a pointer, receives the address of the first character in the string.

The main difference in the definitions of `message1` as an array and `message2` as a pointer is the way the pointer is created. Defining `message1` using the declaration `char message1[80]` explicitly calls for a fixed amount of storage for the array. This causes the compiler to create a pointer constant. Defining `message2` using the declaration `char *message2` explicitly creates a pointer variable first. This pointer is then used to hold the address of a string when the string is actually specified. This difference in definitions has both storage and programming consequences.

From a programming perspective, defining `message2` as a pointer to a character allows string assignments, such as `message2 = "this is a string";`, to be made within a program. Similar assignments are not allowed for strings defined as arrays. Thus, the statement `message1 = "this is a string";` is not valid. Both definitions, however, allow initializations to be made using a string assignment. For example, both of the following initializations are valid:

```
char message1[81] = "this is a string";
char *message2 = "this is a string";
```

From a storage perspective, the allocation of space for `message1` and `message2` is quite different. As illustrated in Figure 9–5, both initializations cause the computer to store the same string internally. In the case of `message1`, a specific set of 81 storage locations is reserved and the first 17 locations are initialized. For `message1`, different strings can be stored, but each string will overwrite the previously stored characters. The same is not true for `message2`.

The definition of `message2` reserves enough storage for one pointer. The initialization then causes the string to be stored in memory and the address of the string's first character, in this case the address of the `t`, to be loaded into the pointer. If a later assignment is made to `message2`, the initial string remains in memory and new storage locations are allocated to the new string. For example, consider the sequence of instructions

```
char *message2 = "this is a string";
message2 = "a new message";
```

The first statement defines `message2` as a pointer variable, stores the initialization string in memory, and loads the starting address of the string (the address of the `t` in `this`) into `message2`. The next assignment statement causes

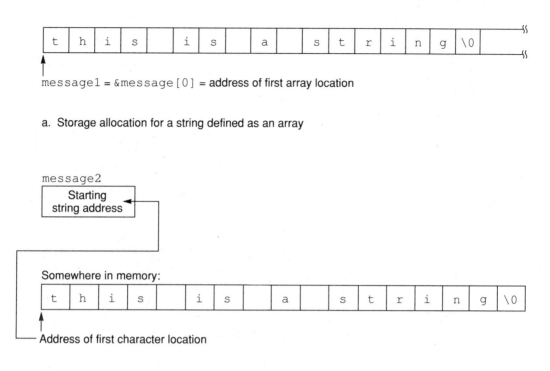

a. Storage allocation for a string defined as an array

b. Storage of a string using a pointer

FIGURE 9–5 String Storage Allocation

the computer to store the second string and change the address in message2 to point to the starting location of this new string.

It is important to realize that the second string assigned to message2 does not overwrite the first string, but simply changes the address in message2 to point to the new string. As illustrated in Figure 9–6, both strings are stored inside the computer. Any additional string assignment to message2 would result in the additional storage of the new string and a corresponding change in the address stored in message2. Doing so also means that we no longer have access to the original memory location.

Pointer Arrays

The declaration of an array of character pointers is an extremely useful extension to single string pointer declarations. For example, the declaration

```
char *seasons[4];
```

creates an array of four elements, where each element is a pointer to a character. As individual pointers, each pointer can be assigned to point to a string using string assignment statements. Thus, the statements

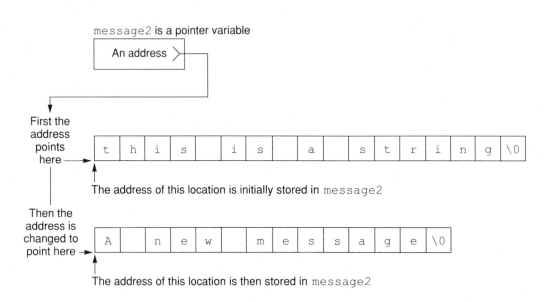

First the
address
points
here

The address of this location is initially stored in message2

Then the
address is
changed to
point here

The address of this location is then stored in message2

FIGURE 9–6 Storage Allocation for Figure 9-5

```
seasons[0] = "Winter";
seasons[1] = "Spring";
seasons[2] = "Summer";
seasons[3] = "Fall";   // note: string lengths may differ
```

set appropriate addresses into the respective pointers. Figure 9–7 illustrates the addresses loaded into the pointers for these assignments.

As illustrated in Figure 9–7, the seasons array does not contain the actual strings assigned to the pointers. These strings are stored elsewhere in the computer in the normal data area allocated to the program. The array of pointers contains only the addresses of the starting location for each string.

FIGURE 9–7 The Addresses Contained in the seasons[] Pointers

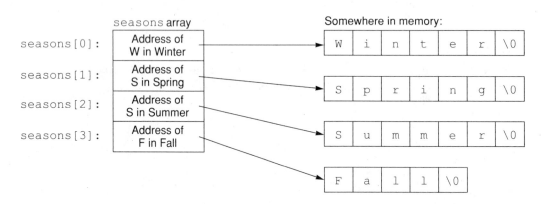

The initializations of the `seasons` array can also be incorporated directly within the definition of the array, as follows:

```
char *seasons[4] = {"Winter",
                    "Spring",
                    "Summer",
                    "Fall"};
```

This declaration both creates an array of pointers and initializes the pointers with appropriate addresses. Once addresses have been assigned to the pointers, each pointer can be used to access its corresponding string. Program 9-5 uses the `seasons` array to display each season using a `for` loop.

 Program 9-5

```
#include <iostream.h>
void main(void)
{
  int n;
  char *seasons[] = {"Winter",
                     "Spring",
                     "Summer",
                     "Fall"};


  for( n = 0; n < 4; n++)
  cout << "\nThe season is " << seasons[n];
}
```

The output obtained for Program 9-5 is:

```
The season is Winter
The season is Spring
The season is Summer
The season is Fall
```

The advantage of using a list of pointers is that logical groups of data headings can be collected and accessed with one array name. For example, the months in a year can be collectively grouped in one array called `months`, and the days in a week collectively grouped in an array called `days`. The grouping of like headings allows the programmer to access and print an appropriate heading by simply specifying the correct position of the heading in the array. Program 9-6 uses the `seasons` array to correctly identify and display the season corresponding to a user-input month.

Program 9-6

```
#include <iostream.h>
void main(void)
{
  int n;
  char *seasons[] = {"Winter",
                     "Spring",
                     "Summer",
                     "Fall"};

  cout << "\nEnter a month (use 1 for Jan., 2 for Feb., etc.): ";
  cin >> n;
  n = (n % 12) / 3;    // create the correct subscript
  cout << "The month entered is a "<< seasons[n] << " month.";
}
```

Except for the expression n = (n % 12) / 3, Program 9-6 is rather straightforward. The program requests the user to input a month and accepts the number corresponding to the month using a cin object call.

The expression n = (n % 12) / 3 uses a common program "trick" to scale a set of numbers into a more useful set. Using subscripts, the four elements of the seasons array must be accessed using a subscript from 0 through 3. Thus, the months of the year, which correspond to the numbers 1 through 12, must be adjusted to correspond to the correct season subscript. This is done using the expression n = (n % 12) / 3. The expression n % 12 adjusts the month entered to lie within the range 0 through 11, with 0 corresponding to December, 1 for January, and so on. Dividing by 3 causes the resulting number to range between 0 and 3, corresponding to the possible seasons elements. The result of the division by 3 is assigned to the integer variable n. The months 0, 1, and 2, when divided by 3, are set to 0; the months 3, 4, and 5 are set to 1; the months 6, 7, and 8 are set to 2; and the months 9, 10, and 11 are set to 3. This is equivalent to the following assignments:

Months	Season
December, January, February	Winter
March, April, May	Spring
June, July, August	Summer
September, October, November	Fall

The following is a sample output obtained for Program 9-6:

```
Enter a month (use 1 for Jan., 2 for Feb., etc.): 12
The month entered is a Winter month.
```

Exercises 9.3

1. Write two declaration statements that can be used in place of the declaration `char text[] = "Hooray!";`.

2. Determine the value of `*text`, `*(text + 3)`, and `*(text + 7)` for each of the following sections of code:

    a. `char *text;`
        `char message[] = "the check is in the mail";`
        `text = message;`
    b. `char *text;`
        `char formal[] = {'t','h','i','s',' ','i','s',' ','a','n',' ',`
                      `'i','n','v','i','t','a','t','i','o','n','\0'};`
        `text = &formal[0];`
    c. `char *test;`
        `char more[] = "Happy Holidays";`
        `text = &more[4];`
    d. `char *text, *second;`
        `char blip[] = "The good ship";`
        `second = blip;`
        `text = ++second;`

3. Determine the error in the following program:

```
#include <iostream.h>
void main(void)
{
  int i = 0;
  char message[] = {'H','e','l','l','o','\0'};

  for( ; i < 5; i++)
  {
    cout << *message;
    ++message;
  }
}
```

4. *a.* Write a C++ function that displays the day of the week corresponding to a user-entered input number between 1 and 7. That is, in response to an input of 2, the program displays the name Monday. Use an array of pointers in the function.
    b. Include the function written for Exercise 4a in a complete working program.

5. Modify the function written in Exercise 4a so that the function returns the address of the character string containing the proper day to be displayed.

6. Write a function that will accept ten lines of user-input text and store the entered lines as ten individual strings. Use a pointer array in your function.

9.4 Common Programming Errors

Three errors are frequently made when pointers to strings are used. The most common is using the pointer to "point to" a nonexistent data element. This error is, of course, the same error we have already seen using subscripts. Since C++ compilers do not perform bounds checking on arrays, it is the programmer's responsibility to ensure that the address in the pointer is the address of a valid data element.

The second common error lies in not providing sufficient space for the string to be stored. A simple variation of this is not providing space for the end-of-string null character when a string is defined as an array of characters, and not including the \0 character when the array is initialized. A more complicated variation of this error is declaring a character pointer, such as `char *p`, and then attempting to copy a string with a statement such as `strcpy(p,"Hello")`. Since no space has been allocated for the string, the string will overwrite the memory area pointed to by `p`.

The last commonly encountered error relates to a misunderstanding of terminology. For example, if text is defined as

```
char *text;
```

the variable `text` is sometimes referred to as a string. Thus, the terminology "store the characters `Hooray for the Hoosiers` into the `text` string" may be encountered. Strictly speaking, calling `text` a string or a string variable is incorrect. The variable `text` is a pointer that contains the address of the first character in the string. Nevertheless, referring to a character pointer as a string occurs frequently enough that you should be aware of it.

9.5 Chapter Summary

1. A string is an array of characters that is terminated by the null character.
2. Strings can always be processed using standard array-processing techniques. The input and display of a string, however, always require reliance on a standard library function.
3. The `cin`, `cin.get()`, and `cin.getline()` routines can be used to input a string. The `cin` object tends to be of limited usefulness for string input because it terminates input when a blank is encountered.
4. The `cout` object can be used to display strings.
5. In place of subscripts, pointer notation and pointer arithmetic are especially useful for manipulating string elements.
6. Many standard library functions exist for processing strings as a complete unit. Internally, these functions manipulate strings in a character-by-character manner, usually using pointers.
7. String storage can be created by declaring an array of characters. It can also be created by declaring and initializing a pointer to a character.

8. Arrays can be initialized using a string assignment of the form

```
char *arr_name[ ] = "text";
```

This initialization is equivalent to

```
char *arr_name[ ] = {'t','e','x','t','\0'};
```

9. A pointer to a character can be assigned a string. String assignment to an array of characters is invalid except for initialization within a declaration statement.

Records as Data Structures

Chapter Ten

In its broadest sense, a structure refers to the way individual elements of a group are arranged and how communication between the elements is to be conducted. For example, a corporation's structure determines how the people and departments in the company are organized and establishes the accepted means of communication between these groups. In its broadest programming form, a structure has a similar meaning: It refers to the way individual data items are arranged to form a cohesive and related unit and establishes the accepted means of communicating and operating with these data items.

A simpler form of structure, and the one presented in this chapter, is a record. A record defines the way individual data items are arranged into a single unit without defining the operations that can be performed on the individual data items. In Chapter 11 we present a more inclusive structure that specifies operations in addition to data and explicitly defines how users can communicate with the data elements.

To make the discussion more tangible, consider the data items typically used in preparing mailing labels, as illustrated in Figure 10–1.

Each of the individual data items listed in the figure is an entity by itself. Taken together, all the data items form a single unit representing a natural organization of the data for a mailing label. This larger grouping of related individual items is a specific example of a record, which in C++ is created as a data structure.

Although there could be thousands of names and addresses in a complete mailing list, the form of each mailing label, or its structure, is identical. In dealing with a data structure it is important to distinguish between the form and the content of the structure.

The form of a data structure consists of the symbolic names, data types, and arrangement of individual data items in the structure. The content of a structure refers to the actual data stored in the symbolic names. Figure 10–2 shows acceptable contents for the structure illustrated in Figure 10–1.

Let us now see how to create, fill, and use data structures.

FIGURE 10–1 Typical Mailing List Components

Name:
Street Address:
City:
State:
Zip Code:

FIGURE 10–2 The Contents of a Structure

Rhona Bronson-Karp
614 Freeman Street
Orange
NJ
07052

10.1 Single Structures

A structure is defined and used in the same manner as any other C++ data
type: It must first be declared and then have specific values assigned to the
individual structure elements. Declaring a structure requires listing the data
types, data names, and arrangement of data items. For example, the definition

```
struct
{
    int month;
    int day;
    int year;
}  birth;
```

gives the form of a structure variable called `birth` and reserves storage for the
individual data items listed in the structure. The `birth` structure variable
consists of three data items, which are called members of the structure.

   Assigning actual data values to the data items of a structure variable is called
populating the structure, and is a relatively straightforward procedure. Each member of a structure is accessed by giving both the structure name and individual
data item name, connected by a period. Thus, `birth.month` refers to the first
member of the `birth` structure, `birth.day` refers to the second member of the
structure, and `birth.year` refers to the third member. Program 10-1 illustrates
assigning values to the individual members of the birth structure variable.

 Program 10-1

```
// a program that defines and populates a data structure
#include <iostream.h>
void main(void)
{
  struct
  {
    int month;
    int day;
    int year;
  } birth;

  birth.month = 12;
  birth.day = 28;
  birth.year = 72;

  cout << "My birth date is " << birth.month << '/'
                              << birth.day   << '/'
                              << birth.year  << '\n';
}
```

The output produced by Program 10-1 is:

My birth date is 12/28/72

As in most C++ statements, the spacing of a structure definition is not rigid. For example, the `birth` structure could just as well have been defined

    struct {int month; int day; int year;} birth;

Also, as with all C++ definition statements, multiple variables can be defined in the same statement. For example, the definition statement

    struct {int month; int day; int year;} birth, current;

creates two structure variables having the same form. The members of the first structure are referenced by the individual names `birth.month`, `birth.day`, and `birth.year`, while the members of the second structure are referenced by the names `current.month`, `current.day`, and `current.year`. Notice that the form of this particular structure definition statement is identical to the form used in defining any program variable: The data type is followed by a list of variable names.

A useful and commonly used modification for defining structure types is listing the form of the structure with no following variable names. In this case, however, the list of structure members must be preceded by a user-selected data type name. For example, in the declaration

    struct Date
    {
        int month;
        int day;
        int year;
    };

the term `Date` is a structure type name: It defines a new type of data that is a data structure of the declared form.* By convention the first letter of a user-selected data type name is uppercase, as in the name `Date`, which helps to identify them when they are used in subsequent definition statements. Here, the declaration for the `Date` structure creates a new data type without actually reserving any storage locations. As such it is not a definition statement. It simply declares a `Date` structure type and describes how individual data items are arranged within the structure. Actual storage for the members of the structure is reserved only when specific variable names are assigned. For example, the definition statement

    Date birth, current;

---

* It is worth noting that this same declaration in C does not create a new data type.

reserves storage for two Date structure variables named birth and current, respectively. Each of these individual structures has the form previously declared for the Date structure.

The declaration of a structure data type, like all declarations, may be global or local. Program 10-2 illustrates the global declaration of a Date data type. Internal to main(), the variable birth is defined as a local variable of Date type.

Program 10-2

```
#include <iostream.h>
struct Date
{
   int month;
   int day;
   int year;
};
void main(void)
{
   Date birth;

   birth.month = 12;
   birth.day = 28;
   birth.year = 72;

   cout << "My birth date is " << birth.month << '/'
                               << birth.day   << '/'
                               << birth.year  << '\n';

}
```

The output produced by Program 10-2 is identical to the output produced by Program 10-1.

The initialization of structures follows the same rules as for the initialization of arrays: Global and local structures may be initialized by following the definition with a list of initializers. For example, the definition statement

```
Date birth = {12, 28, 72};
```

can be used to replace the first four statements internal to main() in Program 10-2. Notice that the initializers are separated by commas, not semicolons.

The individual members of a structure are not restricted to integer data types, as illustrated by the Date structure. Any valid C++ data type can be used. For example, consider an employee record consisting of the following data items:

Name:
Identification Number:
Regular Pay Rate:
Overtime Pay Rate:

A suitable declaration for these data items is:

```
struct Pay_rec
{
  char name[20];
  int id_num;
  float reg_rate;
  float ot_rate;
};
```

Once the `Pay_rec` data type is declared, a specific structure variable using this type can be defined and initialized. For example, the definition

```
Pay_rec employee = {"H. Price",12387,15.89,25.50};
```

creates a structure named `employee` of the `Pay-rec` data type. The individual members of `employee` are initialized with the respective data listed between braces in the definition statement.

Notice that a single structure is simply a convenient method for combining and storing related items under a common name. Although a single structure is useful in explicitly identifying the relationship among its members, the individual members could be defined as separate variables. One of the real advantages to using structures is only realized when the same data type is used in a list many times over. Creating lists with the same data type is the topic of the next section.

Before leaving single structures, it is worth noting that the individual members of a structure can be any valid C++ data type, including both arrays and structures. An array of characters was used as a member of the `employee` structure defined previously. Accessing an element of a member array requires giving the structure's name, followed by a period, followed by the array designation. For example, `employee.name[4]` refers to the fifth character in the `employee.name` array.

Including a structure within a structure follows the same rules for including any data type in a structure. For example, assume that a structure is to consist of a name and a date of birth, where a `Date` structure has been declared as:

```
struct Date
{
  int month;
  int date;
  int year;
};
```

A suitable definition of a structure that includes a name and a `Date` structure is:

```
struct
{
    char name[20];
    Date birth;
} person;
```

Notice that in declaring the `Date` structure, the term `Date` is a data type name; thus it appears before the braces in the declaration statement. In defining the `person` structure variable, `person` is a variable name; thus, it is the name of a specific structure. The same is true of the variable named `birth`. This is the name of a specific `Date` structure. Individual members in the `person` structure are accessed by preceding the desired member with the structure name followed by a period. For example, `person.birth.month` refers to the `month` variable in the `birth` structure contained in the `person` structure.

Exercises 10.1

1. Declare a structure data type named `s_temp` for each of the following records:
   a. a student record consisting of a student identification number, number of credits completed, and cumulative grade point average
   b. a student record consisting of a student's name, date of birth, number of credits completed, and cumulative grade point average
   c. a mailing list consisting of the items previously illustrated in Figure 10–1
   d. a stock record consisting of the stock's name, the price of the stock, and the date of purchase
   e. an inventory record consisting of an integer part number, part description, number of parts in inventory, and an integer reorder number

2. For the individual data types declared in Exercise 1, define a suitable structure variable name, and initialize each structure with the appropriate following data:
   a. Identification Number: 4672
      Number of Credits Completed: 68
      Grade Point Average: 3.01
   b. Name: Rhona Karp
      Date of Birth: 8/4/60
      Number of Credits Completed: 96
      Grade Point Average: 3.89
   c. Name: Kay Kingsley
      Street Address: 614 Freeman Street
      City: Indianapolis
      State: IN
      Zip Code: 07030
   d. Stock: IBM
      Price Purchased: 134.5
      Date Purchased: 10/1/86

e. Part Number: 16879
Description: Battery
Number in Stock: 10
Reorder Number: 3

3. *a.* Write a C++ program that prompts a user to input the current month, day, and year. Store the data entered in a suitably defined structure and display the date in an appropriate manner.

b. Modify the program written in Exercise 3a to accept the current time in hours, minutes, and seconds.

4. Write a C++ program that uses a structure for storing the name of a stock, its estimated earnings per share, and its estimated price-to-earnings ratio. Have the program prompt the user to enter these items for five different stocks, each time using the same structure to store the entered data. When the data has been entered for a particular stock, have the program compute and display the anticipated stock price based on the entered earnings and price-per-earnings values. For example, if a user entered the data XYZ 1.56 12, the anticipated price for a share of XYZ stock is (1.56)*(12) = $18.72.

5. Write a C++ program that accepts a user-entered time in hours and minutes. Have the program calculate and display the time one minute later.

6. *a.* Write a C++ program that accepts a user-entered date. Have the program calculate and display the date of the next day. For purposes of this exercise, assume that all months consist of 30 days.

b. Modify the program written in Exercise 6a to account for the actual number of days in each month.

10.2 Arrays of Structures

The real power of structures is realized when the same structure is used for lists of data. For example, assume that the data shown in Figure 10–3 must be processed.

FIGURE 10–3 A List of Employee Data

Employee Number	Employee Name	Employee Pay Rate
32479	Abrams, B.	6.72
33623	Bohm, P.	7.54
34145	Donaldson, S.	5.56
35987	Ernst, T.	5.43
36203	Gwodz, K.	8.72
36417	Hanson, H.	7.64
37634	Monroe, G.	5.29
38321	Price, S.	9.67
39435	Robbins, L.	8.50
39567	Williams, B.	7.20

Clearly, the employee numbers can be stored together in an array of integers, the names in an array of pointers, and the pay rates in an array of either floating point or double precision numbers. In organizing the data in this fashion, each column in Figure 10–3 is considered as a separate list, which is stored in its own array. The correspondence between items for each individual employee is maintained by storing an employee's data in the same array position in each array.

The separation of the complete list into three individual arrays is unfortunate, since all of the items relating to a single employee constitute a natural organization of data into records, as illustrated in Figure 10–4.

Using a structure, the integrity of the data organization as a record can be maintained and reflected by the program. Under this approach, the list illustrated in Figure 10–4 can be processed as a single array of ten structures.

Declaring an array of structures is the same as declaring an array of any other variable type. For example, if the data type `Pay_rec` is declared as

```
struct Pay_rec {int idnum; char name[20]; float rate;};
```

then an array of ten such structures can be defined as

```
Pay_rec employee[10];
```

This definition statement constructs an array of ten elements, each of which is a structure of the data type `Pay_rec`. Notice that the creation of an array of ten structures has the same form as the creation of any other array. For example, creating an array of ten integers named `employee` requires the declaration

```
int employee[10];
```

In this declaration the data type is integer, while in the former declaration for `employee` the data type is `Pay_rec`.

FIGURE 10–4 A List of Records

	Employee Number	Employee Name	Employee Pay Rate
1st record ⟶	32479	Abrams, B.	6.72
2nd record ⟶	33623	Bohm, P.	7.54
3rd record ⟶	34145	Donaldson, S.	5.56
4th record ⟶	35987	Ernst, T.	5.43
5th record ⟶	36203	Gwodz, K.	8.72
6th record ⟶	36417	Hanson, H.	7.64
7th record ⟶	37634	Monroe, G.	5.29
8th record ⟶	38321	Price, S.	9.67
9th record ⟶	39435	Robbins, L.	8.50
10th record ⟶	39567	Williams, B.	7.20

Once an array of structures is declared, a particular data item is referenced by giving the position of the desired structure in the array followed by a period and the appropriate structure member. For example, the variable employee[0].rate references the rate member of the first employee structure in the employee array. Including structures as elements of an array permits a list of records to be processed using standard array programming techniques. Program 10-3 displays the first five employee records illustrated in Figure 10–4.

Program 10-3

```
#include <iostream.h>
#include <iomanip.h>
struct Pay_rec
{
  long id;
  char name[20];
  float rate;
};         // construct a global template
void main(void)
{
  int i;
  Pay_rec employee[5] = {
                         { 32479, "Abrams, B.", 6.72 },
                         { 33623, "Bohm, P.", 7.54},
                         { 34145, "Donaldson, S.",  5.56},
                         { 35987, "Ernst, T.", 5.43 },
                         { 36203, "Gwodz, K.", 8.72 }
                         };

  cout << '\n';   // start on a new line
  for ( i = 0; i < 5; ++i)
    cout << setiosflags(ios::left) << setw(7)  << employee[i].id
                       << setw(15) << employee[i].name
                       << setw(6)  << employee[i].rate << '\n';
}
```

The output displayed by Program 10-3 is:

```
32479   Abrams, B.      6.72
33623   Bohm, P.        7.54
34145   Donaldson, S.   5.56
35987   Ernst, T.       5.43
36203   Gwodz, K.       8.72
```

In reviewing Program 10-3, notice the initialization of the array of structures. Although the initializers for each structure have been enclosed in inner braces, these are not strictly necessary because all members have been initialized. As with all external and static variables, in the absence of explicit initializers, the numeric elements of both static and external arrays or structures are initialized to zero and their character elements are initialized to nulls. The `setiosflags(ios::left)` manipulator included in the `cout` object call forces each name to be displayed left justified in its designated field width.

Exercises 10.2

1. Define arrays of 100 structures for each of the data types described in Exercise 1 of the previous section.

2. a. Using the data type

```
struct Mon_days
{
  char name[10];
  int days;
};
```

define an array of 12 structures of type `Mon_days`. Name the array `convert[]`, and initialize the array with the names of the 12 months in a year and the number of days in each month.

b. Include the array created in Exercise 2a in a program that displays the names and number of days in each month.

3. Using the data type declared in Exercise 2a, write a C++ program that accepts a month from a user in numerical form and displays the name of the month and the number of days in the month. Thus, in response to an input of 3, the program would display `March has 31 days.`

4. a. Declare a single structure data type suitable for an employee record of the type illustrated below:

Number	Name	Rate	Hours
3462	Jones	4.62	40
6793	Robbins	5.83	38
6985	Smith	5.22	45
7834	Swain	6.89	40
8867	Timmins	6.43	35
9002	Williams	4.75	42

b. Using the data type declared in Exercise 4a, write a C++ program that interactively accepts the above data into an array of six structures. Once the data have been entered, the program should create a payroll report listing each employee's name, number, and gross pay. Include the total gross pay of all employees at the end of the report.

5. a. Declare a single structure data type suitable for a car record of the type illustrated:

Car Number	Miles Driven	Gallons Used
25	1,450	62
36	3,240	136
44	1,792	76
52	2,360	105
68	2,114	67

b. Using the data type declared for Exercise 5a, write a C++ program that interactively accepts the above data into an array of five structures. Once the data have been entered, the program should create a report listing each car number and the miles per gallon achieved by the car. At the end of the report include the average miles per gallon achieved by the complete fleet of cars.

10.3 Passing and Returning Structures

Individual structure members may be passed to a function in the same manner as any scalar variable. For example, given the structure definition

```
struct
{
   int id_num;
   double pay_rate;
   double hours;
} emp;
```

the statement

```
display(emp.id_num);
```

passes a copy of the structure member `emp.id_num` to a function named `display()`. Similarly, the statement

```
calc_pay(emp.pay_rate,emp.hours);
```

passes copies of the values stored in structure members `emp.pay_rate` and `emp.hours` to the function `calc_pay()`. Both functions, `display()` and `calc_pay`, must declare the correct data types of their respective arguments.

Complete copies of all members of a structure can also be passed to a function by including the name of the structure as an argument to the called function. For example, the function call

```
calc_net(emp);
```

passes a copy of the complete `emp` structure to `calc_net()`. Internal to `calc_net()`, an appropriate declaration must be made to receive the structure. Program 10-4 declares a global data type for an employee record. This type is then used by both the `main()` and `calc_net()` functions to define specific structures with the names `emp` and `temp`, respectively.

Program 10-4

```
#include <iostream.h>
#include <iomanip.h>
struct Employee        // declare a global type
{
  int id_num;
  double pay_rate;
  double hours;
};
double calc_net(Employee);   // function prototype

void main(void)
{
  Employee emp = {6782, 8.93, 40.5};
  double net_pay;

  net_pay = calc_net(emp);       // pass copies of the values in emp
  cout << "The net pay for employee " << emp.id_num
       << " is $" << setiosflags(ios::showpoint)
       << setiosflags(ios::left) << setw(10)
       << setprecision(2) << net_pay;
}

double calc_net(Employee temp) // temp is of data type Employee
{
  return(temp.pay_rate * temp.hours);
}
```

The output produced by Program 10-4 is:

```
The net pay for employee 6782 is $361.66
```

In reviewing Program 10-4, observe that both `main()` and `calc_net()` use the same data type to define their individual structure variables. The structure variable defined in `main()` and the structure variable defined in `calc_net()` are two completely different structures. Any changes made to the local `temp` variable in `calc_net()` are not reflected in the `emp` variable of `main()`. In fact, since both structure variables are local to their respective functions, the same structure variable name could have been used in both functions with no ambiguity.

When `calc_net()` is called by `main()`, copies of `emp`'s structure values are passed to the `temp` structure. `calc_net()` then uses two of the passed member values to calculate a number, which is returned to `main()`. Since `calc_net()` returns a noninteger number, the data type of the value returned must be included in all declarations for `calc_net()`.

An alternative to passing a copy of a structure is to pass a reference to the structure. For example, referring to Program 10-4, the prototype of `calc_net()` can be modified to

```
double calc_net(Employee &);
```

If this function prototype is used and the `calc_net()` function is rewritten to conform to it, the `main()` function in Program 10-4 may be used as is. Program 10-4a illustrates these changes in a complete program.

 Program 10-4a

```
#include <iostream.h>
#include <iomanip.h>
struct Employee          // declare a global type
{
  int id_num;
  double pay_rate;
  double hours;
};
double calc_net(Employee &);    // function prototype

void main(void)
{
  Employee emp = {6782, 8.93, 40.5};
  double net_pay;

  net_pay = calc_net(emp);        // pass a reference
  cout << "The net pay for employee " << emp.id_num
       << " is $" << setiosflags(ios::showpoint)
       << setiosflags(ios::left) << setw(10)
       << setprecision(2) << net_pay;
}

double calc_net(Employee &temp)    // temp is a reference variable
{
  return(temp.pay_rate * temp.hours);
}
```

Program 10-4a produces the same output as Program 10-4, except that the `calc_net()` function in Program 10-4a receives direct access to the `emp` structure rather than a copy of it. This means that the variable name `temp` within `calc_net()` is an alternate name for the variable `emp` in `main()`, and any changes to `temp` are direct changes to `emp`. Although the same function call, `calc_net(emp)`, is made in both programs, the call in Program 10-4a passes a reference while the call in Program 10-4 passes values.

Passing a Pointer

In place of passing a reference, a pointer can be used. Using a pointer requires, in addition to modifying the function's prototype and header line, that the call to `calc_net()` in Program 10-4 be modified to

`calc_net(&emp);`

Here the function call clearly indicates that an address is being passed (which is not the case in Program 10-4a). The disadvantage, however, is in the dereferencing notation required internal to the function. However, as pointers are widely used in practice, it is worthwhile to become familiar with the notation used.

To correctly store the passed address `calc_net()` must declare its argument as a pointer. A suitable function definition for `calc_net()` is:

`calc_net(Employee *pt)`

Here, the declaration for `pt` declares this argument as a pointer to a structure of type `Employee`. The pointer variable, `pt`, receives the starting address of a structure whenever `calc_net()` is called. Within `calc_net()`, this pointer is used to directly reference any member in the structure. For example, `(*pt).id_num` refers to the `id_num` member of the structure, `(*pt).pay_rate` refers to the `pay_rate` member of the structure, and `(*pt).hours` refers to the `hours` member of the structure. These relationships are illustrated in Figure 10-5.

The parentheses around the expression `*pt` in Figure 10-5 are necessary to initially access "the structure whose address is in `pt`." This is followed by a reference to access the desired member within the structure. In the absence of the parentheses, the structure member operator `.` takes precedence over the indirection operator. Thus, the expression `*pt.hours` is another way of writing `*(pt.hours)`, which would refer to "the variable whose address is in the `pt.hours` variable." This last expression clearly makes no sense because there is no structure named `pt` and `hours` does not contain an address.

As illustrated in Figure 10-5, the starting address of the `emp` structure is also the address of the first member of the structure.

The use of pointers in this manner is so common that a special notation exists for it. The general expression `(*pointer).member` can always be replaced with the notation `pointer->member`, where the `->` operator is constructed using a minus sign followed by a right-facing arrow (greater-than

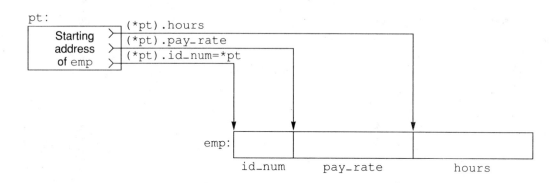

FIGURE 10–5 A Pointer Can Be Used to Access Structure Members

symbol). Either expression can be used to locate the desired member. For example, the following expressions are equivalent:

(*pt).id_num	can be replaced by	pt->id_num
(*pt).pay_rate	can be replaced by	pt->pay_rate
(*pt).hours	can be replaced by	pt->hours

Program 10-5 illustrates passing a structure's address and using a pointer with the new notation to directly reference the structure.

Program 10-5

```cpp
#include <iostream.h>
#include <iomanip.h>
struct Employee    // declare a global type
{
  int id_num;
  double pay_rate;
  double hours;
};
double calc_net(Employee *);    //function prototype

void main(void)
{
  Employee emp = {6782, 8.93, 40.5};
  double net_pay;

  net_pay = calc_net(&emp);        // pass an address
  cout << "The net pay for employee " << emp.id_num
       << " is $" << setiosflags(ios::showpoint)
       << setiosflags(ios::left) << setw(10)
       << setprecision(2) << net_pay;
}

double calc_net(Employee *pt)    // pt is a pointer to a
{                                // structure of Employee type
  return(pt->pay_rate * pt->hours);
}
```

The name of the pointer argument declared in Program 10-5 is, of course, selected by the programmer. When `calc_net()` is called, emp's starting address is passed to the function. Using this address as a reference point, individual members of the structure are accessed by including their names with the pointer.

As with all C++ expressions that access a variable, the increment and decrement operators can also be applied to them. For example, the expression

$$++pt->hours$$

adds one to the `hours` member of the `emp` structure. Since the `->` operator has a higher priority than the increment operator, the `hours` member is accessed first and then the increment is applied.

Alternatively, the expression `(++pt)->hours` uses the prefix increment operator to increment the address in `pt` before the `hours` member is accessed. Similarly, the expression `(pt++)->hours` uses the postfix increment operator to increment the address in `pt` after the `hours` member is accessed. In both of these cases, however, there must be sufficient defined structures to ensure that the incremented pointers actually point to legitimate structures.

As an example, Figure 10–6 illustrates an array of three structures of type `Employee`. Assuming that the address of `emp[1]` is stored in the pointer variable `pt`, the expression `++pt` changes the address in `pt` to the starting address of `emp[2]`, while the expression `--pt` changes the address to point to `emp[0]`.

Returning Structures

In practice, most structure-handling functions receive direct access to a structure by receiving a structure reference. Then any changes to the structure can be made directly from within the function. If you want to have a function return a separate structure, however, you must follow the same procedures for return-

FIGURE 10–6 Changing Pointer Addresses

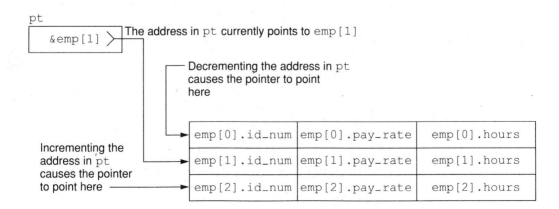

ing complete data structures as for returning scalar values. These procedures include declaring the function appropriately and alerting any calling function to the type of data structure being returned. For example, the function `get_vals()` in Program 10-6 returns a complete structure to `main()`.

Program 10-6

```
#include <iostream.h>
#include <iomanip.h>
struct Employee        // declare a global type
{
  int id_num;
  double pay_rate;
  double hours;
};
Employee get_vals(void);    // function prototype

void main(void)
{
  Employee emp;

  emp = get_vals();
  cout << "\nThe employee id number is " << emp.id_num
       << "\nThe employee pay rate is $" << emp.pay_rate
       << "\nThe employee hours are " << emp.hours << '\n';
}

Employee get_vals(void) // return an employee structure
{
  Employee next;

  next.id_num = 6789;
  next.pay_rate = 16.25;
  next.hours = 38.0;
  return(next);
}
```

The following output is displayed when Program 10-6 is run:

```
The employee id number is 6789
The employee pay rate is $16.25
The employee hours are 38
```

Since the `get_vals()` function returns a structure, the function header for `get_vals()` must specify the type of structure being returned. As `get_vals()`

does not receive any arguments, the function header has no argument declarations and consists of the line

```
Employee get_vals(void)
```

Within `get_vals()`, the variable `next` is defined as a structure of the type to be returned. After values have been assigned to the `next` structure, the structure values are returned by including the structure name within the parentheses of the `return` statement.

On the receiving side, `main()` must be alerted that the function `get_vals()` will be returning a structure. This is handled by including a function declaration for `get_vals()` in `main()`. Notice that these steps for returning a structure from a function are identical to the normal procedures for returning scalar data types previously described in Chapter 6.

Exercises 10.3

1. Write a C++ function named `days()` that determines the number of days from the turn of the century for any date passed as a structure. Use the `Date` structure:

```
struct Date
{
  int month;
  int day;
  int year;
};
```

In writing the `days()` function, use the convention that all years have 360 days and each month consists of 30 days. The function should return the number of days for any `Date` structure passed to it. Make sure to declare the returned variable a long integer to reserve sufficient room for converting dates such as 12/19/89.

2. Write a C++ function named `dif_days()` that calculates and returns the difference between two dates. Each date is passed to the function as a structure using the following global type:

```
struct Date
{
  int month;
  int day;
  int year;
};
```

The `dif_days()` function should make two calls to the `days()` function written for Exercise 1.

3. a. Rewrite the `days()` function written for Exercise 1 to receive a reference to a `Date` structure, rather than a copy of the complete structure.
  b. Redo Exercise 3a using a pointer rather than a reference.

4. a. Write a C++ function named `larger()` that returns the later date of any two dates passed to it. For example, if the dates 10/9/62 and 11/3/62 are passed to `larger()`, the second date would be returned.

b. Include the `larger()` function that was written for Exercise 4a in a complete program. Store the `Date` structure returned by `larger()` in a separate `Date` structure and display the member values of the returned `Date`.

5. a. Modify the function `days()` written for Exercise 1 to account for the actual number of days in each month. Assume, however, that each year contains 365 days (that is, do not account for leap years).

b. Modify the function written for Exercise 5a to account for leap years.

10.4 Linked Lists

A classic data-handling problem is making additions or deletions to existing records that are maintained in a specific order. This is best illustrated by considering the alphabetical telephone list shown in Figure 10–7. Starting with this initial set of names and telephone numbers, we desire to add new records to the list in the proper alphabetical sequence, and to delete existing records in such a way that the storage for deleted records is eliminated.

Although the insertion or deletion of ordered records can be accomplished using an array of structures, these arrays are not efficient representations for adding or deleting records internal to the array. Arrays are fixed and prespecified in size.

Deleting a record from an array creates an empty slot that requires either special marking or shifting up all elements below the deleted record to close the empty slot. Similarly, adding a record to the body of an array of structures requires that all elements below the addition be shifted down to make room for the new entry; or the new element could be added to the bottom of the existing array and the array then resorted to restore the proper order of the

FIGURE 10–7 A Telephone List in Alphabetical Order

Acme, Sam
(201) 898-2392

Dolan, Edith
(213) 682-3104

Lanfrank, John
(415) 718-4581

Mening, Stephen
(914) 382-7070

Zemann, Harold
(718) 219-9912

records. Thus, either adding or deleting records to such a list generally requires restructuring and rewriting the list—a cumbersome, time-consuming, and inefficient practice.

A linked list provides a convenient method for maintaining a constantly changing list, without the need to continually reorder and restructure the complete list. A linked list is simply a set of structures in which each structure contains at least one member whose value is the address of the next logically ordered structure in the list. Rather than requiring each record to be physically stored in the proper order, each new record is physically added wherever the computer has free space in its storage area. The records are "linked" together by including the address of the next record in the record immediately preceding it. From a programming standpoint, the current record being processed contains the address of the next record, no matter where the next record is actually stored.

The concept of a linked list is illustrated in Figure 10–8. Although the actual data for the Lanfrank structure illustrated in the figure may be physically stored anywhere in the computer, the additional member included at the end of the Dolan structure maintains the proper alphabetical order. This member provides the starting address of the location where the Lanfrank record is stored. As you might expect, this member is a pointer.

To see the usefulness of the pointer in the Dolan record, let us add a telephone number for June Hagar into the alphabetical list shown in Figure 10–7. The data for June Hagar is stored in a data structure using the same type as that used for the existing records. To ensure that the telephone number for Hagar is correctly displayed after the Dolan telephone number, the address in the Dolan record must be altered to point to the Hagar record, and the address in the Hagar record must be set to point to the Lanfrank record. This is illustrated in Figure 10–9. Notice that the pointer in each structure simply points to the location of the next ordered structure, even if that structure is not physically located in the correct order.

Removal of a structure from the ordered list is the reverse process of adding a record. The actual record is logically removed from the list by simply changing the address in the structure preceding it to point to the structure immediately following the deleted record.

Each structure in a linked list has the same format; however, it is clear that the last record cannot have a valid pointer value that points to another record, since there is none. C++ provides a special pointer value called NULL that acts

FIGURE 10–8 Using Pointers to Link Structures

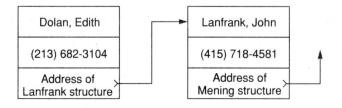

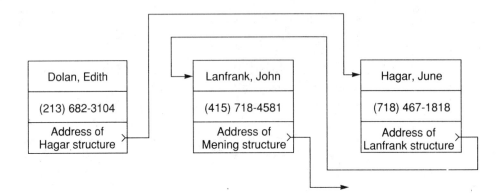

FIGURE 10–9 Adjusting Addresses to Point to Appropriate Records

as a sentinel or flag to indicate when the last record has been processed. The NULL pointer value, like its end-of-string counterpart, has a numerical value of zero.

Besides an end-of-list sentinel value, a special pointer must also be provided for storing the address of the first structure in the list. Figure 10–10 illustrates the complete set of pointers and structures for a list consisting of three names.

The inclusion of a pointer in a structure should not seem surprising. As we discovered in Section 10.1, a structure can contain any C++ data type. For example, the structure declaration

```
struct Test
{
  int id_num;
  double *pt_pay
};
```

declares a structure type consisting of two members. The first member is an integer variable named id_num, and the second variable is a pointer named pt_pay, which is a pointer to a double precision number. Program 10-7 illustrates that the pointer member of a structure is used like any other pointer variable.

FIGURE 10–10 Use of the Initial and Final Pointer Values

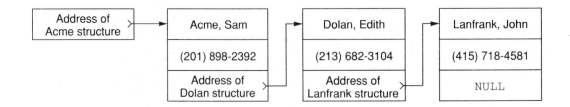

Program 10-7

```cpp
#include <iostream.h>
#include <iomanip.h>
struct Test
{
  int id_num;
  double *pt_pay;
};

void main(void)
{
  Test emp;
  double pay = 456.20;

  emp.id_num = 12345;
  emp.pt_pay = &pay;

  cout << "\nEmployee number " << emp.id_num << " was paid $"
       << setiosflags(ios::showpoint) << setw(6)
       << setprecision(2) << *emp.pt_pay << '\n';
}
```

The output produced by executing Program 10-7 is:

```
Employee number 12345 was paid $456.20
```

Figure 10–11 illustrates the relationship between the members of the `emp` structure defined in Program 10-7 and the variable named `pay`. The value assigned to `emp.id_num` is the number 12345 and the value assigned to `pay` is 456.20. The address of the `pay` variable is assigned to the structure member `emp.pt_pay`. Since this member has been defined as a pointer to a double precision number, placing the address of the double precision variable `pay` in it is a correct use of this member. Finally, since the member operator `.` has a higher precedence than the indirection operator `*`, the expression used in the `cout` call in Program 10-7 is correct. The expression `*emp.pt_pay` is equivalent

FIGURE 10–11 Storing an Address in a Structure Member

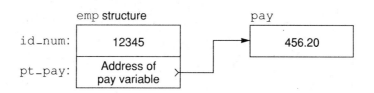

to the expression `*(emp.pt_pay)`, which is translated as "the variable whose address is contained in the member `emp.pt_pay`."

Although the pointer defined in Program 10-7 has been used in a rather trivial fashion, the program does illustrate the concept of including a pointer in a structure. This concept can be easily extended to create a linked list of structures suitable for storing the names and telephone numbers listed in Figure 10–7. The following declaration creates a type for such a structure:

```
struct Tele_typ
{
  char name[30];
  char phone_no[15];
  Tele_typ *nextaddr;
};
```

The `Tele_typ` type consists of three members. The first member is an array of 30 characters, suitable for storing names with a maximum of 29 letters and an end-of-string `NULL` marker. The next member is an array of 15 characters, suitable for storing telephone numbers with their respective area codes. The last member is a pointer suitable for storing the address of a structure of the `Tele_typ` type.

Program 10-8 illustrates the use of the `Tele_typ` type by specifically defining three structures having this form. The three structures are named `t1`, `t2`, and `t3`, respectively, and the name and telephone members of each of these structures are initialized when the structures are defined, using the data listed in Figure 10–7.

Program 10-8

```
#include <iostream.h>
struct Tele_typ
{
  char name[30];
  char phone_no[15];
  Tele_typ *nextaddr;
};

void main(void)
{
  Tele_typ t1 = {"Acme, Sam","(201) 898-2392"};
  Tele_typ t2 = {"Dolan, Edith","(213) 682-3104"};
  Tele_typ t3 = {"Lanfrank, John","(415) 718-4581"};
  Tele_typ *first;     // create a pointer to a structure
```

(continued on next page)

(continued from previous page)

```
   first = &t1;          // store t1's address in first
   t1.nextaddr = &t2;    // store t2's address in t1.nextaddr
   t2.nextaddr = &t3;    // store t3's address in t2.nextaddr
   t3.nextaddr = NULL;   // store the NULL address in t3.nextaddr

   cout << '\n' << first->name
        << '\n' << t1.nextaddr->name
        << '\n' << t2.nextaddr->name
        << '\n';
}
```

The output produced by executing Program 10-8 is:

```
        Acme, Sam
        Dolan, Edith
        Lanfrank, John
```

Program 10-8 demonstrates the use of pointers to access successive structure members. As illustrated in Figure 10–12, each structure contains the address of the next structure in the list.

The initialization of the names and telephone numbers for each of the structures defined in Program 10-8 is straightforward. Although each structure consists of three members, only the first two members of each structure are initialized. As both of these members are arrays of characters, they can be initialized with strings. The remaining member of each structure is a pointer. To create a linked list, each structure pointer must be assigned the address of the next structure in the list.

The four assignment statements in Program 10-8 perform the correct assignments. The expression `first = &t1` stores the address of the `first` structure in the list in the pointer variable named `first`. The expression `t1.nextaddr = &t2` stores the starting address of the `t2` structure into the pointer member of the `t1` structure. Similarly, the expression `t2.nextaddr = &t3` stores the starting address of the `t3` structure into the pointer member of the `t2` structure. To end the list, the value of the NULL pointer, which is zero, is stored into the pointer member of the `t3` structure.

Once values have been assigned to each structure member and correct addresses have been stored in the appropriate pointers, the addresses in the pointers are used to access each structure's name member. For example, the expression `t1.nextaddr->name` refers to the `name` member of the structure whose address is in the `nextaddr` member of the `t1` structure. The precedence of the member operator . and the structure pointer operator -> are equal, and

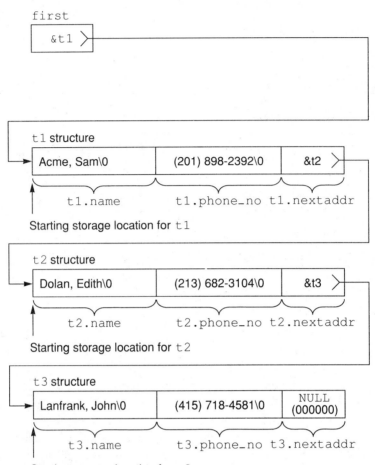

FIGURE 10–12 The Relationship Between Structures in Program 10-8

are evaluated from left to right. Thus, the expression t1.nextaddr->name is evaluated as (t1.nextaddr)->name. Since t1.nextaddr contains the address of the t2 structure, the proper name is accessed.

The expression t1.nextaddr->name can, of course, be replaced by the equivalent expression (*t1.nextaddr).name, which uses the more conventional indirection operator. This expression also refers to "the name member of the variable whose address is in t1.nextaddr."

The addresses in a linked list of structures can be used to loop through the complete list. As each structure is accessed it can be either examined to select a specific value or used to print out a complete list. For example, the display() function in Program 10-9 illustrates the use of a while loop, which uses the address in each structure's pointer member to cycle through the list and successively display data stored in each structure.

Program 10-9

```cpp
#include <iostream.h>
#include <iomanip.h>
struct Tele_typ
{
  char name[30];
  char phone_no[15];
  Tele_typ *nextaddr;
};
void display(Tele_typ *);   // function prototype

void main(void)
{
  Tele_typ t1 = {"Acme, Sam","(201) 898-2392"};
  Tele_typ t2 = {"Dolan, Edith","(213) 682-3104"};
  Tele_typ t3 = {"Lanfrank, John","(415) 718-4581"};
  Tele_typ *first;    // create a pointer to a structure

  first = &t1;        // store t1's address in first
  t1.nextaddr = &t2;  // store t2's address in t1.nextaddr
  t2.nextaddr = &t3;  // store t3's address in t2.nextaddr
  t3.nextaddr = NULL; // store the NULL address in t3.nextaddr

  display(first);     // send the address of the first structure
}

void display(Tele_typ *contents) // contents is a pointer to a structure
{                                // of type Tele_typ
  while (contents != NULL)        // display till end of linked list
  {
    cout << '\n' << setiosflags(ios::left)
              << setw(30) << contents->name
              << setw(20) << contents->phone_no ;
    contents = contents->nextaddr;    // get next address
  }
  cout << '\n';
  return;
}
```

The output produced by Program 10-9 is:

```
        Acme, Sam               (201) 898-2392
        Dolan, Edith            (213) 682-3104
        Lanfrank, John          (415) 718-4581
```

The important concept illustrated by Program 10-9 is the use of the address in one structure to access members of the next structure in the list. When the `display()` function is called, it is passed the value stored in the variable named `first`. Since `first` is a pointer variable, the actual value passed is an address (the address of the `t1` structure). `display()` accepts the passed value in the argument named `contents`. To store the passed address correctly, `contents` is declared as a pointer to a structure of the `tele_typ` type. Within `display()`, a `while` loop is used to cycle through the linked structures, starting with the structure whose address is in `contents`. The condition tested in the `while` statement compares the value in `contents`, which is an address, to the `NULL` value. For each valid address the name and phone number members of the addressed structure are displayed. The address in `contents` is then updated with the address in the pointer member of the current structure. The address in `contents` is then retested, and the process continues while the address in `contents` is not equal to the `NULL` value. `display()` "knows" nothing about the names of the structures declared in `main()` or even how many structures exist. It simply cycles through the linked list, structure by structure, until it encounters the end-of-list `NULL` address. Since the value of `NULL` is zero, the tested condition can be replaced by the equivalent expression `contents`.

A disadvantage of Program 10-9 is that exactly three structures are defined in `main()` by name and storage for them is reserved at compile time. Should a fourth structure be required, the additional structure would have to be declared and the program recompiled. In the next section we show how to have the computer dynamically allocate and release storage for structures at run time, as storage is required. Only when a new structure is to be added to the list, and while the program is running, is storage for the new structure created. Similarly, when a structure is no longer needed and can be deleted from the list, the storage for the deleted record is relinquished and returned to the computer.

Exercises 10.4

1. Modify Program 10-9 to prompt the user for a name. Have the program search the existing list for the entered name. If the name is in the list, display the corresponding phone number; otherwise display this message: The name is not in the current phone directory.

2. Write a C++ program containing a linked list of ten integer numbers. Have the program display the numbers in the list.

3. Using the linked list of structures illustrated in Figure 10–12, write the sequence of steps necessary to delete the record for Edith Dolan from the list.

4. Generalize the description obtained in Exercise 3 to describe the sequence of steps necessary to remove the nth structure from a list of linked structures. The nth structure is preceded by the (*n*–1)st structure and followed by the (*n*+1)st structure. Make sure to store all pointer values correctly.

5. a. A doubly linked list is a list in which each structure contains a pointer to both the following and previous structures in the list. Define an appropriate type for a doubly linked list of names and telephone numbers.

    b. Using the type defined in Exercise 5a, modify Program 10-9 to list the names and phone numbers in reverse order.

10.5   Dynamic Structure Allocation

We have already encountered the concept of explicitly allocating and deallocating memory space using the `new` and `delete` operators (see Section 8.2). For convenience the description of these operators are repeated in Table 10–1.

TABLE 10–1   **Memory Allocation and Deallocation Operators**

Operator Name	Description
new	Reserves the number of bytes required by the requested data type. Returns the address of the first reserved location or NULL if sufficient memory is not available.
delete	Releases a block of bytes previously reserved. The address of the first reserved location is passed as an argument to the function.

This dynamic allocation of memory is especially useful when dealing with a list of structures, because it permits the list to expand as new records are added and contract as records are deleted.

In requesting additional storage space, the user must provide the new function with an indication of the amount of storage needed. This is done by requesting enough space for a particular type of data. For example, the expression `new(int)` or `new int` (the two forms may be used interchangeably) requests enough storage to store an integer number. A request for enough storage for a structure is made in the same fashion. For example, using the declaration

```
struct Tel_typ
{
  char name[25];
  char phone_no[15];
};
```

367

the function calls new Tel_typ and new(Tel_typ) both reserve enough storage for one Tel_typ data structure.

In allocating storage dynamically, we have no advance indication as to where the computer system will physically reserve the requested number of bytes, and we have no explicit name to access the newly created storage locations. To provide access to these locations, new returns the address of the first location that has been reserved. This address must, of course, be assigned to a pointer. The return of a pointer by new is especially useful for creating a linked list of data structures. As each new structure is created, the pointer returned by new to the structure can be assigned to a member of the previous structure in the list.

Program 10-10 illustrates using new to create a structure dynamically in response to a user-input request.

Program 10-10

```cpp
// a program illustrating dynamic structure allocation
#include <iostream.h>
#include <string.h>
struct Tel_typ
{
  char name[30];
  char phone_no[16];
};
void populate(Tel_typ *);   // function prototype
void disp_one(Tel_typ *);   // function prototype

void main(void)
{
  char key;
  Tel_typ *rec_point;      // rec_point is a pointer to a
                           // structure of type Tel_typ

  cout << "Do you wish to create a new record (respond with y or n): ";
  key = cin.get();
  if (key == 'y')
  {
    key = cin.get();       // get the Enter key in buffered input
    rec_point = new Tel_typ;
    populate(rec_point);
    disp_one(rec_point);
  }
  else
    cout << "\nNo record has been created.";
}
```

(continued on next page)

(continued from previous page)

```
// get a name and phone number
  void populate(Tel_typ *record) // record is a pointer to a
  {                              // structure of type Tel_typ
    cout << "Enter a name: ";
    cin.getline(record->name,30);
    cout << "Enter the phone number: ";
    cin.getline(record->phone_no,16);
    return;
  }
// display the contents of one record
  void disp_one(Tel_typ *contents)  // contents is a pointer to a
  {                                 // structure of type Tel_typ
    cout << "\nThe contents of the record just created is:"
         << "\nName: " << contents->name
         << "\nPhone Number: " << contents->phone_no;
    return;
  }
```

A sample session produced by Program 10-10 is:

```
Do you wish to create a new record (respond with y or n): y
Enter a name: Monroe, James
Enter the phone number: (617) 555-1817
The contents of the record just created is:
Name: Monroe, James
Phone Number: (617) 555-1817
```

In reviewing Program 10-10, notice that only two variable declarations are made in `main()`. The variable `key` is declared as a character variable and the variable `rec_point` is declared as being a pointer to a structure of the `Tel_typ` type. Since the declaration for the type `Tel_typ` is global, `Tel_typ` can be used within `main()` to define `rec_point` as a pointer to a structure of the `Tel_typ` type.

If a user enters `y` in response to the first prompt in `main()`, a call to `new` is made for the required memory to store the designated structure. Once `rec_point` has been loaded with the proper address, this address can be used to access the newly created structure. The function `populate()` is used to prompt the user for data needed in filling the structure and to store the user-entered data in the correct members of the structure. The argument passed to `populate()` in `main()` is the pointer `rec_point`. Like all passed arguments, the value contained in `rec_point` is passed to the function. Since the value in `rec_point` is an address, `populate()` receives the address of the newly created structure and can directly access the structure members.

Within `populate()`, the value received by it is stored in the argument named `record`. Since the value to be stored in `record` is the address of a structure, record must be declared as a pointer to a structure. This declaration is provided by the statement Tel_typ *record;. The statements within populate() use the address in record to locate the respective members of the structure.

The disp_one() function in Program 10-10 is used to display the contents of the newly created and populated structure. The address passed to disp_one() is the same address that was passed to populate(). Since this passed value is the address of a structure, the argument name used to store the address is declared as a pointer to the correct structure type.

Once you understand the mechanism of calling new, you can use this function to construct a linked list of structures. As described in the previous section, the structures used in a linked list must contain one pointer member. The address in the pointer member is the starting address of the next structure in the list. Additionally, a pointer must be reserved for the address of the first structure, and the pointer member of the last structure in the list is given a NULL address to indicate that no more members are being pointed to. Program 10-11 illustrates the use of new to construct a linked list of names and phone numbers. The populate() function used in Program 10-11 is the same function used in Program 10-10, while the display() function is the same function used in Program 10-9.

Program 10-11

```
#include <iostream.h>
#include <iomanip.h>
struct Tel_typ
{
  char name[30];
  char phone_no[16];
  Tel_typ *nextaddr;
};
void populate(Tel_typ *);   // function prototype
void display(Tel_typ *);    // function prototype

void main(void)
{
  int i;
  Tel_typ *list, *current; // two pointers to structures of
                           // type Tel_typ

  // get a pointer to the first structure in the list
  list = new Tel_typ;
  current = list;
```

(continued on next page)

(continued from previous page)

```cpp
  // populate the current structure and create two more structures
  for(i = 0; i < 2; ++i)
  {
    populate(current);
    current->nextaddr = new Tel_typ;
    current = current->nextaddr;
  }

  populate(current);          // populate the last structure
  current->nextaddr = NULL;   // set the last address
  cout << "\nThe list consists of the following records:\n";
  display(list);              // display the structures
}

// get a name and phone number
void populate(Tel_typ *record)  // record is a pointer to a
{                               // structure of type Tel_typ
  cout << "Enter a name: ";
  cin.getline(record->name,30);
  cout << "Enter the phone number: ";
  cin.getline(record->phone_no,16);
  return;
}

void display(struct Tel_typ *contents)// contents is a pointer to a
{                               // structure of type Tel_typ
  while (contents != NULL)       // display till end of linked list
  {
    cout << "\n" << setiosflags(ios::left)
         << setw(30) << contents->name
         << setw(20) << contents->phone_no;
    contents = contents->nextaddr;
  }
  return;
}
```

The first time new is called in Program 10-11 it is used to create the first structure in the linked list. As such, the address returned by new is stored in the pointer variable named list. The address in list is then assigned to the pointer named current. This pointer variable is always used by the program to point to the current structure. Since the current structure is the first structure created, the address in the pointer named list is assigned to the pointer named current.

Within main()'s for loop, the name and phone number members of the newly created structure are populated by calling populate() and passing the address of the current structure to the function. Upon return from populate(), the pointer member of the `current` structure is assigned an address. This address is the address of the next structure in the list, which is obtained from new. The call to `new` creates the `next` structure and returns its address into the pointer member of the `current` structure. This completes the population of the `current` member. The final statement in the `for` loop resets the address in the `current` pointer to the address of the next structure in the list.

After the last structure has been created, the final statements in `main()` populate this structure, assign a NULL address to the pointer member, and call `display()` to display all the structures in the list. A sample run of Program 10-11 is provided below:

```
Enter a name: Acme, Sam
Enter the phone number: (201) 898-2392
Enter a name: Dolan, Edith
Enter the phone number: (213) 682-3104
Enter a name: Lanfrank, John
Enter the phone number: (415) 718-4581
The list consists of the following records:

Acme, Sam                         (201) 898-2392
Dolan, Edith                      (213) 682-3104
Lanfrank, John                    (415) 718-4581
```

Just as `new` dynamically creates storage while a program is executing, the delete function restores a block of storage back to the computer while the programming is executing. The only argument required by `delete` is the starting address of a block of storage that was dynamically allocated. Thus, any address returned by new can subsequently be passed to `delete` to restore the reserved memory back to the computer. `delete` does not alter the address passed to it, but simply removes the storage that the address references.

Exercises 10.5

1. As described in Table 10–1, the `new` operator returns either the address of the first new storage area allocated, or NULL if insufficient storage is available. Modify Program 10-11 to check that a valid address has been returned before a call to `populate()` is made. Display an appropriate message if sufficient storage is not available.

2. Write a C++ function named `remove()` that removes an existing structure from the linked list of structures created by Program 10-11. The algorithm for removing a linked structure should follow the sequence developed for removing a structure developed in Exercise 4 in Section 10.4. The argument passed to `remove()` should be the address of the structure preceding the record to be removed. In the removal function, make sure that the value of the pointer in the removed structure replaces the value of the pointer member of the preceding structure before the structure is removed.

3. Write a function named `insert()` that inserts a structure into the linked list of structures created in Program 10-11. The algorithm for inserting a structure in a linked list should follow the sequence for inserting a record illustrated in Figure 10–9. The argu-

ment passed to insert () should be the address of the structure preceding the structure to be inserted. The inserted structure should follow this current structure. The insert () function should create a new structure dynamically, call the populate function used in Program 10-11, and adjust all pointer values appropriately.

4. We desire to insert a new structure into the linked list of structures created by Program 10-11. The function developed to do this in Exercise 3 assumed that the address of the preceding structure is known. Write a function called find_rec () that returns the address of the structure immediately preceding the point at which the new structure is to be inserted. (*Hint:* find_rec () must request the new name as input and compare the entered name to existing names to determine where to place the new name.)

5. Write a C++ function named modify () that can be used to modify the name and phone number members of a structure of the type created in Program 10-11. The argument passed to modify () should be the address of the structure to be modified. The modify () function should first display the existing name and phone number in the selected structure and then request new data for these members.

6. *a.* Write a C++ program that initially presents a menu of choices for the user. The menu should consist of the following choices:

    A. Create an initial linked list of names and phone numbers.
    B. Insert a new structure into the linked list.
    C. Modify an existing structure in the linked list.
    D. Delete an existing structure from the list.
    E. Exit from the program.

Upon the user's selection, the program should execute the appropriate functions to satisfy the request.

b. Why is the original creation of a linked list usually done by one program, and the options to add, modify, or delete a structure in the list provided by a different program?

10.6 Unions[1]

A union is a data type that reserves the same area in memory for two or more variables, each of which can be a different data type. A variable that is declared as a union data type can be used to hold a character variable, an integer variable, a double precision variable, or any other valid C++ data type. Each of these types, but only one at a time, can actually be assigned to the union variable.

The definition of a union has the same form as a structure definition, with the keyword union used in place of the keyword structure. For example, the declaration

```
union
{
  char key;
  int num;
  double price;
} val;
```

[1] This topic may be omitted on first reading with no loss of subject continuity.

creates a union variable named `val`. If `val` were a structure it would consist of three individual members. As a union, however, `val` contains a single member that can be either a character variable named `key`, an integer variable named `num`, or a double precision variable named `price`. In effect, a union reserves sufficient memory locations to accommodate its largest member's data type. This same set of locations is then referenced by different variable names depending on the data type of the value currently residing in the reserved locations. Each value stored overwrites the previous value, using as many bytes of the reserved memory area as necessary.

Individual union members are referenced using the same notation as structure members. For example, if the `val` union is currently being used to store a character, the correct variable name to access the stored character is `val.key`. Similarly, if the union is used to store an integer, the value is accessed by the name `val.num`, and a double precision value is accessed by the name `val.price`. In using union members, it is the programmer's responsibility to ensure that the correct member name is used for the data type currently residing in the union.

Typically a second variable is used to keep track of the current data type stored in the union. For example, the following code could be used to select the appropriate member of `val` for display. Here the value in the variable `u_type` determines the currently stored data type in the `val` union:

```
switch(u_type)
{
  case 'c': cout << val.key;
            break;
  case 'i': cout << val.num;
            break;
  case 'd': cout << val.price;
            break;
  default : cout <<"Invalid type in u_type :" << u_type;
}
```

As they are in structures, a data type can be associated with a union. For example, the declaration

```
union Date_time
{
    long int days;
    double time;
};
```

provides a union data type without actually reserving any storage locations. This data type can then be used to define any number of variables. For example, the definition

```
Date_time first, second, *pt;
```

creates a union variable named first, a union variable named second, and a pointer that can be used to store the address of any union having the form of Date_time. Once a pointer to a union has been declared, the same notation used to access structure members can be used to access union members. For example, if the assignment pt = &first; is made, then pt->date references the date member of the union named first.

Unions may themselves be members of structures or arrays, or structures, arrays, and pointers may be members of unions. In each case, the notation used to access a member must be consistent with the nesting employed. For example, in the structure defined by

```
struct
{
  char u_type;
  union
  {
    char *text;
    float rate;
  } u_tax;
}  flag;
```

the variable rate is referenced as:

```
flag.u_tax.rate
```

Similarly, the first character of the string whose address is stored in the pointer text is referenced as:

```
*flag.u_tax.text
```

Exercises 10.6

1. Assume that the following definition has been made:

```
union
{
  float rate;
  double taxes;
  int num;
} flag;
```

For this union write appropriate cout stream activations to display the various members of the union.

2. Define a union variable named car that contains an integer named year, an array of 10 characters named name, and an array of 10 characters named model.

3. Define a union variable named `lang` that would allow a floating point number to be referenced by both the variable names `interest` and `rate`.

4. Declare a union data type named `Amt` that contains an integer variable named `int_amt`, a double precision variable named `dbl_amt`, and a pointer to a character named `pt_key`.

5. a. What do you think will be displayed by the following section of code?

```
union
{
  char ch;
  float btype;
} alt;
alt.ch = 'y';
cout << alt.btype;
```

b. Include the code presented in Exercise 5a in a program and run the program to verify your answer to Exercise 5a.

10.7 Common Programming Errors

Three common errors are often made when using structures or unions. The first error occurs because structures and unions, as complete entities, cannot be used in relational expressions. For example, even if `Tel_typ` and `Phon_type` are two structures of the same type, the expression `Tel_typ == Phon_typ` is invalid. Individual members of a structure or union can, of course, be compared using any of C++'s relational operators.

The second common error is really an extension of a pointer error as it relates to structures and unions. Whenever a pointer is used to "point to" either of these data types, or whenever a pointer is itself a member of a structure or a union, take care to use the address in the pointer to access the appropriate data type. Should you be confused about just what is being pointed to, remember, "If in doubt, print it out."

The final error relates specifically to unions. Since a union can store only one of its members at a time, you must be careful to keep track of the currently stored variable. Storing one data type in a union and accessing it by the wrong variable name can result in an error that is particularly troublesome to locate.

10.8 Chapter Summary

1. A structure allows individual variables to be grouped under a common variable name. Each variable in a structure is accessed by its structure variable name, followed by a period, followed by its individual variable name. Another term for a structure is a record. One form for declaring a structure is:

```
struct
{
    individual member declarations;
} structure_name;
```

2. A data type can be created from a structure using the declaration form

```
struct Data-type
{
    individual member declarations;
};
```

Individual structure variables may then be defined as this Data-type. By convention, the first letter of the Data-type name is always capitalized.

3. Structures are particularly useful as elements of arrays. Used in this manner, each structure becomes one record in a list of records.

4. Complete structures can be used as function arguments, in which case the called function receives a copy of each element in the structure. The address of a structure may also be passed, either as a reference or a pointer, which provides the called function with direct access to the structure.

5. Structure members can be any valid C++ data type, including other structures, unions, arrays, and pointers. When a pointer is included as a structure member a linked list can be created. Such a list uses the pointer in one structure to "point to" (contain the address of) the next logical structure in the list.

6. Unions are declared in the same manner as structures. The definition of a union creates a memory overlay area, with each union member using the same memory storage locations. Thus, only one member of a union may be active at a time.

Introduction
to Classes

Chapter Eleven

Besides being an improved version of C, the distinguishing characteristic of C++ is its support of object-oriented programming. Central to this object orientation is the concept of a class, which is a programmer-defined data type. In this chapter we explore the implications of permitting programmers to define their own data types and then present C++'s mechanism for constructing classes. As we will see, the construction of a class is based on both structures and functions; structures provide the means for creating new data configurations and functions provide the means for performing operations on the structures. What C++ and other object-oriented languages provide is a unique way of combining structures and functions together in a self-contained, cohesive unit.

11.1 Object-Based Programming

We live in a world full of objects—planes, trains, cars, telephones, books, computers, and so on. Until quite recently, however, programming techniques have not reflected this at all. The primary programming paradigm[1] has been procedural, where a program is defined as an algorithm written in a machine-readable language. The reasons for this emphasis on procedural programming are primarily historical.

When computers were developed in the 1940s they were used by mathematicians for military purposes—for computing bomb trajectories and decoding enemy orders and diplomatic transmissions. After World War II computers were still primarily used by mathematicians for mathematical computations. This reality was reflected in the name of the first commercially available high-level language introduced in 1957. The language's name was FORTRAN, which was an acronym for FORmula TRANslation. Further reflecting this predominant use was the fact that in the 1960s almost all computer courses were taught in either engineering or mathematics departments. The term *computer science* was not yet in common use and *computer science* departments were just being formed.

This situation has changed dramatically, primarily for two reasons. One of the reasons for disenchantment with procedural-based programs has been the failure of traditional procedural languages to provide an adequate means of containing software costs. Software costs include all costs associated with initial program development and subsequent program maintenance. As illustrated in Figure 11–1, the major cost of most computer projects today, whether technical or commercial, is for software.

Software costs contribute so heavily to total project costs because they are directly related to human productivity (they are labor intensive), while the

---

[1] A *paradigm* is a standard way of thinking about or doing something.

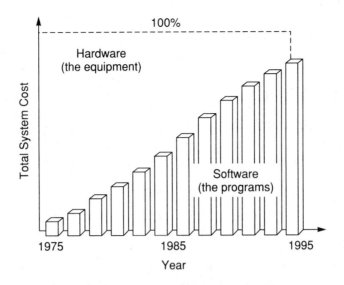

FIGURE 11–1   Software Is the Major Cost of Most Computer Projects

equipment associated with hardware costs is related to manufacturing technologies. For example, microchips that cost over $500 ten years ago can now be purchased for less than $1.

It is far easier, however, to dramatically increase manufacturing productivity a thousand-fold, with the consequent decrease in hardware costs, than it is for programmers to double either the quantity or quality of the code they produce. So as hardware costs have plummeted, software productivity and its associated costs have remained relatively constant. Thus, the ratio of software costs to total system costs (hardware plus software) has increased dramatically.

One way to significantly increase programmer productivity is to create code that can be reused without extensive revision, retesting, and revalidation. The inability of procedurally structured code to provide this type of reusability has led to the search for other software approaches.

The second reason for disenchantment with procedural-based programming has been the emergence of graphical screens and the subsequent interest in window applications. Programming multiple windows on the same graphical screen is virtually impossible using standard procedural programming techniques.

The solution to producing programs that efficiently manipulate graphical screens and provide reusable windowing code was found in artificial intelligence-based and simulation programming techniques. The former area, artificial intelligence, contained extensive research on geometrical object specification and recognition. The latter area, simulation, contained considerable background on simulating items as objects with well-defined interactions between them. This object-based paradigm fitted well in a graphical windows environment, where each window can be specified as a self-contained object.

An object is also well suited to a programming representation because it can be specified by two basic characteristics: a current *state*, which defines how the object appears at the moment, and a *behavior*, which defines how the object reacts to external inputs.

To make this more concrete consider a geometric object, such as a rectangle. A rectangle's current state is defined by its shape and location. The shape is traditionally specified by its length and width, while its location can be specified in a number of ways. One simple way is to list the values of two corner positions. The behavior we provide a rectangle depends on what we are willing to have our rectangle do. For example, if we intend to display the rectangle on a screen we might provide it with the ability to move its position and change either its length or width.

It is worthwhile distinguishing here between an actual rectangle, which might exist on a piece of paper or a computer screen, and our description of it. Our description is more accurately termed a model. By definition, a *model* is only a representation of a real object; it is not the object itself. Very few models are ever complete; that is, a model typically does not reveal every aspect of the object it represents. Each model is defined for a particular purpose that usually only requires representing the part of an object's state or behavior that is of interest to us. To clarify this point further, consider another common object, an elevator.

Like all objects, an elevator can be modeled in terms of a state and a behavior. Its state might be given in terms of its size, location, interior decoration, or any number of attributes. Likewise, its behavior might be specified in terms of its reaction when one of its buttons is pushed. Constructing a model of an elevator, however, requires that we select those attributes and behavior that are of interest to us. For purposes of a simulation, for example, we may only be concerned with the current floor position of the elevator and how to make it move to another floor location. Other attributes and behavior of the elevator may be left out of the model because they do not affect the aspects of the elevator that we are interested in studying. At the end of this chapter we will see how to model an elevator and make our model elevator "move" in C++ using a very simple representation.

It is also important to distinguish between the attributes we choose to include in our model with the values that these attributes can have. The attributes and behavior together define a category or type of object out of which many individual objects can be designated. In object-based programming the category of objects defined by a given set of attributes and behavior is called a *class*. Only when specific values have been assigned to the attributes is a particular object defined.

For example, the attributes length and width can be used to define a general type of shape called a rectangle. Only when specific values have been assigned to these attributes have we represented a particular rectangle. This distinction carries over into C++: The attributes and behavior we select are said to define a general class, or type, of object. The object itself only comes into existence when we assign specific values to the attributes.

As you might expect, attributes in C++ are defined by variables and behaviors are constructed from functions. The set of attributes and behavior defining a class is frequently referred to as the class' *interface*. Once the interface has been specified, creating a particular object is achieved by assigning specific values to the appropriate variables. How all of this is constructed is the topic of the remaining sections.

Exercises 11.1

1. Define the terms:
- *a.* attribute
- *b.* behavior
- *c.* state
- *d.* model
- *e.* class
- *f.* object
- *g.* interface

2. a. In place of specifying a rectangle's location by listing the position of two corner points, what other attributes could be used?
b. What other attributes, besides length and width, might be used to describe a rectangle if the rectangle is to be drawn on a color monitor?
c. Describe a set of attributes that could be used to define circles that are to be drawn on a black and white monitor
d. What additional attributes would you add to those selected in response to Exercise 2c if the circles were to be drawn on a color monitor?

3. a. For each of the following, determine what attributes might be of interest to someone considering buying the item.
- *i.* a book
- *ii.* a can of soda
- *iii.* a pen
- *iv.* a cassette tape
- *v.* a cassette tape player
- *vi.* an elevator
- *vii.* a car

b. Do the attributes you used in Exercise 3a model an object or a class of objects?

4. For each of the following items, what behavior might be of interest to someone considering buying the item?
- *a.* a car
- *b.* a cassette tape player

5. All of the examples of classes considered in this section have consisted of inanimate objects. Do you think that animate objects such as pets and even human beings could be modeled in terms of attributes and behavior? Why or why not?

6. a. The attributes of a class represent how objects of the class appear to the outside world. The behavior represents how an object of a class reacts to an external stimulus. Given this, what do you think is the mechanism by which one object "triggers" the designated behavior in another object? (*Hint:* Consider how one person typically gets another person to do something.)
b. If behavior in C++ is constructed by defining an appropriate function, how do you think the behavior is activated in C++?

11.2 Classes

A *class* is a programmer-defined data type. To understand the full implications of this more clearly, consider the built-in data types supplied by C++: integers, reals, and characters. In using these data types we typically declare one or more variables of the desired type, use them in their accepted ways, and avoid using them in ways that are not specified. Thus, for example, we would not use the modulus operator on two floating point numbers. Since this operation makes no sense it has not been supplied in C++.

In computer terminology, the combination of data and their associated operations is defined as a class. That is, a class defines *both* the types of data and the types of operations that may be performed on the data. Seen in this light it is more correct to speak of the built-in data types provided by C++ as the integer class, the floating point class, and the character class. Such a definition conveys that both a type of data and specific operational capabilities are being supplied. In a simplified form this relationship can be described as:

```
Class = Allowable Data + Operational Capabilities
```

Before seeing how to construct our own classes, let's take a moment to list some of the operational capabilities supplied with C++'s built-in classes. The reason for this is that we will have to provide the same capabilities as part of our own classes. The minimum set of the capabilities provided by C++'s built-in classes is listed in Table 11–1.

TABLE 11–1   Built-in Data Type Capabilities

Capability	Example
Define one or more variables of the class	int a, b;
Initialize a variable at definition	int a = 5;
Assign a value to a variable	a = 10;
Assign one variable's value to another variable	a = b;
Perform mathematical operations	a + b
Convert from one data type to another	a = (int) 7.2;

Although we don't normally think of these capabilities individually when we use them, the designers of C++ clearly had to when they created the C++ compiler. Since C++ allows us to create our own classes we must now be aware of these capabilities and provide them with the classes that we construct.

Construction of a class is inherently easy and we already have all the necessary tools in structures and functions. In C++ structures provide the means of defining new data types and functions provide the means of defining operational capabilities. Using this information we can now extend our equation definition of a class to its C++ representation as follows:

C++ Class = Data Structure + Functions

Thus, in C++ a class provides a mechanism for packaging a data structure and functions together in a self-contained unit. In this chapter we describe how classes are constructed and variables are declared and initialized. The assignment and mathematical capabilities listed in Table 11–1, as they apply to classes, are presented in Chapter 12. Type conversions are presented in Chapter 13.

Class Construction

Unlike a structure, which we have used to define data, a class defines both data and functions.[2] This is usually accomplished by constructing a class in two parts, a declaration section and an implementation section. As illustrated in Figure 11–2, the declaration section declares both the data types and functions of the class. The implementation section is then used to define the functions whose prototypes have been declared in the declaration section.[3]

Both the variables and functions listed in the class declaration section are referred to as *class members*. The data members, as illustrated in Figure 11–2, are also referred to as *instance variables*.

FIGURE 11–2 Format of a Class Definition

```
// class declaration section
class class-name
{
  data members  // instance variables
     and
  function members  // inline and prototypes
};
// class implementation section
function definitions
```

---

[2] The structures presented in Chapter 10 can be expanded to include functions. In this text, however, we will only use classes for this purpose.

[3] This separation into two parts is not mandatory, as the implementation can be included within the declaration section if inline functions are used.

As a specific example of a class, consider the following definition of a class named `Date`:

```
//--- class declaration section

class Date
{
  private:         // notice the colon after the word private
     int month;    // a data member
     int day;      // a data member
     int year;     // a data member
   public:         // again, notice the colon here
     Date(int, int, int);        // a member function - the constructor
     void setdate(int, int, int);  // a member function
     void showdate(void);        // a member function
};

//--- class implementation section

Date::Date(int mm = 7, int dd = 4, int yy = 94)
{
  month = mm;
  day = dd;
  year = yy;
}

void Date::setdate(int mm, int dd, int yy)
{
  month = mm; day = dd; year = yy;
}

void Date::showdate(void)
{
  cout << "The date is " << month << "/" << day << "/" << year << "\n";
}
```

Since this definition may initially look overwhelming, first simply notice that it does consist of two sections—a declaration section and an implementation section. Now consider each of these sections individually.

A class declaration section consists of variable declarations and function prototypes. A commonly used form for this section is:

```
class name
{
  private:
    a list of variable declarations
  public:
    a list of function prototypes
};
```

Notice that this format is followed by our `Date` class, which for convenience we have listed below without any internal comments:

```
//--- class declaration section

class Date
{
  private:
     int month;
     int day;
     int year;
  public:
     Date(int, int, int);
     void setdate(int, int, int);
     void showdate(void);
};  // this is a declaration - don't forget the semicolon
```

The name of this class is `Date`. Although the initial capital letter is not required, it is conventionally used with classes as it is with structures. The body of the declaration section, which is enclosed within braces, consists of variable and function declarations. In this case the variables `month`, `day`, and `year` are declared as integers and three functions named `Date()`, `setdate()`, and `showdate()` are declared via prototypes. The keywords `private` and `public` are access specifiers that define access rights. The `private` keyword specifies that the class members following, in this case the data members `month`, `day`, and `year`, *cannot* be accessed from outside of the class and may only be accessed by other class functions (or friend functions, as will be discussed in Section 12.3). Thus, for example, a statement made outside of the class such as

$$birth.month = 7;$$

where `birth` is a variable of type `Date` is illegal with `private` class members.[4] The purpose of the `private` designation is specifically meant to force all accesses to private data through the provided member functions.[5] Once a class category such as `private` is designated it remains in force until a new category is listed.

Following the `private` class data members, the function prototypes listed in the `Date` class have been declared as `public`. This means that these class functions *can* be called from outside of the class. In general, all class functions should be public; as such they furnish capabilities to manipulate the class variables from outside of the class. For our `Date` class we have initially provided

---

[4] Such statements are clearly acceptable for the data structure members presented in Chapter 10. One of the purposes of a class is to prevent such global type accesses and force all changes to data members to be made through member functions. This is referred to as *information hiding.*

[5] Note that the default membership category in a class is private, which means that this keyword can be omitted. In this text we will explicitly use the `private` designation to reinforce the idea of access restrictions inherent in class membership.

```
return-type    class-name::function-name(argument list)
{
   function body
}
```

FIGURE 11-3 Format of a Member Function

three functions named Date(), setdate(), and showdate(). Notice that one of these member functions has the same name, Date, as the class name. This particular function is referred to as a *constructor* function, and it has a specially defined purpose: It can be used to initialize class data members with values. Also notice that the constructor function has no return type, which is a requirement for this special function. The two remaining functions declared in our declaration example are setdate() and showdate(), both of which have been declared as returning no value (void). In the implementation section of the class these three member functions will be written to permit initialization, assignment, and display capabilities, respectively.

The implementation section of a class is where the member functions declared in the declaration section are written.[6] Figure 11-3 illustrates the general form of functions included in the implementation section. This format is correct for all functions except the constructor, which, as we have stated, has no return type.

As shown in Figure 11-3 member functions defined in the implementation section have the same format as all user-written C++ functions with the addition of the class name and scope resolution operator, ::, that identifies the function as a member of a particular class. Let us now reconsider the implementation section of our Date class, which is repeated below for convenience:

```
//--- class implementation section

Date::Date(int mm = 7, int dd = 4, int yy = 94)
{
   month = mm;
   day = dd;
   year = yy;
}

void Date::setdate(int mm, int dd, int yy)
{
   month = mm; day = dd; year = yy;
}

void Date::showdate(void)
{
   cout << "The date is " << month << "/" << day << "/" << year << "\n";
}
```

---

[6] It is also possible to define these functions within the declaration section by declaring and writing them as inline functions. Examples of inline member functions are presented in Section 11.3.

Notice that the first function in this implementation section has the same name as the class, which makes it a constructor function. As such, it has no `return` type. The `Date::` included at the beginning of the function header line identifies this function as a member of the `Date` class. The rest of the header line `Date(int mm = 7, int dd = 4, int yy = 94)` defines the function as having three integer arguments with default values of 7, 4, and 94, respectively. The body of this function simply assigns the data members `month`, `day`, and `year` with the values of the arguments `mm`, `dd`, and `yy`, respectively.

The next function header line

```
void Date::setdate(int mm, int dd, int yy)
```

defines this as the `setdate()` function belonging to the `Date` class (`Date::`). This function returns no value (`void`) and expects three integer arguments, `mm`, `dd`, and `yy`. In a manner similar to the `Date()` function, the body of this function assigns the data members `month`, `day`, and `year` with the values of its arguments. In a moment we will see the difference between `Date()` and `setdate()`.

Finally, the last function header line in the implementation section defines a function named `showdate()`. This function has no arguments, returns no value, and is a member of the `Date` class. The body of this function outputs the values stored in `month`, `day`, and `year`.

To see how our `Date` class can be used within the context of a complete program, consider Program 11-1. To make the program easier to read it has been shaded in lighter and darker areas. The lighter area contains the class declaration and implementation sections that we have already considered. The darker area

 Program 11-1

```
#include <iostream.h>

// class declaration section
class Date
{
  private:
    int month;
    int day;
    int year;
  public:
    Date(int, int, int);          // constructor
    void setdate(int, int, int);  // member function
    void showdate(void);          // member function to display a date
};
```
(continued on next page)

(continued from previous page)

```cpp
// implementation section
Date::Date(int mm = 7, int dd = 4, int yy = 94)
{
  month = mm;
  day = dd;
  year = yy;
}
void Date::setdate(int mm, int dd, int yy)
{
  month = mm;
  day = dd;
  year = yy;
}
void Date::showdate(void)
{
  cout << "The date is " << month << "/" << day << "/" << year << "\n";
}
```

```cpp
void main(void)
{
  Date a, b, c(4,1,96);    // declare 3 objects - initializes 1 of them

  b.setdate(12,25,95);     // assign values to b's data members
  a.showdate();            // display object a's values
  b.showdate();            // display object b's values
  c.showdate();            // display object c's values
}
```

contains the header and `main()` function. For convenience we will retain this shading convention for all programs using classes.[7]

The declaration and implementation sections contained in the lighter shaded region of Program 11-1 should look familiar to you, as they contain the class declaration and implementation sections that we have already discussed. Notice, however, that this region only declares the class; it does not create any variables of this class type. This is true of all C++ types, including the built-in types such as integers and floats. Just as a variable of an integer type must be declared, variables of a user-declared class must also be declared. Variables defined to be of a user-declared class are referred to as *objects*.

---

[7] This shading is not accidental. In practice the lighter shaded region containing the class definition would be placed in a separate file. A single `#include` statement would then be used to include this class declaration in the program. Thus, the final program would consist of the two darker shaded regions illustrated in Program 11-1 with the addition of one more `#include` statement in the first region. Some programmers separate the lighter shaded region into two files: one for the declaration section and one for the implementation section.

Using this new terminology, the first statement in Program 11-1's `main()` function, contained in the darker area, defines three objects, named a, b, and c, to be of class type `Date`. In C++ whenever a new object is defined, memory is allocated for the object and its data members are automatically initialized. This is done by an automatic call to the class constructor function. For example, consider the definition `Date a, b, c(4,1,96);` contained in `main()`. When the object named a is defined the constructor function `Date` is automatically called. Since no arguments have been assigned to a, the default values of the constructor function are used, resulting in the initialization:

```
a.month = 7
a.day = 4
a.year = 94
```

Similarly, when the object named b is defined, the same default arguments are used, resulting in the initialization of b's data members as:

```
b.month = 7
b.day = 4
b.year = 94
```

The object named c, however, is defined with the arguments 4, 1, and 96. These three arguments are passed into the constructor function when the object is defined, resulting in the initialization of c's data members as:

```
c.month = 4
c.day = 1
c.year = 96
```

The next statement in `main()`, `b.setdate(12,25,95)`, calls b's `setdate` function, which assigns the argument values 12, 25, 95 to b's data members, resulting in the assignment:

```
b.month = 12
b.day = 25
b.year = 95
```

Finally, the last three statements call a, b, and c's `showdate()` function. The first call results in the display of a's data values, the second call in the display of b's data values, and the third call in the display of c's data values. Thus, the output of Program 11-1 is:

```
The date is 7/4/94
The date is 12/25/95
The date is 4/1/96
```

Notice that a statement such as `cout << a;` is invalid within `main()` because `cout` does not know how to handle an object of class `Date`. Thus, we have supplied our class with a function that can be used to access and display an object's internal values.

Terminology

As there is sometimes confusion about the terms classes, objects, and other terminology associated with object-oriented programming, we will take a moment to clarify and review the terminology.

A *class* is a programmer-defined data type out of which objects can be created. *Objects* are created from classes; they have the same relationship to classes as variables do to C++'s built-in data types. For example, in the declaration

```
int a;
```

a is said to be a variable, while in Program 11-1's declaration

```
Date a;
```

a is said to be an object or variable. If it initially helps you to think of an object as a variable, do so.

Objects are also referred to as *instances* of a class and the process of creating a new object is frequently referred to as an *instantiation* of the object. Each time a new object is instantiated (created), a new set of data members belonging to the object is created.[8] The particular values contained in these data members determines the object's *state*.

Seen in this way, a class can be thought of as a blueprint out of which particular instances (objects) can be created. Each instance (object) of a class will have its own set of particular values for the set of data members specified in the class declaration section.

In addition to the data types allowed for an object, a class also defines behavior—that is, the operations that are permitted to be performed on an object's data members. Users of the object need to know *what* these functions can do and how to activate them through function calls, but they do not need to know *how* the operation is done. The actual implementation details of an object's operations are contained in the class implementation, which can be hidden from the user. Other names for the operations defined in a class implementation section are *procedures*, *functions*, *services*, and *methods*. We will use these terms interchangeably throughout the remainder of the text.

---

[8] Note that only one set of class functions are created. These functions are shared between objects. The mechanism for using the same function on different objects' data members is presented in Section 12.3.

Exercises 11.2

1. Define the following terms:

a. class	*g.* data member
b. object	*h.* constructor
c. declaration section	*i.* class instance
d. implementation section	*j.* services
e. instance variable	*k.* methods
f. member function	*l.* interface

2. Write a class declaration section for each of the following specifications. In each case include a prototype for a constructor and a member function named `showdata()` that can be used to display member values.

a. A class named `time` that has integer data members named `secs`, `mins`, and `hours`.

b. A class named `complex` that has floating point data members named `real` and `imaginary`.

c. A class named `circle` that has integer data members named `xcenter` and `ycenter` and a floating point data member named `radius`.

d. A class named `system` that has character data members named `computer`, `printer`, and `screen`, each capable of holding 30 characters (including the end-of-string `NULL`), and floating point data members named `comp_price`, `print_price`, and `scrn_price`.

3. a. Construct a class implementation section for the constructor and `showdate()` function members corresponding to the class declaration created for Exercise 2a.

b. Construct a class implementation section for the constructor and `showdate()` function members corresponding to the class declaration created for Exercise 2b.

c. Construct a class implementation section for the constructor and `showdate()` function members corresponding to the class declaration created for Exercise 2c.

d. Construct a class implementation section for the constructor and `showdate()` function members corresponding to the class declaration created for Exercise 2d.

4. a. Include the class declaration and implementation sections prepared for Exercises 2a and 3a in a complete working program.

b. Include the class declaration and implementation sections prepared for Exercises 2b and 3b in a complete working program.

c. Include the class declaration and implementation sections prepared for Exercises 2c and 3c in a complete working program.

d. Include the class declaration and implementation sections prepared for Exercises 2d and 3d in a complete working program.

5. Determine the errors in the following class declaration section:

```
class employee
{
public:
  int empnum;
  char name[31];
private:
  class(int = 0);
  void showemp(int, char *);
};
```

6. a. Add another member function named `convrt()` to Program 11-1 that does the following: The function should access the `month`, `year`, and `day` data members and display and then return a long integer that is the calculated as *year * 10000 + month * 100 + day*. For example, if the date is 4/1/96, the returned value is 960401 (dates in this form are useful when performing sorts, because placing the numbers in numerical order automatically places the corresponding dates in chronological order).

b. Include the modified `Date` class constructed for Exercise 6a in a complete C++ program.

7. a. Add an additional member function to Program 11-1's class definition named `leapyr()` that returns a 1 when the year is a leap year and a 0 if it is not a leap year. A leap year is any year that is evenly divisible by 4 but not evenly divisible by 100, with the exception that all years evenly divisible by 400 are leap years. For example, the year 1996 is a leap year because it is evenly divisible by 4 and not evenly divisible by 100. The year 2000 will be a leap year because it is evenly divisible by 400.

b. Include the class definition constructed for Exercise 7a in a complete C++ program. The `main()` function should display the message `The year is a leap year` or `The year is not a leap year` depending on the `date` object's year value.

8. a. Add a member function to Program 11-1's class definition named `da_of_wk()` that determines the day of the week for any `date` object. An algorithm for determining the day of the week, known as Zeller's algorithm, is the following:

```
if month is less than or equal to 2
   set the variable mp = 0 and yp = year-1
else
   set mp = int(0.4 * month + 2.3) and yp = year
set the variable t = int(yp/4) - int(yp/100) + int(yp/400)
day-of-week = (365L*year + 31L*(month - 1) + day + t - mp) % 7
```

Using this algorithm the variable `day-of-week` will have a value of 0 if the date is a Sunday, 1 if a Monday, etc.

b. Include the class definition constructed for Exercise 8a in a complete C++ program. The `main()` function should display the name of the day (`Sun`, `Mon`, `Tue`, etc.) for the `Date` object being tested.

11.3 Constructors

A *constructor function* is any function that has the same name as its class. More than one constructor function for each class can be defined. One constructor function is automatically called each time an object is created with the intended purpose of initializing the new object's data members. Constructor functions may also perform other tasks when they are called and can be written in a variety of ways. In this section we present the possible variations of constructor functions and introduce another function, the destructor, which is automatically called whenever an object goes out of existence.

```
class-name::class-name(argument list)
{
   function body
}
```

FIGURE 11–4 Constructor Format

Figure 11–4 illustrates the general format of a constructor. As shown in this figure, a constructor:

- must have the same name as the class to which it belongs
- must have no `return` type (not even `void`)

If you do not include a constructor in your class definition, the compiler will supply one for you. The supplied constructor, however, is a do-nothing constructor. For example, consider the following class declaration:

```
class Date
{
   private:
     int month, day, year;
   public:
     void setdate(int, int, int);
     void showdate(void)
};
```

Since no user-defined constructor has been declared here, the compiler creates a default constructor. For our `Date` class this default constructor is equivalent to the implementation `Date::Date(void){}`—that is, the compiler-supplied default constructor expects no arguments and has an empty body. Clearly this default constructor is not very useful, but it does exist if no other constructor is declared.

The term *default constructor* is used quite frequently in C++. It refers to any constructor that does not require any arguments when it is called. This can be because no arguments are declared, which is the case for the compiler-supplied default, or because all arguments have been given default values. For example, the constructor `Date::Date(int mm = 7, int dd = 4, int yy = 94)` is a valid header for a default constructor also. Here, each argument has been given a default value, and an object can be declared as type `Date` without supplying any further arguments. Using such a constructor, the declaration `Date a;` initializes the a object with the default values 7, 4, and 94.

To verify that a constructor function is automatically called whenever a new object is created, consider Program 11-2. Notice that in the implementation section the constructor function uses `cout` to display the message `Created a new object with data values`. Thus, whenever the constructor is called this message is displayed. Since the `main()` function creates three objects, the constructor is called three times and the message is displayed three times.

Program 11-2

```cpp
#include <iostream.h>
```

```cpp
// class declaration section
class Date
{
  private:
    int month;
    int day;
    int year;
  public:
    Date(int, int, int);    // constructor
};

// implementation section
Date::Date(int mm = 7, int dd = 4, int yy = 94)
{
  month = mm;
  day = dd;
  year = yy;
  cout << "Created a new data object with data values "
       << month << ", " << day << ", " << year << "\n";
}
```

```cpp
void main(void)
{
  Date a;          // declare an ojbect
  Date b;          // declare an object
  Date c(4,1,96);  // declare an object
}
```

The following output is produced when Program 11-2 is executed:

```
Created a new data object with data values 7, 4, 94
Created a new data object with data values 7, 4, 94
Created a new data object with data values 4, 1, 96
```

Although any legitimate C++ statement can be used within a constructor function, such as the cout call made in Program 11-2, it is best to keep constructors simple and use them only for initializing purposes. One further point needs to be made with respect to the constructor function contained in Program 11-2. According to the rules of C++, object members are initialized in the order they are declared in the class declaration section and *not* in the order they may appear in the function's definition within the implementation section. Usually this will not be an issue, unless one member is initialized using another data member's value.

Calling Constructors

As we have seen, constructors are called whenever an object is created. The actual declaration, however, can be made in a variety of ways.

For example, the declaration

```
Date c(4,1,96);
```

used in Program 11-2 could also have been written as:

```
Date c = Date(4,1,96);
```

This second form declares c as being of type Date and then makes a direct call to the constructor function with the arguments 4, 1, and 96. This second form can be simplified when only one argument is passed to the constructor. For example, if only the month data member of the c object needed to be initialized with the value 8 and the day and year members can use the default values, the object can be created using the declaration

```
Date c = 8;
```

Since this resembles declarations in C, it and its more complete form using the equal sign is referred to as the *C style of initialization*. The form of declaration used in Program 11-2 is referred to as the *C++ style of initialization*, and is the form we will use predominantly throughout the remainder of the text.

Regardless of which initialization form you use, in no case should an object be declared with empty parentheses. For example, the declaration Date a(); is not the same as the declaration Date a;. The latter declaration uses the default constructor values while the former declaration results in no object being created.

Overloaded and Inline Constructors

The primary difference between a constructor and other user-written functions is how the constructor is called: Constructors are called automatically each time an object is created, while other functions must be explicitly called by name.[9] As a function, however, a constructor must still follow all of the rules applicable to user-written functions that were presented in Chapter 6. This means that constructors may have default arguments, as was illustrated in Program 11-2, may be overloaded, and may be written as inline functions.

---

[9] This is true for all functions except destructors, which are described later in this section. A destructor function is automatically called each time an object is destroyed.

Recall from Section 6.1 that function overloading permits the same function name to be used with different argument lists. Based on the supplied argument types the compiler determines which function to use when the call is encountered. Let's see how this can be applied to our Date class. For convenience the appropriate class declaration is repeated below:

```
// class declaration section
class Date
{
  private:
    int month;
    int day;
    int year;
  public:
    Date(int, int, int);          // constructor
};
```

Here, the constructor prototype specifies three integer arguments, which are used to initialize the month, day, and year data members.

An alternate method of specifying a date is to use a long integer in the form *year * 10000 + month * 100 + day*. For example, the date 12/24/88 using this form is 881224 and the date 2/5/91 is 910205.[10] A suitable prototype for a constructor that uses dates of this form is:

```
Date(long);    // an overloaded constructor
```

Here, the constructor is declared as receiving one long integer argument. The code for this new Date function must, of course, correctly convert its single argument into a month, day, and year, and would be included within the class implementation section. The actual code for such a constructor is:

```
Date::Date(long yymmdd)     // a second constructor
{
  year = int(yymmdd/10000.0);     // extract the year
  month = int( (yymmdd - year * 10000.0) / 100.00 ); // extract the month
  day = int(yymmdd - year * 10000.0 - month * 100.0); // extract the day
}
```

Do not be overly concerned with the actual conversion code used within the function's body. The important point here is the concept of overloading the Date() function to provide two constructors. Program 11-3 contains the complete class definition within the context of a working program.

---

[10] The reason for specifying dates in this manner is that only one number needs to be used per date and that sorting the numbers automatically puts the corresponding dates into chronological order. For dates after the turn of the century 100 is added to the year. Thus 7/15/03 is represented as the long integer 1030715.

Program 11-3

```
#include <iostream.h>
```

```
// class declaration section
class Date
{
 private:
    int month;
    int day;
    int year;
  public:
    Date(int, int, int);      // constructor
    Date(long);               // another constructor
    void showdate(void);      // member function to display a date
};

// implementation section
Date::Date(int mm = 7, int dd = 4, int yy = 94)
{
  month = mm;
  day = dd;
  year = yy;
}
Date::Date(long yymmdd)      // here is the overloaded constructor
{
  year = int(yymmdd/10000.0);      // extract the year
  month = int( (yymmdd - year * 10000.0)/100.00 ); // extract the month
  day = int(yymmdd - year * 10000.0 - month * 100.0); // extract the day
}
void Date::showdate(void)
{
  cout << "The date is " << month << "/" << day << "/" << year << "\n";
}
```

```
void main(void)
{
  Date a, b(4,1,96), c(970515); // declare three objects

  a.showdate();           // display object a's values
  b.showdate();           // display object b's values
  c.showdate();           // display object c's values
}
```

The output provided by Program 11-3 is:

```
The date is 7/4/94
The date is 4/1/96
The date is 5/15/97
```

Three objects are created in Program 11-3's `main()` function. The first object, a, is initialized with the default constructor using its default arguments. Object b is also initialized with the default constructor but uses the arguments 4, 1, and 96. Finally, object c, which is initialized with a long integer, uses the second constructor in the class implementation section. The compiler knows to use this second constructor because the argument specified, 970515, is a long integer. It is worthwhile pointing out that a compiler error would occur if both `Date` constructors had default values. In such a case a declaration such as `Date d;` would be ambiguous to the compiler, as it would not be able to determine which constructor to use. Thus, in each implementation section only one constructor can be written as the default.

Just as constructors may be overloaded, they may also be written as inline functions. Doing so simply means defining the function in the class declaration section. For example, making both of the constructors contained in Program 11-3 inline is accomplished by the declaration section:

```cpp
// class declaration section
class Date
{
  private:
    int month;
    int day;
    int year;
  public:
    Date(int mm = 7, int dd = 4, int yy = 94)
    {
      month = mm;
      day = dd;
      year = yy;
    }
    Date(long yymmdd)    // here is the overloaded constructor
    {
      year = int(yymmdd/10000.0);    // extract the year
      month = int( (yymmdd - year * 10000.0)/100.00 );  // extract the month
      day = int(yymmdd - year * 10000.0 - month * 100.0); // extract the day
    }
};
```

The keyword `inline` is not required in this declaration because member functions defined inside the class declaration are inline by default.

Generally, only functions that can be coded on a single line are good candidates for inline functions. This reinforces the convention that inline functions should be small. Thus, the first constructor is more conventionally written as:

```
Date(int mm = 7, int dd = 4, int yy = 94)
{ month = mm; day = dd; year = yy; }
```

The second constructor, which extends over three lines, should not be written as an inline function.

Destructors

The counterpart to constructor functions are destructor functions. Destructors are functions having the same class name as constructors, but preceded with a tilde (~). Thus, for our `Date` class, the destructor name is `~Date()`. Like constructors, a default do-nothing destructor is provided by the C++ compiler in the absence of an explicit destructor. Unlike constructors, however, there can only be one destructor function per class. This is because destructors take no arguments—they also return no values.

Destructors are automatically called whenever an object goes out of existence, and are meant to "cleanup" any undesirable effects that might be left by the object. Generally such effects only occur when an object contains a pointer member, which is the topic of Section 12.2.

Arrays of Objects

The importance of default constructors becomes evident when arrays of objects are created. Since a constructor is called each time an object is created, the default constructor provides an elegant way of initializing all objects to the same state.

Declaring an array of objects is the same as declaring an array of any built-in type. For example, the declaration

```
Date thedate[5];
```

will create five objects named `thedate[0]` through `thedate[4]`, respectively. Member functions for each of these objects are called by listing the object name followed by a dot (.) and the desired function. An example using an array of objects is provided by Program 11-4, which also includes `cout` statements within both the constructor and destructor. As illustrated by the output of this program, the constructor is called for each declared object, followed by five member function calls to `showdate()`, followed by five destructor calls. The destructor is called when the objects go out of scope. In this case, the destructor is called when the `main()` function terminates execution.

Program 11-4

```cpp
#include <iostream.h>
```

```cpp
// class declaration section
class Date
{
  private:
    int month;
    int day;
    int year;
  public:
    Date();     // constructor
    ~Date();    // destructor
    void showdate(void);
};

// class implementation
Date::Date()          // user-defined default constructor
{
  cout << "*** A Date object is being initialized ***\n";
  month = 1;
  day = 1;
  year = 95;
}

Date::~Date()         // user-defined default destructor
{
  cout << "*** A Date object is going out of existence ***\n";
}

void Date::showdate(void)
{
  cout << "            "
       << "The date is " << month << "/" << day << "/" << year << "\n";
}
```

```cpp
void main(void)
{
  Date thedate[5];

  for(int i = 0; i < 5; i++)
    thedate[i].showdate();
}
```

The output produced by Program 11-4 is:

```
*** A Date object is being initialized ***
*** A Date object is being initialized ***
*** A Date object is being initialized ***
*** A Date object is being initialized ***
*** A Date object is being initialized ***
                The date is 1/1/95
                The date is 1/1/95
                The date is 1/1/95
                The date is 1/1/95
                The date is 1/1/95
*** A Date object is going out of existence ***
*** A Date object is going out of existence ***
*** A Date object is going out of existence ***
*** A Date object is going out of existence ***
*** A Date object is going out of existence ***
```

Exercises 11.3

1. Determine whether the following statements are true or false:
   a. A constructor function must have the same name as its class.
   b. A class can only have one constructor function.
   c. A class can only have one default constructor function.
   d. A default constructor can only be supplied by the compiler.
   e. A default constructor can have no arguments or all arguments must have default values.
   f. A constructor must be declared for each class.
   g. A constructor must be declared with a return type.
   h. A constructor is automatically called each time an object is created.
   i. A class can only have one destructor function.
   j. A destructor must have the same name as its class, preceded by a tilde (~).
   k. A destructor can have default arguments.
   l. A destructor must be declared for each class.
   m. A destructor must be declared with a `return` type.
   n. A destructor is automatically called each time an object goes out of existence.
   o. Destructors are not useful when the class contains a pointer data member.

2. For Program 11-3, what date would be initialized for object c if the declaration `Date c(15);` was used in place of the declaration `Date c(970515);`?

3. Modify Program 11-3 so that the only data member of the class is a long integer named `yymmdd`. Do this by substituting the declaration

```
long yymmdd;
```

for the existing declarations

```
int month;
int day;
int year;
```

Then, using the same constructor function prototypes currently declared in the class declaration section, rewrite them so that the Date(long) function becomes the default constructor and the Date(int, int, int) function converts a month, day, and year into the proper form for the class data member.

4. a. Construct a Time class containing integer data members seconds, minutes, and hours. Have the class contain two constructors. The first should be a default constructor having the prototype time(int, int, int), which uses default values of 0 for each data member. The second constructor should accept a long integer representing a total number of seconds and disassemble the long integer into hours, minutes, and seconds. The final function member should display the class data members.

b. Include the class written for Exercise 4a within the context of a complete program.

5. a. Construct a class named Student consisting of an integer student identification number, an array of five floating point grades, and an integer representing the total number of grades entered. The constructor for this class should initialize all Student members to zero. Included in the class should be member functions to (1) enter a student ID number, (2) enter a single test grade and update the total number of grades entered, and (3) compute an average grade and display the student ID followed by the average grade.

b. Include the class constructed in Exercise 5a within the context of a complete program. Your program should declare two objects of type Student and accept and display data for the two objects to verify operation of the member functions.

11.4 An Application

Now that you have an understanding of how classes are constructed and the terminology used in describing them, let us apply this knowledge to a particular application. In this application we simulate the operation of an elevator. We assume that the elevator can travel between the 1st and 15th floors of a building and that the location of the elevator must be known at all times.

For this application the location of the elevator corresponds to its current floor position and is represented by an integer variable ranging between 1 and 15. The value of this variable, which we will name cur_floor, for current floor, effectively represents the current state of the elevator. The services that we will provide for changing the state of the elevator will be an initialization function to set the initial floor position when a new elevator is put in service, and a request function to change the elevator's position (state) to a new floor. Putting an elevator in service is accomplished by declaring a single class instance (declaring an object of type Elevator), while requesting a new floor position is equivalent to pushing an elevator button. To accomplish this, a suitable class declaration is:

```
            // class declaration section
            class Elevator
            {
              private:
                int cur_floor;
              public:
                Elevator(int);        // constructor
                void request(int);
            };
```

Notice that we have declared one data member, `cur_floor`, and two class functions. The data member, `cur_floor`, is used to store the current floor position of the elevator. As a private member it can only be accessed through member functions. The two public member functions, `Elevator()` and `request()`, define the external services provided by each `Elevator` object. The `Elevator()` function, which has the same name as its class, becomes a constructor function that is automatically called when an object of type `Elevator` is created. We will use this function to initialize the starting floor position of each elevator. The `request()` function is used to alter the position of the elevator. To accomplish these services a suitable class implementation section is:

```
// class implementation section

Elevator::Elevator(int cfloor = 1)    // constructor
{
.  cur_floor = cfloor;
}

void Elevator::request(int newfloor)   // access function
{
  if (newfloor < 1 || newfloor > MAXFLOOR || newfloor == cur_floor)
    ;  // do nothing
  else if ( newfloor > cur_floor)   // move elevator up
  {
    cout << "\nStarting at floor " << cur_floor << "\n";
    while (newfloor > cur_floor)
    {
      cur_floor++;     // add one to current floor
      cout << "   Going Up - now at floor " << cur_floor << "\n";
    }
    cout << "Stopping at floor " << cur_floor << "\n";
  }
  else  // move elevator down
  {
    cout << "\nStarting at floor " << cur_floor << "\n";
    while (newfloor < cur_floor)
    {
      cur_floor--;    // subtract one from current floor
      cout << "   Going Down - now at floor " << cur_floor << "\n";
    }
    cout << "Stopping at floor " << cur_floor << "\n";
  }
}
```

The constructor function is straightforward. When an `elevator` object is declared it is initialized to the floor specified; if no floor is explicitly given the default value of 1 will be used. For example, the declaration

```
Elevator a(7);
```

initializes the variable `a.cur_floor` to 7, while the declaration

```
Elevator a;
```

uses the default argument value and initializes the variable `a.cur_floor` to 1.

The `request()` function defined in the implementation section is more complicated and provides the class' primary service. Essentially this function consists of an `if-else` statement having three parts: If an incorrect service is requested no action is taken, if a floor above the current position is selected the elevator is moved up, and if a floor below the current position is selected the elevator is moved down. For movement up or down the function uses a `while` loop to increment the position one floor at a time, and reports the elevator's movement using a `cout` object call. Program 11-5 includes this class in a working program.

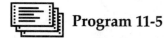 **Program 11-5**

```
#include <iostream.h>
```

```
const int MAXFLOOR = 15;

// class declaration section
class Elevator
{
  private:
    int cur_floor;
  public:
    Elevator(int);        // constructor
    void request(int);
};

// implementation section
Elevator::Elevator(int cfloor = 1)    // constructor
{
  cur_floor = cfloor;
}
```

(continued on next page)

(continued from previous page)

```cpp
void Elevator::request(int newfloor)  // access function

{
 if (newfloor < 1 || newfloor > MAXFLOOR || newfloor == cur_floor)
   ;  // do nothing
  else if ( newfloor > cur_floor)  // move elevator up
  {
    cout << "\nStarting at floor " << cur_floor << "\n";
    while (newfloor > cur_floor)
    {
      cur_floor++;      // add one to current floor
      cout << "  Going Up - now at floor " << cur_floor << "\n";
    }
    cout << "Stopping at floor " << cur_floor << "\n";
  }
  else  // move elevator down
  {
    cout << "\nStarting at floor " << cur_floor << "\n";
    while (newfloor < cur_floor)
    {
      cur_floor--;   // subtract one from current floor
      cout << "  Going Down - now at floor " << cur_floor << "\n";
    }
    cout << "Stopping at floor " << cur_floor << "\n";
  }
```

```cpp
void main(void)
{
  Elevator a;    // declare 1 object of type Elevator

  a.request(6);
  a.request(3);
}
```

The lightly shaded portion of Program 11-5 contains the class construction that we have already described. To see how this class is used, concentrate on the darker shaded section of the program. At the top of the program we have included the iostream.h header file and declared a constant variable MAXFLOOR, which corresponds to the highest floor that can be requested.

Within the main() function three statements are included. The first statement creates an object named a of type elevator. Since no explicit floor has been given, this elevator will begin at floor 1, which is the default constructor argument.

A request is then made to move the elevator to floor 6, which is followed by a request to move to floor 3. The output produced by Program 11-5 is:

```
Starting at floor 1
   Going Up - now at floor 2
   Going Up - now at floor 3
   Going Up - now at floor 4
   Going Up - now at floor 5
   Going Up - now at floor 6
Stopping at floor 6

Starting at floor 6
   Going Down - now at floor 5
   Going Down - now at floor 4
   Going Down - now at floor 3
Stopping at floor 3
```

The basic requirements of object-oriented programming are evident in even as simple a program as Program 11-5. Before the main() function can be written a useful class must be constructed. This is typical of programs that use objects. For such programs the design process is front-loaded with the requirement that careful consideration of the class—its declaration and implementation—be given. Code contained in the implementation section effectively removes code that would otherwise be part of main()'s responsibility. Thus, any program that uses the object does not have to repeat the implementation details within its main() function. Rather the main() function and any function called by main() is only concerned with sending messages to its objects to activate them appropriately. How the object responds to the messages and how the state of the object is retained is not main()'s concern—these details are hidden within the class construction.

Exercises 11.4

1. Enter Program 11-5 in your computer and execute it.

2. Modify the main() function in Program 11-5 to put a second elevator in service starting at the 5th floor. Have this second elevator move to the 1st floor and then move to the 12th floor.

3. Verify that the constructor function is called by adding a message within the constructor that is displayed each time a new object is created. Run your program to ensure its operation.

4. a. Construct a class definition that can be used to represent an employee of a company. Each employee is defined by an integer ID number, a name consisting of no more than 30 characters, a floating point pay rate, and the maximum number of hours the employee should work each week. The services provided by the class should be the ability to enter data for a new employee, the ability to change data for a new employee, and the ability to display the existing data for a new employee.

b. Include the class definition created for Exercise 4a in a working C++ program that asks the user to enter data for three employees and displays the entered data.

c. Modify the program written for Exercise 4b to include a menu that offers the user the following choices:

```
1. Add an Employee
2. Modify Employee data
3. Delete an Employee
4. Exit this menu
```

In response to a choice the program should initiate appropriate action to implement the choice.

5. *a.* Construct a class definition that can be used to represent types of food. A type of food is classified as basic or prepared. Basic foods are further classified as either Dairy, Meat, Fruit, Vegetable, or Grain. The services provided by the class should be the ability to enter data for a new food, the ability to change data for a new food, and the ability to display the existing data for a new food.

b. Include the class definition created for Exercise 5a in a working C++ program that asks the user to enter data for four food items and displays the entered data.

c. Modify the program written for Exercise 5b to include a menu that offers the user the following choices:

```
1. Add a Food Item
2. Modify a Food Item
3. Delete a Food Item
4. Exit this menu
```

In response to a choice the program should initiate appropriate action to implement the choice.

11.5 Common Programming Errors

The more common programming errors initially associated with the construction of classes are:

1. Failing to terminate the class declaration section with a semicolon.

2. Including a `return` type with the constructor's prototype or failing to include a `return` type with the other functions' prototypes.

3. Defining more than one default constructor for a class.

4. Forgetting to include the class name and scope operator, `::`, in the header line of all member functions defined in the class implementation section.

All of these errors will result in a compiler error message.

11.6 Chapter Summary

1. A *class* is a programmer-defined data type. *Objects* of a class may be defined and have the same relationship to their class as variables do to C++'s built-in data types.

2. A class definition consists of a declaration and implementation section. The most common form of a class definition is:

```
// class declaration section
class name
{
  private:
   a list of variable declarations;
  public:
    a list of function prototypes;
};

// class implementation section
class function definitions
```

The variables and functions declared in the class declaration section are collectively referred to as *class members*. The variables are individually referred to as class data members and the functions as class member functions. The terms `private` and `public` are access specifiers. Once an access specifier is listed it remains in force until another access specifier is given. The `private` keyword specifies that the class members following it are private to the class and can only be accessed by member functions. The `public` keyword specifies that the class members following may be accessed from outside the class. Generally all data members should be specified as `private` and all member functions as `public`.

3. Class functions listed in the declaration section may either be written inline or their definitions included in the class implementation section. Except for constructor and destructor functions, all class functions defined in the class implementation section have the header line form:

```
return-type  class-name::function-name(argument list);
```

Except for the addition of the class name and scope operator, `::`, which are required to identify the function name with the class, this header line is identical to the header line used for any user-written function.

4. A *constructor function* is a special function that is automatically called each time an object is declared. It must have the same name as its class and cannot have any `return` type. Its purpose is to initialize each declared object.

5. If no constructor is declared for a class the compiler will supply a *default constructor*. This is a do-nothing function having the definition `class-name::class-name(void){}`.

6. The term *default constructor* refers to any constructor that does not require any arguments when it is called. This can be because no arguments are declared (as is the case for the compiler-supplied default constructor) or because all arguments have been given default values.

7. Each class may only have one default constructor. If a user-defined default constructor is defined the compiler will not create its default constructor. Thus, if any class constructor is user-defined, a default class constructor must also be user-defined.

8. Objects are created using either a C++ or C style of declaration. The C++ style of declaration has the form:

```
class-name list of object names(list of initializers);
```

where the list of initializers is optional. An example of this style of declaration, including initializers, for a class named `Date` is:

```
Date a,b,c(12,25,98);
```

Here the objects `a` and `b` are declared to be of type `Date` and are initialized using the default constructor, while the object `c` is initialized with the values 12, 25, and 98.

The equivalent C style of declaration, including the optional list of initializers, has the form:

```
class-name object-name = class-name(list of initializers);
```

An example of this style of declaration for a class named `Date` is:

```
Date c = Date(12,25,98)
```

Here the object `c` is created and initialized with the values 12, 25, and 98.

9. Constructors may be overloaded in the same manner as any other user-written C++ function.

10. If a constructor is defined for a class, a user-defined default constructor should be written, as the compiler will not supply it.

11. A *destructor function* is called each time an object goes out of scope. Destructors must have the same name as their class, but preceded with a tilde (~). There can only be one destructor per class.

12. A *destructor function* takes no arguments and returns no value. If a user-defined destructor is not included in a class, the compiler will provide a do-nothing destructor.

13. Arrays of objects are declared in the same manner as arrays of C++'s built-in data types. For example, if `Date` is a class name, the declaration

```
Date thedate[5];
```

creates five objects named `thedate[0]` through `thedate[4]`. Member functions for each of these objects are called by listing the object name, such as `thedate[3]`, followed by a dot (.) and the desired member function name.

Additional
Class
Capabilities

Chapter Twelve

The creation of a class requires that we provide the capability to declare, initialize, assign, manipulate, and display data members. In the previous chapter the declaration, initialization, and display of objects was presented. In this chapter we continue our construction of classes and see how to provide assignment between objects and include pointer members within a class declaration.

12.1 Assignment

In Chapter 3 we saw how C++'s assignment operator, =, performs assignment between variables. In this section we see how assignment works when it is applied to objects and how to define our own assignment operator to override the default provided for user-defined classes.

For a specific assignment example, consider the `main()` function of Program 12-1.

Program 12-1

```
#include <iostream.h>
```

```
// class declaration
class Date
{
  private:
    int month;
    int day;
    int year;
  public:
    Date(int, int, int);        // constructor
    void showdate(void);        // member function to display a Date
};
// implementation section
Date::Date(int mm = 7, int dd = 4, int yy = 94)
{
  month = mm;
  day = dd;
  year = yy;
}
void Date::showdate(void)
{
  cout << month << "/" << day << "/" << year << endl;
}
```

(continued on next page)

414

(continued from previous page)

```
void main(void)
{
  Date a(4,1,96), b(12,18,97); // declare two objects

  cout << "The date stored in a is originally ";
  a.showdate();  // display the original date
  a = b;         // assign b's value to a
  cout << "After assignment the date stored in a is ";
  a.showdate();  // display a's values
}
```

Notice that the implementation section of the Date class in Program 12-1 contains no assignment function. Nevertheless, we would expect the assignment statement a = b; in main() to assign b's data member values to their counterparts in a. This is, in fact, the case and it is verified by the output produced when Program 12-1 is executed:

```
The date stored in a is originally 4/1/96
After assignment the date stored in a is 12/18/97
```

This type of assignment is called *memberwise assignment*. In the absence of any specific instructions to the contrary, the C++ compiler builds this type of default assignment operator for each class. If the class *does not* contain any pointer data members, this default assignment operator is adequate and can be used without further consideration. Before considering the problems that can occur with pointer data members, let's see how to construct our own explicit assignment operators.

Assignment operators, like all class members, are declared in the class declaration section and defined in the class implementation section. For the declaration of operators, however, the keyword operator must be included in the declaration. Using this keyword, a simple assignment operator declaration has the form:

```
void operator=(class-name &);
```

Here the keyword void indicates that the assignment returns no value, the operator= indicates that we are overloading the assignment operator with our own version, and the class name and ampersand within the parentheses indicates that the argument to the operator is a class reference. For example, to declare a simple assignment operator for our Date class, the declaration:

```
void operator=(Date &);
```

can be used.

The actual implementation of the assignment operator is defined in the implementation section. For our declaration, a suitable implementation is:

```
void Date::operator=(Date &newdate)
{
  month = newdate.month;   // assign the month
  day = newdate.day;       // assign the day
  year = newdate.year;     // assign the year
}
```

The use of the reference argument in the definition of this operation is not accidental. In fact, one of the primary reasons for adding reference variables to C++ was to facilitate the construction of overloaded operators and make the notation more natural. In this definition `newdate` is defined as a reference to a `Date` class. Within the body of the definition the `day` member of the object referenced by `newdate` is assigned to the `day` member of the current object, which is then repeated for the `month` and `year` members. Assignments such as `a.operator=(b);` can then be used to call the overloaded assignment operator and assign b's member values to a. For convenience, the expression `a.operator=(b)` can be replaced with `a = b;`. Program 12-2 contains our new assignment operator within the context of a complete program.

Program 12-2

```
#include <iostream.h>

// class declaration
class Date
{
  private:
    int month;
    int day;
    int year;
  public:
    Date(int, int, int);       // constructor
    void operator=(Date &);    // define assignment of a date
    void showdate(void);       // member function to display a date
};

// implementation section
Date::Date(int mm = 7, int dd = 4, int yy = 94)
{
  month = mm;
  day = dd;
  year = yy;
}
void Date::operator=(Date &newdate)
{
```

(continued on next page)

(continued from previous page)

```
  month = newdate.month;     // assign the month
  day = newdate.day;         // assign the day
  year = newdate.year;       // assign the year

  return;
}
void Date::showdate(void)
{
  cout << month << "/" << day << "/" << year << endl;
}
```

```
void main(void)
{
  Date a(4,1,96), b(12,18,97); // declare two objects

  cout << "The date stored in a is originally ";
  a.showdate();   // display the original date
  a = b;          // assign b's value to a
  cout << "After assignment the date stored in a is ";
  a.showdate();   // display a's values
}
```

Except for the addition of the overloaded assignment operator declaration and definition, Program 12-2 is identical to Program 12-1 and produces the same output. Its usefulness to us is that it illustrates how we can explicitly construct our own assignment definitions. In the next section, when we introduce pointer data members, we will see how C++'s default assignment can cause troublesome errors that are circumvented by constructing our own assignment operators. Before moving on, however, two simple modifications to our assignment operator need to be made.

First, to preclude any inadvertent alteration to the object used on the right-hand side of the assignment a constant reference argument should be used. For our Date class, this takes the form:

```
void Date::operator=(const Date &secdate);
```

The final modification concerns the operation's return value. As constructed, our simple assignment operator returns no value, which precludes us from using it in multiple assignments such as a = b = c. The reason for this is that overloaded operators retain the same precedence and associativity as their equivalent built-in versions. Thus, an expression such as a = b = c is evaluated in the order a = (b = c). As we have defined assignment, unfortunately, the expression b = c returns no value, making subsequent assignment to a an error. To provide for multiple assignments a more complete assignment operation would return a reference to its class type. Because the implementation of such an assignment requires a special class pointer, the presentation of this more complete assignment operator is deferred until the material presented in Section 12.3 is introduced. Until then, our simple assignment operator will be more than adequate for our needs.

Copy Constructors

Although assignment looks similar to initialization, it is worthwhile noting that they are two entirely different operations. In C++ an initialization occurs every time a new object is created. In an assignment no new object is created—the value of an existing object is simply changed. Figure 12–1 illustrates this difference.

One type of initialization that closely resembles assignment occurs in C++ when one object is initialized using another object of the same class. For example, in the declaration

```
Date b = a;
```

or its entirely equivalent form

```
Date b(a);
```

the b object is initialized to a previously declared a object. The constructor that performs this type of initialization is called a *copy constructor*, and if you do not declare one the compiler will construct one for you. The compiler's *default copy constructor* performs in a similar manner to the default assignment operator by doing a memberwise copy between objects. Thus, for the declaration Date b = a; the default copy constructor sets b's month, day, and year values to their respective counterparts in a. As with default assignment operators, default copy constructors work just fine unless the class contains pointer data members. Before considering the complications that can occur with pointer data members and how to handle them, it will be helpful to see how to construct our own copy constructors.

Copy constructors, like all class functions, are declared in the class declaration section and defined in the class implementation section. The declaration of a copy constructor has the general form:

```
class-name(const class-name &);
```

FIGURE 12–1 Initialization and Assignment

$$c = a \qquad \longleftarrow \text{Assignment}$$

Type definition $\longrightarrow$ Date c = a; $\longleftarrow$ Initialization

As with all constructors, the function name must be the class name. As further illustrated by the declaration, the argument is a reference to the class, which is a characteristic of all copy constructors.[1] To ensure that the argument is not inadvertently altered, it is always specified as a `const`. Applying this general form to our `Date` class, a copy constructor can be explicitly declared as:

```
Date(const Date &);
```

The actual implementation of this constructor, if it were to perform the same memberwise initialization as the default copy constructor, would take the form:

```
Date:: Date(const Date &olddate)
{
   month = olddate.month;
   day = olddate.day;
   year = olddate.year;
}
```

As with the assignment operator, the use of a reference argument for the copy constructor is no accident: The reference argument again facilitates a simple notation within the body of the function. Program 12-3 contains this copy constructor within the context of a complete program.

Program 12-3

```
#include <iostream.h>
```

```
// class declaration
class Date
{
  private:
    int month;
    int day;
    int year;
  public:
    Date(int, int, int);      // constructor
    Date(const Date &);       // copy constructor
    void showdate(void);      // member function to display a date
};
```
(continued on next page)

---

[1] A copy constructor is frequently defined as a constructor whose first argument is a reference to its class type, with any additional arguments being defaults.

(continued from previous page)

```
// implementation section
Date::Date(int mm = 7, int dd = 4, int yy = 94)
{
  month = mm;
  day = dd;
  year = yy;
}
Date::Date(const Date &olddate)
{
  month = olddate.month;
  day = olddate.day;
  year = olddate.year;
}
void Date::showdate(void)
{
  cout << month << "/" << day << "/" << year << endl;
}
```

```
void main(void)
{
  Date a(4,1,96), b(12,18,97); // use the constructor
  Date c(a);   // use the copy constructor
  Date d = b;  // use the copy constructor

  cout << "The date stored in a is ";
  a.showdate();
  cout << "The date stored in b is ";
  b.showdate();
  cout << "The date stored in c is ";
  c.showdate();
  cout << "The date stored in d is ";
  d.showdate();
}
```

The output produced by Program 12-3 is:

```
The date stored in a is 4/1/96
The date stored in b is 12/18/97
The date stored in c is 4/1/96
The date stored in d is 12/18/97
```

As illustrated by this output, c's and d's data members have been initialized by the copy constructor to a's and b's values, respectively. Although the copy constructor defined in Program 12-3 adds nothing to the functionality provided by the compiler's default copy constructor, it does provide us with the fundamentals of defining copy constructors. In the next section we will see how to modify this basic copy constructor to handle cases that are not adequately taken care of by the compiler's default.

Base/Member Initialization[2]

Except for the reference names `olddate` and `newdate`, a comparison of Program 12-3's copy constructor to Program 12-2's assignment operator shows them to be essentially the same function. The difference in these functions is that the copy constructor first creates an object's data members before the body of the constructor uses assignment to specify member values. Thus, the copy constructor does not perform a true initialization, but rather a creation followed by assignment.

A true initialization would have no reliance on assignment whatsoever and is possible in C++ using a *base/member initialization list*. Such a list can only be applied to constructor functions and may be written in two ways.

The first way to construct a base/member initialization list is within a class' declaration section using the form:

```
class-name(argument list) : list of data members(initializing values) {}
```

For example, using this form a default constructor that performs true initialization is:

```
// class declaration section
public:
  Date(int mo=4, int da=1, int yr=96) : month(mo), day(da), year(yr) {}
```

The second way is to declare a prototype in the class' declaration section followed by the initialization list in the implementation section. For our date constructor this takes the form:

```
// class declaration section
public:
  Date(int=4, int=1, int=96);  // prototype with defaults

// class implementation section
Date::Date(int mo, int da, int yr) : month(mo), day(da), year(yr) {}
```

Notice that in both forms the body of the constructor function is empty. This is not a requirement, and the body can include any subsequent operations that you would like the constructor to perform. The interesting feature of this type of constructor is that it clearly differentiates between the initialization tasks performed in the member initialization list contained between the colon and the braces, and any subsequent assignments that might be contained within the

---

[2] The material in this section is presented for completeness only, and may be omitted without loss of subject continuity.

function's body. Although we will not be using this type of initialization subsequently, it is required whenever there is a `const` class instance variable.

Exercises 12.1

1. Describe the difference between assignment and initialization.

2. a. Construct a class named `Time` that contains three integer data members named `hrs, mins,` and `secs,` which will be used to store hours, minutes, and seconds. The function members should include a constructor that provides default values of 0 for each data member, a display function that prints an object's data values, and an assignment operator that performs a memberwise assignment between two `Time` objects.
b. Include the `Time` class developed in Exercise 2a in a working C++ program that creates and displays two `Time` objects, the second of which is assigned the values of the first object.

3. a. Construct a class named `Complex` that contains two floating point data members named `real` and `imag`, which will be used to store the real and imaginary parts of a complex number. The function members should include a constructor that provides default values of 0 for each member function, a display function that prints an object's data values, and an assignment operator that performs a memberwise assignment between two complex number objects.
b. Include the program written for Exercise 3a in a working C++ program that creates and displays the values of two complex objects, the second of which is assigned the values of the first object.

4. a. Construct a class named `Car` that contains the following four data members: a floating point variable named `engine_size`, a character variable named `body_style`, an integer variable named `color_code`, and a pointer named `vin_ptr` to a character. The function members should include a constructor that provides default values of 0 for each numeric data member, 'X' for each character variable, and a `NULL` for each pointer; a display function that prints the engine size, body style and color code; and an assignment operator that performs a memberwise assignment between two `Car` objects for each instance variable except the pointer member.
b. Include the program written for Exercise 4a in a working C++ program that creates and displays two `Car` objects, the second of which is assigned the values of the first object, except for the pointer data member.

5. For a class that contains a pointer data member, such as the one described in Exercise 4, what problems can you anticipate for such a class when a memberwise assignment is performed between two class objects?

12.2 Pointers as Class Members

As we saw in Section 11.2, a class can contain any C++ data type. Thus, the inclusion of a pointer variable in a class should not seem surprising. For example, the class declaration:

```
class Test
{
  private:
    int id_num;
    double *pt_pay;
  public:
    Test(int, double *); //constructor
    void setvals(int a, double *b);
    void display();
};
```

declares a class consisting of two instance variables and three member functions. The first instance variable is an integer variable named id_num, and the second instance variable is a pointer named pt_pay, which is a pointer to a double precision number. We will use the setvals() member function to store values into the private member variables and the display() function for output purposes. The implementation of these two functions along with the constructor function Test() is contained in the class implementation section:

```
// class implementation

Test::Test(int id = 0,  double *pt = NULL)
{
  id_num = id;
  pt_pay = pt;
}

void Test::setvals(int a, double *b)
{
  id_num = a;
  pt_pay = b;
}

void Test::display()
{
  cout << "\nEmployee number " << id_num << " was paid $"
       << setiosflags(ios::showpoint)
       << setw(6) << setprecision(2)
       << *pt_pay << endl;
}
```

In this implementation the Test() constructor initializes its id_num data member to its first argument and its pointer member to its second argument; if no arguments are given these variables are initialized to 0 and NULL, respectively. The display function simply outputs the value pointed to by its pointer member. As defined in this implementation the setvals() function is very similar to the constructor and is used to alter member values after the object has been declared: The function's first argument (an integer) is assigned to id_num and its second argument (an address) is assigned to pt_pay.

The main() function in Program 12-4 illustrates the use of the Test class by first creating one object, named emp, which is initialized using the constructor's default arguments. The setvals() function is then used to assign the value 12345 and the address of the variable pay to the data members of this emp object. Finally, the display() function is used to display the value whose address is stored in emp.pt_pay. As illustrated by the program, the pointer member of an object is used like any other pointer variable.

 Program 12-4

```
#include <iostream.h>
#include <iomanip.h>

// class declaration
class Test
{
  private:
    int id_num;
    double *pt_pay;
  public:
    Test(int, double *);      // constructor
    void setvals(int, double *);   // access function
    void display();                // access function
};

// class implementation
Test::Test(int id = 0, double *pt = NULL)
{
  id_num = id;
  pt_pay = pt;
}
void Test::setvals(int a, double *b)
{
  id_num = a;
  pt_pay = b;
}
void Test::display()
{
  cout << "\nEmployee number " << id_num << " was paid $"
       << setiosflags(ios::showpoint)
       << setw(6) << setprecision(2)
       << *pt_pay << endl;
}
```

(continued on next page)

(continued from previous page)

```
void main(void)
{
  Test emp;
  double pay = 456.20;

  emp.setvals(12345, &pay);
  emp.display();
}
```

The output produced by executing Program 12-4 is:

```
Employee number 12345 was paid $456.20
```

Figure 12–2 illustrates the relationship between the data members of the `emp` object defined in Program 12-4 and the variable named `pay`. The value assigned to `emp.id_num` is the number 12345 and the value assigned to `pay` is 456.20. The address of the `pay` variable is assigned to the object member `emp.pt_pay`. Since this member has been defined as a pointer to a double precision number, placing the address of the double precision variable `pay` in it is a correct use of this data member.

Although the pointer defined in Program 12-4 has been used in a rather trivial fashion, the program does illustrate the concept of including a pointer in a class.

Clearly it would be more efficient to include the `pay` variable directly as a data member of the `Test` class rather than using a pointer to it. In some cases, however, pointers are advantageous. For example, assume we need to store a list of book titles. Rather than use a fixed-length character array as a data member to hold each title, we could include a pointer member to a character array and then allocate the correct size array for each book title as it is needed. This arrangement is illustrated in Figure 12–3, which shows two objects, a and b, each of which consists of a single pointer data member. As depicted, object a's pointer contains the address of ("points to") a character array containing the characters `DOS Primer`, while object b's pointer contains the address of a character array containing the characters `A Brief History of Western Civilization`.

FIGURE 12–2 Storing an Address in a Data Member

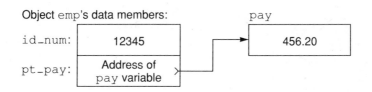

Object emp's data members: pay

id_num: 12345   →   456.20

pt_pay: Address of pay variable

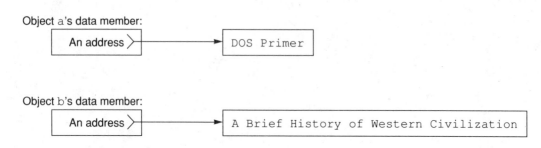

Object a's data member:

An address → DOS Primer

Object b's data member:

An address → A Brief History of Western Civilization

FIGURE 12-3 Two Objects Containing Pointer Data Members

A suitable class declaration section for a list of book titles that are to be accessed as illustrated in Figure 12-3 is:

```
// class declaration
class Book
{
  private:
    char *title;    // a pointer to a book title
  public:
    Book(char *);   // constructor
    void showtitle(void);    // display the title
};
```

The definition of the constructor function, book(), and the display function, showtitle(), are defined in the implementation section as:

```
// class implementation

Book::Book(char *name = '\0')
{
  title = new char[strlen(name)+1];    // allocate memory
  strcpy(title,name);                  // store the string
}

void Book::showtitle(void)
{
  cout << title << endl;
}
```

The body of the Book() constructor contains two statements. The first statement, title = new char[strlen(name)+1];, performs two tasks: First, the right-hand side of the statement allocates enough storage for the length of the name argument plus one, to accommodate the end-of-string null character, '\0'. Next, the address of the first allocated character position is assigned to the pointer variable title. These operations are illustrated in Figure 12-4. The second statement in the constructor copies the characters in the name argument

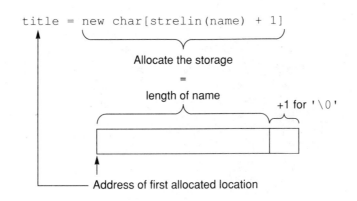

FIGURE 12-4 Allocating Memory for `title = new char[strlen(name)+1]`

to the newly created memory allocation. If no argument is passed to the constructor, then `title` is the empty string; that is, `title` is set to NULL. Program 12-5 uses this class definition within the context of a complete program.

Program 12-5

```
#include <iostream.h>
#include <string.h>

// class declaration
class Book
{
  private:
    char *title;    // a pointer to a book title
  public:
    Book(char *);   // constructor
    void showtitle(void);    // display the title
};
// class implementation
Book::Book(char *strng = NULL)
{
  title = new char[strlen(strng)+1];   // allocate memory
  strcpy(title,strng);                 // store the string
}
void Book::showtitle(void)
{
  cout << title << endl;
}
```

(continued on next page)

(continued from previous page)

```
void main(void)
{
  Book  book1("DOS Primer");    // create 1st title
  Book  book2("A Brief History of Western Civilization");  // 2nd title
  book1.showtitle();    // display book1's title
  book2.showtitle();    // display book2's title
}
```

The output produced by Program 12-5 is:

```
DOS Primer
A Brief History of Western Civilization
```

Assignment Operators and Copy Constructors Reconsidered[3]

When a class contains no pointer data members the compiler-provided defaults for the assignment operator and copy constructor adequately perform their intended tasks. Both of these defaults provide a member-by-member operation that produces no adverse side effects. This is not the case when a pointer member is included in the class declaration. Let's see why this is so.

Figure 12–5a illustrates the arrangement of pointers and allocated memory produced by Program 12-5 just before it completes execution. Let's now assume that we insert the assignment statement book2 = book1; before the closing brace of the main() function. Since we have not defined an assignment operation, the compiler's default assignment is used. As we know, this assignment produces a memberwise copy (that is, book2.title = book1.title) and means that the address in book1's pointer is copied into book2's pointer. Thus, both pointers now "point to" the character array containing the characters DOS Primer, and the address of A Brief History of Western Civilization has been lost. This situation is illustrated in Figure 12–5b.

Since the memberwise assignment illustrated in Figure 12–5b results in the loss of the address of A Brief History of Western Civilization, there is no way for the program to release this memory storage (it will be cleaned up by the operating system when the program terminates). Worse however, is the case where a destructor attempts to release the memory. Once the memory pointed to by book2 is released (again, referring to Figure 12–5b), book1 points to an undefined memory location. If this memory area is subsequently reallocated before book1 is deleted, the deletion will release memory that another other object is using. The results of this can wreck havoc on a program.

---

[3] The material in this section pertains to the problems that occur when using the default assignment, copy constructor, and destructor functions with classes containing pointer members, and how to overcome these problems. On first reading, this section can be omitted without loss of subject continuity.

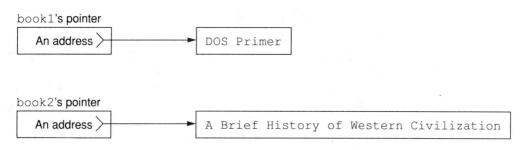

FIGURE 12–5a Before the Assignment

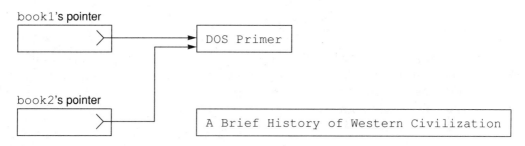

FIGURE 12–5b The Effect Produced by Default Assignment

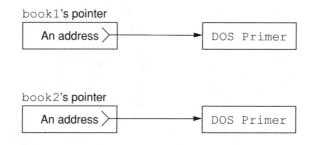

FIGURE 12–5c The Desired Effect

What is typically desired is that the book titles themselves be copied, and their pointers left alone. This situation also removes all of the side effects of a subsequent deletion of any book object. To achieve the desired assignment, we must explicitly write our own assignment operator. A suitable definition for this operator is:

```
void Book::operator=(Book &oldbook)
{
  if(title != NULL)  // check that it exists
    delete(title);   // release existing memory
  title = new char[strlen(oldbook.title) + 1];  // allocate new memory
  strcpy(title, oldbook.title);  // copy the title
}
```

This definition cleanly releases the memory previously allocated for the object and then allocates sufficient memory to store the copied title.

The problems associated with the default assignment operator also exist with the default copy constructor, because it also performs a memberwise copy. As with assignment, these problems are avoided by writing our own copy constructor. For our `Book` class such a constructor is:

```
Book::Book(Book &oldbook)
{
   title = new char[strlen(oldbook.title) + 1];  // allocate new memory
   strcpy(title, oldbook.title);  // copy the title
}
```

Comparing the body of this copy constructor to the assignment operator's function body reveals they are identical except for the deallocation of memory performed by the assignment operator. This is because the copy constructor does not have to release the existing array prior to allocating a new one, since none exists when the constructor is called.

Exercises 12.2

---

1. Include the copy constructor and assignment operator presented in this section in Program 12-5 and run the program to verify their operation.

2. Write a suitable destructor function for Program 12-5.

3. a. Construct a class named `Car` that contains the following four data members: a floating point variable named `engine_size`, a character variable named `body_style`, an integer variable named `color_code`, and a character pointer named `vin_ptr` to a vehicle identification code. The function members should include a constructor that provides default values of 0 for each numeric data member, an 'X' for each character variable, and a `NULL` for each pointer; a display function that prints the engine size, body style, color code, and vehicle identification number; and an assignment operator that performs a memberwise assignment between two `Car` objects that correctly handles the pointer member.

b. Include the program written for Exercise 5a in a working C++ program that creates two `Car` objects, the second of which is assigned the values of the first object.

4. Modify Program 12-5 to include the assignment statement b = a, then run the modified program to assess the error messages, if any, that occur.

5. Using Program 12-5 as a start, write a program that creates five `Book` objects. The program should allow the user to enter the five book titles interactively and then display the titles entered.

6. Modify the program written in Exercise 5 so that the program sorts the entered book titles in alphabetical order before it displays them. (*Hint:* You will have to define a sort routine for the titles).

12.3 Additional Class Features[4]

This section presents several additional features pertaining to classes. These include the scope of a class, creating static class members, granting access privileges to nonmember functions, and a special class pointer named `this` that provides the link between member functions and member variables. Each of these topics may be read independently of the others.

Class Scope

We have already encountered local and global scope in Sections 6.4 and 6.5. As we saw, the scope of a variable defines the portion of a program where the variable can be accessed.

For local variables this scope is defined by any block contained within a brace pair, { }. This includes both the complete function body and any internal subblocks. Additionally, all arguments of a function are considered as local function variables.

Global variables are accessible from their point of declaration throughout the remaining portion of the file containing them, with three exceptions:

1. If a local variable has the same name as a global variable, the global variable can only be accessed within the scope of the local variable by using the global resolution operator, `::`.
2. The scope of a global variable can be extended into another file by using the keyword `extern`.
3. The same global name can be reused in another file to define a separate and distinct variable by using the keyword `static`. `Static` global variables are unknown outside of their immediate file.

In addition to local and global scopes, each class also defines an associated *class scope*. That is, the names of the data and function members are local to the scope of their class. Thus, if a global variable name is reused within a class, the global variable is hidden by the class data member in the same manner as a local function variable hides a global variable of the same name. Similarly, member function names are local to the class they are declared in, and can only be used by objects declared for the class. Additionally, local function variables also hide the names of class data members having the same name. Figure 12–6 illustrates the scope of the variables and functions for the following declarations:

---

[4] Except for the material on the `this` pointer, which is required for the material in Section 13.1, the remaining topics in this section may be omitted on first reading with no loss of subject continuity.

```
float rate;     // global
// class declaration
class Test
{
  private:
    float amount, price, total;   // class scope
  public:
    float extend(float, float);   // class scope
};
```

Static Class Members

As each class object is created it gets its own block of memory for its data members. In some cases, however, it is convenient for every instantiation of a class to share the *same* memory location for a specific variable. For example, consider a class consisting of employee records, where each employee is subject to the same state sales tax. Clearly we could make the sales tax a global variable, but this is not very safe. Such data could be modified anywhere in the program, could conflict with an identical variable name within a function, and certainly violates C++'s principle of data hiding.

This type of situation is handled in C++ by declaring a class variable to be `static`. `Static` data members share the same storage space for all objects of the class; as such, they act as global variables for the class and provide a means of communication between objects.

C++ requires that `static` variables be declared as such within the class' declaration section. Since a `static` data member requires only a single storage

FIGURE 12–6 Example of Scopes

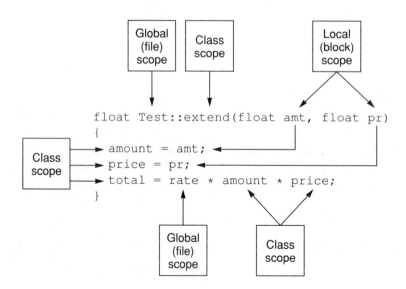

area, regardless of the number of class instantiations, it is defined in a single place outside of the class definition. This is typically done in the global part of the program where the class implementation section is provided. For example, assuming the class declaration

```
//class declaration
class Employee
{
  private:
    static float tax_rate;
    int id_num;
  public:
    Employee(int);    //constructor
    void display();
};
```

the definition and initialization of the static variable tax_rate is accomplished using a statement such as:

```
float Employee::tax_rate = 0.0025;
```

Here the scope resolution operator, ::, is used to identify tax_rate as a member of the class Employee and the keyword static is not included. Program 12-6 uses this definition within the context of a complete program.

Program 12-6

```
#include <iostream.h>

// class declaration
class Employee
{
  private:
    static float tax_rate;
    int id_num;
  public:
    Employee(int);    // constructor
    void display();    // access function
};

// static member definition
float Employee::tax_rate = 0.0025;
```

(continued on next page)

(continued from previous page)

```
// class implementation
Employee::Employee(int num = 0)
{
   id_num = num;
}
void Employee::display()
{
   cout << "Employee number " << id_num
        << " has a tax rate of " << tax_rate << endl;
}
```

```
void main(void)
{
   Employee emp1(11122), emp2(11133);

   emp1.display();
   emp2.display();
}
```

The output produced by Program 12-6 is:

```
Employee number 11122 has a tax rate of 0.0025
Employee number 11133 has a tax rate of 0.0025
```

Although it might appear that the initialization of tax_rate is global, it is not. Once the definition is made, any other definition will result in an error. Thus, the actual definition of a static member remains the responsibility of the class creator. The storage sharing produced by the static data member and the objects created in Program 12-6 is illustrated in Figure 12–7.

In addition to static data members, static member functions can also be created. Such functions apply to a class as a whole rather than to individual class objects and can only access static data members and other static member functions of the class.[5] An example of such a function is provided by Program 12-7.

FIGURE 12–7 Sharing the Static Data Member tax_rate

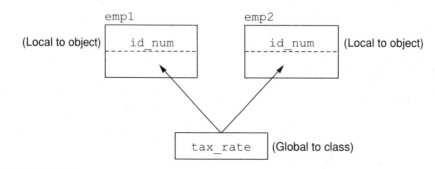

---

[5] The reason for this is that the this pointer, discussed next, is not passed to static member functions.

Program 12-7

```
#include <iostream.h>

// class declaration
class Employee
{
  private:
    static float tax_rate;
    int id_num;
  public:
    Employee(int);     // constructor
    void display();        // access function
    static void disp();  // static function
};

// static member definition
float Employee::tax_rate = 0.0025;

// class implementation
Employee::Employee(int num = 0)
{
  id_num = num;
}
void Employee::display()
{
  cout << "Employee number " << id_num
       << " has a tax rate of " << tax_rate << endl;
}
void Employee::disp()
{
  cout << "The static tax rate is " << tax_rate << endl;
}

void main(void)
{
  Employee::disp();   // call the static functions
  Employee emp1(11122), emp2(11133);

  emp1.display();
  emp2.display();
}
```

The output produced by Program 12-7 is:

```
The static tax rate is 0.0025
Employee number 11122 has a tax rate of 0.0025
Employee number 11133 has a tax rate of 0.0025
```

In reviewing Program 12-7 notice that the keyword `static` is used only when `static` data and function members are declared; it is not included in the definition of these members. Also notice that the `static` member function is called using the resolution operator with the function's class name. Finally, since `static` functions access only `static` variables that are not contained within a specific object, `static` functions may be called before any instantiations are declared.

The `this` Pointer

Except for `static` data members, each class instance contains its own set of member variables, which are stored together in a separate data structure. This permits each object to have its own clearly defined state as determined by the values stored in its member variables.

For example, consider the `Date` class presented in Section 12.1, which is repeated below for convenience:

```
// class declaration
class Date
{
  private:
    int month;
    int day;
    int year;
  public:
    Date(int, int, int);      // constructor
    void showdate(void);      // member function to display a date
};

// class implementation
Date::Date(int mm = 7, int dd = 4, int yy = 94)
{
  month = mm;
  day = dd;
  year = yy;
}
void Date::showdate(void)
{
  cout << month << "/" << day << "/" << year << endl;
}
```

Each time an object is created from this class, a separate structure in memory is set aside for its data members. For example, if two objects named a and b are created from this class, the memory storage for these objects would be as illustrated in Figure 12–8. Notice that each data structure has its own starting

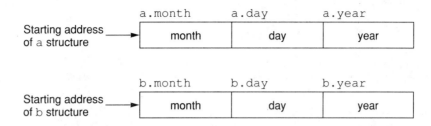

FIGURE 12–8 The Storage of Two `Date` Objects in Memory

address in memory, which corresponds to the address of the first data member in the structure.

This replication of data storage is not implemented for member functions. In fact, for each class *only one copy of the member functions is retained in memory,* and each object uses these same functions.

Sharing member functions requires providing a means of identifying which specific data structure a member function should be operating on. This is accomplished by providing address information to the function indicating where in memory the particular data structure, corresponding to a specific object, is located. This address is provided by the name of the object, which is, in fact, a reference name. For example, again using our `Date` class and assuming a is an object of this class, the statement `a.showdate()` passes the address of the a object into the `showdate()` member function.

An obvious question at this point is how this address is passed to `showdate()` and where it is stored. The answer is that the address is stored in a special pointer variable named `this`, which is automatically supplied as a hidden argument to each nonstatic member function when the function is called. For our `Date` class, which has two member functions, the actual argument list of `Date()` is equivalent to

```
Date(Date *this, int mm = 7, int dd = 4, int yy = 94)
```

and the actual argument list of `showdate()` is equivalent to

```
showdate(Date *this)
```

That is, each member function actually receives an extra argument that is the address of a data structure. Although it is usually not necessary to do so, this pointer data member can be explicitly used in member functions. For example, consider Program 12-8, which incorporates the `this` pointer in each of its member functions to access the appropriate instance variables.

Program 12-8

```
#include <iostream.h>

// class declaration
class Date
{
  private:
    int month;
    int day;
    int year;
  public:
    Date(int, int, int);       // constructor
    void showdate(void);       // member function to display a date
};

// class implementation
Date::Date(int mm = 7, int dd = 4, int yy = 94)
{
  this->month = mm;
  this->day = dd;
  this->year = yy;
}
void Date::showdate(void)
{
  cout << this->month << "/" << this->day << "/" << this->year << endl;
}
```

```
void main(void)
{
  Date a(4,1,96), b(12,18,97); // declare two objects

  cout << "The date stored in a is originally ";
  a.showdate();  // display the original date
  a = b;         // assign b's value to a
  cout << "After assignment the date stored in a is ";
  a.showdate();  // display a's values
}
```

The output produced by Program 12-8 is:

```
The date stored in a is originally 4/1/96
After assignment the date stored in a is 12/18/97
```

This is the same output produced by Program 12-1, which omits using the this pointer to access the data members. Clearly, using the this pointer in Program 12-8 is unnecessary and simply clutters the member function code. There are times, however, when an object must pass its address on to other functions. In these situations, one of which we will see in Section 13.1, the address stored in the this pointer must be used explicitly.

Friend Functions

The only method we currently have for accessing and manipulating private class data members is through the class' member functions. Conceptually, this arrangement can be viewed as illustrated in Figure 12–9a. There are times, however, when it is useful to provide such access to selected nonmember functions.

The procedure for providing this external access is rather simple—the class maintains its own approved list of nonmember functions that are granted the same privileges as member functions. The nonmember functions on the list are called friend functions, and the list is referred to as a friends list.

Figure 12–9b conceptually illustrates the use of such a list for nonmember access. Any function attempting access to an object's private data members is

FIGURE 12–9a Direct Access is Provided to Member Functions

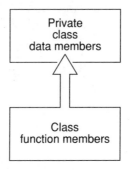

FIGURE 12–9b Access Provided to Non-Member Functions

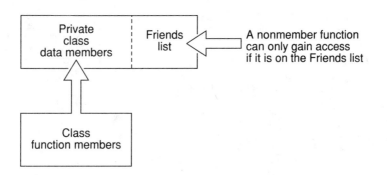

first checked against the friends list: if the function is on the list access is approved, otherwise access is denied.

From a coding standpoint the friends list is simply a series of function prototype declarations that are preceded with the word `friend` and included in the class' declaration section. For example, if the functions named `addreal()` and `addimag()` are to be allowed access to the private members of a class named `Complex`, the following prototypes would be included within `Complex`'s declaration section:

```
friend float addreal(Complex&, Complex&);
friend float addimag(Complex&, Complex&);
```

Here the friends list consists of two declarations. The prototypes indicate that each function returns a floating point number and expects two references to objects of type `Complex` as arguments. Program 12-9 includes these two friend declarations in a complete program.

 Program 12-9

```
#include <stream.h>
#include <math.h>

// class declaration
class Complex
{
  // friends list
  friend float addreal(Complex&, Complex&);
  friend float addimag(Complex&, Complex&);
  private:
    float real;
    float imag;
  public:
    Complex(float, float);  // constructor
    void display();

};

// class implementation
Complex::Complex(float rl = 0, float im = 0)
{
  real = rl;
  imag = im;
}
void Complex::display()
{
  char sign = '+';
```
(continued on next page)

(continued from previous page)

```
        if(imag < 0) sign = '-';
        cout << real << sign << fabs(imag) << 'i';
    }

    // friend implementations
    float addreal(Complex &a, Complex &b)
    {
      return(a.real + b.real);
    }
    float addimag(Complex &a, Complex &b)
    {
      return(a.imag + b.imag);
    }
```

```
    void main(void)
    {
      Complex a(3.2, 5.6), b(1.1, -8.4);
      float re, im;

      cout << "\nThe first complex number is ";
      a.display();
      cout << "\nThe second complex number is ";
      b.display();


      re = addreal(a,b);
      im = addimag(a,b);
      Complex c(re,im);   // create a new complex object
      cout << "\n\nThe sum of these two complex numbers is ";
      c.display();
    }
```

The output produced by Program 12-9 is:

```
The first complex number is 3.2+5.6i
The second complex number is 1.1-8.4i

The sum of these two complex numbers is 4.3-2.8i
```

In reviewing Program 12-9 notice four items. The first is that since friends are not class members, they are unaffected by the access section in which they are declared—*they may be declared anywhere within the declaration section.* The convention we have followed is to include all `friend` declarations immediately following the class header. The second item to notice is that the keyword `friend` (like the keyword `static`) is used only within the class declaration and not in the actual function definition. Third, since a `friend` function is intended to have access to an object's private data members, at least one of the `friend`'s arguments should be a reference to an object of the class that has made it a friend. Finally, as illustrated by Program 12-9, it is the class that grants `friend` status to a function and not the other way around. The function can never confer `friend` status on itself, because to do so would violate the concepts of data hiding and access provided by a class.

Exercises 12.3

1. a. Rewrite Program 12-7 to include an integer `static` data member named `numemps`. This variable should act as a counter that is initialized to zero and is incremented by the class constructor each time a new object is declared. Rewrite the `static` function `disp()` to display the value of this counter.
   b. Test the program written for Exercise 1a. Have the `main()` function call `disp()` after each `Employee` object is created.

2. a. Construct a class named `Circle` that contains two integer data members named `x_cent` and `y_cent`, and a floating point data member named `radius`. Additionally, the class should contain a `static` data member named `scal_factr`. Here the `x_cent` and `y_cent` values represent the center point of a circle, `radius` represents the circle's actual radius, and `scal_factor` represents a scale factor that will be used to scale the circle to fit on a variety of display devices.
   b. Include the program written for Exercise 2a in a working C++ program.

3. Rewrite the `date()` `setdate()`, and `showdate()` member functions in Program 11-1 to explicitly use the this pointer when referencing all data members. Run your program and verify that the same output as produced by Program 11-1 is achieved.

4. a. Could the following three statements in Program 12-9,

```
re = addreal(a,b);
im = addimag(a,b);
Complex c(re,im);   // create a new complex object
```

be replaced by the single statement

```
Complex c(addreal(a,b), addimag(a,b)); ?
```

   b. Verify your answer to Exercise 4a by running Program 12-9 with the suggested replacement statement.

5. Rewrite Program 12-9 to have only one friend function named `addcomplex()`. This function should accept two complex objects and return a complex object. The real and imaginary parts of the returned object should be the sum of the real and imaginary parts, respectively, of the two objects passed to `complex()`.

6. a. Rewrite the program written for Exercise 2a, but include a `friend` function that multiplies an object's radius by the `static` scale factor and then displays the actual radius value and the scaled value.
   b. Include the program written for Exercise 6a in a working C++ program.

7. *a.* Construct a class named `Coord` that contains two floating point data members named `xval` and `yval`, which will be used to store the x and y values of a point in rectangular coordinates. The function members should include appropriate constructor and display functions and a `friend` function named `conv_pol()`. The `conv_pol()` function should accept two floating point numbers that represent a point in polar coordinates and convert them into rectangular coordinates. For conversion from polar to rectangular coordinates use the formulas:

$$x = r \cos \theta$$
$$y = r \sin \theta$$

b. Include the program written for Exercise 7a in a working C++ program.

8. *a.* Construct two classes named `Rec_coord` and `Pol_coord`. The class named `Rec_coord` should contain two floating point data members named `xval` and `yval`, which will be used to store the x and y values of a point in rectangular coordinates. The function members should include appropriate constructor and display functions and a `friend` function named `conv_pol()`.

The class named `Pol_coord` should contain two floating point data members named `dist` and `theta`, which will be used to store the distance and angle values of a point represented in polar coordinates. The function members should include appropriate constructor and display functions and a `friend` function named `conv_pol()`.

The `friend` function should accept an integer argument named `dir`; two floating point arguments named `val1` and `val2`; and two reference arguments named `recref` and `polref`, the first of which should be a reference to an object of type `Rec_coord`, and the second to an object of type `Pol_coord`. If the value of `dir` is 1, `val1` and `val2` are to be considered as x and y rectangular coordinates that are to be converted to polar coordinates; if the value of `dir` is any other value, `val1` and `val2` are to be considered as distance and angle values that are to be converted to rectangular coordinates. For conversion from rectangular to polar coordinates are:

$$r = \sqrt{x^2 + y^2}$$
$$\theta = \ tan^{-1}(y/x)$$

For conversion from polar to rectangular coordinates, use the formulas:

$$x = r \cos \theta$$
$$y = r \sin \theta$$

b. Include the program written for Exercise 8a in a working C++ program.

12.4 Common Programming Errors

1. Using the default copy constructor and default assignment operators with classes containing pointer members. Since these default functions do a memberwise copy, the address in the source pointer is copied to the destination pointer. Typically this is not what is wanted since both pointers end up pointing to the same memory area.

2. Using a user-defined assignment operator in a multiple assignment expression when the operator has not been defined to return an object.

3. Using the keyword `static` when defining either a static data or function member. Here, the `static` keyword should be used only within the class declaration section.

4. Using the keyword `friend` when defining a friend function. The `friend` keyword should be used only within the class declaration section.

5. Failing to instantiate static data members before creating class objects that must access these data members.

6. Forgetting that `this` is a pointer that must be dereferenced using either `*this` or `this->`.

12.5 Chapter Summary

1. An *assignment operator* may be declared for a class with the function prototype:

    void operator=(class-name &);

    Here, the argument is a reference to the class name. The `return` type of `void` precludes using this operator in multiple assignment expressions such as a = b = c.

2. A type of initialization that closely resembles assignment occurs in C++ when one object is initialized using another object of the same class. The constructor that performs this type of initialization is called a *copy constructor* and has the function prototype:

    class-name(const class-name &);

    This is frequently represented using the notation X(X&).

3. Pointers may be included as class data members. A pointer member adheres to the same rules as a pointer variable.

4. The default copy constructor and default assignment operators are typically not useful with classes containing pointer members. This is because these default functions do a memberwise copy in which the address in the source pointer is copied to the destination pointer, resulting in both pointers "pointing to" the same memory area. For these situations you must define your own copy constructor and assignment operator.

5. Each class has an associated class scope, which is defined by the brace pair, { }, containing the class declaration. Data and function members are local to

the scope of their class and can only be used by objects declared for the class. If a global variable name is reused within a class, the global variable is hidden by the class variable. Within the scope of the class variable the global variable may be accessed using the scope resolution operator, ::.

6. For each class object a separate set of memory locations is reserved for all data members, except those declared as static. A static data member is shared by all class objects and provides a means of communication between objects. Static data members must be declared as such within the class declaration section and are defined outside of the declaration section.

7. Static function members apply to the class as a whole, rather than individual objects. As such, a static function member can access only static data members and other static function members. Static function members must be declared as such within the class declaration section and are defined outside of the declaration section.

8. For each class only one copy of the member functions is retained in memory, and each object uses the same function. The address of the object's data members is provided to the member function by passing a hidden argument reference, corresponding to the memory address of the selected object, to the member function. The address is passed in a special pointer argument named this. The this pointer may be used explicitly by a member function to access a data member.

9. A nonmember function may access a class' private data members if it is granted friend status by the class. This is accomplished by declaring the function as a friend within the class' declaration section. Thus, it is always the class that determines which nonmember functions are friends; a function can never confer friend status on itself.

Class Functions, Conversions and Inheritance

Chapter Thirteen

447

This chapter completes our introduction to classes. First we will see how to create operator and conversion capabilities similar to those inherent in C++'s built-in types. With these additions our user-defined types will have all of the functionality of built-in types.

This functionality is then extended by showing how a class designed by one programmer can be altered by another, in a way that retains the integrity and design of the original class. This is accomplished using inheritance, which is a new feature that is central to object-oriented programming. Inheritance permits reusing and extending existing code in a way that ensures the new code does not adversely affect what has already been written. It is the driving force behind the move to object-oriented programming.

13.1 Operator Functions

A simple assignment operator was constructed in Section 12.1. In this section we extend this capability and show how to broaden C++'s built-in operators to class objects. As we will discover, class operators are themselves either member or friend functions.

The only symbols permitted for user-defined purposes are the subset of C++'s built-in symbols listed in Table 13–1. Each of these symbols may be adopted for class use with no limitation as to its meaning.[1] This is done by making each operation a function that can be overloaded like any other function.

The operation of the symbols listed in Table 13-1 can be redefined as we see fit for our classes, subject to the following restrictions:

- Symbols not in Table 13–1 cannot be redefined. For example, the ., ::, and ?: symbols cannot be redefined.
- New operator symbols cannot be created. For example, since %% is not an operator in C++ it cannot be defined as a class operator.
- Neither the precedence nor the associativity of C++'s operators can be modified. Thus, you cannot give the addition operator a higher precedence than the multiplication operator.
- Operators cannot be redefined for C++'s built-in types.

---

[1] The only limitation is that the syntax of the operator cannot be changed. Thus, a binary operator must remain binary and a unary operator must remain unary. Within this syntax restriction an operator symbol can be used to produce any operation, whether or not the operation is consistent with the symbol's accepted usage. For example, we could redefine the addition symbol to provide multiplication. Clearly this violates the intent and spirit of making these symbols available to us. We shall be very careful to redefine each symbol in a manner consistent with its accepted usage.

TABLE 13–1   Operators Available for Class Use

Operator	Description
( )	Function call
[ ]	Array element
->	Structure member pointer reference
new	Dynamically allocate memory
delete	Dynamically deallocate memory
++	Increment
--	Decrement
-	Unary minus
!	Logical negation
~	One's complement
*	Indirection
*	Multiplication
/	Division
%	Modulus (remainder)
+	Addition
-	Subtraction
<<	Left shift
>>	Right shift
<	Less than
<=	Less than or equal to
>	Greater than
>=	Greater than or equal to
==	Equal to
!=	Not equal to
&&	Logical AND
||	Logical OR
&	Bitwise AND
^	Bitwise exclusive OR
|	Bitwise inclusive OR
=	Assignment
+= -= *=	Assignment
/= %= &=	Assignment
^= |=	Assignment
<<= >>=	Assignment
,	Comma

- A C++ operator that is unary cannot be changed to a binary operator and a binary operator cannot be changed to a unary operator.
- The operator must either be a member of a class or be defined to take at least one class member as an operand.

The first step in providing a class with operators from Table 13–1 is to decide which operations make sense for the class and how they should be defined. As

449

a specific example, we continue to build on the Date class introduced previously. For this class a small, meaningful set of class operations is defined.

Clearly the addition of two dates is not meaningful. The addition of a date with an integer, however, does make sense if the integer is taken as the number of days to be added to the date. Likewise, the subtraction of an integer from a date makes sense. Also, the subtraction of two dates is meaningful if we define the difference to mean the number of days between the two dates. Similarly, it makes sense to compare two dates and determine if the dates are equal or one date occurs before or after another date. Let's now see how these operations can be implemented using C++'s operator symbols.

A user-defined operation is created as a function that redefines C++'s built-in operator symbols for class use. Functions that define operations on class objects and use C++'s built-in operator symbols are referred to as *operator functions*.

Operator functions are declared and implemented in the same manner as all member functions, with one exception: It is the function's name that connects the appropriate operator symbol to the operation defined by the function. An operator function's name is always of the form operator<symbol> where <symbol> is one of the operators listed in Table 13–1. For example, the function name operator+ is the name of the addition function, while the function name operator== is the name of the equal to comparison function.

Once the appropriate function name is selected the process of writing the function simply amounts to having it accept the desired inputs and produce the correct returned value.[2] For example, in comparing two Date objects for equality we would select C++'s equality operator. Thus, the name of our function becomes operator==. We would want our comparison operation to accept two date objects, internally compare them, and return an integer value indicating the result of the comparison: 1 for equality and 0 for inequality. As a member function a suitable prototype that could be included in the class declaration section is:

```
int operator==(Date &);
```

This prototype indicates that the function is named operator==, that it returns an integer, and that it accepts a reference to a Date object.[3] Only one Date object is required here because the second date object will be the object that calls the function. Let's now write the function definition to be included

---

[2] As previously noted, this implies that the specified operator can be redefined to perform any operation. Good programming practice, however, dictates against such redefinitions.

[3] The prototype int operator==(Date) also works. Passing a reference, however, is preferable to passing an object because it reduces the function call's overhead. This is because passing an object means that a copy of the object must be made for the called function, while passing a reference gives the function direct access to the object whose address is passed.

in the class implementation section. Assuming our class is named `Date`, a suitable definition is:

```
int Date::operator==(Date &date2)
{
  if( day == date2.day && month == date2.month && year == date2.year)
    return (1);
  else
    return(0);
}
```

Once this function has been defined, it may be called using the same syntax as for C++'s built-in types. For example, if `a` and `b` are objects of type `Date`, the expression `if (a == b)` is valid. Program 13-1 includes the call as well as the declaration and definition of this operator function within the context of a complete program.

Program 13-1

```
#include <iostream.h>
```

```
// class declaration
class Date
{
  private:
    int month;
    int day;
    int year;
  public:
    Date(int, int, int);       // constructor
    int operator==(Date &);    // declare the operator== function
    void showdate(void);       // member function to display a date
};

// implementation section
Date::Date(int mm = 7, int dd = 4, int yy = 94)
{
  month = mm;
  day = dd;
  year = yy;
}
int Date::operator==(Date &date2)
{
  if(day == date2.day && month == date2.month && year == date2.year)
    return (1);
  else
    return(0);
}
```

(continued on next page)

(continued from previous page)

```
void main(void)
{
  Date a(4,1,96), b(12,18,97), c(4,1,96); // declare 3 objects
  if (a == b)
    cout << "Dates a and b are the same." << endl;
  else
    cout << "Dates a and b are not the same." << endl;

  if (a == c)
    cout << "Dates a and c are the same." << endl;
  else
    cout << "Dates a and c are not the same." << endl;
}
```

The output produced by Program 13-1 is:

```
Dates a and b are not the same.
Dates a and c are the same.
```

The first new feature to be illustrated in Program 13-1 is the declaration and implementation of the function named operator==(). Except for its name, this operator function is constructed in the same manner as any other member function: It is declared in the declaration section and defined in the implementation section. The second new feature is how the function is called. Operator functions may be called using their associated symbols rather than in the way other functions are called. Since operator functions are true functions, however, the traditional method of calling them can also be used—by specifying their name and including appropriate arguments. Thus, in addition to being called by the expression a == b in Program 13-1, the call a.operator==(b) could also have been used.

Let's now create another operator for our Date class—an addition operator. As before, creating this operator requires that we specify three items:

1. The name of the operator function
2. The processing that the function is to perform
3. The data type, if any, that the function is to return

Clearly, for addition we will use the operator function named operator+. Having selected the function's name we must now determine what we want this function to do, as it specifically relates to Date objects. As we noted previously, the sum of two dates makes no sense. Adding an integer to a date is meaningful, however, when the integer represents the number of days either before or after the given date. Here the sum of an integer to a Date object is simply another Date object, which should be returned by the addition operation. Thus, a suitable prototype for our addition function is:

```
Date operator+(int);
```

This prototype would be included in the class declaration section. It specifies that an integer is to be added to a class object and the operation returns a `Date` object. Thus, if a is a `Date` object, the function call `a.operator+(284)`, or its more commonly used alternative, `a + 284`, should cause the number 284 to be correctly added to a's date value. We must now construct the function to accomplish this.

Constructing the function requires that we first select a specific date convention. For simplicity we will adopt the financial date convention that considers each month to consist of 30 days and each year to consist of 360 days. Using this convention our function will first add the integer number of days to the `Date` object's day value and then adjust the resulting day value to lie within the range 1 to 30 and the month value to lie within the range 1 to 12. A function that accomplishes this is:

```
Date operator+(int days)
{
  Date temp;  // a temporary date to store the result

  temp.day = day + days;  // add the days
  temp.month = month;
  temp.year = year;
  while (temp.day > 30)    // now adjust the months
  {
    temp.month++;
    temp.day -= 30;
  }
  while (temp.month > 12)  // adjust the years
  {
    temp.year++;
    temp.month -= 12;
  }
  return temp;     // the values in temp are returned
}
```

The important feature to notice here is the use of the `temp` object. The purpose of this object is to ensure that none of the function's arguments, which become the operator's operands, are altered. To understand this consider a statement such as `b = a + 284;` that uses this operator function, where a and b are `Date` objects. This statement should never modify a's value. Rather, the expression `a + 284` should yield a `Date` value that is then assigned to b. The result of the expression is, of course, the `temp` `Date` object returned by the `operator+()` function. Without using the `temp` object the 284 would have to be added to the a object directly, as in the following code:

```
Date Date::operator+(int days)    // BAD CODE - DATE OPERAND IS CHANGED
{

  day = day + days;   // add the days - this changes the date operand

  while (day > 30)    // now adjust the months
  {
    month++;
    day -= 30;
  }
  while (month > 12)  // adjust the years
  {
    year++;
    month -= 12;
  }
  return *this;     // the values in calling object are returned
}
```

Although this function returns the correct value, it also alters the value of its `Date` operand, which is the object making the call. The correct version of this function is included in Program 13-2.

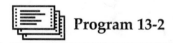 **Program 13-2**

```
#include <iostream.h>
```

```
// class declaration
class Date
{
  private:
    int month;
    int day;
    int year;
  public:
    Date(int, int, int);       // constructor
    Date operator+(int);       // overload the + operator
    void showdate(void);       // member function to display a date
};

// implementation section
Date::Date(int mm = 0, int dd = 0, int yy = 0)
{
  month = mm;
  day = dd;
  year = yy;
}
```

(continued on next page)

(continued from previous page)

```
Date Date::operator+(int days)
{
  Date temp;  // a temporary date to store the result

  temp.day = day + days;  // add the days
  temp.month = month;
  temp.year = year;
  while (temp.day > 30)      // now adjust the months
  {
    temp.month++;
    temp.day -= 30;
  }
  while (temp.month > 12)  // adjust the years
  {
    temp.year++;
    temp.month -= 12;
  }
  return temp;      // the values in temp are returned
}
void Date::showdate(void)
{
  cout << month << "/" << day << "/" << year;
}
```

```
void main(void)
{
  Date a(4,1,96), b; // declare two objects

  cout << "The initial date is ";
  a.showdate();
  b = a + 284;    // add in 284 days = 9 months and 14 days
  cout << "\nThe new date is ";
  b.showdate();
}
```

The output produced by Program 13-2 is:

```
The initial date is 4/1/96
The new date is 1/15/97
```

We can actually improve on the `operator+()` function contained in Program 13-2 by initializing the `temp` object with the value of its calling `Date` object. This is accomplished using either of the following declarations:

```
Date temp(*this);
Date temp = *this;
```

Both of these declarations initialize the `temp` object with the object pointed to by the `this` pointer, which is the calling `Date` object. If the initialization is done, the first assignment statement in the function can be altered to:

```
temp.day += days;
```

Operator Functions as Friends

The operator functions in both Programs 13-1 and 13-2 have been constructed as class members. An interesting feature of operator functions is that, except for the operator functions =, (), [], and ->, they may also be written as friend functions. For example, if the `operator+()` function used in Program 13-2 were written as a friend, a suitable declaration section prototype is:

```
friend Date operator+(Date &, int);
```

Notice that the friend version contains a reference to a `Date` object that is not contained in the member function version. This extra argument is necessary because the implied object argument supplied by a member function's `this` pointer is no longer available. In all cases the equivalent friend version of a member operator function *must* contain an additional class reference that is not required by the member function. This equivalence is listed in Table 13–2 for both unary and binary operators.

Program 13-2's `operator+()` function, written as a friend function, is:

```
Date operator+(Date &op1, int days)
{
   Date temp;   // a temporary date to store the result

   temp.day = op1.day + days;   // add the days
   temp.month = op1.month;
   temp.year = op1.year;
   while (temp.day > 30)      // now adjust the months
   {
      temp.month++;
      temp.day -= 30;
   }
   while (temp.month > 12)   // adjust the years
   {
      temp.year++;
      temp.month -= 12;
   }
   return temp;      // the values in temp are returned
}
```

TABLE 13–2   Operator Function Argument Requirements

	Member Function	Friend Function
Unary operator	1 implicit	1 explicit
Binary operator	1 implicit and 1 explicit	2 explicit

The only difference between this version and the member version is the explicit use of a `Date` argument named `op1` (the choice of this name is entirely arbitrary) in the friend version. This means that within the body of the friend function the first three assignment statements explicitly reference `op1`'s data members as `op1.day`, `op1.month`, and `op1.year`, whereas the member function implicitly makes use of the `this` pointer to reference its arguments as `day`, `month`, and `year`.

In making the determination to overload a binary operator as either a friend or member operator function, the following convention can be applied: *friend functions are more appropriate for binary functions that modify neither of their operands, such as ==, +, −, and etc., while member functions are more appropriate for binary functions, such as =, +=, −= and etc., that are used to modify one of their operands.*

The Assignment Operator Revisited

In Section 12.1 a simple assignment operator function was presented and is repeated below for convenience.

```
void Date::operator=(Date &newdate)
{
  day = newdate.day;      // assign the day
  month = newdate.month;  // assign the month
  year = newdate.year;    // assign the year
}
```

The drawback of this function is that it returns no value, making multiple assignments such as `a = b = c` impossible. Now that we have introduced operator functions with `return` types and have the `this` pointer at our disposal, we can fix our simple assignment operator function to provide an appropriate `return` type. In this case the `return` value should be a `Date`. Thus an appropriate prototype for our operator is:

```
Date operator=(const Date &);
```

Notice that we have declared the function's argument to be a `const` to ensure that this operand will not be altered by the function. A suitable function for this prototype is:

```
Date Date::operator=(const Date &newdate)
{

  day = newdate.day;        // assign the day
  month = newdate.month;    // assign the month
  year = newdate.year;      // assign the year

  return *this;
}
```

In the case of an assignment such as b = c, or its equivalent form b.operator=(c), the function first alters b's member values from within the function and then returns the value of this object, which may be used in a subsequent assignment. Thus, a multiple assignment expression such as a = b = c is possible and is illustrated in Program 13-3.

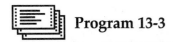 **Program 13-3**

```
#include <iostream.h>
```

```
// class declaration
class Date
{
  private:
    int month;
    int day;
    int year;
  public:
    Date(int, int, int);      // constructor
    Date operator=(const Date &);  // define assignment of a date
    void showdate(void);      // member function to display a date
};

// implementation section
Date::Date(int mm = 7, int dd = 4, int yy = 94)
{
  month = mm;
  day = dd;
  year = yy;
}
Date Date::operator=(const Date &newdate)
{
```

(continued on next page)

(continued from previous page)

```
   day = newdate.day;        // assign the day
   month = newdate.month;    // assign the month
   year = newdate.year;      // assign the year

   return *this;
}
void Date::showdate(void)
{
   cout << month << "/" << day << "/" << year;
}
```

```
void main(void)
{
  Date a(4,1,96), b(12,18,97), c(1,1,98); // declare three objects

  cout << "Before assignment a's date value is ";
  a.showdate();
  cout << "\nBefore assignment b's date value is ";
  b.showdate();
  cout << "\nBefore assignment c's date value is ";
  c.showdate();

  a = b = c;   // multiple assignment

  cout << "\n\nAfter assignment a's date value is ";
  a.showdate();
  cout << "\nAfter assignment b's date value is ";
  b.showdate();
  cout << "\nAfter assignment c's date value is ";
  c.showdate();
}
```

The output produced by Program 13-3 is:

```
    Before assignment a's date value is 4/1/96
    Before assignment b's date value is 12/18/97
    Before assignment c's date value is 1/1/98

    After assignment a's date value is 1/1/98
    After assignment b's date value is 1/1/98
    After assignment c's date value is 1/1/98
```

As noted previously, the only restriction on the assignment operator function is that it can only be overloaded as a member function. It cannot be overloaded as a friend.

Exercises 13.1

1. *a.* Define a *greater than* relational operator function named `operator>()` that can be used with the `Date` class declared in Program 13-1.

   b. Define a *less than* operator function named `operator<()` that can be used with the `Date` class declared in Program 13-1.

   c. Include the operator functions written for Exercises 1a and 1b in a working C++ program.

2. *a.* Define a subtraction operator function named `operator-()` that can be used with the `Date` class defined in Program 13-1. The subtraction should accept a long integer argument that represents the number of days to be subtracted from an object's date and return a date. In doing the subtraction use the financial assumption that all months consist of 30 days and all years of 360 days. Additionally, an end-of-month adjustment should be made, if necessary, that converts any resulting day of 31 to a day of 30, except if the month is February. If the resulting month is February and the day is either 29, 30, or 31, it should be changed to 28.

   b. Define another subtraction operator function named `operator-()` that can be used with the `Date` class defined in Program 13-1. The subtraction should yield a long integer that represents the difference in days between two dates. In calculating the day difference use the financial day count basis that assumes that all months have 30 days and all years have 360 days.

   c. Include the overloaded operators written for Exercises 2a and 2b in a working C++ program.

3. *a.* Determine if the following addition operator function provides the same result as the function used in Program 13-2:

```
Date Date::operator+(int days)    // return a date object
{
  Date temp;

  temp.day = day + days;    // add the days in
  temp.month = month + int(temp.day/30);   // determine total months
  temp.day = temp.day % 30;                // determine actual day
  temp.year = year + int(temp.month/12); // determine total years
  temp.month = temp.month % 12;            // determine actual month

  return temp;
}
```

   b. Verify your answer to Exercise 3a by including the function in a working C++ program.

4. *a.* Rewrite the equality relational operator function in Program 13-1 as a friend function.

   b. Verify the operation of the friend operator function written for Exercise 4a by including it within a working C++ program.

5. *a.* Rewrite the addition operator function in Program 13-2 to account for the actual days in a month, neglecting leap years.

b. Verify the operation of the operator function written for Exercise 5a by including it within a working C++ program.

6. *a.* Construct an addition operator for the Complex class declared in Program 12-9. This should be a member function that adds two complex numbers and returns a complex number.

b. Add a member multiplication operator function in the program written for Exercise 6a that multiplies two complex numbers and returns a complex number.

c. Verify the operation of the operator functions written for Exercises 6a and 6b by including them within a working C++ program.

7. *a.* Create a class named `String` and include an addition operator function that concatenates two strings. The function should return a string.

b. Include the overloaded operator written for Exercise 7a within a working C++ program.

13.2 Two Useful Alternatives—`operator()` and `operator[]`

There are times when it is convenient to define an operation having more than two arguments, which is the limit imposed on all binary operator functions. For example, each of our `Date` objects contains three integer data members: `month`, `day`, and `year`. For such an object we might want to add an integer value to any of these three members, instead of just the `day` member as was done in Program 13-2. C++ provides for this possibility by supplying the parentheses operator function, `operator()`, which has no limits on the number of arguments that may be passed to it.

On the other end of the spectrum, the case illustrated by Program 13-2, where only a single nonobject argument is required, occurs so frequently that C++ also provides an alternative means of achieving it. For this special case, C++ supplies the subscript operator function, `operator[]`, which permits a maximum of one argument. The only restriction imposed by C++ on the `operator()` and `operator[]` functions is that they must be defined as member (not friend) functions. For simplicity, we consider the `operator[]` function first.

The subscript operator function, `operator[]`, is declared and defined in the same manner as any other operator function, but is called differently from the normal function and operator call. For example, if we wanted to use this operator function to accept an integer argument and return a `Date` object, the following prototype is valid:

```
Date operator[](int);  // declare the subscript operator
```

Except for the operator function's name, this is similar in construction to any other operator function prototype. Assuming we want this function to add its integer argument to a `Date` object, a suitable function implementation is:

```
      Date operator[](int days)
      {
        Date temp;   // a temporary date to store the result

        temp.day = day + days;   // add the days
        temp.month = month;
        temp.year = year;
        while (temp.day > 30)      // now adjust the months
        {
          temp.month++;
          temp.day -= 30;
        }
        while (temp.month > 12)   // adjust the years
        {
          temp.year++;
          temp.month -= 12;
        }
        return temp;       // the values in temp are returned
      }
```

Again, except for the initial header line, this is similar in construction to other operator function definitions. Once the function is created, however, it can only be called by passing the required argument through the subscript brackets. For example, if a is a Date object, the function call a[284] calls the subscript operator function and causes the function to operate on the a object using the integer value 284. This call is illustrated in Program 13-4.

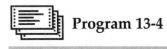 **Program 13-4**

```
#include <iostream.h>
```

```
// class declaration
class Date
{
  private:
    int month;
    int day;
    int year;
  public:
    Date(int, int, int);     // constructor
    Date operator[](int);    // overload the subscript operator
    void showdate(void);     // member function to display a date
};
```

(continued on next page)

(continued from previous page)

```
// implementation section
Date::Date(int mm = 0, int dd = 0, int yy = 0)
{
  month = mm;
  day = dd;
  year = yy;
}
Date Date::operator[](int days)
{
  Date temp;  // a temporary date to store the result

  temp.day = day + days;  // add the days
  temp.month = month;
  temp.year = year;
  while (temp.day > 30)    // now adjust the months
  {
    temp.month++;
    temp.day -= 30;
  }
  while (temp.month > 12)  // adjust the years
  {
    temp.year++;
    temp.month -= 12;
  }
  return temp;      // the values in temp are returned
}
void Date::showdate(void)
{
  cout << month << "/" << day << "/" << year;
}
```

```
void main(void)
{
  Date a(4,1,96), b; // declare two objects

  cout << "The initial date is ";
  a.showdate();
  b = a[284];  // add in 284 days = 9 months and 14 days
  cout << "\nThe new date is ";
  b.showdate();
}
```

Program 13-4 is identical in every way to Program 13-2, except that we have used an overloaded subscript operator function in place of an overloaded addition operator function. Both Programs 13-4 and 13-2 produce the identical output.

Although the expression a[284] used in Program 13-2 *appears* to indicate that a is an array, it is not. It is simply the notation that is required to call an overloaded subscript function.

The parentheses operator function, `operator()()`, is almost identical in construction and calling to the subscript function, `operator[]()`, with the substitution of the parentheses, `()`, for the brackets, `[]`. The difference between these two operator functions is in the number of allowable arguments. Whereas the subscript operator permits passing zero or one argument, the parentheses operator has no limit on the number of its arguments. For example, a suitable operator prototype to add an integer number of months, days, or years to a `Date` object is:

```
Date operator()(int, int, int);
```

Once such a function is implemented (which is left as an exercise) a call such as `a(2,4,3)` can be used to add 2 months, 4 days, and 3 years to the `Date` object named `a`.

These two extra functions provide a great deal of programming flexibility. In the case where only one argument is needed, they permit two different overloaded functions to be written, both of which have the same argument type. For example, we could use the `operator[]` to add an integer number of days to a date object and the `operator()` to add an integer number of months. Since both functions have the same argument type, one function name could not be overloaded for both of these cases.

These two functions also permit us the flexibility to restrict the other operator functions to class member arguments and use these two functions for any other argument types or operations, such as adding an integer to a `Date` object.

Exercises 13.2

1. Replace the subscript `operator[]` function in Program 13-4 with the parentheses `operator()` function.

2. a. Replace the subscript `operator[]` function in Program 13-4 with a member `operator()` function that accepts an integer month, day, and year count. Have the function add the input days, months, and years to the object's date and return the resulting date. For example, if the input is 3,2,1 and the object's date is 7/16/97, the function should return the date 10/18/98. Make sure that your function correctly handles an input such as 37 days and 15 months and adjusts the calculated day to be within the range 1 to 30 and the month within the range 1 to 12.
   b. Include the operator function written for Exercise 2a in a working C++ program and verify its operation.

3. a. Construct a class named `Student` consisting of the following private data members: an integer ID number, an integer count, an array of four floating point grades. The constructor for this class should set all data member values to zero. The class should also include a member function that displays all valid member grades, as determined by the grade count, and calculates and displays the average of the grades. Include the class in a working C++ program that declares three class objects named `a`, `b`, and `c`.

b. Include a member `operator[]` function in the class constructed for Exercise 3a that has a floating point grade argument. The function should check the `count` data member, and if fewer than four grades have been entered the function should store its argument into the `grade` array using the count as an index value. If four grades have already been entered, the function should return an error message indicating that the new grade cannot be accepted. Additionally, a new grade should force an increment to the `count` data member.

c. Include a member `operator()` function in the class constructed for Exercise 3a that has a grade index and grade value as arguments. The function should force a change to the grade corresponding to the index value and update the count if necessary. For example, an argument list of 4,98.5 should change the fourth test grade value to 98.5.

4. *a.* Add a member `operator[]` function to Program 12-9 that multiples an object's complex number (both the real and imaginary parts) by a real number and returns a complex number. For example, if the real number is 2 and the complex number is 3+4i, the result is 6+8i.

b. Verify the operation of the operator function written for Exercise 4a by including it within a working C++ program.

13.3 Data Type Conversions

The conversion from one built-in data type to another was previously described in Section 3.2. With the introduction of user-defined data types the possibilities for conversion between data types expands to the following cases:

- Conversion from built-in type to built-in type
- Conversion from built-in type to user-defined type
- Conversion from user-defined type to built-in type
- Conversion from user-defined type to user-defined type

The first conversion is handled either by C++'s built-in implicit conversion rules or its explicit cast operator. The second conversion type is made using a *type conversion constructor*. The third and fourth conversion types are made using a *conversion operator function*. In this section the specific means of performing each of these conversions is presented.

Built-In to Built-In Conversion

The conversion from one built-in data type to another has already been presented in Section 3.2. To review this case briefly, this type of conversion is either implicit or explicit.

An implicit conversion occurs in the context of one of C++'s operations. For example, when a floating point value is assigned to an integer variable only the integer portion of the value is stored. The conversion is implied by the operation and is performed automatically by the compiler.

An explicit conversion occurs whenever a cast is used. In C++ two cast notations exist. Using the older C notation, a cast has the form *(data-type) expression* while the newer C++ notation has the functionlike form *data-type(expression)*. For example, both of the expressions `(int)24.32` and `int(24.32)` cause the floating point value 24.32 to be truncated to the integer value 24.

Built-In to Class Conversion

User-defined casts for converting a built-in to a user-defined data type are created using constructor functions. A constructor whose first argument is not a member of its class and whose remaining arguments, if any, have default values is a *type conversion constructor*. If the first argument of a type conversion constructor is a built-in data type, the constructor can be used to cast the built-in data type to a class object. Clearly, one restriction of such functions is that, as constructors, they must be member functions.

Although this type of cast occurs when the constructor is invoked to initialize an object, it is actually a more general cast than might be evident at first glance. This is because a constructor function can be explicitly invoked after all objects have been declared, whether or not it was invoked previously as part of an object's declaration. Before exploring this further, let's first construct a type conversion constructor. We will then see how to use it as a cast independent of its initialization purpose.

The cast we will construct will convert a long integer into a `Date` object. Our `Date` object will consist of dates in the form month/day/year and use our by now familiar `Date` class. The long integer will be used to represent dates in the form year * 10000 + month * 100 + day. For example, using this representation the date 12/31/98 becomes the long integer 981231. Dates represented in this fashion are very useful for two reasons: First, it permits a date to be to stored as a single integer, and second, such dates are in numerically increasing date order, making sorting extremely easy. For example, the date 1/1/99, which occurs after 12/31/98, becomes the integer 990101, which is larger than 981231.[4] Since the integers representing dates can exceed the size of a normal integer, the integers are always declared as longs.

A suitable constructor function for converting from a long integer date to a date stored as a month, day, and year is:

```
// type conversion constructor from long to Date

Date::Date(long findate)
{
  year = int(findate/10000.0);
  month = int((findate - year * 10000.0)/100.0);
  day = int(findate - year * 10000.0 - month * 100.0);
}
```

---

[4] For dates after the turn of the century 100 must be added to the year value. Thus, the date 6/15/00 is considered as 6/15/100 and the date 2/12/01 is considered as 2/12/101.

Program 13-5 uses this type conversion constructor both as an initialization function at definition time and as an explicit cast later on in the program.

Program 13-5

```
#include <iostream.h>


class Date
{
  private:
    int month, day, year;
  public:
    Date(int, int, int);   // constructor
    Date(long);            // type conversion constructor
    void showdate(void);
};
// constructor
Date::Date(int mm = 7, int dd = 4, int yy = 94)
{
  month = mm;
  day = dd;
  year = yy;
}
// type conversion constructor from long to date
Date::Date(long findate)
{
  year = int(findate/10000.0);
  month = int((findate - year * 10000.0)/100.0);
  day = int(findate - year * 10000.0 - month * 100.0);
}
// member function to display a date
void Date::showdate(void)
{
  cout << month << "/" << day << "/" << year;
}
```

```
void main(void)
{
  Date a, b(951225), c(4,1,96); // declare 3 objects--initialize 2 of them

  cout << "Dates a, b, and c are ";
  a.showdate();
  cout << ", ";
  b.showdate();
  cout << ", and ";
  c.showdate();
  cout << ".\n";

  a = Date(980101);  // cast a long to a date

  cout << "Date a is now ";
  a.showdate();
  cout << ".\n";
}
```

The output produced by Program 13-5 is:

```
Dates a, b, and c are 7/4/94, 12/25/95, and 4/1/96.
Date a is now 1/1/98.
```

The change in a's date value illustrated by this output is produced by the assignment expression a = Date(980101), which uses a type conversion constructor to perform the cast from long to Date.

Class to Built-In Conversion

Conversion from a user-defined data type to a built-in data type is accomplished using a conversion operator function. A *conversion operator function* is a member operator function having the name of a built-in data type or class. When the operator function has a built-in data type name it is used to convert from a class to a built-in data type. For example, a conversion operator function for casting a class object to a long integer would have the name operator long(). Here the name of the operator function indicates that a conversion to a long will take place. If this function were part of a Date class it would be used to cast a Date object into a long integer. This usage is illustrated by Program 13-6.

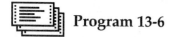 **Program 13-6**

```
#include <iostream.h>
```

```cpp
// class declaration for Date
class Date
{
  private:
    int month, day, year;
  public:
    Date(int, int, int);       // constructor
    operator long();           // conversion operator function
    void showdate(void);
};
// constructor
Date::Date(int mm = 7, int dd = 4, int yy = 94)
{
  month = mm;
  day = dd;
  year = yy;
}
```

(continued on next page)

(continued from previous page)

```
// conversion operator function converting from Date to long
Date::operator long()   // must return a long
{
  long yymmdd;

  yymmdd = year * 10000.0 + month * 100.0 + day;
  return(yymmdd);
}
// member function to display a date
void Date::showdate(void)
{
  cout << month << "/" << day << "/" << year;
}
```

```
void main(void)
{
  Date a(4,1,96); // declare and initialize one object of type Date
  long b;          // declare an object of type long

  b = a;           // a conversion takes place here

  cout << "a's date is ";
  a.showdate();
  cout << "\nThis date, as a long integer, is " << b << '\n';
}
```

The output produced by Program 13-6 is:

```
a's date is 4/1/96
This date, as a long integer, is 960401
```

The change in a's Date value to a long integer illustrated by this output is produced by the assignment expression b = a. This assignment, which also could have been written as b = long(a), calls the conversion operator function long() to perform the cast from Date to long. In general, since explicit conversion more clearly documents what is happening its use is preferred to implicit conversion.

Notice that the conversion operator has no explicit argument and has no explicit return type. This is true of all conversion operators: Its implicit argument will always be an object of the class being cast from, and the return type is implied by the name of the function. Additionally, as previously indicated, a conversion operator function *must be* a member function.

Class to Class Conversion

Converting from a user-defined data type to a user-defined data type is performed in the same manner as a cast from a user-defined to built-in data type—it is done using a member *conversion operator function*. In this case, however, the operator function uses the class name being converted to rather than a built-in data name. For example, if two classes named `Date` and `Intdate` exist, the operator function named `operator Intdate()` could be placed in the `Date` class to convert from a `Date` object to an `Intdate` object. Similarly, the operator function named `Date()` could be placed in the `Intdate` class to convert from an `Intdate` to a `Date`.

Notice that as before, in converting from a user-defined data type to a built-in data type, *the operator function's name determines the result of the conversion*; the class containing the operator function determines the data type being converted from.

Before providing a specific example of a class to class conversion, one additional point must be noted. Converting between classes clearly implies that we have two classes, one of which is always defined first and one of which is defined second. Having, within the second class, a conversion operator function with the name of the first class poses no problem because the compiler knows of the first class' existence. However, including a conversion operator function with the second class' name in the first class does pose a problem because the second class has not yet been defined. This is remedied by including a declaration for the second class prior to the first class' definition. This declaration, which is formally referred to as a *forward declaration*, is illustrated in Program 13-7, which also includes conversion operators between the two defined classes.

 Program 13-7

```
#include <iostream.h>

// forward declaration of class Intdate
class Intdate;

// class declaration for Date
class Date
{
  private:
    int month, day, year;
  public:
    Date(int, int, int);      // constructor
    operator Intdate();       // conversion operator Date to Intdate
    void showdate(void);
};
```

(continued on next page)

(continued from previous page)

```cpp
// class declaration for Intdate
class Intdate
{
  private:
    long yymmdd;
  public:
    Intdate(long);      // constructor
    operator Date();  // conversion operator Intdate to Date
    void showint(void);
};
// class implementation for Date
Date::Date(int mm = 7, int dd = 4, int yy = 94)  // constructor
{
  month = mm;
  day = dd;
  year = yy;
}
// conversion operator function converting from Date to Intdate class
Date::operator Intdate()   // must return an Intdate object
{
  long temp;

  temp = year * 10000.0 + month * 100.0 + day;
  return(Intdate(temp));
}
// member function to display a Date
void Date::showdate(void)
{
  cout << month << "/" << day << "/" << year;
}

// class implementation for Intdate
Intdate::Intdate(long ymd = 0)  // constructor
{
  yymmdd = ymd;
}
// conversion operator function converting from Intdate to Date class
Intdate::operator Date()    // must return a Date object
{
  int mo, da, yr;

  yr = int(yymmdd/10000.0);
  mo = int((yymmdd - yr * 10000.0)/100.0);
  da = int(yymmdd - yr * 10000.0 - mo * 100.0);
  return(Date(mo,da,yr));
}
// member function to display an Intdate
void Intdate::showint(void)
{
  cout << yymmdd;
}
```

(continued on next page)

(continued from previous page)

```
void main(void)
{
  Date a(4,1,96), b;      // declare two date objects
  Intdate c(981215), d;   // declare two intdate objects

  b = Date(c);       // cast c into a date object
  d = Intdate(a);    // cast a into an intdate object

  cout << " a's date is ";
  a.showdate();
  cout << "\n   as an Intdate object this date is ";
  d.showint();

  cout << "\n c's date is ";
  c.showint();
  cout << "\n   as a Date object this date is ";
  b.showdate();
```

The output produced by Program 13-7 is:

```
a's date is 4/1/96
  as an Intdate object this date is 960401
c's date is 981215
  as a Date object this date is 12/15/98
```

As illustrated by Program 13-7, the cast from `Date` to `Intdate` is produced by the assignment `b = Date(c)` and the cast from `Intdate` to `Date` is produced by the assignment `d = Intdate(a)`. Alternatively, the assignments `b = c` and `d = a` would produce the same results. Notice also the forward declaration of the `Intdate` class prior to the `Date` class' declaration. This is required so that the `Date` class can reference `Intdate` in its operator conversion function.

Exercises 13.3

1. a. Define the four data type conversions available in C++ and the method of accomplishing each conversion.
  b. Define the terms *type conversion constructor* and *conversion operator function* and describe how they are used in user-defined conversions.

2. Write a C++ program that declares a class named `Time` having integer data members named `hours`, `minutes`, and `seconds`. Include in the program a type conversion constructor that converts a long integer, representing the elapsed seconds from midnight into an equivalent representation as `hours:minutes:seconds`. For example, the long

integer 30336 should convert to the time 8:25:36. Use a military representation of time so that 2:30 p.m. is represented as 14:30:00. The relationship between time representations is:

*elapsed seconds = hours * 3600 + minutes * 60 + seconds*

3. A Julian date is a date represented as the number of days from a known base date. One algorithm for converting from a Gregorian date, in the form month/day/year, to a Julian date with a base date of 0/0/0 is given below. All of the calculations in this algorithm use integer arithmetic, which means that the fractional part of all divisions must be discarded. In this algorithm M = month, D = day, and Y = year.

```
If M is less than or equal to 2
   set the variable MP = 0 and YP = Y-1
Else
   set MP = int(0.4 * M + 2.3) and YP = Y

T = int(YP/4) - int(YP/100) + int(YP/400)
Julian date = 365 * Y + 31 * (M - 1) + D + T - MP
```

Using this algorithm modify Program 13-6 to cast from a Gregorian date object to its corresponding Julian representation as a long integer. Test your program using the Gregorian dates 1/31/85 and 3/16/86, which correspond to the Julian dates 31077 and 31486, respectively.

4. Modify the program written for Exercise 2 to include a member conversion operator function that converts an object of type `time` into a long integer representing the number of seconds from twelve midnight.

5. Write a C++ program that has a `Date` class and a `Julian` class. The `Date` class should be the same `Date` class as that used in Program 13-7, while the `Julian` class should represent a date as a long integer. For this program include a member conversion operator function within the `Date` class that converts a `Date` object to a `Julian` object, using the algorithm presented in Exercise 3. Test your program by converting the dates 1/31/95 and 3/16/96, which correspond to the Julian dates 34729 and 35139, respectively.

6. Write a C++ program that has a `Time` class and an `Ltime` class. The `Time` class should have integer data members named `hours`, `minutes`, and `seconds`, while the `Ltime` class should have a long data member named `elsecs`, which represents the number of elapsed seconds since midnight. For the `Time` class include a member conversion operator function named `Ltime()` that converts a `Time` object to an `Ltime` object. For the `Ltime` class include a member conversion operator function named `Time()` that converts an `Ltime` object to a `Time` object.

13.4 Class Inheritance

The ability to create new classes from existing ones is the underlying motivation and power behind class and object-oriented programming techniques. Doing so facilitates reusing existing code in new ways without the need for retesting and validation. It permits the designers of a class to make it available to others for additions and extensions, without relinquishing control over the existing class features.

Constructing one class from another is accomplished using a capability called inheritance. Related to this capability is an equally important feature named polymorphism. Polymorphism provides the ability to redefine how member functions of related classes operate based on the class object being referenced. In fact, for a programming language to be classified as an object-oriented language it must provide the features of classes, inheritance, and polymorphism. In this section we describe the inheritance and polymorphism features provided in C++.

Inheritance

Inheritance is the capability of deriving one class from another class. The initial class used as the basis for the derived class is referred to as either the *base, parent,* or *superclass*. The derived class is referred to as either the *derived, child,* or *subclass*.

A derived class is a completely new class that incorporates all of the data and member functions of its base class. It can, and usually does, however, add its own additional new data and function members and can override any base class function.

As an example of inheritance, consider three geometric shapes consisting of a circle, cylinder, and sphere. All of these shapes share a common characteristic, a radius. Thus, for these shapes we can make the circle a base type for the other two shapes, as illustrated in Figure 13–1.[5] Reformulating these shapes as class types we would make the circle the base class and derive the cylinder and sphere classes from it.

The relationships illustrated in Figure 13–1 are examples of simple inheritance. In *simple inheritance* each derived type has only one immediate base type. The complement to simple inheritance is multiple inheritance. In *multiple inheri-*

FIGURE 13–1 Relating Object Types

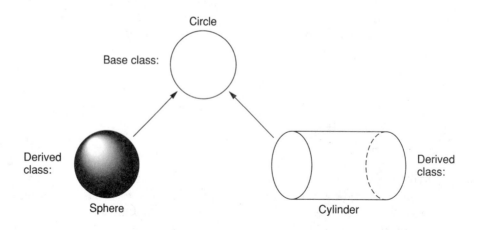

---

[5] By convention, arrows always point from the derived class to the base class.

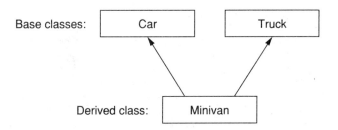

Base classes: Car   Truck

Derived class: Minivan

FIGURE 13–2 An Example of Multiple Inheritance

tance a derived type has two or more base types. Figure 13–2 illustrates an example of multiple inheritance. In this text we will only consider simple inheritance.

The class derivations illustrated in both Figures 13–1 and 13–2 are formally referred to as *class hierarchies*, because they illustrate the hierarchy, or order, in which one class is derived from another. Let's now see how to derive one class from another.

A derived class has the same form as any other class in that it consists of both a declaration and an implementation. The only difference is in the first line of the declaration section. For a derived class this line is extended to include a class-access specification and a base class name and has the form:

class derived-class-name : class-access base-class-name

For example, if `Circle` is the name of an existing class, a new class named `Cylinder` can be derived as follows:

```
class Cylinder : public Circle
{
  // add any additional data and
  // function members in here
};  // end of Cylinder class declaration
```

Except for the class-access specifier after the colon and the base class name, there is nothing inherently new or complicated about the construction of the `Cylinder` class. Before providing a description of the `Circle` class and adding data and function members to the derived `Cylinder` class, we will need to reexamine access specifiers and how they relate to derived classes.

Access Specifications

Until now we have only used private and public access specifiers within a class. Giving all data members private status ensured that they could only be accessed by either class member functions or friends. This restricted access prevents access by any nonclass functions (except friends), *which also precludes access by any derived class functions*. This is a sensible restriction because if it did not exist anyone could "jump around" the private restriction by simply deriving a class.

TABLE 13–3   Inherited Access Restrictions

Base Class Member		Derived Class Access		Derived Class Member
private	——————▶ :	private	——————▶	inaccessible
protected	——————▶ :	private	——————▶	private
public	——————▶ :	private	——————▶	private
private	——————▶ :	public	——————▶	inaccessible
protected	——————▶ :	public	——————▶	protected
public	——————▶ :	public	——————▶	public
private	——————▶ :	protected	——————▶	inaccessible
protected	——————▶ :	protected	——————▶	protected
public	——————▶ :	protected	——————▶	protected

To retain a restricted type of access across derived classes, C++ provides a third access specification—protected. Protected access behaves identically to private access in that it only permits member or friend function access, but it permits this restriction to be inherited by any derived class. The derived class then defines the type of inheritance it is willing to take on, subject to the base class' access restrictions. This is done by the class-access specifier, which is listed after the colon at the start of its declaration section. Table 13–3 lists the resulting derived class member access based on the base class member specifications and the derived class-access specifier.

Using Table 13–3 it can be seen (shaded region) that if the base class member has a protected access and the derived class specifier is public, then the derived class member will be protected to its class. Similarly, if the base class has a public access and the derived class specifier is public, the derived class member will be public. As this is the most commonly used type of specification for base class data and function members respectively, it is the one we will use. This means that for all classes intended for use as a base class we will use a protected data member access in place of a private designation.

An Example

To illustrate the process of deriving one class from another we will derive a Cylinder class from a base Circle class. The definition of the Circle class is:

```
class Circle
{
  protected:
    double radius;
  public:
    Circle(double);  // constructor
    double calcval();
};
```

(continued on next page)

(continued from previous page)

```
// class implementation
Circle::Circle(double r= 1.0)   // constructor
{
   radius = r;
}
double Circle::calcval(void)    // this calculates an area
{
   return(pi * radius * radius);
}
```

Except for the substitution of the access specifier `protected` in place of the usual private specifier for the data member, this is a standard class definition. The only variable not defined is pi, which is used in the `calcval()` function. We will define this as:

```
const double pi = 2.0 * asin(1.0);
```

This is simply a "trick" that forces the computer to return the value of pi accurate to as many decimal places as allowed by your computer. This value is obtained by taking the arcsin of 1.0, which is $\pi/2$, and multiplying the result by 2.

Having defined our base class, we can now extend it to a derived class. The definition of the derived class is:

```
class Cylinder : public Circle   // Cylinder is derived from Circle
{
   protected:
     double length;   // add one additional data member and
   public:            // two additional function members
     Cylinder(double r = 1.0, double l = 1.0) : Circle(r), length(l) {}
     double calcval();
};
```

```
// class implementation
double Cylinder::calcval(void)    // this calculates a volume
{
   return (length * Circle::calcval()); // note the base function call
}
```

This definition encompasses several important concepts relating to derived classes. First, as a derived class, `Cylinder` contains all of the data and function members of its base class, `Circle`, plus any additional members that it may add. In this particular case the `Cylinder` class consists of a radius data member inherited from the `Circle` class, plus an additional `length` member. Thus, each `Cylinder` object contains *two* data members, as is illustrated in Figure 13–3.

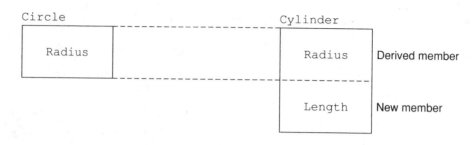

FIGURE 13-3 Relationship Between `Circle` and `Cylinder` Data Members

In addition to having two data members the `Cylinder` class also inherits `Circle`'s function members. This is illustrated in the `Cylinder` constructor, which uses a base member initialization list (see Section 12.1) that specifically calls the `Circle` constructor. It is also illustrated in `Cylinder`'s `calcval()` function which makes a call to `Circle::calcval()`.

In both classes the same function name, `calcval()`, has been specifically used to illustrate the overriding of a base function by a derived function. When a `Cylinder` object calls `calcval()` it is a request to use the `Cylinder` version of the function, while a `Circle` object call to `calcval()` is a request to use the `Circle` version. In this case the `Cylinder` class can only access the class version of `calcval()` using the `scope` resolution operator, as is done in the call `Circle::calcval()`. Program 13-8 uses these two classes within the context of a complete program.

Program 13-8

```
#include <iostream.h>
#include <math.h>

const double pi = 2.0 * asin(1.0);

class Circle
{
  protected:
    double radius;
  public:
    Circle(double);  // constructor
    double calcval();
};

// class implementation
Circle::Circle(double r= 1.0)  // constructor
{
  radius = r;
}
double Circle::calcval(void)    // this calculates an area
{
  return(pi * radius * radius);
}
```

(continued on next page)

(continued from previous page)

```
class Cylinder : public Circle  // cylinder is derived from Circle
{
  protected:
    double length;  // add one additional data member and
  public:          // two additional function members
    Cylinder(double r = 1.0, double l = 1.0) : circle(r), length(l) {}
    double calcval();
};

// class implementation
double Cylinder::calcval(void)   // this calculates a volume
{
  return (length * Circle::calcval()); // note the base function call
}
```

```
main()
{
  Circle circle_1, circle_2(2);  // create two circle objects
  Cylinder cylinder_1(3,4);      // create one cylinder object

  cout << "The area of circle_1 is " << circle_1.calcval() << endl;
  cout << "The area of circle_2 is " << circle_2.calcval() << endl;
  cout << "The volume of cylinder_1 is " << cylinder_1.calcval() << endl;

  circle_1 = cylinder_1;  // assign a cylinder to a circle

  cout << "\nThe area of circle_1 is now " << circle_1.calcval() << endl;
}
```

The output produced by Program 13-8 is:

```
The area of circle_1 is 3.141593
The area of circle_2 is 12.566371
The volume of cylinder_1 is 113.097336

The area of circle_1 is now 28.274334
```

The first three output lines are all straightforward and are produced by the first three cout calls in the program. As the output shows, a call to calcval() using a Circle object activates the Circle version of this function, while a call to calcval() using a Cylinder object activates the Cylinder version.

The assignment statement circle_1 = cylinder_1; introduces another important relationship between a base and derived class: *A derived class object can be assigned to a base class object.*

This should not be surprising because both base and derived classes share a common set of data member types. In this type of assignment it is only this set of data members, which consist of all the base class data members, that are assigned. Thus, as illustrated in Figure 13–4, our Cylinder to Circle assignment results in the following memberwise assignment:

```
circle_1.radius = cylinder_1.radius;
```

479

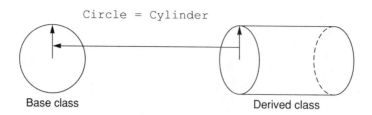

FIGURE 13–4 Assignment from Derived to Base Class

The length member of the Cylinder object is not used in the assignment because it has no equivalent variable in the Circle class. The reverse cast, from base to derived class, is not as simple and requires a constructor to correctly initialize the additional derived class members not in the base class.

Before leaving Program 13-8 one additional point should be made. Although the Circle constructor was explicitly called using a base/member initialization list for the Cylinder constructor, an implicit call could also have been made. In the absence of an explicit derived class constructor the compiler will automatically call the default base class constructor first, before the derived class constructor is called. This works because the derived class contains all of the base class data members. In a similar fashion the destructor functions are called in the reverse order—first derived class and then base class.

Polymorphism

The overriding of a base member function using an overloaded derived member function, as illustrated by the calcval() function in Program 13-8, is an example of polymorphism. *Polymorphism* permits the same function name to invoke one response in objects of a base class and another response in objects of a derived class. In some cases, however, this method of overriding does not work as one might desire. To understand why this is so, consider Program 13-9.

 Program 13-9

```
#include <iostream.h>
#include <math.h>


class One                     // the base class
{
  protected:
    float a;
  public:
    One(float);     // constructor
    float f1(float);    // a member function
    float f2(float);    // another member function
};
```

(continued on next page)

(continued from previous page)

```
// class implementation
One::One(float val = 2)    // constructor
{
  a = val;
}
float One::f1(float num)  // a member function
{
  return(num/2);
}
float One::f2(float num)  // another member function
{
  return( pow(f1(num),2) );  // square the result of f1()
}

class Two : public One  // the derived class
{
  public:
    float f1(float);    // this overrides class One's f1()
};

// class implementation
float Two::f1(float num)
{
  return(num/3);
}
```

```
void main(void)
{
  One object_1;  // object_1 is an object of the base class
  Two object_2;  // object_2 is an object of the derived class

    // call f2() using a base class object call
  cout << "The computed value using a base class object call is "
      << object_1.f2(12) << endl;

    // call f2() using a derived class object call
  cout << "The computed value using a derived class object call is "
      << object_2.f2(12) << endl;
}
```

The output produced by Program 13-9 is:

```
The computed value using a base class object call is 36
The computed value using a derived class object call is 36
```

As this output shows, the same result is obtained no matter which object type calls the f2() function. This result is produced because the derived class does not have an override to the base class f2() function. Thus, both calls to f2() result in the base class f2() function being called.

Once invoked, the base class f2() function will always call the base class version of f1() rather than the derived class override version. The reason for this is because of a process referred to as *function binding*. In normal function calls static binding is used. In *static binding* the determination of which function should be called is made at compile time. Thus, when the compiler first encounters the f1() function in the base class it makes the determination that whenever f2() is called, either from a base or derived class object, it will subsequently call the base class f1() function.

In place of static binding we would like a binding method that is capable of determining which function should be invoked at run time, based on the object type making the call. This type of binding is referred to as *dynamic binding*. To achieve dynamic binding C++ provides virtual functions.

A *virtual function* specification tells the compiler to create a pointer to a function, but not fill in the value of the pointer until the function is actually called. Then, at run time, *and based on the object making the call*, the appropriate function address is used. Creating a virtual function is extremely easy—all that is required is that the keyword virtual be placed before the function's return type in the declaration section. For example, consider Program 13-10, which is identical to Program 13-9 except for the virtual declaration of the f1() function.

Program 13-10

```
#include <iostream.h>
#include <math.h>
```

```
class One                      // the base class
{
  protected:
    float a;
  public:
    One(float);    // constructor
    virtual float f1(float);    // a member function
    float f2(float);    // another member function
};

// class implementation
One::One(float val = 2)    // constructor
{
  a = val;
}
```

(continued on next page)

(continued from previous page)

```cpp
float One::f1(float num)   // a member function
{
  return(num/2);
}
float One::f2(float num)   // another member function
{
  return( pow(f1(num),2) );   // square the result of f1()
}


class Two : public One   // the derived class
{
  public:
    virtual float f1(float);     // this overrides class One's f1()
};

// class implementation
float Two::f1(float num)
{
  return(num/3);
}
```

```cpp
void main(void)
{
  One object_1;   // object_1 is an object of the base class
  Two object_2;   // object_2 is an object of the derived class

    // call f2() using a base class object call
  cout << "The computed value using a base class object call is "
      << object_1.f2(12) << endl;

    // call f2() using a derived class object call
  cout << "The computed value using a derived class object call is "
      << object_2.f2(12) << endl;
}
```

The output produced by Program 13-10 is:

```
The computed value using a base class object call is 36
The computed value using a derived class object call is 16
```

As illustrated by this output the f2() function now calls different versions of the overloaded f1() function based on the object type making the call. This selection, based on the object making the call, is the classic definition of polymorphic function behavior and is caused by the dynamic binding imposed on f1() by virtue of its being a virtual function.

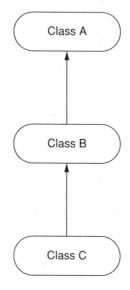

FIGURE 13–5 Inheritance Diagram

Once a function is declared as `virtual` *it remains virtual for the next derived class with or without a virtual declaration in the derived class.* Thus, the second `virtual` declaration in the derived class is not strictly needed, but should be included both for clarity and to ensure that any subsequently derived classes correctly inherit the function. To understand why, consider the inheritance diagram illustrated in Figure 13-5, where class C is derived from class B and class B is derived from class A. In this situation, if function `f1()` is virtual in class A, but is not declared in class B, it will not be virtual in class C.

The only other requirement is that once a function has been declared as virtual the return type and parameter list of all subsequent derived class override versions *must be* the same.

Exercises 13.4

1. Define the following terms:

a. inheritance	*f.* class hierarchy
b. base class	*g.* polymorphism
c. derived class	*h.* static binding
d. simple inheritance	*i.* dynamic binding
e. multiple inheritance	*j.* virtual function

2. Describe the two methods C++ provides for implementing polymorphism.

3. What three features must a programming language provide for it to be classified as an object-oriented language?

4. Describe the difference between a private and a protected class member.

5 a. Modify Program 13-8 to include a derived class named `Sphere` from the base `Circle` class. The only additional class members of `Sphere` should be a constructor and a `calcval()` function that returns the volume of the sphere. (*Note:* volume = $4/3\pi\ radius^3$)

b. Include the class constructed for Exercise 5a in a working C++ program. Have your program call all of the member functions in the `Sphere` class.

6. a. Create a base class named `Point` that consists of an `x` and `y` coordinate. From this class derive a class named `Circle` having an additional data member named `radius`. For this derived class the `x` and `y` data members represent the center coordinates of a circle. The function members of the first class should consist of a constructor, an area function named `area` that returns zero, and a `distance` function that returns the distance between two points, where

$$distance = \sqrt{(x2 - x1)^2 + (y2 - y1)^2}$$

Additionally, the derived class should have a constructor and an override function named `area` that returns the area of a circle.

b. Include the classes constructed for Exercise 6a in a working C++ program. Have your program call all of the member functions in each class. In addition call the base class `distance` function with two `Circle` objects and explain the result returned by the function.

7. a. Using the classes constructed for Exercise 6a, derive a class named `Cylinder` from the derived `Circle` class. The `Cylinder` class should have a constructor and a member function named `area` that determines the surface area of the cylinder. For this function use the algorithm *surface area = 2 π r (l + r)*, where *r* is the radius of the cylinder and *l* is the length.

b. Include the classes constructed for Exercise 7a in a working C++ program. Have your program call all of the member functions in the `Cylinder` class.

c. What do you think might be the result if the base class `distance` function was called with two `cylinder` objects?

8. a. Create a base class named `Rectangle` that contains `length` and `width` data members. From this class derive a class named `Box` having an additional data member named `depth`. The function members of the base `Rectangle` class should consist of a constructor and an `area` function. The derived `Box` class should have a constructor and an override function named `area` that returns the surface area of the box and a volume function.

b. Include the classes constructed for Exercise 8a in a working C++ program. Have your program call all of the member functions in each class and explain the result when the `distance` function is called using two `Circle` objects.

13.5 Common Programming Errors

The common programming errors associated with operator functions, conversions, and inheritance are the following:

1. Attempting to redefine an operator's meaning as it applies to C++'s built-in data types.

2. Redefining an overloaded operator to perform a function not indicated by its conventional meaning. Although this will work, it is an example of extremely bad programming practice.

3. Attempting to make a conversion operator function a friend, rather than a member function.

4. Attempting to specify a return type for a member conversion operator function.

5. Attempting to override a virtual function without using the same type and number of arguments as the original function.

6. Using the keyword `virtual` in the class implementation section. Functions are only declared as `virtual` in the class declaration section.

13.6 Chapter Summary

1. User-defined operators can be constructed for classes using member operator functions. An operator function has the form `operator<symbol>`, where `<symbol>` is one of the following:

```
()  []  ->  new  delete  ++  --  !  ~  *  /  %  +  -
<<  >>  <  <=  >  >=  ++  !=  &&  ||  &  ^  |  =  +=
-=  *=  /=  %=  &=  ^=  |=  <<=  >>=  ,
```

For example, the function prototype `Date operator+(int);` declares that the addition operator will be defined to accept an integer and return a `Date` object.

2. User-defined operators may be called in either of two ways—as a conventional function with arguments or as an operator expression. For example, for an operator having the header line

```
Date Date::operator+(int)
```

if `dte` is an object of type `Date`, the following two calls produce the same effect:

```
dte.operator+(284)
```

```
dte + 284
```

3. Operator functions may also be written as friend functions. The equivalent friend version of a member operator function will always contain an additional class reference that is not required by the member function.

4. The subscript operator function, `operator[]`, permits a maximum of one nonclass argument. This function can only be defined as a member function.

5. The parentheses operator function, `operator()`, has no limits on the number of arguments. This function can only be defined as a member function.

6. There are four categories of data type conversions. They are conversions from

- built-in types to built-in types
- built-in types to user-defined (class) types
- user-defined (class) types to built-in types
- user-defined (class) types to user-defined (class) types

Built-in to built-in type conversions are done using C++'s implicit conversion rules or explicitly using casts. Built-in to user-defined type conversions are done using type conversion constructors. Conversions from user-defined types to either built-in or other user-defined types are done using conversion operator functions.

7. A *type conversion constructor* is a constructor whose first argument is not a member of its class and whose remaining arguments, if any, have default values.

8. A conversion operator function must be a member function. It has no explicit arguments or return type; rather, the return type is the name of the function.

9. *Inheritance* is the capability of deriving one class from another class. The initial class used as the basis for the derived class is referred to as the base, parent, or superclass. The derived class is referred to as either the derived, child, or subclass.

10. Base member functions can be overridden by derived member functions with the same name. The override function is simply an overloaded version of the base member function defined in the derived class.

11. *Polymorphism* is the capability of having the same function name invoke different responses based on the object making the function call. It can be accomplished using either override functions or virtual functions.

12. In *static binding* the determination of which function actually is invoked is made at compile time. In *dynamic binding* the determination is made at run time.

13. A *virtual function* specification designates that dynamic binding should take place. The specification is made in the function's prototype by placing the keyword `virtual` before the function's return type. Once a function has been declared as `virtual` it remains so for all derived classes as long as there is a continuous trail of function declarations through the derived chain of classes.

Data Files

Chapter Fourteen

The data for the programs we have seen so far has either been defined internally within the programs or entered interactively during program execution. This type of data creation and retention precludes sharing data between programs and is a disadvantage in larger systems consisting of many interconnecting programs. For these larger systems, the data used by one program typically must be made available to other programs, without being recreated or redefined.

Sharing data between programs requires that the data be saved independently and separately from any single program. For example, consider the following data:

Code	Description	Price	Amount in Stock
QA134	Battery	35.89	10
QA136	Bulbs	3.22	123
CM104	Fuses	1.03	98
CM212	Degreaser	4.74	62
HT435	Cleaner	3.98	50

This data might be needed by both an inventory control program and a billing program. Therefore, the data would be stored by itself on a floppy diskette, hard disk, or magnetic tape in a data file.

A *data file* is any collection of data that is stored together under a common name on a storage medium other than the computer's main memory. This chapter describes the C++ statements needed to create data files and to read and write data to them.

14.1 Declaring, Opening, and Closing Files

Each data file in a computer is physically stored using a unique file name. Computers operating under the DOS operating system require that a *file name* consist of no more than eight characters followed by an optional period and an extension of up to three characters.[1] Using this convention, the following are all valid computer data file names:

```
balances.dat    records      info.dat
report.bnd      prices.dat   math.mem
```

Computer file names should be chosen to indicate both the type of data in the file and the application for which it is used. Frequently, the first eight characters are used to describe the data itself and the three characters after the decimal point are used to describe the application. For example, the file name `prices.bnd` is useful for describing a file of prices used in a bond application.

---

[1] File names under the traditional UNIX operating system may be a maximum of 14 characters in length.

Within a C++ program a link must be established between the actual file and an object name that must be declared within the program. There are three classes that can be used for the required objects: `ifstream` (from input file stream), `ofstream` (from output file stream), and `fstream` (from file stream) classes. Objects of type `ifstream` can only be used in the creation and input of data from a file, objects of type `ofstream` can only be used in the creation and output of data to a file, while objects of type `fstream` can be used in the creation, input of data from, and output of data to a file. Examples of such object declarations using these classes are:

```
ifstream file_1;   // file_1 can only be used for input
ofstream file_2;   // file_2 can only be used for output
fstream file_3;    // how file_3 is used will be defined later
```

In each of these declarations, the object name is selected by the programmer and is the name of the data file as it will be referenced within the program. This name need not be the same as the external name used by the computer to store the file.

The required header file for the `ifstream`, `ofstream`, and `fstream` classes is the `fstream.h` header file, which must be included at the top of each program that uses a data file. Because the `iostream` class is a base class for the `fstream` class, inclusion of the `iostream.h` header for the `cin` and `cout` objects is not required when the `fstream.h` header file is used.

In the remainder of this section we will rely exclusively on `fstream` class objects for creating files and using them for either input or output. The exact relationship between the `ifstream`, `ofstream` and `fstream` classes, including the internal data structures used by these classes in reading and writing data, is presented in the appendix to this chapter.

Opening a File

Opening a file is a "cookbook" procedure that accomplishes two purposes, only one of which is directly pertinent to the programmer. First, opening a file establishes a physical communications link between the program and the data file. Since details of this link are handled by the computer's operating system and are transparent to the program, the programmer normally need not consider them.

From a programming perspective, the second purpose of opening a file is relevant. Besides establishing the actual physical connection between a program and a data file, opening a file equates the file's external computer name to the name used internally by the program. The function that performs this task is named `open()` and is a member function of the `fstream` class.

It now remains to actually call this function to connect the file's external name to its internal name. In using the member `open()` function, two arguments are required. The first argument is the computer's name for the file; the

TABLE 14–1   Permissible File Modes

Mode	Description
ios::in	Open in input mode
ios::out	Open in output mode
ios::app	Open in append mode
ios::ate	Go to end of file when opened
ios::binary	Open in binary mode (default is text)
ios::trunc	Delete file contents if it exists
ios::nocreate	If file does not exist, open fails
ios::noreplace	If file exists, open for output fails

second argument is the mode in which the file is to be used. Permissible modes for the second argument are listed in Table 14–1. Initially we will only be concerned with the modes ios::in, ios::out, and ios::app, which represent input, output, and append modes, respectively.

A file opened for output creates a new file and makes the file available for writing by the function opening the file. If a file exists with the same name as a file opened for output, the old file is erased. For example, assuming that file1 has been declared as an object of type fstream using the statement

```
fstream file1;
```

then the statement

```
file1.open("prices.dat",ios::out);
```

opens a file named prices.dat that can now be written to. Once this file has been opened the program accesses the file using the internal object name file1, while the computer saves the file under the external name prices.dat.[2]

A file opened for appending makes an existing file available for data to be added to the end of the file. If the file opened for appending does not exist, a new file with the designated name is created and made available to receive output from the program. For example, again assuming that file1 has been declared to be of type fstream, the statement

```
file1.open("prices.dat",ios::app);
```

opens a file named prices.dat and makes it available for data to be appended to the end of the file.

---

[2] The same open statement can be used if file1 had been declared to be of type ofstream. Since the default file mode for ofstream objects is ios::out, this mode can be omitted in the open statement for ofstream objects.

The only difference between a file opened in output mode and one opened in append mode is where the data is physically placed in the file. In output mode, the data is written starting at the beginning of the file, while in append mode the data is written starting at the end of the file. For a new file, the two modes are identical.

For files opened in either output or append mode, the function used to write data to it is similar to the `cout` function used for displaying data on a terminal. This function is described in the next section.

A file opened in input mode retrieves an existing file and makes its data available as input to the program. For example, if `file1` has been declared to be of type `fstream`, the `open` statement

```
file1.open("prices.dat",ios::in);
```

opens the file named `prices.dat` and makes the data in the file available for input.[3] The functions used to read data from a file are similar to the `cin.getline()` and `cin.get()` functions used for inputting data from the keyboard. These functions are also described in the next section.

Notice that in all of the `open` statements the external file name argument passed to `open()` is a string contained between double quotes. If the external file name is first stored in either an array of characters or as a string, the array or string name, without quotes, can be used as the first argument to `open()`.

When a file cannot be opened, for whatever reason, the value assigned to the internal file name is zero. Good programming practice requires that this value always be checked and used to inform the user that a failed open has occurred. For example, the following code attempts to open a file named `prices.dat`, checks the return value, and reports an error message if the file was not successfully opened for input:

```
fstream file1;   // any object name can be used here

file1.open("prices.dat", ios::in);   // open the file
if (file1 == 0)
{
  cout << "The file was not successfully opened!" << endl;
  return;
}
```

Throughout the remainder of the text we will include this type of error checking whenever a file is opened. As a practical matter, however, the test `if (file1 == 0)` is usually expressed in the form `if (!file1)`. We shall use this latter form for all remaining examples.

---

[3] The same `open` statement can be used if `file1` had been declared to be of type `ifstream`. Since the default file mode for `ifstream` objects is `ios::in`, this mode can be omitted in the `open` statement for `ifstream` objects.

Program 14-1 illustrates the statements required to open a file in read mode, including an error-checking routine to ensure that a successful open was obtained. The program prompts the user for the external file name and stores the name in the array f_name[13].

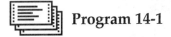 **Program 14-1**

```
#include <fstream.h>
void main(void)
{
  char f_name[13];
  fstream file1;

  cout << "\nEnter a file name: ";
  cin.getline(f_name,12);

  file1.open(f_name,ios::in);    // open the file

  if (!file1)  // check for successful open
  {
    cout << "\nThe file " << f_name << " was not successfully opened"
         << "\n Please check that the file currently exists." << endl;
    return;
  }
  else
    cout << "\nThe file has been successfully opened for reading.";

}
```

Program 14-1 requests that an external data file name be entered by the user. The entered name is stored in the character array f_name and the array name is then passed to the open() function. A sample run using Program 14-1 produced the output:

```
Enter a file name: prices.dat

The file has been successfully opened for reading.
```

Although Program 14-1 can be used to open an existing file in read mode, it clearly lacks statements to read the data in the file and then close the file. These topics are discussed next. Before leaving Program 14-1, however, two items should be noted. First, the iostream.h header file did not have to be included in the program to use the cout object because its definition is incorporated within the `fstream.h` header file. Next, it is possible to combine the declaration of an `fstream` object and its associated `open` statement into one statement. For example, the two statements in Program 14-1,

```
fstream file1;
file1.open(f_name,ios::in);    // open the file
```

can be combined into the single statement

```
fstream file1(f_name,ios::in);
```

In this text we will continue to declare the `fstream` object at the top of the program and explicitly call the `open` statement in a separate statement. You may, however, choose to use the alternative single statement form or encounter it as you progress in your programming experience.[4]

Closing a File

A file is closed using `fstream`'s `close()` function. This function breaks the link between the file's external name and the `fstream` object, which can then be used for another file. For example, the statement

```
file1.close();
```

closes the `file1` file. As indicated, the `close()` member function takes no argument.

Since all computers have a limit on the maximum number of files that can be open at one time, closing files that are no longer needed makes good sense. Any open files existing at the end of normal program execution are also automatically closed by the operating system.

Exercises 14.1

1. Using the reference manuals provided with your computer's operating system, determine:
   a. the maximum number of characters that can be used to name a file for storage by the computer system
   b. the maximum number of data files that can be open at the same time

2. Would it be appropriate to call a saved C++ program a file? Why or why not?

3. Write a suitable declaration statement for each of the following `fstream` objects: `prices`, `fp`, `coupons`, `distance`, `in_data`, `out_data`.

---

[4] The same comment applies to `ifstream` and `ofstream` objects: Rather than declare an object of either of these two types and then explicitly connect an external file to the object using the member `open()` function, the definition and open can be combined into a single statement.

4. Write individual open statements to link the following external data file names to their corresponding internal object names:

External Name	Object Name	Mode
coba.mem	memo	output
book.let	letter	output
coupons.bnd	coups	append
yield.bnd	pt_yield	append
prices.dat	pri_file	input
rates.dat	rates	input

5. Write individual fstream object declarations for each of the files opened in Exercise 4.

6. Write close statements for each of the files opened in Exercise 4.

7. a. Program 14-1 prompts the user for a file name and uses the getline() function to return a string into the character array f_name. Replace the prompt and the getline() statements with the single function call statement get_file(name);. Then write the get_file() function to prompt the user for a file name, accept a file name, and test that a valid file name has been entered. If a valid name has not been entered, print an appropriate message and have the program terminate. If a valid name has been entered, have the program open the file and check that a successful opening has occurred. Consider a valid file name as consisting of at most eight characters, the first of which is a letter.

b. Modify the get_file() function written for Exercise 7a to request a file name continuously until a valid name has been entered. (*Hint:* Include the prompt and the getline() function call in a while or do-while loop that terminates when a valid file name is detected.)

14.2 Reading and Writing Files

Reading or writing to an open file involves almost the identical functions for reading input from a terminal and writing data to a display screen. For writing to a file, the cout object is replaced by the fstream object declared in the program. For example, if out_file is declared as an object of type fstream that is opened for output, the following output statements are valid:

```
out_file << 'a';   // write an a to the file
out_file << "Hello World!";  // write the string to the file
out_file << descrip << ' ' << price;
```

The file name in each of these statements, in place of cout, simply directs the output stream to a specific file instead of to the standard display device. Program 14-2 illustrates the use of a file write function to write a list of descriptions and prices to a file.

Program 14-2

```
#include <fstream.h>
#include <iomanip.h>
void main(void)
{
  float price[] = {39.95,3.22,1.02}; // a list of prices
  char *descrip[] = { "Batteries",   // a list of descriptions
                      "Bulbs",
                      "Fuses"};
  fstream out_file;    // declare the internal file name

  out_file.open("prices.dat",ios::out);  // open the file
  if (!out_file)
  {
    cout << "The file was not successfully opened" << endl;
    return;
  }

  for( int i = 0; i < 3; i++ )
    out_file << setiosflags(ios::left) << ' '<< descrip[i]
             << ' ' << setprecision(2) << price[i];

}
```

When Program 14-2 is executed, a file named prices.dat is created and saved by the computer. The file is a sequential list of characters consisting of the following data:

```
Batteries 39.95 Bulbs 3.22 Fuses 1.02
```

The actual storage of characters in the file depends on the character codes used by the computer. Although only 37 characters appear to be stored in the file, corresponding to the descriptions, blanks, and prices written to the file, the file actually contains 39 characters. The extra characters consist of a blank before the first description and a special end-of-file marker placed as the last item in the file when the file is closed. Assuming characters are stored using the ASCII code, the prices.dat file is physically stored as illustrated in Figure 14-1. For convenience, the character corresponding to each hexadecimal code is listed below the code. A code of 20 represents the blank character. Although the actual code used for the end-of-file marker depends on the system you are using, the hexadecimal code 26, corresponding to Control-Z, is common for the DOS operating system.

```
20 42 61 74 74 65 72 69 65 73 20 33 39 2e 32 35 20 42 75 6c 62 73
   B  a  t  t  e  r  i  e  s        3  9  .  2  5     B  u  l  b  s

20 33 2e 32 32 20 46 75 73 65 73 20 31 2e 30 32 26
   3  .  2  2     F  u  s  e  s     1  .  0  2 ^Z
```

FIGURE 14–1 The `prices.dat` File as Stored by the Computer

Reading data from a file is almost identical to reading data from a standard keyboard, except that the `cin` object is replaced by the `fstream` object declared in the program. For example, if `in_file` is declared as an object of type `fstream` that is opened for input, the input statement

```
in_file >> descrip >> price;
```

will read the next two items in the file and store them in the variables `descrip` and `price`.

The file name in this statement, in place of `cin`, simply directs the input to come from the file rather than the standard input device. Other member functions that can be used for file manipulation are listed in Table 14–2. Each of these functions, however, must be preceded by the file's name.

Reading data from a file requires that the programmer knows how the data appears in the file. This is necessary for correct "stripping" of the data from the file into appropriate variables for storage. All files are read sequentially, so that once an item is read the next item in the file becomes available for reading.

Program 14-3 illustrates reading the `prices.dat` file that was created in Program 14-2. The program also illustrates how the EOF marker can be detected by the `peek()` function. As long as the EOF has not been detected, the program will continue to read characters from the file.

TABLE 14–2 `fstream` Member Functions

Name	Description
`get()`	Extract the next character from the file
`getline(char *,int n,'\n')`	Extract characters from the file until either n-1 characters are read or a newline is encountered (terminates the input with a '\0')
`peek()`	Return the next character in the file without extracting it from the file
`putback(char)`	Push back a character on the file
`eof()`	True if EOF has been reached

Program 14-3

```cpp
#include <fstream.h>
#include <iomanip.h>
void main(void)
{
  int ch;
  char descrip[10];
  float price;
  fstream in_file;

  in_file.open("prices.dat",ios::in);
  if (!in_file)  // check for successful open
  {
    cout << "\nThe file was not successfully opened"
         << "\n Please check that the file currently exists."
         << endl;
    return;
  }
      // now read the file
  while ( (ch = in_file.peek()) != EOF ) // check next character
  {
    in_file >> descrip >> price;  // input the data
    cout << setiosflags(ios::left) << descrip << ' '
         << setprecision(2) << price << '\n';
  }
}
```

Program 14-3 continues to read the file until the EOF marker has been detected. Each time the file is read, a string and a floating point number are input to the program. The display produced by Program 14-3 is:

```
Batteries 39.95
Bulbs 3.22
Fuses 1.02
```

As an alternate to the while loop used in Program 14-3, the following construction could also have been used:

```cpp
    while (1)    // always true
    {
      in_file >> descrip >> price;  // input the data
      if (in_file.eof()) break;
      cout << setiosflags(ios::left) << descrip << ' '
           << setprecision(2) << price << '\n';
    }
```

This latter form attempts to read a description and price first, and then ·checks whether the EOF marker was input instead. If the last input attempt did encounter the EOF the loop is exited, otherwise the data read is displayed.

In place of the in_file extraction, >>, used in Program 14-3, a getline() function call can be used. The getline() requires three arguments: an address where the first character read will be stored, the maximum number of characters to be read, and a terminating character. For example, the function call

```
in_file.getline(line,80,'\n');
```

causes a maximum of 79 characters (one less than the specified number) to be read from the file named in_file and stored starting at the address contained in the pointer named line. getline() continues reading characters until 79 characters have been read or a newline character has been encountered. If a newline character is encountered it is not included with the other entered characters before the string is terminated with the end-of-string marker, \0. Program 14-4 illustrates the use of getline() in a working program.

Program 14-4

```
#include <fstream.h>
#include <iomanip.h>
const int max = 80;
void main(void)
{
  int ch;
  char line[max];
  fstream in_file;

  in_file.open("prices.dat",ios::in);
  if (!in_file)    // check for successful open
  {
    cout << "\nThe file was not successfully opened"
         << "\n Please check that the file currently exists."
         << endl;
    return;
  }
      // now read the file
  while( (ch = in_file.peek()) != EOF )
  {
    in_file.getline(line,80,'\n');
    cout << line << endl;
  }
}
```

Program 14-4 is really a line-by-line text-copying program, reading a line of text from the file and then displaying it on the terminal. The output of Program 14-4 is:

```
Batteries 39.95 Bulbs 3.22 Fuses 1.02
```

If it were necessary to obtain the description and price as individual variables, either Program 14-3 should be used or the string returned by `getline()` in Program 14-4 must be processed further to extract the individual data items.

Standard Device Files

The data file objects we have used have all been logical file objects. A logical file object is one that references a file of logically related data that has been saved under a common name; that is, a data file. In addition to logical file objects, C++ also supports physical file objects. A physical file object is a reference to a hardware device, such as a keyboard, screen, or printer.

The actual physical device assigned to your program for data entry is formally called the standard input file. Usually this is a keyboard. When a `cin` object function call is encountered in a C++ program, the computer automatically goes to this standard input file for the expected input. Similarly, when a `cout` object function call is encountered, the output is automatically displayed or "written to" a device that has been assigned as the standard output file. For most systems this is a CRT screen, although it can be a printer.

When a program is run, the keyboard used for entering data is automatically opened and assigned to the internal `fstream` object name `cin`. Similarly, the output device used for display is assigned to the `fstream` object named `cout`. These objects are always available for programmer use.

Other Devices

The keyboard, display, and error-reporting devices are automatically opened and assigned the internal stream object names `cin`, `cout`, and `cerr`, respectively, by a C++ program using either the `iostream.h` or `fstream.h` header files. Additionally, other devices can be used for input or output if the name assigned by the system is known. For example, most IBM or IBM-compatible personal computers assign the name `prn` to the printer connected to the computer. For these computers a statement such as `out_file.open("prn",ios::out)` opens the printer for output and connects it to the `fstream` object named `out_file`. A subsequent statement, such as `out_file << "Hello World!";`, would then cause the string `Hello World!` to be printed directly on the printer. Notice that as the name of an actual file, `prn` must be enclosed in double quotes in the `open()` function call.

Exercises 14.2

1. a. Write a C++ program that accepts lines of text from the keyboard and writes each line to a file named `text.dat` until an empty line is entered. An empty line is a line with no text—just a new line caused by pressing the Enter (or Return) key.
b. Modify Program 14-4 to read and display the data stored in the `text.dat` file created in Exercise 1a.

2. Determine the operating system command provided by your computer to display the contents of a saved file. Compare its operation with the program developed for Exercise 1b. (*Hint:* Typically the operating system command is called LIST, TYPE, or CAT.)

3. a. Create a file named `employ.dat` containing the following data:

Anthony	A.J.	10031	7.82	12/18/62
Burrows	W.K.	10067	9.14	6/ 9/63
Fain	B.D.	10083	8.79	5/18/59
Janney	P.	10095	10.57	9/28/62
Smith	G.J.	10105	8.50	12/20/61

b. Write a C++ program called `fcopy.c` to read the `employ.dat` file created in Exercise 3a and produce a duplicate copy of the file named `employ.bak`.
c. Modify the program written in Exercise 3b to accept the names of the original and duplicate files as user input.
d. Since the program written for Exercise 3c always copies data from an original file to a duplicate file, can you think of a better method of accepting the original and duplicate file names than prompting the user for them each time the program is executed?

4. a. Write a C++ program that opens a file and displays the contents of the file with associated line numbers. That is, the program should print 1 before displaying the first line, 2 before displaying the second line, and so on for each line in the file.
b. Modify the program written in Exercise 4a to list the contents of the file on the printer assigned to your computer.

5. a. Create a file containing the following names, Social Security numbers, hourly rate, and hours worked:

B. Caldwell	163-98-4182	7.32	37
D. Memcheck	189-53-2147	8.32	40
R. Potter	145-32-9826	6.54	40
W. Rosen	163-09-4263	9.80	35

b. Write a C++ program that reads the data file created in Exercise 5a and computes and displays a payroll schedule. The output should list the Social Security number, name, and gross pay for each individual.

6. a. Create a file containing the following car numbers, number of miles driven, and number of gallons of gas used by each car:

Car No.	Miles Driven	Gallons Used
54	250	19
62	525	38
71	123	6
85	1,322	86
97	235	14

b. Write a C++ program that reads the data in the file created in Exercise 6a and displays the car number, miles driven, gallons used, and the miles per gallon for each car. The output should additionally contain the total miles driven, total gallons used, and average miles per gallon for all the cars. These totals should be displayed at the end of the output report.

7. *a.* Create a file with the following data containing the part number, opening balance, number of items sold, and minimum stock required:

Part Number	Initial Amount	Quantity Sold	Minimum Amount
QA310	95	47	50
CM145	320	162	200
MS514	34	20	25
EN212	163	150	160

b. Write a C++ program to create an inventory report based on the data in the file created in Exercise 7a. The display should consist of the part number, current balance, and the amount that is necessary to bring the inventory to the minimum level.

8. *a.* Create a file containing the following data:

Name	Rate	Hours
Callaway,G.	6.00	40
Hanson,P.	5.00	48
Lasard,D.	6.50	35
Stillman,W.	8.00	50

b. Write a C++ program that uses the information contained in the file created in Exercise 8a to produce the following pay report for each employee:

Name Rate Hours Regular Pay Overtime Pay Gross Pay

Any hours worked above 40 hours are paid at time and a half. At the end of the individual output for each employee, the program should display the totals of the regular, overtime, and gross pay columns.

9. *a.* Store the following data in a file:

5 96 87 78 93 21 4 92 82 85 87 6 72 69 85 75 81 73

b. Write a C++ program to calculate and display the average of each group of numbers in the file created in Exercise 9a. The data is arranged in the file so that each group of numbers is preceded by the number of data items in the group. Thus, the first number in the file, 5, indicates that the next five numbers should be grouped together. The number 4 indicates that the following four numbers are a group, and the 6 indicates that the last six numbers are a group. (*Hint:* Use a nested loop. The outer loop should terminate when the EOF marker is encountered.)

14.3 Random File Access

File organization refers to the way data is stored in a file. All the files we have used have *sequential organization*. This means that the characters in the file are stored in a sequential manner, one after another. Additionally, we have read the files in a sequential manner. The way data is retrieved from the file is called *file access*. The fact that the characters in the file are stored sequentially, however, does not force us to access the file sequentially.

In *random access* any character in the file can be read immediately, without first having to read all the characters stored ahead of it. To provide random access to files, each fstream object establishes a file position marker. This marker is a long integer that represents an offset from the beginning of each file and keeps track of where the next character is to be read from or written to. The member functions that are used to access and change the file position marker are listed in Table 14–3.

The seek() functions allow the programmer to move to any position in the file. In order to understand this function, you must first clearly understand how data is referenced in the file using the file position marker.

Each character in a data file is located by its position in the file. The first character in the file is located at position 0, the next character at position 1, and so on. A character's position is also referred to as its offset from the start of the file. Thus, the first character has a 0 offset, the second character has an offset of 1, and so on for each character in the file.

The seek() functions require two arguments: the offset, as a long integer, into the file; and where the offset is to be calculated from, as determined by the mode. The three possible alternatives for the mode are ios::beg, ios::cur, and ios::end, which denote the beginning, current position, and

TABLE 14–3   File Position Marker Functions

Name[5]	Description
seekg(offset, mode)	For input files, move to the offset position as indicated by the mode
seekp(offset, mode)	For output files, move to the offset position as indicated by the mode
tellg()	For input files, return the current value of the file position marker
tellp()	For output files, return the current value of the file position marker

[5] The suffixes g and p denote get and put, respectively, where get refers to an input (get from) file and put refers to an output (put to) file.

the end of the file, respectively. Thus, a mode of `ios::beg` means the offset is the true offset from the start of the file. A mode of `ios::cur` means that the offset is relative to the current position in the file, and an `ios::end` mode means the offset is relative to the end of the file. A positive offset means move forward in the file and a negative offset means move backward. Examples of `seek()` function calls are shown below. In these examples, assume that `in_file` has been opened as an input file and `out_file` as an output file:

```
in_file.seekg(4L,ios::beg);      // go to the fifth character in the input file
out_file.seekp(4L,ios::beg);     // go to the fifth character in the output file
in_file.seekg(4L,ios::cur);      // move ahead five characters in the input file
out_file.seekp(4L,ios::cur);     // move ahead five characters in the output file
in_file.seekg(-4L,ios::end);     // move back five characters in the input file
out_file.seekp(-4L,ios::end);    // move back five characters in the output file
in_file.seekg(0L,ios::beg);      // go to start of the input file
out_file.seekp(0L,ios::beg);     // go to start of the output file
in_file.seekg(0L,ios::end);       // go to end of the input file
out_file.seekp(0L,ios::end);      // go to end of the output file
in_file.seekg(-10L,ios::end);    // go to 10 characters before the input file's end
out_file.seekp(-10L,ios::end);   // go to 10 characters before the output file's end
```

Notice, in these examples, that the offset passed to `seekg()` and `seekp()` must be a long integer.

As opposed to the `seek()` functions that move the file position marker, the `tell()` functions simply return the offset value of the file position marker. For example, if ten characters have already been read from an input file named `in_file`, the function call

```
in_file.tellg();
```

returns the long integer 10. This means that the next character to be read is offset 10 byte positions from the start of the file, and is the eleventh character in the file.

Program 14-5 illustrates the use of `seekg()` and `tellg()` to read a file in reverse order, from last character to first. As each character is read it is also displayed.

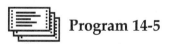 **Program 14-5**

```
#include <fstream.h>
void main(void)
{
  char ch;
  long offset, last;
```

(continued on next page)

(continued from previous page)

```
fstream in_file("test.dat",ios::in);
if (!in_file)    // check for successful open
{
  cout << "\nThe file was not successfully opened"
       << "\n Please check that the file currently exists"
       << endl;
  return;
}

in_file.seekg(0L,ios::end);     // move to the end of the file
last = in_file.tellg();         // save the offset of the last character

for(offset = 1L; offset <= last; offset++)
{
  in_file.seekg(-offset, ios::end);
  ch = in_file.get();
  cout << ch << " : ";
}
}
```

Assuming the file test.dat contains the following data,

Bulbs   3.12

the output of Program 14-5 is:

2 : 1 : . : 3 :   :   :   : s : b : l : u : B :

Program 14-5 initially goes to the last character in the file. The offset of this character, which is the end-of-file character, is saved in the variable last. Since tellg() returns a long integer, last has been declared as long integer.

Starting from the end of the file, seekg() is used to position the next character to be read, referenced from the end of the file. As each character is read, the character is displayed and the offset adjusted in order to access the next character. Note that the first offset used is –1, which represents the character immediately preceding the EOF marker.

Exercises 14.3

1. Rewrite Program 14-5 so that the origin for the seekg() function used in the for loop is the start of the file rather than the end.

2. The seek() functions return 0 if the position specified has been reached, or 1 if the position specified was beyond the file's boundaries. Modify Program 14-5 to display an error message if seekg() returns 1.

3. Write a program that will read and display every second character in a file named test.dat.

4. Using the seek() and tell() functions, write a function named f_chars() that returns the total number of characters in a file.

5. *a.* Write a function named r_bytes() that reads and displays *n* characters starting fromany position in a file. The function should accept three arguments: a file object name, the offset of the first character to be read, and the number of characters to be read. (*Note:* the prototype for r_bytes should be void r_bytes(fstream &, long, long).)

b. Modify the r_bytes() function written in Exercise 5a to store the characters read into a string or an array. The function should accept the address of the storage area as a fourth argument.

6. Assume that a data file consisting of a group of individual lines has been created. Write a function named print_line() that will read and display any desired line of the file. For example, the function call print_line(fstream &f_name, 5); should display the fifth line of the object name passed to it.

14.4 Passing and Returning File Names

File names are passed to a function using the same procedures for passing all function arguments. For passing a file name this requires declaring the passed argument as a reference to an fstream. For example, in Program 14-6 an fstream object named out_file is opened in main() and this object name is passed to the function in_out(). in_out() is then used to write five lines of user-entered text to the file.

Program 14-6

```
#include <fstream.h>
void main(void)
{
  void in_out(fstream &);    // function prototype
  fstream out_file;

  out_file.open("list.dat",ios::out);
  if (!out_file)   // check for a successful open
  {
    cout << "\nThe file was not successfully opened"
         << "\n Please check that the file currently exists."
         << endl;
    return;
  }
```

(continued on next page)

(continued from previous page)

```
   in_out(out_file);   // call the function
}

void in_out(fstream &fname)
{
   int count;
   char line[81];   // enough storage for one line of text

   cout << "Please enter five lines of text:" << endl;
   for (count = 0; count < 5; ++count)
   {
      cin.getline(line,80);
      fname << line << endl;
   }
   return;
}
```

Within main() the file is referenced as out_file. This reference, which is an address, is passed to the in_out() function. The function in_out() stores the address in the reference argument named fname and correctly declares fname to be a reference to an fstream.

In Program 14-7 we have expanded on Program 14-6 by adding a get_open() function to perform the open. Notice that get_open(), like in_out(), accepts a reference to an fstream object as an argument. After the open, this reference is passed to in_out(), as it was in Program 14-6. Although you might be tempted to write get_open() to return a reference to an fstream, this will not work because it ultimately results in an attempt to assign a returned reference to an existing one.

Program 14-7

```
#include <fstream.h>
void main(void)
{
   int get_open(fstream &);   // pass a reference to an fstream
   void in_out(fstream &);    // pass a reference to an fstream
   fstream file1;    // file1 is an fstream object
   char line[81];

   get_open(file1);   // open the file
   in_out(file1);     // write to it
}
```

(continued on next page)

(continued from previous page)

```
int get_open(fstream &fname)
{
  char name[13];

  cout << "\nEnter a file name: " << endl;
  cin.getline(name,12);
  fname.open(name,ios::out);  // open the file
  if (!fname)    // check for successful open
  {
    cout << "Cannot open the file" << endl;
    return 0;
  }
  else
    return 1;
}

void in_out(fstream &fname)
{
  int count;
  char line[81];    // enough storage for one line of text

  cout << "Please enter five lines of text:" << endl;
  for (count = 0; count < 5; ++count)
  {
    cin.getline(line,80);
    fname << line << endl;
  }
  return;
}
```

Program 14-7 is simply a modified version of Program 14-6 that now allows the user to enter a file name from the standard input device. The get_open() function is a "bare bones" function in that it does no checking on the file being opened for output. If the name of an existing data file is entered, the file will be destroyed when it is opened in write mode. To prevent such occurrences the file should be opened in either ios::ate or ios::app modes. Another useful "trick" that you may encounter to prevent this type of mishap is to open the entered file name in read mode. Then, if the file exists, the open() function returns a NULL to indicate that the file is available for input. The NULL acts to alert the user that a file with the entered name currently exists in the system and to request confirmation that the data in the file can be destroyed and the file name used for the new output file. Before the file can be reopened in write mode, of course, it would have to be closed. The implementation of this algorithm is left as an exercise.

For comparison purposes, Program 14-7a illustrates how Program 14-7 would be written using pointers. Notice in Program 14-7a that get_open() can return a pointer to an fstream.

Program 14-7a

```
#include <fstream.h>
void main(void)
{
  fstream *get_open(void); // return an address (pointer)
  void in_out(fstream *);  // pass an address (pointer)
  fstream *file1;
    char line[81];

  file1 = get_open();     // open the file
  in_out(file1);          // write to it
}

fstream *get_open(void)    // get_open() returns a pointer to an fstream
{
  char name[13];
  static fstream file1;    // static is required here

  cout << "\nEnter a file name: " << endl;
  cin.getline(name,12);
  file1.open(name,ios::out);  // open the file
  return(&file1);
}

void in_out(fstream *fname)
{
  int count;
  char line[81];   // enough storage for one line of text

  cout << "Please enter five lines of text:" << endl;
  for (count = 0; count < 5; ++count)
  {
    cin.getline(line,80);
    *fname << line << endl;
  }
  return;
}
```

Exercises 14.4

1. A function named p_file() is to receive a file name as a reference to an fstream object. What declarations are required to pass a file name to p_file()?

2. a. A function named get_file() is to return a pointer to an fstream object. What declarations are required in the function header and internal to the file?

b. What declaration statement is required in each function that calls `get_file()` to ensure correct receipt of the file name returned by `get_file()`? Under what conditions can this declaration be omitted?

3. Write a function named `fcheck()` that checks whether a file exists. The function should be passed a file name. If the file exists, the function should return a value of 1, otherwise the function should return a value of zero.

4. Rewrite the function `get_open()` used in Program 14-7 to incorporate the file-checking procedures described in the text. Specifically, if the entered file name exists, an appropriate message should be displayed. The user should then be presented with the option of entering a new file name or allowing the program to overwrite the existing file.

14.5 Common Programming Errors

Three programming errors are common when using files. The most common error is to use the file's external name in place of the internal object name when accessing the file. The only standard library function that uses the data file's external name is the `open()` function. All the other standard functions presented in this chapter require the object name assigned to the file when it was initially opened.

A second error occurs when using the EOF marker to detect the end of a file. Any variable used to accept the EOF must be declared as an integer variable. For example, if `ch` is declared as a character variable the expression

```
while ( (ch = in.file.peek()) != EOF )
```

produces an infinite loop. This occurs because a character variable can never take on an EOF code. EOF is an integer value (usually –1) that has no character representation. This ensures that the EOF code can never be confused with any legitimate character encountered as normal data in the file. To terminate the loop created by the above expression, the variable `ch` must be declared as an integer variable.

The last error concerns the offset argument sent to the `seekg()` and `seekp()` functions. This offset must be a long integer constant or variable. Any other value passed to these functions can result in an unpredictable effect.

14.6 Chapter Summary

1. A *data file* is any collection of data stored together in an external storage medium under a common name.

2. A data file is opened using `fstream`'s `open()` member function. This function connects a file's external name with an internal object name. After the file is opened, all subsequent accesses to the file require the internal object name.

3. A file can be opened for input, output, or appending. A file opened for output creates a new file or erases any existing file having the same name as the opened file. A file opened for appending makes an existing file available for data to be added to the end of the file. If the file does not exist it is created. A file opened for input makes an existing file's data available for input. An error condition results if the file does not exist.

4. All internal file names must be declared as objects of the fstream class. This means that a declaration similar to

```
fstream f_name;
```

must be included with the declarations in which the file is opened. f_name can be replaced with any user-selected variable name.

5. In addition to any files opened within a function, the standard files cin, cout, and cerr are automatically opened when a program is run. cin is the object name of the physical file used for data entry (usually the keyboard), cout is the object name of the physical file device used for default data display (usually the CRT screen), and cerr is the object name of the physical file device used for displaying system error messages (usually the CRT screen).

6. Data files can be accessed randomly using the seekg(), seekp(), tellg(), and tellp() functions. The g versions of these functions are used to alter and query the file position marker for input files, while the p versions do the same for output files.

7. Table 14–4 lists the member functions supplied by the fstream class for file manipulation.

TABLE 14–4   fstream Member Functions

Name	Description
get()	Extract the next character from the file
getline(char *, int n, '\n')	Extract characters from the file until either n–1 characters are read or a newline is encountered (terminates the input with a '\0')
peek()	Return the next character in the file without extracting it from the file
putback(char)	Push back a character on the file
eof()	True if EOF has been reached

14.7 Chapter Appendix—The **iostream** Library

The input and output library provided as part of each C++ compiler is not part of the C++ language. By convention each C++ compiler provides an input/output library named `iostream` that contains a number of classes that adhere to a common specification originally defined and adopted by AT&T.

In C++ the classes contained within the `iostream` library access files using entities called streams. In this context a *stream* is simply a sequence of data bytes transferred between a program and an open file. For most systems the data bytes represent either ASCII characters or binary numbers.

When the data transfer between a computer and an external data file modifies the data, so that the data stored in the file *is not* an exact representation of the data as it is stored internally within the computer, the file is referred to as a *formatted file*. Examples of this are files that store their data using ASCII codes. Such files are also referred to as text files, and the terms *text* and *formatted* are sometimes used interchangeably.

When the data transfer between a computer and an external data file is done without modification, so that the data stored in the file *is* an exact representation of the data as it is stored internally within the computer, the file is referred to as a *binary or unformatted file*.

The mechanism for reading a byte stream from a file or writing a byte stream to a file, with or without formatting, is always hidden when using a high-level language such as C++. Nevertheless, it is useful to understand this mechanism so that we can place the services provided by the `iostream` library in their appropriate context.

File Stream Transfer Mechanism

The mechanism for transferring data between a program and a data file is illustrated in Figure 14–2.

FIGURE 14–2 The Data Transfer Mechanism

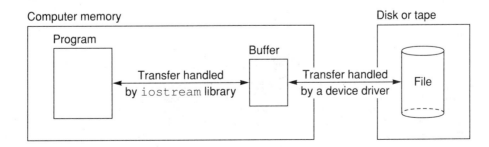

As illustrated in Figure 14–2, transferring data between a program and a file involves an intermediate file buffer contained in the computer's memory. Each opened file is assigned its own file buffer, which is simply a storage area that is used by the data as it is transferred between the program and the file.

From its side, the program either writes a set of data bytes to the file buffer or reads a set of data bytes from the file buffer. The actual transfer of data between the program and the buffer is handled by the iostream library routines.

On the other side of the buffer the transfer of data between the device storing the actual data file (usually a tape or disk unit) and the file buffer is handled by special operating system programs that are referred to as *device drivers*.[6] Typically a disk device driver will only transfer data between the disk and file buffer in fixed sizes, such as 1024 bytes at a time. Thus, the file buffer provides a convenient means of permitting a device driver to transfer data in blocks of one size while the program can access them using a different size (typically as individual characters or as a fixed number of characters per line).

Components of the iostream Library

The iostream library consists of two primary base classes, the streambuf class and the ios class. The streambuf class provides the file buffer illustrated in Figure 14–2 and a number of general routines for transferring data when little or no formatting is required. The ios class contains a pointer to the file buffers provided by the streambuf class and a number of general routines for transferring data with formatting. From these two base classes a number of other classes are derived and included in the iostream library.

Figure 14–3 illustrates an inheritance diagram for the ios family of classes as it relates to the ifstream, ofstream, and fstream classes. The inheritance diagram for the streambuf family of classes is shown in Figure 14–4. As described in the previous chapter, the convention adopted for inheritance diagrams is that the arrows point from a derived class to a base class.

The correspondence between the classes illustrated in Figures 14–3 and 14–4, including the header files that define these classes, is listed in Table 14–5.

Thus, the ifstream, ofstream, and fstream classes that we have used for file access all use a buffer provided by the filebuf class and require the fstream.h header file. Similarly, the cin, cout, and cerr iostream objects that we have been using throughout the text use a buffer provided by the streambuf class and require the iostream.h header file.

---

[6] Device drivers are not stand-alone programs but are an integral part of the operating system. Essentially the device driver is a section of operating system code that accesses a hardware device, such as a disk unit, and handles the data transfer between the device and the computer's memory. It must correctly synchronize the speed of the data transferred between the computer and the device sending or receiving the data. This is because the computer's internal data transfer rate is generally much faster than any device connected to it.

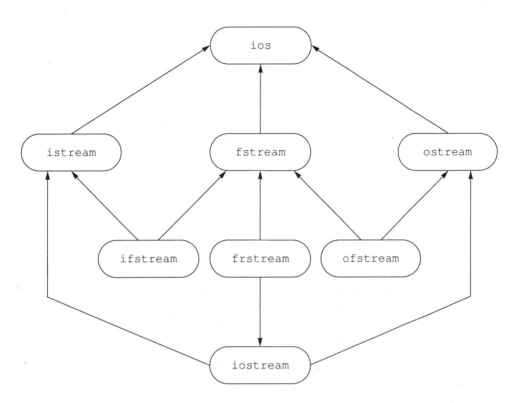

FIGURE 14–3 The Base Class ios and Its Derived Classes (Not all derived classes are shown)

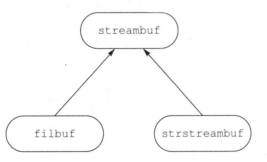

FIGURE 14–4 The Base Class streambuf and Its Derived Classes (Not all derived classes are shown)

TABLE 14–5

ios Class	streambuf Class	Required Header File
istream ostream iostream	streambuf	iostream.h
ifstream ofstream fstream	filebuf	fstream.h

In-Memory Formatting

In addition to the classes illustrated in Figure 14–2, a class named `strstream` is also derived from the `ios` class. This class uses the `strstreambuf` class illustrated in Figure 14–3, requires the `strstream.h` header file, and provides capabilities for writing and reading strings to and from in-memory defined streams.

As an output stream, such a stream is typically used to "assemble" a string from smaller pieces until a complete line of characters is ready to be written, either to `cout` or to a file. Attaching a `strstream` object to a buffer for this purpose is done in a manner similar to attaching an `fstream` object to an output file. For example, the statement

```
strstream inmem(buf, 72, ios::out);
```

attaches a `strstream` object to an existing buffer of 72 bytes in output mode. Program 14-8 illustrates using this statement within the context of a complete program.

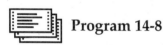 **Program 14-8**

```
#include <strstream.h>
#include <iomanip.h>
void main(void)
{
  int units = 10;
  float price = 36.85;
  char buf[72];   // enough space for one line

  strstream inmem(buf, 72, ios::out);  // open an in-memory stream

  // write to the buffer through the stream
  inmem << "No. of units = "
        << setw(3) << units
        << "  Price per unit = $"
        << setw(8) << setprecision(2) << price << '\0';

  cout << '|' << buf << '|';
}
```

The output produced by Program 14-8 is:

```
|No. of units =  10  Price per unit = $   36.85|
```

As illustrated by this output, the character buffer has been correctly filled in by insertions to the `inmem` stream (note that the end-of-string null, \0, which is the last insertion to the stream, is required to correctly close off the string). Once the desired character array has been filled, it would typically be written to a file as a single string.

In a similar manner a `strstream` object can be opened in input mode. Typically such a stream would be used as a working storage area, or buffer, for storing a complete line of text from either a file or standard input. Once the buffer has been filled, the extraction operator would be used to "disassemble" the string into component parts and convert each data item into its designated data type. Doing this permits inputting data from a file on a line-by-line basis prior to assigning individual data items to their respective variables.

Bit
Operations

Chapter Fifteen

C++ operates with data entities that are stored as one or more bytes, such as character, integer, and double precision constants and variables. In addition, C++ provides for the manipulation of individual bits of character and integer constants and variables. Generally these bit manipulations are used in engineering and computer science programs and are not required in commercial applications.

The operators that are used to perform bit manipulations are called bit operators. They are listed in Table 15–1.

TABLE 15–1   Bit Operators

Operator	Description
&	Bitwise AND
|	Bitwise inclusive OR
^	Bitwise exclusive OR
~	Bitwise one's complement
<<	Left shift
>>	Right shift

All the operators listed in Table 15-1, except ~, are binary operators, requiring two operands. Each operand is treated as a binary number consisting of a series of individual 1s and 0s. The respective bits in each operand are then compared on a bit-by-bit basis and the result is determined based on the selected operation.

15.1 The AND Operator

The AND operator causes a bit-by-bit AND comparison between its two operands. The result of each bit-by-bit comparison is a 1 only when both bits being compared are 1s, otherwise the result of the AND operation is a 0. For example, assume that the following two eight-bit numbers are to be ANDed:

```
1 0 1 1 0 0 1 1
1 1 0 1 0 1 0 1
---------------
```

To perform an AND operation, each bit in one operand is compared to the bit occupying the same position in the other operand. Figure 15–1 illustrates the correspondence between bits for these two operands. As shown in the figure,

```
  1 0 1 1 0 0 1 1
& 1 1 0 1 0 1 0 1
------------------
  1 0 0 1 0 0 0 1
```

FIGURE 15–1 A Sample AND Operation

when both bits being compared are 1s, the result is a 1, otherwise the result is a 0. The result of each comparison is, of course, independent of any other bit comparison.

Program 15-1 illustrates the use of an AND operation. In this program, the variable op1 is initialized to the octal value 325, which is the octal equivalent of the binary number 1 1 0 1 0 1 0 1, and the variable op2 is initialized to the octal value 263, which is the octal representation of the binary number 1 0 1 1 0 0 1 1. These are the same two binary numbers illustrated in Figure 15–1.

Program 15-1

```cpp
#include <iostream.h>
void main(void)
{
  int op1 = 0325, op2 = 0263;

  int op3 = op1 & op2;
  cout << oct << op1 << " ANDed with "<< op2 << " is " << op3 << endl;
}
```

Program 15-1 produces the following output:

```
  325 ANDed with 263 is 221
```

The result of ANDing the octal numbers 325 and 263 is the octal number 221. The binary equivalent of 221 is the binary number 1 0 0 1 0 0 0 1, which is the result of the AND operation illustrated in Figure 15–1.

AND operations are extremely useful in masking, or eliminating, selected bits from an operand. This is a direct result of the fact that ANDing any bit (1 or 0) with a 0 forces the resulting bit to be a 0, while ANDing any bit (1 or 0) with a 1 leaves the original bit unchanged. For example, assume that the variable op1 has the arbitrary bit pattern x x x x x x x x, where each x can be either 1 or 0, independent of any other x in the number. The result of ANDing this binary number with the binary number 0 0 0 0 1 1 1 1 is:

```
op1 =    x x x x x x x x
op2 =    0 0 0 0 1 1 1 1
-------------------------
Result =  0 0 0 0 x x x x
```

As can be seen from this example, the zeros in op2 effectively mask, or eliminate, the respective bits in op1, while the ones in op2 filter, or pass, the respective bits in op1 through with no change in their values. In this example, the variable op2 is called a mask. By choosing the mask appropriately, any individual bit in an operand can be selected, or filtered, out of an operand for inspection. For example, ANDing the variable op1 with the mask 0 0 0 0 0 1 0 0 forces all the bits of the result to be zero, except for the third bit. The third bit of the result will be a copy of the third bit of op1. Thus, if the result of the AND is zero, the third bit of op1 must have been zero, and if the result of the AND is a nonzero number, the third bit must have been a 1.

Program 15-2 uses this masking property to convert lowercase letters in a word into their uppercase form, assuming the letters are stored using the ASCII code. The algorithm for converting letters is based on the fact that the binary codes for lowercase and uppercase letters in ASCII are the same except for bit five, which is 1 for lowercase letters and 0 for uppercase letters. For example, the binary code for the letter a is 01100001 (hex 61), while the binary code for the letter A is 01000001 (hex 41). Similarly, the binary code for the letter z is 01111010 (hex 7A), while the binary code for the letter Z is 01011010 (hex 5A). (See Appendix B for the hexadecimal values of the upper- and lowercase letters.) Thus, given a lowercase letter, it can be converted into its uppercase form by forcing the fifth bit to zero. This is accomplished in Program 15-2 by masking the letter's code with the binary value 11011111, which has the hexadecimal value DF.

Program 15-2

```cpp
#include <iostream.h>
const int TO_UP = 0xDF;
void main(void)
{
  char word[81];        // enough storage for a complete line
  void upper(char *);   // function prototype

  cout << "Enter a string of both upper and lowercase letters:\n";
  cin.getline(word,80,'\n');
  cout << "\nThe string of letters just entered is:\n"
       << word << endl;
  upper(word);
  cout << "\nThis string, in uppercase letters is:\n"
       << word << endl;
}
void upper(char *word)
{
  while (*word != '\0')
    *word++ &= TO_UP;
}
```

A sample run using Program 15-2 follows:

```
Enter a string of both upper and lowercase letters:
abcdefgHIJKLMNOPqrstuvwxyz

The string of letters just entered is:
abcdefgHIJKLMNOPqrstuvwxyz

This string, in uppercase letters is:
ABCDEFGHIJKLMNOPQRSTUVWXYZ
```

Notice that the lowercase letters are converted to uppercase form, while uppercase letters are unaltered. This is because bit five of all uppercase letters is zero to begin with, so that forcing this bit to zero using the mask has no effect. Only when bit five is a one, as it is for lowercase letters, is the input character altered.

15.2 The Inclusive OR Operator

The inclusive OR operator, |, performs a bit-by-bit comparison of its two operands in a similar fashion to the bit-by-bit AND. The result of the OR comparison, however, is determined by the following rule:

The result of the comparison is 1 if either bit being compared is a 1, otherwise the result is a 0.

Figure 15–2 illustrates an OR operation. As shown in the figure, when either of the two bits being compared is a 1, the result is a 1, otherwise the result is a 0. As with all bit operations, the result of each comparison is, of course, independent of any other comparison.

Program 15-3 illustrates an OR operation, using the octal values of the operands illustrated in Figure 15–2.

FIGURE 15–2 A Sample OR Operation

```
  1 0 1 1 0 0 1 1
| 1 1 0 1 0 1 0 1
  ---------------
  1 1 1 1 0 1 1 1
```

Program 15-3

```
#include <iostream.h>
void main(void)
{
   int op1 = 0325, op2 = 0263;

   int op3 = op1 | op2;
   cout << oct << op1 << " ORed with " << op2 << " is " << op3 << endl;
}
```

Program 15-3 produces the following output:

```
325 ORed with 263 is 367
```

The result of ORing the octal numbers 325 and 263 is the octal number 367. The binary equivalent of 367 is 1 1 1 1 0 1 1 1, which is the result of the OR operation illustrated in Figure 15–2.

Inclusive OR operations are extremely useful in forcing selected bits to take on a 1 value or for passing through other bit values unchanged. This is a direct result of the fact that ORing any bit (1 or 0) with a 1 forces the resulting bit to be a 1, while ORing any bit (1 or 0) with a 0 leaves the original bit unchanged. For example, assume that the variable op1 has the arbitrary bit pattern x x x x x x x x, where each x can be either 1 or 0, independent of any other x in the number. The result of ORing this binary number with the binary number 1 1 1 1 0 0 0 0 is:

```
op1   =   x x x x x x x x
op2   =   1 1 1 1 0 0 0 0
          -----------------------
Result =   1 1 1 1 x x x x
```

As can be seen from this example, the ones in op2 force the resulting bits to 1, while the zeros in op2 filter, or pass, the respective bits in op1 through with no change in their values. Thus, using an OR operation a similar masking operation can be produced as with an AND operation, except the masked bits are set to ones rather than cleared to zeros. Another way of looking at this is to say that ORing with a zero has the same effect as ANDing with a one.

Program 15-4 uses this masking property to convert uppercase letters in a word into their respective lowercase form, assuming the letters are stored using the ASCII code. The algorithm for converting letters is similar to that used in

Program 15-2, and converts uppercase letters into their lowercase form by forcing the fifth bit in each letter to a one. This is accomplished in Program 15-4 by masking the letter's code with the binary value `00100000`, which has the hexadecimal value 20.

Program 15-4

```
#include <iostream.h>
const int TO_LOW = 0x20;
void main(void)
{
  char word[81];          // enough storage for a complete line
  void lower (char *);   // function prototype
  cout << "Enter a string of both upper and lowercase letters:\n";
  cin.getline(word,80,'\n');
  cout << "\nThe string of letters just entered is:\n"
       << word << endl;
  lower(word);
  cout << "\nThis string, in lowercase letters is:\n"
       << word << endl;
}
void lower(char *word)
{
  while (*word != '\0')
    *word++ |= TO_LOW;
}
```

A sample run using Program 15-4 follows:

```
Enter a string of both upper and lowercase letters:
abcdefgHIJKLMNOPqrstuvwxyz

The string of letters just entered is:
abcdefgHIJKLMNOPqrstuvwxyz

This string, in lowercase letters is:
abcdefghijklmnopqrstuvwxyz
```

Notice that the uppercase letters are converted to lowercase form, while uppercase letters are unaltered. This is because bit five of all lowercase letters is one to begin with, so that forcing this bit to one using the mask has no effect. Only when bit five is a zero, as it is for uppercase letters, is the input character altered.

15.3 The Exclusive OR Operator

The exclusive OR operator, ^, performs a bit-by-bit comparison of its two operands. The result of the comparison is determined by the following rule:

The result of the comparison is 1 if one and only one of the bits being compared is a 1, otherwise the result is 0.

Figure 15–3 illustrates an exclusive OR operation. As shown in the figure, when both bits being compared are the same value (both 1 or both 0), the result is a zero. Only when both bits have different values (one bit a 1 and the other a 0) is the result a 1. Again, each pair or bit comparison is independent of any other bit comparison.

An exclusive OR operation can be used to create the opposite value, or complement, of any individual bit in a variable. This is a direct result of the fact that exclusive ORing any bit (1 or 0) with a 1 forces the resulting bit to be of the opposite value of its original state, while exclusive ORing any bit (1 or 0) with a 0 leaves the original bit unchanged. For example, assume that the variable op1 has the arbitrary bit pattern x x x x x x x x, where each x can be either 1 or 0, independent of any other x in the number. Using the notation that $\overline{x}$ is the complement (opposite) value of x, the result of exclusive ORing this binary number with the binary number 0 1 0 1 0 1 0 1 is:

```
op1  =    x x x x x x x x
op2  =    0 1 0 1 0 1 0 1
          ----------------
Result =  x̄ x x̄ x x̄ x x̄ x
```

As can be seen from this example, the ones in op2 force the resulting bits to be the complement of their original bit values, while the zeros in op2 filter, or pass, the respective bits in op1 through with no change in their values.

Many encryption methods use the exclusive OR operation to code data. For example, the string Hello there world! initially used in Program 1-1 can be encrypted by exclusive ORing each character in the string with a mask value of 52. The choice of the mask value, which is referred to as the encryption key, is arbitrary, and any key value can be used.

Program 15-5 uses an encryption key of 52 to code a user-entered message.

FIGURE 15–3 A Sample Exclusive OR Operation

```
  1 0 1 1 0 0 1 1
^ 1 1 0 1 0 1 0 1
  ----------------
  0 1 1 0 0 1 1 0
```

Program 15-5

```
#include <iostream.h>
void main(void)
{
  char message[81];      // enough storage for a complete line
  void encrypt(char *); // function prototype
  cout << "\nEnter a sentence:\n";
  cin.getline(message,81,'\n');
  cout << "\nThe sentence just entered is:\n"
       << message << endl;
  encrypt(message);
  cout << "\nThe encrypted version of this sentence is:\n"
       << message << endl;
}
void encrypt(char *message)
{
  while (*message != '\0')
    *message++ ^= 52;
}
```

Following is a sample run using Program 15-5.

```
Enter a sentence:
Good morning

The sentence just entered is:
Good morning

The encrypted version of this sentence is:
s[[P¶Y[FZ]ZS
```

Decoding an encrypted message requires exclusive ORing the coded message using the original encryption key, which is left as a homework exercise.

15.4   The Complement Operator

The complement operator, ~, is a unary operator that changes each 1 bit in its operand to 0 and each 0 bit to 1. For example, if the variable op1 contains the binary number 11001010, ~op1 replaces this binary number with the number 00110101. The complement operator is used to force any bit in an operand to

527

zero, independent of the actual number of bits used to store the number. For example, the statement

```
op1 = op1 & ~07;    // 07 is an octal number
```

or its shorter form,

```
op1 &= ~07;     // 07 is an octal number
```

both set the last three bits of op1 to zero, regardless of how op1 is stored within the computer. Either of these two statements can, of course, be replaced by ANDing the last three bits of op1 with zeros, if the number of bits used to store op1 is known. In a computer that uses 16 bits to store integers, the appropriate AND operation is:

```
op1 = op1 & 0177770;     // in octal
```

or

```
op1 = op1 & 0xFFF8;     // in hexadecimal
```

For a computer that uses 32 bits to store integers, the above AND sets the leftmost or higher order 16 bits to zero also, which is an unintended result. The correct statement for 32 bits is:

```
op1 = op1 & 027777777770;     // in octal
```

or

```
op1 = op1 & 0xFFFFFFF8;     // in hexadecimal
```

Using the complement operator in this situation frees the programmer from having to determine the storage size of the operand and, more importantly, makes the program portable between machines using different integer storage sizes.

15.5 Different-Size Data Items

When the bit operators &, |, and ^ are used with operands of different sizes, the shorter operand is always increased in bit size to match the size of the larger operand. Figure 15–4 illustrates the extension of a 16-bit unsigned integer into a 32-bit number.

As the figure shows, the additional bits are added to the left of the original number and filled with zeros. This is the equivalent of adding leading zeros to the number, which has no effect on the number's value.

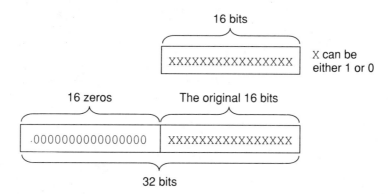

FIGURE 15–4   Extending 16-Bit Unsigned Data to 32 Bits

When extending signed numbers, the original leftmost bit is reproduced in the additional bits that are added to the number. As illustrated in Figure 15–5, if the original leftmost bit is 0, corresponding to a positive number, 0 is placed in each of the additional bit positions. If the leftmost bit is 1, which corresponds to a negative number, 1 is placed in the additional bit positions. In either case, the resulting binary number has the same sign and magnitude of the original number.

FIGURE 15–5   Extending 16-Bit Signed Data to 32 Bits

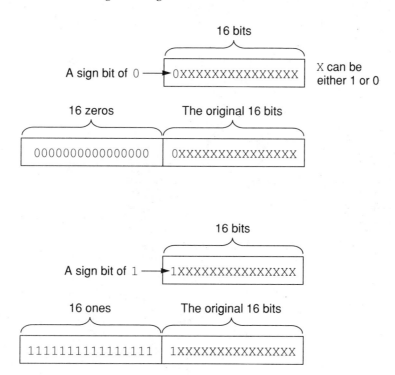

15.6 The Shift Operators

The left shift operator, <<, causes the bits in an operand to be shifted to the left by a given amount. For example, the statement

$$op1 = op1 << 4;$$

causes the bits in op1 to be shifted four bits to the left, filling any vacated bits with a zero. Figure 15–6 illustrates the effect of shifting the binary number 1111100010101011 to the left by four bit positions.

For unsigned integers, each left shift corresponds to multiplication by two. This is also true for signed numbers using two's complement representation, as long as the leftmost bit does not switch values. Since a change in the leftmost bit of a two's complement number represents a change in both the sign and magnitude represented by the bit, such a shift does not represent a simple multiplication by two.

The right shift operator, >>, causes the bits in an operand to be shifted to the right by a given amount. For example, the statement

$$op2 = op1 >> 3;$$

causes the bits in op1 to be shifted to the right by three bit positions. Figure 15–7a illustrates the right shift of the unsigned binary number 1111100010101011 by three bit positions. As illustrated, the three rightmost bits are shifted "off the end" and are lost.

For unsigned numbers, the leftmost bit is not used as a sign bit. For this type of number, the vacated leftmost bits are always filled with zeros. This is the case that is illustrated in Figure 15–7a.

FIGURE 15–6 An Example of a Left Shift

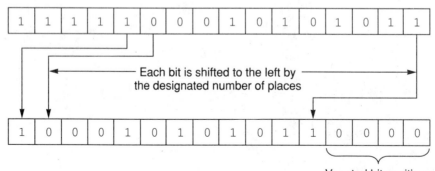

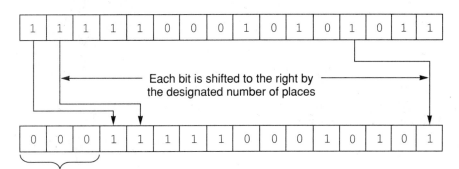

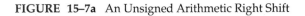

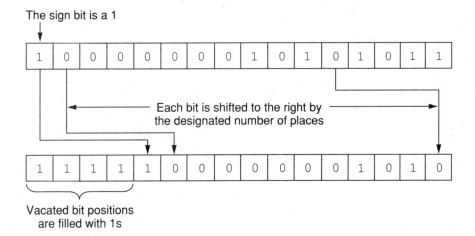

FIGURE 15–7a An Unsigned Arithmetic Right Shift

FIGURE 15–7b The Right Shift of a Negative Binary Number

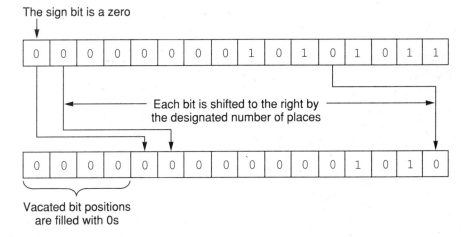

FIGURE 15–7c The Right Shift of a Positive Binary Number

For signed numbers, what is filled in the vacated bits depends on the computer. Most computers reproduce the original sign bit of the number. Figure 15–7b illustrates the right shift of a negative binary number by four bit positions, where the sign bit is reproduced in the vacated bits. Figure 15–7c illustrates the equivalent right shift of a positive signed binary number.

The type of fill illustrated in Figures 15–7b and c, where the sign bit is reproduced in vacated bit positions, is called an arithmetic right shift. In an arithmetic right shift, each single shift to the right corresponds to a division by two.

Instead of reproducing the sign bit in right-shifted signed numbers, some computers automatically fill the vacated bits with zeros. This type of shift is called a logical shift. For positive signed numbers, where the leftmost bit is zero, both arithmetic and logical right shifts produce the same result. The results of these two shifts are only different when negative numbers are involved.

Exercises for Chapter 15

1. Determine the results of the following operations:

a.	11001010	*b.*	11001010	*c.*	11001010
&	10100101	|	10100101	^	10100101

2. Write the octal representations of the binary numbers given in Exercise 1.

3. Determine the octal results of the following operations, assuming unsigned numbers:
   a. the octal number 0157 shifted left by one bit position
   b. the octal number 0701 shifted left by two bit positions
   c. the octal number 0673 shifted right by two bit positions
   d. the octal number 067 shifted right by three bit positions

4. Repeat Exercise 3 assuming that the numbers are treated as signed values.

5. a. Assume that the arbitrary bit pattern xxxxxxxx, where each x can represent either 1 or 0, is stored in the integer variable flag. Determine the octal value of a mask that can be ANDed with the bit pattern to reproduce the third and fourth bits of flag and set all other bits to zero. The rightmost bit in flag is considered bit 0.
   b. Determine the octal value of a mask that can be inclusively ORed with the bit pattern in flag to reproduce the third and fourth bits of flag and set all other bits to one. Again, consider the rightmost bit in flag to be bit 0.
   c. Determine the octal value of a mask that can be used to complement the values of the third and fourth bits of flag and leave all other bits unchanged. Determine the bit operation that should be used with the mask value to produce the desired result.

6. a. Write the two's complement form of the decimal number –1, using eight bits. (*Hint:* Refer to Section 2.8 for a review of two's complement numbers.)
   b. Repeat Exercise 6a using 16 bits to represent the decimal number –1 and compare your answer to your previous answer. Could the 16-bit version have been obtained by sign-extending the 8-bit version?

7. As was noted in the text, Program 15-2 has no effect on uppercase letters. Using the ASCII codes listed in Appendix B, determine what other characters would be unaffected by Program 15-2.

8. Modify Program 15-2 so that a complete sentence can be read in and converted to low-ercase values. (*Hint:* When a space is masked by Program 15-2, the resulting character is \0, which terminates the output.)

9. Modify Program 15-4 to allow a complete sentence to be input and converted to upper-case letters. Make sure that your program does not alter any other characters or symbols entered.

10. Modify Program 15-5 to permit the encryption key to be a user-entered input value.

11. Modify Program 15-5 to have its output written to a file named `coded.dat`.

12. Write a C++ program that reads the encrypted file produced by the program written for Exercise 10, decodes the file, and prints the decoded values on your system's standard output device.

13. Write a C++ program that displays the first eight bits of each character value input into a variable named `ch`. (*Hint:* Assuming each character is stored using eight bits, start by using the hexadecimal mask 80, which corresponds to the binary number `10000000`. If the result of the masking operation is a zero, display a zero; else display a one. Then shift the mask one place to the right to examine the next bit, and so on until all bits in the variable `ch` have been processed.)

14. Write a C++ program that reverses the bits in an integer variable named `okay` and stores the reversed bits in the variable named `rev_okay`. For example, if the bit pattern `11100101`, corresponding to the octal number 0345, is assigned to `okay`, the bit pattern `10100111`, corresponding to the octal number 0247, should be produced and stored in `rev_okay`.

15.7 Chapter Summary

1. Individual bits of character and integer variables and constants can be manipulated using C++'s bit operators. These are the AND, inclusive OR, exclusive OR, one's complement, left shift, and right shift operators.

2. The AND and inclusive OR operators are useful in creating masks. These masks can be used to pass or eliminate individual bits from the selected operand. The exclusive OR operator is useful in complementing an operand's bits.

3. When the AND and OR operators are used with operands of different sizes, the shorter operand is always increased in bit size to match the size of the larger operand.

4. The shift operators produce different results depending on whether the operand is a signed or an unsigned value.

Appendixes

Appendix A   Operator Precedence Table

Table A–1 presents the symbols, precedence, descriptions, and associativity of C++'s operators. Operators toward the top of the table have a higher precedence than those toward the bottom. Operators within each box have the same precedence and associativity.

TABLE A–1   Summary of C++ Operators

Operator	Description	Associativity
() [] -> .	Function call Array element Structure member pointer reference Structure member reference	Left to right
++ -- - ! ~ (type) sizeof & *	Increment Decrement Unary minus Logical negation One's complement Type conversion (cast) Storage size Address of Indirection	Right to left
* / %	Multiplication Division Modulus (remainder)	Left to right
+ -	Addition Subtraction	Left to right
<< >>	Left shift Right shift	Left to right
< <= > >=	Less than Less than or equal to Greater than Greater than or equal to	Left to right
== !=	Equal to Not equal to	Left to right
&	Bitwise AND	Left to right
^	Bitwise exclusive OR	Left to right
|	Bitwise inclusive OR	Left to right
&&	Logical AND	Left to right
||	Logical OR	Left to right
?:	Conditional expression	Right to left
= += -= *= /= %= &= ^= |= <<= >>=	Assignment Assignment Assignment Assignment Assignment	Right to left
,	Comma	Left to right

Appendix B   ASCII Character Codes

Key(s)	Dec	Oct	Hex	Key	Dec	Oct	Hex	Key	Dec	Oct	Hex
Ctrl 1	0	0	0	+	43	53	2B	V	86	126	56
Ctrl A	1	1	1	,	44	54	2C	W	87	127	57
Ctrl B	2	2	2	-	45	55	2D	X	88	130	58
Ctrl C	3	3	3	.	46	56	2E	Y	89	131	59
Ctrl D	4	4	4	/	47	57	2F	Z	90	132	5A
Ctrl E	5	5	5	0	48	60	30	[	91	133	5B
Ctrl F	6	6	6	1	49	61	31	\	92	134	5C
Ctrl G	7	7	7	2	50	62	32	]	93	135	5D
Ctrl H	8	10	8	3	51	63	33	^	94	136	5E
Ctrl I	9	11	9	4	52	64	34	_	95	137	5F
\n	10	12	A	5	53	65	35	`	96	140	60
Ctrl K	11	13	B	6	54	66	36	a	97	141	61
Ctrl L	12	14	C	7	55	67	37	b	98	142	62
RETURN	13	15	D	8	56	70	38	c	99	143	63
Ctrl N	14	16	E	9	57	71	39	d	100	144	64
Ctrl O	15	17	F	:	58	72	3A	e	101	145	65
Ctrl P	16	20	10	;	59	73	3B	f	102	146	66
Ctrl Q	17	21	11	<	60	74	3C	g	103	147	67
Ctrl R	18	22	12	=	61	75	3D	h	104	150	68
Ctrl S	19	23	13	>	62	76	3E	i	105	151	69
Ctrl T	20	24	14	?	63	77	3F	j	106	152	6A
Ctrl U	21	25	15	@	64	100	40	k	107	153	6B
Ctrl V	22	26	16	A	65	101	41	l	108	154	6C
Ctrl W	23	27	17	B	66	102	42	m	109	155	6D
Ctrl X	24	30	18	C	67	103	43	n	110	156	6E
Ctrl Y	25	31	19	D	68	104	44	o	111	157	6F
Ctrl Z	26	32	1A	E	69	105	45	p	112	160	70
Esc	27	33	1B	F	70	106	46	q	113	161	71
Ctrl <	28	34	1C	G	71	107	47	r	114	162	72
Ctrl /	29	35	1D	H	72	110	48	s	115	163	73
Ctrl =	30	36	1E	I	73	111	49	t	116	164	74
Ctrl -	31	37	1F	J	74	112	4A	u	117	165	75
Space	32	40	20	K	75	113	4B	v	118	166	76
!	33	41	21	L	76	114	4C	w	119	167	77
"	34	42	22	M	77	115	4D	x	120	170	78
#	35	43	23	N	78	116	4E	y	121	171	79
$	36	44	24	O	79	117	4F	z	122	172	7A
%	37	45	25	P	80	120	50	{	123	173	7B
&	38	46	26	Q	81	121	51	|	124	174	7C
'	39	47	27	R	82	122	52	}	125	175	7D
(	40	50	28	S	83	123	53	~	126	176	7E
)	41	51	29	T	84	124	54	del	127	177	7F
*	42	52	2A	U	85	125	55				

Appendix C   Program Entry, Compilation, and Execution under the DOS, UNIX, VAX-VMS, and PRIME Operating Systems

In this appendix, we first examine the steps to take to enter, compile, and execute a C++ program. The specific instructions required by the DOS, UNIX, VAX-VMS, and PRIME operating systems are then provided.

General Introduction

As illustrated in Figure C–1, a computer can be thought of as a self-contained world that is entered by a special set of steps called a login procedure. For some computers such as IBM, Apple, and other desktop computers, the login procedure is usually as simple as turning the computer's power switch on. Larger multiuser systems, such as DEC, VAX, and PRIME computers, typically require a login procedure consisting of turning a terminal on and supplying an account number and password.

FIGURE C–1 Viewing a Computer as a Self-Contained World

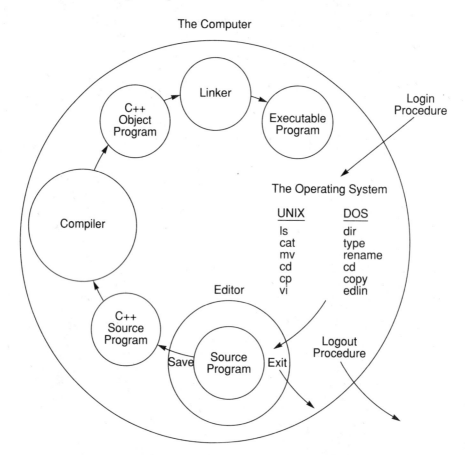

Once you have successfully logged in to your computer system, you are automatically placed under the control of a computer program called the operating system (unless the computer is programmed to switch into a specific application program). The operating system is the program that controls the computer. It is used to access the services provided by the computer, which include the programs needed to enter, compile, and execute a C++ program.

Communicating with the operating system is always accomplished using a specific set of commands that the operating system recognizes. Although each computer system (IBM, Apple, DEC, PRIME, etc.) has its own set of operating system commands, all operating systems provide commands that allow you to log in to the system, exit from the system, create your own programs, and to quickly list, delete, copy, or rename your programs.

The specific operating system commands and any additional steps used for exiting from a computer, such as turning the power off, are collectively referred to as the logout procedure. Make sure you know the logout procedure for your computer at the time you log in to ensure that you can effectively "escape" when you are ready to leave the system. Since the login and logout procedures for each computer are system dependent, determine these procedures for the system you will be using and list them below:

Login Procedure:_____

_____

Logout Procedure:_____

_____

Specific Operating Systems

Each operating system provides a basic set of commands that allow you to list the names of the programs in the system, type the contents of a program, copy programs, rename programs, and delete programs. Table C–1 lists the operating system commands provided by the IBM DOS, UNIX, VAX-VMS, and PRIME operating systems to perform these and other functions. Space has also been left in the table to list the specific operating system command names used by your system to perform these tasks.

The commands listed in Table C–1 to list, copy, delete, or rename programs are all concerned with manipulating existing programs. Let us now turn our attention to creating, compiling, and executing a new C++ program. The procedures for doing these tasks are illustrated in Figure C–2. As shown in this figure, the procedure for creating an executable C++ program consists of three distinct operations: editing (creating or modifying the source code), compiling, and linking. Although every operating system provides an editor program that can be used to create C++ programs, not all operating systems provide a C++

compiler. Fortunately, UNIX, VAX, and PRIME operating systems all have a C++ compiler that is typically installed along with the operating system. For IBM and IBM-compatible PC computers, a separate compiler such as Borland's Turbo C++ or Microsoft's C++ compiler must be purchased and installed to provide the capability of compiling C++ programs.

TABLE C–1 Operating System Commands

Task	DOS	UNIX	VAX	PRIME	Your System
Obtain a directory of programs	dir	ls	dir	LS	
Change to a new directory	cd	cd	cd	DOWN and BACK	
List current directory name	cd	pwd	cd	WHERE	
List a program	type	cat	cat	SLIST	
Copy a program	copy	cp	cp	COPY	
Delete a program	erase	rm	rm	DELETE	
Rename a program	rename	mv	rn	CN	

Editing

Both the creation of a new C++ program and the modification of an existing C++ program require the use of an editor program. The function of the editor is to allow a user to type statements at a keyboard and save the typed statements together under a common name, called a source program file name.

As illustrated in Figure C–1, an editor program is contained within the environment controlled by the operating system. Like all services provided by the operating system, this means that the editor program can only be accessed using an operating system command. Table C–2 lists operating system commands required by the UNIX, DOS, VAX-VMS, and PRIME operating systems to enter their respective editors. Because the UNIX operating system supplies two editor programs, a screen editor named vi and a line editor named ed, two separate commands are provided in UNIX for accessing the desired editor.

TABLE C–2

Operating System	Command to Enter the Editor	Command to Save and Exit	Command to Exit without Saving
DOS	EDLIN	E	q
UNIX (screen editor)	vi	:wq or ZZ	:q!
UNIX (line editor)	e	w and then q or ctrl Z	q
VAX-VMS	E	ctrl E	pfi Q
PRIME	PED	.FILE	.QUIT

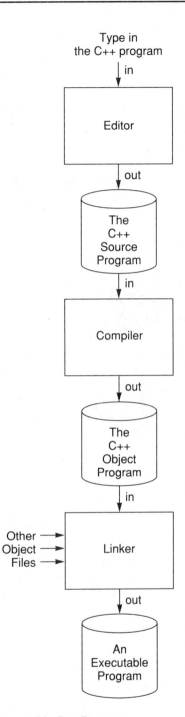

FIGURE C–2 Creating an Executable C++ Program

Once the editor program has been requested, the operating system relinquishes control to this program. Again, as illustrated in Figure C–1, this means that you temporarily leave the world controlled by the operating system and its commands and enter the world controlled by the editor. The editor, like the operating system, has its own set of services and commands. The services provided by the editor include entering C++ statements, modifying and deleting existing statements in a program, listing a program, naming a program, saving a program, and exiting from the editor back into the operating system with or without saving the program.

In using an editor you must carefully distinguish between entering a C++ statement and entering an editor command. Some editors make this distinction by using special keys to alert the editor that what is being typed is a command to the editor rather than the line of a program (for example, in BASIC, the line number informs the editor that the entered line is a program statement and the absence of a line number informs the editor that the entered line is an editor command). Other editors, including those listed in Table C–2, contain two modes: a *text mode* for entering and modifying program statements, and a *command mode* for entering editor commands. Table C–3 lists the commands provided by the UNIX, DOS, VAX-VMS, and PRIME editors for alerting the editor as to whether the text being typed is a command or a program statement.

TABLE C–3 Switching between Command and Text Modes

Editor	Commands to Enter Text Mode from Command Mode	Commands to Enter Command Mode from Text Mode
DOS—EDLIN	i or type at line no.	ctrl and C keys
UNIX—vi	a, i, o, c, s	Esc key
UNIX—ed	a, i, o, c, s	. (period)
VAX—EDT	c	ctrl Z
PRIME—PED	always in text mode	. followed by command

In command mode, each editor permits you to perform the tasks listed in Table C–4. Once you have determined the editor you will be using, fill in Table C–4 (for some of these tasks, the required commands can be found in Tables C–2 and C–3).

Compiling and Linking

Translating a C++ source program into a form that can be executed by the computer is accomplished using a *compiler* program. The output produced by the compiler is called an *object* program. An object program is simply a translated version of the source program that can be executed by the computer system with one more processing step. Let us see why this is so.

Most C++ programs contain statements that use preprogrammed routines, called intrinsic functions, for finding such quantities as square roots, logarithms, trigonometric values, absolute values, or other commonly encountered mathematical calculations. Additionally, a large C++ program may be stored in two or more separate program files. However, multiple files must ultimately be combined to form a single program before the program can be executed. In both of these cases it is the task of the *linker* to combine all of the intrinsic functions and individual object files into a single program ready for execution. This final program is called an executable program.

TABLE C–4   Editor Commands

Task	Command	Example
Save the program and exit from the editor		
Save the program without exiting from the editor		
Exit from the editor without saving the program		
Switch to text mode (if applicable)		
Switch to command mode (if applicable)		
List the complete program from within the editor		
List a set of lines from within the editor		
List a single line from within the editor		
Delete the complete program from within the editor		
Delete a set of lines from within the editor		
Delete a single line from within the editor		
Name a program from within the editor		

Both the compiler and the linker programs can be accessed using individual operating system commands. For ease of operation, however, all operating systems that provide a C++ compiler also provide a single command that both compiles a C++ program and links it correctly with any other required object programs using one command. Table C–5 lists the commands required by the UNIX, VAX-VMS, and PRIME operating systems to either compile only, link only, or compile and link a C++ program to produce an executable program. (Since DOS does not provide a C++ compiler, no entry is included in Table C–5 for this operating system.) Space has been left in the table to enter the command used by your computer for performing these operations.

Finally, once the C++ source program has been compiled and linked, it must be run. In both the VAX-VMS and PRIME operating systems execution of the executable program is begun by simply typing the name of the program in response to the operating system prompt. In the UNIX operating system the executable program produced by the linker is named a.out. Thus, for the UNIX operating system the execution of the last compiled and linked C++ program is initiated by typing a.out in response to the operating system prompt.

TABLE C–5 Specific Operating System Compile and Link Commands

Operating System	Compile and Link Command	Compile Only Command	Link Command
UNIX	cc filename(s)	cc filename(s) -c	ld objectname(s) -lc
VAX-VMS	—	cc filename	lin filename
PRIME	clg c -br l	cc filename	bind :li ccmain :lo filename :li g_lib :li
Your System			

Note: For each operating system listed in Table C–5, every source filename being compiled must end in a .c, and every object filename being linked must end in a .o. The output of a compile-only command automatically produces an equivalent .o object file if the compilation is successful.

Determine and then list the command used by your computer for performing this operation:

Operating system command to
execute a compiled and linked program:_____

Appendix D   Input, Output, and Standard Error Redirection

The display produced by the `cout` object is normally sent to the terminal where you are working. This terminal is called the standard output device because it is where the display is automatically directed, in a standard fashion, by the interface between your C++ program and your computer's operating system.

On most systems it is possible to redirect the output produced by `cout` to some other device, or to a file, using the output redirection symbol, >, at the time the program is invoked. In addition to the symbol, you must specify where you want the displayed results to be sent.

For purposes of illustration, assume that the command to execute a compiled program named `salestax`, without redirection, is:

```
salestax
```

This command is entered after your computer's system prompt is displayed on your terminal. When the `salestax` program is run, any `cout` object activates within it automatically cause the appropriate display to be sent to your terminal. Suppose we would like to have the display produced by the program sent to a file named `results`. To do this requires the command

```
salestax > results
```

The redirection symbol, >, tells the operating system to send any display produced by `cout` directly to a file named `results` rather than to the standard output device used by the system. The display sent to `results` can then be examined by using either an editor program or issuing another operating system command. For example, under the UNIX® operating system the command

```
cat results
```

causes the contents of the file `results` to be displayed on your terminal. The equivalent command under the IBM PC disk operating system (DOS) is:

```
type results
```

In redirecting an output display to a file, the following rules apply:

1. If the file does not exist, it will be created.
2. If the file exists, it will be overwritten with the new display.

In addition to the output redirection symbol, the output append symbol, >>, can also be used. The append symbol is used in the same manner as the redirection symbol, but causes any new output to be added to the end of a file. For example, the command

```
salestax >> results
```

causes any output produced by `salestax` to be added to the end of the `results` file. If the `results` file does not exist, it will be created.

Besides having the display produced by `cout` redirected to a file, using either the > or >> symbols, the display can also be sent to a physical device connected to your computer, such as a printer. You must, however, know the name used by your computer for accessing the desired device. For example, on an IBM PC or compatible computer, the name of the printer connected to the terminal is designated as `prn` and on a UNIX system it is typically `lpr`. Thus, if you are working on an IBM or compatible machine, the command

```
salestax > prn
```

causes the display produced in the salestax program to be sent directly to the printer connected to the terminal.

Corresponding to output redirection, it is also possible to redesignate the standard input device for an individual program run using the input redirection symbol, <. Again, the new source for input must be specified immediately after the input redirection symbol.

Input redirection works in a similar fashion to output redirection but affects the source of input for the `cin` stream. For example, the command

```
salestax < dat_in
```

causes any input functions within `salestax` that normally receive their input from the keyboard to receive it from the `dat_in` file instead. This input redirection, like its output counterpart, is only in effect for the current execution of the program. As you might expect, the same run can have both an input and output redirection. For example, the command

```
salestax < dat_in > results
```

causes an input redirection from the file `dat_in` and an output redirection to the file `results`.

In addition to standard input and output redirection, the device to which all error messages are sent can also be redirected. On many systems this file is given an operating system designation as device file 2. Thus, the redirection

```
2> err
```

causes any error messages that would normally be displayed on the standard error device, which is usually your terminal, to be redirected to a file named `err`. As with standard input and output redirection, standard error redirection can be included on the same command line used to invoke a program. For example, the command

```
salestax < dat_in > show 2> err
```

causes the compiled program named `salestax` to receive its standard input from a file named `dat_in`, write its results to a file named `show`, and send any error messages to a file named `err`.

Because the redirection of input, output, and error messages is generally a feature of the operating system used by your computer and not typically part of your C++ compiler, you must check the manuals for your particular operating system to ensure these features are available.

Appendix E   Command Line Arguments

Arguments can be passed to any function in a program, including the `main()` function. This appendix describes the procedures for passing arguments to `main()` when a program is initially invoked and having `main()` correctly receive and store the arguments passed to it. Both the sending and receiving sides of the transaction must be considered. Fortunately, the interface for transmitting arguments to a `main()` function has been standardized in C++, so both sending and receiving arguments can be done almost mechanically.

All the programs that have been run so far have been invoked by typing the name of the executable version of the program after the operating system prompt is displayed. The command line for these programs consists of a single word, which is the name of the program. For computers that use the UNIX® operating system the prompt is usually the `$` symbol and the executable name of the program is `a.out`. For these systems, the simple command line `$a.out` begins program execution of the last compiled source program currently residing in `a.out`.

If you are using a C++ compiler on an IBM PC, the equivalent operating system prompt is either `A>` or `C>`, and the name of the executable program is typically the same name as the source program with an `.exe` extension rather than a `.cpp` extension. Assuming that you are using an IBM PC with the `C>` operating system prompt, the complete command line for running an executable program named `showad.exe` is `C> showad`. As illustrated in Figure E–1, this command line causes the `showad` program to begin execution with its `main()` function, but no arguments are passed to `main()`.

Now assume that we want to pass the three separate string arguments `three blind mice` directly into `showad`'s main function. Sending arguments into a `main()` function is extremely easy. It is accomplished by including the arguments on the command line used to begin program execution. Because the arguments are typed on the command line, they are, naturally, called *command*

FIGURE E–1 Invoking the `showad` Program

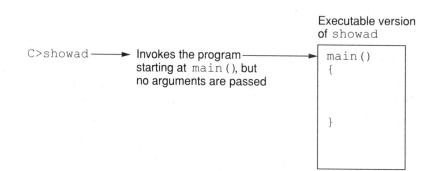

| s | h | o | w | a | d | \0 | t | h | r | e | e | \0 | b | l | i | n | d | \0 | m | i | c | e | \0 |

FIGURE E–2   The Command Line Stored in Memory

line arguments. To pass the arguments `three blind mice` directly into the `main()` function of the `showad` program, we only need to add the desired words after the program name on the command line:

C> showad three blind mice

Upon encountering the command line `showad three blind mice`, the operating system stores it as a sequence of four strings. Figure E–2 illustrates the storage of this command line, assuming that each character uses one byte of storage. As shown in the figure, each string terminates with the standard C++ null character `\0`.

Sending command line arguments to `main()` is always this simple. The arguments are typed on the command line and the operating system nicely stores them as a sequence of separate strings. We must now handle the receiving side of the transaction and let `main()` know that arguments are being passed to it.

Arguments passed to `main()`, like all function arguments, must be declared as part of the function's definition. To standardize argument passing to a `main()` function, only two items are allowed: a number and an array. The number is an integer variable, which must be named `argc` (short for argument counter), and the array is a one-dimensional list, which must be named `argv` (short for argument values). Figure E–3 illustrates these two arguments.

The integer passed to `main()` is the total number of items on the command line. In our example, the value of `argc` passed to `main()` is four, which includes the name of the program plus the three command line arguments. The one-dimensional list passed to `main()` is a list of pointers containing the starting storage address of each string typed on the command line, as illustrated in Figure E–4.

FIGURE E–3   An Integer and an Array Are Passed to `main()`

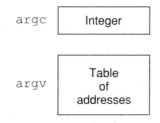

549

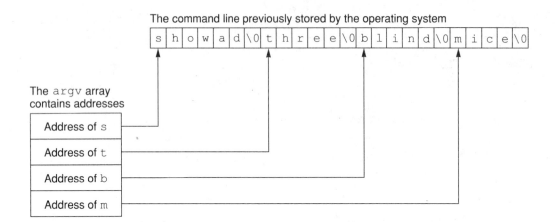

FIGURE E–4 Addresses Are Stored in the `argv` Array

We can now write the complete function definition for `main()` to receive arguments. Since an integer and an array are passed to `main()` and C++ requires that these two items be named `argc` and `argv`, respectively, the first line in `main()`'s definition must be `main(argc,argv)`.

To complete `main()`'s definition, we must declare the data types of these two arguments. Because `argc` is an integer, its declaration is `int argc;`. Because `argv` is the name of an array whose elements are addresses that point to where the actual command line arguments are stored, its proper declaration is `char *argv[];`. This is nothing more than the declaration of an array of pointers. It is read "`argv` is an array whose elements are pointers to characters." Putting all this together, the full function header line for a `main()` function that will receive command line arguments is:

```
void main(int argc, char *argv[])      // complete main() header line
```

No matter how many arguments are typed on the command line, `main()` only needs the two standard pieces of information provided by `argc` and `argv`: the number of items on the command line and the list of starting addresses indicating where each argument is actually stored.

Once command line arguments are passed to a C++ program, they can be used like any other C++ strings. Program E-1 causes its command line arguments to be displayed from within `main()`.

888

Program E-1

```cpp
// A program that displays command line arguments
#include <iostream.h>
void main(int argc, char *argv[])
{
  int i;

  cout << "\nThe following arguments were passed to main(): ";
  for (i = 1; i < argc; i++)
    cout << argv[i] << " ";
  cout << '\n';
}
```

Assuming that the name of the executable version of Program E-1 is a.out, the output of this program for the command line a.out three blind mice is:

    The following arguments were passed to main(): three blind mice

Notice that when the addresses in argv[] are passed to cout, the strings pointed to by these addresses are displayed.

One final comment about command line arguments is in order. Any argument typed on a command line is considered to be a string. If you want numerical data passed to main(), it is up to you to convert the passed string into its numerical counterpart. This is seldom an issue, however, since most command line arguments are used as flags to pass appropriate processing control signals to an invoked program.

Appendix F Floating Point Number Storage

The two's complement binary code used to store integer values was presented in Section 2.8. In this appendix we present the binary storage format typically used in C++ to store single precision and double precision numbers, which are stored as floats and doubles, respectively. Collectively, both single and double precision values are commonly referred to as floating point values.

Like their decimal number counterparts that use a decimal point to separate the integer and fractional parts of a number, floating point numbers are represented in a conventional binary format with a binary point. For example, consider the binary number 1011.11. The digits to the left of the binary point (1011) represent the integer part of the number and the digits to the right of the binary point (11) represent the fractional part.

To store a floating point binary number a code similar to decimal scientific notation is used. To obtain this code the conventional binary number format is separated into a mantissa and an exponent. The following examples illustrate floating point numbers expressed in this scientific notation.

Conventional Binary Notation	Binary Scientific Notation
1010.0	1.01 exp 011
−10001.0	-1.0001 exp 100
0.001101	1.101 exp -011
−0.000101	-1.01 exp -100

In binary scientific notation, the term exp stands for exponent. The binary number in front of the exp term is the mantissa and the binary number following the exp term is the exponent value. Except for the number zero, the mantissa always has a single leading 1 followed immediately by a binary point. The exponent represents a power of 2 and indicates the number of places the binary point should be moved in the mantissa to obtain the conventional binary notation. If the exponent is positive, the binary point is moved to the right. If the exponent is negative, the binary point is moved to the left. For example, the exponent 011 in the number

$$1.01 \text{ exp } 011$$

means move the binary point three places to the right, so that the number becomes 1010. The -011 exponent in the number

$$1.101 \text{ exp } -011$$

means move the binary point three places to the left, so that the number becomes

$$.001101$$

552

TABLE F–1   IEEE Standard 754-1985 Floating Point Specification

Data Format	Sign Bits	Mantissa Bits	Exponent Bits
Single precision	1	23	8
Double precision	1	52	11
Extended precision	1	64	15

In storing floating point numbers, the sign, mantissa, and exponent are stored individually within separate fields. The number of bits used for each field determines the precision of the number. Single precision (32 bit), double precision (64 bit), and extended precision (80 bit) floating point data formats are defined by the Institute of Electrical and Electronics Engineers (IEEE) Standard 754-1985 to have the characteristics given in Table F–1. The format for a single precision floating point number is illustrated in Figure F–1.

The sign bit shown in Figure F–1 refers to the sign of the mantissa. A sign bit of 1 represents a negative number and a zero sign bit represents a positive value. Since all mantissas, except for the number zero, have a leading 1 followed by their binary points, these two items are never stored explicitly. The binary point implicitly resides immediately to the left of mantissa bit 22, and a leading 1 is always assumed. The binary number zero is specified by setting all mantissa and exponent bits to 0. For this case only, the implied leading mantissa bit is also zero.

The exponent field contains an exponent that is biased by 127. For example, an exponent of 5 would be stored using the binary equivalent of the number 132 (127 + 5). Using eight exponent bits, this is coded as 100000100. The addition of 127 to each exponent allows negative exponents to be coded within the exponent field without the need for an explicit sign bit. For example, the exponent –011, which corresponds to –3, would be stored using the binary equivalent of +124 (127 – 3).

Figure F–2 illustrates the encoding and storage of the decimal number 59.75 as a 64-bit single precision binary number. The sign, exponent, and mantissa are determined as follows. The conventional binary equivalent of

$$-59.75$$

is

$$-111011.11$$

FIGURE F–1 Single Precision Floating Point Number Storage Format

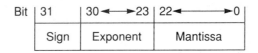

FIGURE F–2 The Encoding and Storage of the Decimal Number 59.75

Expressed in binary scientific notation this becomes

$$-1.1101111 \ \text{exp} \ 101$$

The minus sign is signified by setting the sign bit to 1. The mantissa's leading 1 and binary point are omitted and the 23-bit mantissa field is encoded as

$$11011110000000000000000$$

The exponent field encoding is obtained by adding the exponent value of 101 to 1111111, which is the binary equivalent of the 127_{10} bias value:

$$
\begin{array}{rcl}
1\ 1\ 1\ 1\ 1\ 1\ 1 & = & 127_{10} \\
+\ 1\ 0\ 1 & = & 5_{10} \\
\hline
1\ 0\ 0\ 0\ 0\ 1\ 0\ 0 & = & 132_{10}
\end{array}
$$

Appendix G   Linked Lists Using Classes

Linked lists provides a convenient method for maintaining lists of items, without the need to continually reorder and restructure a list as items are added or deleted. For example, consider the list of names and phone numbers previously introduced in Section 10.4 and reproduced below as Figure G–1.[1]

Constructing a linked list for this case requires that each record have the same format, which includes an address that references the next record in the list. Clearly the last record cannot have a valid address referencing another record, since there is none. So for this last record we will use a NULL address that will act as a sentinel or flag to indicate when the last record has been processed. The NULL address value, like its end-of-string counterpart, has a numerical value of zero.

Besides an end-of-list sentinel value, either a pointer or reference variable must also be provided to store the address of the first record in the list. Figure G–2 illustrates the complete set of addresses and records for the first three names and addresses shown in Figure G–1.

FIGURE G–1   A Telephone List in Alphabetical Order

Acme, Sam
(201) 898-2392

Dolan, Edith
(213) 682-3104

Lanfrank, John
(415) 718-4581

Mening, Stephen
(914) 382-7070

Zemann, Harold
(718) 219-9912

FIGURE G–2   Use of the Initial and Final Address Values

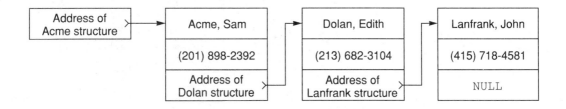

---

[1] Prior to reading this appendix the interested reader should be familiar with the introductory material on linked lists provided in Section 10.4.

This concept can be easily extended to create a linked list of objects suitable for storing any number of names and telephone numbers. The following interface is suitable for such a class:

```
// class declaration (interface)
class Tele_typ
{
  private:
    char name[30];
    char phone[16];
    Tele_typ *nextaddr;
  public:
    Tele_typ(char *, char *);  // a constructor
    Tele_typ *get_addr();  // function returns a pointer to an object of type Tel_typ
    void set_addr(Tele_typ *);
    void display();
};
```

This interface declares three data and four function members, respectively. The first data member is an array of 30 characters, suitable for storing names with a maximum of 29 letters and an end-of-string NULL marker. The next data member is an array of 15 characters, suitable for storing telephone numbers with their respective area codes. The last data member is a pointer suitable for storing the address of an object of the class Tele_typ. The member functions consist of a constructor and three access functions. We will define these functions using the implementation section:

```
// class implementation

Tele_typ::Tele_typ(char *new_name, char *new_phone)
{
  strcpy(name, new_name);
  strcpy(phone, new_phone);
  nextaddr = NULL;
}
Tele_typ *Tele_typ::get_addr()
{
  return nextaddr;
}
void Tele_typ::set_addr(Tele_typ *nextad)
{
  nextaddr = nextad;
}
void Tele_typ::display()
{
    cout << "\n" << setiosflags(ios::left)
         << setw(30) << name
         << setw(20) << phone;
}
```

The constructor and display functions are rather straightforward. The constructor copies its first string argument to the name data member and its second string argument to the phone data member. Finally, it initializes its pointer data member with a NULL address. The display function simply outputs the values contained in the name and phone variables. The remaining two access functions, get_addr() and set_addr(), are used to retrieve and set addresses, respectively, into the pointer data member of an object.

As defined in the implementation, set_addr() expects to receive the address of a Tele_typ object and assigns this address to its pointer member. Similarly, get_addr() simply returns the address stored in its pointer member —that is, it returns a pointer to an object of type Tele_typ.

Program G-1 illustrates the use of the Tele_typ class by specifically creating three objects of this class. The three objects are named t1, t2, and t3, respectively, and each object is initialized with a name and telephone number when the objects are defined, using the data listed in Figure G–1.

Program G-1

```cpp
#include <iostream.h>
#include <iomanip.h>
#include <string.h>
```

```cpp
// class declaration (interface)
class Tele_typ
{
  private:
    char name[30];
    char phone[16];
    Tele_typ *nextaddr;
  public:
    Tele_typ(char *, char *);  // a constructor
    Tele_typ *get_addr();    // function returns a pointer to an object of type Tel_typ
    void set_addr(Tele_typ *);
    void display();
};

// class implementation
Tele_typ::Tele_typ(char *new_name, char *new_phone)
{
  strcpy(name, new_name);
  strcpy(phone, new_phone);
  nextaddr = NULL;
}
```

(continued on next page)

(continued from previous page)

```
Tele_typ *Tele_typ::get_addr()
{
  return nextaddr;
}
void Tele_typ::set_addr(Tele_typ *nextad)
{
  nextaddr = nextad;
}
void Tele_typ::display()
{
    cout << "\n" << setiosflags(ios::left)
         << setw(30) << name
         << setw(20) << phone;
}
```

```
void main(void)
{
  int i;
  Tele_typ t1("Acme, Sam", "(201) 898-2392");
  Tele_typ t2("Dolan, Edith", "(213) 682-3104");
  Tele_typ t3("Lanfrank, John", "(415) 718-4581");
  Tele_typ *first, *current;

  first = &t1;              // store t1's address in first
  t1.set_addr(&t2);         // store t2's address in t1.nextaddr
  t2.set_addr(&t3);         // store t3's address in t2.nextaddr

  current = first;          // set current to first
  while (current != NULL)
  {
    (*current).display();                 // same as current->display()
    current = (*current).get_addr();      // same as current->get_addr()
  }
}
```

The output produced by executing Program G-1 is:

```
Acme, Sam                 (201) 898-2392
Dolan, Edith              (213) 682-3104
Lanfrank, John            (415) 718-4581
```

Since we have already described the class construction, let us now concentrate on the main() function in Program G-1 and see how it creates this output. Figure G–3 illustrates the relationship between the three objects created by the program.

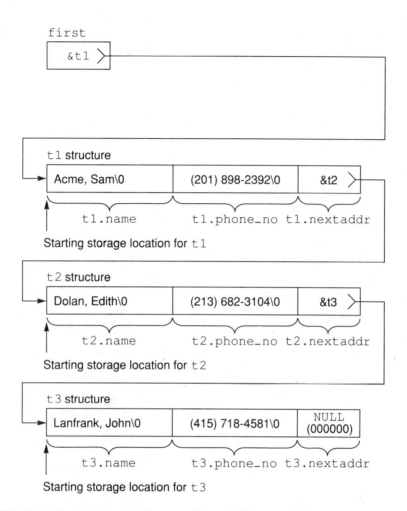

FIGURE G–3   The Relationship Between Objects in Program G-1

From within main(), the three objects illustrated in Figure G–3, t1, t2, and t3, are defined. Each of these objects is of class type Tele_typ. Although each object consists of three members, only the first two members of each object are explicitly initialized. Because both of these members are arrays of characters, they can be initialized with strings. The remaining member of each object is a pointer, which is initialized to a NULL address by the constructor.

To create a linked list from these three objects, each pointer member must be assigned the address of the next object in the list. The three assignment statements in Program G-1 perform the correct assignments. The expression first = &t1 stores the address of the t1 object in the pointer variable named first. The function call t1.set_addr(&t2) uses t1's set_addr() function to store the address of t2 in t1's pointer variable. The result of this call is t1.nextaddr = &t2. Similarly, the function call t2.set_addr(&t3) stores the starting address of the t3 object into the pointer member of the t2 object (that is, t2.next = &t3). The list is automatically terminated by the NULL address placed in t3.next when the t3 object was initialized.

Once values have been assigned to each object member and correct addresses have been stored in the appropriate pointers, the addresses can be used to loop through the complete list for display purposes. As each object is accessed it can either be examined to select a specific value or used to print out a complete list. This is done by main()'s while loop.

The expression (*current).display() in the while loop calls the display() function of the object pointed to by current. Since current is initially set to the address of the t1 object, the function that is called is t1.display(). This display function, as defined in the class implementation section, outputs its object's name and phone number values. t1's get_addr() function is then called, which assigns the address in t1.nextaddr to current. Since t1.nextaddr contains the address of the t2 object, the second time through the loop the t2.display() function is called. This process is repeated until the NULL address in t3.nextaddr is encountered. Note that the expression (*current).display() in the while loop can be replaced by the equivalent expression current->display().

The important concept illustrated by Program G-1 is the use of the address in one object to access members of the next object in the list. Within main(), the while loop is used to cycle through the linked objects, starting with the object whose address is in next. The condition tested in the while statement compares the value in next, which is an address, to the NULL value. For each valid address the name and phone number members of the addressed object are displayed. The address in next is then updated with the address in the pointer member of the current object. The address in next is then retested, and the process continues while the address in next is not equal to the NULL value. The loop "knows" nothing about the names of the objects declared in main() or even how many objects exist. It simply cycles through the linked list, object by object, until it encounters the end-of-list NULL address. Since the value of NULL is zero, the tested condition can be replaced by the equivalent expression !next.

A disadvantage of Program G-1 is that exactly three objects are defined in main() by name and storage for them is reserved at compile time. Should a fourth object be required, the additional object would have to be declared and the program recompiled. This limitation is removed by dynamically allocating and freeing storage for objects at run time, as storage is required. Only when a new object is to be added to the list, and while the program is running, is storage for the new object created. Similarly, when an object is no longer needed and can be deleted from the list, the storage for the deleted record is relinquished and returned to the computer.

Program G-2 illustrates using dynamic storage allocation, using the new routine, which was described in Sections 8.2 and 10.5, to create an object dynamically in response to a user-input request.

Program G-2

```
#include <iostream.h>
#include <iomanip.h>
#include <string.h>
```

```
class Tel_typ
{
  private:
    char name[30];
    char phone[16];
  public:
    Tel_typ(char *, char *);  // a constructor //
    void display();
};

// class implementation
Tel_typ::Tel_typ(char *new_name, char *new_phone)
{
  strcpy(name, new_name);
  strcpy(phone, new_phone);
}
void Tel_typ::display()
{
   cout << "\n" << setiosflags(ios::left)
        << setw(30) << name
        << setw(20) << phone;
}
```

```
void main(void)
{
  char key, new_name[30], new_phone[16];
  Tel_typ *rec_point; // a pointer to an object of type Tel_typ

  cout << "\nDo you wish to create a new record (respond with y or n): ";
  key = cin.get();
  if (key == 'y')
  {
    key = cin.get();  // get the Enter key in buffered input
    cout << "\nEnter a name: ";
    cin.getline(new_name,30);
    cout << "Enter a phone number: ";
    cin.getline(new_phone,16);
    rec_point = new Tel_typ(new_name, new_phone);
    (*rec_point).display();    // same as rec_point->display()
  }
  else
    cout << "\nNo record has been created";
}
```

A sample session produced by Program G-2 is:

```
Do you wish to create a new record (respond with y or n): y
Enter a name: Monroe, James
Enter the phone number: (617) 555-1817
The contents of the record just created is:
Name: Monroe, James
Phone Number: (617) 555-1817
```

In reviewing Program G-2, notice the statement `rec_point` = new `Tel_typ(new_name, new_phone);` in `main()`. This statement calls the new function to create an object of type `Tel_typ`, initializes the newly created object with the strings contained in the character arrays `new_name` and `new_phone` (via the constructor), and stores the address returned by new in the pointer variable `rec_point`. The complete operation of `main()` is as follows:

If a user enters `y` in response to the first prompt in `main()`, the user is requested to enter a name and telephone number. A call is then made to new, as just described.

The newly created object's `display()` function is then called to display the contents of the newly created and initialized object. The mechanism for calling `display()` is identical to that previously described for Program G-2.

Once you understand the mechanism of calling new, you can use this function to construct a linked list of objects. The address in the pointer member of each object in the list must be the starting address of the next object in the list. Additionally, a pointer must be reserved for the address of the first object, and the pointer member of the last object in the list is given a `NULL` address to indicate that no more members are being pointed to.

Program G-3 illustrates the use of new to construct a linked list of names and phone numbers. The `display()` function used in Program G-3 is the same function used in Program G-1.

Program G-3

```cpp
#include <iostream.h>
#include <iomanip.h>
#include <string.h>

// class declaration (interface)
class Tel_typ
{
  private:
    char name[30];
    char phone[16];
    Tel_typ *nextaddr;
```

(continued on next page)

(continued from previous page)

```cpp
  public:
    Tel_typ(char *, char *); // a constructor
    Tel_typ *get_addr();      // function returns a pointer to an object of type Tel_typ
    void set_addr(Tel_typ *);
    void display();
};

// class implementation
Tel_typ::Tel_typ(char *new_name, char *new_phone)
{
  strcpy(name, new_name);
  strcpy(phone, new_phone);
  nextaddr = NULL;
}
Tel_typ *Tel_typ::get_addr()
{
  return nextaddr;
}
void Tel_typ::set_addr(Tel_typ *nextad)
{
  nextaddr = nextad;
}
void Tel_typ::display()
{
  cout << "\n" << setiosflags(ios::left)
       << setw(30) << name
       << setw(20) << phone;
}
```

```cpp
void main(void)
{
  char new_name[30], new_phone[16];
  Tel_typ *first, *current, *newpoint;

  // create the first object in the list
    cout << "\nEnter a name: ";
    cin.getline(new_name,30);
    cout << "Enter a phone number: ";
    cin.getline(new_phone,16);
    current = new Tel_typ(new_name, new_phone);
    first = current;   // save the first address

    for(int i = 1; i <= 2; i++)  // create 2 more objects
    {
      cout << "\nEnter a name: ";
      cin.getline(new_name,30);
      cout << "Enter a phone number: ";
      cin.getline(new_phone,16);
      newpoint = new Tel_typ(new_name, new_phone);
      (*current).set_addr(newpoint);
      current = newpoint;
    }

    current = first;
    while (current != NULL)
    {
      (*current).display();
      current = (*current).get_addr();
    }
}
```

The first time new is called in Program G-3 it is used to create the first object in the linked list. As such, the address returned by new is stored in the pointer variable named newpoint. The address in newpoint is then assigned to the pointer named current. This pointer variable is always used by the program to point to the current object. Since the current object is the first object created, the address in the pointer named list is assigned to the pointer named current.

Within main()'s for loop, the name and phone number members of the newly created object are populated and the pointer member of the current object is assigned an address. This address is the address of the next object in the list, which is obtained from new. The call to new creates the next object and returns its address into the pointer member of the current object. This completes the population of the current member. The final statement in the for loop resets the address in the current pointer to the address of the next object in the list.

After the last object has been created, the while loop in main() displays all the objects in the list. A sample run of Program G-3 is provided below:

```
Enter a name: Acme, Sam
Enter the phone number: (201) 898-2392
Enter a name: Dolan, Edith
Enter the phone number: (213) 682-3104
Enter a name: Lanfrank, John
Enter the phone number: (415) 718-4581
The list consists of the following records:

Acme, Sam                    (201) 898-2392
Dolan, Edith                 (213) 682-3104
Lanfrank, John               (415) 718-4581
```

Just as new dynamically creates storage while a program is executing, the delete function restores a block of storage back to the computer while the programming is executing. The only argument required by delete is the starting address of a block of storage that was dynamically allocated. Thus, any address returned by new can subsequently be passed to delete to restore the reserved memory back to the computer. delete does not alter the address passed to it, but simply removes the storage that the address references.

Appendix H   Solutions

Section 1.1

1. A computer program is a structured combination of data and instructions that is used to operate a computer.

A programming language is the set of instructions, data, and rules that can be used to construct a program.

Programming is the process of using a programming language to produce a computer program.

An algorithm is a step-by-step sequence of instructions that describes how a computation is to be performed.

Pseudocode is a description of an algorithm using short English-like statements.

A flowchart is a description of an algorithm that uses specifically defined graphical symbols.

A procedure is a logically consistent set of instructions that produces a specific result.

An object is a self-contained unit that consists of both data and the specific procedures that can be applied to the data.

A method is another term for the procedures contained within an object.

A message is the means used to activate a particular method within an object.

A response is what is produced by an object in reaction to receiving a message.

A class defines a general set of data and procedural characteristics from which specific objects are created.

A source program consists of the program statements comprising a C++ or other programming language program.

An object program is the result of compiling a source program.

An executable program is a program that can be executed by a computer.

A compiler is a program that translates a source program into an object program.

An interpreter is a program that translates individual source program statements, one at a time, into executable statements. Each statement is executed immediately after translation.

3. Step 1: Pour the contents of the first cup into the third cup.
Step 2: Rinse out the first cup.
Step 3: Pour the contents of the second cup into the first cup.
Step 4: Rinse out the second cup.
Step 5: Pour the contents of the third cup into the second cup.

5. Step 1: Compare the first number with the second number and use the smallest of these numbers for the next step
Step 2: Compare the smallest number found in step 1 with the third number. The smallest of these two numbers is the smallest of all three numbers.

7. a. Step 1: Compare the first name in the list with the name MIXTER. If the names match, stop the search; else go to step 2.
Step 2: Compare the next name in the list with the name MIXTER. If the names match, stop the search; else repeat this step.

Section 1.2

1.
m1234	Valid. Not a mnemonic.
new_bal	Valid. A mnemonic.
abcd	Valid. Not a mnemonic.
A12345	Valid. Not a mnemonic.
1A2345	Invalid. Violates Rule 1; starts with a number.
power	Valid. A mnemonic.
abs_val	Valid. A mnemonic.
invoices	Valid. A mnemonic.
do	Invalid. Violates Rule 3; is a keyword.
while	Invalid. Violates Rule 3; is a keyword.
add_5	Valid. Could be a mnemonic.
taxes	Valid. A mnemonic.
net_pay	Valid. A mnemonic.
12345	Invalid. Violates Rule 1; starts with a number.
int	Invalid. Violates Rule 3; a keyword.
new_balance	Valid. A mnemonic.
a2b3c4d5	Valid. Not a mnemonic.
salestax	Valid. A mnemonic.
amount	Valid. A mnemonic.
$taxes	Invalid. Violates Rule 1; starts with a special character.

3. a.
```
input_bill()       // input the items purchased
calc_ salestax()   // compute required salestax
calc_ balance()    // determine balance owed
```

Section 1.3

1. a.
```
#include <iostream.h>
void main(void)
{
  cout << "Joe Smith";
  cout << "\n99 Somewhere Street";
  cout << "\nNonesuch, N.J., 07030";
}
```

3. a. Six cout statements would be used.

b. One would work, by including newline escape sequences between each two items displayed.

c.
```
#include <iostream.h>
void main(void)
{
  cout << "PART NO.            PRICE\n\n";
  cout << "T1267              $6.34\n";
  cout << "T1300              $8.92\n";
  cout << "T2401              $65.40\n";
  cout << "T4482              $36.99\n";
}
```

Section 1.4

1. a. Yes.

  b. It is not in standard form. To make programs more readable and easier to debug, the standard form presented in Section 1.4 of the textbook should be used.

3. a. Two backslashes in a row causes one backslash to be displayed.

  b. `cout << "\\ is a backslash.\n";`

Section 2.1

1. a. float or double

  b. integer

  c. float or double

  d. integer

  e. float or double

3. 1.23e2   6.5623e2   3.42695e3   4.8932e3   3.21e–1   1.23e–2   6.789e–3

9. a.   64 * 1024 = 65,536 bytes

  b. 128 * 1024 = 131,072 bytes

  c. 192 * 1024 = 196,608 bytes

  d. 256 * 1024 = 262,144 bytes

  e.   64 * 1024 = 65,536 words * 2 bytes/word = 131,072 bytes

  f.   64 * 1024 = 65,536 words * 4 bytes/word = 262,144 bytes

  g. 360 * 1024 = 368,640 bytes

Section 2.2

1. a. 2 * 3 + 4 * 5

  b. (6 + 18) / 2

  c. 4.5 / (12.2 – 3.1)

  d. 4.6 * (3.0 + 14.9)

  e. (12.1 + 18.9) * (15.3 – 3.8)

3. Since all of the operands given are floating point numbers, the result of each valid expression is a floating point number.

  a. 5.

  b. 10.

  c. 24.0

  d. 0.2

  e. 3.6

  f. Invalid expression.

  g. –50.

  h. –2.5

  i. Invalid expression.

  j. 10.

  k. 53.

5. a. 27.0

  b. 8.0

  c. 1.0

  d. 220.0

  e. 22.67

  f. 19.78

  g. 6.0

  h. 2.0

Section 2.3

1. `answer1` is the integer 2

`answer2` is the integer 5

5. *a.* The double quote after the 2nd insertion symbol should come before the symbol and the parentheses at the end of the statement should be a semicolon.

b. The `setw(4)` manipulator should not be enclosed in double quotes.

c. The `setprecision(5)` manipulator should not be enclosed in double quotes.

d. The statement should be `cout << "Hello World!";`

e. The `setw(6)` manipulator should appear before the insertion of the number 47.

f. The `setprecision(2)` manipulator should appear before the insertion of the number 526.768.

Section 2.4

1. The following are not valid:

```
12345       does not begin with either a letter or underscore
while       keyword
$total      does not begin with either a letter or underscore
new bal     cannot contain a space
9ab6        does not begin with either a letter or underscore
sum.of      contains a special character
```

3. *a.* `int count;`

b. `float grade;`

c. `double yield;`

d. `char initial;`

7. *a.*
```
#include <iostream.h>
void main(void)
{
   int num1, num2, total;  // declare the integer variables num1
                           // num2, and num3

  num1 = 25;              // assign the integer 25 to num1
  num2 = 30;              // assign the integer 30 to num2
  total = num1 + num2;   // assign the sum of num1 and num2 to total
  cout << "The total of " << num1 << " and "
       ,, num2 << " is " << total;   // displays the line:
                           // The total of 25 and 30 is 55.
}
```

9.
```
#include <iostream.h>
void main(void)
{
  int length, width, perim;

  length = 16;
  width = 18;
  perim = length + length + width + width;
  cout << "The perimeter is " << perim;
}
```

13. Every variable has a type (e.g., int, float, etc.), a value, and an address in memory where it is stored.

15. a.

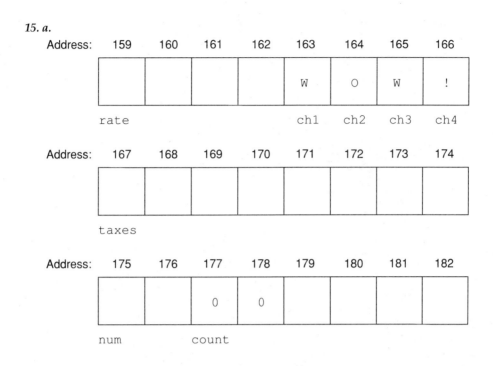

The empty addresses above are usually filled with *garbage* values, meaning their contents are whatever happened to be placed there by the computer or by the previously run program.

Section 2.5

1. a. For an IBM PC or compatible computer, the storage size of a character is one byte and an integer is two bytes.

b. For an IBM PC or compatible computer, two bytes are reserved for short integers, two bytes for unsigned integers, and four bytes for long integers.

3. All that is required to set aside the right amount of storage space for a variable is a definition statement.

Section 3.1

1. a.
```
#include <iostream.h>
void main(void)
{
                // missing declaration for all variables
  width = 15                 // missing semicolon
  area = length * width;    // no value assigned to length
  cout << "The area is " << area   // missing ;
}
```

The corrected program is:

```
#include <iostream.h>
void main(void)
{
  int length, width, area;

  width = 15;
  length = 20;                // must be assigned some value
  area = length * width;
  cout << "The area is " << area;
}
```

b.
```
#include <iostream.h>
void main(void)
{
  int length, width, area;

  area = length * width; // this should come after the
                         // assignment of values to
  length = 20;           // length and width
  width = 15;
  cout << "The area is " << area;
}
```

The corrected program is:

```
#include <iostream.h>
void main(void)
{
  int length, width, area;

  length = 20;
  width = 15;
  area = length * width;
  cout << "The area is " << area;
}
```

c.
```
#include <iostream.h>
void main(void)
{
  int length = 20; width = 15, area; // semicolon after 20
                                     // should be a comma

  length * width = area;  // incorrect assignment statement
  cout << "The area is " << area;
}
```

The corrected program is:

```
#include <iostream.h>
void main(void)
{
  int length = 20, width = 15, area;

  area = length * width;
  cout << "The area is " << area;
}
```

3. a.
```
#include <iostream.h>
void main(void)
{
   float radius, circum;

   radius = 3.3;    // could have been done in the declaration
   circum = 2 * 3.1416 * radius;
   cout << "The circumference is " << circum << "inches";
}
```

5. a.
```
#include <iostream.h>
void main(void)
{
   float length, width, depth, volume;

   length = 25.0;
   width = 10.0;
   depth = 6.0;
   volume = length * width * depth;
   cout << "The volume of the pool is " << volume;
}
```

7. a.
```
#include <iostream.h>
void main(void)
{
   float  total;

   total = 12*.50 + 20*.25 + 32*.10 + 45*.05 + 27*.01;
   cout << "The total amount is $ " << total << '\n';
}
```

9. c.
```
#include <iostream.h>
void main(void)
{
   float speed = 58.0, dist = 183.67, time;

   time = dist/speed;
   cout << "The elapsed time for the trip is " << time " hours";
}
```

11. The second expression is correct because the assignment of 25 to b is done before the subtraction. Without the parentheses the subtraction has the higher precedence, and the expression a – b is calculated, yielding a value, assume 10. The subsequent attempt to assign the value of 25 to this value is incorrect, and is equivalent to the expression 10 = 25. Values can only be assigned to variables.

Section 3.2

1. a. sqrt(6.37)
 b. sqrt(x–y)
 c. sin(30.0 * 3.1416 / 180.0)
 d. sin(60.0 * 3.1416 / 180.0)
 e. abs(pow(a,2.0) – pow(b,2.0)) or abs(a*a + b*b)
 f. exp(3.0)

```
5. #include <iostream.h>
   #include <math.h>
   void main(void)
   {
     float dist, x1 = 7.0, y1 = 12.0 , x2 = 3.0 , y2 = 9.0;

     dist = sqrt(pow((x1-x2),2.0) + pow((y1-y2),2.0));
     cout << "The distance is " << dist << '\n';
   }
```

Section 3.3

```
1. a. cin >> firstnum;
   b. cin >> grade;
   c. cin >> secnum;
   d. cin >> keyval;
   e. cin >> month >> years >> average;
   f. cin >> num1 >> num2 >> grade1 >> grade2
   g. cin >> interest >> principal >> capital >> price >> yield;
   h. cin >> ch >> letter1 >> letter2 >> num1 >> num2 >> num3;
   i. cin >> temp1 >> temp2 >> temp3 >> volts1 >> volts2;
3. a. #include <iostream.h>
      void main(void)
      {
        float fahr, cel;
        cout << "Enter the temperature in degrees Fahrenheit: ";
        cin >> fahr;
        cel = (5.0/9.0)*(fahr - 32.0;
        cout << fahr << " degrees Fahrenheit is "
             << cel << " degrees Celsius\n";
      }
5. a. #include <iostream.h>
      void main(void)
      {
        float miles, gallons, mpg;

        cout << "Enter the miles driven: ";
        cin >> miles;
        cout << "Enter the gallons of gas used: ";
        cin >> gallons;
        mpg = miles/gallons;
        cout << "The miles/gallon is " << mpg << '\n';
      }
```

7. a.
```
#include <iostream.h>
void main(void)
{
    float num1, num2, num3, num4, avg;

    cout << "Enter a number: ";
    cin >> num1;
    cout << "\nEnter a second number: ";
    cin >> num2;
    cout << "\nEnter a third number: ";
    cin >> num3;
    cout << "\nEnter a fourth number: ";
    cin >> num4;
    avg = (num1 + num2 + num3 + num4) / 4.0;
    cout << "\nThe average of the four numbers is "
         << avg << '\n';
}
```
c.
```
#include <iostream.h>
void main(void)
{
    float number, avg, sum = 0;

    cout << "Enter a number: ";
    cin >> number;
    sum = sum + number;
    cout << "\nEnter a second number: ";
    cin >> number;
    sum = sum + number;
    cout << "\Enter a third number: ";
    cin >> number;
    sum = sum + number;
    cout << "\nEnter a fourth number: ";
    cin >> number;
    sum = sum + number;
    avg = sum / 4.0;
    cout << "\nThe average of the four numbers is "
         << avg << '\n';
}
```

11. a. It is easy for a user to enter incorrect data. If wrong or unexpected data is given by the user, either incorrect results will be obtained or the program will *crash*. A crash is an unexpected and premature program termination.

b. In a *data type check* the input is checked to ensure that the values entered are of the correct type for the declared variables. This includes checking that integer values are entered for integer variables, and so on. A *data reasonableness check* determines that the value entered is reasonable for the particular program. Such a check would determine if a large number was entered when a very small number was expected, if a small number was entered when a large number was expected, or if a zero (which could cause problems if the number was the denominator in a division) or a negative number was entered when a positive number was expected, and so on.

c. Data type checks would ensure that the month, day, and year were all entered as integers. Some simple reasonableness checks would ensure that a month was between 1 and 12, a day between 1 and 31, and a year between reasonable limits for the application. More complex reasonableness checks might check that days in months 1, 3, 5, 7, 8, 10, and 12 were between 1 and 31; days in months 4, 6, 9, and 11 were between 1 and 30, and days in month 2 were between 1 and 28 (except for a leap year, in which case the day must be between 1 and 29).

Section 3.4

1.
```cpp
#include <iostream.h>
void main(void)
{
   const float PI = 3.1416;
   float radius,circum;

   cout << "\nEnter a radius: ";
   cin >> radius;
   circum = 2.0 * PI * radius;
   cout << "\nThe circumference of the circle is "
        << circum << '\n';
}
```

3. b.
```cpp
#include <iostream.h>
void main(void)
{
   const float CONVERT = 5.0/9.0;
   const float FREEZING = 32.0;
   float fahren,celsius;

   cout << "\nEnter a temperature in degrees Fahrenheit: ";
   cin >> fahren;
   celsius = CONVERT * (fahren - FREEZING);
   cout << "\nThe equivalent Celsius temperature is "
        << celsius << '\n';
}
```

Section 4.1

1. a. The relational expression is true. Therefore, its value is 1.
  b. The relational expression is true. Therefore, its value is 1.
  c. The final relational expression is true. Therefore, its value is 1.
  d. The final relational expression is true. Therefore, its value is 1.
  e. The final relational expression is true. Therefore, its value is 1.
  f. The arithmetic expression has a value of 10.
  g. The arithmetic expression has a value of 4.
  h. The arithmetic expression has a value of 0.
  i. The arithmetic expression has a value of 10.

3. *a.* age == 30

  c. ht < 6.00

  e. let_in == 'm'

  g. day == 15   month == 1

  i. id < 500   age > 55

b. temp 98.6

d. month == 12

f. age == 30   ht > 6.00

h. age > 50 || employ >= 5

j. len > 2.00   len < 3.00

Section 4.2

1.
```cpp
#include <iostream.h>
void main(void)
{
   const int LIMIT = 20000;
   const float REGRATE = .02;
   const float HIGHRATE = .025;
   const int FIXED = 400;
   float taxable, taxes;

   cout << "Please type in the taxable income: ";
   cin >> taxable;
   if (taxable <= LIMIT)
     taxes = REGRATE * taxable;
   else
     taxes = HIGHRATE * (taxable - LIMIT) + FIXED;
   cout << "\n\nTaxes are $ " << taxes << '\n';
}
```

3. *a.*
```cpp
#include <iostream.h>
void main(void)
{
   float grade;

   cout << "Enter a grade: " ;
   cin >> grade;

   if (grade >= 70.0)
     cout << "A passing grade\n";
   else
     cout << "A failing grade\n";
}
```

5. *a.*
```cpp
#include <iostream.h>
void main(void)
{
   char status;

   cout << "Enter the status: " ;
   cin >> status;

   if (status == 's')
     cout << "The senior person's salary is $400.00\n";
   else
     cout << "The junior person's salary is $275.00\n";
}
```

7. a.
```
#include <iostream.h>
   void main(void)
   {
      int month, day;

      cout << "Enter a month (use a 1 for Jan, 2 for Feb, etc.): ";
      cin >> month;
      cout << "Enter a day of the month: ";
      cin >> day;

      if (month > 12 || month < 1)
         cout << "\nAn incorrect month was entered.";

      if (day < 1 || day > 31)
         cout << "\nAn incorrect day was entered.";
   }
```

b. If a user enters a floating point number, the integer part of the number will be assigned to the integer variable `month`. The month will be correct. The program uses the remaining fractional value for the day input. Since the variable `day` is declared as an integer, a value of zero will be assigned to `day`. A possible solution is to accept the `month` variable as a floating point number, then reassign it to an integer variable to correctly truncate it. No harm is done then if an integer is entered for the month (`scanf()` will first convert it to a floating point number) or if a floating point number is entered. More correctly, a cast should be used, as described in Chapter 14.

9.
```
#include <iostream.h>
   void main(void)
   {
     char in_key;
     int position;

     cout << "Enter a lowercase letter: ";
     cin >> in_key;
     if (in_key >= 'a' && in_key <= 'z')
     {
       position = in_key - 'a' + 1;
       cout << "The character's position is " << position;
     }
     else
       cout << "The character just entered is not a lowercase letter";
   }
```

13. The error is that the intended relational expression *letter* == *'m'* has been written as the assignment expression *letter* = *'m'*. When the expression is evaluated the character m is assigned to the variable letter and the value of the expression itself is the value of *'m'*. Since this is a nonzero value, it is taken as true and the message is displayed.

Realize that, as written in the program, the if statement is equivalent to the following two statements:

```
letter = 'm';
if(letter) cout << "Hello there!";
```

A correct version of the program is:

```
#include <iostream.h>
void main(void)
{
    char letter;

    cout << "Enter a letter: ";
    cin >> letter;
    if (letter == 'm')
        cout << "Hello there!";
}
```

Section 4.3

1.
```
#include <iostream.h>
void main(void)
{
    float grade;
    char letter;

    cout << "Enter the student's numerical grade: ";
    cin >> grade;
    if (grade >= 90.0) letter = 'A';
    else if (grade >= 80.0) letter = 'B';
    else if (grade >= 70.0) letter = 'C';
    else if (grade >= 60.0) letter = 'D';
    else letter = 'F';
    cout << "\nThe student receives a grade of " << letter << '\n';
}
```

Notice that an if-else chain is used. If simple if statements were used, a grade entered as 75.5, for example, would be assigned a "C" because it was greater than 60.0. But the grade would then be reassigned to "D" because it is also greater than 60.0.

```
3. #include <iostream.h>
   void main(void)
   {
      float fahr, cels, in_temp;
      char letter;

      cout << "Enter a temperature followed by"
           << " one space and the temperature's type\n"
           << " (an f designates a fahrenheit temperature\n"
           << " and a c designates a celsius temperature): ";
      cin >> in_temp >> letter;
      if (letter == 'f' || letter == 'F')
      {
         cels = (5.0/9.0)*(in_temp - 32.0);
         cout << in_temp << " degrees Fahrenheit = "
              << cels << " degrees Celsius\n";
      }
      else if (letter == 'c' || letter == 'C')
      {
         fahr = (9.0/5.0)*in_temp - 32.0;
         cout << in_temp << " degrees Celsius = "
              << fahr << " degrees Fahrenheit\n";
      }
      else cout << "The data entered is invalid.\n";
   }
```

5. *a.* This program will run. It will not, however, produce the correct result.

b and c. This program evaluates correct incomes for `mon_sales` less than 20000.00 only. If 20000.00 or more were entered, the first `else-if` statement would be executed and all others would be ignored. That is, for 20000.00 or more, the income for >= 10000.00 would be calculated and displayed.

Had `if` statements been used in place of the `else-if` statements, the program would have worked correctly, but inefficiently.

Section 4.4

```
1. switch (let_grad)
   {
      case 'A':
        cout << "The numerical grade is between 90 and 100";
        break;
      case 'B':
        cout << "The numerical grade is between 80 and 89.9";
        break;
      case 'C':
        cout << "The numerical grade is between 70 and 79.9";
        break;
      case 'D':
        cout << "How are you going to explain this one";
        break;
      default:
        cout << "Of course I had nothing to do with the grade.";
        cout << "\nThe professor was really off the wall.";
   }
```

3.
```
#include <iostream.h>
void main(void)
{
  char marcode;

  cout << "Enter a marital code: ";
  cin >> marcode;

  switch(marcode)
  {
    case 'M':
      cout << "\nIndividual is married.";
      break;
    case 'S':
      cout << "\nIndividual is single.";
      break;
    case 'D':
      cout << "\nIndividual is divorced.";
      break;
    case 'W':
      cout << "\nIndividual is widowed.";
      break;
    default:
      cout << "\nAn invalid code was entered.";
  }   // end of switch
}
```

Section 5.1

1.
```
#include <iostream.h>
void main(void)
{
  int count = 2;

  while (count <= 10)
  {
    cout << count;
    count += z;
  }
}
```

3. *a.* 21 items are displayed, which are the integers from 1 to 21.

   c. 21 items are still displayed, but they would be the integers from 0 to 20 because the cout stream is now activated before the increment.

```
5. #include <iostream.h>
   #include <iomanip.h>
   void main(void)
   {
      int feet = 3;
      float meters;

      cout << "\n";    // start on a new line
      cout << "  Feet    Meters\n";
      cout << "----------------\n";
      while (feet <= 30)
      {
        meters = feet / 3.28;
        cout << setw(5) << feet
             << setiosflags(ios::showpoint) << setw(10)
             << setprecision(2) << meters <<'\n';
        feet += 3;
      }
   }
```

Section 5.2

```
1. #include <iostream.h>
   #include <iomanip.h>
   void main(void)
   {
      int count;
      float num, total;
      const int MAXCOUNT = 8;

      cout << "\nthis program will ask you to enter"
           << " eight numbers.\n";
      count = 1;
      total = 0;

      while (count <= MAXCOUNT)
      {
        cout << "\nenter a number: ";
        cin >> num;
        total = total + num;
        cout << "The total is now " << total;
        count++;
      }
      cout << "\n\nthe final total is " << total;
   }
```

3. a.
```
#include <iostream.h>
#include <iomanip.h>
void main(void)
{
  int num;
  float cels, fahr, incr;

  cout << "Enter the starting temperature in degrees Celsius: ";
  cin >> cels;
  cout << "\n\nEnter the number of conversions to be made: ";
  cin >> num;
  cout << "\n\nNow enter the increment between conversions ";
  cout << "in degrees Celsius: ";
  cin >> incr;
  cout << "\n\n\n";
  cout << "Celsius       Fahrenheit\n";
  cout << "----------------------\n";
  while (count <= num)
  {
    fahr = (9.0/5.0) * cels + 32.0;
    cout << setiosflags(ios::showpoint) << setw(7)
         << setprecision(2) << cels
         << setiosflags(ios::showpoint) << setw(15)
         << setprecision(2) << fahr;
    cels = cels + incr;
  }
}
```

7. This program still calculates the correct values, but the average is now calculated four times. Since only the final average is desired, it is better to calculate the average once outside of the `while` loop.

9. a.
```
#include <iostream.h>
void main(void)
{
  int id, inven, income, outgo, bal, count;

  count = 1;
  while (count <= 3)
  {
    cout << "\nEnter book ID: ";
    cin >> id;
    cout << "\nEnter inventory at the beginning of the month: ";
    cin >> inven;
    cout << "\nEnter the number of copies received during the month: ";
    cin >> income;
    cout << "\nNow enter the number of copies sold during the month: ";
    cin >> outgo;
    bal = inven + income - outgo;
    cout << "\n\nBook #" << id << " new balance is " << bal;
    count++;
  }
}
```

Section 5.3

1. 20 16 12 8 4 0

5.
```
#include <iostream.h>
#include <iomanip.h>
void main(void)
{
  int conv, count;
  float f, c;

  cout << "Enter the number of temperature conversions"
       << "\nfrom Fahrenheit to Celsius to be performed: ";
  cin >> conv;
  cout << '\n';
  cout << "Fahrenheit       Celsius\n";
  cout << "----------       -------\n";
  for (f = 20.0, count = 1; count <= conv; count++)
  {
    c = (f - 32.0) * (5.0/9.0);
    cout << setiosflags(ios::showpoint) << setw(4)
         << setprecision(1) << f
         << "          "
         << setiosflags(ios::showpoint) << setw(5)
         << setprecision(2) << c << '\n';
    f += 4.0;
  }
}
```

7.
```
#include <iostream.h>
#include <iomanip.h>
void main(void)
{
  int count;
  float fahren, celsius;

  for(count = 1; count <= 6; ++count)
  {
    cout << "\nEnter a fahrenheit temperature: ";
    cin >> fahren;
    celsius = (5.0/9.0)*(fahren - 32.0);
    cout << "\nThe corresponding celsius temperature is "
         << setiosflags(ios::showpoint) << setw(5)
         << setprecision(2) << celsius;
  }
}
```

```
11. #include <iostream.h>
    #include <iomanip.h>
    void main(void)
    {
      int yr;
      float total;

      for (total = 1000.00, yr = 1; yr <= 10; yr++)
      {
        total = total * 1.08;
        cout << "The balance at the end of " << n
             << " years is $" << setiosflags(ios::showpoint)
             << setw(8) << setprecision(2) << total << '\n';
      }
    }

15. #include <iostream.h>
    #include <iomanip.h>
    void main(void)
    {
      int i, j;
      float total, avg, data;

      for (i = 1; i <= 4; i++)
      {
        cout << '\n';
        cout << "Enter 6 results for experiment # " << i << ": ";
        for (j = 1, total = 0.0; j <= 6; j++)
        {
          cin >> data;
          total += data;
        }
        avg = total/6;
        cout << "   The average for experiment #" << i
             << " is " << setiosflags(ios::showpoint)
             << setw(6) << setprecision(2) << avg << '\n';
      }
    }
```

```cpp
17. #include <iostream.h>
    #include <iomanip.h>
    void main(void)
    {
      int bowler, game;
      float score, plyr_tot, plyr_avg, team_tot, team_avg;

      for(bowler = 1, team_tot = 0; bowler <= 5; bowler++)
      {
        for(game = 1, plyr_tot = 0; game <= 3; game++)
        {
          cout << '\n';
          cout << "Enter the score for bowler " << bowler << " game "<< game << ": ";
          cin >> score;
          plyr_tot = plyr_tot + score;
        }
        team_tot = team_tot + plyr_tot;
        plyr_avg = plyr_tot/3.0;
        cout << "   The average for bowler " << bowler << " is "
             << setiosflags(ios::showpoint) << setw(5)
             << setprecision(2) << plyr_avg << '\n';
      }
      team_avg = team_tot/15.0;
      cout << "The average for the whole team is "
           << setiosflags(ios::showpoint) << setw(5)
           << setprecision(2) << team_avg;
    }
```

Section 5.4

```cpp
3. a. #include <iostream.h>
      void main(void)
      {
        int num, digit;

        cout << "Enter an integer: ";
        cin >> num;
        cout << "\nThe number reversed is: ";
        do
        {
          digit = num % 10;
          num /= 10;
          cout << digit;
        } while (num > 0);
      }
```

Section 6.1

1. a. `factorial()` expects to receive one integer value.

b. `price()` expects to receive one integer and two double precision values, in that order.

c. An int and two double precision values, in that order, must be passed to `yield()`.

d. A character and two floating point values, in that order, must be passed to `interest()`.

e. Two floating point values must be passed to `total()`.

f. Two integers, two characters, and two floating point values, in that order, are expected by `roi()`.

g. Two integers and two character values, in that order, are expected by `get_val()`.

3. a. The `find_abs()` function is included in the program written for Exercise 3b.

b.
```cpp
#include <iostream.h>
void main(void)
{
  double dnum;
  void find_abs(double);   // function prototype

  cout << "Enter a number: ";
  cin >> dnum;
  find_abs(dnum);
}

void find_abs(double num)
{
  double val;

  if (num < 0)
    val = -num;
  else
    val = num;
  cout << "The absolute value of " << num << " is " << val;
}
```

5. a. The `sqr_it()` function is included in the program written for Exercise 5b.

b.
```cpp
#include <iostream.h>
void main(void)
{
  double first;
  void sqr_it(double);   // function prototype

  cout << "\nEnter a number: ";
  cin >> first;
  sqr_it(first);
}
void sqr_it(double num)
{
  cout << "The square of " << num << " is " << (num*num);
}
```

7. *a.* The function for producing the required table is included in the larger program
written for Exercise 7b.

   b.
```
#include <iostream.h>
  #include <iomanip.h>
  void main(void)
  {
    void table(void);      // function prototype

    table();               // call the function
  }

  void table(void)
  {
    int num;

    cout << '\n'
         << "NUMBER    SQUARE     CUBE\n"
         << "------    ------     ----\n";

    for (num = 1; num <= 10; num++)
      cout << setw(3) << num << "         "
           << setw(3) << num * num << "        "
           << setw(4) << num * num * num << '\n';
  }
```

Section 6.2

1.
```
#include <iostream.h>
  void main(void)
  {
    float firstnum, secnum, max;
    float find_max(float, float);  // the function prototype

    cout << "\nEnter a number: ";
    cin >> firstnum;
    cout << "Great! Please enter a second number: ";
    cin >> secnum;

    max = find_max(firstnum, secnum); // the function is called here

    cout << "\nThe maximum of the two numbers is " << max;
  }
  float find_max(float x, float y)
  {                       // start of function body
    float maxnum;          // variable declaration

    if (x >= y)           // find the maximum number
      maxnum = x;
    else
      maxnum = y;

    return maxnum;        // return statement
  }
```

3. a. `void check(int num1, float num2, double num3)`
   b. `double find_abs(double x);`
   c. `float mult(float first, float second)`
   d. `int sqr_it(int number)`
   e. `int powfun(int num, int exponent)`
   f. `void table(void)`

5. a. The `mult()` function is included in the program written for Exercise 5b.
   b.
```
#include <iostream.h>
void main(void)
{
    double mult(double, double);    // function prototype
    double first, second;

    cout << "Please enter a number: ";
    cin >> first;
    cout << "Please enter another number: ";
    cin >> second;
    cout << "The product of these numbers is "
         << mult(first,second);
}

double mult(double num1, double num2)
{
    return (num1*num2);
}
```

7. The polynomial function is included in the following working program.
```
#include <iostream.h>
void main(void)
{
    float a, b, c, x, result;
    float poly_two(float, float, float, float); // prototype

    cout << "Enter the coefficient for the x squared term : ";
    cin >> a;
    cout << "\nEnter the coefficient for x : ";
    cin >> b;
    cout << "\nEnter the constant: ";
    cin >> c;
    cout << "\nEnter the value for x: ";
    cin >> x;
    result = poly_two(a, b, c, x);
    cout << "\n\n\nThe result is " << result;
}

float poly_two(float c1, float c2, float c3, float x)
{
    return (c1*x*x + c2*x + c3);
}
```

11. *a*. The `fracpart()` function is included in the program written for Exercise 11b.

   ***b*.**
```
#include <iostream.h>
void main(void)
{
  double num;
  double fracpart(double);   // function prototype

  cout << "Enter a number: ";
  cin >> num;
  cout << "\nThe fraction part of " << num
       << " is " << fracpart(num) << '\n';
}

double fracpart(double x)
{
  int whole(double);     // function prototype

  return (x - whole(x));
}
int whole(double n)
{
  int a;

  a = n;    // a = int (n) is preferred - see Section 3.2
  return a;
}
```

Section 6.3

1. a. `float &amount;`
  b. `double &price`
  c. `int &minutes;`
  d. `char &key;`
  e. `double &yield;`

3.
```
#include <iostream.h>
void main(void)
{
  int firstnum, secnum, max;
    void find_max(int, int, int &);  // function prototype

  cout << "Enter a number: ";
  cin >>  firstnum;
  cout << "\nGreat! Please enter a second number: ";
  cin >> secnum;

  find_max(firstnum, secnum, max); // call the function

  cout << "\nThe maximum of the two numbers is " << max << '\n';
```
(continued on next page)

(continued from previous page)

```
  }
  void find_max(int x, int y, int &maxval)
  {
    if (x >= y)
      maxval = x;
    else
      maxval = y;
    return;
  }
```

5.
```
void time(int tot_sec, int &hrs, int &mins, int &secs)
{
  hrs = tot_sec/3600;   // 3600 seconds = 1 hour
                        //  Integer division yields the whole
                        //  number of times 3600 goes into
                        //  tot_sec
  tot_sec -= hrs * 3600;
  mins = tot_sec/60;
  tot_sec -= mins * 60;
  secs = tot_sec;
}
```

Section 6.4

1. a.

Variable Name	Data Type	Scope
price	integer	global to `void main(void)`, `roi()`, and `step()`
years	long integer	global to `void main(void)`, `roi()`, and `step()`
yield	double precision	global to `void main(void)`, `roi()`, and `step()`
bondtype	integer	local to `void main(void)` only
interest	double precision	local to `void main(void)` only
coupon	double precision	local to `void main(void)` only
count	integer	local to `roi()` only
eff_int	double precision	local to `roi()` only
numofyrs	integer	local to `step()` only
fracpart	float	local to `step()` only

Note that although arguments of each function assume a value that is dependent on the calling function, these arguments can change values within their respective functions. This makes them behave as if they were local variables within the called function.

3. All function arguments have local scope with respect to their defined function.

Section 6.5

1. a. Local variables may be automatic, static, or register. It is important to realize that not all variables declared inside functions are necessarily local. An example of this is an external variable.

b. Global variables may be static or external.

3. The first function declares `yrs` to be a static variable and assigns a value of one to it only once when the function is compiled. Each time the function is called thereafter, the value in `yrs` is increased by two. The second function also declares `yrs` to be static, but assigns it the value one every time it is called, and the value of yrs after the function is finished will always be 3. By resetting the value of yrs to 1 each time it is called, the second function defeats the purpose of declaring the variable to be static.

5. The *scope of a variable* tells where the variable is recognized in the program and can be used within an expression. If, for example, the variable years is declared inside a function, it is local and its scope is inside that function only. If the variable is declared outside of any function, it is global and its scope is anywhere below the declaration but within that file, unless another file of the same program extends the scope of the variable by declaring the variable to be external.

Section 7.1

1. a. `int grades[100];`

b. `float temp[50];`

c. `int code[30];`

d. `int year[100];`

e. `float velocity[32];`

f. `float dist[1000];`

g. `int code_num[6];`

3. a. `cin >> grades[0] >> grades[2] >> grades[6];`

b. `cin >> prices[0] >> prices[2] >> prices[6];`

c. `cin >> amps[0] >> amps[2] >> amps[6];`

d. `cin >> dist[0] >> dist[2] >> dist[6];`

e. `cin >> velocity[0] >> velocity[2] >> velocity[6];`

f. `cin >> time[0] >> time[2] >> time[6];`

5. a. `a[1]  a[2]  a[3]  a[4]  a[5]`

b. `a[1]  a[3]  a[5]`

c. `b[3]  b[4]  b[5]  b[6]  b[7]  b[8]  b[9]  b[10]`

d. `b[3]  b[6]  b[9]  b[12]`

e. `c[2]  c[4]  c[6]  c[8]  c[10]`

7.
```
#include <iostream.h>
void main(void)
{
    int grade[8], sum, i;
    float average;

    sum = 0;    // initialize here or in the declaration
    for( i = 0; i <= 7; i++)
    {
        cout << "Enter a value for element number " << i << " : ";
        cin >> grade[i];
        sum = sum + grade[i];
    }
    cout << "\nThe values stored in the array are:\n";
    for (i = 0; i <= 7; i++)
        cout << grade[i] << "   ";
    average = sum / 8.0;

    cout << "\nThe average of these values is "
         << average << '\n';
}
```

9. a.
```
#include <iostream.h>
#include <iomanip.h>
void main(void)
{
   int grades[14], total, i;
   float avg, deviation[14];

   total = 0;
   for(i = 0; i <= 13; ++i)
   {
     cout << "Enter grade # " << (i + 1) << " : ";
     cin >> grades[i];
     total += grades[i];
   }
   avg = total/14.0;
   cout << "\n The average of the grades is " << avg << '\n'
        << "Element      Element       Deviation\n"
        << "Number       Value        from Avg.\n"
        << "-------      -------      ----------\n";
   for(i = 0; i <= 13; ++i)
   {
     deviation[i] = grades[i] - avg;
     cout << setw(4) << i << "     "
          << setw(10) << grades[i] << "      "
          << setiosflags(ios::showpoint) << setw(10)
          << setprecision(2) << deviation[i] << '\n';
   }
}
```

11. a.
```
#include <iostream.h>
void main(void)
{
   double raw[10], sorted[10], min = 1.e5;
   int i, j, index;

   for(i = 0; i <= 9; i++)
   {
     cout << "Enter value # " << (i+1) << " : ";
     cin >> raw[i];
   }
   for(i = 0; i <= 9; i++)
   {
     for(j = 0; j <= 9; j++)   // find the minimum for this pass
     {
       if(raw[j] < min) // look for next min
       {
         min = raw[j];
         index = j;
       }
     }
```

(continued on next page)

(continued from previous page)

```
        sorted[i] = min;        // put min in next sorted element
        min = 1.e5;             // reset min for start of search
        raw[index] = 1.e7;      // don't select this element again
      }
    cout << "The elements in sorted order are:\n";
    for( i = 0; i <= 9; ++i)
      cout << sorted[i] << '\n';
  }
```

b. To locate each minimum, make a complete pass through the array and find the first minimum. Now only nine numbers need be searched since one has been used. After the second lowest element has been selected, only the remaining eight need be searched. Instead of 10 squared passes through the loop, only 10 factorial passes are needed. The number of passes can be reduced using a shell sort rather than a bubble sort.

Section 7.2

1. a. int grades[10] = {89, 75, 82, 93, 78, 95, 81, 88, 77, 82};
b. double amount[5] = {10.62, 13.98, 18.45, 12.68, 14.76};
c. double rates[100] = {6.29, 6.95, 7.25, 7.35, 7.40, 7.42};
d. float temp[64] = {78.2, 69.6, 68.5, 83.9, 55.4, 67.0, 49.8, 58.3, 62.5, 71.6};
e. char code[15] = {'f', 'j', 'm', 'q', 't', 'w', 'z'};

3.
```
#include <iostream.h>
void main(void)
{
  float slopes[9] = {17.24, 25.63,  5.94,
                     33.92,  3.71, 32.84,
                     35.93, 18.24,  6.92};
  int i;
  float max = 0.0, min = 999.9;

  for(i = 0; i <= 8; ++i)
  {
    if (slopes[i] < min) min = slopes[i];
    if (slopes[i] > max) max = slopes[i];
  }
  cout << "\nThe minimum array value is " << min;
  cout << "\nThe maximum array value is " << max << '\n';
}
```

5.
```
char goodstr1[12] = {'G', 'o', 'o', 'd', ' ',
                     'M', 'o', 'r', 'n', 'i', 'n', 'g'};

char goodstr1[] = {'G', 'o', 'o', 'd', ' ',
                   'M', 'o', 'r', 'n', 'i', 'n', 'g'};
char goodstr1[] = "Good Morning";
```

Note: The last declaration creates an array having one more character than the first two. The extra character is the null character.

Section 7.3

1. ```
void sort_arr(double in_array[500])
             or
void sort_arr(double in_array[])
```

5. ```
#include <iostream.h>
void main(void)
{
   float rates[9] = {6.5, 7.2, 7.5, 8.3, 8.6,
                     9.4, 9.6, 9.8, 10.0};
   void show(float []);  // function prototype

   show(rates);
}

void show(float rates[])
{
   int i;

   cout << "\nThe elements stored in the array are:\n";
   for(i = 0; i <= 8; ++i)
     cout << rates[i] << "  \n";
}
```

7. ```
#include <iostream.h>
#include <iomanip.h>
void main(void)
{
   double price[10] = {10.62, 14.89, 13.21, 16.55, 18.62,
                       9.47, 6.58, 18.32, 12.15, 3.98};

   double quantity[10] = {4.0, 8.5, 6.0, 7.35, 9.0,
                          15.3, 3.0, 5.4, 2.9, 4.8};
   double amount[10];

   int i;
   void extend(double [[], double [], double []); // prototype

   extend(price, quantity, amount);
   cout << "The elements in the amount array are:";
   for(i = 0; i <= 9; ++i)
     cout << setiosflags(ios::showpoint)
          << setw(17) << setprecision(3)
          << amount[i] << '\n';
}
void extend(double prc[], double qnty[], double amt[])
{
   int i;

   for(i = 0; i <= 9; ++i)
     amt[i] = prc[i] * qnty[i];
}
```
```

Section 7.4

1. a. `int array[6][10];`
  b. `int codes[2][5];`
  c. `char keys[7][12];`

  d. `char letter[15][7];`
  e. `double vals[10][25];`
  f. `double test[16][8];`

3.
```
#include <iostream.h>
void main(void)
{
  int i, j, total = 0;
  int val[3][4] = {8,16,9,52,3,15,27,6,14,25,2,10};

  for (i = 0; i < 3; i++)
    for (j = 0; j < 4; j++)
      total = total + val[i][j];
  cout << "\nThe total of the values is " << total << '\n';
}
```

5. a.
```
#include <iostream.h>
void main(void)
{
  int i, j, total = 0;
  int max = -999;
  int val[4][5] = {16, 22,  99, 4, 18,
            -258,  4, 101, 5, 98,
             105,  6,  15, 2, 45,
              33, 88,  72, 16, 3};

  for (i = 0; i < 3; i++)
    for (j = 0; j < 4; j++)
   if (val[i][j] > max)
     max = val[i][j];
  cout << "\nThe maximum array value is " << max;
}
```

Section 8.1

1. `&average` means "the address of the variable named average"

3. a.
```
#include <iostream.h>
void main(void)
{
  int num, count;
  long date;
  float yield;
  double price;

  cout << "The address of the variable num is "
       << &num << '\n';
  cout << "The address of the variable count is "
       << &count << '\n';
  cout << "The address of the variable date is "
       << &date << '\n';
  cout << "The address of the variable yield is "
       << &yield << '\n';
  cout << "The address of the variable price is "
       << &price << '\n';
}
```

5. a. `*x_addr`
 b. `*y_addr`
 c. `*pt_yld`
 d. `*pt_miles`
 e. `*mptr`
 f. `*pdate`
 g. `*dist_ptr`
 h. `*tab_pt`
 i. `*hours_pt`

7. a. Each of these variables are pointers. This means that addresses will be stored in each of these variables.
 b. They are not very descriptive names and do not give an indication that they are pointers.

9. All pointer variable declarations must have an asterisk. Therefore, c, e, g, and i are pointer declarations.

11.

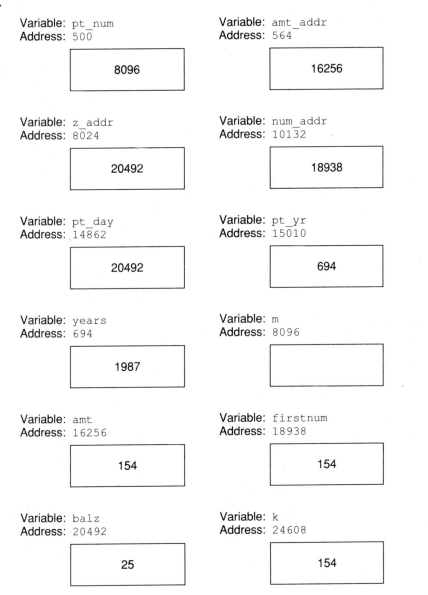

Section 8.2

1. **a.** `*(prices + 5)`
  b. `*(grades + 2)`
  c. `*(yield +10)`
  d. `*(dist + 9)`
  e. `*mile`

  f. `*(temp + 20)`
  g. `*(celsius + 16)`
  h. `*(num + 50)`
  i. `*(time + 12)`

3. **a.** The declaration `double prices [5];` causes storage space for five double precisionnumbers, creates a pointer constant named `prices`, and equates the pointer constant to the address of the first element (`&prices[0]`).

  b. Each element in prices contains eight bytes and there are five elements for a total of 40 bytes.

  c.

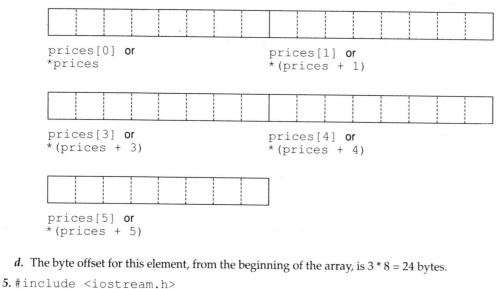

  d. The byte offset for this element, from the beginning of the array, is 3 * 8 = 24 bytes.

5.
```
#include <iostream.h>
void main(void)
{
  float rates[] = {12.9, 18.6, 11.4, 13.7, 9.5, 15.2, 17.6};
  int i;

  cout << "The elements of the array are:\n";
  for(i = 0; i <= 6; i++)
    cout << "   " << *(rates + i);    // The variable pointed
}                                      // to by rates offset by i
```

Section 8.3

3. a.
```
#include <iostream.h>
void main(void)
{
   char strng[] = "Hooray for all of us";
   char *mess_pt;

   mess_pt = &strng[0];    // mess_pt = strng; is equivalent
   cout << "\nThe elements in the array are: ";
   for(   ; *mess_pt != '\0'; mess_pt++)
     cout << *mess_pt;
   cout << '\n';

}
```
b.
```
#include <iostream.h>
void main(void)
{
   char strng[] = "Hooray for all of us";
   char *mess_pt;

   mess_pt = &strng[0];    // mess_pt = strng; is equivalent
   cout << "\nThe elements in the array are: ";
   while (*mess_pt != '\0')  // search for the null character
     cout << *mess_pt++;
   cout << '\n';
}
```

Section 8.4

1.
```
void sort_arr(double in_array[500])
```

```
void sort_arr(double in_array[])
```

```
void sort_arr(double *in_array)
```

5. The problem with this method of finding the maximum value lies in the line

```
if(max < *vals++)   max = *vals;
```

This statement compares the correct value to max, but then increments the address in the pointer before any assignment is made. Thus, the element assigned to max by the expression max = *vals is one element beyond the element pointed to within the parentheses.

9. a. The following output is obtained:

```
33
16
99
34
```

This is why:

```
*(*val) = *(val[0]) = val[0][0] = 33;
*(*val + 1) = *(val[1]) = val[0][1] = 16;
*(*(val + 1) + 2) = *(*(val[1]) + 2) = *(val[1][2]) = 99;
*(*val) + 1 = *(val[0]) + 1 = val[0][0] + 1 = 33 + 1 = 34.
```

In other words, for any two-dimensional array, arr[x][y], what we really have is two levels of pointers. What is meant by *(arr + x) is that there are x number of pointers, each successively pointing to arr[1][0], arr[2][0], arr[3][0],..., arr[x][0]. So an expression such as *(*(arr + x) + y) translates to arr[x][y].

Section 9.1

1. b.
```
#include <iostream.h>
void main(void)
{
   char line[80];
   void vowels(char []); // function prototype

   cout << "Enter a string.\n";
   cin.getline(line,80);
   vowels(line);
}

void vowels(char strng[])
{
   int i = 0, v = 0; // Array element number and vowel counter
   char c;

   while((c = strng[i++]) != '\0')
   switch(c)
   {
     case 'a':
     case 'e':
     case 'i':
     case 'o':
     case 'u':
    cout << c;
    v++;
   }
   cout << '\n';
   cout << "There were " << v << " vowels.\n";
}
```

3. a. The function is included in the program written for Exercise 3b.

  b.
```cpp
#include <iostream.h>
void main(void)
{
  char strng[80];
  void count_str(char []);   // function prototype

  cout << "Enter a line of text\n";
  cin.getline(strng,80);
  count_str(strng);
}
void count_str(char message[])
{
  int i;
  for(i = 0; message[i] != '\0'; ++i);   // The semicolon at
                                         // the end of this
                                         // statement is the
                                         // null statement

  cout << "\nThere number of total characters, "
       << "including blanks,\nin the line just entered is "
       << i << ".\n";
}
```

7.
```cpp
#include <iostream.h>
void main(void)
{
  char word[80];
  void del_char(char [], int, int);   // function prototype

  cout << "Enter a string\n";
  cin.getline(word,80);
  cout << "The word just entered is: " << word << '\n';
  del_char(word, 13, 5); // string, how many to delete, starting position
  cout << word << '\n';  // display the edited string
}
void del_char(char strng[], int x, int pos)
{
  int i, j;

  i = pos-1;   // first element to be deleted (actually, overwritten)
  j = i + x;   // first element beyond delete range
  while (strng[j] != '\0')
    strng[i++] = strng[j++];  // copy over an element
  strng[i] = '\0';   // close off the edited string
  return;
}
```

This program assumes the number of characters to be deleted actually exists. Otherwise the `while` loop would not terminate (unless it just happened to encounter another `null` character somewhere in memory beyond the original string).

9. a. The to_upper() function is included in the program written for Exercise 9c.

c.
```cpp
#include <iostream.h>
void main(void)
{
  char strng[80];
  int i = 0;
  char to_upper(char ch);    // function prototype

  cout << "Enter a line of text\n";
  cin.getline(strng,80);

  while (strng[i] != '\0')  // get the character
  {
    strng[i] = to_upper(strng[i]); // send it to the function
    i++;                           // move to next character
  }
  cout << "The string, with all lower case letters"
       << " converted is:\n";
  cout << strng << '\n';
}

char to_upper(char ch)
{

  if ( ch >= 'a' && ch <= 'z')    // test it
    return(ch - 'a' + 'A');       // change it, if necessary
   else
      return(ch);
}
```

11.
```cpp
#include <iostream.h>
void main(void)
{
  char strng[80];
  int i = 0, count = 1;

  cout << "Enter a line of text\n";
  cin.getline(strng,80);
  if(strng[i] == ' ' || strng[i] == '\0')
     count--;
  while(strng[i] != '\0')
  {
    if(strng[i] == ' ' && (strng[i + 1] != ' ' && strng[i + 1] != '\0'))
       count++;       // encountered a new word
    i++;              // move to the next character
  }
  cout << "\nThe number of words in the line just entered is " << count << '\n';
}
```

The program increases the word count whenever a transition from a blank to a nonblank character occurs. Thus, even if words are separated by more than one space the word count will be incremented correctly. Initially the program assumes the text starts with a word (count = 1). If the first character is either a blank or an end-of-string Null, this assumption is incorrect and the count is decremented to zero.

Section 9.2

1. a. `*text = 'n'`
   `*(text + 3) = ' '`
   `*(text + 10) = ' '`

c. `*text = 'H'`
   `*(text + 3) = 'p'`
   `*(text + 10) = 'd'`

b. `*text = 'r'`
   `*(text + 3) = 'k'`
   `*(text + 10) = 'o'`

d. `*text = 'T'`
   `*(text + 3) = ' '`
   `*(text + 10) = 'h'`

3.
```
#include <iostream.h>
void main(void)
{
   char line[80];
   void vowels(char *);    // function prototype

   cout << "Enter a string.\n";
   cin.getline(line,80);
   vowels(line);
}
void vowels(char *strng)  // strng treated as a pointer variable

{
   int v = 0;    // v = vowel counter
   char c;

   while((c = *strng++) != '\0')  // an address is incremented
   switch(c)
   {
     case 'a':
     case 'e':
     case 'i':
     case 'o':
     case 'u':
       cout << c;
       v++;
   }
   cout << "\nThere were " << v << " vowels.\n";
}
```

```
5. #include <iostream.h>
   void main(void)
   {
     char strng[80];
     void count_str(char *);    // function prototype

     cout << "Enter a line of text\n";
     cin.getline(strng,80);
     count_str(strng);
   }

   void count_str(char *message)    // message as a pointer variable
   {
     int count;

     for(count = 0; *message++ != '\0'; ++count) ; // The semicolon at the
                             // end of this statement is the null statement
     cout << "\nThe number of total characters, including blanks,"
          << "\nin the line just entered is " << count << ".\n";
   }

7. #include <iostream.h>
   void main(void)
   {
     char forward[80], rever[80];
     void reverse(char *, char *); // function prototype

     cout << "\nEnter a line of text:\n";
     cin.getline(forward,80);
     reverse(forward,rever);
     cout << "\nThe text: " << forward;
     cout << "\nspelled backwards is: " << rever << '\n';
   }

   void reverse(char *forw, char *rev)
   {
     int i = 0, j = 0;

     while(*(forw + i) != '\0')        // count the elements
       ++i;                            // in the string
     for(i--; i >= 0; i--)
       *rev++ = *(forw + i);
     *rev = '\0';                      // close off reverse string
     return;
   }
```

9. The function is included within a complete program.

```
#include <iostream.h>
void main(void)
{
  char ch, line[80];
  void append_c(char, char *);   // function prototype

  cout << "\nEnter a line of text: ";
  cin.getline(line,80);
  cout << "Enter a single character: ";
  ch = cin.get();
  append_c(ch,line);
  cout << "The new line of text with the appended "
       << "last character is:\n";
  cout << line;
}

void append_c(char c, char *strng)
{

  while(*strng++ != '\0')     // this advances the pointer
    ;                         // one character beyond '\0 '
  strng--;                    // point to the '\0')
  *strng++ = c;               // replace it with the new char
  *strng = '\0';              // close the new string
}
```

13.
```
void trimrear(char *strng)
  {

    while(*strng != '\0') strng++;   // move to end of string
    strng--;                         // move to char before '\0'
    while(*strng == ' ') strng--;    // skip over blank characters

    *(++strng) = '\0';               // close off string
    return;
  }
```

Section 9.3

1. `char *text = "Hooray!";`
   `char test[] = {'H','o','o','r','a','y','\0'};`

3. message is a pointer constant. Therefore, the statement ++message, which attempts to alter its address, is invalid. A correct statement is

```
cout << *(message + i);
```

Here the address in message is unaltered and the character pointed to is the character offset i bytes from the address corresponding to message.

Section 10.1

1. a.
```
struct s_temp
  {
    int id_num;
    int credits;
    float avg;
  };
```
b.
```
struct s_temp
  {
    char name[40];
    int month;
    int day;
    int year;
    int credits;
    float avg;
  };
```
c.
```
struct s_temp
  {
    char name[40];
    char street[80];
    char city[40];
    char state[2];
    int zip;              // or char zip[5];
  };
```
d.
```
struct s_temp
  {
    char name[40];
    float price;
    char date[8];   // assumes a date in the form XX/XX/XX
  };
```
e.
```
struct s_temp
  {
    int part_no;
    char desc[100];
    int quant;
    int reorder;
  };
```
3. a.
```
#include <iostream.h>
void main(void)
{
  struct
  {
    int month;
    int day;
    int year;
  } date;       // define a structure variable named date
```

(continued on next page)

(continued from previous page)

```cpp
      cout << "\nEnter the current month: ";
      cin >> date.month;
      cout << "Enter the current day: ";
      cin >> date.day;
      cout << "Enter the current year: ";
      cin >> date.year;
      cout << "\nThe date entered is : "
           << date.month << '/' << date.day
           << '/' << date.year << '\n';
   }
```

b.
```cpp
   #include <iostream.h>
   #include <iomanip.h>
   void main(void)
   {
     struct clock
     {
       int hours;
       int minutes;
       int seconds;
     } time;    // define a structure variable named time

     cout << "\nEnter the current hour: ";
     cin >> time.hours;
     cout << "Enter the current minute: ";
     cin >> time.minutes;
     cout << "Enter the current second: ";
     cin >> time.seconds;
     cout << "\nThe time entered is: "
          << setw(2) << setfill('0') << time.hours << ':'
          << setw(2) << time.minutes << ':'
          << setw(2) << time.seconds << '\n';
   }
```

Note the use of the `setw` and `setfill` manipulators. The fill character of 0 forces the field of 2 to be filled with leading zeros.

5.
```cpp
   #include <iostream.h>
   #include <iomanip.h>
   void main(void)
   {
     struct
     {
       int hours;
       int minutes;
     } time;
```

(continued on next page)

(continued from previous page)

```
    cout << "Enter the current hour: ";
    cin >> time.hours;
    cout << "Enter the current minute: ";
    cin >> time.minutes;
    if(time.minutes != 59)
      time.minutes += 1;
    else
    {
      time.minutes = 0;
      if(time.hours != 12)
    time.hours += 1;
      else
    time.hours = 1;
    }
  cout << "\nThe time in one minute will be "
        << setiosflags(ios::showpoint) << setfill('0')
        << setw(2) << time.hours << ':'
        << setw(2) << time.minutes << '\n';
}
```

Note the use of the `setw` and `setfill` manipulators. The fill character of 0 forces the field of 2 to be filled with leading zeros.

Section 10.2

1. a.
```
struct s_temp
{
  int id_num;
  int credits;
  float avg;
};

#include <iostream.h>
void main(void)
{
  s_temp student[100];
```

b.
```
struct s_temp
{
  char name[40];
  int month;
  int day;
  int year;
  int credits;
  float avg;
};

#include <iostream.h>
void main(void)
{
  s_temp student[100];
```

c.
```
struct s_temp
  {
    char name[40];
    char street[80];
    char city[40];
    char state[2];
    int zip;              // or char zip[5];
  };
  #include <iostream.h>
  void main(void)
  {
    s_temp address[100];
```
d.
```
struct s_temp
  {
    char name[40];
    float price;
    char date[8];   // Assumes a date in the form XX/XX/XX
  };
  #include <iostream.h>
  void main(void)
  {
    s_temp stock[100];
```
e.
```
struct s_temp
  {
    int part_no;
    char desc[100];
    int quant;
    int reorder;
  };
  #include <iostream.h>
  void main(void)
  {
    s_temp inven[100];
```
3.
```
struct mon_days
  {
    char name[10];
    int days;
  };
  #include <iostream.h>
  void main(void)
  {
    mon_days convert[12] = {"January", 31, "February", 28, "March", 31,
                            "April", 30, "May", 31, "June", 30,
                            "July", 31, "August", 31, "September", 30,
                            "October", 31, "November", 30, "December", 31};
    int i;
    cout << "\nEnter the number of a month: ";
    cin >> i;
    cout << convert[i-1].name << " has "
         << convert[i-1].days << " days\n";
  }
```

Section 10.3

```
1. struct date
   {
      int month;
      int day;
      int year;
   };

   #include <iostream.h>
   void main(void)
   {
      date present;
      long num;
      long days(date);   // function prototype

      cout << "Enter the month: ";
      cin >> present.month;
      cout << "Enter the day: ";
      cin >> present.day;
      cout << "Enter the year: ";
      cin >> present.year;
      num = days(present);
      cout << "The number of days since the turn"
           << " of the century is " << num << '\n';
   }

   long days(date temp)
   {
      return (temp.day + 30*(temp.month - 1) + 360*temp.year);
   }
```

Note: The reference version of the function `long days()` is written for Exercise 3a, and the pointer version for Exercise 3b.

```
3. a. struct date
      {
         int month;
         int day;
         int year;
      };

      #include <iostream.h>
      void main(void)
      {
         date present;
         long num;
         long days(date &);   // function prototype
```

(continued on next page)

(continued from previous page)

```cpp
   cout << "Enter the month: ";
   cin >> present.month;
   cout << "Enter the day: ";
   cin >> present.day;
   cout << "Enter the year: ";
   cin >> present.year;
   num = days(present);
   cout << "The number of days since the turn"
        << " of the century is " << num;
}

long days(date &temp)
{
   return (temp.day + 30*(temp.month - 1) + 360*temp.year);
}
```

b.
```cpp
   struct date
     {
       int month;
       int day;
       int year;
     };

   #include <iostream.h>
   void main(void)
     {
       date present;
       long num;
       long days(date *);    // function prototype

       cout << "Enter the month: ";
       cin >> present.month;
       cout << "Enter the day: ";
       cin >> present.day;
       cout << "Enter the year: ";
       cin >> present.year;
       num = days(&present);
       cout << "The number of days since the turn"
            << " of the century is " << num;
     }

   long days(date *temp)
     {
       return(temp->day + 30*(temp->month - 1) + 360*temp->year);
     }
```

5.
```
struct date
{
    int month;
    int day;
    int year;
};

#include <iostream.h>
void main(void)
{
    char ch;
    date present;
    long num;
    long days(date);   // function prototype

    cout << "Enter the date as mm/dd/yy: ";
    cin >> present.month >> ch >> present.day >> ch >> present.year;
    num = days(present);
    cout << "The number of days since the turn of the century is "
        << num << '\n';
}

long days(date temp)
{
    long act_days;
    int daycount[12] = { 0, 31, 59, 90, 120, 151,
                        180, 211, 241, 271, 302, 333};

    act_days = temp.day + daycount[temp.month-1] + 364*temp.year;
    return (act_days);
}
```

Section 10.4

1.
```
#include <iostream.h>
#include <string.h>
struct tele_typ
{
    char name[30];
    char phone_no[15];
    tele_typ *nextaddr;
};

#include <iostream.h>
void main(void)
{
```

(continued on next page)

(continued from previous page)

```
    tele_typ t1 = {"Acme, Sam", "(201) 898-2392"};
    tele_typ t2 = {"Dolan, Edith", "(213) 682-3104"};
    tele_typ t3 = {"Lanfrank, John", "(415) 718-4518"};
    tele_typ *first;
    char strng[30];
    void search(tele_typ *, char *); // function prototype

    first = &t1;
    t1.nextaddr = &t2;
    t2.nextaddr = &t3;
    t3.nextaddr = NULL;
    cout << "Enter a name: ";
    cin.getline(strng,30);
    search(first, strng);
    cout << '\n';
  }

  void search(tele_typ *contents, char *strng)
  {

    cout << strng;
    while(contents != NULL)
    {
      if(strcmp(contents->name,strng) == 0)
      {
      cout << "\nFound. The number is " << contents->phone_no;
      return;
      }
      else
      {
      contents = contents->nextaddr;
      }
    }
    cout << "\nThe name is not in the current phone directory.";
  }
```

3. To delete the second record, the pointer in the first record must be changed to point to the third record.

5. a.
```
    struct phone_bk
    {
      char name[30];
      char phone_no[15];
        phone_bk *previous;
        phone_bk *next;
    };
```

Section 10.5

1. The check () function is included below in a complete program used to verify that check () works correctly.

```
struct tel_typ
{
  char name[25];
  char phone_no[15];
  tel_typ *nextaddr;
};

#include <iostream.h>
#include <iomanip.h>
#include <stdlib.h>    // need this for the exit() funciton
void main(void)
{
  int i;
  tel_typ *list, *current;
  int check(tel_typ *);       // function prototype
  void populate(tel_typ *);   // function prototype
  void display(tel_typ *);    // function prototype

  list = new (tel_typ);
  check(list);
  current = list;
  for(i = 0; i < 2; ++i)
  {
    populate(current);
    current->nextaddr = new (tel_typ);

    if (check(current->nextaddr) == 0)
    {
   cout << "No available memory remains. Program terminating";
   exit(0); // terminate program and return to operating system
    }
    current = current->nextaddr;
  }
  populate(current);
  current->nextaddr = NULL;
  cout << "\nThe list consists of the following records:\n";
  display(list);
}
int check( tel_typ *addr)
{

  if(addr == NULL)
    return 0;
  else
    return 1;
  }
```

(continued on next page)

(continued from previous page)

```
void populate( tel_typ *record)
{
  cout << "\nEnter a name: ";
  cin.getline(record->name, 30);
  cout << "Enter the phone number: ";
  cin.getline(record->phone_no,16);
  return;
}

void display( tel_typ *contents)
{
  while(contents != NULL)
  {
    cout << '\n' << setiosflags(ios::left)
         << setw(30) << contents->name
         << setw(20) << contents->phone_no;
    contents = contents->nextaddr;
  }
    return;
}
```

3. The `insert()` function in the complete program below is used to verify that `insert()` works correctly. As written, the function will insert a structure after the structure whose address is passed to it. Since the address of the first structure is passed to it, the new structure is inserted between the first and second structures.

```
struct tel_typ
{
  char name[25];
  char phone_no[15];
  tel_typ *nextaddr;
};

#include <iostream.h>
#include <iomanip.h>
void main(void)
{
  int i;
  tel_typ *list, *current;
  void insert(tel_typ *);    // function prototype
  void populate(tel_typ *);  // function prototype
  void display(tel_typ *);   // function prototype

  list = new (tel_typ);
  populate(list); // populate the first structure
  list->nextaddr = new (tel_typ);
  current = list->nextaddr;
  populate(current); // populate the second structure
  current->nextaddr = NULL;
```

(continued on next page)

(continued from previous page)

```
   cout << "\nThe list initially consists of the following records:";
   display(list);
   insert(list);   // insert between first and second structures
   cout << "\nThe new list now consists of the following records:";
   display(list);
}
void insert(tel_typ *addr)
{
   tel_typ *temp;
   void populate(tel_typ *);   // function prototype

   temp = addr->nextaddr;      // save pointer to next structure
     // now change address to point to inserted structure
   addr->nextaddr = new (tel_typ);
   populate(addr->nextaddr);   // populate the new structure
     // set address member of new structure to saved addr
   addr->nextaddr->nextaddr = temp;
   return;
}

void populate(tel_typ *record)
{
   cout << "\nEnter a name: ";
   cin.getline(record->name,30);
   cout << "Enter the phone number: ";
   cin.getline(record->phone_no,16);
   return;
}

void display( tel_typ *contents)
{
   while(contents != NULL)
   {
     cout << '\n' << setiosflags(ios::left)
          << setw(30) << contents->name
          << setw(20) << contents->phone_no;
     contents = contents->nextaddr;
   }
   return;
}
```

Notice if the `populate` function call is removed from the insert function, then
`insert()` becomes a general insertion program that simply creates a structure and
correctly adjusts the address members of each structure. Also, notice the notation used in
`insert()`. The expression

`addr->nextaddr->nextaddr`

is equivalent to

`(addr->nextaddr)->nextaddr`

This notation was not used in `main()` because the pointer variable `current` is first used to store the address in `list->nextaddr` using the statement

```
current = list->nextaddr;
```

The statement

```
current->nextaddr = NULL;
```

in `void main(void)`, however, could have been written as:

```
list->nextaddr->nextaddr = NULL;
```

An interesting exercise is to rewrite `main()` so that the pointer variable named `current` is removed entirely from the function.

5. The `modify()` function in the complete program below is used to verify that `modify()` works correctly. The driver function creates a single structure, populates it, and then calls `modify()`. `modify()` itself calls the function `repop()`. An interesting extension is to write `repop()` so that an ENTER key response retains the original structure member value.

```
struct tel_typ
{
  char name[25];
  char phone_no[15];
  tel_typ *nextaddr;
};

#include <iostream.h>
#include <iomanip.h>
void main(void)
{
  int i;
  tel_typ *list;
  void populate(tel_typ *);  // function prototype
  void modify(tel_typ *);    // function prototype

  list = new (tel_typ);
  populate(list); // populate the first structure
  list->nextaddr = NULL;
  modify(list);   // modify the structure members
}

void modify(tel_typ *addr)
{
  void display(tel_typ *);  // function prototype
  void repop(tel_typ *);  // function prototype
```

(continued on next page)

(continued from previous page)

```
  cout << "\nThe current structure members are:";
  display(addr);
  repop(addr);
  cout << "\nThe structure members are now:";
  display(addr);
  return;
}

void populate(tel_typ *record)
{
  cout << "\nEnter a name: ";
  cin.getline(record->name,30);
  cout << "Enter the phone number: ";
  cin.getline(record->phone_no,16);
  return;
}

void repop(tel_typ *record)
{
  cout << "\n\nEnter a new name: ";
  cin.getline(record->name,30);
  cout << "Enter a new phone number: ";
  cin.getline(record->phone_no,16);
  return;
}

void display(tel_typ *contents)
{
  while(contents != NULL)
  {
    cout << '\n' << setiosflags(ios::left)
         << setw(30) << contents->name
         << setw(20) << contents->phone_no;
    contents = contents->nextaddr;
  }
  return;
}
```

Section 10.6

1. `cout` stream activations, with the correct control sequences, are contained within the following program.

```
union
{
  float rate;
  double taxes;
  int num;
} flag;
#include <iostream.h>
void main(void)
{
  flag.rate = 22.5;
  cout << "\nThe rate is " << flag.rate;
  flag.taxes = 44.7;
  cout << "\ntaxes are " << flag.taxes;
  flag.num = 6;
  cout << "\nnum is " << flag.num;
}
```

5. Since a value has not been assigned to `alt.btype`, the display produced is unpredictable (the code for a `'y'` resides in the storage locations overlapped by the variables `alt.ch` and `alt.btype`). Thus, either a garbage value will be displayed or the program could crash.

Section 11.1

1. a. An attribute represents a characteristic of an object; specifically, it is a data member of the object.
   b. The behavior of an object defines how the object can be activated and the response that will be produced. It is specified by the object's member and friend functions.
   c. The state of an object defines how the object appears at the moment. It is specified by the values assigned to the object's data member variables.
   d. A model is a representation of a real object.
   e. A class defines the attributes and behavior of a category or set of objects. As such it is a general representation from which specific objects can be created.
   f. An object is a specific instance of a class. As such, values have been assigned to its data members.
   g. The set of attributes and behaviors defining a class is frequently referred to as the class' *interface.*

3. a. i. the title, author, subject, publisher, and date of publication
      ii. the type, size, and cost
      iii. the type (ballpoint, ink cartridge, or ink refillable), the manufacturer, the color, the cost
      iv. the manufacturer of the tape, its length, type, and contents
       v. the manufacturer, cost, size, and capabilities (such as rewind, fast forward, record, etc.)
      vi. its speed, capacity, cost of installation, cost of operation, cost of maintenance, manufacturer
      vii. its manufacturer, overall size, color, cost, engine size, seating capacity, model type, estimated miles per gallon

b. These attributes model a class of objects. Only when specific values are assigned to these attributes is a specific object identified.

5. Animate objects can also be modeled and classified by classes. For example, dogs and cats can be grouped under the category pets, with an attribute of type. In general the attributes included in the class represent characteristics that are of concern for those using the class. For a veterinarian, a more useful attribute might consist of whether the animal has been inoculated or not.

Section 11.2

1. a. A class is a programmer-defined data type. The class specifies both the types of data and the types of operations that may be performed on the data.
b. An object is a specific instance of a class.
c. The declaration section declares both the data types and function prototypes of a class.
d. The implementation section defines the class's functions.
e. An instance variable is another name for a class data member.
f. A member function is a function declared in the class declaration section.
g. A data member is a variable declared in the class declaration section.
h. A member function that has the same name as the class and is used to initialize an object's data members.
i. Class instance is synonymous with an object.
j. Services are synonyms for the functions defined in a class implementation section.
k. Methods are synonyms for the functions defined in a class implementation section.

3. a. The class implementation section is included within the complete program written for Exercise 4a.
b. The class implementation section is included within the complete program written for Exercise 4b.
c. The class implementation section is included within the complete program written for Exercise 4c.

5. The class name should begin with a capital letter (i.e., Employee). The data members should be declared as private and the function members should be declared as public. Additionally, the declaration for the constructor prototype should be `class(int, char *)`.

7.
```cpp
#include <iostream.h>
// class declaration
class Date
{
  private:
    int month;
    int day;
    int year;
  public:
    Date(int, int, int);         // constructor
    void setdate(int, int, int); // member function to assign a date
    void showdate(void);         // member function to display a date
    int leapyr(void);            // the additional member function
};
```

(continued on next page)

(continued from previous page)

```
// implementation section
Date::Date(int mm = 7, int dd = 4, int yy = 94)
{
  month = mm;
  day = dd;
  year = yy;
}
void Date::setdate(int mm, int dd, int yy)
{
  month = mm;
  day = dd;
  year = yy;
}
void Date::showdate(void)
{
  cout << "The date is " << month << '/' << day << '/' << year << '\n';
}
int Date::leapyr(void)
{
  int fullyr;

  fullyr = year + 1900;
  if( (fullyr % 4 == 0 && fullyr % 100 != 0) || (fullyr % 400 == 0) )
    return 1;    // is a leap year
  else
    return 0;    // is not a leap year
}

void main(void)
{
  Date a, b, c(4,1,96);   // declare 3 objects

  b.setdate(12,25,95);    // assign values to b's data members
  a.showdate();
  cout << "  The leap year indicator is " << a.leapyr() << '\n';
  b.showdate();
  cout << "  The leap year indicator is " << b.leapyr() << '\n';
  c.showdate();
  cout << "  The leap year indicator is " << c.leapyr() << '\n';
}
```

Section 11.3

1. a. true
   b. false
   c. true
   d. false
   e. true
   f. false
   g. false
   h. true

   i. true
   j. true
   k. false
   l. false
   m. false
   n. true
   o. false

```
3. #include <iostream.h>

   // class declaration
   class Date
   {
     private:
       long yymmdd;
     public:
       Date(int, int, int);     // constructor
       Date(long);              // default constructor
       void showdate(void);     // member function to display a Date
   };

   // implementation section
   Date::Date(int mm, int dd, int yy)
   {
     yymmdd = yy * 10000L + mm * 100L + dd;
   }
   Date::Date(long ymd = 940704)
   {
     yymmdd = ymd;
   }
   void Date::showdate(void)
   {
     int year, month, day;

     year = (int)(yymmdd/10000.0);      // extract the year
     month = (int)( (yymmdd - year * 10000.0)/100.00 ); // extract the month
     day = (int)(yymmdd - year * 10000.0 - month * 100.0); // extract the day
     cout << "The Date is " << month << "/" << day << "/" << year << "\n";
   }

   void main(void)
   {
     Date a, b(4,1,96), c(970515); // declare three objects

     a.showdate();           // display object a's values
     b.showdate();           // display object b's values
     c.showdate();           // display object c's values
   }
```

Section 12.1

1. Assignment stores a value into an existing variable or object; that is, it occurs after the variable or object has been created by a definition statement. Initialization occurs at the time a new variable or object is created and is part of the creation process.

3. a. The required class is contained within the program solution to Exercise 3b.

b.
```cpp
#include <iostream.h>
#include <iomanip.h>
// declaration section
class Complex
{
 private:
   float real;
   float imaginary;
 public:
   Complex(float, float);    // constructor
   void operator=(Complex &); // overloaded assignment operator function
   void showdata(void);      // display member function
};

// implementation section
Complex::Complex(float re = 0, float im = 0)
{
 real = re;
 imaginary = im;
}
void Complex::operator=(Complex &oldnum)
{
 real = oldnum.real;
 imaginary = oldnum.imaginary;
}
void Complex::showdata(void)
{
  float c;
  char sign = '+';

  c = imaginary;
  if (c < 0)
  {
   sign = '-';
   c = -c;
  }
  cout << "The complex number is "
    << setiosflags(ios::fixed)
    << real << ' ' << sign << ' ' << c << "i\n";

}

void main(void)
{
  Complex a(4.2, 3.6), b;  // declare 2 objects

  a.showdata();     // display object a's values
  b.showdata();     // display object b's values
  b = a;            // assign a to b
  b.showdata();     // display object b's values
}
```

5. A copy of the pointer from object one to object two results in the loss of the address initially stored in object two. The memory space originally pointed to will, however, still contain data. An additional problem results when a destructor is called for object one. The destruction of object one causes the memory space pointed to by object one to be released. Since object two points to the same memory area, this results in object two's pointer member having the address of unallocated memory.

Section 12.2

```
1. #include <iostream.h>
  #include <string.h>

  // class declaration
  class Book
  {
    private:
      char *title;   // a pointer to a book title
    public:
      Book(char *);  // constructor
      Book(Book &);  // copy constructor
      void operator=(Book &);  // overloaded assignment operator
      void showtitle(void);   // display the title
  };
  // class implementation

  Book::Book(char *strng = NULL)   // constructor
  {
    title = new char[strlen(strng)+1];  // allocate memory
    strcpy(title,strng);                // store the string
  }

  Book::Book(Book &oldbook)   // copy constructor
  {
    title = new char[strlen(oldbook.title) + 1];  // allocate new memory
    strcpy(title, oldbook.title);  // copy the title
  }

  void Book::operator=(Book &oldbook)
  {
    if(title != NULL)  // check that it exists
      delete(title);   // release existing memory
    title = new char[strlen(oldbook.title) + 1];  // allocate new memory
    strcpy(title, oldbook.title);  // copy the title
  }

  void Book::showtitle(void)
  {
    cout << title << endl;
  }
```

(continued on next page)

(continued from previous page)

```cpp
void main(void)
{
  Book book1("DOS Primer");    // create 1st title
  Book book2 = book1;          // create a copy
  Book book3("A Brief History of Western Civilization");  // 2nd title

  book1.showtitle();    // display book1's title
  book2.showtitle();    // check the copy worked
  book3.showtitle();    // display the third book title
  book2 = book3;        // assign book3 to book2
  book2.showtitle();    // check the assignment worked
}
```

3. *a.* The required class is contained within the program solution to Exercise 3b.

b.
```cpp
#include <iostream.h>
#include <iomanip.h>
#include <string.h>
// declaration section
class Car
{
 private:
   float engine_size;
   char body_style;
   int color_code;
   char *vin_ptr;
 public:
   Car(float, char, int, char *); // constructor
   void operator=(Car &);      // overloaded assignment operator
   void showdata(void);        // member function to display a time
};

// implementation section

Car::Car(float eng = 0.0, char styl = 'X', int cd = 0, char *pt = NULL)
{
  engine_size = eng;
  body_style = styl;
  color_code = cd;
  vin_ptr = new char[strlen(pt) + 1];  // allocate memory
  strcpy(vin_ptr, pt);                 // store the string
}

void Car::operator=(Car &oldcar)
{
  engine_size = oldcar.engine_size;
  body_style = oldcar.body_style;
  color_code = oldcar.color_code;
  if(vin_ptr != NULL)  // check that it exists
    delete(vin_ptr);   // release existing memory
  vin_ptr = new char[strlen(oldcar.vin_ptr) + 1]; // allocate new memory
  strcpy(vin_ptr, oldcar.vin_ptr);  // copy the vin
}
```

(continued on next page)

(continued from previous page)

```cpp
void Car::showdata(void)
{
  cout << "\nThe values for this object are \n"
       << "  Engine size: " << engine_size << '\n'
       << "  Body style:  " << body_style << '\n'
       << "  Color code:  " << color_code << '\n'
       << "  VIN: " << vin_ptr << '\n';
}

void main(void)
{
  Car a(250.0, 'S', 52, "ABC567YYY"), b;  // declare 2 objects

  a.showdata();    // display object a's values
  b.showdata();    // display object b's values
  b = a;           // assign a to b
  b.showdata();    // display object a's values
}
```

Section 12.3

1. a.
```cpp
#include <iostream.h>
// class declaration
class Employee
{
  private:
    static float tax_rate;
    static int numemps;
    int id_num;
  public:
    Employee(int);     // constructor
    void display();    // access function
};

// static member definition
float Employee::tax_rate = 0.0025;
int Employee::numemps = 0;
// class implementation
Employee::Employee(int num = 0)
{
  id_num = num;
  numemps++;
}
void Employee::display()
{
  cout << "Employee number " << id_num
       << " has a tax rate of " << tax_rate << endl;
  cout << "There are currently " << numemps
       << " Employee objects" << endl;
}
```

(continued on next page)

(continued from previous page)

```cpp
void main(void)
{
  Employee emp1(11122);

  emp1.display();

  Employee emp2(11133);  // create a second object

  emp2.display();
}
```

3.
```cpp
// implementation section
Date::Date(int mm = 7, int dd = 4, int yy = 94)
{
  this->month = mm;
  this->day = dd;
  this->year = yy;
}

void Date::setdate(int mm, int dd, int yy)
{
  this->month = mm;
  this->day = dd;
  this->year = yy;
}

void Date::showdate(void)
{
  cout << "The date is "
       << this->month << '/'
       << this->day << '/'
       << this->year << '\n';
}
```

5.
```cpp
#include <iostream.h>
#include <math.h>
// class declaration
class Complex
{
  // friends list
  friend Complex addcomplex(Complex &, Complex &);
  private:
    float real;
    float imag;
  public:
    Complex(float, float);  // constructor
    void display();

};
```

(continued on next page)

(continued from previous page)

```cpp
// class implementation
Complex::Complex(float rl = 0, float im = 0)
{
   real = rl;
   imag = im;
}

void Complex::display()
{
   char sign = '+';

   if(imag < 0) sign = '-';
   cout << real << sign << fabs(imag) << 'i';
}

// friend implementation
Complex addcomplex(Complex &a, Complex &b)
{
   Complex temp;

   temp.real = a.real + b.real;
   temp.imag = a.imag + b.imag;

   return (temp);
}

void main(void)
{
   Complex a(3.2, 5.6), b(1.1, -8.4), c;
   float re, im;

   cout << "\nThe first complex number is ";
   a.display();
   cout << "\nThe second complex number is ";
   b.display();

   c = addcomplex(a,b);

   cout << "\n\nThe sum of these two complex numbers is ";
   c.display();
}
```

Section 13.1

1. a. The required function is included within the following working program:

```cpp
#include <iostream.h>
// class declaration
class Date
{
  private:
     int month;
     int day;
     int year;
  public:
    Date(int, int, int);       // constructor
    int operator>(Date &);   // declare the operator > function
    void showdate(void);   // member function to display a Date
};

// implementation section
Date::Date(int mm = 7, int dd = 4, int yy = 94)
{
  month = mm;
  day = dd;
  year = yy;
}
int Date::operator>(Date &date2)
{
  long dt1, dt2;

  dt1 = year*10000L + month*100 + day;
  dt2 = date2.year*10000L + date2.month*100 + date2.day;
  if (dt1 > dt2)
    return (1);
  else
    return (0);
}

void main(void)
{
  Date a(4,1,96), b(12,18,95), c(4,1,96); // declare 3 objects
  if (a > b)
    cout << "Date a greater than b \n";
  else
    cout << "Date a less than or equal to b \n";

  if (a > c)
    cout << "Date a greater than c \n";
  else
    cout << "Date a less than or equal to c \n";

}
```

3. a. This operator function provides the same result as the `operator()` function used in Program 13-2.

5. a. The required function is incorporated within the complete program written for Exercise 5b.

b.
```cpp
#include <iostream.h>
// class declaration
class Date
{
  private:
    int month;
    int day;
    int year;
  public:
    Date(int, int, int);     // constructor
    Date operator+(int);     // overload the + operator
    void showdate(void);     // member function to display a Date
};

// implementation section
Date::Date(int mm = 0, int dd = 0, int yy = 0)
{
  month = mm;
  day = dd;
  year = yy;
}
Date Date::operator+(int days)
{
  int daysrem;    // days remaining in the month
  int ds[] = {0,31,28,31,30,31,30,31,31,30,31,30,31};
  Date temp;  // a temporary Date to store the result
  temp.day = day;
  temp.month = month;
  temp.year = year;

  daysrem = ds[month] - temp.day;
  while(daysrem < days)
  {
    temp.month++;
    if(temp.month > 12)
    {
      temp.month = 1;
      temp.year++;
    }
    temp.day = 1;
    days -= (daysrem + 1);
    daysrem = ds[month] - temp.day;
  }
  // now the days remaining is within the current month
  temp.day = temp.day + days;
  return temp;     // the values in temp are returned
}
```

(continued on next page)

(continued from previous page)

```
void Date::showdate(void)
{
  cout << month << "/" << day << "/" << year;
}

void main(void)
{
   Date a(12,15,95), b; // declare two objects

   cout << "The initial Date is ";
   a.showdate();
   b = a + 18;    // add in 18 days
   cout << "\nThe new Date is ";
   b.showdate();
}
```

Section 13.2

1. The function's prototype is:

```
Date operator()(int);     // overload the () operator
```

The function's definition is:

```
Date Date::operator()(int days)
{
  Date temp;  // a temporary Date to store the result

  temp.day = day + days;  // add the days
  temp.month = month;
  temp.year = year;
  while (temp.day > 30)     // now adjust the months
  {
    temp.month++;
    temp.day -= 30;
  }
  while (temp.month > 12)  // adjust the years
  {
    temp.year++;
    temp.month -= 12;
  }
  return temp;      // the values in temp are returned
}
```

Section 13.3

1. a. Conversion from a built-in type to a built-in type is accomplished by C++'s implicit conversion rules or by explicit casting.

Conversion from a built-in type to a user-defined type is accomplished by a type conversion constructor.

Conversion from a user-defined type to a built-in type is accomplished by a conversion operator function.

Conversion from a user-defined type to a built-in type is accomplished by a conversion operator function.

b. A type conversion constructor is a constructor whose first argument is not a member of its class and whose remaining arguments, if any, have default values.

A conversion operator function is a class member operator function having the name of a built-in data type or class.

3.
```
#include <iostream.h>

// class declaration for Date
class Date
{
  private:
    int month, day, year;
  public:
    Date(int, int, int);     // constructor
    operator long();         // conversion operator function
    void showdate(void);
};
// constructor
Date::Date(int mm = 7, int dd = 4, int yy = 94)
{
  month = mm;
  day = dd;
  year = yy;
}
// conversion operator function converting from Date to long
Date::operator long()    // must return a long
{
  int mp, yp, t;
  long julian;

  if (month <= 2)
  {
    mp = 0;
    yp = year - 1;
  }
  else
  {
    mp = int(0.4 * month + 2.3);
    yp = year;
  }
  t = int(yp/4) - int(yp/100) + int(yp/400);
  julian = 365L * year + 31L * (month - 1) + day + t - mp;
  return (julian);
}
```

(continued on next page)

(continued from previous page)

```cpp
// member function to display a Date
void Date::showdate(void)
{
  cout << month << "/" << day << "/" << year;
}

void main(void)
{
   Date a(1,31,85);  // declare and initialize one object of type Date
   long b;           // declare an object of type long

   b = a;            // a conversion takes place here

   cout << "a's date is ";
   a.showdate();
   cout << "\nThis Date, as a long integer, is " << b << endl;
}
```

5.
```cpp
#include <iostream.h>

// forward declaration of class Julian
class Julian;

// class declaration for Date
class Date
{
  private:
    int month, day, year;
  public:
    Date(int, int, int);   // constructor
    operator Julian();     // conversion operator to Julian
    void showdate(void);
};

// class declaration for Julian
class Julian
{
  private:
    long yymmdd;
  public:
    Julian(long);    // constructor
    void showjulian(void);
};

// class implementation for Date
Date::Date(int mm = 7, int dd = 4, int yy = 94)  // constructor
{
  month = mm;
  day = dd;
  year = yy;
}
```

(continued on next page)

(continued from previous page)

```
// conversion operator function converting from Date to Julian class
Date::operator Julian()    // must return a Julian object
{
  int mp, yp, t;
  long temp;

  if (month <= 2)
  {
    mp = 0;
    yp = year - 1;
  }
  else
  {
    mp = int(0.4 * month + 2.3);
    yp = year;
  }
  t = int(yp/4) - int(yp/100) + int(yp/400);
  temp = 365L * year + 31L *s (month - 1) + day + t - mp;
  return (temp);
}

// member function to display a Date
void Date::showdate(void)
{
  cout << month << "/" << day << "/" << year;
}

// class implementation for Julian
Julian::Julian(long ymd = 0)  // constructor
{
  yymmdd = ymd;
}

// member function to display a Julian
void Julian::showjulian(void)
{
  cout << yymmdd;
}

void main(void)
{
  Date a(1,31,95), b(3,16,96);  // declare two Date objects
  Julian c, d;                  // declare two Julian objects

  c = Julian(a);    // cast a into a Julian object
  d = Julian(b);    // cast b into a Julian object
  cout << " a's date is ";
  a.showdate();
  cout << "\n  as a Julian object this date is ";
  c.showjulian();

  cout << "\n b's date is ";
  b.showdate();
  cout << "\n  as a Julian object this date is ";
  d.showjulian();
}
```

Note: There is no conversion operator from `Julian` to `Date`. In general the `Julian` objects are extremely useful for determining actual day count differences between two dates, and for sorting dates. In practice, the `Julian` date would be incorporated as a data member of the `Date` class. Also note that the forward reference to the `Julian` class could be omitted in this program if the `Julian` class were declared prior to the `Date` class.

Section 13.4

1. a. Inheritance is the capability of deriving one class from another class.
   b. A base class is the class that is used as the basis for deriving subsequent classes.
   c. A derived class is the class that inherits the characteristics of a base class,
   d. Simple inheritance is a type of inheritance where the parent of each derived class is a single base class.
   e. Multiple inheritance is a type of inheritance where a derived class has two or more parent base classes.
   f. Class hierarchies are the order in which classes are derived.
   g. Polymorphism is the ability of a function or operator to have multiple forms. The particular form that will be invoked is determined at run time and depends on the object being used.
   h. In static binding the determination of which function will be called is made at compile time.
   i. In dynamic binding the determination of which function will be called is made at run time.
   j. A virtual function is a function that is called by a pointer whose value is determined at run time depending on the object making the call.

3. The three features that must be provided for a programming language to be classified as object-oriented are classes, inheritance, and polymorphism. Object-based languages are languages that support objects but do not provide inheritance features.

5.
```
#include <iostream.h>
#include <math.h>

const double PI = 2.0 * asin(1.0);

class Circle
{
  protected:
    double radius;
  public:
    Circle(double);   // constructor
    double calcval();
};

// class implementation
Circle::Circle(double r= 1.0)   // constructor
{
  radius = r;
}
double Circle::calcval(void)    // this calculates an area
{
  return(PI * radius * radius);
}
```

(continued on next page)

(continued from previous page)

```
class Cylinder : public Circle  // Cylinder is derived from Circle
{
  protected:
    double length;  // add one additional data member and
  public:           // two additional function members
    Cylinder(double r = 1.0, double l = 1.0) : Circle(r), length(l) {}
    double calcval();
};


class Sphere : public Circle  // Sphere is derived from Circle
{
  public:            // two additional function members
    Sphere(double r = 1.0) : Circle(r) {} // base member initialization
    double calcval();
};


// class implementation
double Cylinder::calcval(void)   // this calculates a volume for a cylinder
{
  return (length * Circle::calcval()); // note the base function call
}


double Sphere::calcval(void)    // this calculates a volume for a sphere
{
  return (4.0/3.0 * radius * Circle::calcval()); // note the base function call
}
main()
{
  Circle circle_1, circle_2(2);  // create two Circle objects
  Cylinder cylinder_1(3,4);      // create one Cylinder object
  Sphere sphere_1(4);            // create one Sphere object

  cout << "The area of circle_1 is " << circle_1.calcval() << endl;
  cout << "The area of circle_2 is " << circle_2.calcval() << endl;
  cout << "The volume of cylinder_1 is " << cylinder_1.calcval() << endl;
  cout << "The volume of sphere_1 is " << sphere_1.calcval() << endl;
  circle_1 = sphere_1;  // assign a Sphere to a Circle

  cout << "\nThe area of circle_1 is now " << circle_1.calcval() << endl;
}
```

Section 14.1

1. a. On an IBM PC or compatible, a file name may have up to eight characters, and optionally a decimal point followed by three more characters. If a string is used to hold the file name, an extra character should be provided for the NULL, for a total of 13 characters.

3.
```
fstream prices;
fstream fp;
fstream coupons;
fstream distance;
fstream in_data;
fstream out_data;
```

Note: If these files are in the same program, the single declaration

```
fstream prices, fp, coupons, distance, in_data, out_data;
```

could be used.

5.
```
fstream *memo;
fstream *letter;
fstream *coups;
fstream *pt_yield;
fstream *pri_file;
fstream *rates;
```

Section 14.2

1. a.
```
#include <fstream.h>
void main(void)
{
   fstream out;
   char strng[80];

   out.open("text.dat", ios::out);
   cout << "Enter lines of text to be stored in the file.\n";
   cout << "Enter a carriage return only to terminate input.\n\n";
   cin.getline(strng, 81, '\n');
   while(*strng != '\0')
   {
     out << strng << '\n';
     cin.getline(strng, 81, '\n');
   }
   out.close();
   cout << "End of data input.\n";
   cout << "The file has been written.\n";
}
```

```
b.  #include <fstream.h>
    #include <iomanip.h>
    const int max = 80;
    void main(void)
    {
      int ch;
      char line[max];
      fstream in_file;

      in_file.open("text.dat",ios::in);
      if (!in_file)    // check for successful open
      {
        cout << "\nThe file was not successfully opened"
             << "\n Please check that the file currently exists."
             << endl;
        return;
      }
          // now read the file
      while( (ch = in_file.peek()) != EOF )
      {
        in_file.getline(line,80,'\n');
        cout << line << endl;
      }
    }
```

3. *a.* The data may be entered in a variety of ways. One possibility is to enter the data line by line and write each line to a file. A second method is to use a text editor to write the data to a file. A third possibility is to enter the data as individual items for each line, assemble the items into a complete string, and then write the string. A fourth possibility is to enter the data as individual items and write the file as individual items. The program below uses the last approach.

```
#include <fstream.h>
#include <iomanip.h>
void main(void)
{
  fstream out;
  char name[30], date[30], strng[81];
  int i;
  long id;
  float rate;

  out.open("employ.dat", ios::out);
  for (i = 1; i <= 5; ++i)    // get and write 5 records
  {
   cout << "\nEnter the name: ";
   cin >> name;
   cout << "Enter the ID No: ";
   cin >> id;
```

(continued on next page)

(continued from previous page)

```
        cout << "Enter the rate: ";
        cin >> rate;
        cout << "Enter the date (ex. 12/6/65): ";
        cin >> date;
        out << setiosflags(ios::left) << setw(18) << name
            << setw(7) << id
            << setw(10) << setprecision(2) << rate
            << date << '\n';
    }
    out.close();
    cout << "End of data input.\n";
    cout << "The file has been written.\n";
}
b. #include <fstream.h>
   void main(void)
   {
     fstream in_file, out_file;
     char ch, line[80];

     in_file.open("employ.dat",ios::in);
     out_file.open("employ.bak",ios::out);
     while( (ch = in_file.peek()) != EOF )
     {
       in_file.getline(line,80,'\n');
       out_file << line << '\n';
     }
     cout << "\nFile copy completed.\n";
     in_file.close();
     out_file.close();
   }
c. #include <fstream.h>
   #include <string.h>
   void main(void)
   {
     fstream in_file, out_file;
     char ch, f_name[15], s_name[15], line[80];

     cout << "Enter the name of the file to be copied: ";
     cin >> f_name;
     cout << "Enter the name of the new file: ";
     cin >> s_name;
     if(strcmp(f_name, s_name) == NULL)
     {
       cout << "\nYou have specified the same name for both files.";
       cout << "\nPlease rerun using different names.";
       return;
     }
```

(continued on next page)

(continued from previous page)

```
      in_file.open(f_name,ios::in);
      out_file.open(s_name,ios::out);
      while( (ch = in_file.peek()) != EOF )
      {
         in_file.getline(line, 80, '\n');
         out_file << line << '\n';
      }
      cout << "\nFile copy completed.\n";
      in_file.close();
      out_file.close();
   }
```

Note: The `strcmp()` function checks that you do not try to use the same file name for both input and output. Use of this function requires inclusion of the `string.h` header file. The `exit()` function terminates program execution.

d. A better way would be to enter the source and destination file names on the line used to invoke the executable program. Data entered in this manner are called command line arguments. Command line arguments are described in Appendix E.

5. *a.* The data may be entered in a variety of ways. One possibility is to enter the data line by line and write each line to a file. A second method is to use a text editor to write the data to a file. A third possibility is to enter the data as individual items for each line, assemble the items into a complete string, and then write the string. A fourth possibility is to enter the data as individual items and write the file as individual items. The program below uses the last approach.

```
#include <fstream.h>
#include <iomanip.h>
void main(void)
{
   fstream out;
   char ch, name[30], soc_no[12], strng[80];
   int i;
   float rate, hours;
   out.open("personel.dat", ios::out);
   for (i = 1; i <= 4; i++)    // get and write 4 records
   {
      cout << "\nEnter the name: ";
      cin >> name;
      cout << "Enter the Social Security No: ";
      cin >> soc_no;
      cout << "Enter the rate: ";
      cin >> rate;
      cout << "Enter the hours: ";
      cin >> hours;
```

(continued on next page)

(continued from previous page)

```
        // write the file
        out << setiosflags(ios::left | ios::showpoint | ios::fixed)
            << setw(30) << name << "   "
            << setw(11) << soc_no << "   "
            << setw(6) << setprecision(2) << rate << "   "
            << setw(4) << setprecision(2) << hours << '\n';
    }
    out.close();
    cout << "\nEnd of data input.";
    cout << "\nThe file has been written.\n";
}
```

b.
```
#include <fstream.h>
#include <iomanip.h>
void main(void)
{
    fstream in;
    char ch, line[80], name[30], ss[12];
    float rate, hours, net;

    in.open("personel.dat", ios::in);
    cout << "\nSoc. Sec. No.      Name        Net Pay\n";
    cout << "-------------      ----        -------\n";
    while( (ch = in.peek()) != EOF )
    {
        in >> name >> ss >> rate >> hours;
        net = rate * hours;
        cout << ss << "          " << name << "            "
             << setiosflags(ios::showpoint)
             << setprecision(2) << net << '\n';
    }
    in.close();
}
```

7. *a.* It is assumed that the data has been created using any of the methods mentioned in the solutions to Exercises 3a and 5a and stored in a file named invent.dat.

b.
```
#include <fstream.h>
#include <iomanip.h>
void main(void)
{
    fstream in;
    char p_code[6];
    int i, i_amt, q_sold, m_amt, c_amt, o_amt;

    in.open("invent.dat", ios::in);
    cout << "\n Part      Current     Order";
    cout << "\nNumber    Inventory   Amount";
    cout << "\n------     ---------   ------\n";
    for ( i = 1; i <= 4; i++)
```

(continued on next page)

(continued from previous page)

```
    {
        in >> p_code >> i_amt >> q_sold >> m_amt;
        c_amt = i_amt - q_sold;
        o_amt = m_amt - c_amt;
        if(o_amt < 0)
      o_amt = 0;
        cout << p_code << "    "
                << setw(8) << c_amt
                << setw(8) << o_amt << '\n';
    }
    in.close();
}
```

9. a. It is assumed that the data has been created using any of the methods mentioned in the solutions to Exercises 3a and 5a and stored in a file named `results.dat`.

b.
```
#include <fstream.h>
void main(void)
{
    fstream in;
    int i, num_els, data;
    float total, avg;
    char ch;

    in.open("results.dat", ios::in);
    while( (ch = in.peek()) != EOF)
    {
        in >> num_els;
        cout << "\nThe number of elements in this group is " << num_els;
        cout << "\nThe data in this group is: ";
        for ( total = 0, i = 1; i <= num_els; i++)
        {
            in >> data;     // read in data to be averaged
            cout << " " << data;
            total += data;          // add data to total
        }
      avg = total/num_els;        // compute average
      cout << "\nThe group average = " << avg << '\n';
    }
    in.close();
}
```

Section 14.3

1. The following program displays the data in test.dat, in reverse order (as does Program 14-5), but moves the offset relative to the start of the file.

```
#include <fstream.h>
void main(void)
{
  char ch;
  long offset, last;
  fstream in_file;

  in_file.open("test.dat", ios::in);
  if (!in_file)   // check for successful open
  {
    cout << "\nThe file was not successfully opened"
         << "\n Please check that the file currently exits."
         << '\n';
    return;
  }

  in_file.seekg(0L, ios::end);  // move to the end of the file
  last = in_file.tellg();  // determine the length of the file
  cout << "file length = " << last;
  in_file.seekg(0L,ios::beg);   // move to the start of the file
  cout << "\nThe characters in the file, in reverse order, are:" << '\n';
  for(offset = (last-1); offset = 0; offset--)
  {
    in_file.seekg(offset, ios::beg);
    ch = in_file.get();
    cout << ch << " : ";
  }
  in_file.close();
}
```

5. *a.* The required function is included within the working program listed below. Note that the function does not check that sufficient characters remain in the file for reading.

```
#include <fstream.h>
void main(void)
{
  fstream in;
  char name[13];
  long start, len;
  void r_bytes(fstream &, long, long);  // function prototype

  cout << "\nEnter file name: ";
  cin >> name;
  in.open(name, ios::in);
  cout << "Enter starting position for reading: ";
```

(continued on next page)

(continued from previous page)

```
      cin >> start;
      cout << "Enter number of characters to read: ";
      cin >> len;
      cout << "The characters are: \n";
      r_bytes(in, start, len);
      cout << '\n';
      in.close();
    }
  void r_bytes(fstream &fname, long begin, long num)
  {
    char ch;
    long i;
    --begin;          // the offset is one less than position
    fname.seekg(begin, ios::beg);   // move to the starting char
    for(i = 1; i <= num; i++)
    {
      ch = fname.get();
      cout << ch;
    }
    return;
  }
```

Section 14.4

1. The filename referred to in the exercise is a reference to an object of type fstream. The header line for p_file() is:

```
p_file(fstream &fname)
```

3. The get_open() function is included below with a driver function used to test it.

```
#include <fstream.h>
void main(void)  // driver function to test get_open() function
{
    void get_open(fstream &);      // function prototype
    fstream out_file;

    get_open(out_file);
    if (out_file != NULL)
    {
      cout << "\nThe file has been opened.";
      out_file.close();
    }
    else
      cout << "\nThe file has not been opened.";
}
```

(continued on next page)

(continued from previous page)

```cpp
void get_open(fstream &fname)
{
  char name[13], key;

  cout << "Enter a file name: ";
  cin.getline(name,12);
  // check if the file exists before opening it for writing
  fname.open(name,ios::in);
  if( fname )    // the file exists
  {
    fname.close();
    cout << "\nThe file currently exists. Do you want to"
         << "\nappend to it, overwrite it, or exit."
         << "\nEnter an a, o, or e: ";
    cin >> key;
    switch(key)
    {
  case 'a':
  case 'A': fname.open(name,ios::app);   // append open
          break;
  case 'o':
  case 'O': fname.open(name,ios::out);   // write open
          break;
  default: fname.close();
    }
  }
  else   // the file doesn't exist - create it for writing
          fname.open(name,ios::out);
  return;
}
```

Chapter 15

1. a.
```
  11001010
 &10100101
 ---------
  10000000
```
b.
```
  11001010
 |10100101
 ---------
  11101111
```
c.
```
  11001010
 ^10100101
 ---------
  01101111
```

3. a. $0157 = 001\ 101\ 111;\ 001\ 101\ 111 << 1 = 011\ 011\ 110 = 0336$

  b. $0701 = 111\ 000\ 001;\ 111\ 000\ 001 << 2 = 100\ 000\ 100 = 0404$

  c. 0873 = undefined; there is no octal digit higher than 7.

  d. 087 = undefined.

5. a. The binary number 00001100, which equals octal 014, is the required mask pattern.

  b. Two zeros could be placed in the third and fourth positions to reproduce the flag bits in these positions. However, the inclusive OR operation cannot set the remaining bits to zero.

  c. The binary number 00001100, which equals octal 014, is the required mask pattern.

7. Any character whose sixth bit is zero will be unaffected, which corresponds to characters whose 2nd octal digit (counting from the right) is either 0, 1, 2, or 3. For example, the octal code for the brace character,], is 135. Since its 2nd octal digit is 3, it will be unaffected by Program 12-2.

Any character whose sixth bit is one will be affected by Program 12-2. This includes all characters whose 2nd octal digit is either a 4, 5, 6, or 7, which includes all of the characters from the space (octal 40) to the question mark (octal 77) and all of the characters from the apostrophe (octal 140) through the Del key (octal 177). The latter include the lowercase letters, which are converted to uppercase.

Index